VISUAL COMMUNICATION
images with messages

7th Edition

Paul Martin Lester
University of Texas at Dallas

WritingForTextbooks

WritingForTextbooks

Visual Communication:
Images with Messages, Seventh Edition
Paul Martin Lester

Publisher: Paul Martin Lester
Art Director: xtine burrough
Cover Image: Manchester, England
Courtesy of Paul Martin Lester

ISBN: 978-0-692-92631-4

WritingForTextbooks
Dallas, Texas

for
xtine
allison
parker
martin

Table of Contents

Preface

I think stories can grow
out of the visual.
It can be an engine
for literacy.

Chris Riddell, 1962 –
AUTHOR & ILLUSTRATOR

Because of a feeling of frustration over not finding a textbook for a visual communication class first taught 20 years ago, this seventh edition is in your hands. Between its covers comes a greatly improved and visually expanded textbook that should be used for visual communication classes of course, but also can work well for mass communication and society lecture classes. That's because visual communication is the history of mass communication. Every student in a mass communications program should know of the field's importance in telling stories with words and pictures that educate and persuade.

Where did the idea come from that words communicate better than pictures? Since they were first invented to communicate complex thoughts, words and pictures have been locked in a struggle for dominance, with words throughout history being the clear-cut leader. With the widespread use of Johannes Gutenberg's commercial printing press, words became more important than pictures to convey complex thought. Images were relegated to an occasional medical diagram, a "pretty" border decoration, or a sensational eye-catching picture. Reading and writing became curriculum requirements, but visual literacy wasn't considered a necessary component of an individual's education.

However, with the inventions of motion pictures, television, and the computer with the ubiquitous spread of the web, these media have dramatically changed the role of visual messages in communication. Nowhere on Earth can a person avoid being confronted with some sort of visual message.

The purposes of this edition are the same as all the previous editions. This work is an appreciation that visual messages that are remembered have the greatest power to inform, educate, and persuade, and it is an exploration into why some images are remembered but most are forgotten. Hopefully at the end of the last chapter, your conclusion will be that:

The most powerful, meaningful, and culturally important messages are those that combine words and pictures equally and respectfully.

The first step toward understanding visual communication is to be educated about the many ways that information is produced and consumed in a modern, media-rich society. Typographic, graphic, informational, cartoon, still, moving, televised, computer, and web images are analyzed within a framework of personal, historical, technical, ethical, cultural, and critical perspectives in order to complete this first step.

For hundreds of years technology has kept writers and visual artists separate and unequal. Before Johannes Gutenberg's invention, less than 30 percent of Europeans could read. Seventy years after his printing press became commonplace, 80 percent of the population could read. Seventy years after the introduction of the daguerreotype, almost everyone had a Kodak camera and could see pictures in their local newspapers. And yet, educators never developed a visual grammar for photographs in the same way that a verbal grammar was developed for words after Gutenberg.

We Live in a Visually Intensive Society

Think of all the ways visual messages are displayed—billboards, cell phones, computer monitors, digital cameras, magazines, movie screens, newspapers, packaging, personal digital assistants, photo albums, refrigerator doors, storefronts, T-shirts, tattooed skin, television sets, and wall space. Bombarded daily with a steady, unrelenting stream of visual stimulation from all manner of media, we need to understand pictures. We see mediated images more than we read words. Some experts warn that if the trend continues, civilization will regress to illiteracy and lawlessness. But more optimistic researchers predict that technological advances will merge words and pictures in new ways to create innovative educational possibilities.

In this convergent era, a person cannot afford to know only how to write, to know only how to make an image, or to know only how to make print or web designs. Today, you should be interested in all the ways words and pictures are used—advertising, entertainment, graphic design, journalism, motion pictures, photojournalism, public relations, television, or the web. The artificial walls between the various media imposed by tradition and outdated technology are crumbling.

This book can help you breach those walls and enter the brave new (visual) world on the other side.

Elements of this Textbook
This seventh edition of *Visual Communication: Images with Messages* has 16 chapters divided into two main sections.

Chapter One: Visual Communication
introduces you to the joy of discovery when you really look at pictures and of the philosophy of the author Aldous Huxley, who inspired this book.

Section One comprises five chapters.

Chapter Two: Visual Cues explains the
four visual cues of color, form, depth, and movement and how they can be employed to grab a viewer's attention.

Chapter Three: Visual Theories details
the sensory theories of gestalt and constructivism and the perceptual theories of semiotics and cognition to show how designs and meaning can be improved through a knowledge of these significant theories.

Chapter Four: Visual Persuasion teaches how visual messages are employed to convince others to buy a product, adopt a service, or advocate a point of view.

Chapter Five: Visual Stereotypes gives
a history of "images that injure" as portrayed in all the media, with special emphasis on seven cultural groups—Native Americans, African Americans, Arabs, Asians, Latinos, women, lesbian, gay, bisexual, transgender, and queer persons, and those who use wheelchairs. A section at the end highlights positive examples or "images that heal."

Chapter Six: Visual Analysis takes one,
ordinary photograph used for a public relations purpose of President George W. Bush visiting children, victims of Hurricane Katrina in 2005, to make the point that through a 15-step analysis, any single image is more interesting and memorable if looked at closely.

Section Two contains nine media
chapters that concentrate on the ways we see visual messages. Each chapter in this section is introduced with a detailed description of a significant example from the medium being discussed, followed by a general discussion of the medium from personal, historical, technical, ethical, cultural, and critical perspectives. Each chapter ends with a "Trends to Watch" section and a list of key terms.

Chapter Seven: Typography is a discussion of Johannes Gutenberg's printing press improvements that revolutionized mass communication, a section on the history of writing dating from cave paintings to modern uses, the varying moods and styles of the six typeface families, the use of typography as artwork, Twitter messages, and digital book publishing.

Chapter Eight: Graphic Design features

the work of Saul Bass and his influences on logo designs, motion picture advertisements, and opening title credits, sections on how technology added to a graphic designer's palette, how design considerations are often driven by audience needs, the work of Shepard Fairey within an ethical discussion about appropriation, and how several free-form and grid artistic movements inspired graphic designers and illustrators with an appreciation of aesthetically pleasing word and picture displays.

Chapter Nine: Data Visualizations starts with the colorful weather map from the national newspaper, USA Today, with a discussion about the history of weather graphics for print and screen media, sections that detail the two types of data visualizations—statistical and nonstatistical, the importance of not misrepresenting the visual nature of column charts within an ethical perspective, and the increased use of infographics seen in music videos and art photography.

Chapter Ten: Cartoons is a detailed discussion of one of the most enduring and longest lasting television series, "The Simpsons," from the mind of Matt Groening, the history of cartoons from caricatures scribbled on walls to three-dimensional animated motion pictures, a technical discussion that includes five types of animation production—cel, stop-motion, computer-generated, performance capture, live action/cartoon combinations and virtual.

Chapter Eleven: Photography features the social significance of Dorothea Lange's portrait titled "Migrant Mother" with emphasis on the ethical challenges in the making and distribution of the famous image, a history section that charts the medium's progress from the camera obscura to digital materials, an ethical section that explores the im-

portant issues of using violent images, right to privacy of subjects, and picture manipulations, and a discussion on the significance of the stilled moment.

Chapter Twelve: Motion Pictures discusses what is considered the greatest movie of all time, Citizen Kane, and why it is so admired, a history that took its initial technology from photography and greatly improved upon it, how the industry competed with television through the additions of sound, color, large screens, 3-D projections, and plush seats, and a critical look at the use of stereotypes, the lack of women directors, and the importance of indie productions.

Chapter Thirteen: Television starts with the famous phrase "The tribe has spoken," well-known to fans of Mark Burnett's "Survivor" series, and then moves to a discussion on the genre of reality programs, followed by a historical discussion that starts with the first successful electronic television demonstration and leads to television/web collaborations, and ends with innovations in programs and viewing technologies.

Chapter Fourteen: Computers begins with the work of James Cameron in promoting computer-generated images (CGI) in his critically acclaimed and wildly popular motion pictures, a look at the history of CGI in the movies, a history that begins with a calculator used by ancient Greek astronomers and ends with the successes from the Apple Computer Company, a section on popular, yet violent games, an analyses of the IBM and Apple logos, and a brief description of augmented and virtual reality technologies.

Chapter Fifteen: The Web has an opening discussion that features the lives and work of Sergey Brin and Larry Page, the two graduate students who invented the most popular web search engine in the world, Google, a history of how the internet led to the web, and a section on the importance of the so-called Web 2.0 as it possibly replaces all other media.

Chapter Sixteen: The More You Know, The More You See emphasizes the point that creating designs that use both verbal and visual messages is the best methodology for maximum communicative effectiveness.

Special Features of this Textbook

An informal writing style that explains detailed information in a thorough, yet easily understandable way.

This book includes 739 figures for photographs and illustrations along with weblinks to additional images and videos. Each weblink is accompanied by a graphic symbol alerting you to type the shortened URL provided in the caption into the web browser of your choice. With a total of 191,812 words, each figure is worth 260 words—that seems about right.

Many captions not only identify the image and those responsible for it, but often describe the picture in terms explained in the text.

A glossary at the end contains meaningful definitions of about 200 words and phrases that are introduced in the text.

For the first time, you have the option of purchasing this book as a print or Kindle version from Amazon.com at a drastically reduced price.

Every chapter has been updated and improved with the most relevant and current images obtained from an international pool of photographers for inclusion within these pages.

Finally, with its text, examples, and graphic design, this book exemplifies the best that words and pictures can provide when they combine to tell a compelling and vital story. Wherever you live on this planet and whatever language you choose to use, this book contains a narrative that links each one of us. Visual communication teaches that when messages are respectful, thoughtful, and two-way, they are universal.

Acknowledgements

To all who helped directly to make this edition better and to the rest of you who helped directly to make me better, I offer my heartfelt gratitude and sincere apologies.

Paul Martin Lester
Dallas, Texas

Section 1

The one chapter in this section—the introduction—puts you on a clear path toward your visual communication journey. From an array of five images printed within these pages or available through the provided weblinks one could describe them as everyday, personal, significant, humorous, they all have one aspect in common—they each possess a secret reason for being included in this book. At first glance, their mysterious messages will probably not be fully understood until they are explained at the end of the chapter. That point—the need for words to add definition, refinement, and meaning to images—is an overriding theme in all of the chapters. It is through the careful and respectful combination of words and pictures that lead to what is the ultimate goal of visual literacy as described by the philosopher, author, and teacher, Aldous Huxley. Through analysis of visual messages, a reflective process based on words as thoughts, in print, and/or part of an audio-based presentation, we learn to use our eyes more efficiently, our brain more succinctly, and our minds more completely. Consequently, the process of perceiving the meaning of an image makes us curious, interesting, and ready for more.

1 Visual Communication

A photograph published in the *New York Daily News* in 1963 of construction workers on a building site is almost forgettable except for one redeeming quality—you won't have a clue what's going on in the picture. You could come up with several guesses: Heads bowed for a moment of silence for a fallen comrade, waiting in line for a lunch, or they all have to use the restroom. You would be wrong (Figure 1.1).

An image of an abstract collection of frantic lines and a few shapes that fill the frame on all sides with black, heavy marks is perplexing. You might think a seriously disturbed or perturbed child made the drawing. You would be correct about the age of the artist, but wrong as to her mental state (Figure 1.2).

Consider the painting "A Bar at the Folies Bergère" completed in 1882 by the French master Édouard Manet. The work is a portrait of a young woman bartender

Figure 1.1
Originally published in the New York Daily News *in 1963, these workers are obviously straining for some mysterious reason. If you're a photographer, you may notice clues that others miss.*
***Courtesy of Hal Mathewson and the* New York Daily News**

Figure 1.2
Although seemingly a mish-mash of confusing lines, blobs, and letterforms,
once you know what the child tries to communicate by this drawing, it all makes sense.
Courtesy of Allison Lester

with a mirror behind her reflecting well-dressed patrons and shows her back with a male customer. With a vacant, slightly sad look, she stares into your eyes. This painting helped change the history of art as we know it. But you should be thinking, what's so monumental about this picture? It's simply shows a woman behind a bar. You would be wrong (Figure 1.3).

How about the delightfully engaging Academy Award–winning short animation from British filmmaker Nick Park, *Creature Comforts* (1989)? You might immediately conclude that the film, a brilliant example of the Claymation style

of cartooning that Park spent years making, is concerned with animals that live in a zoo—some like a life of captivity and regulations and others don't. You would be wrong (Figure 1.4).

Finally, a news photograph from one of the most important and far-reaching stories from the first year of the 21st century—the 9/11, 2001 airline attacks on American soil, property, and persons.

The Canadian photojournalist, Lyle Owerko, had just returned from an assignment in Africa, sat in his New York City apartment when he heard the crash from the first airplane hitting one of the Twin Towers. His street-level view was

Figure 1.3
"Un Bar aux Folies Bergère," oil on canvas, 1882, by Édouard Manet. Manet signed his name on the label of the bottle at the left next to a Bass ale, identified by its red, triangular logo. Perhaps there was a tour group from England visiting that evening. The painting was criticized at the time for, among other details, not accurately positioning the bottles reflected in the mirror. Over time, however, the work has become appreciated as one of the most important in the history of the medium.
Courtesy of the Courtauld Institute of Art

W
LINK

Figure 1.4
(Weblink: http://goo.gl/ws8ilu) Aardman Animations and Nick Park produced Creature Comforts *that won an Oscar for Best Animated Film in 1990.*

selected for the cover of the *Time* magazine's special edition. The respectful display has only the name of the magazine at the top and the infamous date carefully located in the space between the two buildings. The cover seems to exemplify the highest form of photojournalism and is an example for the ages of how an art director for a magazine should display important historical images. Nevertheless, the cover was criticized. You might think that some thought it unethical to include a barcode on the cover. You would be wrong (Figure 1.5).

It's hard to imagine how the world has changed since the tragedy of those attacks. One telling effect of those changes has been in visual messages in the me-

Figure 1.5
(Weblink: http://goo.gl/KlgCwg) Lyle Owerko's photograph is a clear example of what the French photojournalist Henri Cartier-Bresson called the "decisive moment" in which composition and content are equally important. The decisions by Time *graphic designers, however, have been criticized.*

dia. Since 9/11 particularly visual news events include:

2001: The U.S. invasion of Afghanistan,

2002: The winter Olympic games held in Salt Lake City, Utah,

2003: The in-flight destruction of the Space Shuttle Columbia, the invasion of Iraq, the fall of Baghdad, and President Bush's "Mission Accomplished" speech on an aircraft carrier,

2004: Janet Jackson's Super Bowl "wardrobe malfunction," the torture of prisoners by U.S. forces in the Abu Ghraib prison captured on soldiers' digital cameras, and the Indian Ocean tsunami that killed almost 300,000 people,

2005: The devastation of Hurricane Katrina (Figure 1.6),

2006: Former President of Iraq Saddam Hussein is executed by hanging,

2007: 32 people killed by a Virginia Tech student,

2008: Cyclone Nargis, which killed more than 100,000 people in Myanmar and the global economic meltdown,

2009: The start of the presidency of Barack Obama, the safe landing of a US Airways flight in the Hudson River in NYC, and the death of Michael Jackson,

2010: An earthquake in Haiti with more than 300,000 deaths, the Eyjafjalla jökull (perhaps pronounced Aya-fi-at-la-yo-gute) volcano eruption, the BP oil spill in the Gulf of Mexico, and Republicans take back the House of Representatives,

2011: The shooting of Representative Gabrielle Giffords with six killed in Tucson, Arizona, the Arab Spring, a Japanese earthquake and tsunami with a radiation leak, deadly tornadoes in the US, and the deaths of Osama bin Laden and Libyan dictator Muammar Gaddafi,

2012: The summer Olympics in London, the election of a president of the

Figure 1.6
Years after Hurricane Katrina struck the gulf coast in 2005 and flooded much of New Orleans many houses within the unique city are still abandoned with yards unkempt and owners desperate to sell.
Courtesy of Paul Martin Lester

United States, and the end of the world on December 21 according to some who follow the pre-Columbian Mayan calendar,

2013: The Boston Marathon bombing and the death of Nelson Mandela,

2014: The conflict in the Ukraine, the thaw of US-Cuba relations, and Robin Williams' death,

2015: *Charlie Hebdo* attack, police shootings, and the Charleston church shooting,

2016: Pulse nightclub shootings in Orlando and Donald Trump elected president, and

2017: President Trump's Administration under investigation by the FBI and several Congressional committees.

These and other stories were mostly told with such powerful images that they were added to our collective memory.

We remember them because of our emotional attachments and because they have been replayed many times on countless news reports. Through repetitive viewing combined with strong mental and emotional associations, over time the images have become permanent in our minds. When you see new images, you make new impressions and comparisons with these previously stored mental pictures. The content of the new and old images constantly bounces back and forth in our minds so that we learn from them. Otherwise, we forget them, as we do most words and pictures that stream across us as we journey through our lives.

Visual communication relies both on eyes that function and on a brain that interprets all the sensory information received. An active, curious mind remembers and uses visual messages in thoughtful and innovative ways. Knowing about the world and the images that it conveys will help you analyze pictures.

And if you can examine pictures critically, you have a good chance of producing high-quality images that others will remember.

All messages, whether verbal or visual, have literal and symbolic components. Many famous and often reproduced images throughout this book have visual messages that are so strong that millions of people who have seen them have memorized them. No doubt, you have seen some of them too. And when you see them again, you will learn something more because you will make new connections in your brain. These images are memorable because they have strong and compelling literal and symbolic messages. You understand what you are looking at (the literal component of a message) and you perceive a deeper, perhaps emotional connection with the message's content (the symbolic component). Consequently, images reproduced in this textbook have helped shape Western culture and how most of us feel about ourselves. Although separate and individual in their intent, content, and medium, all are linked by the inescapable elements common to all visual messages: They are objects that get their life from light (Figure 1.7). That life comes not only from the light of day but also from the light of revelation, the light of understanding, and the light of education.

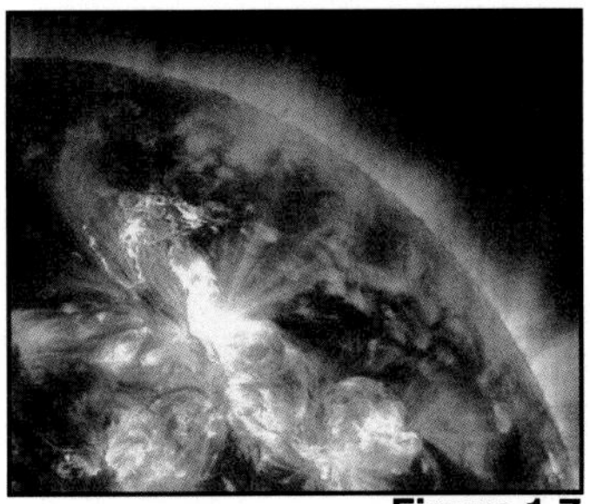

Aldous Huxley, author of the novel *Brave New World* and 46 other books of philosophical and futuristic vision, detailed his efforts to teach himself how to see more clearly in his 1942 work *The Art of Seeing* (Figure 1.8). From the age of 16, Huxley suffered from a degenerative eye condition known as keratitis punctata, an inflammation of the cornea.

One eye was merely capable of light perception and the other could only view an eye chart's largest letter from ten feet away. Today, the condition is rare and attributed most likely to bacterial or a viral infection. It can be treated easily with medications.

In *Seeing*, Huxley described the physical exercises he used to try to

Figure 1.7
Let there be lots of light. In 2012 a massive solar flare from the sun hurled charged particles that made the 93-million-mile journey to Earth in about 34 hours and sparked an aurora borealis light show in Canada and the northern United States.
Courtesy of NASA

Figure 1.8
Aldous Huxley as a young man.
Courtesy of the National Vanguard

overcome his disability without the aid of glasses. However, his main purpose in the book was to convey the idea that seeing clearly is mostly the result of thinking clearly. Huxley summed up his method for achieving clear vision with the formula:

**Sensing plus selecting
plus perceiving equals seeing.**

SENSING

The first stage of clear vision is to sense. To sense simply means letting enough light enter your eyes so that you can see objects immediately around you. Sensing also depends on how well the many parts of the eye work. Obviously, a darkened room and/or damaged or improperly functioning eyes will hamper sensing.

If there is enough light where you are and your eyes are working properly, you will sense light. However, when you are sensing, only your brain is engaged with the outside world—your mind hasn't registered what it is you are sensing. Think of sensing as a camera without a memory card; that is, there is no mental processing of the image during this phase of visual perception.

SELECTING

Huxley's next stage is to select a particular element from a visual array. To select is to focus and look at a specific part of a scene within the enormous frame of possibilities that sensing offers.

That concentration is the result of the combination of the light-gathering and light-focusing properties of the eye with the higher-level functions of the mind. In other words, selecting is a conscious, intellectual act. When you select, you engage more fully the objects in the scene than when you merely look when sensing. Selecting starts the process of classification of objects as harmful, helpful, known, unfamiliar, meaningful, or confusing. To select is to isolate an object within the area where the sharpest

vision takes place in the eye. By selecting individual objects within a scene, you are doing what the eye's physiology is made to do—focus your mental activities on a single area that is isolated from all others.

PERCEIVING

The last stage in Huxley's visual path is the most important—to perceive. That is, you must try to make sense of what you select. If your mind has any chance of storing visual information for long-term retrieval and to increase your knowledge base, you must actively consider the meaning of what you see. To process an image mentally on a higher level of cognition than simply sensing and selecting means that you must concentrate on the subjects within a field of view with the intent of finding meaning and not simply as an act of observation. This process demands much sharper mental activity. Previous experience with specific visual messages is a key in seeing clearly.

Sensing without selecting will often lead to mistakes in perceiving.

The adage "seeing is believing" was first expressed in 1639, and it meant "only physical or concrete evidence is convincing." But the eyes and the mind alike can be easily fooled. Imagine that you are in a car stopped at a traffic light. There's another car stopped in the lane next to you. Although you are staring straight ahead, you notice out of the corner of your eye that there is furious hand motion going on between the two persons in the car next to you. You naturally conclude that the two are having a violent fistfight. Almost afraid to look, you turn your head slightly and look through the open windows and smile at your "aha" moment. The light changes and your attention again is directed to the traffic on the road. The two were simply having an energetic conversation using sign language while waiting for the green light.

Although you can certainly select

Figure 1.9
*(Weblink: http://goo.gl/
DND1S4)
Bloodied and tired and
moments before his death,
replicant Roy Batty played by
Rutger Hauer delivers a moving
speech related to the nature
of visual memory at the end of
Ridley Scott's* Blade Runner.

a particular visual element with little mental processing when it is a new or a surprising occurrence, going to the next level and analyzing a visual message—from an innovative billboard display to two friends talking through the use of their hands—helps ensure that you will find meaning. And if you understand the image, it is likely to become a part of your long-term memory.

Consider for a moment all the visual messages that are a part of your life—a cracked bat given to you by a professional baseball player when you were six-years-old; your fingers on the handlebars during your first bicycle ride; the smile from your favorite teacher during your high school graduation; red blood dripping from a cut on your leg; the sight of a small stream during a quiet walk in the country; a passionate look from a lover. These pictures are all a part of your repertoire of memories.

Images weave themselves into your memory system, sometimes lying dormant for years. You remember and communicate these mental images because they are highly meaningful visual messages.

But think of all the personal visual messages you have experienced but may have forgotten—the billboard advertisements on the outfield wall during the baseball game; where you ended up on your first bicycle ride; the faces of your fellow graduates sitting next to you as you waited for your diploma; the doctor who treated your cut leg; all the colors of the plants as you walked along the trail; the pictures on the wall of your lover's bedroom. Actually, the proportion of remembered to forgotten images is quite small.

One of the most moving soliloquies of any genre of motion picture is at the end of the science fiction movie classic *Blade Runner* (1982) and sums up the fragility of memory. The character played by Rutger Hauer recounts visual memories from his life to Harrison Ford

(Figure 1.9). Hauer starts his speech with, "I've seen things …" and ends with his touching last words when he confesses, "All those moments will be lost in time like tears in rain. Time to die."

Why are a chosen few memories easily recalled whereas a vast array of ambiguous memories is lost?

To answer that question you must know how the brain works. The brain processes three types of visual messages: mental—those that you experience from inside your mind such as thoughts, dreams, and fantasies; direct—those that you see without media intervention; and mediated—those that you see through some type of print (paper) or screen (movie, television, or web) medium.

What you experience and what you remember are products of a mind that actively thinks, with images and words, the mental, direct, and/or mediated visual messages you imagine or experience in your life.

One reason dreams are so often forgotten is that the mental images are not translated into words. You will not remember much through visual messages alone. Memory happens when you think about pictures using words and images. If you immediately tell a friend or write down a dream, you have a better chance of remembering it. That's why a textbook about visual communication takes so many words.

BACK TO THE BEGINNING IMAGES

If you knew something about construction sites and the building techniques that were employed during the 1960s, you might have instantly known what the serious-looking men were doing in the photograph that starts this textbook. But there are other clues as well.

Their sad, downturned faces clearly indicate they are not happy. In fact, they are all struggling. What are they struggling with? Look at their shoulders and their arms. Something is causing their limbs to be pulled down by the extreme weight they all hold. But a lunch plate couldn't possibly be heavy enough to cause such discomfort. If you have photographic experience, there are clues in the picture that only a photographer might notice. For one, a flash bulb was used to take the picture. The shadow of the face of the third man from the right can be seen on the back of the man next to him. The flash's light is at an extreme angle—way off to the left of the frame. Another photographic clue is on the man's head second from the right. See the discoloration of his hair and ear? Two other clues of note: There is a white, vertical line between the third and fourth men from the right, and the man on the upper level in the middle—can you imagine what he is doing?

If you are still stumped, the words that accompanied the picture will explain it all. The caption read, "JOB IS REALLY A PANE. Workmen seem to be faking it for benefit of foreman as they strain under weight of invisible load at 42d St., near Third Ave. They're holding handles of suction cups gripped to huge section of plate glass which was installed in store." The glass appears transparent because the flash is off to the side. The light illuminates the scene but doesn't reflect back into the lens (try to make a portrait of yourself by using a flash with your camera and pointing it straight at a mirror). The slight discoloration on the man's head is a reflection from another light source (probably the sun) on the glass, the vertical line is from the glass pane itself, and the man in the middle is guiding the piece into place.

The child's drawing was made by the author's daughter Allison when she was four years old. She was given a white sheet of typing paper, a thick black marker, and an assignment to draw the story of one of her favorite songs.

The picture contains elements that are meant to be letters and others meant to be images. But since she hadn't yet learned how to write or the icons for simple pictures, the letters and forms seem to merge and are confusing. You might guess the song if you can imagine what the two major dark areas in the frame—top-center and bottom-center—might be and what all the squiggly lines might mean. The popular song is mostly known as "The Itsy Bitsy Spider."

The words are thought to have been first published in a 1910 book, *Camp and Camino in Lower California*, by Arthur Walbridge North. In an account of his travels through the California peninsula and Mexico, North described writing down the words of two pioneer girls he met along the way:

Oh, the blooming, bloody spider went up the water spout,
The blooming, bloody rain came down and washed the spider out,
The blooming, bloody sun came out and dried up all the rain,
And the blooming, bloody spider came up the spout again.

Despite all that blood, the song can be thought of as an optimistic message of hope despite impossible odds. Admittedly, Allison learned a slightly different version, but you get the point. Still, her drawing looks strange. Luckily, she interpreted the elements for us: The little symbol at the top-left corner means that this work is a song, the blob of black near the center is the sun, the blob toward the bottom is the spider and its web, the marks that look like letters contains the message, "Don't get too close to a spider or he might bite you," the seemingly random marks throughout the page designate rain, and the letters in a row at the bottom-right that start with what looks like an "A" is her attempt to write her name. If this assignment were given to you, chances are you would divide the story of the song into separate sections and tell it in narrative form as if seen in a comic book. But Allison, because she didn't know any better, relayed the entire song all in one go. Five years later she repeated the assignment. Sure enough, she had learned the images for a spider, its web, and the sun, with the parts of the song divided by clear borders. She also greatly improved upon her signature (Figure 1.10).

Seven years before the invention of photography was made public, the painter Édouard Manet was born in Paris. By the time he was an adult, artists throughout his country and the world were scared that their profession's days were numbered. Why would anyone pay

this renaissance was the painting of a bored barmaid by Manet.

Take a look at the painting again. It seems straightforward enough, right? A young woman stands behind a marble counter with bottles of alcohol for sale while she, a gentleman customer, and the expansive and raucous Folies Bergère are reflected in the mirror behind her. Look closely. From the mirror's reflection behind her, can you see all the chandeliers and other electric lights, the smoke in the air, the men in the crowd wearing top hats, the woman catching a view with her opera glasses, the woman with long,

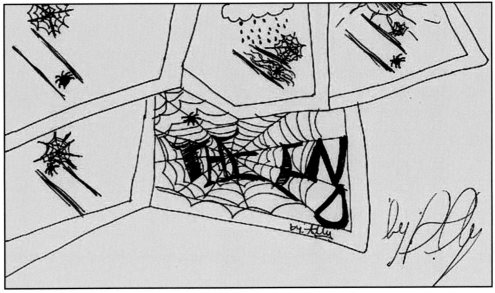

Figure 1.10
The same child who at four-years-old made the drawing of the "The Itsy Bitsy Spider" song in Figure 1.2 repeats the exercise at age nine. But since she learned to read English and became familiar with comic books, the narrative takes place within a storyboard composed of five panels separated by thick borders that are meant to be read left-to-right and top-to-bottom. With less background noise than before, the panels include easily identifiable images of the spider, rain cloud, sun, and cobweb. To solidify the link to motion pictures, the last panel shows a screen filled with the spider resting on its web and an elaborate "The End."
Courtesy of Allison Lester

for a sitting or even buy a painting when the camera recorded exact replicas of people, things, and places at a fraction of the cost? Summing up the artists' frustration was the phrase, "From today, painting is dead!" But of course, painting did not die after photography became popular. In fact, it can be said that painting and its practitioners were reborn and flourished because of photography. One of the chief reasons cited by art critics and others for

yellow gloves distracted by something beside her, and the green stockings of the trapeze artist? Now study the young woman. Notice her golden bracelet, the flowers in her bodice, the jewel-encrusted necklace, her earrings, her bright yellow bangs, and her gaze. She's looking right at you as you stand before her and she awaits your order. Still think all is ordinary in the painting? Wait a minute. The reflection of you and the barmaid should be directly behind her, and yet the image is off to one side showing the backside of the woman and the face that isn't you (of course), but a tall man with a mustache, top hat, and holding a cane.

Manet changed painting by showing through this example that the art world could move away from strict realism. In this work he portrayed a concept that is about as abstract as it gets—two moments in time. In one view he showed the life of a sad, young, bright-blonde barmaid as she thinks about being trapped in a job that she will have until her hair turns gray and her body becomes plump as a much older woman. Her future is depicted in the mirror's view. Manet helped accomplish the transition from realism to a new art form that came to be known as Impressionism. Manet's "Folies Bergère" was his last great work of art and is a key in the transition between the literal and the symbolic as expressed on canvas.

Four-time Academy Award–winning animator Nick Park was born in a small town in northwestern England. As a young boy he was interested in drawing cartoons and making short, experimental movies. After college he worked for a time at a small animation studio, Aardman Animations. His first professional work was for the musician Peter Gabriel's music video for "Sledgehammer," a number one hit in several countries in 1986. Three and a half minutes into the film, you can see headless, dancing chickens brought to life by Park. He became known early on as a master of the stop-motion animation technique using Plasticine, a pliable clay product that brings three-dimensional depth to animated characters. In 1989 he and his fellow staffers completed the five-minute film *Creature Comforts* that won him and his company its first Academy Award.

All forms of animation require a great deal of patience, but manipulating clay figures frame by frame (24 frames usually make up one second of film) requires particular dedication. For *Comfort*, Park worked on and off for about four years. In the motion picture a human reporter (early on you see a hand holding a microphone) conducts a series of interviews with various animals living in the London Zoo at Regent's Park—the oldest in the world, established in 1828 and opened to the public in 1847 (Figure 1.11). The animals have varying opinions about their quality of life. Those that like their life in the zoo include a polar bear male with his two sons, an aardvark, a glasses-wearing koala, and a chicken who makes a point how animals in the circus have to perform. However, a young hippopotamus, a tortoise, a lemur mother with too many children in her tight quarters, a female gorilla who counts the days by making marks on the wall, and a disgruntled jaguar who complains about the lack of space and fresh meat (a microphone attached to a long pole is used for his segment) complain about their environment. The literal message is readily apparent—if animals could talk, you would find out that some like living in a zoo and some don't. Four years' work and an Academy Award to make that obvious point? No.

Andrew, the younger polar bear, gives the point of Park's film away with his first line, "Oh well, the zoos are very important to animals. They're a bit like homes—like nursing homes for poor animals and people like old people."

Most of the dialogue came from interviews Park and his assistants made with persons who lived in housing projects and retirement homes. The short animation is not about zoos at all. It's a commentary on institutional living arrangements—rest homes, prisons, school dorms, military housing, and a parent's or guardian's home. The conclusion that can be made by the movie is that a person living under such regulated conditions should have their individual

Figure 1.11
(Weblink: http://goo.gl/jZ5sQi) Nick Park's patient and tedious technique necessary with stop-motion animation characters created in clay creates a three-dimensional, realistic effect that is difficult to achieve with other forms of animation (See Chapter 10).

needs respected. That's why the film won an Academy Award.

Time's special edition was similar to other magazine covers immediately after 9/11. *People, US News & World Report, Newsweek*, and others featured a single photograph that dramatically showed the inconceivable confluence of fire and smoke after an airplane going full speed smashed into a skyscraper. With such a picture, few words were needed to help clarify the unexplainable. Look in the background of the *Time* cover. There is a hint of how beautiful September 11, 2001 was in New York City as a cloudless blue sky can be seen. In contrast to that tranquility is a fireball surrounded by smoke and a cascading shower of building debris. And yet, you would think that the distracting barcode, a pattern meant to be read by a laser scanner that gives pricing information and other details, could have been placed on the back cover's advertisement just this once.

Perhaps an example of poor etiquette, but it wasn't the barcode that upset media critics and historians. This important photograph was altered to exploit the visual cue of depth for purely commercial reasons.

The background sky behind the stricken tower was removed with a software program so the building could be placed in front of the Time name. The three-dimensional effect is popular with editors for their covers because it can catch a customer's eyes browsing near a bookstore's crowded magazine rack. However, to manipulate a photograph, particularly one with such historical and long-term value for a purely commercial reason, is the height of unethical behavior.

The greatest aid to clear seeing isn't eyes that function with or without glasses or a telescope that brings into sharp focus the craters of the moon. The process of sensing, selecting, and perceiving takes a curious, questioning, and knowledgeable mind. The goal of a visual communicator isn't simply to have an image published or broadcast.

The goal should be to produce powerful pictures so that the viewer will remember their content. Images have little use if a viewer's mind doesn't use them.

As future image consumers and producers, you will want to see images that you remember and make images that will educate others.

The goal of this book is to give you a method for analyzing visual messages regardless of the medium of presentation. Without systematically analyzing an image, you may sense it and not notice the individual elements within the frame. You might not consider its content as it relates to a story. Without considering the image, you will not gain any understanding or personal insights. The picture will simply be another in a long line of forgotten images.

In *The Art of Seeing* Huxley wrote a phrase that sums up visual communication:

The more you know, the more you see.

A former baseball player watches and sees a game much more attentively than someone who is at her first game. The newcomer probably will miss signals from a manager, scoreboard details, the curve of the ball's flight as it speeds from pitcher to batter, and many other details observed by the former player. But the process is more than simply knowing and seeing.

The interim steps between knowing and seeing can be thought of as the visual communication circle dance: The more you know, the more your eyes and brain will sense. The more you sense, the more your mind will select. The more you select, the more you will understand or perceive what you are seeing. The more you perceive, the more you remember, as the images become a part of your long-term memory. The more you remember, the more you learn because you compare new images with those stored in your mind. The more you learn, the more you know. And the more you know, the more you will sense, which starts the circle spinning around again. For clear seeing and knowing, this circle is in constant motion (Figure 1.12).

Analyzing visual messages makes you take a long, careful look at the pictures you see—a highly satisfying intellectual act. Those images become a part of your general knowledge of the world. You discover how images are linked in ways that you never thought of before. You also become a more interesting, curious person. Such is the goal of visual literacy—to sense, to select, yes, but more importantly, to perceive.

KEY TERMS FROM THIS CHAPTER
Abstract • Impressionism • Literal • Long-term memory • News photograph • Realism • Symbolic • Western culture

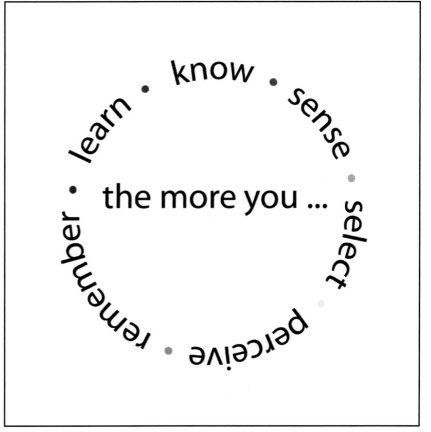

Figure 1.12
As the circle shape implies, the Aldous Huxley's method for clear seeing spins as the more you sense, the more you will come to know.
Courtesy of Paul Martin Lester

Section 1

The five chapters in this section—visual cues, theories, persuasion, stereotypes, and analysis—all make the point expressed by Aldous Huxley that it is the mind—not the eyes—that understands visual messages. Toward that end, we are programmed to notice the four visual cues and how they are employed in print and screen media to attract our attention so that we may learn from pictures. Visual communication theories further refine our understanding of why some pictures are remembered but most are forgotten. And because these visual messages can stimulate both intellectual and emotional responses, they are powerful tools that persuade people to buy a particular product, think a specific way, or learn from a detailed story. A creator of images also has an ethical responsibility to ensure that a picture is a fair, accurate, and complete representation of someone from another culture. Finally, if you don't engage intellectually with a visual message, there is little chance of understanding its meaning and purpose. Consequently, a 15-step methodology for studying any image—still or moving—is included that should change an emotional, short-term, and subjective opinion about a picture into a rational, long-term, and objective response.

2 Visual Cues

In the midst of movement and chaos, keep stillness inside of you.

Deepak Chopra, 1946–
AUTHOR, PHILOSOPHER,
& PHYSICIAN

It sounds like a horrible idea. Put the head of a slightly anesthetized cat into a vice so that it is forced to watch a simple slide show while you poke the back of its brain with a microelectrode.

That scene was not a horror movie plot that would give a member of PETA (People for the Ethical Treatment of Animals) nightmares. Two scientists won a Nobel Prize for that experiment in 1981.

The work of Canadian David Hubel and Swede Torsten Wiesel of the Johns Hopkins University in Baltimore provided clues to how the brain sees images provided by our eyes. The two jabbed a microelectrode into a brain cell in the visual cortex at the back of the brain of an anesthetized cat and connected it to both an amplifier that converted electrical energy to a "put-put" sound and an oscilloscope that turned signals to a blip on a screen so they could measure the response (Figure 2.1).

With the cat's eyes open and focused toward a screen, the scientists flashed simple straight and slanted light patterns. With their set-up, Hubel and Wiesel could see and hear immediately the effect of any nerve cell stimulation by the patterns of light. After they flashed the light on the screen several times and adjusted their equipment, the scientists recorded what they had thought was possible: the stimulated activity of a single brain cell responsible for vision.

The visual cortex is composed of several thin layers of nerve tissue. By this tedious and perhaps ethically disturbing method of placing microelectrodes in various cells within each layer of a cat's brain, Hubel and Wiesel found that some cells responded to a spot of light while others noted the edges of objects, certain angles of lines, specific movements, specific colors, or the space between

Figure 2.1
David Hubel (left) and Torsten Wiesel (combination print) shared a Nobel Prize for attaching a tiny electrode to a cat's visual cortex and identifying the types of brain cells responsible for sight.
Courtesy of the Nobel Prize Organization

lines rather than the lines themselves. In short, each brain cell in the cortex reacts almost in a one-to-one relationship with the type of visual stimulation it receives. From all this information, the brain constructs a map of the outside world, which is projected upside-down on our retinas.

More importantly for visual communicators, it was eventually discovered by other researchers that the brain, through its vast array of specialized cells, most quickly and easily responds to four major attributes of all viewed objects: color, form, depth, and movement. These four visual cues are the major concerns of any visual communicator when designing an image to be remembered by a viewer because they are noticed before a person even realizes what they are. The four visual cues, therefore, are what the brain sees, not the mind. Consequently, the four cues can be used to attract attention to a presentation, whether in print or on a screen.

COLOR

Throughout human history, people have been fascinated by light. Civilizations prayed and celebrated at each new sunrise and invented gods that ruled the sun. Religious leaders equate light with life, and most religions begin with its creation (Figure 2.2). When the light from fire was discovered, probably by accident through a lightning strike, most were awed by its power. Literary references and colloquial expressions about light and vision abound because of the importance placed on seeing. When we want to learn the truth, we say, "Bring light on the subject." After a revelation of some truth, we have "seen the light." If we are concerned that we are not getting the full story, we complain, "Don't keep me in the dark." Performers such

Figure 2.2
Located in Istanbul, Turkey, the Sultan Ahmed Mosque completed in 1616 is also known as the "Blue Mosque" for the tiles that cover its walls. The windows that ring its dome not only help illuminate the vast interior, but also convey religious meaning.
Courtesy of Paul Martin Lester

as Daft Punk and Radiohead, among others, know the power of light to attract attention so they produce expensive light shows to accompany their concert performances (Figure 2.3). Light can intrigue, educate, and entertain, but nowhere is light so exquisitely expressed as through color.

Various philosophers, scientists, and physicians throughout recorded history have attempted to explain the nature of color. Aristotle reasoned correctly that light and color were different names for the same visual phenomenon. Much later, Leonardo da Vinci proposed that there were six primary colors—white, black, red, yellow, green, and blue. He came to that conclusion simply by reasoning that the six colors were wholly independent and unique. Da Vinci showed that by mixing these six colors

in the form of paints in varying degrees, all the other colors capable of being seen by a normal human eye could be created. His interest in and theories on the mixing of colors came directly from his experience as one of the great masters of painting. Although all the colors desired by painters can be made by mixing those six color pigments together in varying degrees, this property of paints doesn't explain how light is mixed.

Thomas Young, a British physician and scientist, was the first to link color and the human eye. In 1801 he suggested that nerve fibers in the retina respond to the colors red, green, and violet. Twenty years later, the great German physiologist and physicist Hermann von Helmholtz was born. In 1851 he invented the ophthalmoscope, which enabled doctors to see inside a person's eye. In

Figure 2.3
With traditional and laser stage lighting effects, this set-up is not typical for a classical music concert. The Classical Spectacular in the Rod Laver Arena, Melbourne, 2005.
Courtesy of Fir0002/ Flagstaffotos

1867 he published his greatest work, a handbook on optics, in which he refined Young's ideas on how humans see color. Their combined work became known as the Young-Helmholtz theory, or the tri-chromatic theory, and explained how the eye physically sees color. Their theory became a fact in 1959 after their idea was experimentally proven. Sir John Herschel, the scientist who invented the word "photography," praised Young as a "truly original genius." The immortal physicist Albert Einstein had kind works for von Helmholtz as well when he remarked, "I admire ever more the original, free thinker Helmholtz" (Figure 2.4).

Every color we see can be made with three basic, primary colors—red, green, and blue. When these colors are mixed, it is called additive color. Equal amounts of these colored lights will add together to produce white light. The additive mixing of colors is the basis for color we

see from our eyes and in photography, television and computer monitors, and stage lighting.

Some students get confused because they are taught that the primary colors are magenta, yellow, and cyan. But those colors are the primaries used for paint pigments and printing presses—not light. When paints are mixed together, the colors in the paint absorb every color except the wavelength that we see reflected back. This method of color mixing is called subtractive color because as they are mixed they become darker. Subtractive color is used in offset printing, in which four colors are used to create color photographs and illustrations on paper—magenta, yellow, cyan, and for added definition, black (Figures 2.5 and 2.6).

Three different methods can be used to describe color: objective, comparative, and subjective. The objective method

Figure 2.4
Hermann von Helmholtz's statue in front of Humboldt University in Berlin.
Courtesy of Christian Wolf

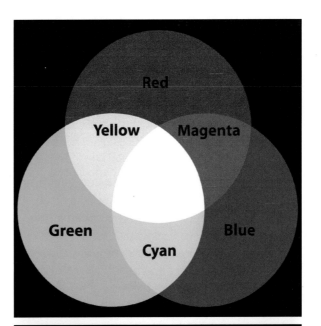

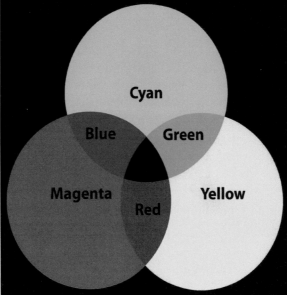

Figures 2.5 & 2.6
These simple graphs illustrate the primary (red, green, and blue) and secondary (magenta, yellow, and cyan) colors.
Courtesy of Paul Martin Lester

for describing colors depends on known standards of measurement. The comparative and subjective methods rely on the evaluation of the person who sees the color.

Objective Method The objective, or scientific, method for describing colors rests on the assumption that the perception of color is a result of various light wavelengths stimulating the cones along the back of the eyes' retinas. A color can be accurately measured by the location of its wavelength on the electromagnetic spectrum. The length of an energy wave is measured in parts per millimeter. The wavelength of the visible light spectrum is 300 nanometers wide. That's about one one-hundredth of an inch. Blue shows up on the visible spectrum at about 430 nanometers, green has a wavelength that starts at about 530 nanometers, and red has a wavelength beginning at 560 nanometers.

The objective method can also be used to measure a color's unique temperature that distinguishes it from every other color. The color red, for example, is about 1,000°K, and a deep blue color is a much hotter 60,000°K. Sunlight at noon, depending on the time of year, is between 4,900° and 5,800°K. The next time you look at logs burning in a fireplace, note the various colors produced. Yellow and red colors are cooler on the temperature scale than green or blue colors.

Because of its long wavelength and quick recognition by the eye, red is used for signal lights, stop signs, and other warning or attention- getting purposes. There are two reasons that the eye notices red more easily—one has to do with the length of the color's wavelength, and the other with the physiology of the eye. Since red has a longer wavelength, it is noticed from farther away and stays inside a person's eyes longer than any of the other visible colors. Plus, the slightly yellow-colored cornea protects the eye from harmful ultraviolet rays and also absorbs the shorter wavelength colors of blue and green, letting the longer wavelengths of red pass through to the retina easier.

Comparative Method The second technique for describing colors is less accurate than the objective method, but more useful. As with a dictionary definition, the color red might be compared to the color of blood, green with healthy plants, and blue with the sky on a clear, sunny day. But one person's conception of the color red isn't always the same as someone else's. Blood red is dark, but the red of poinsettia plant leaves and traffic lights are slightly different. For the comparative method to be of use, the color that another color is compared with must be accepted universally as a standard. A problem arises when the word for a color is not understood. Paints used for canvases, house walls, and automobiles are sometimes hard to compare if you are unfamiliar with their names. Automobile paint from the Dulux company used for Volkswagen cars from 1954 to 1982 could come in 28 shades of blue—andorra, bahai, bahama, baltic, belgrave, commercial, diamond, flipper, gemini, gulf, horizon, lavender, miami, mountain, neptune, ocean, pacific, pastel, pigeon, regatta, sea, seeblau, slate, space, strato, summer, tasman, and zenith. It should be clear that the

comparative method could only be used to give a rough estimate of what a color might look like.

Subjective Method This third technique for describing color is the most symbolic. A person's mental state or association with an object strongly affects the emotional response to a color. In their drawings, children tend to prefer abstract colors to shapes and lines. Girls generally use more intense colors than boys in their early picture-making. Educational psychologists consider such use of color to indicate enjoyment of social interactions and possession of higher reasoning abilities. Painters have known for years that the warm colors—reds and yellows—appear closer than the cooler colors—blues and greens. The terms *warm* and *cool* are psychological distinctions and are not related to the actual temperature of the color. Lighter colors tend to be viewed as soft and cheerful, and darker colors have a harsh or moody emotional quality about them. A room painted a light color will appear larger than the same room painted a dark color. Colors or hues that are tinted (made lighter) tend to recede, whereas shaded (made darker) colors advance toward the viewer, making the room look smaller. Because people associate colors with objects and events, this visual attribute is highly subjective and emotional.

We tend to associate a memorable experience, whether pleasant or bad, with the colors of the objects that constitute the event. Do you relate it to a specific object? Most people never associate color with a formless blob, but with a definite object. For that reason, memory of an object affects the perception of its color.

For green, the color symbolizes fertility, youth, nature, money, jealousy, and hope. In 1434 the painter Jan Van Eyck painted, "The Arnolfini Portrait." A woman wears a green dress and looks pregnant by her pose (Figure 2.7).

Figure 2.7
"The Arnolfini Portrait," oil on oak panel, 1434 by Jan van Eyck. The Dutch artist Jan van Eyck's painting is a seemingly simple portrait of a man with his wife, and yet it is considered to be one of the most complex in Western art. The image is actually a memorial. It shows Giovanni di Nicolao Arnolfini and his first wife Costanza Trenta who had died the year before. With its use of natural, realistic lighting, a perspective probably achieved from the use of a camera obscura visual aid to create an illusion of depth, and numerous objects displayed throughout the work that have symbolic meanings, the work is a favorite of art history students. Although it is often mistakenly thought that the woman is pregnant, it was fashionable at the time for dresses to make their wearers appear to be with child. In the 15th century, the color green symbolized hope— in this case, hope that the couple would have a child by the green dress she wears. But as signified by the one lit candle in the chandelier on his side and the burned out candle on hers, their hope was dashed when she died.
Courtesy of the National Gallery, London

The puppet Kermit was a logical choice as the spokesfrog for Ford's line of hybrid cars. Green is a favorite color of those who are outgoing and have large appetites. Emerald green connotes versatility and ingenuity, whereas a grayish green signifies deceitful behavior. Green stones worn around the neck were thought to promote fertility. Green also is believed to have a calming effect. Many backstage waiting rooms in theaters are called "greenrooms" because of the color of their painted walls.

Another artist, the New York born Edward Hopper became a leader in the realist style of oil painting. A tall, shy, introspective person, Hopper often captured lonely people who were unable or unwilling to communicate with each other. His use of lighting and colors often gave an eerie, otherworldly spookiness to his works such as "Early Sunday Morning," "Chop Suey," "New York Movie," "Hotel Room," and his masterpiece, "Nighthawks" (Figure 2.8).

Graphic designers in print and screen media know the power of color to attract attention. Logo and poster designers are careful about their use of color. They must consider not only the possible symbolic meanings of color, but also how color should be used to make a logo memorable and prominent in a crowded media market. Two colors that are distinct but not too similar should be used (Figure 2.9). A website that uses too many colors that are too bright runs the risk of looking amateurish. Care should also be taken in choosing colored copy and backgrounds so that persons with low vision or color deficiencies can read the words. Since green and red colors are sometimes hard to see, a designer should avoid highlighting text in those colors. Many times newspapers that must compete with other publications on a newsstand's rack for a reader's eyes often display red banners and photographs with the color prominently displayed.

Figure 2.8
"Soir Bleu," oil on canvas, 1914 by Edward Hopper. When the American Edward Hopper was 32-years-old he painted this Parisian scene: A sex worker with heavy makeup surveys possible prospects while her pimp sits alone, his eyes focused on another view. During this blue evening lit by oriental lanterns, she considers the strange trio of a bearded Vincent van Gogh look-alike in a beret, a military officer, and a "classically attired" clown in white, while an upper-class couple enjoys a late-night drink. Hopper's use of color is an "early attempt to create, rather than merely record, a sophisticated, anti-sentimental allegory of adult city life" that he duplicated later in "Nighthawks" (1942).
Courtesy of the Whitney Museum of American Art

Figure 2.9
A poster created by graphic designer Crystal Adams announces a design competition. Overlapping silhouettes of common household objects are set large and in the center of the poster, with a subtle gradated color scheme over a black background, for maximum viewer effect.
Courtesy of Crystal Adams

The use of color on the front page of a newspaper can be controversial. In 1984, the worst mass murder in the history of America up to that time occurred when a gunman opened fire and killed 22 and wounded 19 at a McDonald's restaurant outside San Diego. The front page of *The Tribune* showed a ghastly pair of color photographs. In one, blood streams down the leg of a young victim sitting on an ambulance, and the other has a yellow "Golden Arches" logo and arrow pointing to rescue workers trying to save the life of a boy on the ground. Readers wrote letters and made phone calls to the editor of the San Diego newspaper complaining about the gruesome nature of the images. If the pictures had been printed in black and white, it is doubtful readers would have complained (Figure 2.10).

Color in the hands of an inspired movie director should be studied. British director Sir Ridley Scott's science fiction classic *Blade Runner* (1982) was one of many standout directorial achievements in his career, alongside *Alien* (1979), *Thelma & Louise* (1991), and *Gladiator* (2000), which won a Best Picture Academy Award. Two scenes from *Blade Runner* show why it earned two Oscar nominations for best art direction and visual effects. The scenes are similar in content—they both show a character taking a type of lie detector test that determines whether or not the subject is a robot, called a "replicant" in the film. In the first scene, the two characters don't like each other much. In fact, at the end of the scene, one of them is murdered. To show the animosity they feel for each other, the set is filled with a cold, blue, unemotional light. The other scene shows two characters meeting for the first time. They will later fall in love. The set for this one is bathed in a warm, golden color indicating their love interest.

Color is a highly subjective and powerful means of communicating ideas.

W LINK

Figure 2.10
(Weblink: http://goo.gl/pEcjOk)
In San Ysidro, California, a mass murder at a McDonald's restaurant on July 18, 1984, resulted in 22 deaths with 19 injured. Part of the horror of these front-page images comes from the added information supplied by color. The brightly colored and usually benign McDonald's "golden arches" and entrance sign points to an emergency worker struggling to the save the life of a young victim.

James Maxwell, the Scotsman who gave the electromagnetic spectrum its name and invented color photography in 1861, once wrote that the "science of color must be regarded essentially as a mental science" (Figure 2.11).

FORM

The brain responds to another common attribute of images, which is the recognition of three types of forms: dots, lines, and shapes.

Dots The dot is the simplest form that can be written with a stylus. A dot anywhere within a framed space demands immediate attention. In the center, it becomes the hub of visual interest. If off to one side, it creates tension since the layout appears out of balance. Two dots within a framed space also create tension, since the viewer is forced to divide attention between the two forms. When three or more dots appear in an image, the viewer naturally tries to connect them with an imaginary line. It may be a straight or curved line, or it may take the basic shape of a square, triangle, or circle.

Hundreds of small dots grouped together can form complex pictures (Figure 2.12). Georges Seurat in the 19th century used a technique called pointillism in which he peppered his paintings with small colored dots that combined in the viewer's mind to form an image. His most famous work, "Un dimanche aprè-midi à l'Île de la Grande Jatte"

Figure 2.11
Although a black and white photograph conveys a documentary feel, the same picture in color communicates important visual information including the colors on the scoreboard, the green of the grass, and the pink of the cotton candy.
Courtesy of xtine burrough

Figure 2.12
"Bottle House, Rhyolite, Nevada," 2002, by Gerry Davey. The thousands of beer, whiskey, soda, and medicine bottles that create a pattern of circles—besides being a relatively inexpensive alternative to lumber—provide a visually pleasing aesthetic and has been an eye-catching photographic subject since this house was built in 1906.
Courtesy of Gerry Davey

(1884-1886), is an invigorating concert of colored dots. If a security guard at the Chicago Institute of Art lets you get a few inches from the canvas, you can appreciate the technique involved, but you won't be able to tell the work's subject. But if you view this work from 20 feet away, you see a scene of pleasant relaxation on a sunny day (Figure 2.13). Seattle-based photographer Chris Jordan produced a variation of Seurat's painting in which the surprising "points" that compose the image are revealed upon a close-up view. In "Cans Seurat," instead of dots of paint, Jordan used photographs of 106,000 tiny soda cans—"the number used in the U.S. every thirty seconds" (Figure 2.14).

Lines When dots of the same size are drawn so closely together that there is no space between them, the result is a line. According to anthropologist Evelyn Hatcher, straight lines convey a message of stiffness and rigidity, and they can be horizontal, vertical, or diagonal. Horizontal lines, especially when low in the frame, remind viewers of a horizon with plenty of room to grow (Figure 2.15). If the horizontal line is high in the frame, the viewer feels confined, as the layout seems heavy. Vertical lines bring the eye of the viewer to a halt in a layout. The eye attempts to travel around the space created by the line. Diagonal lines have a strong, stimulating effect in a field of view. The most restful diagonal line is one that extends from one corner to its diagonal opposite. It is a perfect compromise between horizontal and vertical forces. Any other diagonal line strongly moves the eye of the viewer in the line's direction. Several diagonal lines within a composition create a nervous dynamic energy. Curved lines convey a mood of playfulness, suppleness, and movement. Curves have a gracefulness about them that softens the content of their active message (Figure 2.16). If lines are thick and dark, the message is strong and confident. If lines are thin and light with a clear separation between them, the mood is delicate, perhaps a bit timid.

Grouped lines form blank spaces that the eyes naturally want to inspect. When drawn as part of an object, they combine to simulate the sensation of touch. The lines that form the surface of an object may be part of an illustration or part of the natural lighting where the object is located. A rough surface has several small curved lines that make up its bumpy exterior. A smooth surface has few lines that mark its coating. Texture stimulates the visual sense by the image itself and the tactile sense through memory. For example, previous experience with the sharp points of the needles of a cactus transfers to a picture of the plant.

Lines can be controversial when a graphic artist or photographer uses a Photoshop tool to stretch the legs of models to make them appear thinner and perhaps more attractive. Lines can also be powerful tools in conveying complex messages.

Commercials for AT&T's wireless network service cleverly repeat its logo, which comprises rising vertical lines. In "Sweet Pea," with music by Amos Lee, the logo can be seen as palm trees, buildings, newspapers, bread sticks, and playground equipment (Figure 2.17). Likewise, a public service announcement (PSA) for the Peace Corps starts with a hand's life line and continues the theme of a horizontal journey in its "Life is Calling" commercial narrated by Matthew McConaughey (Figure 2.18).

Shapes The third type of form, shapes, is the combination of dots and lines into patterns that occur throughout nature and in graphic design. Shapes are figures that sit on the plane of a visual field without depth and define the outside edges of objects. They can be as simple as a beach ball and as complex as the side of a person's face. A shape that is quickly recognized is clearly separated from

Figure 2.13
"Un Dimanche après-midià l'Île de la Grande Jatte," 1884–1886, by Georges-Pierre Seurat. The 19th century French pointillist constructed his paintings by using a series of dots and only twelve separate colors, never mixing one color with another. This tedious, mathematically based painting technique found few advocates because the style lacked spontaneity. Nevertheless, this Sunday Parisian scene, his most famous work, can be appreciated on a technical level when the thousands of tiny dots are clearly discerned from a close up view while its sunny optimism is communicated by its inherent vibrancy viewed from a few yards back.
Courtesy of the Art Institute of Chicago

Figure 2.14
"Cans Seurat," 2007, by Chris Jordan. Viewed from far away, the photograph seems like a faithful reproduction of Seurat's famous painting. However, as you get closer to the work, the "dots" are revealed for what they are—soda pop cans. According to Jordan, the photograph contains "106,000 aluminum cans, the number consumed in the United States every 30 seconds." For Seurat, taking a faraway view of the work reveals the subject of his paintings. Jordan's photographs require the opposite focus—you need to put your eyes right up to them to understand the point.
Courtesy of Chris Jordan

Figure 2.15
The world is an optimistic place when a patron of a cruise ship from the Bahamas notices the low horizon line of the ocean under a sunny day.
Courtesy of Paul Martin Lester

Figure 2.16
Conceived by Danish architect Jørn Utzon and completed in 1973, the spherical rooflines and sail-like vaults of the Sydney Opera House constitute one of the most famous curved shapes in the world.
Courtesy of Paul Martin Lester

Figure 2.17
(Weblink: http://goo.gl/q3iSs1)
The joy of watching this commercial is enhanced by the clever ways the vertical bar motif is incorporated into the backgrounds of the scenes.

Figure 2.18
(Weblink: http://goo.gl/MqBP30)
Except for one scene, the graphic narrative of a life's journey is communicated by a variety of horizontal lines.

the background of the image. The three basic shapes are parallelograms, circles, and triangles. From these three shapes, variations that make all known or imagined forms can be created. The name of a form created by a combination of shapes is polygon. As with all visual attributes, cultural meaning is assigned to each shape. In 1987 American animator Bill Plympton was nominated for an Academy Award for his short cartoon, *Your Face.* In its short time frame, Plympton shows how a creative and talented mind can make variations on the shapes that combine to form a human face. In 2005 he collaborated with Kanye West on a music video of the song "Heard 'Em Say." Four years later Plympton drew illustrations for 12 of West's songs for the book *Through the Wire.*

Parallelograms The parallelogram is a four-sided figure with opposite sides that are parallel and equal in length. The two major types of parallelograms are squares and rectangles. "Be there or be square" is often a challenge given by those organizing a party. In Western culture, a *square* is defined as an unsophisticated or dull person. Similarly, a square shape, with its formally balanced, symmetrical orientation, is the dullest and conventional shape (Figure 2.19). But strength also comes from its plain appearance. A square is considered sturdy and straightforward. In language, the equivalents are a *square deal* or a *square shooter.* The implication from the phrases is that the business transaction or person so described may not be flamboyant but that you can trust that the person or transaction is fair. Rectangles are the slightly more sophisticated cousins of squares. Of all the geometric figures, rectangles are the most common and are the favored shape of the frame for mediated images. High-definition television (HDTV) changed the shape of television screens from squares to the wide-screen rectangular form used in movie theaters. Composition in motion picture and still photography formats often takes advantage of the horizontal sides that a rectangle naturally creates. In a rectangular frame, the chief object of focus does not have to be in the center for the work to appear balanced. A clever commercial for a Volkswagen Beetle aired in 2003. It compared the modern, oval shape of the car with everyday square objects—a clock, house, piece of toast, sponge, and so on, which made the point that you didn't want to drive just

Figure 2.19
The dull square shape of a table during a conference in Helsinki, Finland is made more interesting by the turned perspective, the casual arrangement of discarded objects, and the harsh side lighting that distorts the shadows.
Courtesy of Paul Martin Lester

another box (Figure 2.20).

W LINK **Figure 2.20**
(Weblink: http://goo.gl/C1XtsE)
The contrast of everyday square-shaped objects and the sleeker design of the VW automobile is made clear in a witty way.

Circles The first shapes primitive humans probably took notice of were the bright, circular forms in the sky (the sun and the moon), the round shape of another person's head, and the two circular eyes staring at them. As Leonardo da Vinci once wrote, "The sense which is nearest to the organ of perception functions most quickly, and this is the eye, the chief, the leader of all other senses" (Figure 2.21).

Circles have always been important attention getters. No wonder advertisers of video games, picture agencies, and motion pictures use the human

Figure 2.21
Window to the soul: The eye not only absorbs light but also reflects it, while its round shape catches the eye of a viewer.
Courtesy of Paul Martin Lester

doing something wrong, whether it's Mel Gibson in a nice shirt and a glowing smile in 2006 or Nick Nolte in 2002 with disheveled hair and a much too colorful Hawaiian shirt (Figures 2.22).

A person might close their eyes or hide them behind hands, sunglasses, or a veil. Such gestures could mean that the person wants to block out the world, to hide the extent of grief from others, to look fashionable, or to obey culturally bound religious restrictions against showing their eyes in public. Secret Service members and many security guards like to wear sunglasses so you can't see what their eyes are watching (Figure 2.23). The Dublin-born singer Sinéad O'Connor gained tremendous popularity early in her career with a 1990 music video directed by John Maybury, a British filmmaker known for his films *The Jacket* (2005) and *The Edge of Love* (2008). "Nothing Compares 2 U," written and originally performed by Prince with his 1980s band The Family, showed arresting, close-up images of O'Connor singing with her eyes mainly looking into the camera's lens. The intimate filmmaking technique allowed a viewer to feel her pain after losing a love (Figure 2.24).

Triangles These are the most dynamic and active of shapes. As energetic objects, they convey direction, but they can burden a design with the tension they can create. The two types of triangles—equilateral and isosceles—have vastly different symbolic meanings. All three sides of an equilateral triangle are the same length. Its shape conveys a serene mood because of symmetrical balance. Think of the silent stone pyramids of Egypt. They calmly watch the passing of each millennium and tourist with a camera. Seen from a distance, they are an abrupt change in the naturally sloping sand dune–filled horizon. Seen up close, their power obviously comes from their stable bases. The triangle juggles its two parts—the base and the apex—to create

eye in ad campaigns. To emphasize the form of the red Target logo, a television commercial featured eyes, a door's peephole, a ball, and other circle shapes. Photojournalists also know how telling a person's eyes are in understanding a subject's personality. If the subject stares straight into a camera's lens, the message might be one of bewilderment, defiance, innocence, happiness, or concentration. A specific genre of photography, the police mug shot, in which the person arrested must look into the lens, often reveals a hidden side of a celebrity caught

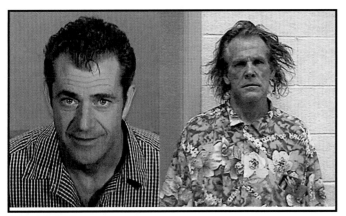

Figures 2.22

In their booking photographs by patrol and sheriff officials for being under the influence, actors Mel Gibson (left) and Nick Nolte are contrasts in demeanor, hair styles, and shirt choices. But they do have one thing in common—they look straight into the camera's lens, a requirement of such pictures. Gibson's eyes reveal playfulness and vulnerability, whereas Nolte's eyes show defiance and anger.
Courtesy of the Los Angeles County Sheriff's Department/ California Highway Patrol

Figure 2.24
(Weblink: http://goo.gl/BEobpx) The agony of a lost love is enhanced by the close-up view of Sinéad O'Connor's face that emphasizes the misery in her eyes.

Figure 2.23
Although looking right at the camera's lens, this New England bench sitter reveals little about his personality since a pair of sunglasses covers his eyes. Rather than an attempt to look cool, the man probably wears them to avoid harmful ultraviolet rays of the sun.
Courtesy of Paul Martin Lester

a dynamic energy. From its base comes stability, but from its peak comes tension (Figure 2.25). In contrast, the isosceles triangle draws its power not from its base but from its sharp point. Think of the Washington Monument in Washington, D.C. When the point is vertical and used in architecture, the shape is called a steeple and symbolizes a religious person's hoped-for destination. But pointed in any direction, isosceles triangles invite the eyes to follow. When using the isosceles shape, a visual communicator must be sure to give the viewer something to see at the end (Figure 2.26).

DEPTH

If humans had only one eye and confined their visual messages to drawings on the walls of caves, there would be no need for more complex illustrations that could be made from dots, lines, and shapes. But because we have two eyes set slightly apart, we naturally see in three dimensions—width, length, and depth—rather than only the first two. In 1838, Sir Charles Wheatstone presented a paper to the Royal Society of London detailing his views on binocular vision. He concluded that our two eyes give different views and create the illusion

Figure 2.25
The Temple of Kukulcan, known as "El Castillo," "The Castle" at Chichén Itzá, Mexico, is a Mayan structure built about 800CE. At 30 meters high, the terraced pyramid with a temple on top is a masterwork that demonstrates precise architectural and construction skills. As with the pyramids in Egypt, its shape causes passersby to notice its silent, solemn dignity.
Courtesy of Daniel Schwen

Figure 2.26
A gift from the people of Japan, cherry trees in full blossom ring the Tidal Basin in Washington, D.C., and frame the Washington Monument in the background. The powerful and striking shape of the monument against the clear sky is in contrast to the stable and constant pyramid shapes found in Mexico and Egypt.
Scott Bauer, U.S. Department of Agriculture

of depth. The images are projected onto each two-dimensional (2-D) retinal screen at the back of each eye and travel to the brain, which interprets the difference between the images as depth.

Wheatstone used his studies in depth perception to discover the stereoscopic process. Based on his findings, the 3-D photographic illusion printed on stereocards was introduced to the public. Each card had two slightly different photographs mounted side by side on a cardboard backing. When each eye viewed them simultaneously through a viewer called a stereoscope, the brain merged the images into one, 3-D image. The difference between looking at an ordinary photograph and an image through a stereoscope is striking. Stereoscopically enhanced views were enormously popular as educational and entertainment sources from about 1860 until 1890. Before the invention of the halftone method for printing pictures in publications, stereocards viewed through stereoscopes were the main source of pictorial news for wealthy patrons (Figure 2.27).

In the 1990s Magic Eye Inc. started a fad using random dot stereogram images that gave most viewers a 3-D effect from color patterns. Advertisers from the Ford Motor Company to the U.S. Army Corps of Engineers have commissioned stereograms using Magic Eye's computer process (Figure 2.28).

Eight Depth Cues

Since perception is such a complicated combination of eye and brain properties, researchers have identified eight possible factors, used singly or in combination, that give viewers a sense of depth: space, size, color, lighting, textural gradients, interposition, time, and perspective. All of these cues, when combined with our two eyes, help us to notice when one object is near and another farther away.

Space This cue depends on the

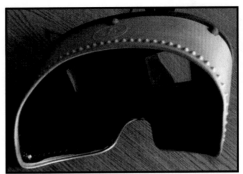

Figure 2.27
After British scientist Charles Wheatstone published a paper in 1838 detailing the principle that creates a 3-D view from our two eyes slightly apart, Sir William Brewster invented an inexpensive viewer for seeing the 3-D effect. With Queen Victoria's interest in stereocards during the Great Exhibition in 1851 at the Crystal Palace in London, the public took notice of the effect. The American physician Oliver Wendell Holmes spread the fad further with his handheld viewer shown here. Home users subscribed to a stereocard company and received sets of images in the mail. Before photographs could be published in newspapers, stereocards were the main source for visual news.
Courtesy of Paul Martin Lester

Figure 2.28
Autostereograms produced by such companies as Magic Eye Inc. are images that create the illusion of a 3-D picture floating on a graphic background. If you focus your attention at an imaginary point behind the picture, you may see a figure swimming above the frog. Such images were popular in the 1990s for fun and in advertising, but interest has waned since then.
Courtesy of the U.S. Army Corps of Engineers

frame in which an image is located. With a natural scene, the illusion of space depends on how close you are to a subject. Standing in an open field gives the feeling of a large amount of space and enhances the feeling of depth. If an object is close to the eyes, depth perception is limited. Likewise, the placement of content elements is important for an image. Often, beginning photographers are told to add interest to their pictures by including a tree limb or some other object in the foreground of the frame (Figure 2.29).

Size If a viewer is aware of an object's actual size, it can help in the illusion of depth perception. An airliner seen from a distance is a small size on the viewer's retina. If someone had no idea what the flying object was, she might conclude that it was quite small. But because we are familiar with the actual size of the aircraft, we know that it is far away and not as small as an insect (Figure 2.30). Size, consequently, is closely related to our ability to determine an object's distance. Distance is related to space and helps in our perception of depth. Size also is related to scale and mental attention. Without knowing an object's size, we have to view it next to an object of known size. Archaeologists take pictures of artifacts found at historical sites with a ruler in the frame so that viewers will know how large the recovered object is. Tourists often are disappointed when they travel to Mount Rushmore in South Dakota because, with no frame of reference, the presidential faces carved in the rock do not convey a sense of their enormous size. Educational psychologist Jean Piaget found that if much attention is given to an object, its size will be overestimated. A small figure often attracts attention within a visual frame because the viewer must concentrate on it. Scale and attention are related to depth perception because there is no illusion of depth if objects are all viewed as the same size.

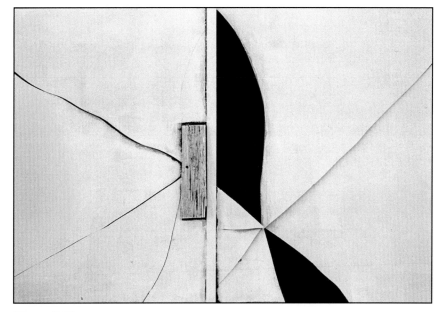

Figure 2.29
"Abandoned Restaurant Window, Pecos, Texas," 2005, by Gerry Davey. A cloudy day without direct sunlight makes it hard to determine which forms are in the foreground and which ones are in the back. Are the dark shapes on the right side the eyes of a space alien looking at you?
Courtesy of Gerry Davey

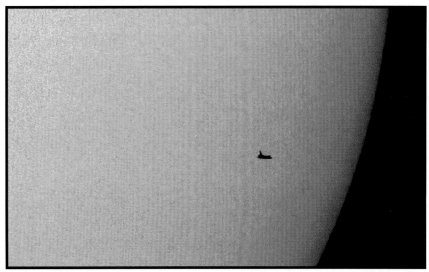

Figure 2.30
Captured via telescope, the space shuttle Atlantis is seen in flight in front of the sun in 2009. Knowing the relative size of objects helps determine the foreground from the background. The extreme telephoto effect also makes it appear that the spacecraft is quite close to the star.
Courtesy of NASA/Thierry Legault

Color As indicated at the start of this chapter, an object's color can communicate depth. Because of their high electromagnetic frequency, warm-colored objects appear closer than those that are cool-colored. High-contrast pictures with great differences between light and dark tones seem closer than objects colored with more neutral colors (Figure 2.31).

Figure 2.31
The muralist who painted this scene on a wall near the Pacific Ocean in Long Beach, California understands the power of the color red to help viewers notice the objects in the background.
Courtesy of Paul Martin Lester

Lighting Differences in light intensities can communicate depth. A television studio technician will position a light above and behind a news announcer. Called a "hair light," the brightness level is slightly higher than the lights in front in order to separate the person from the background. The prevalence of shadows also indicates an object's volume and gives the viewer another depth cue. The light's brightness and position create shadows that the viewer notices (Figure 2.32).

Textural Gradients The ripple effect seen in a still pond suddenly disturbed by a rock or the ridges from the wind on a sand dune are called textural gradients. With water, the ridges appear closer together as they move away from a viewer's point of view. With sand, shadows in the foreground are larger than the shadows in the craters that are farther away. The difference in their size contributes to the illusion that the scene fades into the background (Figure 2.33).

Interposition Graphic designers for *Sports Illustrated* magazine regularly use interposition for their covers with a picture of a player in front of a headline or the publication's name. The 3-D effect often shows a player seemingly leaping off the page. Such a graphic technique is employed so that the cover catches the eye of a potential customer within a crowded bookstore (Figure 2.34).

Time As a depth cue, time refers to a viewer's attention to a particular element within an image. When something interests us, we tend to stare at it for a longer amount of time than other parts of a visual array. Examples might be someone you know or something you are attracted to because of past associations. To an outsider, the element may technically be considered in the background. In a magazine advertisement, for example, words, a model's face or clothing, or an unusual

Figure 2.32
Electric lights along the walls and sunlight through a window in the background help create the illusion of depth and an eerie feeling in this hallway in a Taos, New Mexico hotel.
Courtesy of Paul Martin Lester

Figure 2.33
Our eyes can sense the illusion of depth in the photograph of this Southern California beach because the shadows within the footprints in the sand in the foreground are large compared with those farther back in the picture.
Courtesy of Paul Martin Lester

Figure 2.34
The close-up view of the spelling-challenged Occupy Wall Street protestor in New York City is an example of interposition as the sign and the Guy Fawkes' mask fill the foreground.
Courtesy of Paul Martin Lester

object in the background that triggers a memory might propel that element to the foreground for you (Figure 2.35).

Perspective The most complex depth cue is perspective. That's because it is equal parts brain function and learned behavior. A person's cultural heritage has more bearing on the interpretation of perspective attributes than any other cue. The concept of perception as used in Western art is relatively new compared with the entire history of art. In Europe during the Renaissance, visual communicators usually were artists and scientists. Probably the most famous during this era was Leonardo da Vinci. His paintings reflect an early attention to

Figure 2.35

The Taos, New Mexico, Pueblo is an archeological site where Native Americans lived almost one thousand years ago. Presently, about 150 persons still live there. Depending on your personal interest, you may spend more time looking at the adobe structure, the store "OPEN" sign, the window frame, the sleeping dog, the handwritten sign with the "F" letters drawn as two "7s," the elaborate smiley face, the parched ground, the play of light and shadow in the background, or some other detail. Consequently, whichever element you spend more time looking at becomes the foreground.

Courtesy of Paul Martin Lester

duplicating on a 2-D surface the illusion of depth as viewed in the real world. One of Leonardo's most famous works, "The Last Supper," uses perspective to express the social importance of the Christ figure. His "Leonardo box" aided painters in duplicating depth by tracing a scene on a sheet of paper (later on glass) with the artist's eye remaining in the same position. Using this method, a painter could be sure that the drawn lines accurately mimicked an actual scene (Figure 2.36). But the "box" most commonly used by artists of the day to

draw accurate landscapes was the *camera obscura*, or "dark chamber." A small hole in a box projects an upside-down view of the outside scene if lighting conditions are favorable. Artists inside a large camera obscura traced the outside view on a thin sheet of paper to replicate depth cues. Much later, light-sensitive material replaced paper and became the basis for modern photography. The medium, more than any other invention, spurred artists to render scenes in their proper perspective.

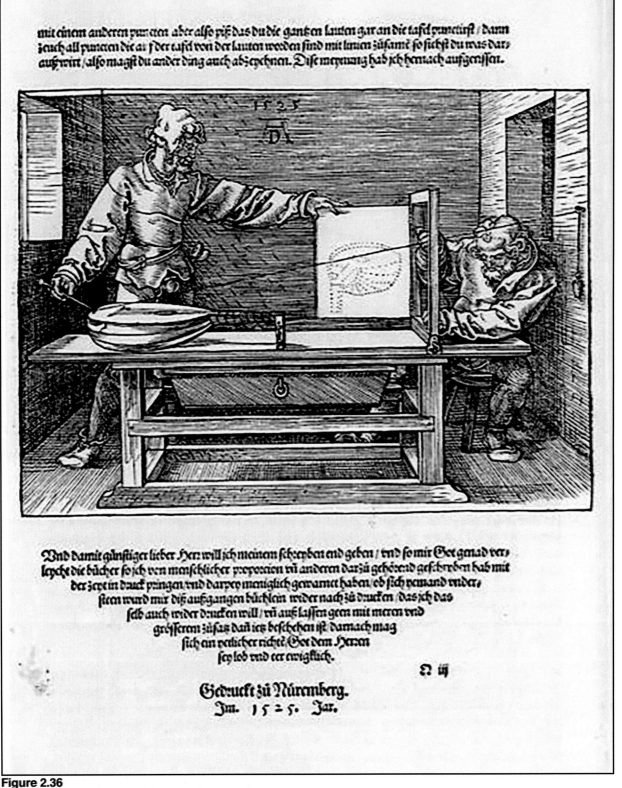

Figure 2.36

The woodcut by Albrecht Dürer from his 1525 book, Introduction in the Art of Measurement with Compass and Ruler, shows an example of an apparatus for translating 3-D objects into 2-D drawings. No doubt a best seller. The perspective tool uses a frame to achieve an accurate linear perspective of an object.
Courtesy of the estate of Albrecht Dürer

In her book *Visual Metaphors: A Methodological Study in Visual Communication*, Evelyn Hatcher identifies four major forms of perspective: illusionary, geometrical, conceptual, and social.

Illusionary Perspective An illusionary perspective can be achieved through size, color, lighting, interposition, and linear perspective. When you stand on a railroad track and look down the ties, the steel rails seem to converge into a single area, or vanishing point, in the distance. This trait of parallel lines when seen at a distance is called linear perspective and provides the illusion of 3-D depth in a painting, photograph, film, or other flat surface (Figure 2.37).

Some artists played with the illusion of depth by having their subjects appear to be escaping from their frames. Called *trompe l'oeil*, or "trick of the eye" artists such as Titian, Pere Borrell del Caso, Edward Collyer, and George Henry Hall used techniques that gave the illusion of 3-D depth (Figure 2.38). Contemporary British artist Julian Beever creates pavement chalk drawings that delightfully trick and intrigue the eyes (Figure 2.39), and the Italian artist known as Blu further advances the artform with his large, 3-D animated drawings. In his piece named "Muto," Blu makes a drawing, a camera records the frame, he erases it, makes a new drawing, and repeats the process. When edited, the result is a captivating animated film of the 3-D public artwork (Figure 3.40).

Those who make 3-D motion pictures and television shows are currently enjoying a renaissance of the genre. Instead of the poor quality sci-fi and horror 3-D pictures of the 1950s seen with red-and-blue cellophane pasted

Figure 2.37
Delta Airlines flight attendant Katherine Lee, dubbed "Deltalina" by her fans who think she resembles the actress Angelina Jolie, is placed within the center of the frame of the pre-flight safety video to maximize passenger interest and the linear perspective effect.
Courtesy of Paul Martin Lester

Figure 2.38
"Escaping Criticism," 1874. The Spanish painter Pere Borrell del Caso used the trompe l'oeil effect to make it appear the wide-eyed peasant boy is leaving the frame.
Courtesy of the Collection of the Bank of Spain

Figure 2.39
(Weblink: http://goo.gl/w1YccY)
Julian Beever travels the world as an invited artist to create his three-dimensional drawings during art shows and street festivals. His anamorphic illusions are necessarily distorted and should be viewed from only one perspective.

Figure 2.40
(Weblink: http://goo.gl/nsugtr)
Produced by the street artist Blu, the edgy, scratchy drawing style requires erasing and creating count-less images for this thoroughly engaging animation.

Figure 2.41
Sri Lalitā-Tripurāsundari enthroned with her left foot upon the Sri Chakra, also known as Sri Yantra, holds her traditional symbols, the sugarcane bow, flower arrows, noose, and goad. She is seated on a chair supported by Brahma, Vishnu, Rudra, Maheswara and Sadashiva. Lakshmi and Saraswati are fanning her. Contrary to Western traditions, this geometrical perspective uses the size and placement of Lalitā in the frame to signify supremacy over the other gods.
Courtesy of Arjunkrishna90

on cheap cardboard frames, audience members now are able to watch motion pictures originally produced in 3-D such as *Hugo* (2011), *A Very Harold & Kumar 3D Christmas* (2011) *Avatar* (2009), and *Coraline* (2009) and previously released 2-D movies converted into 3-D such as Disney's *Beauty and the Beast* (2012), *Top Gun* (1986), *Jurassic Park* (1993), and all six *Star Wars* films. With comfortable glasses in theaters equipped to show digitally projected 3-D movies producers expect new box office life from their past efforts.

Advertisers also produce commercials using 3-D technology. In 2006 a Norwegian animation studio named BUG created the first 3-D commercial for the Mitsubishi car company. In 2009, about 150 million glasses were handed out to viewers so that commercials for *Monsters vs. Aliens* and SoBe's Lifewater drink could be seen during the Super Bowl. Home watchers are also able to enjoy the effect with 3-D TV, which is particularly popular for sports and action movies.

Geometrical Perspective This type of perspective is common among traditional Japanese and Mayan artwork. The goddess Lalitā-Tripurāsundari is higher and larger in the frame so is considered in the foreground (Figure 2.41). So-called "naïve" wall murals as seen in Belfast, Northern Ireland, in the 1980s often showed the main subject of a painting in the same way (Figure 2.42). Young children without artistic training also often exhibit this type of perspective in their drawings. The child's drawing in Chapter 1 is an example.

Conceptual Perspective This element of perspective is a compositional trait that relies on a more symbolic definition of depth perception. It can be divided into two types: multiview and social. With the multiview perspective, a viewer can see many different sides of an object at the same time. The picture is like an X-ray, or transparent view of the object. Near objects overlap far objects only by the outside edges or lines that make up their shapes. Pablo Picasso often used this type of perspective in which the subject's various moods and angles are seen all at the same time. Photographer Clarence John

Figure 2.42
After the Glorious Revolution of 1688, the Dutch Protestant Prince William III of Orange overthrew the Catholic King James II of England to become King of England, Scotland, and Ireland. Two years later, William's Protestant troops conquered the Catholic army in Ireland at the Battle of the Boyne. What followed was almost three hundred years of discrimination and attempted genocide of the Catholics in Northern Ireland. Despite recent progress in relations between the two religious groups, districts in Belfast are still segregated. With a simply drawn wall mural showing William of Orange on a white steed large in the frame, his dominance over the land is celebrated on an abandoned building within a Protestant neighborhood.
Courtesy of Paul Martin Lester

W LINK
Figure 2.43
(Weblink: goo.gl/vgLxDE) *Louisiana born poet and photographer Clarence John Laughlin often wrote lengthy captions for his photographs. For his "The Masks Grow to Us" created in 1947 he wrote an apt description of the conceptual perspective, "In our society, most of us wear protective masks (psychological ones) of various kinds and for various reasons. Very often the end result is that the masks grow to us, displacing our original characters with our assumed characters. This process is indicated in visual, and symbolic, terms here by several exposures on one negative—the disturbing factor being that the mask is like the girl herself, grown harder, and more superficial."*

Laughlin in "The Masks Grow to Us" (1947) employed a multiple exposure technique in which the hard, cold stare of a mannequin's face starts to cover the soft features of a live model. His point was to say that if a person is not truthful, she might become permanently phony (Figure 2.43).

Social Perspective In social perspective, the most important person in a group picture is often larger in size, centrally located, or separated from other, less important people (Figure 2.44). A viewer often assumes power relationships because of social perspective. A group picture of a large family often has older adults in the center with the children surrounding them on the edges. The owners and partners of a law firm may pose for an advertising photograph in the center. In advertising images, a man nearer and larger in the frame with his hand resting or with an arm wrapped around a woman's shoulder often signifies his dominance over her. Over the past three decades, the feminist movement has made advertisers and others more sensitive to nonverbal, negative stereotypes such as these. Erving Goffman's content analysis *Gender Advertisements* is a classic collection of visual sexism in advertising.

One of the reasons the motion picture *Citizen Kane* (1941), directed by Orson Welles, is considered the greatest movie ever made is because of its technical innovations. One advance that particularly impressed director Roger Corman was the use of depth. Ordinarily, action within a film takes place along the so-called x-axis, an imaginary line along the horizontal plane, and the y-axis, a line that represents the vertical plane. But when the illusion of depth is introduced to an image, the *z*-axis, a line that moves into the frame, is introduced. With special lenses, lighting, and films, Gregg Toland, the cinematographer for *Kane*, created deep-focus photography—characters were in focus far into a scene, adding more information and the illusion of depth to the picture.

MOVEMENT

Color, form, and depth join movement to constitute the principal qualities of images that make the cells in the visual cortex respond quickly to a stimulus. Recognizing movement is one of the most important traits in the survival of an animal. Knowing whether an object or other animal is moving closer or farther away helps the animal avoid potentially harmful encounters. There are four types of movement: real, apparent,

graphic, and implied.

Real Movement This type of movement is motion not connected with an image presented in the media. It is actual movement as seen by a viewer of some other person, animal, or object. Because real movement does not involve mediated images, we don't emphasize it in this textbook.

Apparent Movement The most common example of this type of movement is motion picture films. Moving images are a series of still images put together sequentially for film, videotape, or digital media and moved through a viewing device at a fast speed. Each single picture is shown only for a fraction of a second. Movement is perceived in the brain because of a phenomenon called *persistence of vision*. In 1824 Peter Mark

Figure 2.44
The position of these friends emphasizes that the man in front is the boss—an example of social perspective.
Courtesy of Allison Lester

Roget, who later became famous for his popular *Thesaurus*, proposed that this phenomenon resulted from the time required for an image to fade from the cells of the retina. Scientists now know that persistence of vision, or *diligence of foresight* if a *Thesaurus* is handy, is a result of the time needed for the brain to receive and recognize the picture. It takes about one-tenth of a second for an image to enter the eyes and register in the mind. Consequently, at 24 frames a second, a character or object in a film appears to move because of a blurring between individual frames as they pass through a projection device at that speed.

Graphic Movement Graphic movement can be the motion of the eyes as they scan a field of view or the way a graphic designer positions elements so that the eyes move throughout a layout. Visual communicators often position the graphic elements in a design to take advantage of the eyes' movement around a picture and layout. A viewer's eyes will move through and notice elements in an image based on previous experiences and current interests, seeing certain parts of the picture and ignoring others. Nevertheless, a visual communicator can direct a viewer's eyes in a preconceived direction. The eye will usually follow a line, a slow curve, or a horizontal shape before it follows other graphic elements. Of course, colors, sizes of individual pieces, and placement of elements against a frame's white or background colored space also are crucial (Figure 2.45).

Implied Movement Implied movement is motion that a viewer perceives in a still, single image without any actual movement of an object, image, or eye. Some graphic designs purposely stimulate the eyes with implied motion in order to attract attention. Optical or "op" art has been used in advertisements and in psy-

chedelic posters of the 1960s to achieve frenetic, pulsating results. Visual vibration is the term used for these images. Through high-contrast line placement or the use of complementary colors, moiré (wavy) patterns seem to move as if powered by an unseen light source (Figure 2.46).

Implied movement also has roots in the beginnings of human communication. Outside the village of Montignac in southwestern France, the entrance to the Lascaux Cave was discovered in 1940 by 18-year-old Marcel Ravidat. Much later in 1994, while exploring a cave on his family's land in southern France, Jean-Marie Chauvet discovered the oldest known cave etchings and paintings. *Le Grotte Chauvet* contains 416 cave paintings of extraordinary detail and cultural significance dating from approximately 30,000 years ago. Many paintings

Figure 2.45
At a newsstand in Los Angeles, magazine covers are prime examples of graphic movement that attracts the eyes.
Courtesy of Paul Martin Lester

in several of the caves discovered have views of animals in which they appear to be running. For example, one of the drawings in the *Chauvet* cave shows a bison running but with additional legs. With so many other animals accurately displayed, archeologists puzzled why this one was not anatomically correct. Speculation about the artist's intent ended after someone brought in a flaming torch to see the drawing as the cave dwellers themselves would have seen it. With the aid of a fire's light, it could easily be seen that the extra legs gave the viewer the illusion that the bison was actually galloping across the cave. Perhaps this example of implied movement is evidence that early humans longed for motion pictures (Figure 2.47). Unfortunately (or fortu-

nately) for these cave dwellers, buttered popcorn and flavored carbonated sugar water were invented much later.

New York City born director Martin Scorsese won Academy Awards for Best Director and Best Picture for *The Departed* (2006). In 1990 he made a critically acclaimed mobster movie, *Goodfellas*. The action leading up to a drug bust scene is a clinic in camera and actor movements synchronized to make an audience member feel the tension and paranoia that the characters have when taking drugs and performing other illegal acts. The scene starts with the character played by Ray Liotta snorting a line of cocaine and ends with him being busted in the driveway of his house. In between, the camera zooms in

Figure 2.46
"A Hand for Riley," 2009, by xtine burrough. The British artist Bridget Riley is one of the most influential painters of the Op Art movement. After earning her degree from the Royal College of Art in London, she worked as a teacher and illustrator for the J. Walter Thompson advertising agency. In the 1960s she developed her distinctive style of black and white geometrical forms that created an internal, vibrant, visual energy and helped launch the Op Art movement. This piece is based on Riley's "Movement in Squares," 1961.
Courtesy of xtine burrough

and out, pans left, right, up, and down, and moves in and out. The shots are quickly edited for maximum tension. The musical selections also enhance the frenetic feeling. The actors are constantly moving, talking, and looking for surveillance helicopters. It is not only a brilliant example of the visual cue of movement, it is also a powerful anti-drug message (Figure 2.48).

David Hubel, Torsten Wiesel, and other scientists who built on their work through experiments with rats, monkeys, and people with brain injuries demonstrated that the cells in the visual cortex respond primarily to color, form, depth, and movement. But even without the knowledge of research, for many millennia visual communicators have used these four visual cues in their work, whether it has appeared on cave walls or on computer screens. An important lesson for image producers who want to make memorable messages is to understand that brain cells are complex "difference detectors." They are stimulated more by the relative differences between visual elements than by the intensity of each one. Consequently, a gaudy, colorful presentation may lose much of its impact if all its graphic elements have the same intensity. Differences between the visual cues detected by brain cells are only part of the reason that some messages are noticed and others are ignored. The content of a visual message, which we discuss next, also plays a vital role.

Figure 2.47
Zach Zorich of Nautilus magazine writes that these "Five stag heads in the Nave region of Lascaux cave might represent a single stag in different stages of motion."
Courtesy of Norbert Aujoulat

KEY TERMS FROM THIS CHAPTER
Binocular vision • Composition • Cortex (Visual) • Electromagnetic spectrum • Feminist movement • Genre • Gesture • Halftone • Layout • Logo • Microelectrode • Moiré pattern • Mug shot • Multiple exposure • Pan • Photoshop • Public Service Announcement (PSA) • Random dot stereogram • Renaissance • Retinas • Shot • Visual array • Wavelength • Zoom

Figure 2.48
(Weblink: http://goo.gl/7pnSUy)
The frenetic lifestyle of Ray Liotta's drug selling character in Goodfellas *is enhanced by the directorial choices made by Academy Award winner Martin Scorsese.*

3 Visual Theories

Students and practitioners of visual communication are often intimidated by the word "theory." But remember: Theories are simply best guesses made from a series of carefully considered observations.

A theory is not cut in stone; it is not a fact. As such, a theory should be questioned and rigorously defended without passion and with an open-minded attitude from both sides so that the exchange leads to its improvement, rejection, or elevation to an established fact. Over the centuries, psychologists, philosophers, and professionals have proposed many theories trying to explain how we see and how we learn from images.

The four theories we discuss in this chapter were selected for their direct connection to mass communications. They can be divided into two fundamental groups: sensory and perceptual. Those who advocate the sensory theories (gestalt and constructivism) maintain that direct or mediated images are composed of light objects that attract or repel us. They are more concerned with what the brain sees—the visual cues of color, form, depth, and movement—but not so much of how the mind considers them. The perceptual theories (semiotics and cognitive) are concerned mainly with the meaning that humans associate with images—what the mind sees.

The two sets of theories can be summed by the difference between what something looks like and what it actually is. To understand any of these approaches to visual communication, you must first know the difference between visual sensation and visual perception.

A sensation is a stimulus from the outside world that activates nerve cells within your sense organs. Wood burning in a fireplace activates the cells in your ears because you can hear the logs cracking and hissing, in your nose because you can smell the rich aroma of the wood, in your hands and face because you can feel the warmth of the fire, in your mouth if you pop a hot toasted marshmallow into it, and in your eyes as you watch the hypnotizing glow of the yellow flames. Sensations are lower-order, physical responses to stimuli and alone convey no meaning. Nerve cells in your ears, nose, hands, mouth, and eyes do not have the capacity to make intelligent thoughts. They are simply conveyors of information to the brain. Our minds make meaning of all the sensory input. Conclusions based on those data are almost instantaneous. Our minds interpret the noises, smells, temperatures, tastes, and sights as a fire. Visual perception concentrates on the conclusions that are made from information gathered by our eyes (Figure 3.1).

Figure 3.1
Sitting before such a fire, your brain registers its heat, colors, and sounds while your mind notices the artificial logs and natural gas jets, but if you are cold, the brain wins.
Courtesy of Paul Martin Lester

SENSORY THEORIES OF VISUAL COMMUNICATION

Researchers and theorists who concentrate on sensory theories of visual communication are mainly concerned with how the brain notices or fails to see the visual cues of color, form, depth, and movement. A useful motion picture that helps you imagine what it's like to be a brain cell is the documentary *Koyaanisqatsi* (1982) directed by Godfrey Reggio (Figure 3.2). With the thousands of slow- and fast-motion images and quick and frenetic cuts between scenes of everything from crowded freeways to women who work on a snack cake assembly line, there are too many images to process and remember. Scenes in the film become a blur composed not of content but of the four visual cues. The film shows what being a brain cell in your visual cortex at the back of your brain is like—the cell notes the stimulation and passes it on to your mind without considering it. As a general rule, sensory theories are not concerned with the literal meaning of what is possible to be seen. They help us understand how we can be attracted and distracted from visual messages.

Gestalt The gestalt theory of visual perception emerged from a simple observation. German psychologist Max Wertheimer received his inspiration during a train trip in the summer of 1910. As he looked out the windows as the train moved through the sunny German countryside, he suddenly realized that he could see the outside scene even though the opaque wall of the train and the window frame partially blocked his view.

He left the train in Frankfurt, went to a toy store, and bought a popular children's toy of the day—a stroboscope, similar to what we call a flipbook today. The flipbook is a simple form of cartoon animation. On the first page of the book, a drawing—say, of a cartoon character in a running position—is displayed on the right-hand side of the page. On each subsequent page, the drawing of the figure is slightly different depending on the actions intended by the artist. To see the effect of the moving character, a viewer uses a thumb to flip the pages rapidly. A modern example of this animation technique can be seen in a music video from the Dutch pop group Kraak & Smaak for their 2007 hit, "Squeeze Me" (Figure 3.3).

Figure 3.2
(Weblink: http://goo.gl/gT6X6H) Turn the volume up high and turn off all the lights in the room and get absorbed in the hypnotic artistry of Koyaanisqatsi, a Hopi word that means, "Life out of Balance."

Figure 3.3
(Weblink: http://goo.gl/sTcXfb) As a child's toy the simply drawn flipbook has its own charm, but when a series of photographs are flipped to correspond with the music video's background, the effect is arresting.

Wertheimer's observations during the train trip and using the flipbook led to more research at the University of Frankfurt. Wertheimer concluded that the eye merely takes in all the visual stimuli, whereas the brain arranges the sensations into a coherent image. Without a brain that links individual sensory elements, the phenomenon of movement would not take place. His ideas led to the famous statement:

The whole is different from the sum of its parts.

In other words, perception is a result of a combination of sensations and not of individual sensory elements. The word *gestalt* comes from the German noun that means form or shape. Gestalt psychologists further refined the initial work by Wertheimer to conclude that visual perception is a result of organizing sensory elements or forms into various groups. Discrete elements within a scene are combined and understood by the brain through a series of four fundamental principles of grouping that are often called laws: similarity, proximity, continuation, and common fate.

Similarity This gestalt law states that objects that look similar will be automatically grouped together by the brain. Simple experiments with the basic shapes of filled-in circles and square forms made that clear to gestalt researchers. Whether for print or screen media, words are easily separated from images. However, when a page is composed of nothing but similarly sized words or pictures, the viewing of it can be tedious. Visual interest comes from dissimilarity, not similarity (Figure 3.4).

Proximity The brain more closely associates objects close to each other than it does an object that is farther apart. Likewise, two friends standing near each other will be viewed as being more closely related than a third person standing 20 yards from the couple. Proximity is also a factor with the visual cue of depth. The illusion is enhanced if an object is perceived as being close to the viewer while another seems farther away. If two objects appear to be on the same horizontal plane or are the same size, their proximity is equal and the sensation of depth is reduced (Figure 3.5).

Continuation The brain does not prefer sudden or unusual changes in the movement of a line. In other words, the

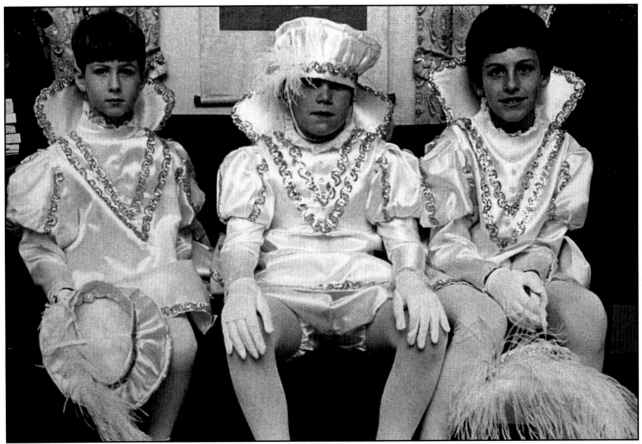

Figure 3.4
Three boys dressed in similar Mardi Gras costumes pose for a picture while they wait to be photographed with the queen of a ball in New Orleans. One of the reasons the brain links the boys as a single unit is because of their similarity. Regardless, look at their expressions closely— they have quite different personalities--innocent, cynical, and friendly.
Courtesy of Paul Martin Lester

Figure 3.5
A poster produced by the Federal Art Project in the 1930s is used to promote education and civic activity. It also is an example of proximity—the brain naturally divides the two sets of penguins because of their closeness to each other.
Courtesy of the Library of Congress

Figure 3.6
A billboard for a Target department store in Adelaide, Australia, demonstrates continuation as you continue the circles that make up the store's logo in your mind. This image also demonstrates that non-American advertisers can get away with more than their U.S. counterparts.
Courtesy of Paul Martin Lester

brain seeks as much as possible a smooth continuation of a perceived movement (Figure 3.6). The line can be a drawing, or it can be several objects placed together along an imaginary line. Objects viewed as belonging to a continuous line will be mentally separated from other objects that are not a part of that line. Continuation also refers to objects that are partially blocked by a foreground object with a viewer's mind continuing the line in order to achieve a kind of graphic closure.

Common Fate Finally, another principle of gestalt psychology is common fate. A viewer mentally groups five arrows or five raised hands pointing to the sky because they all point in the same direction. An arrow or a hand pointed in the opposite direction will create tension, because the viewer will not see it as part of the upwardly directed whole. Again, a visual communicator can use this principle to direct a viewer's eyes toward or away from a graphic element in a picture or design (Figure 3.7). The placement of a warning label in a cigarette ad is made through research by tobacco industry graphic designers to be the least viewed part of a page.

Danish gestalt psychologist Edgar Rubin developed the principle of camouflage when he made patterns with little or no separation between the foreground and the background. Understanding and manipulating this trait of visual perception led directly to military applications of merging the colors of uniforms and equipment with those of surrounding backgrounds in order to hide them (Figure 3.8). This principle also influenced the work of artists M. C. Escher and Paul Klee, both of whom were influenced by the writings and findings of several gestalt psychologists.

Visual communicators learned at least two important lessons from the gestalt theory—studying individual elements of a picture helps you to better

Figure 3.7
A Work Progress Administration poster from the 1930s promotes the early treatment of syphilis with the use of the gestalt principle of common fate. Happily dancing men free of the disease move up while those who waited for treatment sadly trudge downward.
Courtesy of the Library of Congress

Figure 3.8
The Danish psychologist Edgar Rubin used the gestalt principles to draw conclusions about how the mind tells the difference between a foreground and a background (also known as figure and ground). Noting how we see differences led to the idea of creating similarities and camouflage clothing for military uses. PFC Joel Graham applies camouflage paint as his unit prepares to board a ship that will take him to the verdant countryside of Puerto Rico for a military exercise.
U.S. Department of Defense

understand its whole meaning, and the theory helps you create more noticeable print and screen media designs.

When analyzing a visual message, tiny details within a frame should be studied first to discover how they create a different and often surprising whole. For example, a photographic craze in the 1990s used a computer to mesh the exposures and compositions of hundreds of similarly themed single images into a gestalt whole. As a student at the Massachusetts Institute of Technology, Robert Silvers invented a photographic technique called "photomosaic" that can arrange hundreds of single photographs by their exposures into one picture. Through his company Runaway Technologies, he creates examples such as a picture of the Earth comprising single images from the ground, Leonardo da Vinci's "Mona Lisa" that is a composite of paintings from the artist's notebooks and the Renaissance period, and a close-up portrait of Nazi Holocaust victim Anne Frank as a combination of pictures from that era (Figure 3.9). Silvers has also produced images for use in advertisements for Audi, Coca Cola, Master-Card, and other corporations.

In addition, gestalt helps to focus on a tiny, cropped version of a photograph so that additional insights can be learned when attention is turned to the entire image. Diane Arbus was an inspired portrait photographer who helped invent a genre of photography known as the "snapshot aesthetic." Many times she took pictures of unusual-looking persons—circus performers, nudists, identical twins, a giant, and so on—and photographed them in such a way as to make the portrait look like an ordinary picture you would find in a family's photo album. If you look at just the face of Arbus's portrait titled "A Woman with her Baby Monkey, N.J., 1971," you won't see any signs of the animal that sits on her lap dressed like a baby (Figure 3.10). What you might notice with the close-up view, however, is the broken slat in the blinds and reflective wood paneling behind her, the cut and style of her hair, and her plain clothes that all indicate economic status. Studying her face, you will see her slight, closed-mouth smile is belied by the sadness evident in her eyes. Finally, the turn of her head and the distracting shadow in the background caused by a flash are indications of the snapshot aesthetic style. After that concentrated and focused view, seeing the entire photograph confirms and also expands the initial observations. Poignancy is added to the photograph when it is also considered that the portrait was made the year Arbus killed herself.

Figure 3.9
*(Weblink: http://goo.gl/pwvo5H)
The photographic work of Robert Silvers is a demonstration of the gestalt phrase, "The whole is different from the sum of its parts." If you have no idea who this person is, looking closely at the individual images that compose the whole picture reveals clues to the subject of this portrait. Holocaust identification photographs, German officials, and prison camp views are placed within the work depending on their exposures. Once the whole image is revealed, it is obvious the portrait is of a smiling and vibrant Annelies "Anne" Frank, who hid with her family from the Germans within a house in Amsterdam until they were discovered in 1944. Seven months later she died of typhus at the Bergen-Belsen concentration camp at the age of 15. In 1952 the English translation of her* The Diary of a Young Girl *was published to international critical acclaim.*

Figure 3.10
*(Weblink: http://goo.gl/Gfww6F)
Diane Arbus' "A Woman with her Baby Monkey, N.J., 1971" is a study in how the gestalt visual communication theory can teach how to better study images—concentrate on small details and put them together into a whole.*

Gestalt research radically changed the design philosophy of graphic artists. The strength of gestalt is its attention to the individual forms that make up a picture's content. Any analysis of an image should start by concentrating on those forms that naturally appear in any picture. Recall that color, form, depth, and movement all are basic characteristics of an image that the brain notices. Gestalt teaches a visual communicator to combine those basic elements into a meaningful whole. The approach also teaches the graphic artist to focus attention on certain elements by playing against the gestalt principles. For example, a company's logo (or trademark) will be noticed in an advertisement if it has a dissimilar shape, size, or location in relation to the other elements in the layout.

Gestalt also helped alter the front-page layouts of newspapers. Before the theory was advanced, newspapers were a mind-numbing collection of gray words on a page separated by six to eight long, vertical columns that ran the length of the page. The main story's small headline, followed by smaller subheads, and then even smaller body copy, started at the top-left of the page and continued on without breaks or pictures. These designs, intended for highly literate readers, were dull and unattractive. In gestalt terms, the page was an example of similarity, the columns showed equal proximity, continuation was imposed as the reader's eyes finished the bottom of one column to advance to the top of the next, and all the columns were meant to be read in the same direction, indicating a common fate (Figure 3.11). Today, a newspaper's front page is a varied, sometimes desperately cacophonous collection of different sized headlines, columns, and pictures. In gestalt terms, the page is now dissimilar, because separate stories are easily differentiated, proximity is noted when two photographs for the same story are printed closely together, continuation is indicat-

Figure 3.11
This first edition of the Daily Globe *(St. Paul, Minnesota), published on January 1, 1880, illustrates how the four gestalt laws of similarity, proximity, continuation, and common fate do not necessarily create a graphic design that holds much visual interest for a reader.*
Courtesy of the Library of Congress

ed by both a vertical and a horizontal flow of the eyes depending on the layout, and the relative importance of each story is shown by its position and size on the page (Figure 3.12). Modern newspaper design is a lesson in the application of the gestalt theory. Most experts agree, however, that gestalt design won't be enough to save the delivery of news on paper.

The work of gestalt theorists clearly shows that the brain is a powerful organ that classifies visual material in discrete groups. What we see when looking at a picture is modified by what we are directed to see or miss by photographers, filmmakers, and graphic designers.

Figure 3.12
Modern newspaper design creates visual interest by displaying contrasts in headline, picture, and story styles, sizes, and locations, as shown by the front pages taped to a wall as editors for the German publication Bild *work on the next issue in 1977.*
Courtesy of George Louis

Constructivism In 1970, Julian Hochberg, a professor of psychology at Columbia University, found that the eyes of his experimental subjects were constantly in motion as they scanned an image. These quick fixations all combined within the viewer's short-term memory to help build a mental picture of a scene. For Hochberg, a viewer constructs a scene with short-lived eye fixations that the mind combines into a whole picture. If memorable, the scene will be added to a person's long-term memory. The gestalt approach described a viewer as being passive. In contrast, constructivism emphasizes the viewer's eye movements in an active state of perception.

Hochberg had his subjects use eye-tracking machines in his visual perception experiments. These devices can chart the way a viewer looks at an image. Since the area of sharpest focus that we see is about the size of the letter "e" printed on this page, the eye constantly moves in order to maintain focus. Eye-tracking machines simply made obvious the eyes' frenetic journey across a direct or mediated image (Figure 3.13).

Two graphic designers and researchers helped make Hochberg's theory practical for visual communicators by showing how viewers notice elements on a page or screen.

In 1990, Dr. Mario García of the Poynter Institute and García Media and Dr. Pegie Stark Adam of Poynter used an eye-track testing machine to record on videotape the eye movements of participants as they read different versions of a newspaper. Participants wore special glasses that "contained two small cameras—one that recorded eye movement and another that recorded where the reader looked." The time spent on each element of a page could also be recorded. As expected, researchers found that readers noticed the largest picture on a page first and a headline before a story. Captions under photographs were the third most viewed element on a page. Clearly, the results indicated how important graphic designs are in capturing a reader's attention.

Subsequent eye-track studies looked at the reading habits of online readers. One study found that web users noticed text on a screen first, unlike their print counterparts who noticed images first. For García it was clear that online "is more like reading a book, where one concentrates on the text and prefers photos to appear separately."

In 2007 a more elaborate study tried to find differences in readers as they navigated the various elements that make up print and online pages. Studying more than 350 elements that could be found

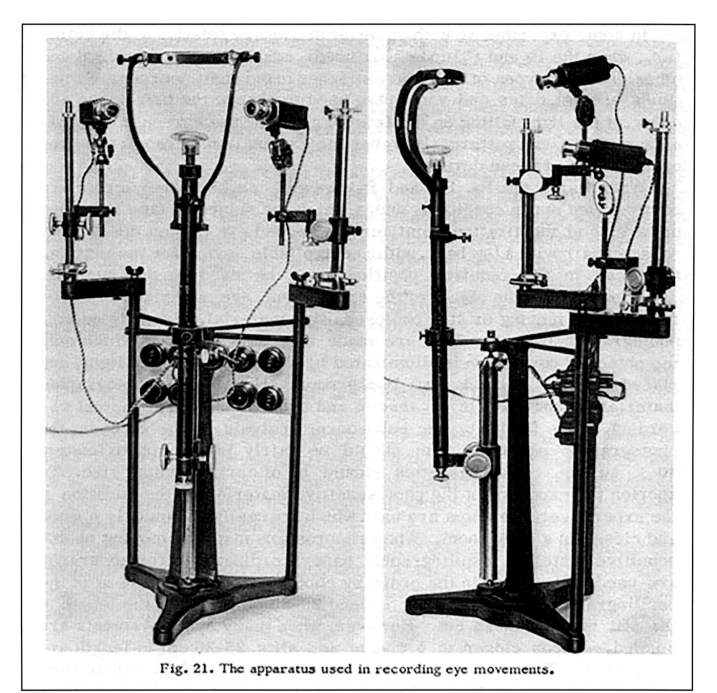

Fig. 21. The apparatus used in recording eye movements.

Figure 3.13
In order to conduct research on graphic design attributes for print and online publications, subjects were asked to wear head-sets that recorded eye movements and time spent viewing various elements. This elaborate set-up was used by eye-tracking researchers in the 1960s and perhaps later to gain information from terrorists--JK.
Courtesy of A.L. Yarbus

W
LINK
Figure 3.14
(Weblink: http://goo.gl/glKfDd)
A typical record from an
eye-tracking set-up shows the
sweeping right, left, up, and
down movements as the subject was attracted by graphic
elements presented on a
computer monitor.

on pages—headlines, stories, pictures, briefs, advertisements, podcasts, blogs, teasers, and so on—the study was an exhaustive use of the eye-track proce- dure. The research discovered several differences between online and print readers. Online users read more of a story than readers in broadsheet and tabloid formats. Online users scanned through various stories whereas print readers tended to start at the beginning and read to the end. More attention by readers of all graphic formats was given if stories also contained information- al graphics, sidebars, and lists. Bigger headlines and photographs got a lot of attention in print, but online readers noted navigational elements and links. Photojournalistic images of real people were preferred over studio set-up shots. Both groups liked color over black and white (Figure 3.14).

Ironically, the news organizations that participated in the study in order to find out how to keep the readers they have and attract new ones included the *Star Tribune* of Minneapolis and the Philadelphia *Daily News*, whose parent companies filed for bankruptcy in 2009, and the *Rocky Mountain News*, which quit publishing altogether the same year. This downward trend for news- papers is why analysts with the Future Exploration Network predict that "newspapers in the U.S. will become insignificant by 2017 and the rest of the world by 2040" while academics at USC's Annenberg School for Commu- nication and Journalism in the Center of the Digital Future predict that most U.S. newspapers will be gone in five years.

Although limited by their emphasis on "what the brain sees" and not what the objects seen mean, sensory theories can be thought to be limited in their application for visual communicators. Nevertheless, the gestalt and construc- tivism theories both have important uses for print and/or screen media graphic

designers. No work is useful if readers, viewers, and users do not notice it.

PERCEPTUAL THEORIES OF VISUAL COMMUNICATION

The semiotics and cognitive theories of visual perception can be considered to be content driven. Although recognizing that vision cannot happen without light illuminating, structuring, and sometimes creating perceptions, these two theories stress that humans are unique in the ani- mal kingdom because we assign complex meaning to the objects we see.

Semiotics The flag that is raised high above a baseball stadium and is watched reverently during the singing of the national anthem by those in the stands and on the field is a sign. The right hand placed over the approximate location of the heart during the singing of the anthem is a sign. The words printed in a program about the players on the field are signs. The close-up photograph of a player holding a bat awaiting a pitch are signs. The refs' black outfits and the managers' hand signals are signs. The illuminated numbers on the scoreboard are signs. Even cleat marks in the dirt are signs. The "high-five" slap with a friend after a team's home run is a sign. The simple silhouette illustration of a woman on a restroom door is a sign. The green traffic light as you make your way home from the game is a sign (Figure 3.15).

A sign is simply anything that stands for something else. After reading the preceding list of signs you might well ask: What is *not* a sign? That's a good question, because almost any action, object, or image will mean something to someone somewhere. Any word or physical presentation, from a yelled comment to an orange jacket, is a sign if it has meaning beyond the object itself. Consequently, the meaning behind any sign must be learned. In other words, for something to be a communicated sign, the viewer must understand its meaning.

Figure 3.15
Fans of the Los Angeles Angels wear a fake Mohawk and standard red baseball caps along with a jersey to support their team.
Courtesy of Paul Martin Lester

But if you don't understand the meaning behind the orange color of a jacket, it isn't a sign for you. It's just a jacket.

Semiotics (called *semiology* in Europe) is the study or science of signs. The field is the culmination of Aldous Huxley's mantra: The more you know, the more you see. Images will be much more interesting and memorable if signs that are understood by many are used in a picture. The study of semiotics is vital because signs permeate every message, whether verbal or visual. The academic study of semiotics attempts to identify and explain the signs used by every society in the world.

Although semiotics has gained popularity relatively recently, it is an old concept. In 397 CE, Augustine of Hippo, a Roman philosopher, linguist, and bishop of the Roman Catholic Church,

first proposed the study of signs. He recognized that nature is filled with universally understood entities that afforded communication on many nonverbal levels. For Augustine, signs were the link between nature and humans—between the outer and inner worlds. More importantly, signs from nature also linked individuals to form cultural meaning that could be transferred to future generations. The word semiotics comes from the language of his country: *Semeion* is the Greek word for sign.

Contemporary semiotics emerged through the work of two theorists just before World War I. Swiss linguist Ferdinand de Saussure developed a general theory of signs while a professor at the University of Geneva (Figure 3.16). We know about his work in semiotics because of the notes written by his students during his lectures, which were later published. A lesson: Listen closely to your instructors and take good notes. At about the same time, American philosopher Charles Sanders Peirce (pronounced "purse") published his own ideas about the effect of signs on society (Figure 3.17). De Saussure and Peirce inspired others to concentrate in this field of study. The Americans Arthur Asa Berger, Charles Morris, and Thomas Sebeok, the Italian Umberto Eco, the French Roland Barthes, and many others have contributed greatly to the study of semiotics. Eco's novels *The Name of the Rose, Foucault's Pendulum*, and *The Island of the Day Before* are fascinating and amusing explorations of symbolic meaning.

De Saussure and Peirce weren't particularly interested in the visual aspects of signs. They were traditional linguists who studied the way words were used to communicate meaning through narrative structures. However, over the years semiotics has evolved into a theory of perception that involves the use of images in unexpected ways. For example, Sebeok, a professor emeritus at Indiana University who died in 2002, identified some of the topics that semiotics researchers have studied. Besides the obvious subject of visual signs and symbols used in graphic designs, they include the semiotics of the theater, where performance elements are analyzed; the semiotics of puppetry, in which the colors, costumes, gestures, and staging of the characters are studied; the semiotics of television and commercials; the semiotics of tourism; the semiotics of the signs used in Boy Scout uniforms and rituals; the semiotics of notational systems used in dance, music, logic, mathematics, and chemistry; and urban semiotics, in which the growth and physical attributes of cities are seen as social symbols. The field has become so popular that journals, international conferences, and academic departments at universities are

Figure 3.16
Ferdinand de Saussure (flipped horizontally so he and Pierce could stare at each other) was a Swiss linguist who was monumental in establishing the symbolic interpretation of signs through his course in general linguistics taught at the University of Geneva. After his death in 1913, two former students published his lectures from their notes which led to the founding of the field of semiotics, the study of signs.

devoted to semiotics.

Peirce's contribution to semiotics was in the formulation of three different types of signs: iconic, indexical, and symbolic. All signs must be learned, but the speed of comprehension of each type of sign varies. Thinking about iconic, indexical, and symbolic signs is a way to really look and study a visual message in a much more thorough and critical manner. Once this process is done, you soon realize that even the simplest image has complex cultural meaning. However, it is important to realize that the three categories of signs are not mutually exclusive. The written and visual examples given in this section are meant to focus your attention on one particular type of sign.

A napkin from Hof's Hut, a popular chain of southern California restaurants, portrays the three types of signs through pictures and words and will be used as an example for this section (Figure 3.18).

Figure 3.17
Charles Sanders Peirce was an American philosopher and scientist considered to be the founder of the field of semiotics, but he led a troubled life. Appointed to teach logic courses at Johns Hopkins University, he was dismissed after it was learned he lived with a woman while he was separated but still married to his first wife. After the scandal, he could no longer find employment in academia. In 1887 he lost his family inheritance after purchasing 2,000 acres of farmland in Pennsylvania that never returned the investment. Wanted by the authorities for assault and failure to pay his debts, he was saved from prison by sympathetic friends and family members. To support himself until he died in 1910, he wrote articles for journals and gave lectures. From his articles, lectures, and correspondence, the field of semiotics was established in America.
Courtesy of the National Oceanic and Atmospheric Administration

Iconic Signs Icon, from the Greek word *eikenai*, means "to be like" or "to seem." Iconic signs are the easiest to interpret because they most closely resemble the thing they are meant to represent. Examples of icons are the accurate cave paintings of animals by prehistoric humans, the simple drawings above restroom doors that communicate the gender allowed inside, the trash can, printer, and home images on the desktops of many computers, street signs that indicate dangerous road conditions, and—the most common of all—pho-

Figure 3.18
The Hof's Hut restaurant napkin is a study of many different types of semiotic signs—iconic, the illustration of a pot pie; indexical, the "heat" lines emanating from the crust; and symbolic, the words and colors.
Courtesy of Paul Martin Lester

tographs and motion pictures that are meant to be representations of what they depict.

Almost any documentary photographer's images would be good examples of iconic signs. The portraits of German August Sander work well. Looking at his many images you cannot doubt that at some time the persons pictured resembled their portraits (Figure 3.19). *For the restaurant's napkin, the tilted, brown illustration of a chicken pot pie in the top-left corner is an iconic sign—the drawing is meant to represent a pie similar to one you can order at the restaurant.*

Indexical Signs Indexical signs have a logical, common sense connection to the thing or idea they represent rather than a direct resemblance to the object. Consequently, their interpretation takes a

Figure 3.19
(Weblink: http://goo.gl/tL4viI) August Sander was given a camera when he was 15-years old in 1892. He taught himself photography and to develop and print his pictures in a darkroom. He would become an expert in the medium with a popular photographic studio. He also hosted a radio broadcast about photography and wrote five books. However, after his son, a Communist, was arrested by the Nazis, many of Sander's images were destroyed. Nevertheless, he salvaged many of his negatives so that his prints are in collections throughout the world.

Figure 3.20
This 19th century drawing presents good examples of indexical signs. There are two possible sources for the smoke—a steam engine on the horse-drawn fire engine and a fire inside the house. But is there a blaze on the fire engine or is the man at the window simply smoking a (rather large) cigar? Experience helps us decipher indexical signs. But as with all images, there are other signs to analyze. The photographic quality of the image makes it an iconic sign, and the buildings, clothing, and horses are symbolic signs of an earlier age.
Courtesy of *Uncensored Situations*, 1966, The Dick Sutphen Studio, Inc.

LINK
Figure 3.21
(Weblink: http://goo.gl/NJAjir) Besides being an excellent portrait photographer, John Loengard was the photo editor for Life *magazine for 14 years. He is also the author of several books about photography.*

little longer than that of icons. We learn indexical signs through everyday life experiences. Peirce used a sundial as an illustration of an indexical sign. The sun's shadow implied the movement of time. Other indexical signs can be a footprint on the beach or on the surface of the moon, smoke spewing out of a high smokestack or an automobile exhaust pipe, or the high temperature reading of a sick patient. Footprints stand for the person who impressed them. Smoke represents the pollution generated by the furnace or engine. Fever indicates that the patient has an infection (Figure 3.20). A famous portrait of trumpeter Louis Armstrong taken in 1965 by John Loengard of *Life* magazine is a tightly cropped image that shows lines on two fingers and his lips, which are indexical signs of his age. The portrait captures him rubbing petroleum jelly to his lips to soften them before a concert (Figure 3.21).

Back to the napkin, we have learned through our experiences that the six lines trailing from the pot pie are meant to represent heat. Someone's food is fresh and right out of the oven. However, to someone else, those lines might indicate that the pie is falling, a common visual device used in printed cartoons. More bizarre, a creative person might think that the lines mean that the pie is a marionette, a type of puppet controlled by strings, or even stranger, a pie full of rats, with the brown lines representing the tails showing through the crust. All of these interpretations come from the indexical sign on the napkin of lines exuding from the pie.

Symbolic Signs The third type of sign is the most abstract. Symbols have no logical or representational connection between them and the things they represent. Symbols, more than the other types of signs, *have* to be taught (Figure 3.22). For that reason, social and cultural considerations influence them greatly. Words, numbers, colors, gestures, flags,

costumes, most company logos, music, and religious images all are considered symbols (Figure 3.23). Because symbols often have deep roots in the culture of a particular group, with their meanings being passed from one generation to the next, symbolic signs mean more than iconic or indexical signs (Figure 3.24). The burning of a country's national flag as a protest gesture is a powerful symbol of defiance and anger. It isn't simply an act to create heat through the burning of a piece of fabric.

The meaning one gets from a symbol is highly personalized and often distinct. In the novel *The Da Vinci Code* by Dan Brown, a main character attempts to explain this fact of human nature: "Telling someone what a symbol 'meant' was like telling them how a song should make them feel—it was different for all people. A white Ku Klux Klan headpiece conjured images of hatred and racism in the United States, and yet the same costume carried a meaning of religious faith in Spain."

Symbols tied to religious faith often evoke the strongest emotional responses. After burned copies of the Qura'n, a holy book revered by Muslims as the literal word of God, were found at NATO's Bagram Air Base in Afghanistan in 2012, Kabul citizens erupted in rioting. The violence resulted in many civilians killed and wounded along with American troops that included a colonel and a major. Despite an apology from President Obama and a call for restraint by Afghan leader Hamid Karzai, the extreme reaction to the symbolic slight caused added resentment of America's occupation of the country and a public relations crisis.

Closer to home, after cleaning fluid reacted to the surface of windows of the Seminole Finance Corp. building in Clearwater, Florida, in 1996, many claimed to see a 60-foot apparition of the Virgin Mary (Figure 3.25). Consequently, a shrine was established that included a large, wooden crucifix, an area where

Figure 3.22
In 1981 the Ulster Defense Association (UDA) was an ultraconservative paramilitary organiza-
tion in Belfast, Northern Ireland. The sans serif typeface urges Irish hunger strikers in 1981 to
starve themselves in the prison wing known as "H-Block." The cross for the "I" in "DIE" is an
ironic religious symbol when it is associated with this violent message.
Courtesy of Paul Martin Lester

Figure 3.23
Clasped hands symbolize prayer or contemplation in many cultures. The unusually tight cropping of the
top of the image emphasizes the importance of the gesture by a doctor who treats young patients who
have been paralyzed from gunshots.
Courtesy of Paul Martin Lester

Figure 3.24
A black cloth over the head of a person symbolizes death in many cultures. In reality, this man is simply avoiding the sun or the photographer on the boardwalk of Atlantic City.
Courtesy of Paul Martin Lester

persons could light candles, and white, plastic chairs where you could sit and meditate. With the thousands that came to see the window's image, the building was abandoned by its owners and later sold to the Shepherds of Christ Ministries, which sold bibles and other religious works in its bookstore. But such a popular icon can be a tempting target. In 2004 a high school student admitted that he broke out the window and destroyed the giant "head" with a powerful slingshot (the author is not certain whether the perpetrator's name was David).

In 2011 the 30,000-member Sons of Confederate Veterans sued the state of Texas after it was unsuccessful in having the Department of Motor Vehicles approve its specialty license plate that featured a graphic design with a

Confederate flag. Backers claimed it honored veterans while opponents said it supported a culture of bigotry. Either way, the debate over the "stars and bars" was an example of how a symbol can be emotionally charged. After a white supremacist terrorist murdered nine persons attending a gathering at the Emanuel African Methodist Church in Charleston, South Carolina in 2015, officials and citizens of mostly southern cities started to rethink honoring the Confederacy with statues of Civil War leaders prominently displayed in their towns. The New Orleans City Council voted that its four Confederate monuments be removed and in 2017 the last one, that of Gen. Robert E. Lee was taken off the 60-foot pedestal of Lee Circle. Visual symbolism often provides power-

Figure 3.25
*The power of symbolic signs to emotionally connect persons with them is
evident in this picture. After a cleaning solvent accidentally stained the outside
glass of a building in Clearwater, Florida, in 1996, for many the result resembled
the head of the religious figure, the Virgin Mary. Thousands came to the site
seeking inspiration and comfort. Eventually, the window was broken.*
Courtesy of Paul Martin Lester

Figure 3.26
*On the Denton (Texas) County Courthouse square is a monument erected by the Daugh-
ters of the Confederacy in 1918. All attempts to have the statue removed have so far been
unsuccessful.*
Courtesy of Paul Martin Lester

ful messages whether they are displayed or imagined (Figure 3.26). Another controversy that involves the Civil War comes from Texas. The Six Flags amusement park company, with its headquarters in Grand Prairie, was named for the number of flags flown over what is now the state: Spain, France, Mexico, the Republic of Texas, the Confederate States of America, and the United States. Time will tell if any protests force the company to change its name to Five Flags Over Texas.

The printed words on the napkin are all examples of symbolic signs. Notice the typeface choice for "Hof's Hut." You will learn in Chapter 7 how a designer's typographic choices can provide additional meaning to a presentation. The typeface family used for the name of the restaurant is called blackletter. It originated from the first commercial printing press by the German Johannes Gutenberg in 1455. Consequently, over the years the typeface's symbolic meaning includes concepts such as German, religious, traditional, and long established. Although not a German restaurant, the Hofman family who owns the chain wanted to honor their German roots. Under the name is the word "R E S T A U R A N T S" presented with a much different typeface, a sans serif. It has a clean and modern symbolic meaning enhanced by the extra space or kerning between the cheery blue letters. A goldenrod rule enhances the bright mood. Hof's Hut, then, has been around for a long time, their kitchen is tidy and sanitary, and their restaurant is a pleasant place, despite what may be interpreted by its pot pie picture.

An example of all three types of signs used in portraits of the same person over several centuries can be seen in the portraits of Christopher Columbus. Since no portraits of him were made during his lifetime, a study of his pictures is an example of cultural relativism—different people from various times in history have a range of

portraits of the famous seaman. After his death and when his exploits became known, the portraits were iconic—the public simply needed to know what the explorer looked like. Hundreds of years after his explorations, Italian American commercial interests used Columbus as a symbol for their own purposes. They wanted to use his name and history to promote the Columbian Exhibition in Chicago in 1892 and to try to change the name of America to Columbia. Consequently, his portraits were indexical—he was seen being guided by the light or voice of God. At the 500th anniversary, however, when opinions of Columbus and his voyages were severely critical, the portraits were symbolic—they showed his face as a collection of jigsaw puzzle pieces or as a sailing ship that had a death mask on its bow (Figures 3.27 and 3.28).

New Orleans photographer and poet Clarence John Laughlin made pictures of objects that for him had complex symbolic meanings. One image is of a statue by the side of a grave he named "Figure from the Underworld, 1951." His typically lucid and elaborate caption directs the viewer to notice all three types of signs. Iconic: "A horrible little stucco figure, probably turned out by the thousands in a mold, and found in a Louisiana country garden." Indexical: "The fierce suns and heavy rains of Louisiana have eaten it as though by acid." Symbolic: "Leaving it as though with its brain exposed, and with a sweet smile turned sickly and defeated. It rises as if from some nether plane—the dark and ragged American world of the 1930s." His image becomes a powerful metaphor that makes a comment about our present economic times (Figure 3.29).

Besides iconic, indexical, and symbolic signs, Roland Barthes described another way to think of individual elements within an image. He developed the concept of a *chain of associations* that make up a picture's narrative. To under-

Figure 3.27
"Portrait of a Man, Said to be Christopher Columbus," 1519, by Sebastiano del Piombo (Sebastiano Luciani). This portrait is highly regarded and has been used in many descriptions and articles about the Admiral, but it is not Columbus. Born around 1485, Piombo would have been 21 years old when Columbus died, but there was no indication he knew him. Moreover, Piombo took up painting later in his life, having devoted his early years to music. As a portrait, it is a bit unusual because the subject wears a hat with a curled border. A deep-edged and ornate sleeveless coat or mantle hangs from his shoulders. His fingers are long and delicate. His face is round, his eyes blue, and a dimple is barely visible in his chin. Most striking about this painting is the legend that runs along the top. The inscription that identifies the sitter as Columbus was included much later to increase the value of the painting.
Courtesy of the Metropolitan Museum of Art

Figure 3.28
"Christopher Columbus," oil on canvas, 1866, by Karl von Piloty. A German painter of considerable skill and reputation, Piloty was known for his historical works. He later was appointed keeper of the Munich Academy, was ennobled by the King of Bavaria, and was a respected educator. This painting is a good example of indexical signs. While a crewman sleeps, the bearded Admiral is seen on deck late at night, bags under his eyes from worry, and checking his progress on a map when a heavenly light rivets his attention as he nears land.
Courtesy of *Visual Anthropology*

Figure 3.29
(Weblink: http://goo.gl/qkWfB4)
New Orleans photographer Clarence John Laughlin's "Figure from the Underworld, 1951" is a visual metaphor for the degradation of society and a clear example of an indexical sign in semiotics.

Figure 3.30
As one of the few traffic signs that originated in the United States, the first stop sign was erected in Michigan, the home of the American automobile industry, in 1915 and showed the word "STOP" in black letters against a yellow octagon background. A common stop sign stands for a complicated set of legal specifications and codes. In 1954 the design was changed to a standard 30 inches across each side of its octagonal area with a three-quarter-inch white border. The white uppercase sans serif letters forming the word "STOP" are ten inches high. The height of a sign from the base must be at least five feet. The color red was chosen because the same color is used for traffic lights. The sign is also retroreflective. It reflects headlights back with a minimum of scattering. But the traffic sign also stands for a complex set of legal codes—for example, if you arrive first at an intersection you can proceed first, but if two or more drivers arrive at the junction at the same time, the one on the left must yield to the one on the right.
Courtesy of Paul Martin Lester

stand this concept, we must first discuss how we communicate through words.

In verbal language, the narrative or story we are telling/reading/hearing is linear. One word follows the next in a specific rule-based order known as its syntax, or grammar. These rules of syntax have been established and agreed upon over centuries for a language and its people. Pictures, on the other hand, are presentational. All the elements of an image, whether still or moving, are presented all at once with a viewer free to look at them in any order. Signs within an image are presented in various ways for a variety of media, many times depending on the style of the image maker. But since most of us think of images through thoughts composed of words within our minds, we usually link individual elements within a picture into a narrative whole. For Barthes, each element is a link that forms a chain of associations, or meaning. The common term for Barthes's chain of associations is codes. A code is an amalgamation of hundreds of ideas and/or elements into one, convenient concept. The next time you are stopped at a street corner and see a stop sign, think of all the underlying statutes and laws that regulate the sign itself—its color, location, shape, size, height, and so on—and its meaning—to stop, of course, but also where, for how long, and in which order if other cars are present (Figure 3.30). Asa Berger elaborated on Barthes and suggested four types of codes: metonymic, analogical, displaced, and condensed.

Metonymic Code A collection of signs that cause the viewer to make assumptions about what is seen is a metonymic code. In that way, this type of code is closely associated with indexical signs. You assume something about what you see. Most advertisers, whether working in commercial, non-profit, or political venues, want the viewer to make assumptions about a particular product

or service. A viewer of a studio set-up portrait of a smiling family—father, mother, daughter, and dog—playfully wrapped in bed linens used in an advertisement shown in a magazine makes a number of assumptions about the picture—that this is a real family, that they are actually happy, and that their choice of cotton comforters has brought them to this blissful state. Furthermore, it is hoped that when you see this pleasant quartet of good-looking models, you will

W LINK Figure 3.31
(Weblink: http://goo.gl/NB2Huu) Most metonymic codes reveal themselves in advertisements as this collection of images makes clear.

think that if you had the same products on your bed you would be just as satisfied with your life (Figure 3.31).

Analogical Code This type of code is a group of signs that cause the viewer to make mental comparisons. Examples, often called figures of speech, might compare an old tree to a human face, a live mouse to a computer device, and lined yellow paper to a lemon peel. A large piece of equipment, such as a blast furnace in a steel mill, might have shapes and patterns that when seen at a particular angle and under specific lighting conditions resembles the face of a robot. It is unlikely that the architect of the factory positioned parts of the furnace to resemble the eyes, nose, and mouth of a face, but it is likely that an observant photographer would take a picture in such a way to show those features because it adds interest to the picture (Figure 3.32). During the 2009 U.S. Open tennis tournament, American Express introduced a commercial for its charge card that showed everyday objects, singularly and in combination that resembled human faces when sad or happy. Produced by WPP's Ogilvy & Mather advertising agency, it puts the analogical code to creative commercial use.

Figure 3.33
*(Weblink: http://goo.gl/SlOsUY)
Stanley Kubrick's* Dr. Strangelove or: How I Learned to Stop
Worrying and Love the Bomb
*(1964) is a classic study of the
displaced code. The nuclear
warhead prop that actor Slim
Pickens rides at the end of the
movie is the ultimate phallic
symbol.*

Figure 3.32
*In the summer of 1976, the Viking Orbiter 1 took photographs of the Cydonia region of Mars
in the planet's northern hemisphere to find possible landing sites for its sister spaceship, the
Viking Lander 2. One of the images revealed what a NASA public relations person described
as a "huge rock formation . . . which resembles a human head . . . formed by shadows giving
the illusion of eyes, nose and mouth." The so-called "Face on Mars" became an instant
popular culture phenomenon, with some using it as evidence of life on the planet. In 2001 the
Mars Global Surveyor took another picture of the rock cropping. There was no face, but the
analogical code lives on.*
NASA Jet Propulsion Laboratory

Displaced Code Whenever there is a
transfer of meaning from one set of signs
to another, a displaced code is used. In
the classic movie *Dr. Strangelove or: How
I Learned to Stop Worrying and Love
the Bomb* (1964) directed by Stanley
Kubrick, rifles, missiles, airplanes, and
other phallic shapes were photographed
purposely to communicate the idea of
sexual tension among certain military
characters. The film's climax shows
the character Major T.J. "King" Kong
played by Slim Pickens gleefully riding
the bomb to his and the world's doom
(Figure 3.33).

Images of penises are not acceptable
pictures for most members of society
and so are displaced by their phallic
equivalents. Liquor, lipstick, and cigarette advertisers also commonly use
phallic imagery in the form of their
products' shapes in the hope that potential customers will link the use of their
products with possible sexual conquest. Ads from Skyy vodka, Tom Ford
eyewear, and Sisley clothing regularly
employ such symbolism. To attract attention and to link sex with their products,
"shock ads" from these companies have
used the shape of a tie, the placement
of a bottle, a man's middle finger in the
mouth of a woman, and a female model
holding a snake and attempting to lick its
head.

Condensed Code In many respects,
this type of code is the most interesting. Condensed codes are several signs
that combine to form a new, composite
message. Televised music videos and the
advertisements inspired by them have
unique and often unexpected meanings.

Figure 3.34
(Weblink: http:// goo.gl/Xnnfcq)
In his 1980 photograph "Untitled," Jerry Uelsmann creates a cloud-filled sky contained within a box is suspended above the edge of an ocean with crashing waves. Without much help from the title, any meaning from this set of elements must come from the viewer.

Figure 3.35
(Weblink: http://goo.gl/HSHflF)
With its mandolin-based, folksy sound, "Losing My Religion" was a surprise hit for the rock band REM. Michael Stipe wanted the video to be in a similar style as Sinéad O'Connor's "Nothing Compares 2 U." However, director Tarsem Singh based the film on the short story by Gabriel Garcia Marquez, "A Very Old Man with Enormous Wings" about an angel that falls into a village. At the 1991 MTV Music Video Awards it won six trophies including best music video.

The signs of musicians, dancers, music, quick-editing techniques, graphics, colors, and so on all form a complex message. Within the culture a message is intended for, a condensed code has relevant meaning. For those outside that culture being represented, the images can be confusing, random, and without purpose. But the way individuals combine signs and form their own meaningful messages often cannot be controlled by the creators of the signs. The photographic work of American Jerry Uelsmann combines elements from several images to make intriguing composite pictures (Figure 3.34).

Semiotics teaches the importance of symbolism in the act of visual perception and communication. A viewer who knows the meaning behind the signs used in a complex picture will gain insights from it, making the image more memorable. The motion pictures of American director David Lynch (*Blue Velvet*, 1986; *Lost Highway*, 1997; *Mulholland Dr.*, 2001) are often examples of complex semiotic signs. For example, the opening scene from *Twin Peaks: Fire Walk with Me* (1992) has a strange woman wearing a red dress and a blue rose who communicates through gestures important information to the characters played by Chris Isaak and Kiefer Sutherland.

The 1991 music video from the rock group REM for their song "Losing My Religion" is a rich and potentially confusing collection of signs (Figure 3.35). Its overall meaning is aided by knowing the history of the band and the biography of its members, the lyrics of the song, the fact that the director, Tarsem Singh is from India, the "Myth of Icarus," the history of fascism, and the paintings of Italian Michelangelo Merisi da Caravaggio, particularly his 1601-02 oil, "The Incredulity of Saint Thomas" (Figure 3.36).

The problem in using complex signs as a part of an image is that they may be misunderstood, ignored, or interpreted the wrong way. Nevertheless, the challenge for visual communicators, expressed in the study of semiotics, is that signs can enhance the visual experience and educate, entertain, and persuade a viewer.

Cognitive Theory According to the cognitive theory, what is going on in a viewer's mind is just as important as the images that can be seen. Mental activities focus attention on a visual element, but they can also distract a viewer. The cultural anthropologist Carolyn Bloomer identified several mental activities that affect visual perception: memory, projection, expectation, selectivity, habituation, salience, dissonance, culture, and words.

Memory Arguably the most important mental activity involved in accurate visual perception, memory is our link with all the images we have ever seen. A historic photograph of President Lincoln's funeral in Washington, D.C. in 1865 or a crowd shot from the 1969 Woodstock, New York music concert might be of interest to you as they trigger memories and associations because of a funeral you have attended, a visit to America's capitol, something you read about the 16th president, someone you know who was at the historic concert, or a music festival you attended. Someone else might have no associations with either picture and quickly turn the page (Figure 3.37).

Projection Creative individuals see recognizable forms in Cheerios floating in a bowl of milk in the morning or in rock patterns while sitting near a pool in Palm Springs, California. Others make sense out of clouds or trees, or find comfort in the messages learned from tarot cards, astrological forecasts, and the I-Ching. One reason the common inkblot test developed in 1921 by the Swiss Freudian psychologist Hermann

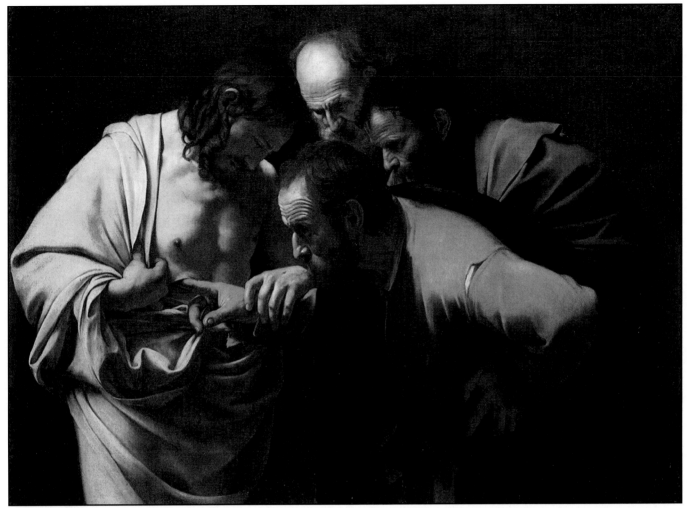

Figure 3.36

"The Incredulity of St. Thomas," 1601–1602, by Caravaggio. The Italian painter Michelangelo Merisi da Caravaggio popularized a technique called selective illumination that became a signature of the Baroque school of art that he initiated. His use of spot lighting and dark shadows added dramatic interest to his works. He also preferred to use ordinary people he met on the streets as models in his paintings to give them a realistic quality, unlike the idealized religious works of the day. "The Doubting of St. Thomas," hanging in the former summer palace of Frederick the Great, captures the moment told in the Bible when St. Thomas investigates the wounds of Jesus and no longer doubts that he has returned to life after his crucifixion.

Courtesy of the Sanssouci Picture Gallery

Rorschach is used is that individuals often reveal personality traits by deriving meaning from the oddly formed shapes. A person's mental state of mind is thus "projected" onto an inanimate object or generalized statement. Someone may spend hours marveling at the humanlike face formed by the curves and shadows in a tree trunk while another will walk past. The difference between the two may be in the mental processes that affect what they see (Figure 3.38).

Expectation Having preconceived expectations about how a scene should appear often leads to false or missed visual perceptions. Italian artist Guido Daniele (Figure 3.39) paints images of zebras, elephants, eagles, and snakes on human hands. The intriguing visual result is that a viewer often forgets that the animal paintings use a hand as the substrate for the work. Daniele lives and works in Milan, Italy where he produces photo-realistic paintings for private collectors and advertising agencies.

A clever magazine advertisement and commercial for Johnnie Walker's Blue Label whisky is at first an artistic collection of wavy lines—until a full-

Figure 3.37

President Lincoln's funeral procession in New York City, with 11,000 members of the military and about 75,000 civilians marching along, was as elaborate in real life as it is shown here in this lithograph based on a photograph attributed to Matthew Brady and published in Harper's Weekly *on May 13, 1865. If you are a history buff interested in Lincoln, or have been to funeral or parade recently, this image may be of interest to you because it might trigger memories.*
Courtesy of the Library of Congress

length image of a man standing before a woman sitting in a chair holding a bottle suddenly is noticed under the catch phrase, "For those who know what to look for" (Figure 3.40). Researchers Robert Becklen and Daniel Cervone devised an experiment in 1983 in which subjects were asked to count the number of times a three-person team wearing black T-shirts passed a basketball. In a recent recreation, Daniel J. Simons substitute an umbrella with someone in an ape costume walking casually through the room (Figure 3.41).

Selectivity Aldous Huxley discussed this cognitive element when he wrote of combining selecting with sensing and perceiving. Most of what people see within a complicated visual experience is not part of conscious processing. For example, rarely do people think about their own breathing unless made aware of it. Most of visual perception is an unconscious, automatic act by which large numbers of images enter and leave the mind without being processed. We usually focus only on significant details within a scene. If you are trying to locate a friend sitting in packed bleachers during a baseball game, all the other unknown faces in the crowd will have little significance. When you see your friend, your mind suddenly locks on that person as if with the help of a spotlight in a darkened room. Concentrating on people observing a funeral procession in a documentary photograph taken during the violent era of 1981 in Belfast, Northern Ireland, you might miss the covered face of an Irish Republican Army (IRA) soldier (Figure 3.42).

Figure 3.38
Projection is in the mind of the beholder. Whether you see a seemingly random and meaningless pattern created by a plant climbing the wall of a building in Santa Monica, California or a representation of the Statue of Liberty depends on your mental state.
Courtesy of Paul Martin Lester

Figure 3.42
Expectation is a mental condition that can lead to heightened observation if a scene matches your mental imaginings or to poor visual perception if your preconceived idea of what you will see is not matched by reality. A casual viewer would most likely overlook the masked Irish Republican Army (IRA) soldier at the lower right of the frame during a funeral for a hunger striker in Belfast, Northern Ireland, in 1981.
Courtesy of Paul Martin Lester

Habituation To protect itself from overstimulation and unnecessary images that might fatigue and confuse, the mind tends to ignore visual stimuli that are a part of a person's everyday, habitual activities. When you walk or drive to school or work the same way every day, your brain will ignore the sights along your route. Many people like to travel to new areas because the images experienced in an unfamiliar place often are striking and interesting. One way to prevent your mind from thinking habitually is to search for new ways to think about familiar objects or events in your daily life so that you save money on a flight to Amsterdam. Practicing creative thought readies your mind to think actively about new images when you see them. Walker Evans, one of the most famous photographers in the medium's history, produced a series of pictures of everyday tools—a pair of pliers, a wrench, and so on—using high-quality studio lighting

and camera techniques to celebrate their often overlooked designs. Accompanying his 1955 portfolio in *Fortune* magazine titled "Beauties of the Common Tool," Walker wrote, "Almost all the basic small tools stand, aesthetically speaking, for elegance, candor, and purity" (Figure 3.43). Likewise, another master of photography, Edward Weston, photographed ordinary objects such as a seashell, a bell pepper, and a toilet seat for the same reason (Figure 3.44). Looking at their images, you can't help but find the sublime in their banality.

Salience A stimulus will be noticed more if it has meaning for an individual. If you recently met someone you like whose favorite food is from India, whenever you smell curry, hear other people talking about the country, or watch *Slumdog Millionaire* (2008), you will be reminded of that person. If you are hungry you will notice the smells of cooking food emanating from an open window. A

W LINK
Figure 3.39
(Weblink: http://goo.gl/xJLLNO) As demonstrated by the work on his website, Guido Daniele is a versatile artist with hand and body painting as well as traditional illustrations for personal and commercial purposes.

W LINK
Figure 3.40
(Weblink: http://goo.gl/sLXf3S) The irony of Johnnie Walker's "For those who know what to look for" campaign is that most viewers will miss the hidden visual message in the advertisement because they don't know what to look for.

W LINK
Figure 3.41
(Weblink: http://goo.gl/wTNCVL) Show this video to your friends and see if they notice the unexpected addition.

W LINK
Figure 3.43
(Weblink: http://goo.gl/IPLm3t) Two pages from Fortune magazine with photographs by Walker Evans. Former Farm Security Administration (FSA) photographer Evans made a series of pictures of everyday objects under studio lighting that demonstrate the cognitive element of habituation. Without being able to study Evan's photographs, you might miss the metal texture of the trowel and the crescent wrench, the contrast of curved versus straight lines, and the shadows that define their thickness.

W
LINK
Figure 3.44
*(Weblink:
http://goo.gl/QKcqRz)
American photographer
Edward Weston transforms
an ordinary bell pepper into
a symbol masculinity in his
"Pepper, 1930."*

trained biologist will see more in a slide under a microscope than the average person will; both individuals see all there is to see under the microscope, but what the biologist sees is consciously processed in the mind (Figure 3.45).

Dissonance For many, trying to read while a television or stereo is loudly playing in the same room is difficult be-

understand because of all the competing formats. A classic example of dissonance came from the cable network CNN when it introduced in August 2001 its new version of the 1982 staple "Headline News." Television critics across the country voiced their negative opinion about the format because of all the competing bits of information—an anchorperson talking on camera or as a voice-over, still

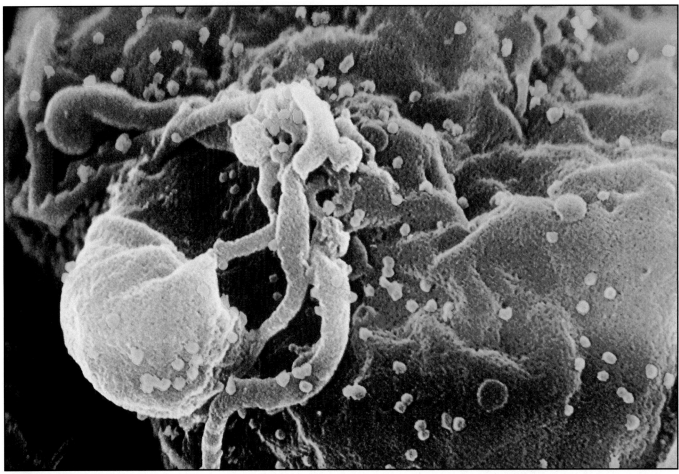

Figure 3.45
The cognitive element of salience refers directly to Aldous Huxley's famous phrase, "The more you know, the more you see." If you are a medical research, you will more likely find meaning from this electron microscope view of the HIV virus (small green spheres) attacking a white blood cell. As a general rule, the more salience you bring to any visual message the more interesting it will be to you.
Courtesy of the Centers for Disease Control and Prevention

cause the mind tends to concentrate on only one activity at a time. A book is set aside the moment a television program or the lyrics of a song become interesting. Television programs that combine written and spoken words, multiple images, and music run the risk of creating visual messages that the viewer cannot

and/or moving images, graphics with headlines, stock details, weather reports, news "crawls" that updated news events, and advertising logos. Because of the negative feedback, CNN toned down most of its visual display, but kept the crawl along the bottom of the screen.

Dissonance can also happen if a

room is too warm or too cold, if there is a personal matter that you cannot stop thinking about, or if there are too many road sign advertisements competing for your attention on a highway. Too many distractions and you will find it difficult to concentrate on a single visual message (Figure 3.46).

Culture As a manifestation of the

a particular culture you also will comprehend some of the underlying reasons behind their use. Culture isn't simply the concept of a country's borders or the idea of high-class or upper-class "culture." It spans ethnicity, economic situations, places of work, gender, age, sexual orientation, physical disability, geographic location, and many other aspects of a person's life. Franc Boas, a leader in the

Figure 3.46
"Little Chapel," Las Vegas, 1999, by Gerry Davey. Sandwiched between the Yucca Motel with its "UEEN" beds and the Oasis Motel with its adult movies, fantasy rooms, and Jacuzzis, you might miss the fact that if you get married in the Little Chapel of the Flowers you can get your wedding webcast FREE. Dissonance is a result of so many elements within a visual array that important details are missed.
Courtesy of Gerry Davey

way people act, talk, dress, eat, drink, behave socially, and practice their religious beliefs, cultural influences have a tremendous impact on visual perception. Religious icons, state and country flags, T-shirt designs, and hairstyles all have individual and cultural meanings. If you are aware of the signs that are a part of

field of anthropology in his book *Anthropology and Modern Life* explained that culture is "the community of emotional life that rises from our everyday habits." Boas thought that culture was more important than race. Culture determines the importance of the signs that affect the people who live with and among us

Figure 3.47
One of the most important determinants of what you notice and what you miss visually is your cultural identity. For this group of persons waiting for an Easter parade in the French Quarter of New Orleans, what each person notices may be a factor of race, age, gender, weight, and alcohol intake.
Courtesy of Paul Martin Lester

(Figure 3.47).

Words Although we see with our eyes, most of us think with words. Consequently, words, like memory and culture, profoundly affect our understanding and subsequent long-term recall of an image (Figure 3.48). One of the strongest forms of communication is when words and images are combined in equally respectful ways. That is why magazines, newspapers, and websites regularly have captions for each photograph and news anchors and broadcast journalists use voice-overs to explain what is being shown.

Semiotics and cognitive approaches to visual communication state that the human mind is an infinitely complex living organism that science may never fully understand. But meaningful con-

nections between what people see and how they use those images arise when mental processing is viewed as a human rather than an automatic, mechanical process.

The sensory theories of gestalt and constructivism and the perceptual theories of semiotics and cognitive teach visual communicators to look closely at their world, create designs that attract attention, be mindful of the varied messages that come from images, and understand the possible mental enhancers and distractions to anything that might be attempted graphically.

Figure 3.48
A photograph of a haphazard stack of snow skis of various lengths and conditions has little meaning without the addition of the sign posted on a building at the Snakedance Condominiums in the Taos Ski Valley. Skiers are free to take whatever they want. However, with no evidence of snow anywhere in the picture, perhaps it is not the best time to enjoy that outdoor activity.
Courtesy of Paul Martin Lester

KEY TERMS FROM THIS CHAPTER

Blogs • Broadsheet • Closure • Cultural Relativism • Fascism • Ku Klux Klan • Podcasts • Rituals • Short-term memory • Shrine • Sidebars • Social symbols • Substrate • Syntax • Tabloid • Teasers • Visual perception

4 Visual Persuasion

*Character may almost be called
the most effective means of
persuasion.*

*Aristotle, 384-322BCE
SCIENTIST, PHILOSOPHER,
& TEACHER*

A newborn baby lies alone with an umbilical cord still attached; a black horse mates with a docile white; a young, attractive priest kisses a young, attractive nun romantically on the lips; a car engulfed in flames; sensitive portraits of death row inmates—the connection between these and other striking images is that they were all used as advertisements to sell clothing. They also generated an enormous amount of controversy in newspapers, magazines, and television news reports throughout the world (Figure 4.1).

There is a trite saying sometimes uttered by those slightly burned by the media's too glaring light, "Any publicity is good publicity." For even though most of the news articles and televised reports about the Benetton clothing company's advertising campaigns were negative, business boomed. The company started by the Italian magnate and politician Luciano Benetton, 82, sells about 100 million sweaters, shirts, and pants through some 6,000 outlets in 120 countries, and employs more than 7,000 persons. Total sales in 2015 were more

Figure 4.1
Two models employed by Benetton wear the clothing of a priest and nun who kiss for the camera in this studio image. The picture upset many Catholics because it seemed to mock their religious beliefs.
Courtesy of United Colors of Benetton 1991 spring/summer advertising campaign, Oliviero Toscani

than $1.7 billion, a decline from previous years. The strategy of using shocking images to generate editorial condemnation backfired when the company went too far portraying death row inmates as fashion models. Sears' executives decided to cancel a contract to sell Benetton sweaters on its shelves. After the controversy, Benetton apologized and promptly terminated the employment of Oliviero Toscani, who had been the creative director for the company and responsible for its campaigns for almost two decades.

SHOCK ADVERTISING

Because of photography's ability to arouse viewer interest and occasional condemnation, controversial and unusual pictures are sometimes used to shock potential customers to get attention. Although a sometimes risky marketing strategy, company officials recognize the impact of images to shock viewers.

Brooke Shields probably began the manifestation of "soft porn" advertisements when she posed at age 14 in tight-fitting Calvin Klein jeans in 1980 and cooed, "Nothing comes between me and my Calvins." Klein has consistently used shock advertising as a way of generating enormous controversy and

publicity. But sometimes he goes too far. A $6 million campaign was withdrawn in 1996 in response to a public outcry when teenage boys and girls were photographed in sexually provocative poses by Stephen Meisel, who took pictures of Madonna for her 1992 book *Sex*. Nevertheless, the Klein brand name made it on news reports that acted like free advertising for the company (Figure 4.2).

Some art directors know that shock advertising can make a company a media standout for the moment and give a fresh, edgier look to a traditional company. Former *Playboy* magazine model Jenny McCarthy sat on a toilet, her panties below her knees, for the shoe company Candies. Media critic Collin Brooke noted that the ad's "taboo nature brought it attention." The 2009 spokesperson for Candies was Britney Spears, who has had her own personal dramas played out in the media (Figure 4.3). After Christian Dior introduced its "Addict" cosmetic line with perfume-crazed, open-mouthed, scantily clad, and sweaty models in 2002, the campaign was called "outrageous and irresponsible" by a member of Congress (Figure 4.4). But the 2005 "Addict 2" campaign with emaciated models was barely noticed

Figure 4.2
"We Know What You Want, New York City," 2000, by Gerry Davey. If the larger-than-life size of the billboard doesn't attract attention, the advertiser hopes the topless model will. And yet, the potentially shocking picture seems to attract only the attention of a photographer.
Courtesy of Gerry Davey

Figure 4.3
(Weblink: http://goo.gl/22vttl)
Even Jenny McCarthy must sit on a toilet to conduct business.

Figure 4.4
(Weblink: http://goo.gl/cc6Ua7)
Christian Dior profited from the addict look through negative publicity about its campaign.

Figure 4.5
(Weblink: http://goo.gl/noOtJ9)
Not to be outdone by Dior, Sisley created a much more obvious connection to addiction in their advertisement.

Figure 4.6
(Weblink: http://goo.gl/m5BRSP)
With studio lighting and sitcom camera techniques, the web-only commercial for Absolut looks ordinary, except when the comedians start talking. Whether the humor is appreciated or not is not as important as the attention a viewer gives to this unusual video.

Figure 4.7
(Weblink: http://goo.gl/Ag-4wDm)
Although explained as a visual coincidence, the reaction to Gilbey gin's advertisement was hot enough to melt the ice cubes.

Figure 4.8
(Weblink: http://goo.gl/56QEn8)
Probably few consumers linked sex with a sugar drink, but when Pepsi cans were stacked, some did.

Figure 4.9
(Weblink: http://goo.gl/Qzfmxj)
Abercrombie & Fitch executives were not content to arrange their clothing to spell, "Sex," but instead used young models to promote the idea.

Figure 4.10
(Weblink: http://goo.gl/GO7PDT)
This Paris Hilton commercial for Carl's Jr. burgers has been called soft porn as she glides over the top and washes a Bentley automobile. Some have complained that parents cannot easily control for the content of advertisements as can be done with regular broadcast programs.

Figure 4.11
(Weblink: http://goo.gl/fbK5FT)
The job recruiting company Accolo cleverly and humorously parodied the Paris Hilton Carl's Jr. commercial to gain attention for its service.

Figure 4.12
(Weblink: http://goo.gl/DFlzx4)
At first the video is a bit confusing. Two young persons in separate rooms timing themselves as they put on their clothes is supposed to be unexplained. It's only when the end of the commercial is reached is the mystery explained in this JCPenney commercial that never ran on commercial television.

by media critics. Sisley, a clothing brand owned by Benetton, showed young women with dark rings around their eyes "snorting" the white straps of a slinky dress from straws for its Junkie campaign, misspelled by its Chinese advertising company as "Fashioin" (Figure 4.5). Humorous commercials can also get a company's product noticed. The Swedish vodka company Absolut, known for its advertising campaign in which it commissions artists to produce posters that incorporate the shape of the bottle in clever ways, asked comedian Zack Galifianakis (*Comedians of Comedy*, 2005, *The Hangover*, 2009, and *The Hangover 2*, 2011) to produce a series of web-only commercials with the comedy duo Tim Heidecker and Eric Wareheim, known for their television show, "Tim and Eric Awesome Show, Great Job!" and their motion picture, *Tim and Eric's Billion Dollar Movie* (2012), that were as bizarre as they were funny and became a popular YouTube download (Figure 4.6).

Linking sexual activity with products is a long-established tactic for advertisers. Ice cubes in a glass next to a bottle of Gilbey's gin spelled the word "SEX" and caused a brief uproar (Figure 4.7). Likewise, if you stacked two particular Pepsi cans produced in 1990 you could see the word "SEX," although a spokesperson said it was just a coincidence (Figure 4.8). Executives of the preppy clothier Abercrombie & Fitch (A&F) discovered that sometimes controversy sparked by an advertising campaign does not sell more clothes. Nudity and sexual themes, some involving group sex, were depicted in the company's 2003 *Christmas Field Guide* (Figure 4.9). Many parents became enraged and boycotted the store. A&F quietly withdrew the catalog. Meanwhile, Paris Hilton exploited her sex-crazed celebrity reputation in a 2005 commercial for the Carl's Jr. hamburger chain (Figure 4.10), which was hilariously parodied in an Accolo job-recruiting ad (Figure 4.11).

In 2008, a commercial that was leaked to the web, not produced or approved by JC Penney executives was titled "Speed Dressing." It showed two teenagers removing their clothes and then dressing quickly in anticipation of doing the same in the girl's basement while her mother watched TV upstairs (Figure 4.12). Saatchi & Saatchi, JCPenney's advertising agency, apologized for the spot.

Shockingly violent or sexual images used in ads are the culmination of corporate cynicism in which almost any sensational still or moving image is justified if it gets the attention of potential customers. But not all shock advertising is used for commercial reasons. Barnardo's, a London-based charity that aids more than 50,000 children and their families in about 300 projects across Great Britain, is known for its striking and controversial campaigns. In 2000, an ad showed a baby about to inject heroin (Figure 4.13). Despite the fact that donations grew by five percent and surveys showed public awareness of the charity had doubled, criticism of the graphic content of the ads caused Barnardo's executives to withdraw the campaign.

Other activist individuals and groups use shock images to get noticed. To protest invasive surgery as a cure for breast cancer, photographer Joanne Matuschka, who had a mastectomy, posed in 1993 for a cover story in the *New York Times Magazine* and created a series of posters showing her naked body from the waist up (Figure 4.14). People for the Ethical Treatment of Animals (PETA) often creates controversial advertising in order to gain the media's attention. The Anti-Defamation League and Germany's highest court denounced a campaign in 2003 produced by PETA that included photos of 60-square-foot panels of animals in cages next to photos of Jewish concentration camp victims behind barbed wire, with the slogan "Holocaust on your plate." The German court called the campaign "an offense against human

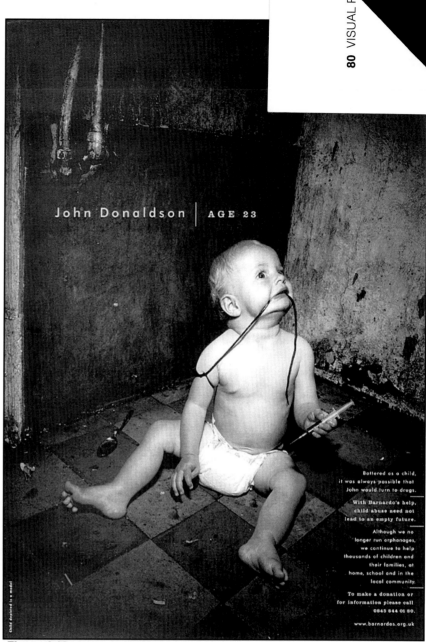

Figure 4.13

"John Donaldson Age 23." With harsh lighting and tilted frame amid a stark and dingy backdrop, the baby shocks a viewer and potential donor to Barnardo's charity by its striking reality. Even though the child was a model, the campaign was called off because many were offended.

Courtesy of Barnardo's

Figure 4.14
*(Weblink:
http://goo.gl/V5CbRk)
Joanne Matuschka strikes an
elegant pose on the cover of
the* New York Times Magazine.

Figure 4.15
*(Weblink: http://goo.gl/V6osGV)
Any link with Nazis and the
Holocaust is controversial in today's society and sure to bring
attention to a public service
campaign.*

Figure 4.16
*(Weblink:
http://goo.gl/R1ELVw)
The PETA organization is
known for its shocking public
service announcements. The
scenes shown in this ad probably weren't considered in the
animation 2016 hit* The Secret
Life of Pets.

Figure 4.17
*(Weblink: http://goo.gl/Jb6uWh)
Once again, PETA found itself
in hot water, this time because
of steamed vegetables.*

dignity" (Figure 4.15). A PSA (Public Service Announcement) commercial called "Sex and the Kitty," which was intended to promote animal birth control, was considered too racy for network television (Figure 4.16). In 2009 PETA was again in the news for a PSA intended to promote vegetarianism, after NBC prohibited the spot from being shown during the Super Bowl telecast because it was considered too sexually suggestive (Figure 4.17).

The reason shock advertisements are prevalent is because they work. Controversial ad campaigns generate stories in the news media and sales. If a media firestorm is the result, the age-old saying is invoked, "It is easier to ask for forgiveness than permission." This adage applies to political campaigns as well. For the 2016 presidential race, the websites FactCheck.org and Polit-Fact.com worked overtime to publicize errors, minor and major, they found in campaign commercials regardless of party affiliation. When a charge in an advertisement against a rival is particularly egregious, the websites inform media organizations. On occasion, pressure to "do the right thing" compels a campaign spokesperson or a candidate to apologize for the misrepresentation. If the piece came from a so-called independent SuperPAC, a contender will ask that it be discontinued. Regardless, the damage is typically done when "fake news" and "alternative facts" become the norm.

A particularly egregious example of fake news happened during the 2016 presidential election campaign. A fictionalized story from True Pundit caught the attention of the traditional news media after the content was retweeted by retired Lt. General Michael Flynn, the first national security advisor for President Trump. Flynn resigned his position after it was discovered he misrepresented the subject of a telephone conversation with Russian Ambassador Sergey Kislyak to Vice President Pence. Nevertheless, Flynn's tweet content read:

U decide—NYPD Blows Whistle on New Hillary Emails: Money Laundering, Sex Crimes w Children, etc…MUST READ!
Weblink: https://t.co/O0bVJT3QDr

—General Flynn (@GenFlynn) November 3, 2016

The weblink goes to the True Pundit news site that detailed sexual allegations by Bill and Hillary Clinton supposedly being investigated by police officials. About a month later a man armed with a loaded assault rifle, inspired by the phony information, entered a Washington DC pizza restaurant and fired shots in order, he thought, to save children that were inside and used as Hillary sex slaves. Luckily no one was hurt and he was arrested. Nevertheless, this incident should act as a cautionary tale about fake news accounts—there are many who read stories on blogs and retweeted on Twitter that believe the reports must be true because they fit their view of the world.

BENETTON AND SHOCK ADVERTISING
Benetton's target audience has always been 18- to 24-year-olds, who are perhaps more socially conscious clothing buyers than other age groups. Beginning in 1989, Benetton used photographs in catalogs, store posters, and billboards to promote the company's idea of multicultural harmony. In all the advertising pictures, the only copy on the page was the Benetton logo. Later, a telephone number was added so that those interested could order a subscription to Benetton's monthly magazine *Colors*. Images of models from different races are shown breast-feeding a baby, with hands that are cuffed together, and as two children sitting side by side on matching toilets symbolically emphasized racial harmony and equivalence for Benetton (Figure 4.18).

Figure 4.18
Benetton has long maintained that its advertising campaigns attract attention and promote racial harmony. However, many have criticized their choice of images. Dr. Bette Kauffman, a professor at the University of Louisiana at Monroe, writes, "The black woman's face is completely confined, contained, imprisoned by the white man's hands and forceful kiss. Indeed, for his hand to cover her forehead like that, he has to have her entire head trapped in his left arm. This would be a problematic image if the woman were white! The goofy 'smile' on her face does nothing to combat the impression that she has no say in this matter."
Courtesy of United Colors of Benetton 1991 spring/summer advertising campaign, Oliviero Toscani

In 1991, the Benetton campaign switched to more overtly political images. One ad showed a picture of several rows of crosses in a cemetery. The ad was banned in Italy, France, Great Britain, and Germany. Arab countries refused to print a picture of African, Anglo, and Asian children sticking their tongues out at the camera. Members of the Catholic Church were outraged that a picture of a priest and nun kissing was used in an advertisement. During this era, though, no picture received as much attention as that of a child photographed fresh from the womb of her mother. This image was printed on billboards, but was banned in Italy and Great Britain.

Never one to rest on previous publicity-seeking achievements, creative director Oliviero Toscani embarked on other Benetton campaigns that used previously published news photographs. The long list of disturbing images without context or explanation included a woman sobbing over the bloody body of a Mafia victim that was published only in Italy, a mercenary soldier holding the thigh bone of a human, the image of Albanian refugees escaping on an Italian ship, a red-eyed duck coated with oil after a recent spill, a Zulu woman with albinism who appeared embarrassed next to two

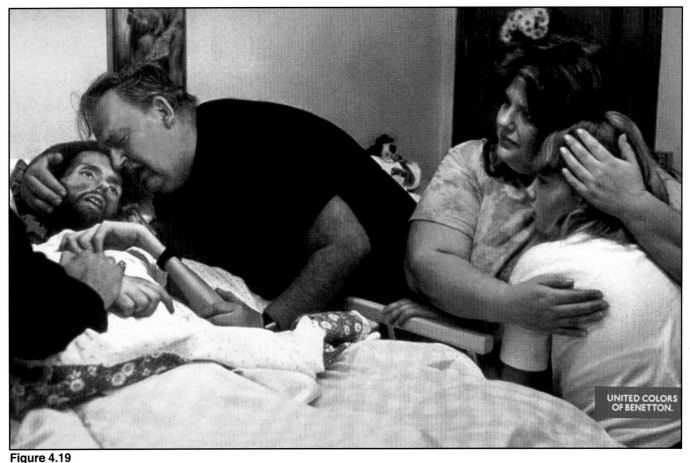

Figure 4.19
David Kirby, 32, is on his deathbed surrounded by grieving family members. Therese Frare's photograph is an unforgettable emotional moment. But the green logo of Benetton makes it clear that the image is intended not only to make people care but to remind viewers to buy clothing.
Courtesy of United Colors of Benetton

brown-skinned women who appear to shun her, an Indian couple wading through flood waters, South American children working as laborers, a man sprawled on the ground while being forced to submit to a radio interview by men on top of him, and the picture that has been called "the most shocking photo used in an ad," David Kirby surrounded by family members shortly before his death due to HIV/AIDS (Figure 4.19).

Ohio University student Therese Frare had been photographing in the Pater Noster House in Columbus, a hospice care home where Kirby received treatment. Kirby allowed her to take pictures of him that were to accompany a story for a school project. Their relationship eventually led to the moving, deathbed image that caused little reaction as

an editorial picture in *Life*. Benetton executives saw the picture after it won the World Press Photo Budapest Award and came in second place in the association's general news category. Kirby's parents, Bill and Kay, gave permission to Benetton to use the image in its ad campaign because they thought it would raise HIV/AIDS awareness around the world. Benetton executives donated $50,000 to the Pater Noster House to furnish and renovate the facilities.

David Kirby was from Stafford, Ohio, a small town of only 94 residents. Lured by the prospect of a better life, he traveled west after high school and eventually ended up in California in the 1980s. He soon lost touch with his family. But after contracting HIV/AIDS, Kirby telephoned his parents and asked if he could return home. He wanted to die with family members around him. Although there is no known cure, medications can extend the length and quality of life of those with the disease today. Kirby's parents immediately welcomed him back. His return to the town, however, caused panic among many residents who were uneducated about the disease. The emergency workers who took him to the hospital later burned everything in the ambulance that Kirby had touched. Schoolchildren screamed in horror about an "AIDS monster" living near them. But Kirby didn't shrink from the cruel characterizations. He often went door to door to educate neighbors about himself and HIV/AIDS. As an activist, he did much to calm the fears of Stafford's residents.

When the disease progressed to its conclusion, the 32-year-old Kirby was at the hospice with his family. Frare took the picture of Kirby surrounded by his father, sister Susan, and niece Sarah openly weeping over the loss of their loved one. His mother was in the next room crying.

The picture is a riveting moment in which a family faced with unspeakable tragedy is united by their grief. Barb Cordle, who was the volunteer director at the Pater Noster House and who helped care for Kirby, said that "the picture in the ad has done more to soften people's hearts on the AIDS issue than any other I have ever seen. You can't look at that picture and hate a person with AIDS. You just can't." But others, particularly HIV/AIDS activists, looked at the picture and felt horror, anger, and outrage over the image being used in an advertisement. They cite the use of the picture as another example of a large corporation exploiting a personal tragedy to sell a product. They wondered why a phone number for HIV/AIDS information could not be included in the ad if an 800 number was printed so that customers could obtain the company's

new catalog. Critics asked whether using such an emotionally powerful image for commercial purposes without written copy in the advertisement to explain the meaning of the picture is ever morally acceptable.

The picture generated much discussion about shock advertising on television talk shows and in newspaper and magazine articles. The controversy over the image swirled around its use in the advertisement. Such a narrow discussion ignored the fact that Frare's image was a sensitive example of the best photojournalism could offer. Nevertheless, because of all the media attention, more than one billion people around the world probably saw the Kirby family scene. But interest in the controversy didn't necessarily mean that more people became educated about HIV/AIDS around the world.

Peter Fressola, Benetton's director of communications and responsible for the company's publicity, asserted that the reason for the ad campaign was to make people think, to get them to talk about serious issues, and to promote worldwide multiculturalism. Toscani also wanted to expand the way advertisements were used. He believed that ads could be used to inform and spark commentary about serious issues. "Advertising can be used to say something that is real about things that exist," said Toscani. Both Fressola and Toscani admitted that they also wanted to create advertising that broke traditional banal presentations in order to focus more attention on the company. Without doubt, the campaign was a tremendous success. Estimated worldwide sales jumped 10 percent, or by more than $100 million, from 1991 to 1992 during the controversy.

END OF AN ERA FOR BENETTON

But it was a $20 million advertising campaign launched in an issue of *Talk* magazine in January 2000 that caused Benetton to rethink the philosophy behind shock advertising. *Talk* contained a

W
LINK

Figure 4.20
*(Weblink: http://goo.gl/f7W1oc)
The video shows close-up interviews of death row inmates who were featured in Benetton's "We, on Death Row" advertising insert. They tell about their hard life in prison, the foods they miss, the dreams they've had, and their opinions about the death penalty.*

96-page booklet entitled "We, on Death Row." With the bright green Benetton logo interspersed on several pages, photographer Toscani posed 26 death row inmates from across the United States like models (Figure 4.20). None wore Benetton clothing. They simply answered questions about their favorite foods, activities, their mothers, and fear of execution. Benetton expressed hope that the campaign, which included billboards and pages in other national magazines, would draw attention to the issue of executions in America. With its death penalty, the United States is a member of an exclusive group of countries that includes Afghanistan, China, Iran, Iraq, and North Korea. Regardless, many were outraged by the advertising supplement, particularly the families of those killed by the inmates.

Benetton was accused of glamorizing the murderers while ignoring their crimes. One outraged couple decided to fight back. Donata and Emery Nelson saw the image of Victor Dewayne Taylor on a billboard. Taylor kidnapped, sodomized, and murdered their teenage son along with his friend. The Nelsons started a petition and began picketing branches of the Sears department store that had recently begun selling Benetton clothing. Donata Nelson explained, "I know they have strange ads for Benetton, but how low can they go? They've sunk about as low as the men on death row." Sears executives canceled the multimillion-dollar deal with Benetton and quit selling its clothing in about 800 outlets. In addition, the attorney general of Missouri, Jay Nixon, filed a lawsuit against the company, alleging that Benetton misrepresented its intent when gaining access to four murderers within a Missouri prison.

Faced with an enormous blitz of unfavorable publicity and a trial, the case was settled when Benetton paid $50,000 to a fund for victims of crimes in Missouri. Benetton also sent letters to the families of victims of the Missouri inmates in which the company expressed its regret for any pain the campaign may have caused them. Nevertheless, defending the campaign, Benetton said, "We wanted to attack the policy of the death penalty. We knew that a debate could emerge from our advertising but nevertheless we wanted to test and see what type of debate would emerge. A debate, as with our previous AIDS pictures, emerged." After 18 years of a controversial yet creative partnership, art director Toscani and Benetton parted ways.

Perhaps to rehabilitate the company's image, Benetton worked with the United Nations (U.N.), which has no advertising budget, to bring social issues through media campaigns to the attention of consumers. In 2001, Benetton produced images for the "International Year of Volunteers," and in 2003 a $15 million campaign called "Food for Life" showed portraits of people from around the world who received food from the U.N. (Figure 4.21).

Since 2005, Toscani has been in the news. His photographs of men "participating in homosexual behavior" were used in a campaign for Ra-Re, an Italian clothing brand. The next year he ran unsuccessfully for a seat in the Italian parliament, perhaps inspired by Benetton, who was an Italian senator. In 2007 he introduced a new campaign called "No-l-ita," meant to be associated with the Vladimir Nabokov novel *Lolita* about a young seductress. The campaign featured French model Isabelle Caro, who has suffered from anorexia nervosa since she was 13 years old. At one point her five-foot, five-inch frame weighed only 55 pounds (Figure 4.21). An Italian media watchdog group said it "breached its code of conduct" and banned billboards of her nude, emaciated body. However, Italian health minister Livia Turco said the billboards promoted "responsibility towards the problem of anorexia."

In 2011 Benetton sparked controver-

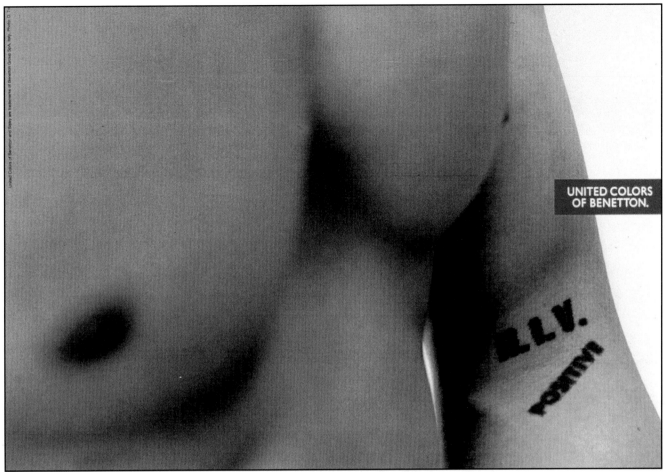

UNITED COLORS
OF BENETTON.

Figure 4.21
An HIV/AIDS reference in this studio photograph for Benetton using a male model provoked protests from various Jewish groups upset over the use of a tattoo that resembled a Holocaust victim's markings.
Courtesy of United Colors of Benetton 1993 fall/winter advertising campaign, Oliviero Toscani

sy with its Unhate campaign that showed manipulated photographs of world leaders (the Pope and al-Tayeb, sheik of the al-Azhar mosque, Mahmoud Abbas, President of the Palestinian National Authority and Benjamin Netanyahu, Prime Minister of Israel, and Paramount Leader of the Republic of China Hu Jin-tao and President Obama) kissing each other on the lips. Alessandro Benetton, executive deputy chairman explained that the company was trying to spread "brotherhood with a kiss." An Obama White House spokesperson disapproved of the president's "name and likeness for commercial purposes" (Figure 4.22).

THE FINE LINE BETWEEN
PERSUASION AND PROPAGANDA
Regardless of how you assign motives to actions, the Benetton campaigns that use editorial pictures in advertisements to generate enormous publicity highlight an important feature of mass communication: The fields of advertising, public relations, and journalism always have been closely related. The blurring between corporate and editorial interests is one of the most pressing concerns of media critics today.

Persuasion uses factual information and emotional appeals to change a person's mind and to promote a desired behavior. In contrast, propaganda uses one-sided and often nonfactual information or opinions that appear to be facts, along with emotional appeals, to change

LINK

Figure 4.21
(Weblink: http://goo.gl/dwZ861) Although combating anorexia nervosa is a worthy cause, Oliviero Toscani's in your face, shock advertisement style offended more than it helped.

LINK

Figure 4.22
(Weblink: http://goo.gl/VgjvMy) Political figures from 2011 are pictured being amorous with their ideological opposites in Benetton's Unhate campaign.

a person's mind and promote a desired behavior. Most information, whether factual or not, is communicated through the mass media. More and more, that information relies on the emotional appeal inherent in visual presentations.

In 1922 the journalist and media critic American Walter Lippmann published *Public Opinion*. It stressed the need for images to change a person's attitude. "Pictures have always been the surest way of conveying an idea," wrote Lippmann, "and next in order, words that call up pictures in memory." Recognizable symbols used in visual presentations will become long-lasting memories with the power to change attitudes if viewers have a chance to actively think about the content of the image and relate it to their own situation. All human communication—whether advertising layouts, lectures from parents and professors, closing arguments by lawyers in a trial, or campaign speeches—uses persuasion and sometimes propaganda in an attempt to mold or change a listen-

Figure 4.23
As with the Benetton image of David Kirby, the advertising photograph for the Kenar clothing company is meant to alert the public about HIV/ AIDS. But what is the connection between supermodel Linda Evangelista, seven older women wearing black dresses, an empty wooden chair, and the HIV/AIDS issue? The striking image attracts attention, but says nothing about the disease to most people walking along Times Square in New York City.
Courtesy of Paul Martin Lester

er or viewer's attitude. Communications educator James Carey says that "communication is fundamentally and essentially a matter of persuasion, attitude change, behavior modification, and socialization through the transmission of information" (Figure 4.23).

The Role of Persuasion In the 4th Century BCE, Aristotle was the first to write about the art of persuasion. He defined it as communication designed to influence listeners' choices. According to Aristotle, persuasion has three components: ethos, logos, and pathos. Ethos refers to a source's credibility. A professor for a well-known university will usually be more believable speaking about the state of the economy than an ordinary citizen found by a journalist on the street. Logos refers to the logical arguments used to persuade an individual. Whatever is being communicated should fit your personal view of how the world works. If the information seems far-fetched, you may reject the argument from the onset. Pathos refers to emotional appeals used in the persuasive argument. Testimonials from those with direct knowledge of a situation are often the most effective statements. Images of animals and children suffering, if used sparingly, also can be persuasive. Aristotle thought that if a speaker is believable or imbued with authority, uses factual arguments in a reasoned presentation, and gains an audience's attention through emotional means, persuasion is possible. The Canadian singer Sarah McLachlan participated in an effective PSA video to help prevent animal cruelty, which featured sad-eyed cats and dogs looking right in the camera with her song "Angel" playing in the background (Figure 4.24). Since the ad began airing in 2006, the American Society for the Prevention of Cruelty to Animals (ASPCA) has received more than $30 million in donations.

Persuasion is a socially accepted way of attempting to change individuals' attitudes. In a pluralistic, democratic society, the government most commonly attempts to persuade the public through the news media. When the president introduces a new budget, the government mobilizes its huge public relations bureaucracy to "sell" the plan to the U.S. Congress and the American people. The president and the administration use the print, broadcast, and web media to communicate their ideas. Such a system naturally leads to tension between the government and the media, especially if independent journalists disagree with the government's message and report their findings.

Charlie Fisher of MoveOn.org created a PSA commercial, "Child's Play," that was turned down for airing by CBS executives for showing during the Super Bowl game in 2004. Because of the controversy, CNN aired the spot as part of a news segment. The short film is an excellent example of Aristotle's pathos because children are portrayed working dead-end, boring jobs in order to pay off the country's trillion-dollar deficit (Figure 4.25).

The Role of Propaganda The word propaganda started out as a neutral term, without negative connotations. It simply meant a way to spread or *propagate* an idea to a large population. In the 17th century, the Roman Catholic Church set up the *Congregation for Propagating the Faith* as an effort to add more members to the church. But subsequently, its use by governments intent on conveying their version of the truth to citizens and enemies alike has given the term a pejorative connotation that can't be ignored. Whereas persuasion is the art of convincing someone that your position is correct through factual information, propaganda is thought of as the duping of an unsuspecting public through misleading or false information. The word has long been associated with the thought-control

Figure 4.24
(Weblink: http://goo.gl/fyD6yy) With its music, direct eye-contact, and images of abused animals, this ASPCA public service announcement is a classic example of pathos.

Figure 4.25
(Weblink: http://goo.gl/Loip6T) While most of the world was watching Janet Jackson's controversial "wardrobe malfunction" during her performance at the 2004 Super Bowl halftime show, CNN broadcast this video concerned with the national debt and who would have to pay it off.

techniques used by totalitarian regimes, but critics have expanded the definition to include many of the persuasion techniques utilized by all governments and large corporations to persuade an unsuspecting public. Sociologist Harold Lasswell said that "both advertising and publicity fall within the field of propaganda." Media critic John Merrill enlarged the definition to include journalism, saying that "three-fourths of all media content . . . contains propaganda for some cause, idea, institution, party or person." In the end, the best definition of propaganda may be the use of spoken, written, pictorial, or musical representations to influence thought and action through debatable techniques.

Political Propaganda

Beginning in earnest from the beginning of the 20th century, visual propaganda could be found in colorful and visually eye-catching political posters. Above the banner "TOGETHER WE WIN," a World War I sailor and soldier are arm-in-arm with a brawny steel worker carrying a sledgehammer by the American illustrator James Montgomery Flagg (Figure 4.26). Another popular recruiting poster showed the British military leader Lord Kitchener pointing his finger at a potential recruit created by illustrator Alfred Leete (Figure 4.27). Flagg appropriated the idea for a stern Uncle Sam pointing his finger at a viewer (Figure 4.28). The Lord Kitchener and Uncle Sam finger motif is so popular it is common to see it used in advertisements throughout the world. During World War II, a poster of a strong and confident woman under the words "We Can Do It!"—which was created by J. Howard Miller and modeled on a photograph of Geraldine Doyle—symbolized factory workers who helped the war effort (Figure 4.29). After the popular American artist Norman Rockwell painted a similar woman, she became known as "Rosie the Riveter" (Figure 4.30).

In 1933 the Third Reich of Nazi Germany established the Ministry of Propaganda with Joseph Goebbels as its head. Probably most known for its classic propaganda movie *Triumph of the Will* by filmmaker Leni Riefenstahl, dramatizing Adolph Hitler during the 1934 Nazi Party Congress in Nuremberg, the Ministry was also responsible for poster production. Typical was one that showed a photograph of Hitler in a heroic stance in front of an army of swastika flag carriers, guided by light from the heavens, with, ironically, the dove of peace and the words, "Long live Germany!" (Figure 4.31). Another, labeled "LIBERATORS," is a complicated collection of visual symbols. A Ku Klux Klan hooded robotic giant meant to be the United States is in the act of destruction. With two muscular arms, one holding an LP record and the other a money bag, and two additional arms with one holding a machine gun and the other a grenade, the poster alludes to America's presumed racism, Jewish sympathies, and obsession with beauty, consumerism, and entertainment (Figure 4.32).

The Vietnam War sparked a different genre of the art form, the anti-war poster. An anonymous British artist created "Vietnam Skeleton," a clever variation of Flagg's Uncle Sam with the poster torn open to reveal a menacing skeleton (Figure 4.33). On the opposite end of the anti-war continuum is the simple graphic of a flower that includes the text "War is not healthy for children and other living things." Created by printmaker Lorraine Schneider, it became a powerful icon for the anti-war movement (Figure 4.34). In 2005, Schneider's daughter Carol gave a necklace with the design to anti-Iraq War protestor Cindy Sheehan.

VISUAL PERSUASION IN ADVERTISING

Media critic and educator Everette Dennis defines advertising as "any form of non-personal presentation and promotion of ideas, goods, and services by

Figure 4.26
"Together We Win," c. 1917, by James Montgomery Flagg. This World War I propaganda poster shows men of the Army, Navy, and industry in lockstep, with clenched fists and eager smiles, ready to wage war in Europe. More than 116,000 American members of the military were killed in the war, and more than 200,000 wounded. Although a serious artist, illustrator, and cartoonist, the American James Flagg is best known for his poster work.
Courtesy of the Library of Congress

Figure 4.28
"I Want You for U.S. Army," c. 1917, by James Montgomery Flagg. Considered to be Flagg's most famous poster because it introduced Uncle Sam, a symbol of America to the public, it was an appropriation of an earlier work by the British illustrator Alfred Leete.
Courtesy of the Library of Congress

Figure 4.27
Created in 1914 by Alfred Leete, the striking face of Field Marshal Horatio Herbert Kitchener was so recognizable to British citizens of the day, his name did not need to be included on the World War I recruitment poster. As with the Flagg version, the steely and direct eye contact and pointing finger is effective as it personalizes the message. The number of British military killed in World War I was more than one million, with over two million wounded. On a diplomatic mission to Russia in 1916, the armored cruiser was struck by a mine and sank. Only 12 crewmen of the 655 on board survived. The field marshal's body was never found. Here, he is resurrected to attract attention to a poster in Helsinki, Finland.
Courtesy of Paul Martin Lester

Figure 4.29
"We Can Do It!" 1942, by J. Howard Miller. Since the reasons for Americans to enter World War II were clearer than those for WWI—after all, the country had been attacked at Pearl Harbor—recruiting posters were not as vital to the war effort as works that bolstered morale and home front efforts. J. Howard Miller, an American graphic artist employed by the Westinghouse Company, created one of the most enduring images from the era. Based on a picture taken by a United Press International (UPI) photographer of Geraldine Doyle working in a factory, it was little seen during the war, as it was only shown for two weeks at Westinghouse. However, the image is widely used today as a symbol of feminism.
Courtesy of the National Archives

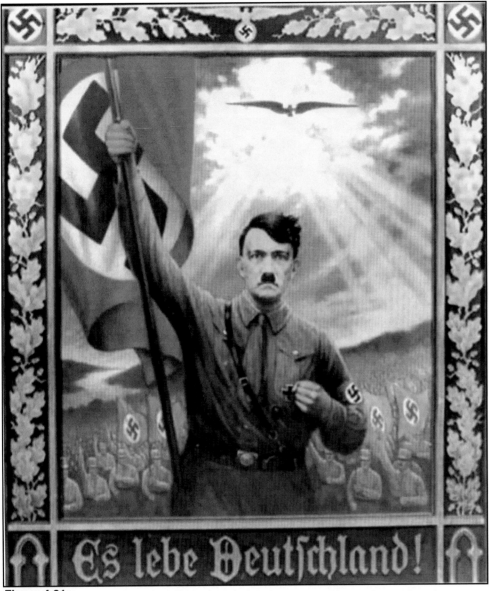

W LINK

Figure 4.30
(Weblink: http://goo.gl/THp4Sb)
"Rosie the Riveter," 1943, by Norman Rockwell. Rockwell, one of the most beloved American illustrators created cover images for the Saturday Evening Post *for more than 50 years. With her name painted on her riveter, the Rockwell painting is a powerful symbol of a woman's role in manufacturing military equipment during World War II. The redheaded and muscular Rosie on her lunch break casually sits on a metal post before an American flag with her foot on Adolf Hitler's autobiography Mein Kampf. And yet, when the men came home after the war, women were asked to replace their riveters with vacuum cleaners.*

Figure 4.31
"Es lebe Deutschland!" (Long live Germany). Adolf Hitler, the leader of Germany's Nazi Party, resolutely carries the party's flag and stands ahead of and above his soldiers. The title of the poster is printed in a blackletter, German-style typeface. The tilted horizon indicates the struggle will be hard, but the bird and the streaks of sunlight bursting through the clouds that frame Hitler's head are indexical signs that at least he believed that God sanctified his mission of world dominance. The swastika symbol dates back to the Neolithic prehistoric period from about 5,000BCE in the Middle East and Europe. Over the centuries it has been used by Indian cultures as a symbol for Hinduism and Buddhism. Today, its use is outlawed in Germany, except for religious purposes.
Courtesy of K. Stauber

Figure 4.32
"Liberators," 1944 (Following page). *In this symbolic-laden World War II German propaganda poster, American culture is feared as much as its might if Germany loses the war. Prone citizens near a town's traditional water fountain await the onslaught of American music, superficial beauty, racism, Jewish interests, and violence. The little figure in the foreground with the large ears holds a sign that sarcastically reads in Dutch, "The USA will save European culture from extinction."*
Courtesy of Harald Damsketh

W LINK

Figure 4.34
(Weblink:
http://goo.gl/S6D4qU)
Drawn in a simple style a child might produce, Lorraine Schneider's anti-war poster is a powerful and enduring message of peace.

Figure 4.33
"I Want You for U.S. Army" (after James Montgomery Flagg), offset lithograph, United Kingdom, c. 1972. During the Vietnam War, an anonymous British illustrator composed an anti-war poster in which the Uncle Sam in James Flagg's World War I recruiting poster is supplanted by a symbol of death.
Courtesy of the Library of Congress

Figure 4.35
More than 50 years after the Japanese seaport town of Hiroshima was devastated by an atomic bomb, the city is a vibrant commercial municipality with large billboards hawking products just as in most other downtown districts.
Courtesy of Paul Martin Lester

an identified sponsor." The advertising industry in the United States employs more than 400,000 people and generates more than $650 billion in annual billings worldwide. According to Dennis, advertising benefits society because it funds most of the media, provides consumer information in the form of public service announcements, and stimulates the economy (Figure 4.35).

It is estimated that the average television viewer spends three years of her total life watching commercials. As such, visual messages are vital in those communications. Effective advertisers, therefore, make use of the semiotic code of metonymy. Through words, images, and situations, they want the potential customer to make assumptions about the ads they see related to their own behavior. A Johnny Walker Black Label Scotch ad that shows the opened gate of a long lawn headed to the front door of a three-story mansion is meant to convey the assumption that if you buy the alcohol you will be living like those inside the house. Likewise, other alcohol manufacturers, particularly Skyy vodka out of San Francisco, pose models in sexually suggestive scenarios to link consumption with sex.

Out of necessity, advertisers are also becoming more creative about where their ads are placed. With digital video recorders (DVRs) such as those made by TiVo and built-in systems available to satellite users, viewers can control what they watch and skip traditional commercials. As more and more consumers use the device, advertisers have to find clever ways to plug their products. For the show "How I Met Your Mother," CBS put life-sized pictures of two main characters on elevator doors. The networked also stenciled ads for such shows as "CBS Mondays," "The Amazing Race," and "CSI" on eggshells. The rum brand Captain Morgan produced a small poster to stick to the door of a men's room in a bar that read, "Got a little CAPTAIN in you?" In 2009, the fast-food chicken chain KFC paid $3,000 to fill 350 potholes on the streets of Louisville, Kentucky, and was allowed to stamp each smooth surface with a chalk stencil that read, "Re-freshed by KFC."

Motion picture and television cross promotions are popular as well. Print ads for milk featured the Incredible Hulk. Hugh Jackman's Wolverine character in *X-Men: The Last Stand* (2006) was placed on a Diet Dr. Pepper can. Angelina Jolie's face hovered over a Jeep like the one she drove in *Lara Croft: Tomb Raider* (2001). The staff of NBC's "The Office" met at a Chili's restaurant. Tom Hanks worked for Federal Express in *Cast Away* (2000), with the movie acting like a long commercial for the shipping company. During the 2003 Super Bowl telecast, FedEx did one better and used a Hanks stand-in actor to recreate a plot line from the film for a commercial (Figure 4.36).

Having a celebrity spokesperson will almost always assure viewer interest, but if the message is not accurate the ploy can backfire. Australian actress Kerry Armstrong (*Mind the Gap*, 2005 and *Reservations*, 2008) and Coca-Cola were criticized for a 2009 magazine advertisement which claimed it was a myth that the sugar water soda "makes you fat, rots your teeth, and is packed with caffeine." The Australian Competition and Consumer Commission, which oversees accuracy in advertisements, forced the cola company to print retractions in all of the major newspapers.

From 1913, the name of Camel cigarettes and the picture of a dromedary on the pack were meant to symbolically link the use of Turkish paper and tobacco. Joe Camel or "Old Joe," created in 1974 by the British graphic artist Billy Coulton for a French tobacco company, had been the cigarette mascot for the R. J. Reynolds Tobacco Company in the United States since 1987. However, in 1997 the cartoon character, criticized for at-

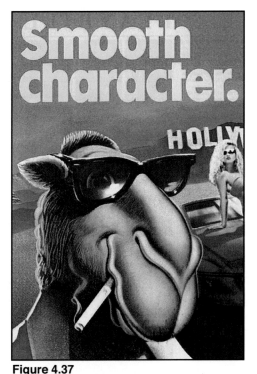

Figure 4.37
Although denied by R. J. Reynolds Tobacco Company officials, the cartoon character Joe Camel, or "Old Joe," was criticized for enticing young people to smoke by making the habit look fun and sophisticated. In 1997, under pressure from the U.S. Congress and anti-tobacco groups, Reynolds voluntarily ended its Joe Camel campaign in America. After the U.S. Congress enacted strict anti-tobacco legislation in 2009, Senator Richard Durbin of Illinois remarked, "Joe Camel has been sentenced and put away forever."
Courtesy of Paul Martin Lester

tracting underage smokers to the brand, was discontinued (Figure 4.37). With more than 400,000 deaths attributed to smoking and those inhaling secondhand smoke every year in America, the Food and Drug Administration (FDA) introduced new, visually graphic warning messages on packages (Figure 4.38).

Product placement (showing a product) and product integration (having the product part of a show's plot) in motion pictures and television programs have long been effective staples of advertising. Experts predict by 2014, income from product placements in movies, on television, and in other media will amount to more than $6 billion.

W LINK

Figure 4.36
(Weblink: http://goo.gl/RCq9Fy) Parodies are almost always attention getters for sophisticated viewers who have seen the referent image. In this FedEx commercial, the music from Cast Away *plays as the stranded man character returns a package. However, shouldn't he deliver it to the recipient rather than the sender?*

Figure 4.38
Margaret Hamburg, the Administrative Commissioner for the FDA called the visual messages placed on cigarette packs in the fall of 2012 "an important and powerful tool" to reduce the number of deaths from tobacco-related diseases. She estimated that the advertising campaign would compel more than 200,000 smokers out of the 46 million in the U.S. to quit. Critics note that the messages may violate the First Amendment rights of companies selling a legal product and that the graphic nature of the pictures would have to increase to continue to shock consumers.
Courtesy of the U.S. Food and Drug Administration

Motion pictures and television shows are filled with commercial messages that are often accepted without criticism from viewers. *Wings* (1927), the first movie given the Best Picture Academy Award, contained an ad for Hershey's chocolate. The silent World War I epic from Paramount directed by William Wellman was restored in 2012 in a DVD, Blu-ray release on its 85th anniversary. The consummate spy James Bond often drove fast cars provided by Aston-Martin and BMW. Sales of Reese's Pieces candies increased by 65 percent after moviegoers watched the alien in *E.T.: The Extra-Terrestrial* (1982) follow the candy trail. Seagram's, the parent company for Mumm's champagne, paid $50,000 for Cher to drink that brand in the movie *Moonstruck* (1987). Interestingly, the 1950s-era drama *Revolu-*

tionary Road (2008), in which many of the actors smoked heavily in the movie, contained an ending credit message that explained tobacco companies gave no money toward the production. Apple is a leader in product placements. In movies and in television shows, Apple products are seen being used by stars ranging from Jerry Seinfeld to Sarah Jessica Parker. In *Iron Man 2* (2010) there were 64 Apple products shown in the movie. Almost 70 promotional partners were part of Universal's environmental tale, *Dr. Seuss' The Lomax* (2012) including government agencies and companies wanting to advance their Earth-friendly attitudes or green products. Some environmentalists criticized the tie-in with the Mazda CX-5 SUV. In 2012 a Volkswagen Passat was an essential plot feature for an episode of ABC's "The Middle," an Outback Steakhouse in NBC's "30 Rock," and a Sprint smartphone on ABC's "Desperate Housewives." Reality TV shows, however, are the real masters of the strategy called "advertainment." The *Wall Street Journal* reported that "The Biggest Loser" and "American Idol" combined had more than 10,000 brand name placements on their shows. Justin Osborne of Volkswagen approves of the process: "We're very into authentic and organic integrations that don't seem too heavy-handed or obvious." However, the Writers Guild of America would like to see a printed message on the bottom of screens alerting viewers to the ad pitch.

Documentary filmmaker Morgan Spurlock, most known for his Big Mac and fries chow-fest in *Super Size Me* (2004) produced a motion picture about product placements in his 2011 film, *POM Wonderful Presents: The Greatest Movie Ever Sold*. Not surprisingly, Spurlock had trouble finding companies to pay to have their products included in a movie that criticized the practice (Figure 4.39). Although he understands that producers often need the extra income provided by companies, Spurlock admits, "There has to be a balance between the creative forces and the marketing forces. Otherwise it's just one big commercial."

To help television executives and advertisers work more closely together, digital imaging technology can be used to place products into old television shows. Princeton Video Image Inc., the company that created the imaginary scrimmage and first down lines for televised football games, now produces "virtual product placements" for marketers. Besides being able to place ads only the television audience can see behind goal posts, home plates, soccer fields, and on NASCAR racetracks, the technology can be used to put products in scenes. Imagine a rerun of "Grey's Anatomy" in which the characters gather at "Joe's Bar" to be seen drinking Miller beer. Media

critic Jeff Smith explains, "Product placement is one of the ways to reach a captive audience. If you work your product into a TV show or a film, it's impossible for the viewer to zap it out."

Clever website marketers use a variety of methods to get their advertising message noticed. Since studies show that most people ignore banner ads on websites or set web browsers to block such ads, so-called webitisers (advertisers on websites) are creating more obtrusive "in-your-face ads." David Hallerman, an industry analyst, explained, "the inherent nature of advertising is to annoy people enough so that they pay attention. Advertising rarely doesn't irritate." In addition to the usual "pop up" windows that appear over the intended information and "pop under" windows that are placed under a website's window so you see them after you think you have closed down your browser, three new types of ads were introduced in 2009: The "fixed panel," in which the ad moves up or down the page as a user scrolls, the "XXL box" that allows users to see video commercials, and "pushdown" ads that open to show a larger ad. These types of windows are sometimes effective in attracting customers because it is difficult to ignore the message.

Another type of ad that is difficult to ignore is the billboard displayed on an entire side of a multi-story building. These so-called "supergraphics" produced by SkyTag and other companies can be as much as 20 stories high. However, city governments and anti-billboard activists are working together to try to prevent these visual eyesores (Figure 4.40).

Ads on a different scale can attract attention as well. A clever way to get a reader's attention was seen within a small, one-column space in *The New Yorker* magazine. The overhead view showed the results of a Mini Cooper that had just run into an ad for the canoe/kayak hybrid Poke Boat below it. No one

W LINK

Figure 4.39
*(Weblink: http://goo.gl/wlTF8R) Morgan Spurlock wears a "NASCAR style" advertising-heavy suit while he holds bottles of POM to promote his documentary P*OM Wonderful Presents: The Greatest Movie Ever Sold.*

Figure 4.40
Workers on a platform lift change an advertisement on a building in Hollywood from Disney's G-Force *(2009) to the musical* Mary Poppins. *These huge, multi-story ads are controversial; some say they are urban eyesores and distractions for drivers.*
Courtesy of Paul Martin Lester

was injured in the collision. Likewise, an ad for Quaker instant oatmeal showed a bike ramp with the logo printed on it in the lower-left corner of a newspaper page, and a boy shown from the shoulders down on a bicycle at the top-right of the same page. Without text of any kind, the boy on the bike is suspended in white space. It is an arresting image with a satisfying "aha" moment when you put the two sections together and read the tagline, "Give your kids a boost."

Other techniques blur the line between editorial and advertising. Stick-on ads and foldout flaps can be found on *ESPN The Magazine* covers and the *Los Angeles Times* front page, whereas *Esquire* magazine used mix-and-match covers with famous faces on its cover for an ad. Voicing concern for this practice was Sid Holt, chief executive of the American Society of Magazine Editors, "Everyone has to be able to tell the difference between advertising and editorial, and if you can't tell there's a difference, there's a problem." Trouble is, advertisers don't want you to tell the difference.

Another ploy by marketing directors that blurs the line between reality and fiction for motion pictures is to create a website that strongly implies a movie's fictional content is real. Producers of *The Blair Witch Project* (1999) generated enormous interest in their movie before its release by providing information on its website that made many moviegoers believe that the film was a recreation of actual events. Likewise, for the forgettable film *Godsend* (2004), a science fiction/supernatural story about a distraught couple who agrees to have their dead son cloned, its website looked so

real and sincere that many didn't make the connection with the motion picture and believed there really was an American institution where human cloning took place. When parents who had lost a child called a number provided on the site, they were told of the hoax. Negative publicity about the film generated more viewer interest because of the controversy.

Technology can also bridge the analog and digital worlds. Augmented reality (AR) or Mixed Reality (MR) is the term used to describe a variety of computer and/or web-based applications that can link smartphone and tablet users with product information, coupons, and store locations. One of the first examples of augmented reality for advertising purposes was based on a process first developed by the Japanese company Denso-Wave in 1994. Quick Response (QR) graphic codes can be put on billboards, print ads, and websites and then photographed by a user with a cell phone that has an application that can process the image. Product information, a discount coupon, website, or an e-mail or telephone number can be displayed on a user's cell phone. The company 2D Sense (2Dsense.com) offers a free application for smartphones that allows users to read these graphic codes and create their own. These two-dimensional codes are now a common sight (Figure 4.41). In 2012 Garry Trudeau's "Doonesbury" cartoon strip feature a QR code in a mailbag segment featured. With a smartphone reader app, you could scan the code and see the cartoon's website.

AR is much more than simple QR codes. In the 2002 summer blockbuster hit *Minority Report* Tom Cruise's character tries to elude police officials by walking briskly through a shopping mall, but he cannot hide from iris-recognition scanners located near each digital wall poster for products as Lexus and American Express. As he passes an ad, a flash registers a scan of his eyes. Suddenly,

Figure 4.41
Two friends pose for a photograph. On the T-shirt of the man on the right is a QR code created from the application 2D Sense. If you take a picture of it using the program, a web browser will show his webpage. Initiated by Japanese inventors, QR codes are common in newspaper, magazine, and billboard advertisements.
Courtesy of Allison Lester

W
LINK
Figure 4.42
(Weblink: http://goo.gl/soQua9) Perhaps advertisements that can quickly scan individual iris patterns and adjust its message accordingly is a bit far-fetched, but many innovations come from the minds of science picture writers.

a friendly man's voice calls out, "John Anderton. You can use a Guinness right about now." If you saw the movie, the last thing he wants or needs at that point in the film is to stop off at the pub and have a pint of the slow-pouring, dark Irish brew (Figure 4.42).

If you think such augmented reality technology is at least 40 years away, you may be surprised to learn that from 2008 digital storefronts and mall displays in Japan have used facial recognition technology to identify your age and gender as you walk pass. Today, along the Grand Canal and Palazzo shops within the Venetian resort in Las Vegas, entertainment ideas are projected at you through the technology while such diverse companies as Adidas and Kraft Foods have similar presentations. Common are locative apps for smartphones that can direct a user to movie theaters, bars, restaurants, and so on based on a current location. Either a map will display on the screen or arrows will overlay the actual view from a smartphone's camera lens. Through augmented, value added, interactive techniques and technologies, passive readers and viewers become engaged users that are entertained, persuaded, and educated by the content.

VISUAL PERSUASION IN PUBLIC RELATIONS

Opinion makers, whether in government or business, long ago learned that what is reported in a news story sometimes isn't as important as how it is presented. Public relations specialists try to influence news reporters in the hope that favorable coverage will result. Public relations people also attempt to influence public opinion positively about a particular product, company, or issue. The public relations industry helps gain the public's support for issues and services identified as important by corporate executives. As part of that process, public relations employees contact journalists to help them identify

important stories by giving them tips. Media ethicist John Merrill asserts that 50 percent of all the stories presented in the media—whether print or broadcast—probably are generated initially by a public relations person.

The 2016 race to the White House demonstrated that politicians and their publicity handlers have readily embraced what has been called a photographic opportunity, shortened to "photo op." The photo op is a stage-managed, highly manipulated still or moving image. A successful photo op appears to look real but is actually a contrived fiction in which the source, his or her handlers, and sometimes the photographers themselves orchestrate the timing, location, subject, props (telephone, pen and paper, podium, and so on), lighting, foreground and background elements (banners, signs, supporters, and so on), and sometimes even the selection and placement of the photographers covering the "event." Although traditionally the photo op is thought of as a way to get positive publicity for a politician, the photographic genre can include all types of so-called media or pseudo-events that might include owners celebrating their store openings to portraits of corporate leaders in their offices. As the writer and political commentator George F. Will wrote, "A photo opportunity, properly understood, is someone doing something solely for the purpose of being seen to do it. The hope is that those who see the resulting pictures will not see the elements of calculation (not to say cunning) that are behind the artifice."

One of the most infamous photo ops devised by the George W. Bush administration probably sounded like a good idea at the time, but it backfired. Less than two months after the invasion of Iraq by American and coalition forces in March 2003, President Bush gave a rousing speech announcing the end of all major combat operations aboard the aircraft carrier *USS Abraham Lincoln* un-

Figure 4.43
With a banner that read "Mission Accomplished" and Navy personnel carefully arranged on the deck of the USS Abraham Lincoln, President Bush participates in what came to be one of the most embarrassing photo ops of his presidency.
Courtesy of Paul Morse, the White House

Figure 4.44
In a photo op arranged by Senior Advisor Karl Rove, President Bush looks out the window from Air Force One at the damage to New Orleans and the Gulf Coast two days after Hurricane Katrina struck land in 2005. For many, the picture symbolized the ineffectual response from government officials following the catastrophe.
Courtesy of Paul Morse, the White House

Figure 4.45

In the first photo op controversy of the Obama Administration, a low-flying Air Force aircraft (it is only called "Air Force One" when the President is aboard) was photographed in 2009 over the Statute of Liberty, but not before frightening residents of Manhattan who thought another 9/11-type terrorist attack was taking place. The White House official responsible for the photo op later resigned from his position.
Courtesy of the White House

der a large banner that read "Mission Accomplished." But after the war dragged on for years with American soldiers and Iraqi civilians killed and wounded by the thousands, the visual stunt was criticized (Figure 4.43). Later, after Hurricane Katrina slammed into the Gulf Coast and flooded New Orleans in August 2005, Bush was pictured flying over the stricken land from the comfort of Air Force One (Figure 4.44). The photo op made him look detached and clueless, and helped send his approval rating to the low level he maintained until the end of his presidency.

In 2009 the Obama Administration was embarrassed by negative publicity over an ill-advised photo op. Air Force One, but without the president on board,

flew low over Manhattan accompanied by two military jets in order to take a photograph of the aircraft. It caused many residents and onlookers in New York City, site of the World Trade Center's twin towers destruction on 9/11, to panic (Figure 4.45). President Obama, who had no knowledge of the flight ahead of time, was reportedly infuriated by the photo shoot that cost American taxpayers $328,835. The director of the White House Military Office who was responsible resigned his position.

The public relations profession is criticized because it sometimes hides its commercial intent from unsuspecting readers and viewers. It can rarely be determined whether a persuasive public relations person originally suggested a news story to a reporter. More often than not, because of time constraints, budget cutbacks, and the history of commercialism of the mass media, a public relations person's information in printed and video news releases are published or aired with little criticism or cross-checking of facts. Moreover, social media websites such as Facebook, Digg, Twitter, and popular blogs are being used by savvy public relations personnel to get the word out to influential networkers to announce a birthday party, an innovative technology, a political campaign, or a website.

Fortunately, the public relations industry is filled with many bright, articulate, and caring individuals who work hard to overcome the historical stereotypes of the publicity hounds who spend their time glad-handing at cocktail parties and hacks who churn out press releases dictated by management. Concern about negative perceptions of the industry led to the 1948 formation of the Public Relations Society of America (PRSA), with student chapters around the world. The society established a code of ethics, accredits public relations professionals and academic programs, promotes scholarly research in the field, and showcases successful public relations activities. Consequently, the public relations profession gets better publicity.

VISUAL PERSUASION IN JOURNALISM

Large, bold headlines with big, dramatic pictures, and short, easy-to-read stories are tactics used by newspaper graphic designers to attract new readers and hold onto the ones they have. Such displays are not new. When Tom Howard snuck a camera into the death chamber in 1928 and photographed Ruth Snyder, the first woman executed in the United States since 1899, New York's *Daily News* devoted about one fifth of the front page to the word, "DEAD!" and the rest of the page for the chilling photograph (Figure

4.46). Equally dramatic were the word and picture choices by the New York *American* after the German airship, the *Hindenburg* exploded in 1937. These displays are not only sensational and catch a customer's eye, they also act as advertisements for the publication. The message is: We present the news in exciting visual ways better than our competition. Television news stations engage in the same practice when they lead a newscast with dramatic live digital video and then later use that footage in a commercial for itself. With subscriptions and advertising dollars dwindling, newspaper executives, journalists, and readers are seriously concerned whether the near future will still have the news on paper. What is clear is that simply altering the typography and making photographs larger will not be sufficient to save the news(paper) industry.

Many media critics and journalists look to the web for examples of the future of newspapers and serious, investigative stories. Almost every traditional newspaper in the world, from a large, metropolitan daily to a small, weekly publication, has a website that either copies a version of its print edition or creates exclusive content for its online editions. Journalists take pictures, shoot digital video, and record digital audio to include with copy and links to additional information. This type of display is designed for those who have lost, or never had, the news*paper* reading habit and are comfortable with gaining information from a computer monitor.

BACK TO DAVID KIRBY

Look at the Benetton advertisement of David Kirby on his deathbed surrounded by family members one more time (Figure 4.47). The original caption in *Life* magazine read, "THE END. After a three-year struggle against AIDS and its social stigma, David Kirby could fight no longer. As his father, sister and niece stood by in anguish, the 32-year-old

Figure 4.46
After Ruth Snyder was convicted of arranging for the murder of her husband, she became the second woman executed by the electric chair at Sing Sing prison in New York. The picture is blurry because Tom Howard, a Chicago Tribune photographer brought in by the Daily News so state officials wouldn't know him, made at least two exposures with a hidden camera strapped to his leg. The newspaper's illustrator also retouched it. Nevertheless, the front page, with its dramatic headline and large photograph, is an iconic symbol of journalistic sensationalism. As an attention-getting combination of word and picture, it also acts as an advertisement for the publication.
Courtesy of the New York Daily News

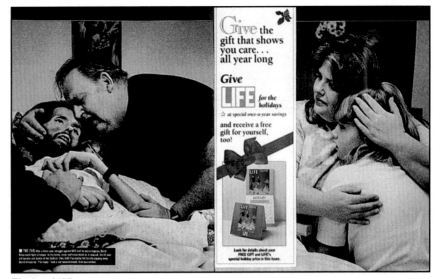

Figure 4.47
David Kirby's private family tragedy was published originally in a November 1990 issue of Life *magazine. The black and white tones give a documentary look to the photograph but contrast starkly with the brightly colored holiday advertisement insert.*
Courtesy of Therese Frare

founder and leader of the Stafford, Ohio, AIDS foundation felt his life slipping away. David whispered, 'I'm ready,' took a labored breath, then succumbed."

The caption for the Benetton ad read, "United Colors of Benetton."

The words in the journalistic context of *Life* magazine are meant to stir the reader's emotions, to educate the reader about a family's courage and love for each other, and perhaps to persuade the reader to do something tangible about the HIV/AIDS crisis. The words in the advertising context for Benetton are meant to sell sweaters.

Before assigning nothing but positive motives to the editors of *Life* magazine, take a look at what else is on the page with the Kirby family. Therese Frare's black-and-white image is on a double-page spread inside a black border framed by a thin, white rule. In 2003 the image was included in *Time* magazine's collection, "The Most Influential Images of All Time," along with Joseph Nicéphore Niépce's first photograph and Dorothea Lange's "Migrant Mother" (Figure 4.48).

The cutline is at the lower left of the picture. The text is printed in white and set inside a black box. But stuck between the two pages—attached between the image of Kirby and his father on the left page and his sister and niece on the right—is a cheery, insert printed with

colorful holiday graphics. It is a promotion to get the reader to subscribe to the magazine. "Give the gift that shows you care . . ." the copy reads, "all year long. Give LIFE." When you turn the little card over it reads next to the crying face of David Kirby's father, "With LIFE your holiday shopping's a snap." Except, of course, if you are dead. Although explained away by a *Life* executive as a coincidence, the placement of the card that must be turned by a reader in order to see the entire Kirby photograph is a perfect location to get maximum attention for its own advertisement.

Advertising and journalism once again merge in a shockingly ironic and insensitive way.

KEY TERMS FROM THIS CHAPTER
Advertising campaign • Anorexia nervosa • Augmented or mixed reality • Blogs • Caption • Copy • Death penalty • Editorial picture • HIV/AIDS • Hospice • *Life* magazine • Locative • LP record • News photograph • Pater Noster House • PSA • World Press Photo

W
LINK
Figure 4.48
(Weblink: http://goo.gl/5e7kir) Starting with Joseph Niépce's photograph in 1826, the powerful collection of photographs ends with the 2015 image of the body of three-year-old Aylan Kurdi who drowned in the Mediterranean Sea. Unfortunately, the picture next to it is a selfie of the smiling and beautiful stars of Hollywood during the 2014 Academy Awards ceremony.

5 Visual Stereotypes

Portrayed as bloodthirsty savages, alcoholic indigents, romantic princesses, and silent but wise sidekicks, Native Americans have long been a staple of paperback, movie, and television stereotypes. But the practice of stereotyping Native Americans probably goes as far back as the 17th century. In *Publick Occurrences Both Forreign and Domestick*, the first English-language newspaper in America, there were two stories concerning Native Americans: One praised "their industry and communal spirit in staving off starvation" and the other accused them of "kidnapping white children, presumably to ravage or eat them" (Figure 5.1). It seems the dominant culture has always wanted to portray Native Americans both ways—as noble savages and as feared adversaries—in order to pigeonhole their culture and justify the treatment of Native peoples throughout American history (Figure 5.2).

There is always debate, it seems, whether Hollywood and other portrayals honor or marginalize Native peoples. "Cowboys versus Indians," despite Americans encroaching on Native lands, was a staple of early Hollywood films. D. W. Griffith, infamous for his flawed classic *Birth of a Nation* (1915), made the first picture that had the classic scene of a wagon train being terrorized in *The Last Drop of Water* (1911) (Figure 5.3). He also directed *Fighting Blood* (1911) and *The Battle of Elderbrush Gulch* (1913). The famed director Cecil B. De-Mille's first movie was named *The Squaw Man* (1913) (Figure 5.4). The word "squaw" is a derogatory word for a woman's vagina. Other angry Native movies followed, including the box office hit *The Covered Wagon* (1923), *Northwest Passage* (1940) that starred Spencer Tracy, and *Red River* (1948) with John Wayne. After 1950 the cowboy/Indian genre lost popularity among movie producers, as audiences became more interested in gunslinger westerns. In 1973 actor Marlon Brando refused to accept his Academy Award for Best Actor in *The Godfather* because of the way Hollywood had portrayed Native Americans in the movies.

University of Alaska professor Dan Rearden cited *Eskimo* (1933), *On Deadly Ground* (1994), and Disney's *Snow Dogs*

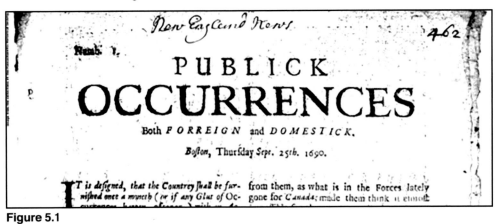

Figure 5.1
The September 25, 1690 edition of Publick Occurrences Both Forreign and Domestick *included positive and negative stories about Native Americans.*
Courtesy of the Massachusetts Historical Society

Figure 5.2

First published in 1919, The Open Road for Boys *was a typical magazine for boys that promoted camping, hiking, and shooting things with air rifles. In this 1934 cover story, a "Medicine Man," one of the most sacred leaders responsible for the tribe's spiritual and physical health, is distorted in this common, violent stereotype.*

Courtesy of Open Road Publishing

W
LINK
Figure 5.3
*(Weblink: http://goo.gl/
F2t8UG)*
Directed by D.W. Griffith, who later became infamous for his The Birth of a Nation, The Last Drop of Water or The Story of the American Desert, shows wagon trains attacked by Native American warriors.

Figure 5.4
A magazine advertisement for the 1914 silent film, The Squaw Man *co-directed by Cecil B. DeMille, his first motion picture production.*
Courtesy of the Chalmers Publishing Company

(2002) as offensive. In *Dogs*, the character played by Cuba Gooding, Jr., tells of a nightmare in which he was an Eskimo. "Children are watching this in a Disney film," Rearden said. "The message is, if you're Eskimo, that's a nightmare. What's at stake with kids watching movies like this?"

In 1995 Disney released an animated movie about a Powhatan woman named Pocahontas. In defending the romantic princess stereotype in the movie, Roy Disney wrote that the film is "responsible, accurate, and respectful." However, Chief Roy Crazy Horse said, "It is unfortunate that with this sad story, which Euro-Americans should find embarrassing, Disney makes 'entertainment' and perpetuates a dishonest and self-serving myth at the expense of the Powhatan Nation." Native American stereotypes have been seen in such popular television shows as "My Favorite Martian," "Star Trek," and "Quantum Leap." In one episode of the popular 1990s television sitcom "Seinfeld," Jerry is considered a racist by his friends when he buys a cigar

store Indian for his Native American girlfriend (Figure 5.5).

No debates, however, are as heated as those outside huge professional sports arenas and small-town grass fields played under Friday night lights. Groups such as the National Indian Education Association, the National Congress of American Indians, the American Civil Liberties Union, the U.S. Commission on Civil Rights, and others have condemned the use of Native American symbols as sports mascots. Nevertheless, the use of Native mascots is still popular. Almost 2,000 school athletic programs around the United States still have Native mascots.

Alumni of schools and universities and fans of professional teams throughout the United States use the same defense: "Indian people should be proud that there are people who want to represent them and follow in their footsteps and conduct themselves with dignity and honor." But names like the Washington Redskins, which is a racial slur on par with the n-word; cartoon

Figure 5.5
Wearing a skirt depicting an American flag, this wooden sculpture outside a cigar store shows a Native American scout with one hand shading his eyes and the other holding a package of cigars. Since Native Americans introduced tobacco to European explorers and settlers, the use of "cigar store Indians" became an advertisement symbol. Today, however, use of these statues is limited, since many compare the figure with African American racist lawn ornaments and other stereotypical representations that are seen as demeaning.
Courtesy of Paul Martin Lester

Figure 5.6
Named in 1933, the Redskins, the team mascot for the Washington, D.C., NFL football team is defended by team boosters as it "refers to the red paint used on the skin of Indian warriors." Bill Plaschke, sports columnist for the Los Angeles Times *writes "How does a team from the nation's capital, supported by a fan base of some of the nation's greatest thinkers, maintain a nickname that is the Native American equivalent to the N-word?"*
Courtesy of Paul Martin Lester

images like the toothy grin of Chief Wahoo, the Cleveland Indians' mascot; the "tomahawk chop" employed by fans of the Atlanta Braves; and the "Sacred Ground" at the Kansas City Chiefs end zone are not honoring Native peoples and are denounced by experts who offer a variety of reasons for ending such depictions (Figure 5.6). About the Redskins' NFL mascot, Suzan Shown Harjo, executive director of the Morning Star Institute, a non-profit advocacy group for Native American rights, said that Redskins "is the most derogatory thing Native Peoples can be called in the English language."

Another argument against the use of mascots is because of "collateral use." Fans from opposing teams often use racial slurs and obscene cartoon depictions based on a Native mascot (Figure 5.7). Lucy Ganje, then Professor of Communications with the University of North

Figure 5.7
An example of "collateral use" of Native American school mascots is this T-shirt worn by fans of North Dakota State University, a football rival of the University of North Dakota. Allison Two-Bears who attended State admitted, "'Sioux suck.' That's what my fellow classmates were chanting. That's what rivals do and I understand that. But being from that culture, I felt there was no respect behind that name." The red color was added for emphasis.
Courtesy of Lucy Ganje

Dakota, writes, "Native children have the right to grow up believing they're more than mascots for products and sports teams. They have the right to attend a football game without standing next to someone yelling, 'Scalp the Indians!'"

In 2005 the National Collegiate Athletic Association (NCAA) announced that it would ban from postseason play any team that used a Native American mascot. Consequently, sensitivity to the mascot issue seems to be gaining ground. Faced with sanctions from the National Collegiate Athletic Assn., in 2010 the North Dakota Board of Higher Education voted to retire the Fighting Sioux mascot. In retaliation, the North Dakota Senate passed a law, signed by Governor Jack Dalrymple, which mandated the university to keep the divisive image. However, in 2012 the NCAA compelled the university to change its logo. Three years later a public vote was allowed with five possible mascot candidates: Fighting Hawks, Roughriders, Nodaks, Sundogs, and North Stars.

The Fighting Hawks won with 57 percent of the vote. Robert Kelley, the school's president explained, "I think this name underscores the tremendous competitive spirit of our athletic teams, our student-athletes and the entirety of the University of North Dakota, expressing our state spirit and the fact that UND continues to ascend to newer heights."

Because of pressure from the NCAA, alumni, and other concerned citizens, educational institutions around the United States have changed from their Native mascots in recent years. The Redmen of St. John's University in New York became the Red Storm; Southern Nazarene University in Oklahoma were once the Redskins and are now the Crimson Storm; Ohio's Miami University changed their mascot from the Redskins to the RedHawks; and Marquette changed from the Warriors to the Golden Eagles.

REINFORCING STEREOTYPES WITH IMAGES

Whether an individual is identified

Figure 5.8
It was rare for President Franklin Roosevelt to be photographed using a wheelchair because it was thought he would look weak, especially during wartime. He agreed to this picture because it was a family snapshot.
Courtesy of the FDR Library

Figure 5.9
At at early age children learn, probably from the media and parents who accept too easily the social conventions, that girls are pretty in pink. This one poses for a photographer in a Southern California neighborhood and reflects her age and social group. But she goes against the stereotype of a pretty girl in a pink dress by holding a toy (let's hope) submachine gun.
Courtesy of Paul Martin Lester

W
LINK

Figure 5.10
(Weblink: http://goo.gl/6RmdiK)
Reading the News *published by Michael Shaw is one of the best websites to read serious analyses of news images. Shaw also sponsors online discussions with experts on selected topics.*

because of gender, age, cultural heritage, economic status, sexual orientation, or physical disability, the visual message generally communicated about that person often is misleading and false (Figures 5.8 and 5.9). Because pictures affect a viewer emotionally more than words alone do, pictorial stereotypes often become misinformed perceptions that have the weight of established facts. These pictures can remain in a person's mind throughout a lifetime.

When pictorial stereotypes are repeated enough times, they become part of a society's culture. Culture is a culmination of learned, mutually accepted rules that define communication for a group of people during a particular time period. People form attitudes about others, both within and outside their own culture, through direct experiences, interactions with family members and friends, educational institutions, and the media. Culture tells us what we should do to get along within a particular society as well as what our actions mean to others. Communication is easier when people share the same cultural meanings (e.g., speak the same language or use the same visual symbolism).

Through everyday experiences, a person acquires a certain set of beliefs and attitudes about other people, places, objects, and issues. Perhaps as a youth you were punished by a high school principal and thus dislike all persons in authority. Maybe you have heard that Mexico City has high pollution levels so you never want to visit. Perhaps your father doesn't like to eat broccoli and so neither do you. Maybe someone you admire opposes capital punishment, influencing you to adopt that same attitude. What you believe, what you think is true, forms your attitudes. Attitudes are general and long-lasting positive or negative feelings. If information is limited or its source isn't trusted, a belief can become an enduring attitude that can lead to stereotypical generalizations. The

goal of education is to teach an individual how to seek factual information and base beliefs and attitudes on reasoned conclusions.

To be successful, communication (from the Latin word for *commonness*) requires mutual understanding of the symbols used. By definition, different cultures attribute different meanings to similar actions. Consequently, members of one culture often are easy to identify and have trouble communicating with members of another culture. In a multicultural society, members of some cultures often are stigmatized because of their inability to use the symbols of the dominant culture. Dominant cultures are not designated by having the most members, but by having the most economic and political influence over an entire society. Dominant cultures can also have individual members who cross ethnic, racial, gender, and other lines. Michael Shaw, publisher of a popular visual analysis website Reading the Pictures recently wrote, "Visual persuasion and bias is typically the device and luxury of those in and with power, whatever branch of government, media entity, industrial corporation, or, yes, political party, we happen to be talking about" (Figure 5.10).

Throughout the world, an estimated 17,000 distinct cultural groups almost never receive media attention within their societies. In Latin America, for example, 600 separate tribes live in lowland regions alone. In the United States, some 20 million people belong to so-called "fringe" religious groups, and 75 million classify themselves as belonging to more than 120 separate ethnic cultures. But the faces that most often appear in still photographs and moving images are Anglo. The dominant cultural groups—those with the most power and influence in the social structure, including the media—are the ones that control which images get seen. It is always to the advantage of the dominant groups to stereotype other groups in order to secure dominance.

One of the chief functions of the brain is to categorize visual information into basic units that can be easily and quickly analyzed. That's why early scientists and engineers called the brain a "difference engine." Unfortunately, this trait of the brain also leads to instant categorization of people. Noticing a person's gender, age, ethnic background, and the like is perfectly natural. But having preconceived attitudes that may or may not be true about that person are learned and often misguided.

Stereotypical media coverage manifests itself as a sin of admission or omission. Media coverage of individuals who belong to a specific cultural group usually presents them as special cases to be pitied for their terrible living situations, admired for bettering themselves, or, most often, reviled for their violent criminal actions. The stories of hardworking, decent members of various cultural groups often are ignored. Accounts of their lives simply are not considered to be "news."

Part of the problem with the media's portrayals of diverse groups is that few practicing journalists are from those groups. At least 86 percent of the daily newspapers in the United States do not have any diverse staff members and 78 percent have no diverse group members in management positions. Sensitivity to the stereotyping of ethnic and other groups isn't a high priority when newsrooms all exhibit the same skin color. In addition, schools of communication have few if any culturally diverse professors or students. A test for your own school or workplace is easily conducted—find the racial/ethnic percentages for your geographical area. If there is no discrimination, the number for those you see at school or work should be the same. In professional sports, however, the percentages are reversed. Although the percentage of African Americans men

in the US is about six percent, almost 70 percent of those who play for the National Football League is African American. Such a finding often leads to almost all African Americans playing for an almost all-Anglo audience. Unfortunately, this statistic is far too common across gyms and arenas in America. Obviously, such a large discrepancy indicates a racial issue that should be addressed for society.

SPECIFIC EXAMPLES OF STEREOTYPING

Every form of prejudice is based on the assumption that members of one group are better than members of another because of false opinions about physical, intellectual, and social characteristics. Throughout history, the dominant groups in societies have discriminated against various ethnic and other groups. Some groups have managed to overcome discrimination and become a part of the dominant societal force. Most others have not been so successful.

Almost any group you can think of has been the target of prejudice and discrimination at some time—children, older people, religious zealots and atheists, people who are homeless, those who have disabilities, students, professionals, unemployed people, the poor and the rich, foreigners, city and country dwellers, people with southern accents, people with Brooklyn accents—and on and on until every person can find his or her own category. Men must always be strong, have well-endowed pecs, and be interested in women, hunting, and—as Full Throttle's "Get Your Man Out" commercial would want you to believe—energy drinks. Religious fundamentalists are fanatics. News photographers and paparazzi are "animals." Anglos are racists. Blind persons cannot live successfully alone, as reflected in a scene with Gene Hackman and Peter Boyle in Mel Brooks' *Young Frankenstein* (1974). Intellectually disabled individuals are easy fodder for jokes in motion pictures. The former

First Lady of California, Maria Shriver, denounced a character named Simple Jack played by Ben Stiller in the movie *Tropic Thunder* (2008). In the movie, "retard" is repeated several times and refers to the character. With an estimated eight million intellectually disabled Americans, Shriver says that the word is "equal to the impact of the 'N-word' on an African American."

African Americans, Arabs, Asians, Latinos, women, lesbian, gay, bisexual, transgender, and queer (LGBTQ) persons, and persons who use wheelchairs are examples of groups that have long been discriminated against. Pictorial stereotypes presented in the media of all these cultural groups shape the public's perception of them.

African American Stereotypes

African American history is directly tied to past U.S. government-sanctioned enslavement. Consequently, African Americans have faced tremendous difficulty in overcoming stereotypes, despite legal, economic, and social reforms. Racism is the belief that one race is better than another because of the genes in a person's chromosomes. When European explorers came into contact with Africans in the 16th century, many concluded that Africans must not have European mental processing abilities because African societies lacked the technological advances common in Europe. Later, evolutionary theory became a scientific justification for racism, with western Europeans thought to be on a higher evolutionary plane than other races. Those with economic interests in the slave trade used all these rationalizations. Thinking of Africans simply as animals on the same level as apes often was used as an excuse for severe treatment during capture, transport to the New World, enslavement, and forced labor (Figure 5.11).

Unlike other ethnic groups that immigrated voluntarily and retained their own cultures, African Americans were not allowed to re-create their own African cultures in the slave colonies. The master-slave mentality also made assimilation extremely difficult even after the Thirteenth Amendment outlawed slavery following the American Civil War. Few in the North had ever had any contact with African Americans. Until 1860, there were more than 500,000 free African Americans living in the South. They had been born of free mothers, had paid for their own freedom, or had been set free by their owners. In the South these freed slaves had occupations as diverse as architects and hotel clerks. But in the North, discrimination in jobs, housing, and education was much more common and institutionalized, making the assimilation of African Americans into the dominant culture particularly difficult. Nevertheless, separate and unequal treatment, demonstrated though different water fountains, theater entrances, restaurants, schools, and businesses, existed in both the North and South (Figure 5.12).

Prejudice and discrimination continue to this day. In a study of 700,000 cases in which officers of the Los Angeles Police Department stopped pedestrians or drivers in 2003 and 2004, conducted by the Southern California branch of the American Civil Liberties Union (ACLU), it was found that African Americans were 127 percent more likely to be stopped than Anglos. The study brought criticisms of racial profiling to the department (Figure 5.13). In a 2011 study from the College Board Advocacy & Policy Center it was found that 28 percent of African Americans had obtained a college associate degree or higher compared with 44 percent for Anglo men. The study also found that 34 percent of African American men with high school diplomas are unemployed and 10 percent of all African American men ages 15 to 24 are in jail. Prejudice reared its head in 2012 after Trayvon

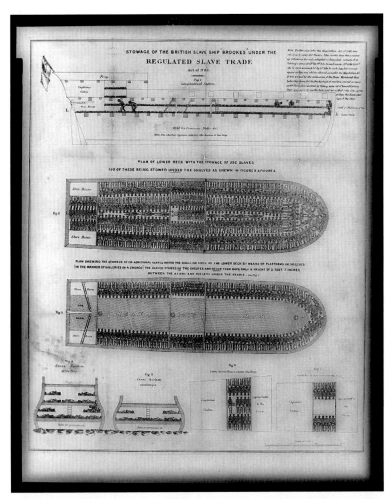

Figure 5.11
Stowage of the British slave ship Brookes under the regulated slave trade act of 1788. This diagram of a typical slave ship that crossed the Atlantic Ocean to America in the 18th and 19th centuries can only hint at the horrific travel conditions of the kidnapped Africans. It has been estimated that up to 30 percent of the victims from each voyage died, their bodies left to decay next to the living.
Courtesy of the Library of Congress

Figure 5.12
"Colored Entrance, New Orleans, Louisiana," 1997, by Gerry Davey. Evidence of racial discrimination against African Americans is noticed on the wall of this French Quarter structure. It has since been painted over.
Courtesy of Gerry Davey

Figure 5.13
*(Weblink:
http://goo.gl/cKcym2)
A Los Angeles Police Depart-
ment officers search an African
American man.*

Figure 5.14
*(Weblink: http://goo.gl/dr7vbG)
Several websites have been
created to document the controversial shootings by police
and upon law enforcement officials. Although not graphically
interesting, Killed By Police
is an impressive example of
spreadsheet documentation.*

Figure 5.15
*(Weblink: http://goo.gl/b0bZpJ)
"Saturday Night Live" performer Eddie Murphy plays multiple
characters in the 2007 Norbit
motion picture—all stereotypes
in one form or another.*

Figure 5.16
*(Weblink: http://goo.gl/kU5YhY)
The two photographs show
three persons trying to survive
as best as they can during one
of the worst natural disasters
in American history. However,
according to the caption writers, two European Americans
find while an African American
man loots.*

Figure 5.17
*(Weblink:
http://goo.gl/M4XAho)
Red Cross officials should
have been more aware of the
image choices made in this
public service announcement.*

Martin, an African American teenager was killed by a neighborhood watch volunteer in Florida. After protest marches around the country, President Obama noted, "If I had a son, he'd look like Trayvon." Meanwhile, since Martin's death and largely because of the rise in citizen journalism, smartphone technology, and social media, mostly European American police officers have been filmed making violent arrests and killing mostly African American suspects. The website Killed By Police maintains, unfortunately, a long list (Figure 5.14).

Recent studies of African American pictorial coverage in print and broadcast media have noted the pictorial legacy of discrimination based on stereotyping. Although more African Americans are seen in the media, the most common pictures of them still relate to crime, sports, and entertainment. Having African American entertainment and sports heroes is important for children, but the message being sent is that they can "make it" in society only if they excel in those fields.

Motion pictures and television have come a long way in eliminating many of the most blatant stereotypical portrayals of African Americans. Yet despite a few exceptions, African American representations in movies and music videos present a stereotypical pattern that concentrates on sexual and violent acts. Many critics are concerned that television's situation comedies also continue false impressions about African Americans.

Male actors wearing wigs, makeup, and heavy body suits to portray overweight, insensitive, and crass women are a recent trend in African American stereotypes. Martin Lawrence in *Big Momma's House* (2000), *Big Momma's House 2* (2006) and *Big Mommas: Like Father, Like Son* (2011), Tyler Perry in *Madea's Family Reunion* (2006), *Madea Goes to Jail* (2009), and *A Madea Christmas* (2011), and Eddie Murphy in *Norbit* (2007) all perpetuate the loud, large

woman stereotype through their distorted, oversimplified images (Figure 5.15). They reinforce prejudicial thinking that continues social discrimination.

Other negative examples are unfortunately easy to find. After Hurricane Katrina slammed into the Gulf Coast in 2005, the captions for two news pictures taken in New Orleans made the images controversial. The photographs showed survivors performing the same action—wading in chest-high polluted water while carrying food and drinks from a store. The African American man in one picture was categorized as "looting" the store, whereas the Anglo couple had left the store after "finding" their items. Besides showing how racial profiling can creep into a caption, they also show that images in themselves are ethically neutral—it is the words that accompany visual messages that cause misrepresentations and misunderstandings (Figure 5.16). The Red Cross apologized for a public service illustration meant to promote pool safety, but almost all of the "Not Cool" activities seen in the advertisement were performed by African American children (Figure 5.17).

President Barack Obama's election to the presidency triggered unfortunate racial stereotypes. Soon after he signed an economic stimulus bill into law, a tragic news story was reported in 2009 of a woman severely mauled by a pet chimpanzee. The animal was shot and killed. Sean Delonas of the *New York Post* drew a cartoon depicting a police officer killing a chimpanzee and the other saying "They'll have to find someone else to write the next stimulus bill." Critics immediately decried the cartoon as racist and inflammatory. One said, "To compare the nation's first African American commander in chief to a dead chimpanzee is nothing short of racist drivel."

Since the 19th century, motion pictures and cartoons have portrayed African Americans as apes. Social psychologists Phillip Goff and Jennifer Everhardt call this attitude "a kind of racial programming, a legacy even something as progressive as Obama's election cannot obliterate." The editor of the *Post* defended the work by calling it a parody and claiming that it simply mocked "Washington's efforts to revive the economy." Nevertheless, the newspaper printed an unusual apology, not for the cartoon itself, but to those whom the cartoon might have offended (Figure 5.18).

Arab Stereotypes

Unlike many other groups, Arab culture is not only a social construct that comprises Arab-speaking peoples, but is distinct from others by differences in shared histories, religion, music, culinary specialties, and artworks. As such, those who identify themselves as Arab can have light or dark hair and skin and identify themselves as Muslim, Christian, or any other religion. In the United States, most Arabs are Christians who immigrated from Lebanon and Syria. Nevertheless, in news and entertainment media, the prevalent stereotypes of Arabs as convenience store counter workers, unintelligible taxicab drivers, and cold-blooded religious fanatics are commonly featured. The Arab Face website is a collection of Arab stereotypes that includes the sheik, Bedouin, maiden, haggler, and terrorist (Figure 5.19). Well before the events of 9/11, stereotypical generalizations, discrimination, and assaults against Arabs had occurred. The list of media examples is long and injurious.

The folk tales of Aladdin and his lamp and Ali Baba and his 40 thieves are ancient stories that were included in a collection called *One Thousand and One Nights*. Unfortunately, these stories, as well as the equally popular Sinbad the Sailor, are examples of powerful popular culture positive icons that were turned into stereotypes by Hollywood and

others (Figure 5.20). From such motion pictures as *Aladin and the Wonderful Lamp* (1900) came *The Thief of Bagdad* (1924), starring Douglas Fairbanks, and its parody *Grief In Baghdad* (1925), with the principal actors strangely played by chimpanzees. Cartoons such as *Gypped in Egypt* (1930), *Popeye the Sailor Meets Sinbad the Sailor* (1936), *Popeye and Ali Baba's Forty Thieves* (1937), and Porky Pig in *Ali-Baba Bound* (1940) added to the notion that Arabs were dumb-headed and money-crazy (Figure 5.21). More recently, Disney's *Aladdin* (1992) sparked controversy. Marvin Wingfield and Bushra Karaman wrote, "The film's light-skinned lead characters, Aladdin and Jasmine, have Anglicized features and Anglo-American accents. This is in contrast to the other characters who are dark-skinned, swarthy and villainous—cruel palace guards or greedy merchants with Arabic accents and grotesque facial features."

Without a doubt, the depiction of Arabs as maniacal terrorists is hard to shake. Jack Shaheen, a Lebanese American writer, laments, "There is never an Arab hero for kids to cheer." In such pre-9/11 films as *Raiders of the Lost Ark* (1981), *Back to the Future* (1985), *True Lies* (1994), and *The Siege* (1998), Shaheen's assertion is supported. The director of the Islamic Council of New England said, "*The Siege* hideously distorts the religion of Islam." Many protested the linking of Islam and violence. After the 9/11 attacks, motion pictures and television programs such as *Team America: World Police* (2004), *American Dreamz* (2006), *You Don't Mess with Zohan* (2008), *Iron Man* (2008), and most episodes of the FOX television series "24" were criticized for their portrayal of Arabs as terrorists. In *Iron Man*, Egyptian-born actor Sayed Badreya played an arms dealer who kidnaps the character played by Robert Downey, Jr. In a *Los Angeles Times* story Badreya explained that when he first arrived in Hollywood

Figure 5.18
(Weblink: http://goo.gl/iC8ccg) For many, Sean Delonas' editorial cartoon depicted President Obama as a chimpanzee killed by police officers.

Figure 5.19
(Weblink: http://goo.gl/EFoJBn) The Arabface website, "refers to the creation and propagation of racist Arab stereotypes and caricatures." Several examples in many categories are shown.

W
LINK

Figure 5.21
(Weblink: http://goo.gl/4ALDQl)
Intruder Porky Pig vanquishes Arab citizens with stereotypical gusto in their home country turning their village into an Ali Baba's "Auto Camp."

Figure 5.20
From an illustration by Albert Robida in an 1895 edition of Ali Baba and the Forty Thieves, *Hollywood directors later exploited the violent nature of Arab swordsmen. The son of a French carpenter, Robida escaped his humble beginnings by becoming a renowned caricaturist, illustrator, and the editor of his own magazine,* La Caricature.
Courtesy of ArabSaga

in 1986 "I couldn't work. I was too handsome. So I put on some weight and grew a beard, and suddenly I was working every day and playing the angry Arab."

After the Oklahoma City bombing in 1995 that killed 168, numerous assaults were reported by those who looked Arab to the attackers, because news agencies repeated a false rumor that Arab terrorists were involved. In fact, it was homegrown Anglo terrorist Timothy McVeigh who was responsible for the bombing. Fast forward six years and not much had changed. Less than a month after 9/11, the U.S. Justice Department issued a report that the agency had "received numerous reports of violence, threats of violence, and discrimination against Arab-Americans and other Americans of Middle Eastern and South Asian descents. Any threats of violence or discrimination against Arab or Muslim Americans or Americans of

South Asian descents are not just wrong and un-American, but also are unlawful and will be treated as such."

Violent behavior against those who appear Arab is not limited to real world assaults. Dr. Tom Denson, a communications researcher at the University of New South Wales, conducted a study with students regarding their stereotypes of Arabs. In a first-person shooter video game, "innocent figures in the game were more likely to be shot at if they were wearing turbans or hijabs." Denson called this response the "turban effect" and noticed it in both male and female players. He concluded, "People learn about negative stereotypes from their parents, their peers, their education and the media. Muslims tend to be portrayed negatively in the media so the findings make sense, even in an otherwise tolerant western society like Australia." He also warned that such negative behavior might be more prevalent in the United States and Great Britain. A Gallup poll of Muslim Americans taken in 2008 showed that although they have achieved high levels of education and employment, they report "feelings of unease" with increased stereotypical media coverage and a suspicion of Islam since the terrorist attacks of 9/11. An Amnesty International report identified prejudice intensified since 2009 after legislative actions in France, Belgium, Spain, Turkey, and Switzerland restricted Muslims from practicing their faith in public. Ibrahim Hooper, a spokesperson for the Council on American-Islamic Relations said, "The bizarre bans on Islamic attire and efforts to target mosques in Europe have great similarities to what we see here in the United States."

On the plus side, although former president, Barack Obama is not Muslim, the fact that his middle name is Hussein and was elected president of the United States heartened many Arab and Muslim Americans that there might be a spirit of tolerance evolving within the country. Yet in 2011 the TLC series, "All-American Muslim" that features several Muslim families from Dearborn, Michigan, home to the largest Muslim population in the United States, became controversial when the home improvement chain Lowe's pulled its advertising. The Florida Family Association, a group that has campaigned against the show identified "All-American Muslim as "propaganda" that is "clearly designed to counter legitimate and present-day concerns about many Muslims who are advancing Islamic fundamentalism and Sharia law." However, U.S. Representative Keith Ellison, who is Muslim, said in a statement that Lowe's had "chosen to uphold the beliefs of a fringe hate group" (Figure 5.22). However, the positive spirit was short-lived after presidential candidate Donald Trump's tough talk against Muslims during the 2016 campaign and his later efforts to impose a travel ban to the

US for citizens of predominately Muslim countries. In 2017 the Supreme Court agreed to prohibit entry into the US, with restrictions, persons from six Muslim majority countries, Iran, Libya, Somalia, Sudan, Syria, and Yemen, initially named in a Trump Executive Order, but put on hold through lower court decisions. The Court will hear the case this fall.

Figure 5.22
A Muslim woman poses for a photograph at a teashop inside the Grand Bazaar, the oldest shopping mall in the world dating from 1461, located in Istanbul, Turkey.
Courtesy of Paul Martin Lester

Asian Stereotypes

Asian American students often tell personal anecdotes in which they have been stereotyped as being good at math, bad drivers, golf obsessed, and wealthy. More serious and embedded stereotypes are discussed by academics Farah

Figure 5.23
Many of the early stereotypes of evil and diabolical Asian villains seen in Hollywood films come from actual portraits of warriors, a noble and honored profession. This 1760 hanging silk scroll shows a portrait of Wu Fu, Brigadier General of the Gansu Region of north central China.
Courtesy of the Library of Congress

Mahdzan and Norlinda Ziegler in their analysis of Asian American stereotypes in the media. They identify the "exaggerated depictions of exotic, sex-hungry Asian women to the gangster-involved, sexually abusive characteristics of Asian men" in mainstream motion pictures. The evil and diabolical crime genius Fu Manchu, first featured in the books by English author Sax Rohmer in the 1910s, was often a character in motion pictures (Figure 5.23).

Various media perpetuate engrained Asian stereotypes. In print cartoons, Marvel comic books featured anti-heroes such as Mandarin and the Yellow Claw, and DC Comics' Wonder Woman battled the giant Egg Fu, who closely resembled Jabba the Hutt from *Star Wars: Episode VI–Return of the Jedi* (1983). In films, *The Mysterious Dr. Fu Manchu* (1929) starred the Swedish actor Warner Oland who later was better known for his portrayal of detective Charlie Chan. Fu Manchu inspired a host of "Yellow Peril" characters in various media in which Asian criminals were out to dominate the world. Ming the Merciless was an evil influence in the *Flash Gordon* serials of the 1930s. James Bond's first nemesis was Dr. No played by Canadian actor Joseph Wiseman. The opposite of the male gangster is the "Dragon Lady" stereotype exemplified in Lucy Liu's character O-Ren Ishii in Quentin Tarantino's *Kill Bill: Vol. 1* (2003). In *The Joy Luck Club* (1993), Asian men were portrayed as being cheap, ego-driven, and bad sexual partners. In *Year of the Dragon* (1985), the "China Doll," a "sexually active, exotic, overly feminine and eager to please" female stereotype was shown (Figure 5.24). On television, Asian actors are hard to find. Doctor Zin, voiced by Anglo Jeffery Tambor, was shown in the 1960s "Jonny Quest" (Figure 5.25) while another Anglo actor, David Carradine starred in the eponymous series "Kung Fu" in the 1970s. In the final "Newhart" episode in 1982, for example, Japanese

investors bought the entire town and turned it into a golf course. A "South Park" episode titled "The China Problem" featured the children uncovering a plot to take over the world hatched at a P.F. Chang's restaurant. Han Lee, a Korean diner owner played by Matthew Moy in the 2012 CBS sitcom "2 Broke Girls" has been criticized as a retro-stereotype with his broken English and greedy personality.

Media stereotypes often lead to hurtful actions. In 2009, after the first Asian American was named the president of Ivy League Dartmouth College, hate e-mails circulated among students. Jim Yong Kim, a South Korean-born health expert in HIV/AIDS with the World Health Organization, grew up in Iowa since the age of five. In high school he was the class valedictorian and quarterback for the football team. In 2006 he was named one of *Time* magazine's 100 most influential people for his work in helping the world's poor. But a daily e-mail update sent to about 1,000 students run by a group not associated with the college called him a "Chinaman" and warned of the "Asianification" of the campus. The writer of the e-mail reportedly "is full of regret" and "did not mean to offend anyone." In 2012 President Obama named Kim to head the World Bank, the first physician and Asian-American named to that position.

In 2012 professional basketball enthusiasts, especially New York Knicks fans were overtaken with "Linsanity." While the young Harvard-educated NBA point guard Jeremy Lin scores more than 25 points a game, his popularity has also exposed, as *Los Angeles Times* writer Bill Plaschke notes, America's "causal prejudice and lazy stereotypes of Asian Americans." For example, the MSG network showed Lin's face on top of a fortune cookie, A WNYW New York morning television show host made a joke about the shape of his eyes, and ESPN fired an employee for describing a Knick's loss

Figure 5.24
(Weblink: http://goo.gl/ljdaCm) Directed by Michael Cimino, Year of the Dragon *stars Mickey Rourke who plays Stanley White, a racist New York City cop with Ariane Koizumi as Tracy Tzu who changes his opinion about Asians.*

Figure 5.25
(Weblink: http://goo.gl/yhaqZR) Dr. Zin, voiced by "Transparent" actor Jeffrey Tambor, is up to no good in the 1993 animated television movie, Jonny's Golden Quest *produced by Hanna-Barbera studios.*

as a "Chink in the armor." As Plaschke wrote a call for other sports journalists, "Jeremy Lin's heritage is a wonderful part of this story and should not be ignored. But can't we do that without being ignorant?"

Latino Stereotypes

As with Asians, the Latino culture is wonderfully diverse with members from Cuba, Puerto Rico, Mexico, Central and South America, and Spain. And yet, even though about 16 percent of the American population is Latino, a recent study sponsored by the National Association of Hispanic Journalists reported that less than one percent of the stories on network newscasts feature Latinos. Out of that small percentage, the overwhelming topics covered are crime, terrorism, poverty, welfare, and illegal immigration.

The Hispanic American Culture website noted a study in which high school students were asked to come up with words to describe Latinos: "Taco. Cactus. Poverty. Welfare. Sombrero. Mules. Lots of children. Chicken. Farmers. Tequila. Migrant workers. Illegal aliens. Chips-n-dip. Pollution. Ponchos. Limited variety of food. Markets. Gangs. Camaros. Field workers." Most if not all of these negative generalizations stem from media portrayals (Figure 5.26). Such stereotypes can lead to examples of bad behavior. In 2012 fans of a predominantly Anglo high school in San Antonio chanted "USA" after its basketball team won over a predominantly Latino high school. Officials immediately apologized for what was considered racist taunts.

Latinos portrayed in motion pictures, live-action commercials, and on television have created controversy. In film, *Viva Max* (1969), about the retaking of the Alamo by a gang of inept soldiers, and *¡Three Amigos!* (1986) played up the Mexican bandit stereotype and sparked protests. Kristy Acevedo offered a critique of the animated film *Happy Feet* (2006) that was produced by

the Australian animation house Animal Logic for Warner Bros. In the film, the character Mumble is banished by the Emperor penguins and forced to live in a penguin ghetto where the males speak with "heavy Mexican accents, including Ramon, played by the Anglo Robin Williams." Writes Acevedo, "The messages embedded in the film are undeniable. The tall Emperor penguins, white, sometimes stodgy, are definitely the haves, and the Latino misfit penguins are the have-nots. Why should cartoon penguins ever be sorted into ethnic communities in a children's film? Are we trying to teach children that 'birds of a feather flock together?' We are teaching children segregation, not the integration Martin Luther King, Jr. dreamed about." *Happy Feet 2* (2011) offered more of the same with Robin Williams reprising his Latino character, Ramon. To its credit, Disney's *Beverly Hills Chihuahua* (2008) has voices of Latino stars Edward James Olmos, George Lopez, and Andy Garcia, but the plot of the film "shows an ignorance of Mexican culture that could offend Latinos." For example, a statue that is shown as a history lesson of the Mexican Aztec culture is actually Machu Picchu, an Inca structure in Peru.

In commercials, a Chihuahua used as a spokesperson for Taco Bell offended many in the Latino community because fast food is not considered "home cooking" by most Latinos. The little dog was pulled in 2000. From 1967 to 1971 a cartoon character created by the famous Warner Bros. animator Tex Avery and voiced by Mel Blanc, who also played Bugs Bunny, Elmer Fudd, and Speedy Gonzalez, offended many for its stereotype of Latinos. The Frito Bandito, a creation of the Foote, Cone & Belding advertising agency for Fritos corn chips, was a short bandit with a gold tooth, a long, thin mustache, sporting two pistols with crossed ammunition belts and a huge, yellow sombrero who tried to steal your corn chips. The commercials ran

Figure 5.26
A Mexican stereotypical figure is meant to attract attention to a restaurant in Old Town, outside San Diego.
Courtesy of Paul Martin Lester

from 1967 until pressure from protest groups caused the end of the character in 1971 (Figure 5.27).

The Warner Bros. character Speedy Gonzalez was noted as "the fastest mouse in Mexico." In his second appearance in 1955, he stole cheese from security guard Sylvester the Cat for his fellow drunken mice friends and his lazy and slow-witted cousin Slowpoke Rodriguez (Figure 5.28). After the Cartoon Network obtained the Speedy collection, the episodes were taken off the air in 1999 "for perpetuating stereotypes about Mexicans." A more recent example comes from "Saturday Night Live" alum Rob Schneider. His 2012 sitcom on CBS,

"Rob" is loosely based on his marriage to a Latina television producer. It has been called the "worst Latino stereotype on television" with jokes about large families, siestas, leaf blowers, and guacamole. "Rob" actor Cheech Marin defends the series with, "I don't think you want to stay away from the stereotypes, I think you want to confront them and deal with them." But as one critic wrote, "Dealing with stereotypes and exploiting them are two different things."

Women Stereotypes

Males in almost every culture in the world and throughout the history of social interaction have thought that they

Figure 5.27
(Weblink: http://goo.gl/tSa2KR) This rare black and white commercial for Frito corn chips featured the stereotypical Mexican bandit, "The Frito Bandito."

Figure 5.28
(Weblink: http:// goo.gl/zo6vx6) In this Speedy Gonzalez cartoon clip, two stereotypical Mexican cat characters lament over the fact that they should have avoided Speedy and instead tried to catch Slowpoke Rodriguez.

Figure 5.29
Many women throughout the world are forced by cultural restrictions— including religious and/or social customs—to cover their faces while in public, as this 19th century woodcut demonstrates.
Uncensored Situations, 1966,
The Dick Sutphen Studio, Inc.

are the dominant and more important gender. Such patterns of thought have led to prejudice and pervasive discrimination against women (Figure 5.29). At birth, girls are treated more gently than boys. Historically, girls were taught to stay home and attend to household duties. Boys were encouraged to be adventurous and active. Women were expected to find happiness in marriage and motherhood. Men were expected to find fulfillment in their careers. Women were valued for their appeal as sexual objects. Men were valued for their intelligence, strength, and energy. Watch any episode of the critically acclaimed AMC series "Mad Men," set in a 1960s advertising agency to see this stereotype in action.

During the Industrial Revolution in the 19th century, many poor women were allowed to work in the factories for the first time because of labor shortages. Despite this advance in social thinking, women were still not allowed to vote, own property, testify in court, make a legal contract, spend their wages without getting permission from their husbands, or even retain guardianship over their children. In the U.S., abolitionist activism on behalf of freedom for slaves in the South led many also to consider freedom for women in the North. Eventually, Wyoming became the first state to give women the right to vote. In 1920, the Nineteenth Amendment, which gave women national voting rights, was ratified. Although voting reform was an important step, efforts to reform other discriminatory practices were unsuccessful. The late Texan columnist Molly Ivins noted that women's rights were especially slow in coming to Texas, for example. "Until June 26, 1918," she writes, "the Texas Constitution mandated that all Texans had the right to vote except 'idiots, imbeciles, aliens, the insane and women.'" Women weren't allowed to serve on juries in Texas until 1954.

Throughout World War II women again were needed in the factories, this time to produce armaments, to replace the men serving in the armed forces. When the war ended, these "Rosie the Riveters" succumbed to tremendous social pressure to take care of their returning men, have babies, and let the male "breadwinners" have the jobs they needed in order to support their families (See Chapter 4). The result was the "baby boom," named for the large number of children born during the late 1940s and the 1950s.

In spite of this social progress for women in the 1960s and beyond, media stereotypes of women in news, entertainment, and advertising contexts constantly remind viewers of society's male-dominated view. On television, women often are portrayed as sex objects designed only for a man's pleasure, as wives whose chief duty is to serve their husbands, and as mothers who often must rear children without a husband's help. In the 1950s, women were portrayed as being less intelligent than men, being dependent on men for support, and thus being inferior. Obviously, such stereotypes do not portray men and women equally (Figure 5.30). Early television situation comedies such as "I Love Lucy," "The Adventures of Ozzie and Harriet," "Father Knows Best," "The Donna Reed Show," and "Leave It to Beaver" reinforced the view that the women should stay home and take care of the house and children. Although today's women sitcom characters are mostly out of the house, in programs such as "2 Broke Girls," "Modern Family," and "The Big Bang Theory" any thought of a serious career is second to punchy jokes about sex.

Nowhere is the unequal status of men and women as obvious as in advertising. Images in magazine ads and in television commercials show women as sexual objects to attract the attention of potential customers to the product. Hair care, clothing, and makeup advertisements regularly give women the impression that they are inferior if they do not

measure up to the impossible beauty standards demonstrated by high-priced models. Research on television commercials has revealed that men are used as voice-overs when an authority figure is desired, women are portrayed mainly in a family setting in which men are benefited, women often are noticeably younger than their male counterparts, and fewer girls and women are used in advertisements than boys and men. Although never the only cause for gender discrimination, print, television, movie, and web images that show bikini-clad models holding phallic-shaped beer bottles reinforce the idea that women are mentally inferior to men and good only for sexual pleasure (Figures 5.31 and 5.32). Major female actresses such as Nicole Kidman and Sarah Jessica Parker as well as female cast members for the television shows "Gossip Girls" and "The Hills" have posed while wearing only their underwear for such magazines as *Vanity Fair* and *Rolling Stone*. Such objectification of women, although seemingly innocent, can lead to degradation, intimidation, stalking, assault, rape, and murder.

Lesbian, Gay, Bisexual, Transgender, and Queer (LGBTQ) Stereotypes

If someone were to advocate that people with disabilities or Native Americans, African Americans, or women should be forced to suffer the physical and emotional scars of discrimination, most people would roundly condemn that person as a crackpot. That's because prejudice and discrimination generally are opposed on legal and moral grounds. However, the approximately 25 million LGBTQ members of our society belong to one of the few groups that can be discriminated against legally.

Ironically, lesbians and gays are the most diverse of any cultural group. In fact, data from the 2010 U.S. Census showed that same-sex married and

W LINK

Figure 5.30
(Weblink: http://goo.gl/NuUdtF) Since the father always knows best, he is in the center of attention in this publicity photograph of the cast of the situation comedy "Father Knows Best" that ran from 1954 until 1963. The picture is also an excellent example of social perspective (See Chapter 2).

Figure 5.31
In this advertisement for Cointreau liqueur, the shape and position of the models' fingers and the bottle itself are meant to link drinking the alcoholic beverage to sexual conquest.
Courtesy of Neil Chapman

Figure 5.32
Although at first glance the man appears to be holding the woman's breasts in the Seagram's billboard, she is actually touching herself. Media critic Irving Goffman has written that such a gesture by women connotes subservience to men. The metonymic code of dress style, jewelry, and background details communicates an upscale environment. Ironically, the JVC advertisement displays the words that Seagram executives hope male buyers of their gin will believe: "Hold everything."
Courtesy of Neil Chapman

unmarried couples make up 646,464 households in the United States, which puts on average about 206 same-sex couples in every county in America. LGBTQ persons cannot be isolated by race, gender, economic situation, social position, region of the country, religious belief, political orientation, or any other physical attribute. Many are extremely hesitant to admit their sexuality, fearing an employment, housing, and/or social backlash.

When the HIV/AIDS crisis became known in the early 1980s, homosexuals were cast as either victims or villains, with little concern about an objective presentation. Independent and well-financed videos produced and distributed by conservative religious organizations that operated their own cable networks played on the fear of disease. Such programs included "The Gay Agenda" and "Gay Rights/Special Rights." For example, in "Gay Rights," an HIV/AIDS patient talked of having 50 sexual partners in one night—hardly representative of homosexuals as a group. Pro-gay rights commercials—one featuring a gay soldier who was killed in Vietnam with the message "End Discrimination"—are seldom seen, as the major networks refuse to air most political advertisements.

Discrimination continues. In 2009, after a Microsoft Xbox Live game user identified herself as a lesbian in her profile, she was subjected to offensive comments from other gamers. Instead of an investigation by Microsoft officials, her account was canceled. In a classic "shock advertising" strategy (See Chapter 4), after news of this story was made public, the company apologized. In 2012 a jury convicted a former Rutgers University student of hate crimes and other charges after he secretly videotaped his dorm mate having sex with another man. When the video was discovered, the roommate killed himself. Rutgers officials altered its housing policy to better accommodate LGBTQ students, but it was learned through the trial that 87 percent of college campuses do not include sexual orientation in their policies that bar discrimination.

Despite President Obama's decision to allow transgender persons to openly serve in the military, President Trump in a series of Tweets announced in 2017 that he would not allow transgender individuals to serve "in any capacity in the U.S. military." The issue is complicated by the fact that there were thousands already serving—some in dangerous combat situations. The tweets were a disappointing setback for those interested in overcoming social discrimmination.

Wheelchair Users

For many, Labor Day marks the end of the summer season. It is a U.S. holiday that recognizes the transition between lazy days full of relaxation and the start of a new season of productivity for students and workers alike. As that last picnic, last stroll along a trail, or last dive into a pool begins to fade into a pleasant memory, about 750 million viewers worldwide settle into comfortable chairs, turn on their television sets, and watch some or all of the 23-hour Jerry Lewis Muscular Dystrophy Association (MDA) telethon, the annual fund-raising program that has become a staple of the medium. The only other televised program that gets more viewers is the NFL's Super Bowl.

Jerry Lewis had been the national chairman of the MDA since 1952 and the emcee for the telecast since 1966. With his professional charm and slicked-back black hair, he introduces each performance, from acrobats to zoo animals, with the same level of enthusiasm, despite the many hours he has worked on the show (Figure 5.34).

Many Las Vegas performers are interspersed with filmed spots about muscular dystrophy (MD) research and people afflicted with the disease. Between dancers, singers, magicians, and comedians in the old theater tradition known as vaudeville, we see scientists in white lab coats mixing chemicals in test tubes, doctors talking passionately into the camera of the need for more money to further their research, and children in wheelchairs being pushed to their next physical therapy session. On stage, parents and other family members of these children talk with tears in their eyes about the shock of learning of their child's illness.

Filmed segments or cutaways to a local station's activities usually end with emotional monologues from Lewis. The "poster child" for the year usually arrives in a wheelchair to the front of the small stage and recites a brief, if a bit self-conscious and awkward, message. Lewis then delivers an emotional appeal for money. At the end of his performance, a spokesperson for a large corporation walks on stage, introduces a slickly produced video about the company's role in the fight against MD, and delivers a check in true photo op fashion. Lewis hoots with joy and announces that the check has a number "followed by lots of zeros." The lights flash, the audience applauds, and the camera zooms in to reveal the dancing numbers on the electronic tote board high above the stage as it registers a new total (Figure 5.35).

The Jerry Lewis/MDA telethon almost always starts with an ironic twist. As a fundraiser that exists to help many

Figure 5.33
*(Weblink: http://goo.gl/A0PtfP)
The lead characters played by Jake Gyllenhaal and Heath Ledger in Brokeback Mountain show their love for each other in this scene from the motion picture.*

Figure 5.34
*(Weblink: http://goo.gl/m9sSlM)
Longtime sidekick for Johnny Carson's "The Tonight Show," Ed McMahon and host Jerry Lewis look fresh at the start of a Labor Day MDA telethon.*

Figure 5.35
*(Weblink: http://goo.gl/SYcmJO)
Jerry Lewis reacts happily at the end of the 44th annual MDA Telethon at the South Point Hotel & Casino in 2010. The tote board displays the total amount raised that year.*

W
LINK

Figure 5.36
(Weblink: http://goo.gl/yGmv8j)
There was always a disconnect at the start of a Jerry Lewis/ MDA telethon because it was a show that raised money for those who need wheelchairs but the opening acts almost always featured one of the most strenuous activities one can perform with legs—dancing.

who do not have full muscle function or who have other mobility challenges, the program usually begins with the most energetic activity that one can possibly do with two healthy legs–dance. Over the years the opening has been a production of men and women tapping, kicking, clogging, and hopping. For example, the 2009 opening featured the Trinity Irish Dancers, a troupe of clogging, clapping, smiling girls (Figure 5.36). Imagine that you are watching the performance while sitting in a wheelchair, and you might start to understand why the telethon is criticized every year for insensitivity toward those whom it supposedly supports.

It is the "pity approach" to fund-raising that most irks many who use wheelchairs to navigate through their daily lives. In 1990, an essay Lewis wrote for *Parade* magazine caused controversy when he characterized persons with MD as "half a person." Although he later apologized for his remarks after a public outcry, Jerry Lewis made clear the connection between making money and exploiting pity. In 1994, former telethon poster children calling themselves "Jerry's Orphans" started to publicly object to the pity campaign by calling it a "pity-thon." Lewis also showed his contempt for those who criticize this Aristotle-based pathos tactic during an interview on the show "CBS Sunday Morning." In 2000 Lewis told correspondent Martha Teichner, "I'm telling about a child in trouble. If it's pity, we'll get some money. I'm giving you facts. Pity. You don't want to be pitied for being a cripple in a wheelchair? Stay in your house." Harriet Johnson, a lawyer from South Carolina with a neuromuscular disease, said that Lewis's remark was an example of "shocking bigotry."

He has also sparked outrage by remarks on other subjects. In 2000, as he was receiving an award from the U.S. Comedy Arts Festival (now known as the Comedy Festival), he admitted

that he didn't like female comics because each one is "a producing machine that brings babies in the world" and by implication shouldn't be telling jokes and performing skits. In 2007, during a telethon he jokingly described the son of a camera operator using an anti-gay slur. After news reports criticized him, he apologized.

In 2011, after 45 years of service, Jerry Lewis was no longer affiliated with MDA or the telethon. Perhaps MDA executives were weary of Lewis' offhand remarks that caused public relations headaches or grew tired of the telethon having his name in its title. Whatever the reason, it was suddenly announced before the annual show that Jerry Lewis would no longer host the annual fund-raiser. It was reported that executives unceremoniously fired Lewis without an opportunity to host one last time because they were concerned what the entertainer might say. Comedian Paul Rodriguez voiced the opinion of many when he said, "It's really crappy the way they treated him. The man is an institution."

For those who use wheelchairs, the telethon is an annual reminder of how mainstream media communicate stereotypical attitudes, even for a good cause. Those in wheelchairs aren't seen as active, independent, and normal. They are viewed as helpless and fragile individuals to be pitied—and who can exist only if a viewer picks up the telephone and pledges a donation.

WHERE DO WE GO FROM HERE?
Reverend Martin Luther King, Jr., wrote those words as the title of his last book. He also used them as the title of a speech he gave to the Tenth Anniversary Convention of the Southern Christian Leadership Conference in Atlanta on August 16, 1967, eight months before he was assassinated. In the speech he said:

When our days become dreary with low

hovering clouds of despair, and when our nights become darker than a thousand midnights, let us remember that there is a creative force in this universe, working to pull down the gigantic mountains of evil, a power that is able to make a way out of no way and transform dark yesterdays into bright tomorrows. Let us realize the arc of the moral universe is long but it bends toward justice.

During the historic 2009 inauguration of President Obama, the first African American elected president, Reverend Joseph Lowery, who founded the Southern Christian Leadership Conference with King, gave the benediction. Later, Lowery delivered a sermon to contemporary civil rights leaders including Eric Holder, the nation's first African American attorney general, on the anniversary of "Bloody Sunday," when civil rights marchers were beaten in Selma, Alabama, in 1965. Lowery related how during the inauguration he tried to see the site where King made his famous "I Have a Dream" speech in 1963 (Figure 5.37):

But I couldn't make out the Lincoln Memorial," Lowery said. *"These old eyes have grown dim. But the eyes of my heart saw the Lincoln Memorial and the ears of my soul heard a 34-year-old preacher standing on the steps, issuing a summons to a nation to climb out of the pits of racism to a higher ground of character and competence. And there I was, never dreaming that I would even see a black president. And here I was not only seeing, but participating. And I was glad to be there to say that today, January 20, is the nation's response to that summons issued by that 34-year-old preacher in 1963.*

In his book *A Theory of Justice*, John Rawls writes of the "veil of ignorance." He asserts that members of all cultural groups must retreat to an "original position" in which cultural rules and social differences disappear (See Chapter 6).

Figure 5.37
The Rev. Martin Luther King, Jr. acknowledges the crowd at the Lincoln Memorial for his "I Have a Dream" speech during the March on Washington, D.C., on Aug. 28, 1963. King founded the Southern Christian Leadership Conference in 1957, advocating nonviolent action against America's racial inequality.
Courtesy of the National Archive

Figure 5.38
(Weblink: http://goo.gl/J4RvGi)
The "American Idol" 2011 final-
ists are a picture of diversity.

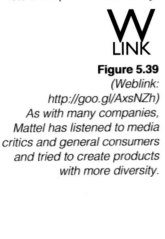

Figure 5.39
(Weblink:
http://goo.gl/AxsNZh)
As with many companies,
Mattel has listened to media
critics and general consumers
and tried to create products
with more diversity.

When all barriers between individuals are lifted, everyone is freed to experience what it is like to be in the "other person's shoes." At that point, Rawls believes, everyone in a society will have equal status and access to the goods and services produced by that society. The need is to build solid bridges between people that are not based on superficial, stereotypical, and visible symbols.

The only place where people regularly and over a long time see members from other cultural groups is in the pages of newspapers and magazines, on television, in the movies, and on computer screens. But when most of those media images are misleading, viewers aren't challenged to examine the basis of their prejudices and do something about them. To change people's minds about diversity may require far-reaching changes in the entire society.

Images That Heal
There are signs of progressive visual messaging. One particularly positive change is the many contestants of singing competition shows that come from diverse backgrounds (Figure 5.38). Above the slogan, "Not all blind people sell pencils," a public service advertisement from the American Foundation for the Blind shows portraits of a successful professor, wrestling coach, district attorney, and sports announcer. Whether for credit cards, jewelry, or automobiles, advertisers are using more and more actors from diverse cultures. In 2017 Mattel announced a change in Ken, the 56-year-old companion to Barbie. The doll now comes in "different body types, skin tones and hairdos, including a man-bun and a cornrow" (Figure 5.39). As a hopeful sign, it is possible to find images in the media that are positive examples from all the groups mention below.

Native Americans Native groups praised Chief Dan George in *Little Big Man* (1970), Rodney A. Grant

and Michael Spears in *Dances with Wolves* (1990), Arthur Redcloud in *The Revenant* (2015), Michael Horse in Showtime's 2017 version of David Lynch's "Twin Peaks," Wes Studi in *Avatar* (2009), Benjamin Bratt in *Traffic* (2000), *Miss Congeniality* (2000), and *Despicable Me 2* (2013), Adam Beach in *Smoke Signals* (1998) and *Flags of Our Fathers* (2006), Graham Greene in *The Green Mile* (1999), and Cree Summer in *Inspector Gadget* (1999) for their honest portrayals. However, the list needs to be expanded (Figure 5.40).

African Americans From 1984 to 1992 television viewers saw the challenges an upper middle class African American family faced in "The Cosby Show." Photographer Bruce Davidson produced a coffee table book in 1970, *East 100th Street*, which documented the everyday lives of persons living in Harlem, New York City, and returned almost 30 years later to update his work. The Black Coaches and Administrators organization reported that for 2011 there were 28 African American men who were head coaches among the 119 NCAA Division 1 college football teams or 24 percent, a commendable number since the overall African American population the U.S. is about 13 percent. In a 1997 Volkswagen commercial, two young men, one Anglo and the other African American, ride in a car, pick up a smelly chair, and get rid of it set to the tune of "Da Da Da" by the German band Trio (Figure 5.41). The commercial was praised for showing an everyday lifestyle activity in which the races of the two men didn't matter.

More significantly, TV One, a cable network begun in 2004 that concentrates its programming on the "authentic, rich, and diverse experience of African American life, history, and culture" is perhaps best known for its show "Find Our Missing." With about 13 percent of the U.S. population, 40 percent of African Americans are missing. Hosted by "Law

Figure 5.40
A page from the Nordisk Familijebok, a Swedish encyclopedia from 1904, shows Native and South Americans from 33 tribes, from the Aleuts in Alaska to the Fuegians from the southern tip of Tierra del Fuego. Studying the diversity of their headdresses, hairstyles, facial attributes, expressions, and clothing, it is difficult to imagine anyone lumping them together as one cultural group.
Courtesy of Project Runeberg

& Order" actress S. Epatha Merkerson, the program attempts to find lost family members in a "dramatic and emotional" fashion with viewer assistance. Advertising giant BBDO New York for Procter & Gamble's, My Black is Beautiful produced "The Talk" in which parents warn children about racism in thier lives (Figure 5.42)

During 2017 television shows available that feature mostly African American casts that are popular include "Power," "Empire," "Black-ish," "Scandal," and "How to Get Away with Murder."

Episodes have storylines that appeal to a wide swath of viewers. Another indication of movement toward progressiveness is that for the first time in the history of the ABC game show, "The Bachelor" and "The Bachelorette," the woman desired by the men is a 32-year-old lawyer from Dallas who happens to be African American, Rachel Lindsay (Figure 5.43).

Arabs Director Cherien Dabis's *Amreeka* (2009) tells the sensitive and real-life story of a divorced Palestinian woman

W
LINK
Figure 5.41
(Weblink: http://goo.gl/IWoUqC) Volkswagen was praised for its lifestyle-type commercial in which two friends drive along city streets, as any two friends.

W
LINK
Figure 5.42
(Weblink: http://goo.gl/ qM8MMu) "The Talk" is an example of advertisers using their skills to communicate tolerance.

Figure 5.43
(Weblink: http://goo.gl/qYB9ZV)
The 2017 bachelorette, Rachel Lindsay holds a rose for one of her suitors.

Figure 5.44
(Weblink: http://goo.gl/i3SRra)
The American television series "Fresh Off the Boat" debuted on ABC in 2015. Created by Iranian-American Nahnatchka Khan and based on celebrity chef Eddie Huang's memoir, early on he voiced concerns about the portrayals.

Figure 5.45
(Weblink: http://goo.gl/52cvBp)
Simple compositions and a direct perspective in black and white videos that act as still photographs give the portraits of people at the end of The Motorcycle Diaries even more dignity.

who immigrates to the United States with her son after the invasion of Iraq in 2003. Iranian stereotypes are slowly being countered by such motion pictures as *Persepolis* (2007), an animated film based on Marjane Satrapi's graphic novel and Academy Award winner for Best Foreign Language Film *A Separation* (2011), about a married couple that must decide to stay in Iran or leave the country for the sake of their child. In 2012 the journalism profession was shocked to learn of the death of two-time Pulitzer Prize winner Anthony Shadid, an Arab-speaking Lebanese American known for his sensitive reporting of civilians trapped by the ravages of war.

Asians Actors with Asian backgrounds received roles on television that include Linda Liu in "Ally McBeal," Margaret Cho in "All American Girl," Sandra Oh, a Canadian, in "Grey's Anatomy," and Ken Jeong in "Community." The ABC sitcom "Fresh Off the Boat," inspired by the life of chef Eddie Huang, features a Taiwanese American family living in Orlando to run a restaurant (Figure 5.44). In motion pictures (Ben Kingsley, born Krishna Bhanji, won the Best Actor Academy Award in 1982 for *Gandhi* and Keanu Reeves in *The Matrix* trilogy. Acclaimed Asian directors include Ang Lee of *The Ice Storm* (1997), *Crouching Tiger, Hidden Dragon* (2000), and *Brokeback Mountain* (2005), M. Night Shyamalan with his eerie tales in *The Sixth Sense* (1998), *Signs* (2002), and *After Earth* (2013), and Mira Nair for *Salaam Bombay* (1988), *Mississippi Masala* (1991), and *Monsoon Wedding* (2001). Other Asian role models include Maya Lin, a landscape artist and sculpture best known for her Vietnam Veterans Memorial in Washington, DC, Dr. Jim Yong Kim, and Jeremy Lin, discussed earlier.

Latinos In 2009 the Latino community was gladdened after Puerto Rican American Sonia Sotomayor was inducted as the first Latina to become a member of the Supreme Court of the United States. In addition, many actors popular with all audiences have Latino roots including Jessica Alba, Catherine Bach, Lynda Carter, Cameron Diaz, Eva Longoria, Freddie Prinze, Jr., Jimmy Smits, and Sofia Vergara. According to author and academic Dr. Henry Puente, "Well-known Latino actors have little incentive to play the stereotypical or underdeveloped Latino characters that frequent current U.S. motion pictures." Also, the black & white portraits of many of the Latinos encountered along the journey of Ernesto "Che" Guevara and Alberto Granado shown at the end of *Diarios de Motocicleta* (2004) demonstrated a deep respect for the individuals and their culture (Figure 5.45). Television programs that have included Latino actors as positive portrayals include Stephanie Beatriz in "Brooklyn Nine-Nine," Jon Huertas in "Castle," Dascha Polanco in "Orange is the New Black," and Aubrey Plaza in "Parks and Recreation."

Women Many times over-the-top parodies teach important lessons about sexism. A popular faux commercial on "Saturday Night Live" showed a boy and girls playing two different versions of chess in "Chess for Girls." The boy became frustrated after the girls were provided with pieces that resembled toys and dolls being quieted because a Queen piece holds a sleeping baby (Figure 5.46). Another example of an artist showing stereotypes in order to make a point against stereotypes is the music video "Stupid Girls" by Alecia Moore (aka P!nk). A girl is offered two ways of life—conforming to traditional standards of behavior and beauty that leads to breast enhancement and bulimia or being socially aware, intelligent, articulate, and playing the male-dominated sport of football (Figure 5.47). In 1995, the Nike sports clothing company launched its "If You Let Me Play" advertising cam-

Figure 5.49
Female Marines pose for the camera in Afghanistan.
Courtesy of the Department of the Navy

paign, in which mostly pre-teen girls spoke directly into the camera. They told of the benefits of playing sports, which included statements such as "I will be more likely to leave a man who beats me" and "I'll be less likely to get pregnant before I want to." Although criticized for the adult themes the girls addressed, the statistics and social issues in the ad were important (Figure 5.48). After these girls are allowed to play sports, many grow into strong women who serve their country (Figure 5.49).

Considered a groundbreaking advertising promotion in combating stereotypical thinking was the "Real Beauty" campaign by the personal product manufacturer Dove, which was founded in 1955 with a popular line of soaps and skin creams. In 2004 ordinary-looking women posed for British fashion photographer John Rankin Waddell and American photographer Annie Leibovitz. The images were used in billboard and magazine advertisements created by Ogilvy & Mather, Canada. Dove

also started the "Self-Esteem Fund" to promote various projects related to positive self-awareness and anti-mainstream advertising messages directed at women. Several short videos that were produced received international praise. *Evolution* (2006) (Figure 5.50) and *Onslaught* (2007) (Figure 5.51) won awards at the prestigious Cannes Lions Advertising Festival. In *Evolution*, a "pretty, but ordinary girl," the model Stephanie Betts, is transformed into a billboard beauty through lighting, makeup, hair products, and Photoshop. But before too many accolades are given to the Dove campaigns, it should be noted that the British and Dutch company Unilever that owns Dove also promotes its Axe line of men's fragrances with commercials that are considered stereotypical and misogynistic.

In 2017 women and their stories have been featured in several television shows with mostly critical and audience support. Such episodic programs with feminist themes presented by

Figure 5.46
(Weblink: http://goo.gl/NeNGyX)
One of the most enduring commercial spoofs created for "Saturday Night Live" is "Chess for Girls." With its pink palette, sleeping baby, and little boy angst, the fake ad educates others about gender stereotyping.

Figure 5.47
(Weblink: http://goo.gl/BfJ0a9).
As with Rejlander's "Two Ways of Life" (See Chapter 11), Alecia Moore offers choices that many girls and women must face as they age.

Figure 5.48
(Weblink: http://goo.gl/9ywEFL)
Nike was criticized for this commercial when it was first introduced in 1995, but the message is still important.

Figure 5.50
(Weblink: http://goo.gl/gzCFXe)
The transformative power of makeup, hair styling, lighting, and Photoshop is the theme of this Dove film.

Figure 5.51
(Weblink: http://goo.gl/7teIOF)
Onslaught is an excellent title for this short film in which a girl is bombarded with media messages that harm. The piece is a powerful criticism of the beauty industry.

W
LINK
Figure 5.52
*(Weblink: http://goo.gl/1Q2TNe)
Still not a fan of this type of
hard sell advertising, but some
media critics appreciate that a
boy model has been included
in the commercial.*

W
LINK
Figure 5.54
*(Weblink: http://goo.gl/1xphfp)
Murderball, a documentary
about players of wheelchair
rugby has its brutal moments,
but most of the film is a sensitive portrait of those who use
wheelchairs.*

non-broadcast networks include "Girls," "Crazy Ex-Girlfriend," "Broad City," "Fleabag," "I Love Dick," and "Glow."

LGBTQ *The Advocate*, a monthly magazine established in 1967, continues to be a valuable resource for LGBTQ issues and entertainment. Among the many activities that support civil rights for the LGBTQ community, GLAAD (Gay and Lesbian Alliance Against Defamation) showcases work through its annual media awards. For example, singled out as worthy of praise in 2017 were "The Rachel Maddow Show" on MSNBC, "Anderson Cooper 360" on CNN, and the "PBS NewHour." Also honored were the motion pictures *Moonlight* and *Star Trek Beyond* and the television shows "Brookly Nine-Nine" and "Transparent." The marriage between the Australian actress Portia de Rossi and the popular daytime talk show host Ellen DeGeneres in 2008 publicized the positive relationship between the two women. Young lesbian and gay characters have come out in such television shows as "90210," "Degrassi," "Glee," "Gossip Girl," "Greek," "Hellcats," "Pretty Little Liars," and "Skins." Mark Burnett of "Survivor" fame (See Chapter 13) is also the executive producer for the Primetime Emmys award show and has chosen the popular lesbian actress Jane Lynch to be the host. In addition, the gay actor Neil Patrick Harris reprised his role as host for the Tony Awards. In 2012 Canadian transsexual Jenna Talackova was initially told she could not participate in the Miss Universe beauty pageant. President Donald Trump when he was only known as a real estate magnate and reality television personality, owned the Miss Universe and Miss USA pageants. After negative publicity, the decision was reversed so Talackova could participate in the Canadian contest.

There is evidence that advertisers are responding to criticisms of stereotypical gender appeals. "Gender-neutral marketing" is the term for producing products and advertising campaigns primarily for members of Generation Z, those 19-years-old and younger that resist the "blue is for boys and pink is for girls" mindset and demonstrate a more "gender-fluid" approach in their lifestyles. For example, toy manufacturer Mattel introduced its Moschino Barbie doll with a boy among the girl models in the promotional video (Figure 5.52), model James Charles applies makeup for Coty's CoverGirl, and the Target Corp. removed all of its gender-based signs within their stores. Media critics have noted interest in this issue after the role-model efforts of Jill Soloway, producer and writer for Amazon's critically acclaimed "Transparent," public personality Caitlyn Jenner, and Laverne Cox, an actress on Netflix's "Orange Is the New Black."

Overcoming ingrained stereotypes takes many years for a culture to achieve. The process could be speeded up if the images of culturally diverse groups, including LGBTQ individuals showed them as respected people who have ordinary needs, fears, and hopes and lead ordinary lives (Figure 5.53).

Wheelchair Users Motion pictures and television programs occasionally feature an actor who uses a wheelchair, but as with Native Americans, the list is short. Unlike Native media examples, however, most portrayals are made by actors who personally do not need that mode of transportation. Movies that have featured actors who use wheelchairs include *Coming Home*, (1978), *Born on the Fourth of July* (1989), *My Left Foot* (1989), *The Waterdance* (1992), *Rory O'Shea Was Here* (2004), and *Avatar* (2009). Television examples include "Glee," "Friday Night Lights," "My Name is Earl," and "The Family Guy." *Murderball* (2005), is a documentary film about paraplegics who play the grueling game of full-contact rugby on basketball

Figure 5.53
Two women publicly proclaim their love for each other by gestures and signs during an International Women's Conference in Houston, Texas. Images of lesbian, gay, bisexual, transgender, and queer individuals can depict sweet, personal, and universal moments, just as with everyone else.
Courtesy of Laurie Williams

courts that has been critically acclaimed, if not widely seen (Figure 5.54).

Unequal power, ownership, privilege, and respect are at the core of communication problems between cultural groups. When the media regularly celebrate cultural diversity with words and images instead of concentrating on conflict and stereotypes, the goal of ending prejudice, racism, and discrimination will come a little closer to being reached.

KEY TERMS FROM THIS CHAPTER
9/11 • Assimilation • Aztec culture • Discrimination • Gallup poll • Hijab • HIV/AIDS • Islam • Muslims • Poster child • Prejudice • Racial profiling • Sharia law • Terrorists • Vaudeville

6 Visual Analysis

British critic and artist John Ruskin, who died in 1900, was best known for initiating the Arts and Crafts movement that celebrated handiwork. The Bolshevik revolutionary Leon Trotsky called him "one of those rare men who think with their heart." Ruskin once wrote, "The greatest thing a human soul ever does in this world is to see something …. To see clearly is poetry, prophecy, and religion, all in one." As you have learned by now, the first step in seeing clearly is to think clearly. Analysis is a way the mind not only engages with the outside world, but also internalizes its lessons and learns from them.

Critics throughout the history of literature have used many methods to analyze works created by others. Although this textbook advocates a visual analysis method, there is no single process that is correct in every situation. For example, David Lodge, in his book *Small World: An Academic Romance* (1984), lists 14 different analytical perspectives: allegorical, archetypal, biographical, Christian, ethical, existentialist, Freudian, historical, Jungian, Marxism, mythical, phenomenological, rhetorical, and structural. Although most analyses don't require so many approaches, you must be able to use some sort of critical method to analyze pictures to fully appreciate visual communication. Any type of analysis is always a journey of personal investigation. As Lodge wrote, "Analysis reveals the person making the analysis—not really the piece itself."

Image analysis teaches two important lessons about the creation of memorable pictures: A producer of messages should have an understanding of the diversity of cultures within an intended audience and she should also be aware of the symbols used in images so that they are understood by members of those cultures.

Although visual analysis is vital in understanding a picture's place within a cultural context, the concept of visual analysis is fairly new given the long history—more than 30,000 years of visual message production. But from the dawn of modern typography—Johannes Gutenberg's commercial printing press—the visual media were rarely employed for any purpose other than as margin drawings or as sensational, attention-getting devices to attract the non-reading public to performances. At best, images might be used as maps or medical diagrams. Consequently, those who produced pictures were often regarded with less worth than their written word counterparts. For example, newspaper photographers in the first half of the 20th century were often considered to be "reporters with their brains knocked out." However, later in the century, critics and educators such as Rudolf Arnheim, John Berger, Roland Barthes, Susan Sontag, and others took image production and visual communicators seriously. Consequently, visual literacy gradually developed into a serious study.

John Berger is a British critic, artist, and novelist. He is best known for his landmark book on visual culture, *Ways of Seeing* (1972), which was developed into a television series for the BBC. For Berger, an image must be analyzed within its presentational context. A quick-click photograph viewed on an iPhone, a somber and respectful gallery exhibit with viewers enjoying cheese and drinks, a series of travel images on Facebook or Flickr, murals sprayed on subway trains, any photograph published in this book, a newspaper front page or magazine cover, a movie in a theater or shown on television or a computer monitor, a large advertisement on a billboard—all create unique contexts of meaning and, thus, of analysis. But as varied as the contexts are for viewing images, so too should be the varied ways in which images are analyzed (Figure 6.1).

Figure 6.1
Whether images are considered graffiti seen on a street, as part of a Facebook album from a trip to Istanbul, Turkey, or seen at the Museum of Modern Art in New York City, each venue requires a unique set of analytical considerations.
Courtesy of Paul Martin Lester

Historian and educator David Perlmutter identifies eight ways to help understand an image:

Production (how was the image physically produced and how are elements combined within a frame),
Content identification (what are the major elements and what is the story being told),
Functional (what is the context for the image and how was it put to use),
Expressional (what emotions are conveyed by the content and how are those feelings translated across cultures),
Figurative (how are the symbols and metaphors employed and what are any culturally sensitive elements),
Rhetorical-moral (what are the philosophical justifications for making and showing the work and what are any responsibilities the producer has to the subject and viewers),
Societal or period (how does the image reflect the culture and mores of the time it was produced and what does it communicate to future generations), and

Comparative (how is the image similar to previously created works and how does it fit within the body of work of the image creator).

Not surprisingly, Perlmutter admits that such an analysis "involves a great deal of effort."

Analytical approaches, although time-consuming, are valuable because they help you notice the smallest details that make up an image, which often leads to greater, universal truths. Meaning/perceiving should be the goal of any type of visual analysis—whether for personal, professional, or cultural reasons. The process also requires that you become familiar with the biography of an artist, the details of her culture and her life that led to the picture's creation. Analysis should come after a detailed viewing of the work itself and the impact, if any, the work had on the artist, other artists, the subjects, the viewers, the genre, the culture, and society. As such, an analysis of *any* image, whether still or moving, seen in print or screen media, should not be taken lightly.

As you will note in the subsequent chapters, six perspectives for analysis—

personal, historical, technical, ethical, cultural, and critical—will help explain a wide variety of presentation media, from the use of typography to the way websites present almost unlimited links. But before using any of these six analytical perspectives, there are nine preliminary steps you should take in order to prepare yourself for a thorough analysis. These nine steps include:

Make a detailed inventory list of all you see in a picture,

Note the unique compositional elements within the frame,

Consider how the visual cues of col form, depth, and movement work singly and in combination to add interest and meaning,

Look at the image in terms of the gestalt laws of similarity, proximity, continuation, and common fate,

Identify any iconic, indexical, and symbolic signs,

Think of how the four semiotic codes of metonymy, analogy, displaced, and condensed contribute to its understanding,

Isolate any cognitive elements that may be a part of the image,

Consider the purpose the work might have, and

Determine whether the image is aesthetically pleasing.

A picture taken by U.S. Army Corps of Engineers photographer Keith Matthews of President George W. Bush greeting children and teachers at the DeLisle Elementary School in DeLisle, Mississippi after Hurricane Katrina in 2005 is used as an example of visual analysis. For a more in-depth analysis of this image, see *On Floods and Photo Ops: How Herbert Hoover and George W. Bush Exploited Catastrophes* by Paul Martin Lester and published by the University Press of Mississippi. Before you read the author's analysis, study the image yourself and come up with your own interpretation. Your response may be quite different. Also, even though a photograph is used for this demonstration, the procedure described here should be used with any form of visual message (Figure 6.2).

1. Inventory List Make a list of all you see—animal, vegetable, and mineral—in the picture. If it helps, imagine a grid with horizontal and vertical lines superimposed upon the picture so that you actively consider every possible part of the picture.

In the photograph, President Bush is in the foreground to the left in front of children and adults configured in a receiving line. The president appears to be moving from the left to the right in front of the children. He smiles and looks at something off camera to the right. His right shoulder is toward the camera. His arms are at his sides, but appear to be moving upward to make a gesture. He slouches slightly forward with his back arched. He does not wear a hat. The top and back of his head are lit by bright sunlight. His gray hair is trimmed above his ears. He is cleanly shaved. Bush wears a blue, long-sleeved striped business shirt with vertical and horizontal dark blue lines that form a grid pattern. President Bush's shirt in the photograph has no buttons on the collar. The top button of the shirt is undone. He does not wear a tie. However, his sleeves are buttoned at the wrists. His left pocket on his shirt appears empty. A white short-sleeve undershirt can be seen under the President's dress shirt. There is a glint from the sun's reflection off a plain gold wedding band on President Bush's left

Figure 6.2
The original caption for the photograph read: "President Bush is greeted by students at DeLisle Elementary School where portable classrooms provided by the FEMA and the Army Corps of Engineers have allowed students to resume some degree of normalcy in this devastated community (USACE Photo by Keith Matthews)."
Courtesy of Keith Matthews and the U.S. Army Corps of Engineers

ring finger. He wears a black leather woven belt with leaf-like embossed patterns. A small silver five-point star is the belt's buckle.

To the president's left and configured horizontally along the photograph's plane are approximately twenty Anglo and seven African American children. There are ten boys (seven Anglo and three African American) and seventeen girls (thirteen Anglo and four African American). Sixteen of the children look directly at President Bush, three look at the photographer, and the others look elsewhere; fourteen children smile, two students seem to laugh, and one child attempts to touch the president's arm. The light from the sun is reflected in some of the children's eyes, giving the illusion that an electronic flash

was used in the picture. Thirteen of the children wear T-shirts of various colors. One girl at the right has on a pink, blue, and yellow horizontally striped shirt printed with the words "I Love My Bug," and an illustration of a Volkswagen car, known as the "Beetle" and nicknamed the "Bug." The girl wearing the Bug shirt also has a nametag attached that has "My name is" printed and "Jettie" handwritten on the tag (Figure 6.3). Two other girls in the front row also wear nametags, but their names cannot be read. No other nametags can be seen on any other children. Jettie also has a slightly reddish scrape or scar visible on her cheek. Another girl in the middle of the group who smiles at the camera has a cut on her upper lip. Four of the children wear dress shirts. One boy has an unbuttoned shirt that shows a T-shirt underneath. Two of the girls wear earrings. One girl in the front row has a clip in her hair. Two African American girls wear their hair tied in the back by plastic colored balls. None of the other girls have their hair tied behind them. One tall African American girl in the center and toward the back has her hair in a cornrow style.

There are approximately twelve adults standing behind the children. The women are all Anglo. Two women seem to be laughing, while the others appear to smile. Two hold inexpensive cameras. All have unassuming hairstyles. Nine of the women wear white T-shirts that include "PASS CHRISTIAN SCHOOLS" in an uppercase blue sans serif typeface. Two of the women show an identification card attached to a blue strap around their neck. Four women wear necklaces. Two of the necklaces have crucifix symbols attached. One laughing woman to the left of the president has long brown hair, a dress shirt open that shows a white "PASS CHRISTIAN" T-shirt underneath, and a dragonfly pin. Three women wear eyeglasses, and one sports sunglasses.

In the background approximately thirty feet from the photographer are eight men, although two might be older boys. One of the men might be a Latino, one is African American, and the rest are Anglo. Three of the men wear sunglasses. One man appears to be dressed in a police uniform. The African American man wears a white T-shirt that has "MBI" printed on the left side.

There is a school structure at the back and right that has "T-4" printed on a building. To the left, there is at least one portable trailer in the back.

2. *Composition* Actively notice the picture's elements. How do the individual parts contribute or distract from the picture as a whole?

Figure 6.3
Jettie's name tag and t-shirt with "I Love My Bug" can be seen in this detail.
Courtesy of Keith Matthews and the U.S. Army Corps of Engineers

The camera angle is slightly higher than the president's height and with a horizontal view. With the president, children, teachers, and security personnel in the background, there are four rows of persons in the photograph. Three sides of the picture are filled to the edges with people. The top contains space between the men and the edge of the frame (Figure 6.4).

3. *Visual Cues* Study the visual cues of color, form, depth, and movement within the image. Note how they interact and conflict. How are colors used? Look for the source and direction of light in the picture. Does light come from a natural or artificial source? How are shapes and lines utilized within the frame of the image? If there are persons in the image, take notice of their eyes to see whether they are looking at or away from the camera or are hidden from view. How is the illusion of depth achieved? Are your eyes actively moving around the frame?

Figure 6.4
Because the photographer is tall, a high perspective reveals four rows of people—president, children, teachers, and security personnel.
Courtesy of Keith Matthews and the U.S. Army Corps of Engineers

Color: *The photograph is taken in color. The intense sunlight on the president's hair and shirt indicate the picture was taken near noon. Pink is the dominant color worn by the girls. The white t-shirts worn by the teachers help to link them.*

Form: *As the photograph was taken with a horizontal perspective, the arrangement of those in the picture creates a strong rectangle form.*

Depth: *With Bush in the front and larger than the others combined with the backlight from the sun, he is clearly in the foreground while everyone is in the back (Figure 6.5).*

Movement: *There is a sense of movement from left to right as President Bush greets the static children. Also, since his gaze is concentrated upon someone off camera to the right, there is graphic movement in that direction.*

4. Gestalt laws How does the visual communication theory of gestalt contribute to the understanding of the image?

Similarity: *The different sizes of the four rows of people tend to divide each one into separate bands.*

Proximity: *President Bush, the children, and the teachers seem closely connected because of how near they are to each other. Conversely, the security personnel in the background have gaps between them and are not as coherent (Figure 6.6).*

Continuation: *Bush's eye contact off the frame leads a viewer's eyes in that direction.*

Common fate: *The children and teachers that look toward the president are separated from those that look in some*

Figure 6.5
The backlight on Bush helps to separate him from the others.
Courtesy of Keith Matthews and the U.S. Army Corps of Engineers

Figure 6.6
Working for different government agencies, the security men in the background probably do not know each other well as indicated by the space between them.
Courtesy of Keith Matthews and the U.S. Army Corps of Engineers

other direction.

5. Semiotic Signs What are any iconic, indexical, and symbolic signs that can be identified in the image?

Iconic Signs: *The photograph itself is an example of an iconic sign, since there is little doubt that the individuals pictured lived and are accurately portrayed.*

Indexical Signs: *The fact that most of the subjects are wearing casual clothes is an indexical sign that the weather was warm.*

Symbolic Signs: *President Bush is dressed casually except for his buttoned sleeves. He has a belt buckle with a silver star and wears a wedding ring. These are symbolic signs that he is still treating this event a bit formally, is from Texas, and is married (Figure 6.7).*

6. Semiotic codes Do any of the metonymy, analogy, displaced, or condensed codes contribute to its understanding?

Metonymy: *Since almost everyone is smiling, the assumption is that this is a pleasant event for all pictured.*

Analogy: *The group of excited school children is similar to any politician visiting children during a public event (Figure 6.8).*

Displaced: *Unlike followers during a political rally who reach for a politician's handshake, these children are more subdued and perhaps respectful of the office of the president. Instead of shaking Bush's hand, they offer him support with their eye contact and smiles.*

Condensed: *Although seemingly a simple picture to document the President's visit to those affected by Hurricane Katrina, the image also is a contrived media event meant to show that Bush cares about children.*

7. Cognitive Elements How do the cognitive concepts of memory, projection, expectation, selectivity, habituation, salience, dissonance, culture, and words contribute to the image's understanding?

Memory: *This photograph may be more meaningful if it helps you recall a time when you were as close to someone famous.*

Projection: *You might assume that the only woman wearing sunglasses is blind.*

Expectation: *With any gathering of typical school children, it is a bit unusual to see the President of the United States.*

Selectivity: *Obviously, because of his placement in the foreground, one notices the president first.*

Habituation: *The security personnel in the background seem distant and a bit bored probably because they have seen this type of media event many times in their careers.*

Salience: *If you are a student of history, curious about how Hurricane Katrina affected the Gulf Coast, or a fan of President Bush, this picture will mean more to you.*

Dissonance: *The woman behind Bush's back with her mouth open and*

Figure 6.7
Buttoned sleeves, a belt buckle, and a ring reveal much about the man.
Courtesy of Keith Matthews and the U.S. Army Corps of Engineers

dragonfly pin may be a distraction (Figure 6.9).

Culture: *Given the demographics of southern Mississippi, African Americans are under-represented as students and as teachers.*

Words: *The original caption for the photograph (See Figure 6.2) gives a positive review of the work from FEMA and the U.S Army Corps of Engineers, but does not explain why the children are so happy to see Bush.*

8. Purpose of the Work Where do you think the picture was made? What do you think is the image's purpose? Is it news, art, scientific, a personal snapshot, or some other type of image?

The photograph was a part of a collection of photographs on a government's website documenting the good work performed by various Federal agencies after Hurricane Katrina. It was never printed in a newspaper or magazine. It has found additional "life" however, by being part of a visual communication analysis.

9. Image Aesthetics Is there anything about the image that makes it particularly compelling to look at? Does it have formal and/or creative elements that make it particularly beautiful? Does the image make you want to see more of the creator's work?

Although there is a certain charm to this

Figure 6.8
U.S. President George W. Bush meets patients and their families in the reception room of the Amana District Hospital in Dar es Salaam, Tanzania.
Courtesy of Eric Draper, the White House

image because of the way a politician can "work" a row of school children, its utilitarian purpose—to make a politician look helpful in the eyes of the public—any formal determination of the picture's aesthetic worth is tempered. The picture is perhaps one step from a family snapshot, but has little value.

Now you are ready for the six perspectives:

Personal: An initial reaction to the work based on your subjective opinions.
Historical: A determination of the importance of the work based on the medium's time line.
Technical: The relationship between light, the method used to produce the work, and the context in which the work is shown.
Ethical: The moral and ethical responsibilities that the producer, the subject,

and the viewer of the work have and share.
Cultural: An analysis of the metaphors and symbols used in the work that convey meaning within a particular society at a particular time.
Critical: The issues that transcend a particular image and shape a reasoned personal reaction.

The goal of this analysis is to move from a subjective, quick, and emotional opinion, often expressed from a personal perspective, to an objective, long-term, and reasoned judgment reflected by the critical perspective.

Personal Perspective
Upon first viewing any image, everyone draws a quick conclusion about a picture based entirely on a personal response. When asked about a movie, words and phrases such as "good," "bad," "I like it,"

Figure 6.9
With her flowing hair, big smile, over-shirt, and large dragonfly pin, this woman stands out from the rest of the crowd, but is she a distraction?
Courtesy of Keith Matthews and the U.S. Army Corps of Engineers

or "I don't like it" are the usual quick responses. These answers indicate that a person initially analyzes the picture on a superficial, cursory level. Personal perspectives are important because they reveal much about the person making the comments. But such opinions have limited use simply because they are so personal. These comments cannot be generalized beyond the individual, nor do they reveal much in the way of how others in the present or future should think of the work. A memorable image, perhaps one that is considered a masterpiece by critics and the public alike, always sparks strong personal reactions, either negative or positive, and also reveals much about the culture from which it was made. A viewer who rests a conclusion about an image on only a personal perspective denies the chance of perceiving the image in a more meaningful way.

It is not surprising that the photograph was never published in a newspaper or magazine. The picture at first glance is not worth a second look. The picture is obviously a set-up and stage-managed photo op or media event so that the politician can show his concern and advance his own political self-interest. Consequently, an initial reaction of the picture is rather negative.

Historical Perspective
Each medium of presentation—from typography to the web—has a unique history of circumstances that were set in motion by individuals interested in promoting the medium. For typography, the history of writing dates from the dawn of recorded history. For the web, the developments are relatively recent. Knowledge of a medium's history allows you to understand current trends in terms of their roots in techniques and philosophies of the past. Innovative and aesthetically pleasing visual messages come from an awareness of what has

been produced before while contemporary pictures will influence future image creation. Since images are artifacts that immediately preserve past events, an historical analysis is of utmost importance in understanding the present meaning of any image.

Ask yourself: When do you think the image was made? What major developments were happening when the image was produced? Is there a specific artistic style that the image imitates?

In 2005 Hurricane Katrina was the costliest natural disaster to ever hit the United States. Total damages topped $81.2 billion ($91 billion today). More than 169,000 homes, 350,000 automobiles, and 35,000 boats were destroyed. It was the third strongest hurricane to make landfall on American soil and the fifth deadliest storm, with more than 1,800 known deaths. It also sparked widespread criticism of the U.S. Army Corps of Engineers for the design and maintenance of its failed flood protection system and criticism of the slow local, state, and federal responses to the emergency, including that from FEMA. On May 19, 2006, the name "Katrina" was official retired for use as a hurricane and replaced by Katia (Figure 6.10).

At the time the picture was taken, mass circulation newspapers and magazines were beginning to be overshadowed by web-based publications. The style of photography is common to most media events—a clear picture of a politician in the foreground and seemingly unaware of the camera.

Technical Perspective
You must know something about how each medium of presentation works. A thorough critique of any visual presentation requires knowledge of how the creator generated the images you see. Whether clay for stop-motion animated films, camera settings with still and moving pictures, or software controls for

Figure 6.10
With the New Orleans skyline in the distance, a portion of the more than 169,000 homes flooded by Hurricane Katrina can be seen in the foreground.
National Oceanic and Atmospheric Administration

computer-generated images, knowing the ways they are produced gives you a clearer understanding of the meaning and purpose of a work. With an understanding of the techniques involved in producing an image, you are also in a better position to know when production values are high or low, when great or little care has been taken, or when much or little money was spent to make the images. Ask yourself: How was the image produced? What techniques were employed? Is the image of good quality?

During Bush's visit to the DeLisle school at about 10:30 A.M., using a Canon EOS digital camera, Keith Matthews, a photographer and graphic designer for the U.S. Army Corps of Engineers for almost thirty years, took a picture of the president standing amid schoolchildren. Matthews's digital single-lens reflex (SLR) camera is the most commonly used camera by professional photojournalists because, with its small size and through-the-lens viewing system, the camera is easily maneuvered up and down and right and left, is quickly zoomed and focused, and has an almost unlimited capacity of high-quality images that can be taken. The "snapshot," off-the-cuff, and informal style of this image is directly attributable to the use of the SLR camera. The color photograph was made using a wide-angle lens, a medium-size aperture, without fill-in flash, and less than ten feet away from the president. The original technical specifications for the image provided by Matthews included the file name as "bush2000.jpg" (the number designation refers to the number of pixels [picture elements] along its horizontal edge and not the year); size: 2,000 by 1,333 pixels (27.778 x 18.514 inches); and the dots per inch (dpi): 72, an acceptable setting for images designated for web presentations.

Ethical Perspective

Ethics is the study of how persons, other sentient beings (those that can feel pain), and systems (such as governmental agencies and the environment) behave (known as *descriptive ethics*) and how they *should* behave (known as *normative ethics*). You should try as much as possible to concentrate your analyses on normative, rather than descriptive, ethics. You want to come to a conclusion of what someone should do rather than simply describe what someone did.

Anyone considered to be practicing ethical behavior should abide by all the role-related responsibilities that a job requires and should not during the execution of those duties cause unjustified harm. Every profession, from graphic design to website production, has a unique set of requirements or role-related responsibilities that combine to form the concept of a person's "job." For example, a visual journalist for a news organization develops sources, conceives stories, takes images, records audio, interviews sources, writes captions, voice-overs, and copy, edits the words and pictures, checks to make sure all facts are accurate, and arranges to display the work in print, on television, and/or the web.

Doing your job and not causing unjust harm has been called the "ethics mantra." As long as those professional obligations are met, the first part of the mantra is satisfied. But to be considered

ethical, you must also make sure that any harm that may ensue must be justified. A nurse causes some discomfort that might be interpreted as harm with a needle stick, but the pain is justified in order to get well. A professor assesses your exams and papers that may cause harm to your GPA, but it is justified to help you learn. Showing a video of a celebrity in an embarrassing situation on a local newscast may be harmful to that person's reputation, but as long as the airing is deemed acceptable for reasonable, objective persons, the harm can probably be justified. Any action that causes physical or mental harm without adequate justification is unethical.

Six principal ethical philosophies can and should be used to analyze a picture. Knowledge of philosophies is important because they help explain how actions can or cannot be justified. In chronological order, they are golden rule, hedonism, golden mean, categorical imperative, utilitarianism, and veil of ignorance. Although there are many more useful philosophies that could be discussed, these are the principal theories that have survived for more than 2,500 years of Western moral philosophy. Even if the names are new to you, their basic ideas should be familiar to all who have grown up in the United States or other European-influenced cultures. Aspects of these theories are used to justify our public policies, laws, and social conventions.

Golden Rule The golden rule, or the ethic of reciprocity, teaches people to "love your neighbor as yourself." This theory has been attributed to ancient Greek philosophers such as Pittacus of Mytilene (died 568BCE), considered one of the "Seven Sages of Greece," who wrote, "Do not to your neighbor what you would take ill from him;" Thales of Miletus (died 546BCE), another Sage of Greece who said, "Avoid doing what you would blame others for doing;" and

Epictetus (died 135CE), a Stoic philosopher who wrote, "What thou avoidest suffering thyself seek not to impose on others." In fact, every major religion has some variable of the golden rule as a part of their scriptures and/or teachings. This philosophy holds that an individual should be as humane as possible and never harm others by insensitive actions (Figure 6.11).

A television producer who decides not to air close-up footage of family members mourning the loss of a loved one at a funeral decides not to run the video because it might compound their grief and make viewers feel bad. She invokes the golden rule.

For the Bush image, it is a positive "feel good" moment despite the reality of what life must be like under such living conditions. As such, it probably made those who saw the picture smile to see children entertained by a powerful and famous member of their government.

Hedonism From the Greek word for pleasure, hedonism is closely related to the philosophies of nihilism and narcissism. A student of Socrates, Aristippus (who died in Athens in 366BCE) founded this ethical philosophy on the basis of pleasure (Figure 6.12). Aristippus believed that people should "act to maximize pleasure now and not worry about the future." His phrase sums up the hedonistic philosophy: "I possess; I am not possessed." The Renaissance playwright and poet Ben Johnson, a contemporary of William Shakespeare, once wrote one of the best summaries of the hedonistic philosophy, "Drink today, and drown all sorrow; You shall perhaps not do it tomorrow; Best, while you have it, use your breath; There is no drinking after death." Phrases such as "live for today" and "don't worry, be happy" currently express the hedonistic philosophy. If an opinion or action is based purely on a personal motivation—money, fame,

relationships, and the like—the hedonistic philosophy is at work.

When an image maker considers *only* the aesthetic pleasure, monetary gain, or possible awards a picture might bring, hedonism is the dominant philosophy. It is rare for a visual communicator or anyone else to admit to a purely hedonistic justification for an act that others might judge unethical.

A freelance professional photographer, known as a paparazzo after a character in the movie *Irma la Douce* (1963), who stands in wait for a celebrity to exit a concert, restaurant, or home so that a picture can be made solely for the purpose of making money from it uses the hedonism philosophy. As such, this philosophy is probably the least admitted to by practitioners out of the six principal ethical philosophies.

The photograph demonstrates hedonism because the photographer wanted to feature the notable person in the picture, George W. Bush and his work in aiding those affected by the hurricane in the most positive light possible. The president is using hedonism too as he wanted to be seen with children to seem more compassionate.

Golden Mean The Greek philosopher Aristotle was born near the city Thessaloniki in 384BCE. As his parents were wealthy, he studied at the Athens-based Academy led by the renowned Greek philosopher Plato (Figure 6.13). After learning and teaching at the educational institution for 20 years, he traveled throughout the region studying the biology and botany of his country. He was eventually hired as a tutor for Alexander the Great and two other kings of Greece, Ptolemy and Cassander. When he was about 50 years old he returned to Athens and began his own educational institution, the Lyceum, where he wrote an astounding number of books on diverse subjects that made breakthroughs in sci-

Figure 6.11
A brown terracotta statuette recovered from the house of Julia Felix of Pompeii shows the Greek philosopher Pittacus of Mytilene, one of the first to write about the golden rule during the 1st centuryBCE.
Courtesy of Marie-Lan Nguy-

Figure 6.12
The Greek philosopher Aristippus as seen on a Roman coin. A native of Cyrene, Aristippus was born of wealthy parents and studied under Socrates. Aristippus viewed pleasure as the ultimate goal of life. He reportedly never turned down an opportunity to indulge himself before a table or in the company of sex workers.
Courtesy of the University of Düsseldorf

Figure 6.13
This marble bust of Aristotle was created by the sculptor Lysippos about 330BCE during the philosopher's lifetime. Note the extensive comb-over.
Courtesy of the photographer, Jastrow

ence, communications, politics, rhetoric, and ethics. He was the earliest known writer to describe the phenomenon of light noticed in a camera obscura that eventually led to a further understanding of how the eyes and the photographic medium work.

Although the golden mean was originally a neo-Confucian concept first espoused by Zisi, the only grandson of the Chinese philosopher Confucius, Aristotle elaborated on it for Western readers in his book *Nicomachean Ethics*. The golden mean philosophy refers to finding a middle ground or a compromise between two extreme points of view or actions. The middle way doesn't involve a precisely mathematical average but is an action that approximately fits that situation at that time.

When using the golden mean philosophy, you must first think of the two most extreme examples. For a particularly violent or controversial news photograph or video, there are two extreme choices. The first is to take and then use the picture large and in color on a front page of a newspaper, the cover of a magazine, in the lead for a news broadcast, or the top of a web page. The other extreme choice is not to use the image at all. A compromise or middle way might be to use the image in black and white, small, on an inside page, as a short, edited video, or on a website where users are warned before clicking a link to it. Generally speaking, most ethical dilemmas are solved with the golden mean approach.

The school picture is a compromise or golden mean between images of the children in their harsh day-to-day living conditions and not taking any pictures at all.

Categorical Imperative Immanuel Kant was born in Königsberg, the capital of Prussia (now Kaliningrad, Russia) in 1724 (Figure 6.14). The fourth of 11 children, at an early age he showed intellectual promise and escaped his crowded household to attend a special school.

At the age of 16 he graduated from the University of Königsberg, where he stayed and taught until his death. Kant never married and never traveled farther than 100 miles from his home during his lifetime. Thirteen years before his death in 1804, he published *Critique of Pure Reason*. It is considered one of the most important works in philosophical history. Kant established the concept of the categorical imperative. *Categorical* means unconditional and *imperative* means that the concept should be employed without any question, extenuating circumstances, or exceptions. Right is right and must be done even under the most extreme conditions. Consistency is the key to the categorical imperative philosophy. Once a rule is established for a proposed action or idea, behavior and opinions must be consistently and always applied in accordance with it. But for Kant, the right action must have a positive effect and not promote unjustified harm or evil. Nevertheless, the categorical imperative is a difficult mandate to live up to.

If a visual reporter's rule is to document any situation and take pictures regardless of whether she thinks her newspaper will print them because she considers that action to be part of her job and to be performed without objections, then this decision becomes a categorical imperative. She takes photographs because it is her duty to do so, and it leads to a positive conclusion—the pictures document an activity for historical purposes if for no other reason.

As a photographer for the U.S. Army Corps of Engineers, Keith Matthews had little choice but to take a picture of President George Bush with a group of children. Regardless, Matthews no doubt felt it was part of his professional role-related responsibility to take the picture in order to document the event. Therefore, *his categorical imperative would be to perform the same act under any similar set of circumstances.*

Utilitarianism This philosophy is usually considered the combined work of British thinkers Jeremy Bentham, John Stuart Mill, and Harriet Taylor. The legal scholar and philosopher Jeremy Bentham developed his theory of utility, or the greatest happiness principle, from the work of Joseph Priestley, who is considered one of the most important philosophers and scientists of the 18th century. Bentham acknowledged Priestley as the architect of the idea that "the greatest happiness of the greatest number is the foundation of morals and legislation." John Stuart Mill was the son of the Scottish philosopher James Mill and was tutored for a time by Bentham. When he was three years old, he was taught to read Greek; by the time he was 10 he read Plato's works easily. With the aid of his wife Harriet Taylor, he developed the philosophy of utilitarianism expressed in his books *On Liberty* (1859) and *Utilitarianism* (1863). He gave credit to Taylor for her influence but, as was the custom of the time, did not give her co-authorship credit (Figure 6.15).

Mill expanded on Priestley and Bentham's idea of utilitarianism by separating different kinds of happiness. For Mill, intellectual happiness is more important than the physical kind. He also thought that there is a difference between happiness and contentment, which is culminated in his phrase, "It is better to be a human being dissatisfied than a pig satisfied; better to be Socrates dissatisfied than a fool satisfied." In utilitarianism, various consequences of an act are imagined, and the outcome that helps the most people is usually the best choice under the circumstances. However, Mill specified that each individual's moral and legal rights must be met before applying the utilitarian calculus. According to Mill, it is not acceptable to cause great

Figure 6.14
The German philosopher Immanuel Kant.
Courtesy of the Museum Stadt Königsberg in Duisburg

harm to a few persons in order to bring about a little benefit to many. However, if everyone is being treated justly, then it is acceptable to do something that might provide a large benefit to the community as a whole.

Editors and news directors frequently use and misuse utilitarianism to justify the printing of disturbing accident scenes in their newspapers, magazines, on television, and websites. Although the image may upset a few because of its gruesome content, it may persuade many others to drive more carefully. That action is acceptable under the utilitarianism philosophy because people do not have a moral right to be sheltered from sad news on occasion. For many, the educational function of the news media—from the typographical and graphic design displays that can be easily read to informational graphics that explain a complex concept—is most often expressed in the utilitarian philosophy.

Keith Matthews most likely thought that by taking a picture of President Bush's visit with school children he would be educating others that although the flooding from Hurricane Katrina destroyed most of their homes, the children looked reasonably well fed and happy to be visited.

Veil of Ignorance Articulated by the American philosopher John Rawls in his book *A Theory of Justice* in 1971, the veil of ignorance philosophy considers all people equal as if each member wore a veil so that such attributes as age, gender, ethnicity, and so on could not be determined. No one class of people would be entitled to advantages over any other. Imagining oneself without knowing the positions that one brings to a situation results in an attitude of respect for all involved. The phrase "walk a mile in someone's shoes" is a popular adaptation of the veil of ignorance philosophy. It is considered one answer to prejudice and discrimination. Rawls taught at Harvard

Figure 6.15
John Stuart Mill and Harriet Taylor.
Courtesy of Wisepress Publishing

University for almost 40 years (Figure 6.16). In 1999 he received the National Humanities Medal from President Bill Clinton, who said that he "helped a whole generation of learned Americans revive their faith in democracy itself."

A viewer of a print or screen display might invoke this philosophy in an e-mail of thanks to a visual communicator or journalist, if the viewer were made to think of her own loved ones after seeing a picture of subjects of a visual message.

A viewer of this photograph might think of a child she knows and imagine the living conditions at home after a terrible environmental catastrophe. Thinking of such a connection with "the other" and feeling empathy for those affected by Hurricane Katrina might result in contributions to the Red Cross and Salvation Army.

After a thorough study of the six ethical philosophies briefly described above, an analysis of the Bush picture might also include the following:

George W. Bush was an American politician who understood the power of positive publicity. Five days before President Bush's visit to DeLisle Elementary, a CBS News poll revealed that his "overall job approval rating reached the lowest ever measured in this poll." Bush needed to be seen by sympathetic and energetic children excited by a visit from the President to their small town after his administration's disastrous non-reaction to Hurricane Katrina. He and his publicity handlers thought the photo op would show Bush, the compassionate conservative, as a politician who cares. But the picture demonstrates the exploitation of the good graces, best wishes, and innocent hopes of those most vulnerable—the children—who naively looked up to a powerful adult visiting them (Figure 6.17).

Cultural Perspective

Here is your chance to further refine your analysis given the influences from the historical, technical, and ethical perspectives. Cultural analysis of a picture involves identifying the symbols and metaphors used in an image and determining their meaning for the society as a whole. Symbolism may be analyzed through the picture's use of heroes and villains, by the form of its narrative structure, by the style of the artwork, by the use of words that accompany the image, and by the attitudes about the subjects and the culture communicated by the visual artist. The cultural perspective is closely related to the semiotics approach.

Metaphors combine a viewer's experiences with the meaning of a visual message. Aristotle, in *Rhetoric*, wrote, "It is a great thing, indeed, to make proper use of poetic forms, . . . But the greatest thing by far is to be a master of metaphor." Real world experiences infuse an image under analysis with special meaning for the viewer so that underlying metaphors can be discovered. Educator Stuart Jay Kaplan defines metaphors as

Figure 6.16
(Weblink: http:// goo.gl/XKRAqY) The philosopher John Bordley Rawls poses for a picture.

"combinations of two or more elements in which one element is understood or experienced in terms of the other." For Kaplan and others, "Metaphors serve as interpretive frameworks for organizing information about the world and making sense of experiences." George Lakoff and Mark Johnson, in *Metaphors We Live By*, expand the point when they write, "No metaphor can ever be comprehended or even adequately represented independently of its experiential basis." The American anthropologist Evelyn Payne Hatcher, author of *Art and Culture: An Introduction to Anthropology of Art* (1999), wrote that metaphors "are a matter of trying to understand and comment upon what is going on [within a picture] in terms of our previous experience." Metaphors that are commonly understood across time and cultures "rest on the common experiences of the human." For Hatcher, "Visual art is not merely a matter of aesthetics, but one of visually

Figure 6.17
President George W. Bush spends a moment Tuesday, Oct. 11, 2005, with bored and distracted students at Delisle Elementary School in Pass Christian, Miss. The school reopened Tuesday for the first time since Hurricane Katrina devastated the Gulf Coast region.
Courtesy of Eric Draper, the White House

developed ideas, usually conceived in some metaphorical form."

Ask yourself: What is the story and the symbolism involved in the elements of the visual message? What do they say about current cultural values? What metaphors can be expressed through the work?

The symbolism of power and dominance as expressed through social perspective is clearly evident in the photograph. Bush is in the front and slightly separated from the others who do not dare to shake the politician's hand. Although he removed his coat and tie in the photo op with the children, his buttoned sleeves indicate a business-like demeanor and purpose for his visit. Several of the children look up at him with awe, and yet all his attention is directed off camera.

The children seem at ease in their familiar environment, whereas Bush, a symbol of technological progress and an urbane attitude, looks out of place. As seen by his clothing and pose, the government versus ordinary citizen conflict is a metaphor for modernism that divides those who are content and secure from those who have lost everything and must begin anew.

Critical Perspective

The final step in analyzing a picture is to apply a critical perspective. In this last step, you should attempt to transcend a particular image and draw general conclusions about the medium, the culture from which it is produced, and the viewer. A critical perspective allows the viewer to use the information learned about a medium, its practitioner, and the image produced to make more general comments about the society that accepts or rejects the images. As such, a critical perspective redefines a person's initial personal perspective in terms of universal conclusions about human nature.

Ask yourself: What do I think of this image now that I've spent so much time looking at and studying it? What lessons does it have for those who view the image?

As an artifact that illustrates the public relations profession, the Bush elementary school photograph has value for visual communicators who study the photo op genre. It also is useful for biographers of George W. Bush, who may use the image to illustrate an aspect of his personality and media savvy. Consequently, an initial negative opinion of the picture is changed to one of positive worth through the analytical process.

Whether it is a still or moving image, if you study it by first making an inventory list, then by noting its compositional elements, include a discussion on the gestalt laws, visual cues, semiotic signs and codes, cognitive elements, possible purposes, and aesthetic qualities, and then from personal, historical, technical, ethical, cultural, and critical perspectives, you become intellectually engaged with the picture. Using the six perspectives will encourage you to base conclusions about images on rational rather than emotional responses. You will find that all images have something to tell you because every picture created, no matter how banal or ordinary it may be at first glance, have some meaning to communicate. The producer of the image took the time to frame and make the picture for a reason. The message that the artist wants to communicate may be simply a literal story, the hope that the viewer will appreciate the image's aesthetic beauty, or an underlying political agenda. Just because you cannot initially see any purpose for an image is no reason to discard it. Many large lessons are lost because of a failure to study small, captured moments. An image, regardless of its medium of presentation, is forgotten if it isn't analyzed. A forgotten image simply becomes another in a long stream of meaningless pictures that seem to flood

Figure 6.18
Hopefully after a careful analysis of President Bush's visit to see schoolchildren and their teachers in DeLisle, Mississippi, you have a fuller appreciation of the photograph. Time spent really looking can turn a banal photo op into an object of wonder.
Courtesy of Keith Matthews and the U.S. Army Corps of Engineers

every aspect of our lives. Meaningless pictures entertain a viewer only for a brief moment and do not have the capacity to educate. But an analyzed image can affect a viewer for a lifetime.

The nine chapters on typography, graphic design, informational graphics, cartoons, photography, motion pictures, television, computers, and the web are analyzed within the six-perspective analytical framework described above. Although analysis is time-consuming at first, practice reduces the amount of time required. It is up to you, and only you, to find meaning and use for a picture. If you take the time to study images carefully, you will become a much more interesting and knowledgeable person. You will also be more likely to produce images that have greater meaning for more people. These images are also remembered longer than unconsidered pictures.

Your ultimate goal with regard to any analysis of a picture is to understand your own reaction to the image. Through this analytical process, you review, refine, and renew your personal reaction to an image. Being critical is a highly satisfying intellectual exercise (Figure 6.18).

KEY TERMS FROM THIS CHAPTER
Archetypal • Bolshevik • Existentialist • Freudian • Jungian • Marxism • Mythical • Phenomenological • Rhetorical • Structural

Section 2

The previous chapters gave you vital background information and a procedure for analyzing visual messages. However, you are only halfway to fully being able to articulate why some images are remembered and most others are forgotten. The following chapters will complete your journey by detailing how pictures are used within various media. With each chapter there is a quotation from an innovator of the field, an introductory section that details a famous example with an analysis, a concentrated breakdown of the chapter's topic in terms of the six personal, historical, technical, ethical, cultural, and critical perspectives, a section that discusses trends to look out for now and in the future for the medium, and a list of terms that you can find in the glossary. Plus, as with the subsequent chapters, be sure and study the still images printed alongside the copy. Seek out the weblinks within the text included with the figures. Read closely the captions associated with each picture. Many times valuable information is conveyed about visual communication through the captions.

7 Typography

For less than $50, you can download the typeface "textur" from the Linotype.com website. That's the one Johannes Gutenberg used to print his Bibles. He took about four years and more than he could afford to complete the process from typeface to the printed page, but in minutes you can copy and paste a King James version of the Bible found on the Electronic Text Center website provided by the University of Virginia Library into a word processing program. With the command "Select All," replace the typeface with the one Gutenberg used. Send the file to your laser printer and your version is complete. If you want to save the trouble, you could have bought a single page of Gutenberg's Bible at the 45th California International Antiquarian Book Fair in 2012 for only $85,000. A complete copy would set you back about $35 million.

Gutenberg chose to make copies of the Bible, printed in Latin and set in a style later known as textura, not because he was a religious person, but because he was a smart businessperson (Figure 7.1). He knew that once church officials heard of the product of his printing invention, which used the language they preferred in the style of handwritten copies, he would be rich.

Gutenberg labored in his workshop and eventually produced a marvel in technology with a commercial printing press that ushered in a revolution in mass communications. In four years he produced 140 Bibles on paper and 40 on vellum, or leather. The two-volume, mostly 42-line double-column book, with hand-painted borders and enlarged letters, measured 11 × 16 inches, and weighed more than 50 pounds. The work was introduced in 1455, 100 years before William Shakespeare wrote his first sonnet.

But there were two flaws in Johannes' get-rich plan—he couldn't pay back the money he borrowed to support his lifestyle, experiments, and printing operation. Plus, he never included a personal logo or printer's mark on a single printed page.

From early childhood, Johannes must have been a precocious, problem child. For one thing, he didn't like his last name. Believed to be the third son of wealthy Mainz, Germany parents, he was born Johannes Gensfleisch, German for *goose bumps*. Maybe because he was teased as a child, he changed his name to the town of his mother's birth. His uncle was the master of the mint at Mainz, so he learned the skills of metalworking, engraving, mirror making, and decorating objects with precious stones—all crafts he would put to good use later in life.

Unfortunately for his family's economic status, around 1430 there was an uprising of the working class against the aristocracy. Gutenberg's upbringing and outgoing personality earned him a leadership role in the dispute, but he and his father were forced to leave Mainz when they feared for their lives. The two settled in Strasbourg, France, then a German city, about 100 miles southwest of Mainz. They left his mother behind to manage the family's home.

In Strasbourg, Johannes developed a reputation for being quick tempered and a borrower of large sums of money. In 1437 he asked for a woman's hand in marriage. All was well and good until he changed his mind and called the wedding off. Her family promptly sued him for breach of contract. At his trial, he so berated one of her witnesses that the man later sued him for slander. The experience must have soured him on marriage, for he remained a bachelor his whole life (Figure 7.2).

The funds required to support his printing experiments were enormous, and trying to secure enough money to continue his work caused most of the troubles in Gutenberg's life. When he

Figure 7.1
Johannes Gutenberg's Bible doesn't start with the Old or New Testaments. The first page of his printing masterpiece comes from the Epistle of St. Jerome, an introduction written in the 5th century by the saint who translated the religious book into Latin, called the Vulgate. In his introduction he mainly defends his reasoning for using a Hebrew Bible as the base for his translation into Latin rather than a Greek version. Besides using the language of the Catholic Church of the day, Latin was a good choice because of the many ways it can be abbreviated. Nevertheless, a reader is helped through the rigid, two-column page by painted red markers for the start of each sentence. Plus, Gutenberg left space for artists to later add colored text and fanciful enlarged.
Courtesy of Kevin Eng

needed more money to continue his printing experiments, he agreed to a five-year contract to teach two partners his secret method. After one of his associates died, his former partner's sons sued for the advance their father had given to Gutenberg. Court documents reveal that he won that case. An important part of the official court document, an inventory of his workshop, shows that it included a press, various examples of type, and a "mysterious instrument" that was probably a device for casting type molds in metal. For historians, this record is crucial in establishing the fact that Gutenberg was indeed a printer. Also interesting was the court's inventory of his personal property that revealed he had

the equivalent of 2,000 bottles of wine.

After he borrowed a large sum of money from the Church of St. Thomas in Strasbourg, and failed to repay the loan, church elders sued him for the money. Gutenberg fled back to Mainz in 1443 where he lived the rest of his life (Figure 7.3).

Seven years later Gutenberg borrowed money from a wealthy Mainz gold merchant, Johannes Fust. This transaction would cause his downfall because he used his printing equipment as collateral for the loan. In 1455 with the work nearly completed on the Bibles that could easily pay off his debt, Fust grew impatient or greedy and brought suit against him. Fust won the case and was

Figure 7.2
Since no portraits were made during his lifetime, Johannes Gutenberg's likeness is based on written descriptions. Here, he wears traditional garb and inspects a printed page from his commercial press.
Courtesy of the Library of Congress

Figure 7.3
Mainz, Germany.
Courtesy of Martin Bahmann

awarded the presses and all of the work in progress.

Gutenberg was locked out of his own print shop while Fust traveled to several European capitals selling the books that he called his own and that included his printer's mark. In a perhaps fitting development, while on his book tour, he caught the plague and died. It has been assumed that the German legend of Faust, a man who sells his soul to the devil has been retold throughout history, was inspired by Fust's life.

Gutenberg went bankrupt but was saved by Archbishop Adolf of Mainz who bestowed the rank of nobleman to him with an annual pension that allowed him to live the last years of his life in relative comfort. Gutenberg is believed to have died in 1468 and was buried somewhere in the cemetery of the Franciscan church in Mainz. No marker was erected to identify his grave because no one knew the importance of his invention during his lifetime.

Although the popular assumption is that Gutenberg invented printing, that isn't quite the case. His genius was in combining what was known at the time with some of his own ideas. He combined a type mold acceptable for printing, a suitable metal alloy, ink that would easily adhere to metal, paper and parchment, the construction of books, and a printing press.

Metal Type Gutenberg was not the first to use movable type as a substitute for writing by hand. Pi-Sheng, a Chinese alchemist, invented movable type with characters made from heat-hardened clay and glue in the 11th century. The oldest known printed book, the *Diamond Sutra*, a collection of Buddhist teachings, was a roll of paper 16 feet long printed with writing from wooden blocks (Figure 7.4). In Korea, an unknown inventor developed separate bronze and copper type characters that were used for printing almost 80 years

before Gutenberg's book. The first known work printed with movable metal type was titled *Jikji*, another book of Buddhist teachings, produced in a Buddhist temple in Korea in 1377 (Figure 7.5).

Gutenberg most likely used his metalworking skills and borrowed funds to eventually develop an alloy that was soft enough to cast as an individual letter, hard enough to withstand several thousand impressions on sheets of paper, and would not shrink when it cooled in a type mold. Through hundreds of extremely expensive experiments, Gutenberg developed a mixture of lead, tin, and antimony that satisfied his strict requirements.

Ink Fortunately, printing inks were common by that time and easier to adapt. The Egyptians and Chinese had used writing ink as early as 2600 BCE. Gutenberg probably used ink that was developed by the Dutch artist Jan Van Eyck. His formula called for the boiling of linseed oil and soot, which produced a thick, tacky ball that could be smeared on metal type.

Paper The Egyptians had long used papyrus, a crude paper made from reeds that grew along the banks of the Nile River as a substrate for their writing. The eunuch Ts'ai Lun for the emperor's court in 105 CE probably invented paper in China. Paper as a medium for writing gradually made its way to the West. By Gutenberg's time, paper mills were well established in Germany, Spain, France, and Italy.

Although it was vastly more expensive, Gutenberg preferred the use of parchment as a printing substrate. Vellum is the name for the highest-quality material made from the skins of young or stillborn calves, goats, or sheep. The Old French word *velin* means "calf" and is the basis for the English word veal. Vellum is a long-lasting leather that can be printed on both sides. Because inks

Figure 7.4
Printed in the year 868CE, the Diamond Sutra is the world's earliest surviving printed book. It is one of the most sacred works of the Buddhist faith. The words of the document run along a column to the left, while an elaborate image featuring the Buddha large and high in the frame fills the rest of the page.
Courtesy of the British Library

are better preserved on its surface, it was used for the most colorful illustrations. Another reason for Gutenberg's money woes, however, was that he had to maintain a herd of cattle to supply animal skins for his copies.

Press Printing also requires a press. The machine had to be sturdy enough to withstand the weight of the platen and the type itself. Presses at the time were used to produce wine and cheese. With his interest in wine, not surprisingly, Gutenberg's printing press was a modification of a wine press in use at that time. His press was simply a large screw that lowered a weight onto a sheet of paper or parchment against a plate of inked type.

This basic design remained the same until the invention of steam-powered presses about 350 years later.

After Gutenberg's invention became well known, print shops opened in France and Italy and quickly spread throughout Europe. By 1500, there were 1,120 print shops in 260 towns in 17 European countries. More than 10 million copies of 40,000 different works had been printed by that year. As books became plentiful and inexpensive, literacy and educational opportunities quickly grew. Societies moved from oral presentations to reading as the primary method of teaching. As people became better educated, democratic ideas spread. Secularism challenged traditional ideas about

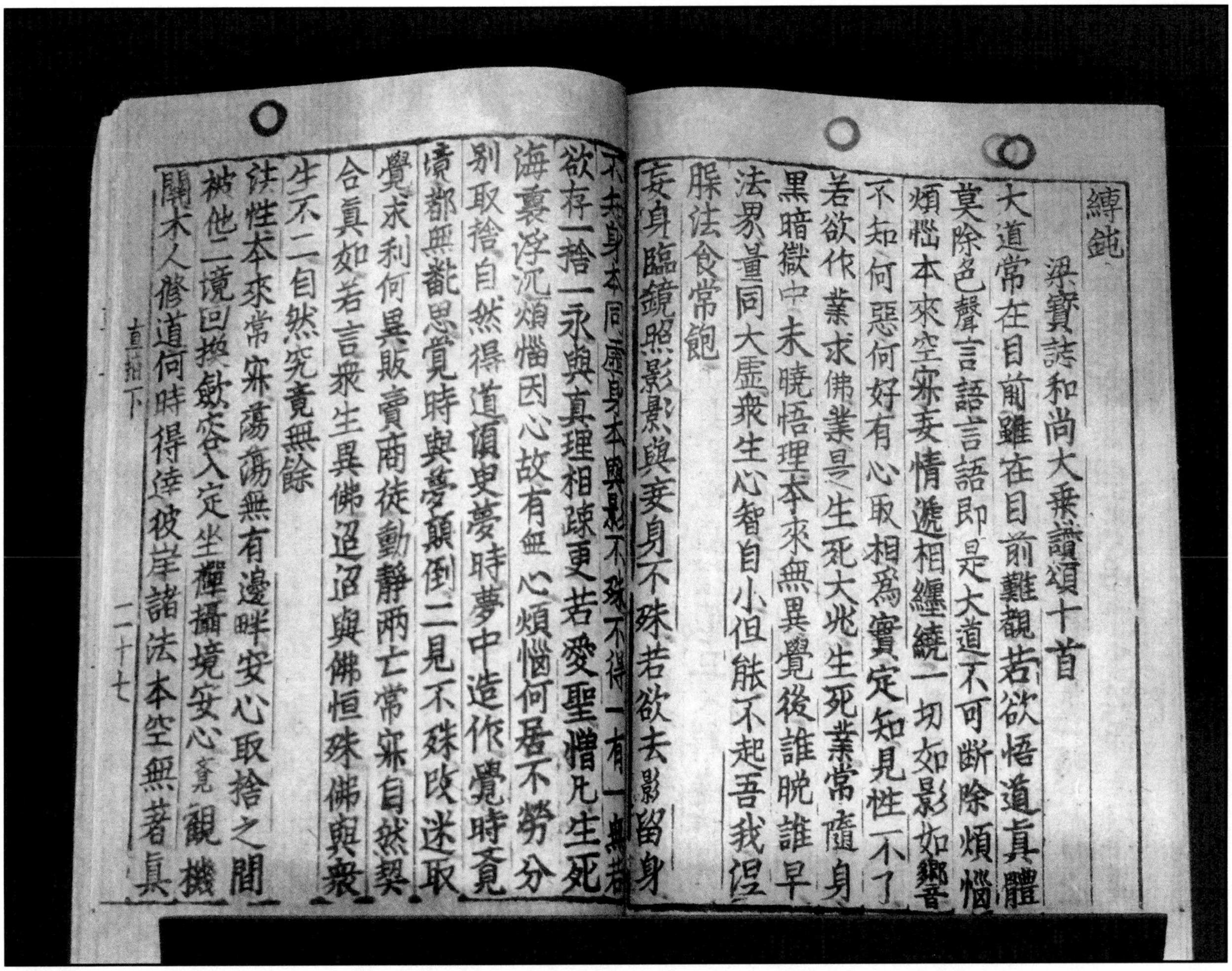

縛鈍
梁寶誌和尚大乘讃頌十首
大道常在目前雖在目前難覩若欲悟道真體
莫除色聲言語言語即是大道不可斷除煩惱
煩惱本來空寂妄情遞相纏繞一切如影如響
不知何惡何好有心取相爲實定知見性不了
若欲作業求佛業是生死大兆生死業常隨身
黒暗獄中未曉悟理本來無異覺後誰晩誰早
法界量同大虚衆生心智自小但能不起吾我涅
槃法食常飽
妄身臨鏡照影影與妄身不殊若欲去影留身
不知身本同虚身本與影不殊不得一有一無若
欲存一捨一永與真理相踈更若愛聖憎凡生死
海裏浮沉煩惱因心故有無心煩惱何居不勞分
別取捨自然得道須臾夢時夢中造作覺時覺
境都無翻思覺時與夢顛倒二見不殊改迷取
覺求利何異販賣商徒動靜兩亡常寂自然契
合真如若言衆生異佛迢迢與佛恒殊佛與衆
生不二自然究竟無餘
法性本來常寂蕩蕩無有邊畔安心取捨之間
被他二境回換斂容入定坐禪攝境安心覺觀
機關木人修道何時得達彼岸諸法本空無著真
直指下 二十七

Figure 7.5

"The Monk Baegun's Anthology of the Great Priests' Teachings on Identification of the Buddha's Spirit by the Practice of Seon," known as the Jikji, *is the world's oldest book printed with metal type. It was produced in Korea about 80 years before Gutenberg's invention. Vertical grid lines on the pages are a result of the metal type process.*

Courtesy of the Bibliotheque Nationale de France

religious attitudes. Business opportunities and cities expanded as printing sped the recording of transactions. More than any other single invention, the printing press signaled an end to the Dark Ages that followed the collapse of the Roman Empire and the beginning of the Renaissance.

The Gutenberg Bible not only showed the world the potential of the print medium, it also signaled the start of typography—the reproduction of words through a mechanical process. Typography, as exemplified in Gutenberg's work, put printed words on an equal artistic footing with hand-lettered words.

Within a few decades after Gutenberg's achievement, artists who were specialists in the creation and use of various typographical styles combined the craft of sculpture with the art of graphic design to produce lettering that was both practical and beautiful. Typography reminds us that words are graphic elements with pictorial and emotional qualities as important as any illustration.

Johannes Gutenberg will always be credited for inventing the first commercially viable printing press. But he was a person with all-too-human frailties. Despite the events in his life, or because of them, he accomplished what he set out to do. Perhaps in the end he dedicated so many years of his life to printing a Bible as an act of contrition for his

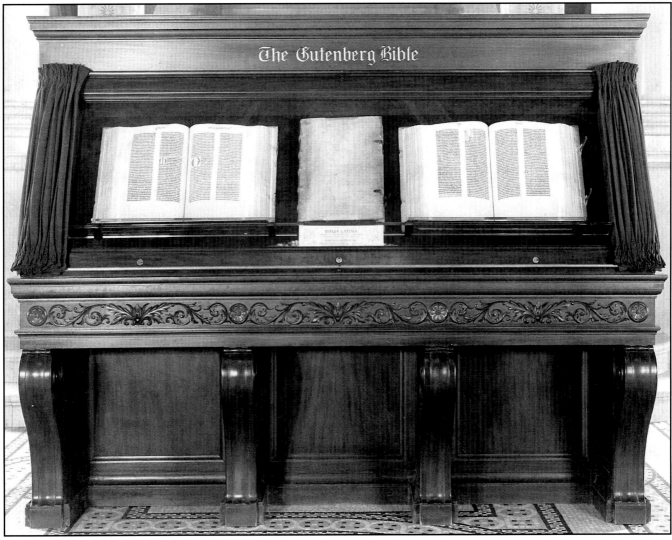

Figure 7.6
The three-volume Gutenberg Bible on display within the elaborate and respectful case in the east corridor of the Library of Congress is only one of three surviving perfect vellum copies in the world.
Courtesy of the Library of Congress

relationships with other people. We will never actually know his motives because, ironically, the inventor of commercialized printing left no printed record of his own life (Figure 7.6).

TYPOGRAPHY AND THE SIX PERSPECTIVES

Because words are so important in communicative messages, the way those words are presented form a vital link between what they mean and how they are viewed. The study of typography is vital for students of communication because poor typographical use in print

and screen media is often an indication of amateurish presentations. In addition, not being aware of the many typographical choices available to a designer is like only watching for the plot of a motion picture—much is missed.

Personal Perspective

Typographical designer Jonathan Hoefler once remarked, "Typography is to writing as soundtracks are to movies." If the music for a motion picture is too loud or too soft, too intense or too calm, or in an inappropriate style, an audience member is distracted. Typographical choices can guide a viewer toward understanding the literal message of the words and toward perceiving symbolic meaning. But the wrong choices can make words hard to read and distract from their message. *How* words are presented, then, are just as important as *what* those words are.

A graphic designer has many variations of type at her disposal. In addition to the obvious choice of the particular typeface style, a single word or a block of copy varies in its size, placement, color of the letters, the background, column width, length, and justification style. If a designer is working in a screened media either for television, motion pictures, or online, other variables can include pacing, the length of time letters are shown on a screen, and direction, the placement of where the words enter and exit a frame. Unless the letters are the main thrust of a presentation, it is a safe bet that most typographic choices made for print and screen media go unnoticed by an untrained viewer.

Artists, however, seldom want their work to have a neutral reaction. They want their choices seen and responded to by a viewer. American Barbara Kruger has been exhibiting found images with provocative text messages since 1979. She studied art and design from the photographer Diane Arbus and worked for several Condé Nast magazines as a graphic designer (Figure 7.7).

San Francisco–based typographical artist Tauba Auerbach (Figure 7.8) uses letterforms in her pieces that often demonstrate how the same word can have different messages depending on the typographic choices employed (Figure 7.9). The Seoul, Korea, artist duo of Marc Voge and Young-Hae Chang of Young-Hae Chang Heavy Industries (Figure 7.10) work primarily with online animated typographical forms set to music that make statements about social customs and practices. In their piece called "The End," they demonstrate

through mostly large, uppercase sans serif letters that breaking up is hard to do. Voge and Chang vary the music and pacing depending on the letterforms inherent within each language. Again, the literal message remains the same, but the effect on viewers is quite different. New York artist Yael Kanarek, perhaps more well known for the integrated media piece "World of Awe" (Figure 7.11), also works with word sculptures made from rubber cutouts. In "Lemon," the word is displayed in 32 languages in a collage of rubber characters glued together to form a crocheted piece in order to investigate the "territorial properties of language."

Historical Perspective

Although the art of typography officially began with the first edition of Gutenberg's Bible, typography is linked directly to the history of writing. And even though anatomically modern humans have been on the Earth for about 180,000 years, the practice of placing symbolic messages on a medium of presentation is at least 30,000 years old.

Drawing

As evidence of higher intelligence over other animals, early humans began to preserve images of animals by drawing or carving petroglyphs on the walls of caves, on smooth mountain spaces, on desert plateaus, and on the bones of slaughtered animals (Figure 7.12). Paintings and petroglyphs were a realization by early humans that they could make their thoughts permanent by preserving them. Later, drawings of human figures and symbols for the sun and moon abounded, but overwhelmingly the main subjects were the animals that were hunted in the part of the world where the drawings were found. The drawings represent two kinds of visual messages: pictographs and ideographs. Pictographs are pictures that stand for objects, plants, or animals. Ideographs are images that represent abstract ideas. Most modern

Figure 7.7
(Weblink: http://goo.gl/xAzmbl)
Barbara Kruger is known for her layered photographs that include strong typographic examples in her films, books,

Figure 7.8
(Weblink: http://goo.gl/dvAXmp)
"Blah, blah, blah," 2006, by Tauba Auerbach. The New York–based typographic artist Tauba Auerbach shows in this work how the same word can have different symbolic and emotional meanings depending on the choice of typeface.

Figure 7.9
(Weblink: http://goo.gl/g9b621)
Tauba Auerbach's website not only shows examples of her work, but is also fun to navigate.

Figure 7.10
(Weblink: http://goo.gl/pWrRNq)
Although the centered column filled with links to Heavy Industry typographical work is not that attractive, the animated pieces are always interesting and entertaining.

Figure 7.11
(Weblink: http://goo.gl/wTc1Y2)
Yael Kanarek has a modern and traditional website that showcases the typographical work.

Figure 7.12
Written words evolved from cave paintings on walls in prehistoric times. Over the millennia the wall space on caves of the Lascaux region of southern France gradually became limited. This photograph was taken in France's Lascaux Grotto.
Courtesy of Professor Saxx

Figure 7.14
(Weblink: http://goo.gl/GeJoVY) Werner Herzog, as with his other documentaries, created a mesmerizing portrait of the Chauvet cave paintings in Cave of Forgotten Dreams.

humans can easily understand ancient pictographs, but the ideographs created by early humans remain a mystery (Figure 7.13).

In the Lascaux and Chauvet caves in southern France, for example, early artists mixed charcoal or colors from the soil with animal fat or their own saliva. They spread these paints with their fingers, spit them from their mouth, or used crude reed brushes to produce paintings of animals with remarkable clarity and artistry. These drawings represent the first known attempts to create a written language. Sadly, because of all the attention, many cave drawings are in danger of being taken over by a creeping fungus, caused by rising temperatures from high-powered lights, poor circulation, and human contact. The aesthetic beauty and timeless awe of 32,000-year-

old cave drawings are evident in the 2011 documentary by the German filmmaker Werner Herzog in his *Cave of Forgotten Dreams*. His 3-D exploration of the Chauvet cave is a rare peek inside the minds of ancient humans (Figure 7.14).

Writing

Since the earliest written messages, writing has transitioned from drawing to mechanical and then digital production throughout history and by many literate cultures wishing to preserve their heritage, particularly, the Sumerians, the Egyptians, the Chinese, the Phoenicians, the Greeks, and the Romans.

The Sumerians Like the animals they hunted, for thousands of years, early humans were wanderers who constantly searched for food, shelter, and water in small tribes of individuals with similar interests. But around 12,000BCE in what is now Iraq, thousands of these nomads started to congregate in the lush valleys that formed an arc from Lower Egypt to the Persian Gulf known as the Fertile Crescent (Figure 7.15). Between the Tigris and Euphrates rivers, the Sumerians lived in Mesopotamia, or the "Land Between the Rivers" for more than 10,000 years. They planted crops, domesticated animals, initiated the Bronze Age when they mixed copper with tin for stronger tools and weapons, invented the wheel, created a complex system of religious and social discipline, buried their dead in organized services, and invented the first system of writing.

At the temple in Uruk, Iraq in about 3500BCE, scribes wrote on clay tablets for the first time in history. This monumental step in human development took the form of crude pictographic text arranged in columns from right to left. The pictures described the agricultural lives of the people and reported the number of cattle, sacks of grain, and barrels of beer that people possessed (Figure 7.16). Specially educated scribes used a sharp-edged stylus to make impressions in damp clay tablets that they later dried in the sun or in kilns. In about 2800BCE, the scribes started to turn the pictures over on their sides to ease in their production. Three hundred years later, they replaced their pointed sticks with triangular-tipped styluses that they pushed into, rather than dragged through, the clay. Unfortunately, many historical and irreplaceable ancient pieces remain missing after the looting of the museum in Uruk following the U.S. invasion of Iraq in 2003.

This innovation, along with more abstract representations of objects and ideas, meant that those with less artistic skill than earlier pictographic scribes could produce Sumerian writing.

Figure 7.13
"Petroglyph, Rural New Mexico," 2002, by Gerry Davey. Human, animal, and symbolic forms scratched in rocks have been found throughout the world.
Courtesy of Gerry Davey

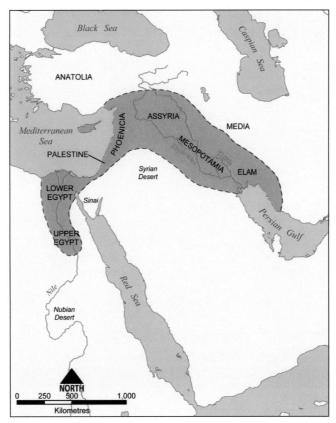

Figure 7.15
The Fertile Crescent is the name for the arc-like region of the Middle East where humans about 14,000 years ago quit being nomads and started to settle in large numbers. The Crescent included Ancient Egypt, the Levant, or the eastern Mediterranean, and the "Land Between the Rivers," Mesopotamia.
Courtesy of Norman Einstein

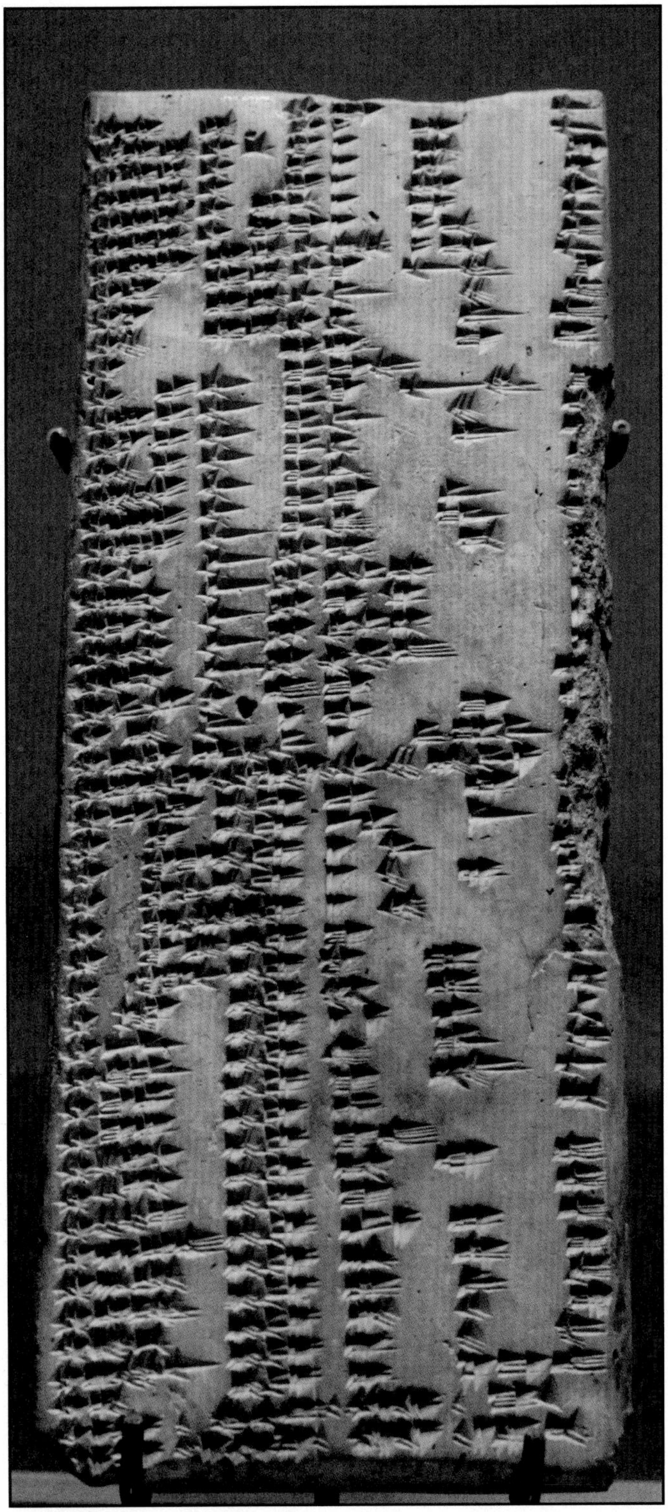

Figure 7.16
Over several centuries, highly stylized cuneiform writing, which employed a slanted wooden stylus pressed into soft clay, became the norm for the Sumerian scribes.
Courtesy of Paul Martin Lester

Nevertheless, this writing style called *cuneiform* (Latin for "wedge-shaped") required strict schooling from childhood on, because there were hundreds of characters to learn. One of the oldest written stories is the *Epic of Gilgamesh*. In 12 tablets using cuneiform, believed to be written in 2700BCE, it told of a devastating flood. The cuneiform story became known because of a later Akkadian-language version of the story. Akkadian was a Semitic language, later replaced by Aramaic (Figure 7.17).

The Egyptians Stretching more than 4,000 miles, the Nile is the longest river in the world. Sometime in 3100BCE, Sumerian ideas about writing reached the Egyptians. Hieroglyphs remained the chief written language of the civilization until the Romans conquered the area in 390CE. The name is derived from the Greek words *hieros* for "holy" and *gluphein* for "engrave." This "writing of the gods" reveals that the Egyptians were much more sensitive to the pictorial qualities of writing than the Sumerians. Egyptian hieroglyphics not only told the story of their culture, but also did so in a poetic, beautifully visual way (Figure 7.18).

From an initial symbol set of 700, hieroglyphs eventually expanded to more than 5,000 characters. By 1500BCE, hieroglyphic writing divided into two forms: hieratic and demotic scripts. The hieratic form is the most familiar style of writing and was used for official business, religious documents, and the pyramids. The demotic script was more popular for everyday types of writing because it was less illustrative. Its characters were also more abstract and symbolic.

For hundreds of years, the meaning of Egyptian hieroglyphs remained a mystery for researchers. But in 1799, during Napoleon's expedition to Egypt, the Rosetta Stone was found near the port city of Rashid. Written in 196BCE,

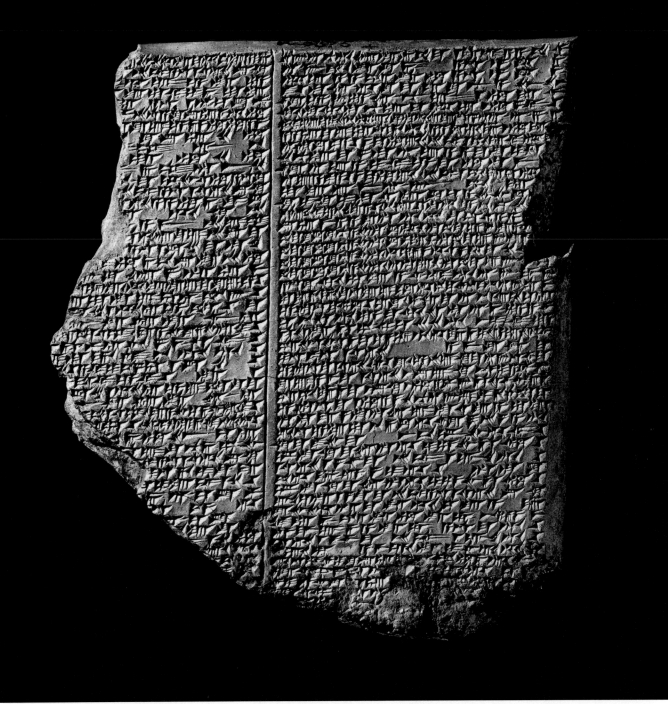

Figure 7.17
The Epic of Gilgamesh *is the oldest surviving literary work in the history of civilization. Written in Sumerian and Akkadian, the vertical line denotes the two versions of the cuneiform classic. Shown here is the 11th or "Deluge" tablet that tells of a great flood. Many believe it is the basis for the story of Noah in the Bible.*
Courtesy of the British Museum

Figure 7.18
"The Obelisk of Theodosius," erected in 390CE can be found in Istanbul, Turkey. The aesthetically beautiful Egyptian hieroglyphics immediately indicates how much more labor intensive the writing style was than cuneiform writing because of its larger and detailed symbol set.
Courtesy of Paul Martin Lester

the stone, named for the color of the rock, contained the same information in hieroglyphic, demotic, and ancient Greek. The message carved into the stone came from the king of Egypt, Ptolemy V Epiphanes, who proclaimed that the priesthood was exempt from various taxes and set forth an order to erect statues in his likeness in their temples. In 1808 the French scholar Jean-François Champollion was able to translate most of the Rosetta Stone with the help of others, including Thomas Young, who also helped developed the tri-color theory. The stone is now on exhibit in the British Museum in London (Figure 7.19). By 1822, Champollion could translate any hieroglyphic text. Just before his death at age 42, he published a dictionary to enable Egyptologists to learn about the ancient culture.

The Chinese In 1800BCE, Tsang Chieh, after noticing tracks left behind by a bird, supposedly invented calligraphy. Chinese calligraphy is one of the most complicated forms of communication known (Figure 7.20). It was never reduced to abstract symbols, as were many of the other systems. It has remained a written language comprising more than 44,000 individual symbols for centuries.

By royal decree in 210BCE, the Chinese writing system was simplified to about 1,000 basic characters that are still in use today. Such a writing system made the use of the language in mechanical presses difficult. Devising metal typefaces, as Gutenberg had done for every Chinese character was simply too costly and time consuming. Chinese printers would spend all their time finding and sorting symbols. Consequently, the Chinese developed a pictorial calligraphic style that is praised as an art form throughout the world.

Figure 7.19
This is a rare view of the front (left) and back of the Rosetta Stone in this combined picture on display in the British Museum in London. Named for the color of the rock the texts were carved into, it was created in the year 196BCE. Its horizontal lines divide the telling of the same edict in three different languages—ancient hieroglyphics, a more modern style called demotic, and classical Greek. Discovered in 1799 by a French Army engineer in preparation of Napoleon Bonaparte's attempt to seize Egypt, the sight of the historical treasure, which measured 45 inches high, 28.5 inches wide, and 11 inches thick, stunned the army officers. After Napoleon gave up his quest to capture the country, British troops seized the stone and brought it to London in 1802, where it resides today in the British Museum. The English medical doctor Thomas Young, who, with Hermann von Helmholtz, developed the tri-chromatic theory of color perception, was the first to translate the demotic text, while the French scholar Jean-François Champollion expanded on the translations and created a dictionary for future researchers. Although the message of the stone is somewhat banal—it gives the temple priests a tax break—the reason modern anthropologists know so much about ancient Egyptian culture is because the Rosetta Stone could be used to translate the hieroglyphic writings found written on papyrus and engraved on the pyramids.
Courtesy of Paul Martin Lester

Figure 7.20
"Poem Written on a Boat on the Wu River," Mi Fu, ca. 1095. The flowing, delicate lines that comprise the calligraphic words have an aesthetic pleasure as beautiful as any image.
Courtesy of the Metropolitan Museum of Art

Figure 7.21
Although the idea of an alphabet, a highly symbolic symbol set of letters consisting of the sounds one makes when speaking, was discovered earlier in the region, the Phoenicians are credited with spreading the concept throughout the known world. Consequently, the word phonetic is a tribute to the Phoenicians, as the alphabet became the basis of almost all modern languages.
Courtesy of Paul Martin Lester

W
LINK
Figure 7.22
(Weblink: http://goo.gl/K64r6P) "How to Spell the Alphabet," 2005, by Tauba Auerbach. The artist provides her own take on the English 26-letter phonetic alphabet.

The Phoenicians Between Egypt to the west and Sumer to the southeast, the great society of merchants known as Phoenicia prospered along the Mediterranean Sea in the area now known as Lebanon, Syria, and Israel. By about 2000BCE, the Phoenicians possessed some of the fastest sailing ships known and traded goods throughout the region. They learned the Egyptian and Sumerian writing systems in order to trade with them successfully, but cultural pride led them to develop their own.

The Phoenician culture is forever linked to one of the greatest advances in the history of communication: the alphabet (Figure 7.21). Derived from the first two words of the Greek alphabet, *alpha* and *beta*, an alphabet is a collection of symbols in a specified order that represents the sounds of spoken language.

The genius of an alphabet was that it reduced to a handful the number of characters needed to write a language. The Egyptians used about 5,000 symbols, the Phoenicians only 22. Found in the limestone of a sarcophagus in the Phoenician city-state of Byblos, the 22 abstract symbols represent the final phase in the transition from pictorial to purely symbolic characters. The English language alphabet uses 26 letterforms that represent the sounds made while speaking (Figure 7.22). However, a close inspection of a dictionary reveals that in reality, 26 letter symbols are not enough. More than 40 characters are needed for a more complete pronunciation of all the words.

The Greeks Because the Greeks obtained their papyrus from the Phoenician capital of Byblos, they gave their papyrus writing paper the same name. The English word *bible* is from the Greek phrase that means "a papyrus book." The Greeks also learned the Phoenician alphabet sometime between 1000 and 700BCE. The Phoenicians had little use for vowel sounds, but the Greeks

did. They changed five consonants to the vowels *a, e, i, o,* and *u* and added two other vowel sounds for a total of 24 characters. The Greeks introduced uppercase and lowercase letters. Capitals were reserved for writing on stone, while lowercase letters were used on papyrus (Figure 7.23).

The Romans Roman society was one of the largest and most influential in the history of Western civilization. Growing from a sleepy little village in 750BCE on the Tiber River in what now is central Italy in a region known as Latium, the "Latins" built and ruled an empire in about 700 years that stretched from England to the north to Egypt to the south, and from Spain to the west to Mesopotamia to the east. As they did with all the peoples they conquered, when they overwhelmed the Greeks, the Romans absorbed much of their culture, including its alphabet. The Romans made many adjustments to the Greek writing system. Late in the 10th century CE, the Latin letter W, a variation of the common letter V, was added. Finally, in the 14th century, some 400 years after Latin had died as a spoken language, the 26th letter, J, was added to complete the alphabet.

As the Greeks had done, the Romans used uppercase letters (usually painted red) on buildings and lowercase characters when writing on papyrus rolls or wax tablets (Figure 7.24).

Other civilizations around the world had their own histories and writing styles. In 2006 a stone block about 1,000 years old contained drawings believed to be a writing system developed by the pre-Columbian Olmec civilization in Mexico. It is the oldest such find on the continent. Zapotec and Maya cultures developed writing styles 500 years later. However, for all these writing examples, no translation has been found (Figure 7.25).

By Gutenberg's era, the Venetian

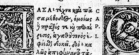

Figure 7.23
Part of the first page of Aristotle's Nicomachean Ethics,
printed in August 1566 in Greek and Latin.
Courtesy of Future Perfect at Sunrise

Figure 7.24
*For writing on stone, Romans used all uppercase letters, as
seen in this example displayed in the Louvre Museum in Paris.*
Courtesy of Paul Martin Lester

Figure 7.25
*Maya glyphs in
stucco at the Museo
de sitio in Palenque,
Mexico.*
**Courtesy of Kwami-
kagami**

Figure 7.26
Jean Grolier, the viscount d'Aguisy, the Treasurer-General of France and biblio-phile, sits in the house of Aldus Manutius, the location of his Aldine Press.
Courtesy of the Collection of the Grolier Club, New York

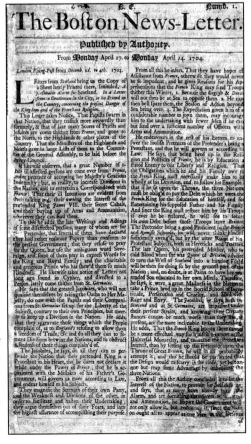

Figure 7.27
An issue of the Boston News-Letter, *printed April 24, 1704, was the first American newspaper with a regular circulation. With its two columns of aligned type introduced by an enlarged letter, it is similar in style to Gutenberg's Bible.*
Courtesy of the Massachusetts Historical Society

Aldus Manutius and his Aldine Press published high-quality works by Greek and Roman philosophers and illustrated works of fiction. In 1498 he finished a five-volume set of Aristotle's works. He also published *The Dream of Poliphilus*, a curious tale about a young man searching for his lover. The book is noted for its sexually explicit illustrations. Aldus also was known for promoting italic type. Unlike today, when the slanted script is reserved for titles of books or movies, Aldus used italic to save money—it allowed pages to be filled with more characters, thus using less paper (Figure 7.26).

Evidence of Gutenberg's legacy is found throughout the world. In 1704, the *Boston News-Letter* became the first single-sheet American newspaper (Figure 7.27). When the French Revolution erupted in 1789, a call for the freedom of the press was answered with the establishment of more than 300 newspapers in France the next year.

Johannes Gutenberg's quaint converted wine press became a historical relic in 1814 when the German Frederich Koenig used the steam engine to power a press in London that could print 1,110 sheets a day. In 1828, a four-cylinder press that could handle 4,000 sheets a day for *The Times* of London was invented. Later improvements increased that output to 8,000 sheets per hour. The American Richard Hoe made an important advance when he introduced the rotary press in 1847 (Figure 7.28). With the invention of lithography and the halftone photo-engraving screen, color illustrations and photographs could be printed during the same press run as the type. By the late 1880s, most high-circulation publications used a web perfecting press with coated papers that allowed high-quality, fast-paced printing on both sides of a long roll of paper. The advent of stereotype plates further sped up the printing process, as several duplicate pages could be printed on different

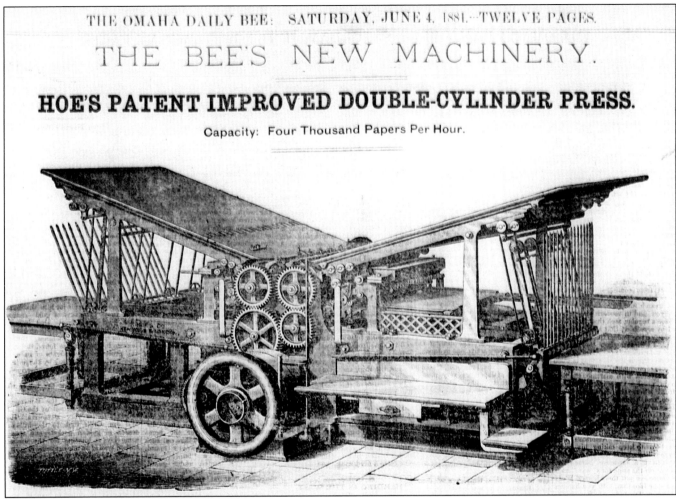

THE OMAHA DAILY BEE: SATURDAY, JUNE 4, 1881.—TWELVE PAGES.

THE BEE'S NEW MACHINERY.

HOE'S PATENT IMPROVED DOUBLE-CYLINDER PRESS.

Capacity: Four Thousand Papers Per Hour.

Figure 7.28
Readers of the Omaha Daily Bee *in 1881 read the announcement of the arrival of a new Hoe press that could print 4,000 papers an hour. The Hoe press was used primarily to publish Sunday newspapers that used color. Richard March Hoe grew up in New York City as a printer as his father Robert built presses for sale. The two worked on steam-driven presses in which one cylinder held the type while another held the paper. Gradually, more cylinders were added for faster speed.*
Courtesy of the Library of Congress

presses at the same time.

With computers, digital typesetting allowed an operator to use the machine to generate letters. In 1984, Apple introduced its Macintosh computer with on-screen controls for the production of words and graphics on the same system. The next year the inexpensive LaserWriter printer from Apple was launched, and the desktop computer revolution officially started.

Technical Perspective

In order to analyze the use of typefaces in print or screen communications, you must be aware of the various choices available to a typographer. A designer who uses words also must make choices about various typeface styles in relation to overall size, color, fonts, text block size, justification, space, and animation.

Typeface Families

Typography is a big business. It is estimated that computer companies, typesetters, printers, publishers, advertising agencies, and writers spend more than $300 million a year to purchase typefaces. Johannes Gutenberg had an easy time selecting the typeface style for his Bible because there was only one—textur. Since Gutenberg's day, at least 40,000 different typeface styles have been created, with more than 176,000 attri-

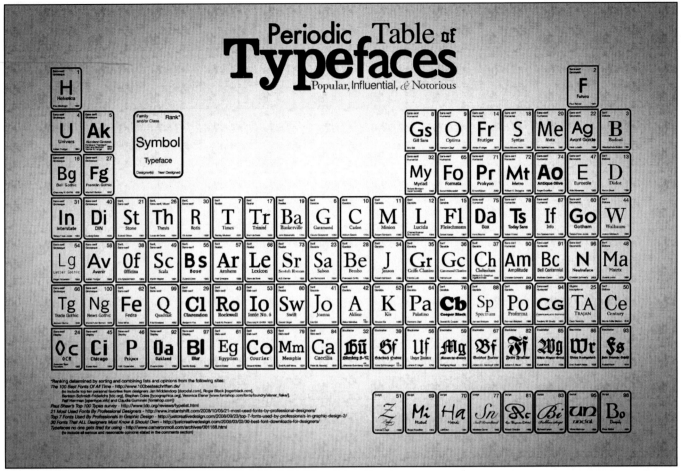

Figure 7.29
"Periodic Table of Typefaces Popular, Influential, & Notorious," by Camdon Wilde. Arranged as a periodic table for chemical elements, Wilde sorted and arranged 100 typefaces based on lists generated by typographical experts. The sans serif typeface family seems to be the winner with more than 30 examples on the table.
Courtesy of Camdon Wilde

bute variations. With so many choices, a method was devised to group all of the typefaces into categories or families. The resulting six basic typeface families became blackletter, roman, script, miscellaneous, square serif, and sans serif. Think of each typeface family as separate colors or musical styles, each with their own mood and purpose (Figure 7.29).

Blackletter Sometimes called gothic, old style, old English, renaissance, or medieval, the blackletter typeface family is highly ornate and decorative. Individual strokes that make up the letters are thick and have sharp diagonal lines. Many of the strokes in capital letters are connected with thinner supporting lines. The ends of the letters usually have small

stylized strokes that were early predecessors of the serif. Because it happened to be the style that scribes in monasteries used for their handwritten works, Gutenberg fashioned his metal type characters accordingly. Consequently, the family is associated with traditional, conservative, religious, or German content. A newspaper's name was often set in this typeface family to communicate to readers that the publication had traditional values and was long established (Figure 7.30). The cartoonist Jules Feiffer, for example, used the typeface to illustrate the voice of God. For the motion picture *Inkheart* (2008), makeup artist Jenny Shicore was asked to simulate blackletter tattooed text on some of the characters' faces.

Figure 7.30
Like this 1902 issue of The Washington Times, *the blackletter typeface family is still used for the modern version, but over time the period at the end of the name was removed.*
Courtesy of the Library of Congress

Roman The roman typeface family is the most commonly used of them all. Body copy in books, magazines, and newspapers use roman because it is familiar to readers and exceedingly legible. The gently curved serifs create lines that are easy to read (Figures 7.31). Development of the style of roman used today took approximately 300 years from the time it was introduced in 1465. During that period, three forms were introduced: *old style*, created by two Venetian printers, Nicolaus Jenson and Aldus Manutius, and the French Claude Garamond, who shaved the metal of the blackletter characters so that the strokes were not quite as thick or ornate, *transitional*, for which William Caslon and John Baskerville of England in the 18th century made the letters more vertical and allowed a bit more contrast between the thin and thick strokes with less ornate serifs, and *modern*, from the Italian Giambattista Bodoni, who produced more than 100 different alphabet collections. As a result, roman lost its early link to blackletter and became a distinctive family, with letter strokes changed from thick lines with little contrast to thinner strokes with a noticeable difference in width.

Figures 7.31
The urgency of the upper-case warning posted on a dock outside Leesburg, Florida is diminished by the choice of a roman typeface family for the sign. A sterner sans serif family typeface would have been a better choice. However, if you have to worry about snakes hiding in a boat, perhaps your typeface choice should not be your first concern.
Courtesy of Paul Martin Lester

Figure 7.32
In this advertisement for the health resort town of Saratoga Springs, New York published in a 1922 issue of the New York Tribune, *the script typeface family seen in "Saratoga Springs" and "The Washington Baths" lends an air of sophistication to the famous place.*
Courtesy of the Library of Congress

Script Cursive writing is defined as letters that are linked. In 1557, Robert Granjon of France introduced the first typeface designed to mimic the hand-writing of ordinary people. Ironically, the script typeface family is now used almost exclusively for documents and publications that want to promote a high-quality, high-class appearance (Figure 7.32). Wedding invitations and licenses, for example, commonly are printed in script because the fine letters, perhaps more than any other family's style, give the piece an air of handmade attention to detail.

Miscellaneous Sometimes referred to as novelty or display type, the members of the miscellaneous typeface family, as the name suggests, cannot easily be sorted into the other families. Miscellaneous type first began appearing for advertising purposes during the Industrial Revolution. As more people made more money because of the efficiency of new machines, they needed more products and services. Printing came to be thought of as not simply a means of disseminating information and news through books, magazines, and newspapers, but also as a way to attract potential customers through advertising. The miscellaneous family's unique feature is that its style purposely draws attention to itself (Figure 7.33). For example, creative typographers designed typefaces with letters formed by collections of flowers or contorted human figures.

The Industrial Revolution also spurred the final two typeface families discussed.

Square Serif In 1815, probably inspired by architecture and other sights reported after Napoleon's conquest of Egypt, Vincent Figgins designed a typeface similar to the modern roman but with right angle curves jutting from the letter strokes. Sometimes called 3-D, slab, or Egyptian, the square serif

Figure 7.33
Although the main typeface used by this 1937 Works Progress Administration poster by Richard Floethe has roots in the sans serif family, it is considered an example of a miscellaneous typeface because it looks like it was made with a stencil—a good choice for a poster about posters.
Courtesy of the Library of Congress

typeface family is intended, as is the miscellaneous family, to draw attention to itself and the product it is helping to advertise. Square serif is the least used typeface family today because of its bricklike appearance, which gives it an unpleasant rigid look. Curiously, in American culture this typeface family is associated with the Wild West because it was used commonly on storefronts in pioneer towns in western movies made in Hollywood. It is also a favorite choice, for some reason, of college graphic designers for university initials on caps and sweatshirts (Figure 7.34).

Sans Serif In 1832, William Caslon IV introduced the first member of this family. It was immediately controversial. The French word *sans* means "without." Caslon simply took existing letters and trimmed off all their serifs. The result was a typestyle that Caslon named "block type." Typographical critics of the day immediately voiced their objections to the type family as being too simple

Figure 7.34
"Restaurant Bar, Austin, Nevada," 2003, by Gerry Davey. The seldom used typeface family of square serif is nevertheless popular for signs that evoke a spirit of the old American West. The connection probably comes from Hollywood westerns that often used the family for its storefront sets.

Figure 7.35

The famous "J'accuse" front page written by Émile Zola related to the Dreyfus case on January 13, 1898 in L'Aurore *is an early example of the sans serif typeface family.*
Courtesy of *L'Aurore*

Figure 7.36

The sans serif typeface family is used to communicate a serious message. Since 9/11, this warning sign has appeared on the cabin door of some airlines. By the way, flight attendants get really nervous when you take a picture like this one. Best to leave it to a professional.
Courtesy of Paul Martin Lester

and without style.

Despite the early criticism, sans serif typefaces have enjoyed several periods of popularity. Printers in the 1880s liked the new style, because many felt that the streamlined, clean-looking letter strokes fit the new machine age. Plus, they saved money. Typefaces with serifs often snapped off because of fast-moving presses. Printing had to be stopped to replace letters, and flawed pages were discarded. With sans serif types, printers didn't have to stop the presses to replace broken letters. But the sans serif fad eventually faded. During the 1920s there was a rebirth in interest. Architectural and graphic design styles of de stijl, bauhaus, and art deco revived the type family, as artists thought the simple lines matched the illustrations they created (See Chapter 8). In the 1970s, newspaper publishers asked designers to modernize their front pages. Many turned to the sans serif family for headlines and photo captions to offset the roman type of the body copy for their print and online editions (Figure 7.35).

Without serifs, the type style connotes a no-nonsense, practical approach to lettering in which a viewer isn't distracted by the addition of serifs. For that reason, stop, warning, and exit signs most often are printed in the sans serif style (Figure 7.36). Screen media presentations have demonstrated the importance of the sans serif style, as it is easy to read. Consequently, these typefaces are used most often in motion picture titles and credits, in captions for television news programs, and for computer, tablet, and smartphone screens.

Austrian graphic designer Stefan Sagmeister stunned the art world in his 1996 poster for Lou Reed's "Set the Twilight Reeling," with inked text on the musician's face (Figure 7.37). Three years later he upped the ante for an AIGA (American Institute of Graphic Arts) poster for a lecture he gave in Cranbrook, Michigan. An assistant scratched the title, location, subject, day, and time of his lecture with a sharp blade on Sagmeister's naked torso (Figure 7.38).

The MTV Music Video of the Year award for 1992 was presented to director Mark Fenske for his one and only music video of the Van Halen song "Right Now." The visual interpretation of the song uses mostly sans serif, with some miscellaneous typefaces for sentences such as "Right now science is building a better tomato" and "Right now your parents miss you" (Figure 7.39).

One of the most enduring and universally used sans serif typefaces is Helvetica, created in 1957 by the Swiss designer Max Miedinger. In 2007 Gary Hustwit released a documentary of the same name that featured interviews with many of the most famous designers in the world (Figure 7.40).

Typeface Attributes

Whether for print or screen presentations, a graphic designer must make choices about seven major type attributes: size, color, font, column, justification, space, and animation.

Size Type is measured in points. A single point is 0.0138 inch. For printed text blocks, the best type sizes are between 9 and 12 points. Display type is considered to be anything larger than 14 points. Banner newspaper headlines for some significant event are 72 points or larger (Figure 7.41). Screen presentations require a type size twice that of printed body copy.

Color Actually two colors are implied—the color of the type and the color of the background, sometimes called, regardless of the actual color, "white space." Research on type consistently shows that the most legible combination of colors for long blocks of copy is black type against a white background. For eye-catching headlines, designers occasionally use white type against a

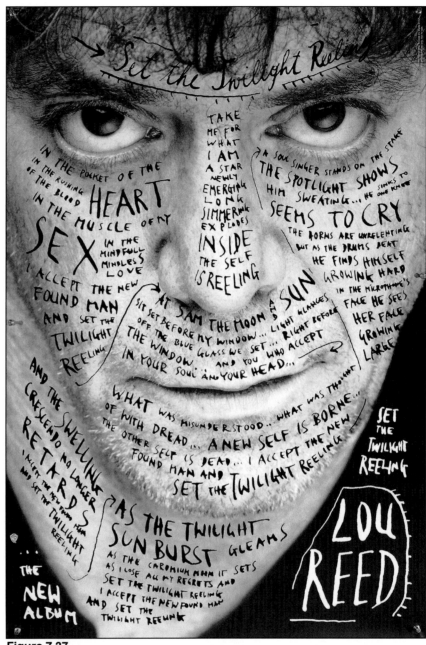

Figure 7.37

"Lou Reed Poster," 1996, by Stefan Sagmeister. Born in Austria, Stefan Sagmeister is one of the most respected typographers and graphic designers in the world. After studying at Pratt Institute in New York City and working for advertising agencies, he formed his own design studio in 1993. In 2005 he received a Grammy Award for Best Boxed or Special Limited Edition Package for art directing the Talking Heads album, "Once in a Lifetime." Examples of his work can be found in galleries throughout the world. In this striking poster for Lou Reed's "Set the Twilight Reeling," hand-drawn sans serif song titles were used because, as Sagmeister explains, "The lyrics are extremely personal. We tried to show this by writing those lyrics directly over his face."

Courtesy of Stefan Sagmeister, photography by Timothy Greenfield Sanders

Figure 7.39
*(Weblink: http://goo.gl/8orWq7)
Directed by Mark Fenske, the
music video for Van Halen's
"Right Now" is a rich collection
of typographical examples that
with the images enhance the
lyrics of the song. Lead singer
Sammy Hagar was opposed
to the concept stating, "People
ain't even going to be listening
to what I'm saying because
they'll be reading these sub-
titles." Despite Hagar's angry
protestations, the video has
been called one of the greatest
of all time.*

Figure 7.40
*(Weblink: http://goo.gl/lgffyg)
If you love typography, you
should see the documentary,
Helvetica, one of the most
readable and popular sans
serif typefaces in the world. By
the way, helvetica is the typeface used for the captions.*

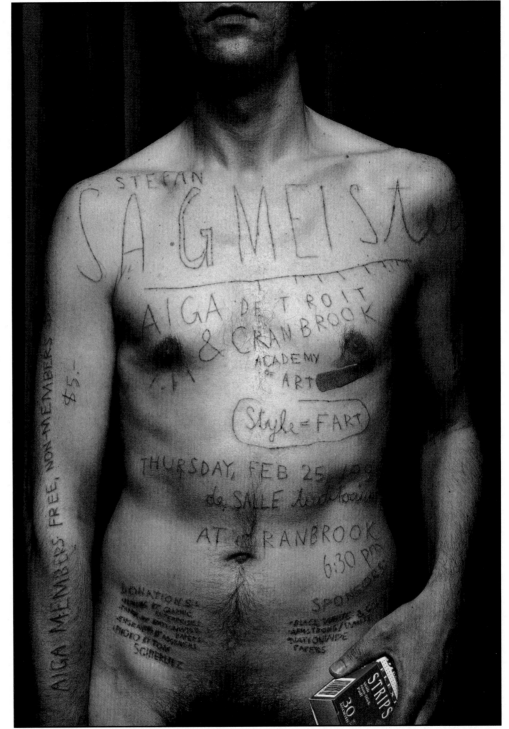

Figure 7.38
*"Sagmeister AIGA Detroit Poster," 1999, by Stefan Sagmeister. For a poster announcing the
details of a lecture, Sagmeister had an intern scratch the details on his body in a sans serif
typeface. Says Sagmeister, "We tried to visualize the pain that seems to accompany most of
our design projects." Then he added, "Yes, it did hurt real bad."*
Courtesy of Stefan Sagmeister, photography by Tom Schierlitz

Figure 7.41

Similar to most other newspaper front pages for the news, Armistice Day, November 11, 1918, the end of World War I, "The War to End All Wars," is celebrated by the large banner headlines.

Courtesy of *The Erie Daily Times*

Figure 7.42
To attract attention to an advertisement, each business in this vertical strip on the front page of a 1908 issue of the Daytona Gazette-News *features boldface in the typography. The top one for "Continuous Moving Pictures," the phrase we now call movies, has pictures for 10 cents each ($2.40 in today's dollars). If that's not enough of an enticement, there is a live alligator in the window.*
Courtesy of the Library of Congress

Figure 7.43
As with most newspapers of the era, this 1849 issue of the New York Daily Tribune *presented a conservative layout meant for those who wanted to read long, in-depth stories.*
Courtesy of the Library of Congress

black background (called reverse type), colored type against a white background, or white type against a colored background. Motion picture title artists often make movie credits white and the title of the movie, the most significant part of the copy block, another color. Television graphic artists often place white text on top of a colored box, banner, or a shadow to identify the person speaking.

Font Often substituted for the word *typeface*, a font typically refers to all of the letters and symbols that are possible with an individual typeface. For many graphic designers, a typeface's font also means the attributes of plain text, **boldface**, *italic*, underline, and any other attention-grabbing graphic devices available (Figure 7.42). Most designers, whether for print or screen mediums, use such fonts conservatively.

Column Two factors are involved with a column's size: line width and col-

umn length. For the best reading width, lines should contain no more than 12 words. While two columns in print or online are more readable than one wide column, books are set in one column, magazines usually in two to four, and newspapers can have up to eight columns on a page (Figure 7.43).

Justification Text may be presented with margins that are aligned left and/or right, or centered. Left justified text is the most common style, with the right side of the text not justified (also called ragged right). Right justified, called ragged left, and centered types are seldom used for long passages because a viewer has trouble determining where the next line starts. Completely justified type, as used by Gutenberg, has a rigid, conservative, but organized appearance.

Space Kerning is the term used to describe the space between individual letters. A modern, informal appearance can be achieved if the kerning is made an obvious design factor. When kerning is too little, too much, or uneven, the copy may be difficult to read. Leading (pronounced "ledding") describes the space between horizontal lines of type. The space between two columns of type is called the alley, and the space between the pages of a book or magazine is called the gutter (Figure 7.44).

Animation Besides all the other considerations mentioned above, a visual artist who works with typography in motion for screen media must also consider such variables as position, the location of the entrance and exit points for the text, timing—at what point words appear or disappear, pacing—how fast or how slowly words appear and disappear, and other visual effects such as fades, dissolves, wipes, and so on. With screen media, the choices for a graphic designed with regard to typography become much more complex and

Figure 7.44
In this 1910 advertisement for Postum, a caffeine-free coffee substitute, the black and white illustration, the subdued lighting, the symmetrical layout, and the leading between the lines of type help reinforce the calming effect of the product.
Courtesy of the *Technical World Magazine*

Figure 7.45
(Weblink: http://goo.gl/jXpRdw)
Media artist and professor xtine burrough's entrancing video is a tribute to typography and the dada spirit (See chapter 8).

potentially rewarding. The online media artist xtine burrough creates visual poems with animated text set in a roman typeface over edited video. In *Nighght*, a tribute to Aram Saroyan's 1965 dada poem "lighght," the soft quality of the roman typeface matches the revolving and weaving letterforms of her poem (Figure 7.45).

Ethical Perspective
Typographical designers usually invent and use typefaces that combine the philosophies of utilitarianism with the golden rule. In other words, a design is both useful, the words can be easily read, and it adds beauty to our lives with an aesthetically pleasant design. But if typefaces are made to draw attention or to satisfy a designer's personal needs, hedonism may be at work. Graphic artist Milton Glaser, responsible for the design of *New York* magazine and the "I [HEART] NY" logo, among others, warns, "There's a tremendous amount of garbage being produced under the heading of new and innovative typographical forms." Despite the criticism of typefaces being designed solely for the amusement of a particular graphic artist, the prevalent use of typographical computer programs produce ways of thinking about the use of type never before imagined. Glaser could be referring to graphic designer David Carson, for many years the innovative art director for *Ray Gun* magazine. He has been called the founder of grunge typography because of his non-traditional displays of text on a page that includes lines of type that overlap, columns of varying lengths on the same page, and an interview with the musician Brian Ferry he considered so boring that he set the text in the symbol set known as Zapf Dingbats (Figure 7.46).

Jonathan Hoefler, who created typefaces for *Sports Illustrated* and other magazines, likes "unusual fonts that challenge typographical assumptions. After all, design is about breaking the rules. Rule-breakers become rulers." The world is certainly large enough to support both dynamic, cacophonous displays and quiet, traditional typographical presentations.

Cultural Perspective
Because typography gives the artist's style to a text, it is linked, as is any art form, to a particular culture at a particular time. The history of typography may be divided into five major eras: pre-Gutenberg, Gutenberg, industrial, artistic, and digital.

Pre-Gutenberg (before 1455)
During this era, words and images were linked as equal partners in communication. Scribes, with their power to shape what future readers of their texts thought of their civilizations, had enormous power and were pampered by their leaders. One example is the 950 fragments known as the Dead Sea Scrolls, originally discovered in 1947 within 11 caves along the shore of the Dead Sea east of Jerusalem dated between 150BCE and 70CE. These documents were hand written biblical tracts written on vellum and papyrus. Later, beautifully aesthetic illustrated manuscripts combined words and images in the tradition of the Egyptians. Ireland's *Book of Kells* contained four Gospels of the New Testament and was printed about 800CE. As well as lushly illustrated works from Persian and European crafters, the work elevated the concept of aesthetic beauty when applied to printed materials in the form of scrolls, maps, manuscripts, and books (Figure 7.47).

Gutenberg (1456–1760) This era is marked by its influence of the printed word in typographically heavy designs with practitioners that often thought of images as afterthoughts. The rise in literacy and the need for books of all types produced a tremendous explosion in the number of publishing houses. Unfortu-

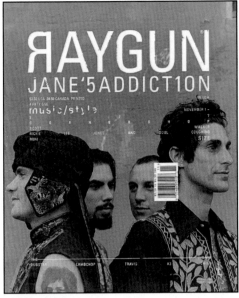

Figure 7.46

The cover of Ray Gun #51 *exudes playful irreverence to the so-called rules of typographical display with a reversed "R" in the name, cutout letters for music/style, and extreme kerning. Published from 1992 until 2000, Chris Ashworth was the art director for the cover who placed the typography on the layout without seeing the portrait of the band first. Ashworth explains, "As always with* Ray Gun *the process was wonderfully dysfunctional which was a joy. I loved the experience of seeing how elements juxtaposed against one another without it all being deliberately and methodically built as one communication. After it came out we had to create a special large format version of the cover and frame it for the Janes' drummer because he was upset that the barcode had landed on his head. The masthead had a nice relationship to the band pose, which was totally unintentional as I'd created the type prior to seeing the image." Ashworth is now the Executive Global Creative Director for Getty Images. His work can be seen at chris-ashworth.com.*
Courtesy of Chris Ashworth

nately, pictures were reserved for illustrative decorations around text blocks or for medical and other scientific textbooks and not appreciated for their own unique communicative value.

Industrial (1761–1890) This period is known as the "dark ages" of typographical design. Machine mentality ruled style. Efficiency in design and the ability to attract attention to advertisements, rather than the appearance of a typeface, were praised. The increase in all kinds of printed advertising called for typefaces that customers noticed. Elaborately shaped typefaces, often used in combination with several others and sprinkled around the images of products in an advertisement, gave the appearance of a "typographical car wreck." The style was popular in an era of fast-paced efficiency (Figure 7.48).

Artistic (1891–1983) Artists such as the French master Henri de Toulouse-Lautrec elevated typography into a respected art form through their painted posters for theatrical openings and other purposes. The movement brought advertising's use of typography out of the dark ages. The art nouveau decorative style, inspired from Asian calligraphy and designs on screens and vases, revolutionized the combination of words and images on a page. Later, several modern art styles of the 20th century (dada, de stijl, bauhaus, art deco, pop art, punk, new wave, and hip-hop) were linked with specific cultures and expressed messages related to political content, architecture, and product design. These art movements used typography as an integral part of their graphic design.

Digital (1984–present) The introduction of relatively inexpensive Macintosh computers with on-screen user controls by Apple in 1984, combined with high-quality laser printers with networking capabilities, allowed graphic artists to

Figure 7.47

The Irish Book of Kells *printed around 800CE is an excellent example of early illuminated manuscripts. This figure shows the illustrations on the opening page of the Gospel of John.*
Courtesy of Trinity College, Dublin

Figure 7.48

An 1867 advertisement for a package of potash from which soap could be made is a collection of typeface families—script, roman, miscellaneous, and sans serif. They are meant to attract a viewer's attention but the combination makes the author want to wash his eyes.

Courtesy of the Library of Congress

more easily match their original design concepts with tools that were relatively inexpensive and easily mastered, for a global audience. Consequently, designers have learned to create typefaces for print and screen media, whether for a small circulation flyer or for a web presentation that receives several million user hits a day.

Critical Perspective

The field of typography reminds us that what is considered acceptable or good is when the text choices match the expectations of an intended audience. The typographical choices for a tin of McVitie & Price's digestive biscuits is an excellent example (Figure 7.49). With its conservative presentation, it is obviously not meant as a treat for a younger audience. If this product were intended

for children, the box would show words in various colors, typefaces, and off-centered in a dynamic, three-dimensional, page-jumping, and exciting layout. Think of any cereal box meant for children (Figure 7.50). A website for an upcoming concert with the Cincinnati Symphony Orchestra (Figure 7.51) will employ much different typographical choices than one for the indie band The Chainsmokers (Figure 7.52).

Early scribes lost much of their political power when alphabets were invented and anyone could easily learn to write. But when artists developed calligraphic and illustrative skills, they turned words into works of art. Today's scribes are the graphic designers who can use a computer to make sure that the words match the style of the illustrations, the content of the piece, and the intended audience.

Figure 7.49
Many of the typographical choices in this old advertisement—lack of color, the use of a roman typeface, and a centered, justified column—indicate that the product was not marketed to children.
Courtesy of McVitie & Price

W
LINK
Figure 7.51
(Weblinks: http://goo.gl/
Kwf9cW)
The website for the Cincin-
nati Symphony Orchestra is
an information heavy collec-
tion of aligned typographi-

W
LINK
Figure 7.52
(Weblinks: http://goo.gl/
YFqDvW)
The Chainsmokers' website
has the same amount of information as Cincinnati's but
has songs and videos with
easy-to-navigate typographical choices.

Figure 7.50
With a colorful name, cartoon characters, and sugared rice, how could any parent or guardian
resist the demands from young children to purchase this dessert in a box?
Courtesy of Paul Martin Lester

Figure 7.53

As shown by the covers of these zines, homemade publications offer a variety of typographical and graphic design layout choices for producer and viewer.

Courtesy of Paul Martin Lester

*TRENDS TO WATCH
FOR TYPOGRAPHY*

Every medium of presentation—from typography to the web—is dominated by computer technology. Fewer artists prefer the analog crafts of handset type printing and chemical-based photographic darkrooms. Most work today is all digital. With individuals linked with others around the world, computer technology has sparked a rebirth in writing and reading, just as Gutenberg's printing press did 50 years after its invention.

For example, an estimated 20,000 homemade magazines are produced in the United States alone every year in garages, dens, and bedrooms with pens, typewriters, copy machines, and computers. With names like *Official Facilities Meeting Guide, Tight Fit, Return Whence You Came,* and *Fever,* creators of these specialty publications called *zines* (pronounced "zeens") comment on fringe culture, creative products, political and social issues, and alternative lifestyles with a freestyle, hand-drawn typographical and visual exuberance (Figure 7.53). The modern roots of these publications date back to 1930s science fiction comic books and Hollywood fan magazines of the 1950s. Sold in bookstores, record shops, and through mail orders, zines typically have low circulations, are under

20 pages, and have irregular issue dates. They nevertheless often make important contributions to the global environmental and anti-consumerism movements expressed in the DIY (Do-It-Yourself) ethic. With the advent of web logs, shortened to "blogs," and online magazines, the web version of the printed zine makes it possible for anyone with a wireless computer connection to have her views, both in words and images, showcased for a world of users to comment. Creative typographical choices are a vital part of the success of a zine or blog. Once on the margin of popular culture, zines are now in the mainstream with such web-based publications as *Slate* and *Salon* and blogs such as *The Huffington Post* and *Reading the News*.

One of the most accomplished new artists working with the typographical medium for online presentations is Evan Roth, aka fi5e. Created with partner Max Asare, such works as "Typographic Illustration," "Graffiti Taxonomy," and "Typoactive" expand and challenge established rules regarding traditional typographic displays. In "Illustration" (Figure 7.54), users are allowed to select a typeface, which is then used for images on a screen. If Garamond is selected, an image of Bob Dylan is formed with the typeface as his song "Don't Think Twice It's Alright" plays. For Century Gothic, a map of California is created as Jose Feliciano sings "California Dreamin.'" "Graffiti Taxonomy" as Roth notes, "presents isolated letters from various graffiti tags, reproduced in similar scales and at close proximity. The intent of these studies is to show the diversity of styles as expressed in a single character." For "Typoactive," you can type in your own text that pulsates on the screen in a hyperactive, dynamic dance of letters that you can capture with a screen saver and save to your computer to print (Figure 7.55).

Book publishing and reading have been dramatically changed by recent

Figure 7.54
(Weblink: http://goo.gl/ScTgq3)
Use Evan Roth's "Typoactive" software to create your own message.

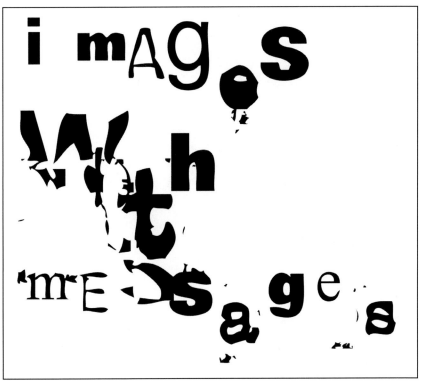

Figure 7.55
"images with messages." Using Evan Roth's online "Typoactive" program, any combination of letters can be turned into a modern form of a kidnapper's ransom note.
Courtesy of Paul Martin Lester

technological advances. What has been called the "ATM of books," OnDemand-Books' Espresso Book Machine is in use at bookstores, libraries, and museums around the world. Per a user's demand, it can print an entire paperback book with a cover in a matter of minutes. Someday this technology may be available for customers at convenience stores and coffee shops.

With print-on-demand self-publishing companies such as authorHOUSE, iUniverse, Lulu.com, Scribd.com and Amazon.com, an author can skip many of the traditional steps in the editorial process and make a book available to readers as an electronic and/or printed

Figure 7.56
An independent bookstore in Saratoga, New York is crowded with used books and many other items. While browsing the shop, serendipity can lead to unusual finds that are seldom discovered through online book websites.
Courtesy of Paul Martin Lester

version. With Lulu, authors can publish works such as paperbacks, hard covers, photography books, and calendars. An ISBN assignment, professional cover design, and marketing services increase the cost. When completed, an author can charge as much as she wants for the work, and it can be ordered through bookstores and online companies such as Amazon and Barnes and Noble. With Scribd, authors set their own price for the books. Readers can purchase the entire work or any portion of it, just as is common with music on iTunes. Perhaps this model may be employed by the newspaper industry some day. Another innovation comes from the Massachu-

setts Institute of Technology (MIT). Through its OpenCourseWare, textbooks from more than 1,800 courses in 33 disciplines can be accessed by a student and read on a computer screen or printed if desired.

With portable readers such as Amazon's Kindle, Touch, and Fire, Sony's Reader, and Apple's iPhone and iPad, downloaded books, newspapers, magazines, and websites can be listened to or read off the screen via wireless connections. Herman Melville's *Moby Dick*, for example costs 80 cents from Amazon's Kindle book site. Transferred to an iPhone, it takes as many as 9,461 screens to get through the classic. A user of the

Sony Reader can download more than 500,000 free books in the public domain that have been digitized by Google. In 2011 the digital publisher Vook made available Anne Rice's novella *The Master of Rampling Gate* for the iPad 2. In addition to the basic text, there are links to interviews and additional information embedded in the work. In 2012 Apple announced three products to help students: iBooks 2, for interactive textbooks for iPads, iBooks Author, for publishers and authors to create textbooks for the iBookstore, and iTunes U, for students to download syllabi, textbooks, and presentations. The apps are free with most books costing $14.99.

Another text-based system is the online service Twitter.com, which began its service in 2006. Through "mobile texting, instant message, or the web," short text updates of no more than 140 characters called "tweets" in a clean, sans serif typeface can be sent to your "followers" while you can follow friends and celebrities. In 2011 Twitter and Facebook messages helped mobilize the so-called "Arab Spring" with protestors in various Middle East countries coordinating activities and spreading news and information between readers all over the world. But many fans were disappointed in 2012 when Twitter announced it would block tweets from a country that required it to do so. Democracy movements might be thwarted without social media communications.

In 1913 the inventor of motion pictures Thomas Edison famously predicted, "Books will soon be obsolete in the schools." In a classic conflict of interest argument, he thought films would replace books. But as more and more computer users become comfortable reading text on a screen, will there be a need for paper and ink, manufactured from two precious natural resources? In 2012 the venerable *Encyclopaedia Britannica*, its multi-volume and expensive set of books once a symbol of wealth and class on a

shelf of a person's home, announced it would no long make a print version. In addition, large chain bookstores were blamed for the demise of many small and independent bookshops as featured in the movie *You've Got Mail* (1998). Anyone remember B. Dalton and Waldenbooks? Ironically, in 2011 the superchain Borders closed its stores and online website leaving Barnes & Noble as the last brick and mortar store standing (Figure 7.56). It remains to be seen if its reader tablet Nook will prevent a similar demise. However, in 2012 the company got a boost from the computer giant Microsoft Corp. when it invested $605 million in the bookseller's digital reader business.

Kevin Kelly, writing in *The New York Times Magazine*, believes the switch from analog to digital is good for the book medium. He thinks that as Google, the Library of Congress, the Chinese, and countless other entities and individuals gradually complete the process of turning all analog print books into digitalized versions, they will become more valuable as an intellectual resource. Readers will learn of unknown and once isolated works, discover connections between them, and share them with others. Regardless of the future of printed material, the proper use of typography is just as vital in the analog as the digital realms (Figure 7.57).

KEY TERMS FROM THIS CHAPTER

AIGA • Alloy • Analog • Banner • Blogs • Bronze Age • Calligraphy • Dark Ages • DIY • Engraving • Lithography • Maya • Olmec • Petroglyphs • Pictographs • Platen • Ptolemy V • Renaissance • Roman Empire • Sarcophagus • Scribe • Secularism • Serif • Slander • Stereotype plate • Stylus • Substrate • Type mold • Uruk, Iraq • Vellum • Web perfecting press • Zapf Dingbats • Zapotec

Figure 7.57
The cover of Visual Communication Images with Messages *as seen on an iPhone 7 with a Kindle app. The author took a screenshot, mailed the picture to himself, retrieved it from his mail server on his MacBook Pro, used Photoshop to crop the edges, and inserted it into position. Many think that in the future all printed material will be delivered and read entirely through digital rather than analog means.*
Courtesy of Paul Martin Lester

8 Graphic Design

Graphic design will save the world right after rock and roll does.

David Carson, 1955-
GRAPHIC DESIGNER, ART
DIRECTOR, & SURFER

Although you may not know it, your life is unavoidably connected to a Bronx-born graphic designer you might not have heard about, Saul Bass (Figure 8.1).

Figure 8.1
Saul Bass was the first designer to create a visual style that was used in an advertisement in conjunction with an opening title sequence for a movie—the poster for The Man with the Golden Arm.
Courtesy of Saul Bass

You see his pictures in your kitchen, on your television screen, on charities' stationery letterheads, on grocery store shelves, in magazines and newspapers, in gas stations, in movie theaters, atop corporate buildings, and on airplanes. Bass has designed packages for everyday food products and corporate trademarks for Fortune 500 companies. He has designed gasoline stations for major oil companies. He has made an Oscar-winning film and has produced the titles and ending credits for numerous well-known motion pictures. Unlike many other designers, Saul Bass was equally at home with print and screen media presentations.

Born in 1920 to immigrant parents in New York, Bass earned an early reputation for spending all his free time drawing whatever he saw and reading whatever he could find. He trained at the Art Students' League and Brooklyn College. At the age of 18, he worked as an apprentice in the art department of the New York office of Warner Bros. Studio. His job was to help create movie posters ("one sheets") used to promote motion picture releases. Movie posters in the late 1930s and 1940s tried to show as much of the content of a film as possible, considering the limited space. Large, miscellaneous typeface family lettering usually identified the movie's title. Close-up colorful paintings of the film's stars captured during an emotional moment usually were surrounded by smaller drawings of other scenes from the movie. These posters were important marketing pieces before the advent of television. They were used in newspaper advertisements and adorned the front of movie theaters to attract ticket buyers. Almost always they were graphically extravagant and appealed to emotions.

While Bass attended Brooklyn College, he was fortunate to have as an instructor one of the leaders of the bauhaus graphic art movement, György Kepes. One of the books that Bass read on his daily commute to work changed his life. It was *Language of Vision: Painting, Photography, Advertising-Design* by Kepes (Figure 8.2). The bauhaus art movement advocated focusing on essentials. For movie posters, the philosophy implied that instead of throwing in every possible significant scene in a movie, as in many previous and modern-day previews or trailers, a poster should feature a single idea or theme expressed in the film that would catch the imagination of potential customers. Bass decided to follow the bauhaus design philosophy for movie posters and title sequences and in all the other graphic work he produced.

In 1949 Bass moved to Los Angeles. He soon landed a job working for Howard Hughes and his movie studio, RKO. But Bass became frustrated when he realized that Hughes controlled every aspect of his company and allowed few ideas other than his own to be used. By 1955 he quit and formed his own design studio. His first employee, Elaine Makatura, later became his wife.

For the next 30 years, the team of Bass and Makatura, with their employees for their firm Bass/Yager & Associates, produced company logos, product packaging, and title sequences for many major motion pictures. His work inspired generations of graphic designers in print and for the screen.

CONTRIBUTIONS OF SAUL BASS TO GRAPHIC DESIGN

With such a stunningly diverse portfolio of work in all manner of media, Saul Bass is an able follower of Johannes Gutenberg and his commercial printing press.

Film Work Bass' early interest in motion pictures translated into print advertisements and opening title credits—he worked on several movies as a storyboard artist and director. He was responsible for one of the most memorable visual messages in the history of motion pictures—the "shower murder

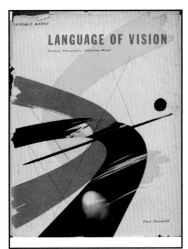

Figure 8.2
György Kepes was a Hungarian-born artist, educator, and theorist. While living in Berlin in 1930 he became involved in the bauhaus movement through his friend Laszlo Moholy-Nagy. In 1937 Moholy-Nagy and he moved to Chicago to teach at the New Bauhaus school. Kepes headed the study of light and color that he later used for his published works in which he explained his ideas on design theory. In 1943 he took a teaching position at Brooklyn College. One of his students was Saul Bass. After World War II, Kepes taught at the Massachusetts Institute of Technology (MIT) until he retired in 1974.
Courtesy of Paul Martin Lester

W LINK

Figure 8.3

*(Weblink: http://goo.gl/3SG4yu)
Storyboards, a cartoon version
of a motion picture or a complicated scene as the murder
of the Janet Leigh character in
Psycho, offer a clear path into
the mind of a filmmaker.*

W LINK

Figure 8.9

*(Weblink: http://goo.gl/Mj2fzQ)
The Art of the Title website is
one of the best locations to find
opening title credits for a variety of motion pictures including
the Saul Bass classic, Carmen
Jones.*

scene" with Janet Leigh and Anthony Perkins in the movie *Psycho* (1960). As a storyboard artist, Bass produced a kind of comic book version of the film that showed the characters within each scene of the movie. Although the famous director Alfred Hitchcock controlled the actual shooting of the scene, Bass's 48 drawings included such features as the torn shower curtain and the famous transition from the drain to a close-up of Leigh's eye (Figure 8.3).

Bass also produced short movies about the creative process. In 1968 he won an Academy Award in the short subjects category for his film about human creativity, *Why Man Creates.*

Packaging and Logos Bass designed the visual elements seen on such diverse products as Wesson oils, Lawry's season-ings, Northern towels, Kleenex tissues, and Ohio Blue Tip matches. In 1970, he redesigned the logo for the Quaker Oats Company to give it a more modern look (Figure 8.4). Before being acquired by Philip Morris, General Foods had Bass redesign its logo. The leaf pictograph within a thick, black, open-ended line symbolizes wholesomeness, growth,

strength, and dynamism (Figure 8.5). He has also designed logos for United Way, the YWCA, Continental Airlines, United Airlines, Warner Communica-tions, and Minolta (Figure 8.6). His logo for the Girl Scouts manages to convey a sense of diversity within the organiza-tion using only one color (Figure 8.7). When U.S. District Judge Harold Green ordered AT&T to break up into regional telephone companies in 1983, he also de-manded that the parent company change its "bell in a circle" logo (designed by Bass in 1969). He came up with a blue globe encircled by white lines varying in width that connotes a worldwide network that cares about its customers (Figure 8.8).

Advertisements, Posters, and Title Credits In 1954, Bass met famed film director Otto Preminger and designed a poster for his movie *Carmen Jones* (Fig-ure 8.9). Preminger liked it so much that he used it as part of the title sequence for the movie. Until that time, the titles for motion pictures rarely set the mood of a picture. Exceptions were epic dramas that showed a well-manicured hand turning the pages of a book that con-

Figure 8.4
The Quaker graphic reminds the consumer of the company's historic link to its oats breakfast cereal product, but also con-veys a modern, forward-looking message.
Courtesy of Saul Bass

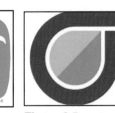

Figure 8.5
The round shape of the General Foods logo conveys wholesomeness and natural good-ness.
Courtesy of Saul Bass

Figure 8.6
Bass' United Airlines logo used long, curved lines that simulate flight.
Courtesy of Saul Bass

Figure 8.7
Bass employs an optical illusion technique to pres-ent three faces in his Girl Scouts logo.
Courtesy of Saul Bass

Figure 8.8
The AT&T logo created by Bass with its pulsating horizontal lines within a circular shape connotes the worldwide communication network of the telephone com-pany.
Courtesy of Saul Bass

tained the title and credits.

At first, Bass was nervous about designing for the motion picture medium. He once admitted that "I . . . found myself confronted with a flickering, moving, elusive series of images that somehow had to add up to communication." But the success of his work, as noted by historian Estelle Jussim, demonstrates "the ingenuity of a brilliant graphic designer conquering the difficulties of a new medium."

In 1955, Bass inspired the creative design of future movie titles with the opening sequence for the film *The Man with the Golden Arm* (Figure 8.10). Bass admits that he used the title sequence "to create a little atmosphere." The mood that Bass established in the animated sequence perfectly matched the storyline for the movie. In the film, Frank Sinatra plays a drug-addicted poker dealer. Backed by Elmer Bernstein's staccato jazz score, white bars with text moved across the screen in a tense, abstract dance, eventually forming a jagged pictographic arm that became the symbol of heroin addiction (Figure 8.11). In 1959, Bass again used jazz music, this time by Duke Ellington, to introduce another Preminger movie, *Anatomy of a Murder* (Figure 8.12).

Besides creating the title sequences, Bass also designed the advertising posters for the movies, using minimal pictographs that symbolically presented the essence of the plot. Theater owners were uncomfortable with the posters because they wanted traditional works with large, close-up images of the stars. But when director Otto Preminger threatened to pull the movie from theaters that didn't use the posters, the owners capitulated. The public had no objections to the new poster presentations and title sequences.

In 1960, Bass created the emotionally charged title sequence for the film *Exodus*, with raised arms holding a rifle in triumph. In a 1962 movie, *Walk on the Wild Side*, the opening sequence showed

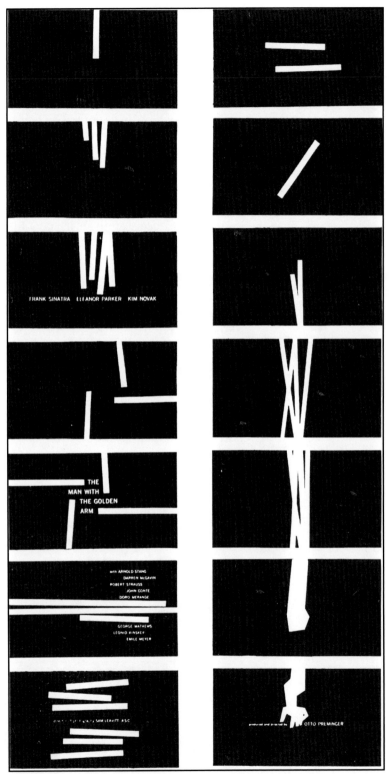

Figure 8.10
The opening sequence for The Man with the Golden Arm *conveys the desperation and confinement of drug addiction. As Bass explains, "The intent of this opening was to create a mood . . . spare, gaunt, with a driving intensity. The staccato movement of white bars against a black background creates a strident geometry that finally forms 'The Arm,' the symbol of the distorted, disjointed life of a drug addict."*
Courtesy of Saul Bass

Figure 8.11
(Weblink: http://goo.gl/7ZES5G)
In The Man with the Golden Arm, *Saul Bass combines his love for music with his skill at animation sequences.*

Figure 8.12
(Weblink: http://goo.gl/4ebSZ2)
Saul Bass was known for matching the onesheet print advertisement with the graphic choices of a movie's title sequence. His work in Anatomy of a Murder *is an excellent example of this agreement.*

Figure 8.13
(Weblink: http://goo.gl/PC1iw7)
If the Academy Awards offered an Oscar for Best Title Sequence, which they should, Saul Bass would win easily for his work in the opening of Casino. *Beginning with a live action sequence, the Robert DeNiro character is propelled into the fires of Hell that transform into the neon lights of Las Vegas.*

a catfight that was a metaphor for the street life of New Orleans portrayed in the motion picture. He also made the titles for the movies *Broadcast News* (1987), *War of the Roses* (in which the titles are supposedly in front of a red, satin sheet, which turns out to be Danny DeVito's handkerchief, 1989), Martin Scorsese's *Goodfellas* (1991), *Cape Fear* (1992), *The Age of Innocence* (1993), and his last, *Casino* (1995) (Figure 8.13).

Scorsese said of Bass that he "fashioned title sequences into an art, creating in some cases, like *Vertigo*, a mini-film within a film. His graphic compositions in movement function as a prologue to the movie—setting the tone, providing the mood and foreshadowing the action." For Bass "Titles can be sufficiently provocative and entertaining to induce the audience to sit down and look because something is really happening on screen." Bass inspired several generations of title designers for movies—Susan Bradley (*Monsters, Inc.*, 2001), Josh Comen (*Napoleon Dynamite*, 2004), and Kyle Cooper (*Se7en*, 1995) and television—Ellen and Lynda Kahn of TwinArt ("Arrested Development" and "The Ellen DeGeneres Show") and Digital Kitchen ("Six Feet Under," "True Blood," and "True Detective") (Figure 8.14).

GRAPHIC DESIGN AND THE SIX PERSPECTIVES

Graphic design is the art and craft of bringing organized structure to a group of diverse elements, both verbal and visual. Although graphic design is usually thought of as an art form for print, because of the spread of design applications to all the media, its meaning has expanded to include the use of words, pictures, and sounds in motion pictures, on television, and through computers.

Personal Perspective

Saul Bass once said, "Design is thinking made visual." The next time you look at a print page or view a screen presentation, take the time to note the various graphic elements within your field of view. As with typography, most people are unaware of the many decisions a graphic designer makes in order to communicate the literal message of the design and also to convey the emotional quality or mood of the piece. Selecting and placing all the word and image elements of a presentation is the task of the graphic designer.

Historical Perspective

William Addison Dwiggins first used the term *graphic design* in 1922. During his career he created more than 300 book

Figure 8.14
Lynda Kahn and her twin sister Ellen have designed opening title credits since 1987. In 2006 the team won an Emmy for the main title design and graphics package for "The Ellen DeGeneres Show." In this partial storyboard of the opening of the critically acclaimed yet canceled Fox television network's "Arrested Development," the quirky characters and plot lines are communicated through asymmetrical image placement, tilted text lines, colors, and arrows.
Courtesy of TwinArt

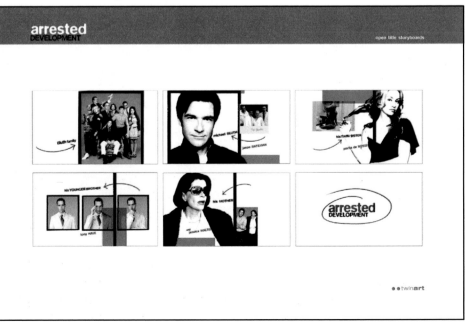

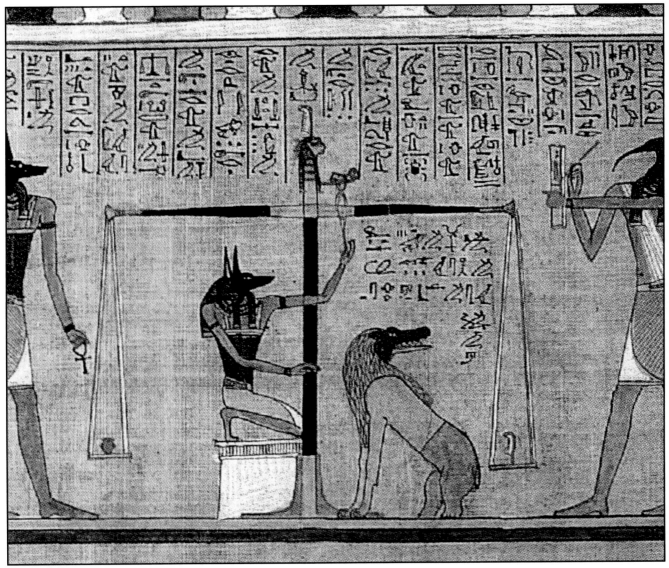

Figure 8.15
This scene from the Papyrus of Hunefer (c. 1275BCE), shows a typical Book of the Dead *theme. The heart of the scribe Hunefer is weighed on a scale against the feather of truth, by the jackal-headed Anubis on the left. The ibis-headed Thoth, scribe of the gods and on the right, records the result. If Hunefer's heart equals exactly the weight of the feather, Hunefer is allowed to pass into the afterlife. If not, he is eaten by an Ammit composed of a crocodile, a lion, and a hippopotamus.*
Courtesy of the British Museum

designs for the Alfred A. Knopf publishing company. Although the term may be relatively new, the practice is as old as recorded history. As with the history of typography, the history of graphic design may be divided into five eras: pre-Gutenberg, Gutenberg, industrial, artistic, and digital.

Pre-Gutenberg (before 1455) The Egyptians were the first culture to produce illustrated manuscripts and wall decorations that combined their writing system with illustrations. *The Books of the Dead* (2300–1200BCE) are excellent examples of illustrated scrolls that were commonly used for both exalted and less well known members of Egyptian society who could pay for the service (Figure 8.15).

Another important pre-Gutenberg development was the combination of nature and art by the Greeks. The founder of the Academy in Athens and one of the most important figures in Western philosophical thought, Plato, and the writer,

Figure 8.16
Natural forms inspired many of the letter and graphic design concepts invented by the Greeks. Note how the shell of a nautilus can be divided into eye-pleasing divisions or "golden sections."
Courtesy of Ole Skaug

Figure 8.17
Much of Greek architecture exhibited scroll-like spirals, called volutes, *that were inspired by the natural forms in the environment.*
Courtesy of Time-Freeze

architect, and engineer Marcus Vitruvius Pollio expressed a "dynamic symmetry" composed of natural shapes found in the world: the square, the triangle, and the circle. In architecture, typography, and graphic design, naturally occurring objects inspired Greek designers who were particularly drawn to the similar shapes found in the shell of a nautilus, pinecones, pineapple scales, daisies, and sunflowers (Figures 8.16 and 8.17).

Gutenberg (1456–1760) With the invention of the commercial printing press, less time was needed for the actual production of lettering by hand. Consequently, more care could be given to typography, illustrations, and graphic design. A publisher or art director for a book had assistants design pleasing typefaces, arrange the text in functional and aesthetically ways, draw elaborate cover, border, and whole-page illustrations, and put all these elements together in a unified format. In Germany, enlarged letters, colored borders, and wide alleys and margins were the common stylistic elements in books. In Italy and France, roman typefaces were commonly used to improve readability. Pages were illustrated with floral decorations or drawings related to the story (Figure 8.18).

Industrial (1761–1890) Steam-powered printing presses, mechanical typesetting machines, and a great need for advertising materials promoted the idea that graphic design's sole purpose was to attract the attention of potential customers through advertising. An important invention—lithography—expanded the range of graphic design by making easier the use of images with words. Before that invention, pictures could be included with their verbal counterparts in print material only through hand-drawn illustrations or crudely fabricated drawings in wood or metal.

Aloys Senefelder of Munich in 1800 patented the lithographic process,

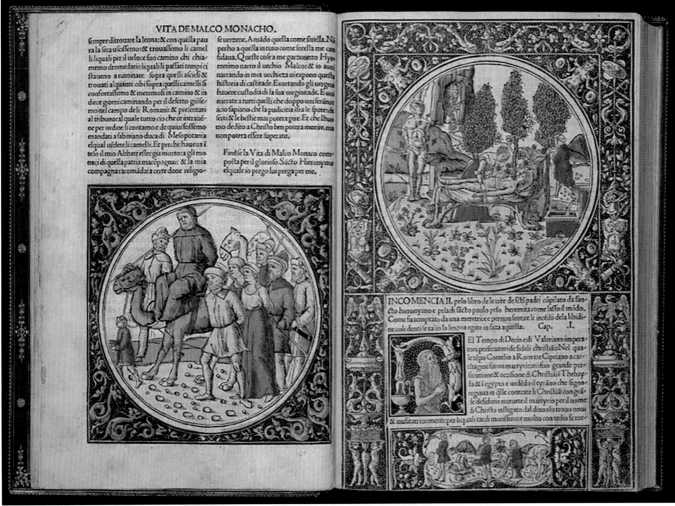

Figure 8.18
Typical of 16th Century books is this page from a Venetian work from 1501 that shows colored woodcuts and printed roman text. The image on the left depicts the capture and enslavement of Malchius by the Bedouins while the right side depicts a series of events from the life of Saint Paul the Hermit.
Courtesy of the Library of Congress

which is a printing method based on the principle that oil and water don't mix. The word lithography means "writing on stone" (from the Greek *lithos*, for "stone," and *grapho*, "to write"). In 1837, Godefroy Engelmann of France invented color lithography. Magazines soon began to exploit this new technology, combining words and images in a single press run (Figure 8.19). In 1857, one of the first illustrated magazines, *Harper's Weekly*, employed the first "visual artist," Thomas Nast. He was famous for his sketches of Civil War battles that were published on the cover of the magazine (Figure 8.20). Nast later became one of the most noted American cartoonists in history (See

Chapter 10).

In 1868, Richard Hoe made improvements to his steam-powered press so that color lithographs could be easily and economically reproduced in great numbers. From 1860 to 1900, lithography was used to place images on paper and tin containers for art reproductions, political posters, all kinds of novelty items used as souvenirs, and for greeting and business cards. Printed, colored cards became enormously popular gifts when the American printing firm of Currier & Ives distributed them in the middle of the 19th century. Nathaniel Currier and James Ives published more than 4,000 color drawings that pictured everyday

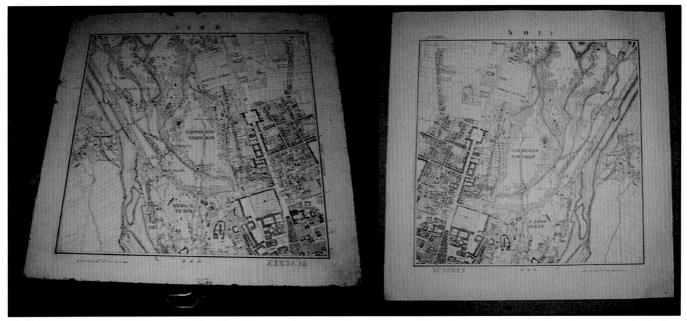

Figure 8.19
Invented by the German Aloys Senefelder in 1796, lithography became the main way in which text and artwork was printed on paper. The technique relies on the principle that water and oil don't mix. A lithographer makes a drawing with a greasy crayon on a smooth section of limestone. The stone is then coated with water. Because it is porous, the limestone soaks up the water. Oil-based ink is rolled on the stone, which attaches itself to the greasy drawing. After paper is pressed on the stone, the image is transferred. The two photographs show the negative lithography stone and the resulting positive print of an old map of Munich.
Courtesy of the Wikimedia Foundation

Figure 8.20
Before the use of the halftone printing process for photographs was introduced, engraving artists for newspapers and magazines often made images more dramatic through "artistic license." The horror of the dead soldiers and horses after a Civil War battle, is intensified because the image is a composite of a photograph taken by Timothy H. O'Sullivan and eyewitness accounts.
Courtesy of Harper's Weekly

Maj. Rathbone.   Miss Harris.   Mrs. Lincoln.   President.   Assassin.
THE ASSASSINATION OF PRESIDENT LINCOLN,
AT FORD'S THEATRE WASHINGTON. D.C. APRIL 14TH 1865.

Figure 8.21
After the assassination of President Lincoln by John Wilkes Booth in 1865, Currier & Ives, the largest printer of postcards in the United States at that time, commissioned an artist to make an engraving of the murder based on eyewitness reports and photographs of the participants. Despite the gruesome nature of the image, the cards were enormously popular.
Courtesy of the Library of Congress

and historic American events. These early postcards are valued collectors' items today. But until the invention of the halftone engraving process, printing high-quality photographs along with text on a press was still impossible (Figure 8.21).

American Stephen Horgan introduced the first crudely reproduced photograph using a printing press. On December 2, 1873, an advertisement in the New York *Daily Graphic* for Steinway Hall, a popular concert venue of the day, included what is considered to be the first printed photograph (Figure 8.22). Eighteen years later, the first color photographs were reproduced in a Paris magazine, *L'Illustration*, but the process

Figure 8.22
Although Stephen Horgan is credited with inventing an early form of halftone printing, the photograph of Steinway Hall was reproduced through a lithographic process and then transferred to an engraving plate for the printing press.
Courtesy of the *Daily Graphic*

was much too complicated and costly for widespread use. Frederic Ives of Philadelphia introduced a halftone screen composed of horizontal and vertical lines printed on a sheet of film in 1885. When a photoengraved plate was used with such a screen, the result was a much higher quality image than Horgan was able to reproduce. Two other Philadelphians, Max and Louis Levy, introduced a halftone plate in 1893 that reproduced even higher quality printed images. Advances in photoengraving and halftone techniques allowed the regular use of photographs in print media by World War I, which continues to this day.

Artistic (1891–1983) The artistic period merged graphic design art styles with various technological advances, including the halftone photographic screen process, color lithography, motion pictures, and television. This important period in the history of graphic design will be discussed in depth in the cultural perspective section.

Digital (1984–present) A machine that changed the face and practice of graphic design, whether for print or screen media—the computer—marks the digital era. The combination of small, inexpensive, easy-to-use computers and high-quality laser printers and networking innovations led to a proliferation in the use and presentation of words and images. For example, because of the computer, methods for working with and presenting photographs have radically changed. Halftone screens can now be simulated with computer programs that sidestep the entire photoengraving process. Furthermore, with the global distribution possible with the web, still and moving pictures can be taken with digital cameras or smartphones and uploaded to a server so that a worldwide audience can see the images minutes after they are taken.

Television news graphic artists have learned to organize complicated visual messages. They make bold presentations that combine the on-screen elements of announcer or reporter, moving video shot at a story scene, icons or logos, and textual information, all within the small television format. Web presentations for commercial, educational, and entertainment programs have introduced sound and user interactivity as design elements that graphic designers must also incorporate into their work.

Technical Perspective
Attempting to identify "good" graphic design is always dangerous because, like beauty, it is a highly subjective determination. What is considered good design changes over time and varies among cultures. Styles, as do fads, can capture immediate interest but become outdated just as quickly. But humans are rational and need to quantify all types of things, including what constitutes good graphic design. One method for determining good design is to be aware of the visual cues that the brain most readily responds to and the sensory and perceptual theories. Without question, some designs are noticed more than others are, some designs are remembered longer than others are, and some arrangements of words and images soothe while others cause nervous tension.

Out of that mix of sensory and perceptual elements, most graphic design experts have come up with four suggestions that lead to the concept of good design: contrast, balance, rhythm, and unity. Because good graphic design can follow or challenge them, they are called suggestions, not rules or principles. The discussion of the four suggestions that follows is in accordance with mainstream graphic design thought. A designer should always have a clear reason for using each one in a presentation. It's rare that a design is more important than the literal message it is supposed to communicate.

Contrast The design suggestion of contrast refers to differences in color, size, symbolism, time, and sound in print or screen designs. A lot of contrast among elements signifies a busy and youthful design. Little contrast usually indicates a no-nonsense and conservative approach. For screen media, little time between the showings of images indicates highly dynamic displays. A good design will usually use colors that complement each other slightly, rather than contrast with each other greatly. For example, a colored rule used to separate a headline from body copy should be close in hue to the dominant color in a photograph that accompanies the story. A design with colors that contrast with each other (e.g., yellow and blue) will create tension in the viewer. Of course, if that kind of an emotional reaction is desired, such a design strategy is warranted.

The size of the graphic elements should vary but be proportional to the overall frame of the design. Proportion, or scale, refers to the spatial relationship between design elements and the size of the page or frame. Sometimes a small element within a large frame has more visual impact than a large element that fills the frame (Figure 8.23). Designer and educator Mario García asserts that every design should have a "center of visual impact." A design should have one element that is emphasized, most often by its dominant size. That is the element the viewer notices first. For the most part, viewers prefer a design that presents the most important element in an obvious way because it minimizes the frustration that occurs when they must hunt for the significant elements.

Space is related to size because the scale of the elements determines how much space is available. Spaces among the various elements keep the eye from becoming fatigued. The front pages of most daily newspapers have little white space because they are filled with stories

and pictures. Space is sacrificed in order to fit as many important news stories as possible on a page. Inside each section the stories tend to be more feature oriented and thus allow the designer more freedom in using layouts with space separate from typographical space (kerning and leading). As a general rule, space should be present around the edges of a frame and not trapped in the center. A design with a lot of space is considered modern or classy, whereas a crowded design with little space is viewed as traditional and serious (Figure 8.24).

Designers of screen presentations also have to deal with decisions related to contrasting lengths of time and sounds. An element shown on the screen for a long time gains emphasis over one that flashes on the screen and quickly disappears. Transitions between various segments may be long slow fades or quick editing cuts. A long, fading transition from one scene to another has a romantic, restful connotation; quick cuts signify action and energy.

When designers work with screen presentations, sound becomes an important consideration. Sound refers to all the audio aspects involved with a presentation—music, narration, dialogue, and sound effects. Sometimes television commercials are slightly louder than the program in order to gain the attention of potential customers. The late Robert Altman, director of *M*A*S*H* (1970), *The Player* (1992), *A Prairie Home Companion* (2006) was known for his use of sound to make smooth transitions between scenes. Graphic designers who use computers have a wide variety of sound options for their educational and entertainment programs. Digital music and sound effects add drama, realism, and explanations to web presentations.

Balance This design suggestion refers to the placement of elements within a design's frame. A design is considered balanced if it equalizes the weight be-

Figure 8.23
(Weblink: http://goo.gl/UaKKE8)
The Volkswagen Beetle in this advertisement from the 1960s gets noticed because of its small size relative to the frame.

Figure 8.24
In this advertisement for Eastman Kodak's two-dollar Brownie camera (adjusted for inflation the price is $24) published in the New York Tribune *in 1921, the images are too similar in size and seem to be floating on the page rather than linked into a coherent whole. Plus, the eyes become trapped in the white space between the pictures.*
Courtesy of the Library of Congress

tween the *x* (horizontal) and *y* (vertical) axes. A single design element set in a square, rectangle, or circle midway along both axes results in a perfectly symmetric design. The frame, like the human face, may be divided into two similar parts. A balanced design is most appropriate for formal and classy presentations in which a traditional or conservative approach is desired. Like the square from which it comes, a symmetrical design is stable, but a bit dull. William Dwiggins once remarked, "Symmetry is static, that is to say, quiet; that is to say, inconspicuous." Stefan Lorant, picture editor for *Lilliput* and *Picture Post* magazines in the 1930s, used a symmetrical grid to showcase what he called "the third effect." Two photographs printed the same size and side-by-side created a new meaning in the mind of the reader that each photograph alone could not achieve (Figure 8.25). For example, because Lorant had escaped Nazi Germany, he expressed his criticism of the appeasement policy of the British government just before World War II when he ran a picture of Prime Minister Neville Chamberlain next to that of a braying llama (Figure 8.26). A contemporary version of the third effect can be found in Lawrence Weschler's beautifully illustrated book, *Everything that Rises*, in which he compares the similarities of such works as photographs of American Civil War Army engineers lounging at a campsite in 1861 to firefighters resting in a break room after 9/11.

Asymmetric designs are less formal and create dynamic tension within the frame by a visual tilt toward one element over another. This design approach is used to add interest to a dull collection of visual elements or to attract attention, particularly with younger viewers (Figure 8.27).

Rhythm The way design elements are combined to control movement of the viewer's eye from one element to another is called rhythm. Sequencing and simplicity help determine a viewer's path through a piece. Sequencing is the positioning of individual elements so that a viewer naturally views one and then another element in the order desired by the designer. Placing material on separate pages naturally sequences newspapers and magazines in print and for the web. Because motion pictures are a collection of moving, single frames, they are automatically sequenced as well. But within a single page or frame, elements can be positioned to lead the viewer through the design. A large, banner headline attracts a reader's attention, and the placement of a photograph and the story close to the headline provides a sequence for the three elements. A sequence also can be initiated within an image. The direction of a person's eyes or hands in a picture will cause the viewer's gaze to move toward that part of the frame. A designer should be sure that it makes sense for a viewer to look in that direction.

Simplicity is part of the rhythm of a design. A simple design—one that contains few elements—will attract little viewer eye movement. But a complex design with several units will create tension as the viewer's eye dances from one element to another. The front page of *The New York Herald* announcing the sinking of the luxury ocean liner *Titanic* is a classic example of a clash of design elements—a large three-row headline, the photo album display of portraits of the rich and famous passengers, and an artist's re-creation of what the ship might have looked like going down. The frenetic display matches the event (Figure 8.28). Contrast the front page with *The New York Times'* treatment of art and copy—a much more conservative and dignified graphic design approach. (Figure 8.29).

Unity This design suggestion is composed of related content as well as

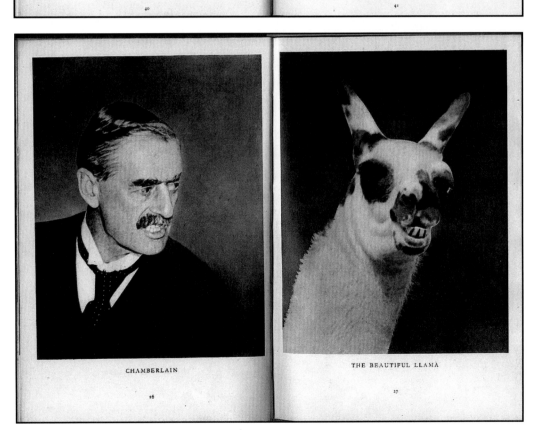

THE RIPE PEAR

40

THE JOLLY PUBLICAN
(But don't tell me the caption is wrong on this page)

41

Figure 8.25
As a regular feature of Lilliput *magazine that Stefan Lorant founded in 1937, he would usually juxtapose a popular politician with an animal for comedic or political intent. Lorant teaches a viewer something about visual communication—some faces can be compared with common objects. His "third effect" is evidence because the visual comparison between the two would not be possible without showing both photographs.*
Courtesy of Lilliput

CHAMBERLAIN

26

THE BEAUTIFUL LLAMA

27

Figure 8.26
As a German citizen briefly jailed after Adolph Hitler came to power, Stefan Lorant did not appreciate the "non-agression pact," known as the Munich Agreement, signed by Neville Chamberlain, the Prime Minister of Great Britain in 1938. Consequently, Lorant made a political "third effect" combination.
Courtesy of Lilliput

Figure 8.27
In this Works Progress Administration poster created by Christopher DeNoon, the symmetrical placement of the tagline attracts parents while the dynamic, asymmetrical location of the buildings and playground is meant to attract children to the Ohio housing unit.
Courtesy of the Library of Congress

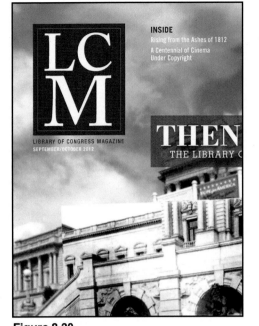

Figure 8.30
Any editorial staff for any publication, including the Library of Congress Magazine, *makes typographical and illustration choices that express the unique style of the publication. The conservative placement of the sparce elements on the cover is meant to reflect the editorial stance of the magazine.*
Courtesy of the Library of Congress

stylistic consistency. Elements within a design should all be similar in content, with words and pictorial elements fitting the same mood. For example, a bright color used as a background for a somber subject may not be appropriate. Stylistic consistency refers to a design concept in which multiple pages or frames of a piece appear to be unified. Graphic designers take great care in organizing typographical and pictorial elements so the pages form a unified look (Figure 8.30). *The New Yorker, Wired, USA Today*, and *The New York Times* all express different styles. For example, the table of contents page is radically different for *The New Yorker* as compared with that of *Wired* magazine. Traditional black type on a white background typifies *The New Yorker*'s conservative graphic style (even though the editorial content of the publication is considered liberal), while many colors and images fill the *Wired* display.

Contrast, balance, rhythm, and unity

are guidelines for designers to either follow or challenge. When used traditionally, they are design considerations that can result in clear, noticeable, pleasing, and useful visual messages. But when the rules are bent or broken, exciting results can happen. Remember that good design is audience dependent—what works in one context may be confusing or silly in another.

Ethical Perspective
A graphic designer must balance three conflicting approaches—utilitarianism, hedonism, and the golden mean. The philosophy of utilitarianism stresses the educational benefits of a publication. In the context of graphic design, it means that a design should be readable, legible, and useful. Concentrating on the hedonism philosophy may lead to designs that attract attention only for the purpose of satisfying commercial interests, shocking viewers, or expressing a personal statement. As Saul Bass said, "Sometimes we design for our peers and not to solve communications problems." Between those two extremes is the golden mean approach, which advocates design decisions based on a "middle way" between the two extreme display styles. To achieve Aristotle's golden mean philosophy, then, the designer must reach a difficult compromise by juggling the purpose of the piece, the need for it to be noticed, the idea that it should be pleasing to look at, and the desire to create a unique style. But because innovation seldom comes from designers who follow this compromising approach, being sensitive to conflicting ethical philosophies is one of the reasons that the field of graphic design is challenging and rewarding.

Other Issues of Concern
Graphic designers and all other visual communicators also must be sensitive to other ethical considerations besides stereotypes discussed in Chapter 5:

Figure 8.28
The New York Herald*'s front page is a cacophonous collection of a large headline, a sensational artist's drawing of the sinking ocean liner, and the portraits of the rich and famous within variously shaped borders that are scattered haphazardly as pictures in a family photo album. All of these elements contribute to a chaotic rhythm that adds dramatic interest to one of the most important stories of the century.*
Courtesy of the Library of Congress

Figure 8.29
The New York Times*' front page of the sinking of the Titanic is a more subdued and traditional combination of words and pictures than the* New York Herald*'s display. The front page contains only two photographs and a careful alignment of text modules. The difference between the two can be ascribed to the fact that the two newspapers had two different constituents that they attempted to please.*
Courtesy of the Library of Congress

Product promotions, appropriation, and editorial decisions.

Product Promotions Because the combination of text, graphic elements, and images forms a powerful communications link, a print or screen media message can easily persuade a viewer by its content. A graphic designer's choices can reinforce stereotypes in the media that can leave lasting impressions. Many products that are sold legally to consumers are harmful if used regularly and over a long period of time. Cigarettes, alcohol, and other drugs certainly fall in that category. The production and use of

some products harms the environment. Every graphic designer must decide whether to work for a company that sells such products to consumers. There is a growing trend among graphic designers to pay attention to this issue when selecting clients. For example, Saul Bass and his associates made a conscious effort not to work for companies that make harmful products.

Appropriation The concept of fair representation involves giving credit for a design when credit is due. Most graphic designers are not geniuses suddenly inspired to produce a completely new style

Figure 8.31
Shepard Fairey's "Obey" sticker is attached to an electrical box on a college campus. The image comes from a likeness of the seven-foot, 500-pound wrestler and actor, André René Roussimoff, better known as André the Giant.
Courtesy of Paul Martin Lester

W
LINK

Figure 8.32
(Weblink: http://goo.gl/Sz85S6)
"Obama 'Hope' Portrait" by Shepard Fairey.

of design. Many ideas are appropriations of previously created compositions, but with an artist's unique style added to create a new piece. South Carolinian graphic designer and so-called "street artist" Shepard Fairey borrows from popular culture images and phrases for his reconstituted art. His "Obey" campaign that became a meme came from slogans on billboards from John Carpenter's *They Live* (1988), and his graphic version of "The Medium is the Message" is a famous phrase attributed to the Ca-

nadian media critic Marshall McLuhan (Figure 8.31).

In 2008, Fairey received additional notoriety after he made a poster that featured a head-and-shoulders portrait of Barack Obama over the word "HOPE" from a photograph taken by Associated Press (AP) photographer Manny Garcia in 2004. Garcia believed he should have been compensated for the work, whereas Fairey argued that the appropriation is a form of "fair use." Although Fairey and the AP settled out of court, in 2012 the illustrator pleaded guilty in a New York court to one count of criminal contempt as he destroyed and manufactured evidence in the case. Nevertheless, the U.S. National Portrait Gallery acquired the poster in 2009 for its permanent collection (Figure 8.32).

A graphic designer who reproduces wholesale someone else's work without credit or compensation is acting unethically and courting legal problems. Designers should be inspired by other work, but not copy it exactly. Because Fairey's changes in colors and textures of the original photograph greatly alter the image, he is within the parameters of ethical behavior. In a competition organized by the London Design Museum, Fairey's poster with "PROGRESS" under the image won the design of the year award. In 2011 Fairey substituted a Guy Fawkes mask for President Obama's face to honor the Occupy Wall Street movement.

Editorial Decisions Graphic designers sometimes need to make difficult image selection and placement choices when a news event has more than one storyline. The Elián González story, the young boy rescued off the coast of Florida in 1999 and later involved in a highly public custody battle between U.S. and Cuban relatives, is a good example. After several months of highly public but unsuccessful negotiations, in the early morning of April 22, 2000, a

SWAT team of federal agents came into the house where Elián was staying. A Pulitzer Prize–winning photograph by Alan Diaz shows a SWAT team member with a submachine gun about to take the screaming child (Figure 8.33). He was shortly returned to his father. Editors had a difficult choice—emphasize the taking of Elián in a large photograph, as on the cover of *Newsweek* magazine; feature his reunion with his father, as on the *Time* cover; or try to balance the two storylines with images about the same size side-by-side, as on the *Washington Post* front page. Whichever choice is made, an editor should make a decision after a reasoned discussion with fellow journalists and not for sensational, economic, or political considerations.

Cultural Perspective

Most of the trends in graphic design initially began as styles for political and advertising posters that were nailed to walls in cities with large numbers of pedestrians. After a time, other designers and mainstream media outlets adopted the technique. Nine of the art movements discussed here have had the most influence on graphic design. They may be divided into two main groups: free form and grid. Leading proponents of both groups have expressed not only aesthetic foundations for their art but political intent as well. These and other art movements used words and pictures in equally respectful ways and saved design from the "car wreck" styles of the industrial era.

The free form artistic styles of art nouveau, dada, art deco, pop art, punk, new wave, and hip-hop are noted for their free-flowing placement of text and other graphic elements within a design's frame. In many of their graphic messages, designers communicated angry rebellion and frustration over political and social structures that allowed world wars and injustice to flourish. They hoped that calling attention to obvious hypoc-

risies of society would prompt people to act to change such conditions. Other designers, however, created works that were meant to be commercially successful.

The grid artistic approach, exemplified by the de stijl and bauhaus styles, was less obvious in its political message. The grid styles attempted to give objective, unemotional organization to graphic design. Designers developed a geometric approach based on horizontal, diagonal, and vertical lines and the basic forms of squares, rectangles, and circles, and usually combined the use of the colors red, yellow, and blue with black, gray, and white. They carefully placed each design element within a frame to ensure unity in the gestalt tradition—individual elements are not as important as the whole design.

Free form and grid approaches are not limited to print design. It is important to consider how these two approaches also apply to television and film messages. An example of the free form approach for moving images is seen in the opening title sequences of a television series as HBO's "True Blood" in which the camera constantly moves through a set or location as if it were a character itself (sometimes referred to as a "single-camera" technique). Conversely, almost any situation comedy with characters in a tightly controlled and choreographed theater set (e.g., CBS's "The Big Bang Theory" and FOX's "New Girl") in which a director uses one to four cameras and quickly cuts between actors in a scene (sometimes called a "multicamera" style) is an example of the grid approach (Figure 8.34).

Free Form Approaches

Graphic designs that use the free form approach exhibit an organic, flowing style noticed by the use of lines, colors, and typography.

Art Nouveau Modern graphic design was saved from the crass commercialism

W LINK
Figure 8.33
(Weblink: http://goo.gl/aoRgrU) Photojournalist Alan Diaz worked hard to gain Elián González's Miami family's trust. The result was a Pulitzer Prize winning news photograph of a government official taking the boy from the home to be reunited with his father.

W LINK
Figure 8.34
(Weblink: http://goo.gl/dwgySB) Most situation comedy television shows use a multicamera style with actors and camera movements carefully choreographed by a director who employs a grid approach as with NBC's classic sitcom "Seinfeld."

of the Industrial Era designs with the introduction of the art nouveau (or "new art") style around 1890. Art nouveau was the first commercial art style intended to make products and their advertisements more beautiful. Art nouveau was highly influenced by traditional Asian vases, paintings, and screens, particularly from Japan and Korea (Figure 8.35). Borders were marked by stylized, plantlike vines, and typography mimicked the flowing curves of the graphic elements. At first, critics severely criticized art nouveau, using such phrases as "linear hysteria," "strange decorative disease," and "stylistic free-for-all" to describe the art style. Eventually, however, the movement gained credibility after Henri Marie Raymond de Toulouse-Lautrec-Monfa gained popularity for his posters for var-

ious performances (Figure 8.36). A child of two first cousins, Toulouse-Lautrec suffered from a number of health problems. As a teenager he broke his right and then his left leg, which failed to heal properly. As a consequence, he grew to be only five feet tall, was unable to walk easily, but threw himself into creating artwork. He died at the age of 36 in 1901 as a result of alcoholism and syphilis. In 2005 one of his early paintings was sold for $22.4 million.

Although much more popular in Europe, the movement was best demonstrated in the United States on the covers of *Harper's Monthly*. Artists such as Maxfield Parrish and Will Bradley produced graphic designs for advertisements in the mid-1890s that were so praised for their beauty that they soon became collectors' items. Besides cover and poster work, Parrish was also known for his dreamy landscapes filled with golden nymph-like characters (Figure 8.37). Bradley started as an errand boy and apprentice to a printer in Chicago and went on to become art director for the literary journal *The Chap-Book*, where he worked with other art nouveau artists such as Toulouse-Lautrec and Aubrey Beardsley, the controversial British illustrator known for his erotic drawings (Figure 8.38). Bradley also created his own striking covers for the publication (Figure 8.39). He later became art director for *Collier's* magazine and in the 1920s he supervised all the graphic production for William Randolph Hearst's newspapers, magazines, and motion pictures.

The art nouveau movement inspired other designers to link artistry with functionalism for the first time since Gutenberg's time. It was a revolutionary art movement because it rejected the Victorian traditions of commercial excesses and a machine mentality.

Dada In 1916 Europe was preoccupied with the horrors of World War I. Dada emerged as a critical examination of the social structures that allowed such an event to occur. It expressed artists' rage with political leaders by the use of absurd, asymmetric designs. Writings and graphics were intended to confuse, educate, and gain attention. One of the founders of the movement, Romanian-born poet Tristan Tzara, said simply, "Dada means nothing." The name supposedly came out of a meeting of

Figure 8.37
"Princess Parizade Bringing Home the Singing Tree" from the book, Arabian Nights *published in 1906. Maxfield Parrish was clearly influenced by art nouveau as evident in the flowing lines of the work. The son of an engraver and painter, Parrish was encouraged to create art at an early age. After earning a degree in fine arts from the Pennsylvania Academy, he found work illustrating books and magazine covers and producing illustrations for various advertisements. Parrish eventually developed a unique style of artistic expression using luminous colors in thick layers that produced a three-dimensional quality with dramatic use of lighting for his often fantastical subject matter.*
Courtesy of the Pennsylvania Academy of the Fine Arts

Figure 8.38

"Jokanaan and Salomé" by Aubrey Beardsley for Oscar Wilde's play Salomé,
published in 1893. Born to middle-class parents in Brighton, England, Aubrey
Beardsley had to quit school at the age of 16 to work as a clerk for an insurance
company. Encouraged by the British painter Edward Burne-Jones, Beardsley
attended art classes and became an illustrator. The gracefully flowing lines
and high contrast drawing style of his pen and ink artwork helped define and
promote the art nouveau movement. His illustrations for magazines and plays
were often controversial for their exaggerated erotic features. His career was
cut short due to his early death at the age of 25 from tuberculosis.
Courtesy of Dmitry Rozhkov

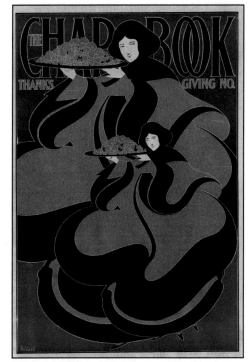

Figure 8.39

"Cover for The Chap-Book," 1895, by Will
Bradley. Nicknamed the "Dean of American Designers," Will Bradley has also been
called the "American Aubrey Beardsley" for
his similar flowing style that helped define
the U.S. art nouveau movement. Born in
Boston, he became a printer at an early age
and eventually an illustrator most famous for
his poster work after he moved to Chicago.
At one point it was said he was the highest
paid graphic designer in the early 20th century. In this Thanksgiving cover, his distinct
style is evident as twin women beckon the
reader with trays of food.
Courtesy of the Library of Congress

poets, painters, and graphic designers at the Cabaret Voltaire in Zurich, Switzerland, in 1916. The German refugee and poet Hugo Ball sponsored the social gathering. Opening a French dictionary at random, one of the members quickly pointed to the word for a child's hobbyhorse: *dada*. Its practitioners viewed harmony and symmetry as stifling. For the dada artists, graphic design elements reflected the way modern life actually was lived—quickly paced and tense. It was hoped that by using such designs they could communicate criticism of the many hypocrisies they perceived during and after the "War to End All Wars." Politicians and wealthy individuals were particular targets of dada publications.

Dada graphic designs consisted of typography of different sizes and styles randomly distributed on a page (Figure 8.40). At first glance, such designs are extremely difficult to read. However, Marshall McLuhan argued that dada showed a way to escape the confines of the Western tradition of reading from left to right in tightly controlled rows as the only way to present verbal messages. He preferred the "words in liberty" demonstrated by dada artists. Dada later went on to inspire artists such as "Walt Whitman, Allen Ginsberg, yippies, hippies, and punks."

Painters, graphic designers, filmmakers, and cartoonists experimented with nontraditional image-making. Painters Jean Arp, Max Ernst, and Marcel Duchamp, famous for his *Nude Descending a Staircase, No. 2* (1912) and *Bicycle Wheel* (1913), stretched the boundaries of acceptable fine art. Graphic designers introduced montage or composite techniques in which they cut out and arranged pieces of pictures on a page. In film, this innovation was demonstrated by Sergei Eisenstein's classic 1925 film *Battleship Potemkin*, in which more than one image was presented on the screen. Director Abel Gance went farther two years later with his 5½ hours silent

Figure 8.40
"Kleine Dada Soirée," 1922 by Theo van Doesburg and Kurt Schwitters. Although he would later be named the founder of the de stijl art movement, Theo van Doesburg also was an unconventional Dadaist. In 1931 he moved to Switzerland to hopefully improve his failing health, but he died that year of a heart attack. Born in Hanover, Germany, Kurt Schwitters was fearless in experimenting with all kinds of artistic expressions that included the styles of dada, constructivism, and surrealism and the media of painting, graphic design, typography, sculpture, and music. Although never officially a member of the dada art group, he nevertheless incorporated its free spirit to his work. For nine years starting in 1923 he published the influential art journal Merz. *One issue was edited and typeset by El Lissitzky. Barely escaping the Nazis, Schwitters fled to Norway and then England, where he remained until his death in 1948. This mish-mash of text, overlapping torn and pasted poster parts, and colors by Schwitters is a classic dada art expression of the time. It is no wonder that the American collage artist Robert Rauschenberg counts Schwitters as one of his influences.*
Courtesy of the Centraal Museum, Utrecht, The Netherlands

masterpiece *Napoleon*. The film required three projectors that showed different images at the same time. Consequently, it was a financial disaster because no theater could show it. In 2012 a restored version was screened at Oakland's Paramount Theatre.

In 1970, an engineer for General Dynamics, Sidney Laverents, made a humorous film called *Multiple SIDosis* with a 16-millimeter film camera and a two-

W
LINK
Figure 8.41
(Weblink: http://goo.gl/Wb1f7g)
The quirky indie film, Multiple
SIDosis *by Sidney Laverents*
is not for every taste, but the
early use of multiple image
tracks should be appreciated
for its historical value.

track, reel-to-reel tape recorder, which featured multiple images of him playing various instruments on the screen at the same time. The short film was selected for the prestigious National Film Registry collection (Figure 8.41). Finally, American George Herriman's comic strip "Krazy Kat," which ran in William Randolph Hearst's newspapers from 1913 to 1944, featured the tribulations of Krazy Kat, who was in love with a mouse named Ignatz, who in turn couldn't stand him and threw bricks at his head. Herriman's dada-like strip probably inspired the rule-breaking, adult-themed line of cartoonists that includes Friz Freleng of Looney Tunes and Matt Groening of "The Simpsons," as opposed to the "family values" cartoons from the Walt Disney Studios (See Chapter 10).

Art Deco Called "the last of the total styles," art deco united buildings, objects, fashions, and typographical and graphic designs by its stylish and distinctive look. Art deco (called *art moderne* in Europe) takes its name from a 1925 exhibition in Paris titled *Exposition Internationale des Arts Décoratifs et Industriels Modernes*, which covered both banks of the Seine River.

The distinctive art deco style was noted for its streamlined shapes and curved sans serif typographical lettering that presented a modern graphic look. Advertisers at first didn't like the style because the conservative nature of U.S. design at the time favored function over form. Critics viewed art deco as anti-utilitarian. Nevertheless, *Harper's Bazaar* signed one of the most famous art deco artists, Erté, to a ten-year contract to make erotically styled drawings for its covers (Figure 8.42). Today his posters are valuable collectors' items. As the public embraced the style, advertisers started using art deco designs. Use of the style spread to department stores, corporate headquarters, and even automated vending machines. The Chrysler

Building in New York City is a classic example of art deco architecture, as are the multicolored hotels and apartment buildings on Miami Beach (Figure 8.43).

Pop Art The pop art movement combined the organic vines of art nouveau designs and the rebellious philosophy of dada. Pop art gets its name from a group of London artists and designers who met in the mid-1950s. *Pop*, short for "popular," was the label given to objects—from sensational movie posters to the tail fins of Detroit automobiles—that were viewed as unworthy of serious artistic attention and yet were a part of a society's popular culture.

The style was connected with alternative lifestyles and rebellion against authority demonstrated by the "beatnik" culture. The poem *Howl* by Ginsberg, the novel *On the Road* by Jack Kerouac, the peace sign designed by Gerald Holtom in 1956 as a nuclear disarmament symbol, and the photographs published in Robert Frank's *The Americans* (1956) were verbal and visual examples of artists questioning traditional cultural values. In 2009 an expanded edition of the Swiss photographer's portrait of America was published with an accompanying exhibit at the National Gallery of Art in Washington, D.C.

In the 1960s, pop art combined grassroots political movements concerned with civil rights and anti–Vietnam War opinions with the "hippie" culture, centered on the corner of Haight and Ashbury streets in San Francisco. Posters that advertised rock concerts and political rallies displayed psychedelic art that tried to represent the visual sensations people experienced after taking a hallucinogenic drug. Intensely contrasting colors in vinelike forms with hand-drawn lettering in the same style were visually arresting but hard to read for a viewer who was not part of the culture. Consequently, the designs were a symbolized code that relayed factual

Figure 8.42

The French art deco master Erté poses with a model and examples of his graphic design work. Romain de Tirtoff was born in St. Petersburg, Russia, to a wealthy and influential family in 1892. He moved to Paris to become a graphic designer when he was 18 years old. To avoid embarrassing his family, he took up the pseudonym of Erté, the pronunciation of his initials, R.T. He worked regularly for Harper's Bazaar *magazine as an illustrator. He also created costumes and set designs for the famous Parisian dance hall Folies Bergère (the site of the famous Manet painting from Chapter 1).*

Courtesy of Paul Martin Lester

Figure 8.43

With its sleek lines, curved shapes, and sans serif name, the Chrysler Building in New York City is an example of the art deco graphic design movement as an architectural expression. The American architect William Van Alen designed the building that is considered one of the most beloved by residents and tourists.

Courtesy of Paul Martin Lester

information but also served to link those within the culture. Artist Peter Max brought pop art into the mainstream with his colorful posters, as did New York artist Andy Warhol, who used innovative printing techniques on common American icons (e.g., Campbell's soup cans and Marilyn Monroe) to create strikingly visual works of art (Figure 8.44). By the early 1970s, pop art had reached its peak, but not before influencing fast food restaurants, comic books, and supermarket product packaging. San Francisco Bay area artist Jason Munn, a graphic designer who works in the pop art style, was inspired by the movie posters of Saul Bass. Using images of everyday objects such as paint buckets, bicycle wheels, and 45-rpm records, Munn has created concert posters for the bands Why?, Built to Spill, the Decembrists, and the musician Beck (Figure 8.45).

Figure 8.44

(Weblink: http://goo.gl/c7hVKh) Campbell's Soup Cans. 1962. Synthetic polymer paint on thirty-two canvases. Andy Warhol. According to popular reports, the author Muriel Latow suggested Warhol paint something he sees every day like a can of Campbell's soup. The key to understanding popular culture as a movement is that the artist elevates the ordinary to a level of high aesthetic value.

Figure 8.45

"Record Release for Why?," 2008, by Jason Munn. Jason Munn's clever use of the gestalt law of continuation creates a dynamic visual pun for the indie band Why? His use of vinyl record parts is also a trademark of pop culture artists—showing viewers new ways to think of ordinary objects. Munn, originally from Wisconsin, lives outside San Francisco. He started The Small Stakes studio in 2003, which produces book covers, album packaging, T-shirt designs, screen-printed posters, and illustrations. His work has appeared in Print, Communication Arts, and Creative Review. His posters are also part of the permanent collection at the San Francisco Museum of Modern Art.

Courtesy of Jason Munn

Figure 8.46

"Upcoming Genocide, El Monte, California," 2005, by Kevin McCarty. With roots in the rule-breaking and angry artists of the dada movement, punk can be an anti-establishment expression through music, artwork, and fashion. And yet, photographer and educator Kevin McCarty captures the dual personalities of a young punk advocate with his shaved head, heavily gelled, bird-like hair style, and leather jacket that is in contrast with his soft facial features, curious expression, and a framed studio portrait in the background of the treasurer of an Elks Lodge, the site of a punk music show.

Courtesy of Kevin McCarty

Punk In the late 1970s, a new form of graphic design, initially called neo-dada and then punk, emerged. Creators of punk placed typographical and other visual elements on pages in angry, rebellious, and random ways in the style of "ransom note" cutouts. In that way, punk was greatly influenced by the earlier dada movement. Underground comic books and zines as well as music and fashion styles were the first outlets for this art form (Figure 8.46). Punk artists were critical of the lavish spending habits of the wealthy, as were their dada predecessors.

New Wave Punk, as with other art movements, quickly became absorbed into mainstream culture. Cartoonist Gary Panter decried the transition into respectability when he said, "Punk was an honest expression, while new wave is a packaging term." New wave, founded by the Swiss Wolfgang Weingart and American April Greiman, was highly influenced by the ease of typographical and visual manipulations made possible by computer technology. It was connected with a youthful culture that viewed all new technology as exciting. The colorful cutout titles that Tiber Kalman and Alexander Isley made for the movie *Something Wild* (1986) were examples of new wave that have been critically praised (Figure 8.47). The design was also influenced by the music and the fashions of such bands as Depeche Mode, Devo, and the Pet Shop Boys.

Hip-hop Started as a fashion, graphic design, graffiti art, and dance accompaniment to rap music in the 1970s, hip-hop eventually gained mainstream attention (Figure 8.48). The quick editing of visual messages to the beat of pulsating rhythms is combined with pictographic images on walls, clothing, and within the pages of such magazines as *Blaze and Vibe* until they quit publication, *Blaze* in 2000 and *Vibe* in 2009. Musically, hip-hop diversified to include various forms of rap (alternative, gangsta, jazz, and Southern). The high mark of hip-hop was 2004, when OutKast's album *Speakerboxxx/The Love Below* won Best Album of the Year at the Grammy Awards, and the movie *You Got Served* about a dance contest was a surprise hip-hop hit. Since then, however, albums by hip-hop artists have declined in sales.

Grid Approaches
The idea of a grid came from graphic designers who wanted to create organized and efficient presentations— whether for print or for architecture. The approach is represented by two art movements—de stijl and bauhaus.

De Stijl In the summer of 1917 several Dutch painters, including Theo van Doesburg and Piet Mondrian, perceived the use of a grid as a way to search for universal harmony in the wake of World War I (Figure 8.49). Unlike dada artists, de stijl designers believed that an unemotional use of lines, common shapes, and the colors of red, yellow, and blue would usher in a new utopian spirit of cooperation among the people of the world. De stijl, translated as *the style*, introduced contemporary graphic designers to the grid format through a journal of the same name.

Figure 8.47
(Weblink: http://goo.gl/0qMa2W) Although there certainly are wild moments in the movie Something Wild, *the new wave graphic style of the opening title credits by Tiber Kalman and Alexander Isley assures a viewer that the events all work out in the end.*

Figure 8.48
As with other graphic design and art movements, hip-hop is evidenced in music, fashion, typography, and spontaneous forms of expression. A hip-hop artist communicates the exuberance of the art form with multi-colored, spray-painted bold, sans serif-based miscellaneous typeface family letters and cartoon characters.
Courtesy of Chico Iwana

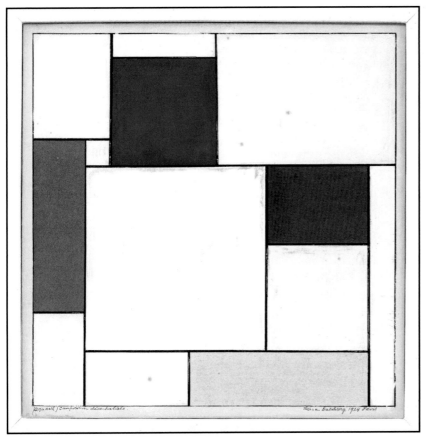

Figure 8.49
"Composition Décentralisée, 1924" by Theo van Doesburg. Born Christian Emil Marie Küpper, he took the surname of his stepfather after he started to paint professionally. After seeing Piet Mondrian's work, van Doesburg contacted him and the two helped found the de stijl movement. As with many duos in the history of visual communications, Mondrian was the shy creator of original work and van Doesburg, although a respected painter, was more outgoing and did much to promote de stijl.
Courtesy of the Solomon R. Guggenheim Museum

Like Mondrian, Doesburg composed abstract paintings of thick black horizontal and vertical lines that divided his canvases into basic shapes, which he filled in with colors. His artwork inspired graphic designers to use the same system with text and images.

Architect and designer Le Corbusier made an important contribution to the use of the grid in architecture with his 1948 book *Modulor* and the design system of the same name. Le Corbusier was a pseudonym, taken from the name of a maternal relative, of Swiss-born Charles-Édouard Jeanneret. By the 1960s modular design, named after Le Corbusier's book, became the dominant force in modernizing the front pages of news-

papers around the world. In modular design, text and images for each story are placed within rectangular shapes called *modules.* A newspaper redesigned modularly has more of a horizontal than vertical orientation and is meant to remind readers and potential customers that its stories and pictures are as easy to read as those found on television.

In his 1981 book *Contemporary Newspaper Design* and workshops at newspapers around the world, Mario García spread the modular design approach. When the national newspaper *USA Today* was introduced in September 1982, its design was heavily influenced by the philosophies of García and other modular advocates (Figure 8.50).

Bauhaus In 1919, architect Walter Gropius headed a design workshop and think tank in Weimar, Germany, called the *Das Staatliches Bauhaus.* Bauhaus comes from the German words *bauen,* "to build," and *haus,* "house." Bauhaus was originally intended as an architectural school; the grid-like look of skyscrapers with their individual cubicles for similarly dressed office workers comes from bauhaus architectural design (Figure 8.51). The design style quickly embraced the de stijl concept of creating harmony in the world by unifying art and technology. Bauhaus is characterized by its emphasis on useful, simple, and clearly defined forms. Abstract painter Paul Klee, designer and photographer Laszlo Moholy-Nagy, and his assistant, designer Gyorgy Kepes, who is the author of ten books including *The Language of Vision* (1944) and *Sign, Image, Symbol* (1966), which inspired the work of Saul Bass, were important bauhaus designers and educators.

Critical Perspective
What is considered "good" graphic design almost always depends on the audience. As with different generations that often do not appreciate the musical

Figure 8.51
From 1925 until 1932, the bauhaus school, founded by Walter Gropius, was located in Dessau, Germany, shown here. During part of that time, the famed German architect Ludwig Mies van der Rohe, also known for his catchphrases "Less is more" and "God is in the details," was its director. Although typography and graphic design were taught at the school, bauhaus is recognized more as an architectural movement. With typography by Herbert Bayer, the entrance to the workshop block at the school is a study in a soothing symmetrical grid of similarly sized window panes.
Courtesy of Jim Hood

Figure 8.50
As a demonstration of modular design that was influenced by the grids of de stijl artists, this mock newspaper contains four discrete rectangular modules, two with and two without a photograph. The visual effect is a more horizontal and modern-looking layout than early 20th century newspaper front pages.
Courtesy of Paul Martin Lester

tastes of younger or older generations, design sensibilities are shaped by the values expressed from other cultures. Designer Milton Glaser is concerned about the prevalence of poorly designed websites. He observes, "There's a whole mess of very ugly things on the web. And to some extent that's because technicians are doing the design." Web design has been greatly improved by designers who appreciate the constraints of grid construction in the organized alignment of words, pictures, links, and navigational elements on a page.

Graphic design education is a key in using computer technology to produce work that is functional and aesthetically pleasing. But because the dominant, product-oriented culture in the United States relies on television and other screen media for educational and entertainment purposes, marketers, not artists or their fans make many of the decisions

that determine whether a graphic design style remains popular. As more and more persons are educated about good design, computer technology, which allows everyone to produce works that are sensitive to graphic design issues, may take style decisions out of the hands of the commercial interests. If not, graphic design may revert to the consumerism popular during the Industrial era.

TRENDS TO WATCH FOR GRAPHIC DESIGN

Computer programs make it possible for every individual to create a graphic design for any purpose. Whether the style is free form, grid, or a totally new kind of graphic innovation, a person's selection and placement of pictorial elements within a frame will express that individual's personality. With the computer, television, and telephone merging into the same machine through smartphones

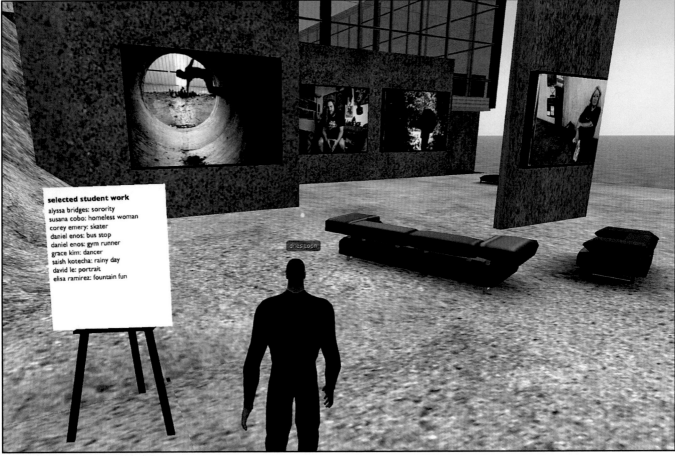

selected student work
alyssa bridges: sorority
susana cobo: homeless woman
corey emery: skater
daniel enos: bus stop
daniel enos: gym runner
grace kim: dancer
saish kotecha: rainy day
david le: portrait
elisa ramirez: fountain fun

dries loon

Figure 8.52
A Second Life avatar stands before a gallery that shows photographs from students of a visual reporting class.
Courtesy of Paul Martin Lester

and digital television sets, sophisticated home design studios are linked to other workshops throughout the world producing programs and applications for these innovative communicative devices.

Virtual reality presentations, either dedicated systems with elaborate helmet and body-suit gear or simulated online communities found in such games as World of Warcraft and the social networking site of Second Life, will further revolutionize interpersonal communications by creating "cyberspace" worlds in which the designer actually becomes a visual element within the frame (Figure 8.52).

KEY TERMS FROM THIS CHAPTER
Banner • Consumerism • Functionalism • Halftone • Lithography • Meme • Montage • Rule • Situation comedy • Storyboard • Virtual reality

9 Data Visualizations

Whether a national tragedy on the scale of 9/11 or a local story concerned with crimes within specific neighborhoods, words written and spoken and images still and moving can't tell the whole story to a waiting, curious world. With such complicated news stories, a third tool used by visual journalists is necessary—data visualizations.

Data visualizations (also called informational graphics, infographics, information design, and news graphics) are visual displays that can be anything from a pleasing arrangement of facts and figures in a table to a complex, animated interactive diagram with accompanying text and audio that helps explain a story's meaning. With headlines, copy, and photographs in print as well as video, audio, and interactive features online, examples of data visualizations are included in media presentations in order to explain aspects of a story that words, traditional pictures, and video alone could not explain fully.

David McCandless is a London-based author, educator, and data visualizer. His book, *Information is Beautiful* is a pleasing combination of statistics and aesthetics concerned with societal interactions and social media

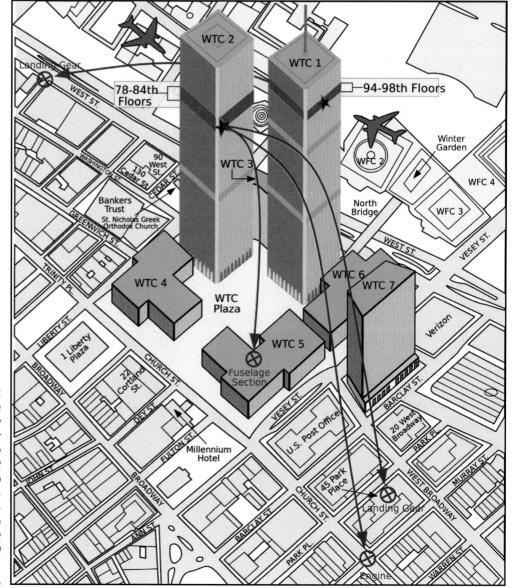

Figure 9.2
A diagram and a locator map show where landing gear and other airplane parts fell after two jet airliners crashed into the World Trade Center towers on September 11, 2001. Such information could not be visually conveyed in any other way.
Courtesy of FEMA

that add flavor and insight to drab, ordinary facts and figures. In his work and through his public presentations, he is a member of a new professional group, the data journalist. In one of his TED talks, he describes how through data mining, an analytical technique that can identify social trends, he can answer such questions as when most breakups between couples occur and how news events illuminate and frighten the public (Figure 9.1).

Typical of news organizations worldwide, soon after the airliners crashed into the twin towers of the World Trade Center in 2001, researchers and graphic artists for print and screen media as well as for the U.S. government were at work completing several informational graphics that showed the airliners' flight paths, the location of the planes' hits upon the towers, and the reason for the collapse of the buildings, among other details of the story (Figure 9.2).

USA Today, once the country's undisputed national newspaper, offered visualization displays during the 2016 presidential election with links to infointeractive displays such as "Presidential Poll Tracker" (Figure 9.3), with polling data provided for each state at various points in time and "Candidate Match Game" (Figure 9.4), which allowed users to compare their own views with each candidate.

It is no accident that the newspaper's website offers such advanced communication techniques. *USA Today* has been at the forefront of the use of informational graphic design and has inspired countless other media entities since the newspaper was introduced on Wednesday, September 15, 1982.

The Gannett newspaper chain, headed by Allen Neuharth until he retired in 1989, saw an unfilled niche in the newspaper market. After being an editor for the *Miami Herald* and working for the Knight newspaper chain, later named Knight-Ridder, Neuharth took over as

head of the Gannett chain of publications. At the time the United States had no national, general interest daily publication. In 1979, Neuharth sent some of his key staff members to a covered-window bungalow (to avoid spies) a few blocks from his Cocoa Beach, Florida, home to develop the national newspaper. One of the experts in the early days was graphics editor George Rorick who had been recruited specifically to create the stunningly aesthetic and technologically advanced national weather map.

From the start, the newspaper was created to attract the attention of the generations brought up on television. *USA Today* is a kind of printed version of the Cable News Network (CNN) channel. Its brief story treatment, combined with multicolored graphic illustrations, pays tribute to the printing industry's chief rival—television. Even the paper racks designed by Fred Gore resemble television sets. But it was the *look* of the newspaper that attracted the most attention. George Cotliar, managing editor of the *Los Angeles Times*, admitted that *USA Today*'s "major contribution to journalism is, of course, its graphics. And it has helped bring a lot of newspapers into the twentieth century." The most striking graphic feature in the newspaper is the data visualization on the back page of the first section (Figure 9.5).

The large weather map received universal acclaim since its introduction. Media critic Peter Boyle called the map "the most imitated feature in American journalism." In a 1987 poll of newspaper editors, more than half had increased their weather coverage since the introduction of *USA Today*, and 25 percent of them admitted that it was because of the popularity of the large, colorful weather map (Figure 9.6). Before its introduction, newspapers around America printed their own maps. After *USA Today*, other publications began dropping their drab, black-and-white satellite photographs and introduced color graphic elements,

Figure 9.1
(Weblink: http://goo.gl/SQh7sq) With a casual style and compelling examples, David McCandless is a competent advocate of data visualizations that amaze and instruct viewers.

Figure 9.3
(Weblink: http://goo.gl/sgMYCD) During the 2016 election, the "Presidential Poll Tracker" from USA Today *allowed users to see which candidate was winning the primary. Obviously, Donald Trump ended up with a higher percentage than his Republican opponents.*

Figure 9.4
(Weblink: http://goo.gl/FiKqKs) With USA Today's *"Candidate Match Game," users could input their opinions about a variety of issues and see which 2016 presidential candidate coordinates.*

Figure 9.5
Designed by Fred Gore, the paper racks for USA Today *were designed to look like the newspaper's chief competition—television sets, although it is rare to see a TV on a sidewalk that accepts quarters. Except for cooler temperatures in Colorado, the weather map indicates through its use of color that most of America experienced warm air on the day this photo was taken.*
Courtesy of Paul Martin Lester

color pictures, and a variety of illustrations in order to attract more readers (Figure 9.7).

WEATHER MAPS

The *USA Today* weather graphic would not have been possible had it not been for many factors in weather map–making history. No other kind of map—printed or broadcast—enjoys such a favorable and persistent following or is so dependent on the telecommunications industry for the delivery of its data.

Newspaper Use The first printed weather map did not show high and low temperatures or warm and cold fronts. Drawn by Edmond Halley in 1686, its symbols simply indicated wind directions over the oceans (Figure 9.8). Based on reported observations, his map was

crudely drawn and showed the direction of trade winds and monsoons. As such, it was an early aid to mariners. Halley is best known for the comet that bears his name. In 1682 he accurately predicted that the comet would return every 75–76 years. If you were born after 1986, you missed it, but take heart. You get another chance in 2061.

Introduction of the telegraph in 1848 allowed weather observations from around the country (and later the world) to be depicted on a map. It wasn't until April 1, 1875, that *The Times* of London printed the first daily weather map, which was composed by a pioneer of statistical presentations, Francis Galton, cousin of Charles Darwin. Because of the large landmass of the United States, getting weather reports for the entire country was much more difficult than it

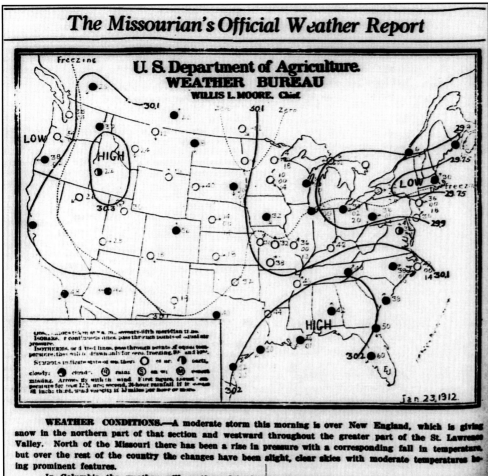

W LINK

Figure 9.6
*(Weblink: http://goo.gl/EOwU6S)
The online version of USA Today has a similar appearance of most web-based news outlets with easy navigation, simple alignment of elements, and still and moving image links.*

Figure 9.7
Typical of many small newspapers of the day, this weather map printed in the Missourian *in 1912 was supplied by the U.S. Department of Agriculture and shows high temperatures, fronts, and present conditions.*
Courtesy of the Library of Congress

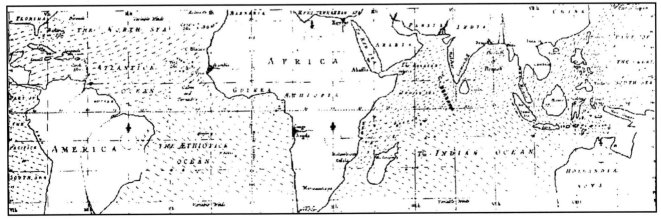

Figure 9.8
One of the first data maps in which a map was combined with statistical information was this 1686 data visualization by Edmond Halley. Prevailing wind currents throughout the world are indicated by the direction of the tiny strokes.
Courtesy of Edward Tufte, Graphics Press LLC, Cheshire, CT

Figure 9.9
Web users can find detailed weather information supplied by the U.S. National Oceanic and Atmospheric Administration (NOAA). The colors alert residents of numerous warnings, including those for floods, fogs, and freezes.
Courtesy of NOAA

was in Great Britain. However, the U.S. Weather Service, formed in 1870 as a branch of the U.S. Army Signal Office, supplied weather information to the *New York Herald* and the *New York Daily Graphic*. As a one-time experiment in 1876, the *Herald* published America's first weather map. Three years later, the *Daily Graphic* began regular publication of a weather map. Stephen Horgan, inventor of an early halftone engraving screen, made the weather maps for the *Daily Graphic*.

It was 55 years later, however, before *The New York Times* signaled the beginning of the weather map's regular use when it published its first map in 1934. The next year, the Associated Press (AP) Wirephoto network began transmitting weather maps electronically via telephone lines to its member newspapers across the country. Publishers liked the maps from the AP because they could use them in local newspapers without alteration.

In 1960, NASA launched the first geosynchronous weather satellite, TIROS-1, which sent back pictures of the United States from 22,000 miles in space. The National Weather Service provided the images to newspapers and television stations for use in their weather coverage (Figure 9.9).

Television Weather Segments Before the 1970s, weather segments of local TV news programs were intended as light-hearted diversions from the other, more important news and sports segments. Sexy women with no apparent qualifications other than their appearance or people dressed up in clown suits read the weather reports in comical ways. CBS talk show host David Letterman began his television career explaining the weather for an Indianapolis station and Fritz Coleman, the weather reporter for the NBC affiliate in Los Angeles started as a stand-up comedian and disc jockey. Today the trend is toward more professionalism among weather personnel. Many now have degrees in meteorology and receive the "seal of approval" from the American Meteorological Society after finishing a training session for television meteorologists.

The epitome of thorough weather presentations with an often folksy, informal, and some say, tedious delivery is Chicago-based WGN-TV's Tom Skilling III. Brother of Jeffrey, the jailed former CEO of the disgraced Enron Corporation, Tom is a member of both the American Meteorological Society and the National Weather Association. His weather segments during the hour-long newscast often last several minutes and are filled with numerous computer-generated maps that flood the chroma keyed effects screen behind him with colorful numbers and isobar lines.

Another indication of the popularity of weather information is The Weather Channel, the first nationally broadcast 24-hour cable weather service, which was launched by John Coleman, the weather personality for ABC's "Good Morning America," during the same year as *USA Today*. The channel and its reporters are particularly valuable during severe weather conditions such as hurricanes.

USA Today is a cheery, easily readable example on paper of what is offered on a portable computer screen. Many communications experts think that the future of newspapers is a move to web-only presentation. If so, *USA Today* may be considered to be a transition between print and computer, between the analog and digital eras. The stories are written in a short, feature-oriented style that could easily fit on a few computer frames. The headlines are easily distinguished from the other elements on the page and are written in a light, casual style. The typography is a mixture of sans serif and roman typeface families, which creates variety on the page and is eminently readable. Photographs, data visualizations, and most lines are in color to maximize visual impact. Graphic elements are selected for their eye-catching impact. Consequently, a reader needs to expend only a little more effort than when watching thirty minutes' worth of national news on television.

But faced with a plunge in circulation and loss advertising revenue, in 2010 newspaper executives announced that its business model would deemphasize its traditional print version and concentrate on its digital operations. In fact, *USA Today* can no longer boast that it is the country's highest circulation publication—that distinction now goes to *The Wall Street Journal*. Toni Locy, a former reporter for the paper said, "*USA Today* used to be the trendsetter in the business. Nobody had color before *USA Today*. Nobody had a weather map. And *USA Today* has lost a step in the last five or six years. So I think they're right to try to regain the ground they've lost." Since fewer potential customers have a newspaper reading habit, the industry overall has tried to tap into the web and tablet apps to attract new readers. Since *USA Today* is known for its innovations, perhaps it will show how other newspapers can be successful.

DATA VISUALIZATIONS AND THE SIX PERSPECTIVES

Statistical designer, author, and former Princeton University professor Edward Tufte (pronounced *tough-tea*) has been called the "da Vinci of data." He estimates that between 900 billion and two trillion informational graphics are printed annually worldwide in print and screen media. Television meteorologists stand before colorful animated weather maps. Presidential candidates use multiple-colored graphics when making campaign infomercials. Business executives and educators put charts they created with an Excel spreadsheet within a PowerPoint page. Magazines, newspapers, corporate annual reports, and textbooks are filled with examples. The informational graphic helps tell a story that is too tedious for words, yet too complex for photographs alone.

Personal Perspective

Besides creating a record of a society's major news and trends, the media also provide a place for corporations to advertise their goods and services. But one of the main utilitarian missions of the media is to educate. Reporters attempt to construct stories that answer the six journalistic questions of who, what, when, where, why, and how. The first four satisfy the basic requirements for most news stories, but *why* and *how* are part of the educational function of journalism and require more space or time. Research indicates that a reader or viewer learns and remembers better if the journalistic questions are answered with a combination of words, images, and data visualizations.

In this increasingly visual age, communicators find that images and graphics often help clarify factual accounts that in the past were the domain of word descriptions alone. As Tim Harrower reports in the sixth edition of his popular workbook *The Newspaper Designer's*

Handbook, "When we want information, we say show me—don't tell me."

Data visualizations combine the aesthetic sensitivity of artistic values with the quantitative precision of numerical data in a format that is both understandable and dramatic. A company's growth and decline over several years can be communicated simply with a line chart that replaces several thousand words. It may be impossible for a photographer to capture the scene of a late-breaking news story in some remote part of the world, but a locator map can at least let a reader know where the event occurred. The best combine the intellectual satisfaction of words with the emotional power of visual messages.

Three Innovative Examples

Data visualizations can be powerful and even life altering. Three informational designs helped change the way persons saw themselves, their place in history, and the environment. We would not have a clear visualization of evolution without Charles Darwin's 1859 drawings of finches. We would not have a mental representation of our genetic makeup without the diagram of DNA's double helix structure, formulated by Francis Crick and James Watson from X-ray images by Rosalind Franklin and incorporating additional research by Maurice Wilkins in 1953. We are better able to understand our contribution to global warming because of Charles Keeling's elegantly simple and alarming graph that shows the rise of carbon dioxide in the atmosphere since 1958 (Figures 9.10–9.12).

Informational graphics is concerned with using sometimes dry, statistical data for visual presentations that engage the viewer and help her to understand the information in a new way. One of the best practitioners in the field is Nigel Holmes, a British information designer who worked for *Time* magazine for 16 years and the author of *Wordless Dia-*

grams (2005) and *On Information Design* (2006) with Steven Heller as well as four other books. Holmes wrote, "Information graphics should be GRAPHIC. A reader or new media user should SEE the subject and the data." Holmes once gave a seemingly simple exercise to conference attendees: Explain in a meaningful way the difference between a million, a billion, and a trillion. With the 2013 U.S. national debt estimated to be more than $10 trillion, understanding the meaning of these numbers is important. But simply adding zeros, or creating an inaccurate chart with three vertical columns at different heights, will not suffice. Holmes told his audience to covert the numbers to seconds. With 86,400 seconds in a day and 31,556,926 seconds in a year, one million seconds is about 12 days. One billion seconds is about 32 years. And one trillion seconds is about 32,000 years. As with Holmes' demonstration, the best informational graphics cause the viewer to rethink set assumptions (Figure 9.13).

Historical Perspective

Some anthropologists have noticed that around the neck and head areas of animal cave paintings from 30,000 years ago (about one trillion seconds in the past) are chips in the stone that appear to be made from spears. Such observations lend credence to the hypothesis that perhaps the paintings were early diagrams to help cave residents practice their aim.

The first clear-cut use of informational graphics by an advanced civilization took the form of maps. Carved in the Sumerian clay in about 3800BCE, crude maps showed a vast agricultural estate in Mesopotamia. Two thousand years later, the craft of map making had not improved much. The Egyptians used simple maps to denote boundaries between properties.

After the Greeks invented the concepts of longitude and latitude for

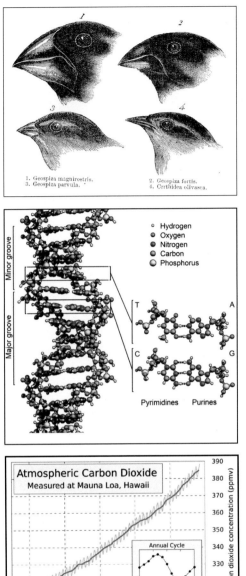

Figure 9.10
"Darwin's finches," 1845, by John Gould. During Charles Darwin's second voyage on the HMS Beagle from 1831 to 1836, he collected what turned out to be about 14 separate species of finches while exploring the Galápagos Islands. Significant were the alterations in the birds' beaks—each one was slightly different, having adapted to the unique food sources they had on their home islands. With drawings by the ornithologist John Gould, Darwin used this example as proof of his theory of evolution detailed in his 1859 book The Origin of the Species.
Courtesy of the estate of John Gould

Figure 9.11
Deoxyribonucleic acid (DNA) is a large molecule that contains the genetic instructions for the development and functioning of all living creatures. It exists as a pair of entwined molecules in the shape of a double helix. The DNA molecule is composed of two spiraling sugar phosphate backbones that support the four chemical base pairs (like steps on a ladder). A human has about three billion bases with more than 99 percent of them the same in all persons. Although the Swiss physician Friedrich Miescher first discovered DNA in 1869, the double helix structure wasn't identified until an article written by James Watson and Francis Crick was published in Nature *in 1953.*
Courtesy of Zephyris

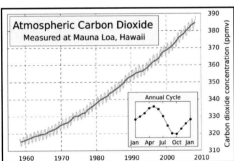

Figure 9.12
From 1958 until his death in 2005, the Pennsylvania-born scientist Charles Keeling made recordings of carbon dioxide levels from the Mauna Loa Observatory atop the volcano of the same name on the Big Island of Hawai'i. He discovered a trend of rising atmospheric concentrations of carbon dioxide, with dips in the levels each year during the spring and early summer in the northern hemisphere, when plant growth increases and consumes the gas. The rise is correlated with an increase in fossil fuel emissions. In 1997 Keeling was given a special achievement award from Vice President Al Gore, who used his work in his 2006 Academy Award–winning documentary An Inconvenient Truth.
Courtesy of Sémhur

dividing the world into a grid of set coordinates in about the 6th Century BCE, their maps became much more accurate. That innovation enabled mariners to explore farther regions of the world with the confidence that they could find their way home. Much later, in 1137CE, a three-foot-square stone was the medium for a detailed map of the eastern coast of China. The map called the "Yü Ji Tu" ("Map of the Tracks of Yü the Great") was produced with a sophisticated grid system for a highly accurate representation (Figure 9.14).

With the spread of printing during the Renaissance, maps and detailed medical illustrations were regularly included with text. Middle Ages sketch artists often used a camera obscura to render accurate diagrams of the human skeletal system. In his notebooks, Leonardo da Vinci often illustrated his innovative ideas with infographics. A diagram in one of his notebooks, estimated to be drawn in 1510, purportedly shows a fetus in the womb. The artist and scientist was also a cartographer as he produced accurate maps (Figure 9.15). A 1546 edition of Petrus Apianus's *Cosmographia* con-

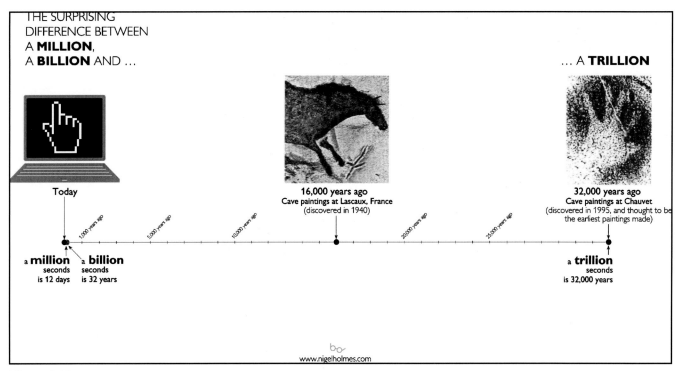

Figure 9.13

The reason there is no such word in the English language as trillionaire *because no one could ever amass that much money. The reason is obvious when the numbers are translated into this time line.*

Courtesy of Nigel Holmes for *Time* magazine, 1979

Figure 9.14
"Yü Ji Tu" or "Map of the Tracks of Yü the Great", 1137 (inverted to match the scene as printed). Unearthed in the Forest of Steles in Xi'an, capital of northwest China's Shaanxi Province, this early map carved in stone shows a portion of China's geography, emphasizing its river systems, with incredible accuracy using a grid. The map was rubbed on paper to produce a positive image about 650 years before the invention of lithography.
Courtesy of Eric Connor

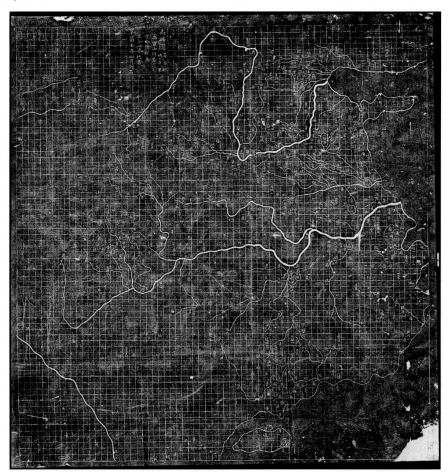

tained a map that showed many details of the European continent (Figure 9.16).

Besides location maps, so-called "concept maps" use a tree structure with roots, trunk, branches, and leaves as a popular metaphor for presentations of genealogical and known knowledge. One of the earliest examples was an engraving published in 1649 called "THE TREE OF MANS LIFE," written by the English author Richard Dey and engraved by John Goddard (Figure 9.17). The point of this tree infographic is made clear by the piece's subtitle (with spelling not corrected): "Or an Emblem declareing the like, and unlike, or various condition of all men in their estate of Creation, birth, life, death, buriall, resurrection, and last Judgment, with pyous observations out of the Scriptures upon the severall branches." Much later, John Venn, an English mathematician added to the contribution of concept maps when he published his way of organizing data within simple oval sets he modestly called Venn diagrams in a 1880 article titled "On the Diagrammatic and Mechanical Representation of Propositions and Reasonings" (Figure 9.18).

Data Visualization Pioneers

Informational graphics might forever have been limited to simple maps or diagrams if not for individuals who had the creative intelligence to understand that graphics could be more than simple drawings. The power of a graphic representation of empirical data lies in its explanation of complex processes by an immediate visual message. William Playfair, Dr. John Snow, and Charles Minard, in particular, had the insight to link numbers with traditional graphic forms to tell complex stories with eloquent simplicity.

William Playfair

A Scottish political economist, Playfair is considered by many to be the founder of data visualizations. He was educated by his brother,

a mathematician at the University of Edinburgh, and learned drafting while working for an engineering company. In his 1786 publication *The Commercial and Political Atlas*, he printed 44 charts that gave details about the British economic system. But one of his charts was unlike any graphic previously seen (Figure 9.19).

To show one year's data for Scottish exports and imports, Playfair invented a graph that used black bars for exports and ribbed bars for imports. He showed dollar amounts at the top and listed individual countries down the right side. His innovation became the first bar chart, showing that infographics could convey complex messages powerfully and simply. Today, bar charts are one of the most common elements found in publications. Playfair is also credited with inventing the pie chart—a graphic representation of 100 percent of some quantity within separate pie wedges. His 1801 chart showed the extent of the Turkish Empire in Africa, Europe, and Asia (Figure 9.20).

Dr. John Snow

Another innovative use of data visualizations was a result of mass deaths from disease. London in the 1850s, like many overly crowded and unsanitary cities of the day, was often ravaged by outbreaks of cholera, which could kill thousands of people. Dr. John Snow, a physician concerned about the cause of the dreaded disease, obtained the names and addresses of about 500 of those who had died during an 1854 epidemic. When faced with all the street numbers written on several sheets of paper, Snow could make little sense of the data and could see no patterns. But when he plotted each death on a street map of a tiny section of central London, the visual representation of the data clearly showed the deaths clustered around the Broad Street water pump and not any other source (Figure 9.21). Snow asked that the pump be dismantled. The plague ceased (Figure 9.22).

Figure 9.15
"Studies of Embryos," c. 1510, pen over red chalk on paper, by Leonardo da Vinci (Next page). Although da Vinci helped in dissections of human bodies with the anatomical expert Marcantonio della Torre, this drawing of a four-month-old fetus was based on a cow and not from direct experience.
Courtesy of Luc Viatour

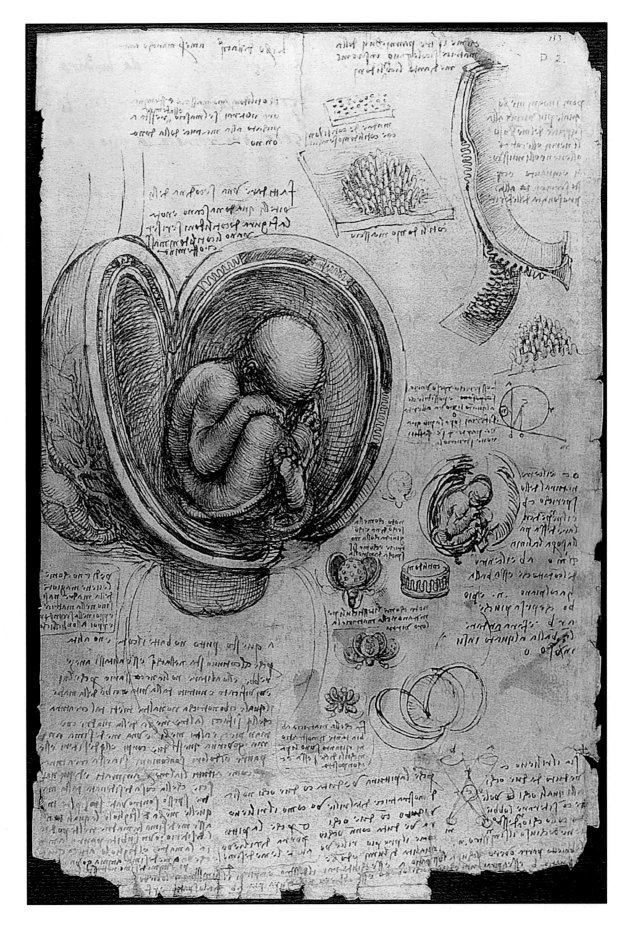

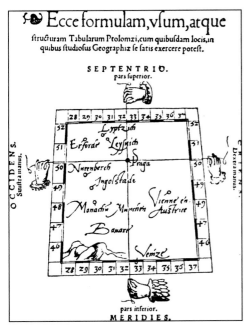

Figure 9.16
Western map accuracy improved greatly when locations were superimposed on a grid representing latitude and longitude—an innovation from the Greeks but a technique perfected by the Chinese more than 400 years earlier. In his 1546 edition of Cosmographia, *the German mathematician, astronomer, and cartographer Petrus Apianus plotted the location of various European cities with the help of bodiless hands holding threads.*
**Courtesy of Edward Tufte,
Graphics Press LLC, Cheshire, CT**

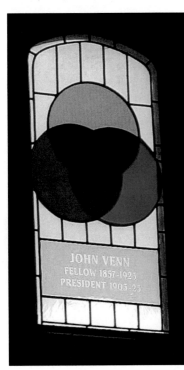

Figure 9.17
"The Tree of Mans Life," 1659, engraved by John Goddard. The heavens shine down upon the leaves, branches, trunk, and roots of all humankind. Christ with the saved in heaven and angels seated on a semi-circle of clouds; intertwined branches of the tree form two ovals, the upper containing the figure of Death with a funeral scene, the lower the feast of Dives with Lazarus looking on, holding crutches and a begging bowl; at lower left, a poor woman sits outside her house nursing her baby; at lower right, a rich woman nurses her child, in swaddling bands, beside a curtained bed. Typical of science of the day was to mix religious views with natural observations to create infographic metaphors for the assumed steady and positive progress of human civilization.
Courtesy of the British Museum

Figure 9.18
To honor John Venn, the inventor of the simple circular infographic named for him, the dining hall of Gonville and Caius College in Cambridge, England, displays a stained glass window designed by Maria McClafferty. With his father and grandfather both reverends for a sect of evangelical Christians who advocated prison reform and the end of slavery, John Venn naturally became a priest of the church in 1859. While teaching "moral sciences" at Gonville and Caius College where he had graduated, he wrote three books on logic and philosophy. His Symbolic Logic, *published in 1881 contains examples of his famous diagram.*
Courtesy of Frederic Schutz

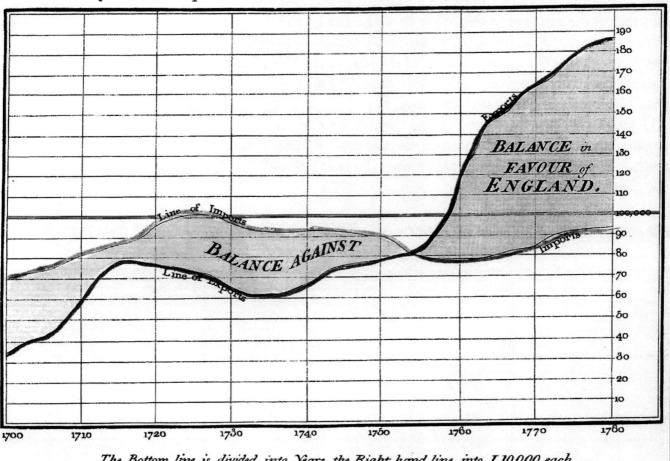

Exports and Imports to and from DENMARK & NORWAY from 1700 to 1780.

The Bottom line is divided into Years, the Right hand line into L10,000 each.

Published as the Act directs, 1st May 1786, by Wm Playfair

Neele sculpt 352, Strand, London.

Figure 9.19

The Scottish engineer William Playfair is an important figure in the history of informational graphics because he was one of the first to substitute time and money data for the latitude and longitude coordinates of Western maps. Charts, then, may be thought of as maps that plot economic positions against time rather than geographic locations. With years represented by the x axis and monetary amounts by the y axis, this area chart shows visually that England exports more goods to Denmark and Norway—a favorable economic condition that began in 1754.

Courtesy of Rich Farmbrough

Figure 9.20

Although noted for his advancements in informational graphics, William Playfair never seemed to be able to keep a job. In 1777 at the age of 18, he became an assistant to the renowned Scottish inventor, James Watt, whose improvements to the steam engine advanced the Industrial Revolution. Five years later he left to start his own silversmith shop, but it failed. In 1787 he moved to Paris where he helped bring down the Bastille during the French Revolution. Returning to London, he opened a bank that failed. To make ends meet he wrote books and political pamphlets. His 1801 book Commercial and Political Atlas and Statistical Breviary *is credited with the publication of the first pie chart. The chart shows the relative influence of the Turkish Empire in Africa, Asia, and Europe. Asia wins.*

Courtesy of Schutz

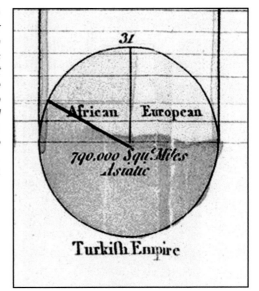

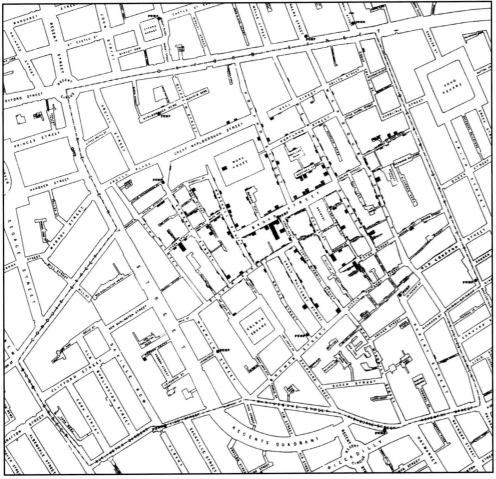

Figure 9.21
*British physician Dr. John Snow was one of the first to study the use of ether and chloroform
for surgical operations. He also is responsible for the medical field known as epidemiology,
or the science of population health and illness. A close-up of a London street map from 1854
shows the dots that Dr. John Snow marked to indicate a death from the latest outbreak of
cholera. His data visualization clearly showed a problem with the Broad Street pump. However, city officials refused to believe that fecal pollution of the water, as was later proved to
be the case, caused cholera. A vegetarian and teetotaler who never married, Snow died of a
stroke four years after his water pump finding.*
Courtesy of Edward Tufte, Graphics Press LLC, Cheshire, CT

Figure 9.22
*Although the actual site of the water
pump that Dr. John Snow asked to be
replaced is at another location, the City of
London erected a replica for tourists. The
pub behind the pump is named the John
Snow, an ironic honor since he never
drank alcohol.*
Courtesy of Paul Martin Lester

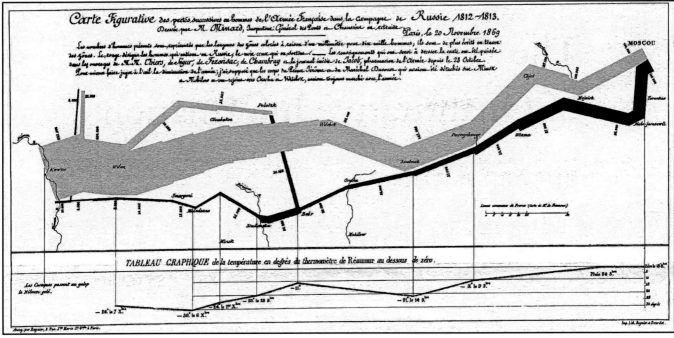

Figure 9.23

Charles Minard eloquently portrays Napoleon's disastrous military advance on Moscow in 1812 in an informational graphic that has been called the best ever produced. The width, shading, and position of the horizontal lines indicate troop strength, direction, and position. This single visual message shows that Napoleon started with 422,000 troops and ended with 10,000.
Courtesy of Jeff Dahl

Charles Minard As with Snow, French engineer Charles Minard in 1869 combined statistical information and a map to tell a complicated story in a simple, direct way (Figure 9.23). Minard created a data visualization of Napoleon's disastrous march to Moscow and retreat during the War of 1812 that has been called "the best statistical graphic ever drawn." Historian E. J. Marey complimented the piece as "seeming to defy the pen of the historian by its brutal eloquence." Minard told the incredible story of the loss of about 400,000 soldiers and support staff in one military campaign through an illustration that combined five different series of information. He showed the size and the location of the army and the direction of its movements on a two-dimensional surface, as well as the temperature on various dates. Minard proved that a complex story could be reduced to its simplest elements in a compelling visual format.

Continuing with the 19th century, highly skilled visual artists fashioned maps and illustrations from eyewitness accounts and photographs for numerous publications. In the United States, two leaders in the use of illustrations were publications established in 1850—*Frank Leslie's Illustrated Newspaper* and *Harper's Weekly*. With the halftone engraving process for photographs not becoming standard practice until decades later, *The Philadelphia Inquirer* and other newspapers used maps mostly to tell about important Civil War battles (Figure 9.24). These data visualizations had a side benefit for graphic design generally. Large, horizontal maps caused front-page designers to rethink the customary rigid, vertical column look of newspapers of the day. Because these horizontal, hand-drawn maps had to extend across more than a single column, designers of front pages eventually let headlines and stories follow that same pattern.

Maps always have been the chief infographic in wartime. During the two world wars, hand-lettered maps and diagrams dominated the pages of newspapers and magazines as readers eagerly sought information about military

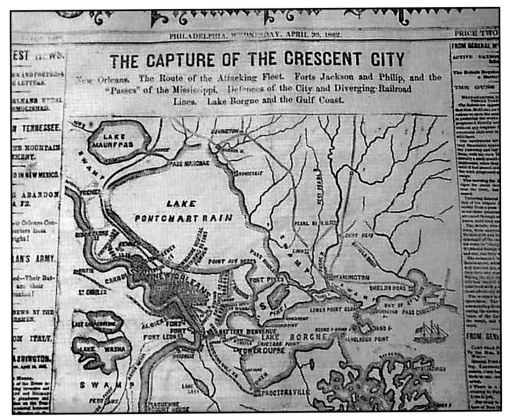

Figure 9.24
"The Capture of the Crescent City," April 30, 1862, The Philadelphia Inquirer. *New Orleans falls to the Yankees. Before the halftone printing process, photographs could not be used to illustrate news stories. Only words and engravings could be used to describe the latest news.*
Courtesy of the Library of Congress

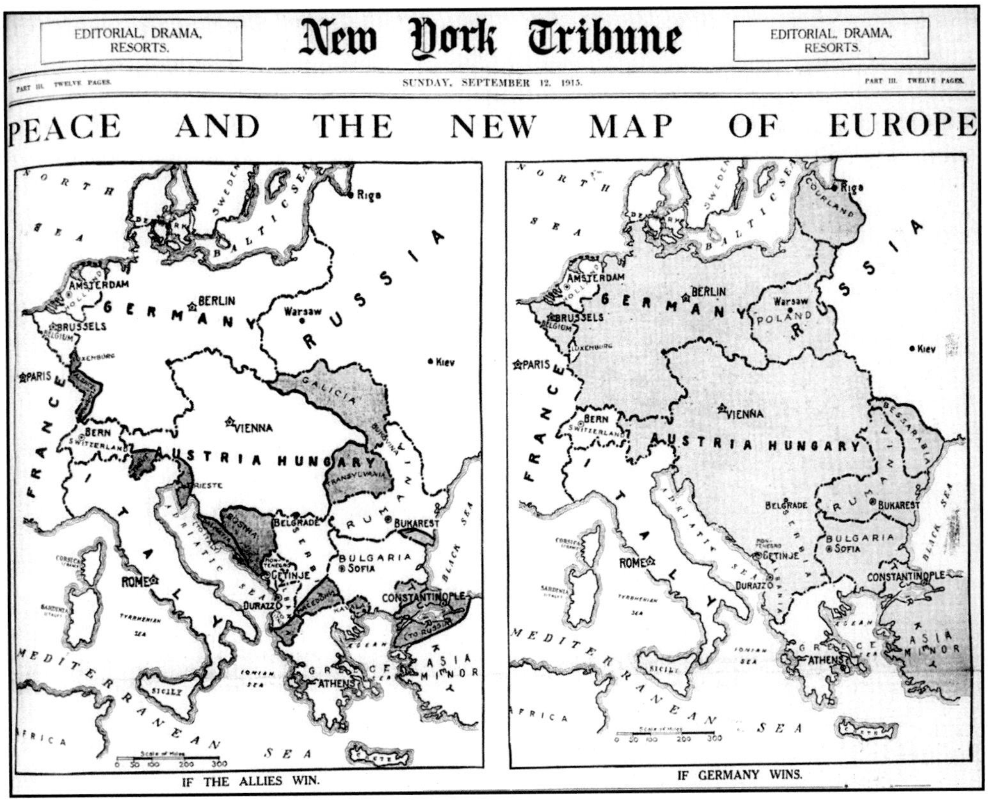

Figure 9.25
The importance of maps to help tell the many stories related to wars is indicated by the placement of these two on the front page of the New York Tribune, *printed about two years before America declared war on Germany during World War I.*
Courtesy of the Library of Congress

actions around the world. With many unsure about the location of battles during the world wars and later the geography of Korea, Vietnam, Afghanistan, and Iraq, maps were the main type of news graphic used during those conflicts (Figure 9.25).

With computer technology becoming affordable and easily manageable, newsrooms could produce custom-made illustrations. Television stations and graphics firms under contract made logos, titles, and other graphics for TV shows. As a result of the new emphasis on graphic design for television, newspaper editors saw a need to give their newspapers a more modern appearance. Graphics editors were hired to oversee both the photography and graphics departments.

Technical Perspective

There are two main types of informational graphics: statistical and nonstatistical. Statistical data visualizations are visual displays that present empirical, quantitative data. Nonstatistical are visual displays that rely on a visually pleasing arrangement of verbal and visual qualitative information.

Statistical Data Visualizations

The four main types of statistical infographic elements are charts (also called graphs), data maps, infofilms, and infointeractives. Line, relational, pie, and pictographs are the primary examples of charts, but other variations include bubble, doughnut, radar, surface, and scatter plots. Data maps usually combine numeric data and locations within a simple locator map to form a powerful story-telling combination. Infofilms combine the visual cue of movement with statistical information. Infointeractives are usually web-based data sources that allow users to engage with the presented facts in an interactive format.

Charts Much of the news contains numeric information. The president's budget, the value of the U.S. dollar compared with the values of currency in other countries, the increase or decrease in criminal activity, and election results are examples of stories that are primarily about numbers. Reading a story that simply listed in sentence form all the figures generated by such stories would be tedious and mind-numbing. Charts (graphs) were invented to display numerical information concisely and comprehensibly and to show trends visually.

A line chart contains a rule that connects points plotted on a grid that correspond to amounts along a horizontal, or *x*-axis and a vertical, or *y*-axis. Designers often use line charts to show variations in quantities over a period of time. They are most effective when the quantities change dramatically over time. A significant upsurge or decline in a company's sales or a politician's rise and fall, for example, can be easily shown on a line chart (Figure 9.26). Occasionally, information designers will color the area below the line of the chart for a more dramatic effect. The graph then is called an area chart.

Although it depends on the type of data used, the *y*-axis for line charts should begin at zero. Intervals of time usually are displayed along the *x*-axis and should be consistent and evenly spaced to avoid visual misrepresentation of the data.

In contrast to line charts, which best show broadly based trends over time, relational charts show significant changes in two or more specific items during a particular time period. For example, two bars of different heights would best represent gold and silver prices for a particular year. When horizontal boxes present the amounts, the chart is called a bar chart. When vertical bars represent the amounts, the chart is called a column chart. Whether the graphic is a bar or column chart depends on a designer's

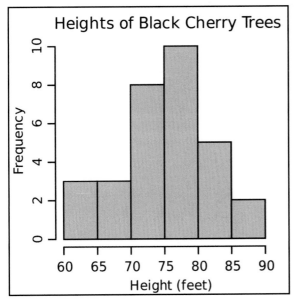

Figure 9.26
A simple column chart reveals the relationship between the number of black cherry trees and their height. It turns out that the majority of trees are also the tallest. Why this information is important to know is anyone's guess.
Courtesy of *The Minitab Student Handbook*

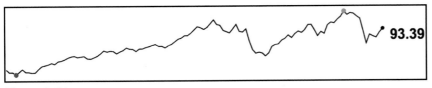

Figure 9.27
Data visualizations advocate Edward Tufte in his book Beautiful Evidence *(2006) argues for charts with fewer distractions from unnecessary grid lines, words, and numbers. Consequently, his sparkline charts, especially useful for long-range stock market data, present the information without getting in the way of it.*
Courtesy of Edward Tufte, Graphics Press LLC, Cheshire, CT

preference.

Edward Tufte proposed a stripped-down and elegant type of chart he dubbed the "sparkline." Similar to a Kagi chart, first seen in the 1870s in Japan to show changes in the price of rice, a sparkline reduces the dissonance of too much text and numbers accompanying a typical chart. It can reduce a complicated and busy series of numbers to an elegant, visual-only display (Figure 9.27).

A pie chart compares amounts individually and for the whole (Figure 9.28). The only way that pie charts can be used to show complex trends is to use several pie charts, which isn't effective. Design-ers usually avoid pie charts because they often can get crowded with too much information to show. A pie chart should have no more than five slices and no slice should be smaller than one percent of the total. A pie chart with too many or with skinny, low percentage slices is difficult to read. Colors of individual slices should contrast, and each slice should be labeled clearly. Finally, all the wedges should be drawn accurately to correspond to the percentages they represent. Use of computer graphics software ensures pie-slice accuracy. Although pie charts are distinctive and immediately attract attention by their round shape, as

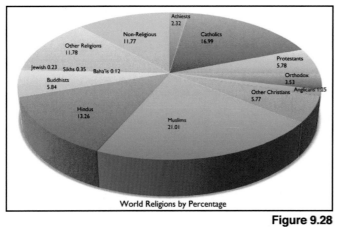

Figure 9.28

This pie chart created through an Excel spreadsheet shows the percentages of the major world religions as of 2007 according to The World Factbook from the Central Intelligence Agency (CIA). A pie chart can be useful as a way of splitting 100 percent of some entity. However, if the slices get too small, as they are in this example, a table is a better choice.
Courtesy of Paul Martin Lester

Figure 9.29

A pictograph is a chart, but instead of lines or columns that stand for numbers, a picture is used. Hopefully, the image chosen will be conceptually linked to the subject of the chart. In this German illustration concerned with the percentage of feeds to give to pigs in order for them to gain the most weight, the three different figures at the bottom are in the form of pictographs of lead weights representing each column.
Courtesy of the German Federal Archive

Tufte points out, "a table should almost always be used over a dumb old pie chart."

A pictograph is a type of graph that uses illustrations that represent the items or concepts compared. For example, imagine an example concerned with the price of computers. Instead of showing the lowering costs of hardware with a line or relational graph, the designer shows the cost differences by using columns composed of smaller and smaller computer monitors. Pictographs are the most criticized of all graph forms because they often employ cute, content-deprived drawings to represent numerical information for the sole purpose of attracting the reader's attention. These visual representations often are misleading and wrong. Although pictographs are dismissed for insulting the intelligence of readers, they are widely used (Figure 9.29).

Data Maps Maps that combine geographic information with numeric data can be the most eloquent type of data visualization produced. Data maps can represent hundreds of figures in a visual format that an unsophisticated reader can instantly analyze. They combine the drawing techniques used in diagrams with quantitative data to help tell a complicated story in a simple presentation (Figure 9.30). The *USA Today* weather map with colored strips representing different temperatures is the type of data map most commonly used in the media. The maps produced by Dr. Snow and Charles Minard are classic examples of the use of numbers combined with simple geographic maps.

Investigative reporters have discovered the power of visually combining numeric data and geographic locator maps in telling their stories. For example, cancer death or crime statistics overlaid on a city's map enable readers to notice patterns that words alone could not emphasize as well (Figure 9.31).

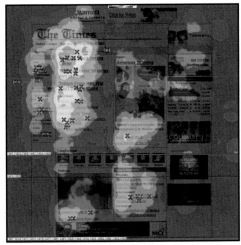

Figure 9.30
From the Poynter Institute's EyeTrack III study of 2003, a heat map reports where and for how long an experimental subject looked at a web version of a fictitious newspaper. The red color indicates the most interest in a page element while the blue color the least. The "X" marks are mouse clicks. From this example it can be seen that this subject was interested in the headline links, but didn't look that much at the pictures presented on the page.
Courtesy of the Poynter Institute for Media Studies

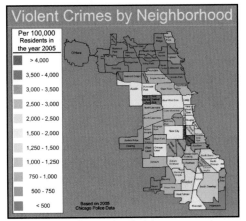

Figure 9.31
When maps are combined with complex data, they provide viewers with a more complete picture of an area. From a 2005 Chicago Police annual report, this data map shows the total incidences of violent crimes for Chicago neighborhoods. Depending on where you live, you may feel ease or discomfort at the visual display.
Courtesy of Peter Fitzgerald

Infofilms The industrial and graphic design team of Charles and Ray Eames produced one of the most powerful short science films. Based on the book *Cosmic View* by Kees Boeke, *Powers of Ten* is a nine-minute documentary that takes a viewer from a close-up of a couple enjoying a picnic into deep space and back again through logarithmic zooms. Originally made for IBM in 1968, it was rereleased in 1977. In 1998 it was added to the U.S. National Film Registry of the Library of Congress (Figure 9.32).

Many infofilms employ animation techniques to express complex data that is difficult to visualize. During the first O. J. Simpson trial in 1995, Failure Analysis, Inc., created a realistic animated diagram based on evidence collected after the murders of Nicole Simpson and Ron Goldman for the software distribution and technical information company CNet. Although the jury never saw the video, it was shown on national television on the tabloid journalism show "Hard Copy." A short film compares the size of the Earth with other known objects in space (Figure 9.33) while students and faculty of the Vancouver Film School created an infofilm to help explain the power of tsunamis (Figure 9.34). ABC News calls its computer-generated mannequin-like infofilms "Virtual Views." These quickly produced displays can be made viewer-ready in a matter of hours for television and web news shows. Companies such as Z-Axis Corporation in Denver and Decisionquest in Torrance, California, produce courtroom graphics in still and animated platforms.

Infointeractives The FlowingData website created by UCLA student Nathan Yau is a popular source to discover the latest use of informational graphics from designers located around the world. The site "explores how designers, statisticians, and computer scientists are using data to understand ourselves better—mainly

Figure 9.32
(Weblink: http://goo.gl/RP0c2x) From a couple enjoying the day at a Chicago park, the viewer is led on a wondrous journey beyond the stars and then back again in the Powers of Ten. *Not only visual arresting, the motion picture teaches how a logarithmic scale can drastically change perspective.*

Figure 9.33
(Weblink: http://goo.gl/a4wC0S) The sensational aspects of the murders of Nicole Simpson and Ron Goldman are enhanced in this realistic infofilm by repeated images, slow motion, and a serious music score. Based on an interpretation of the evidence by its producers, it was only shown to television viewers and not the jury.

Figure 9.34
(Weblink: http://goo.gl/qlaoja) With simple illustrations and animation techniques, low cost professional infofilms can be produced by students at universities.

W
LINK
Figure 9.35
(Weblink:
http://goo.gl/Q3xlhm)
One of the best websites to
learn of current trends and
critiques of data visualizations with examples from
around the world presented
in a clear, elegant graphic
design is Flowing Data created by Nathan Yau.

through data visualization." The website was inspired by the work of data analysis expert John W. Tukey, who was a professor at Princeton University and a researcher for AT&T Bell Laboratories. While at Princeton, Tukey gave joint seminars on information design with a young professor, Edward Tufte. Besides his interest in visualizing statistical results, in 1958 he coined the word "software" to refer to computer programs.

Out of the hundreds of infointeractive examples Yau makes known through his Twitter account and his website features what he considers to be the top 15 uses of data visualization for 2011 (Figure 9.35). The top five are below with his descriptions:

Dear Data A year-long project by Stefanie Posavec and Giorgia Lupi. Each tracked everyday things during a week, such as how many times each picked up the phone, and then visualized the data on a postcard. Then they mailed the postcards to each other, with Lupi currently in New York and Posavec in London.

You Draw It: How Family Income Predicts Children's College Chances Gregor Aisch, Amanda Cox, and Kevin Quealy for the Upshot asked readers to draw a line that plotted family income against the percent of children who attended college. So you had your line, reality, and what other people thought the correlation looked like.

Hack Your Way To Scientific Glory The point of the FiveThirtyEight piece by Christie Aschwanden and Ritchie King wasn't so much a disbelief that something so absurd could make it through the rigor of peer review. Rather, it was that science (and interpreting data) is hard.

Making of "Where Are Ü Now" The music visualization that plays along the sides of the video help you understand what the musicians are talking about.

Watch how the measles outbreak spreads when kids get vaccinated – and when they don't Rich Harris, Nadja Popovich, and Kenton Powell for the *Guardian* showed what happens when counties don't get kids vaccinated.

Nonstatistical Data Visualizations
Although not as numerically sophisticated as the statistical elements, nonstatistical informational graphics are a vital part of story-telling in this visual age. They comprise fact boxes, tables, nondata maps, diagrams, and miscellaneous formats.

Fact Boxes These infographics contain a series of statements that summarize the key points of a story (Figure 9.36). These boxes catch the reader's attention in a graphic and entertaining way. They closely resemble the journalistic sidebar—a short article that elaborates on a specific topic mentioned in a longer story. Fact boxes rarely stand alone; they usually are part of a story. However, television and presentation graphic frames often use a variation of the fact box as subject headings for voice-overs by announcers. Fact boxes in print media are also used with photographs, icons, and other elements in an attempt to attract new readers.

Tables If you simply want to display numbers or words, a table puts them in an orderly format of rows and columns, with enough white space for readability. The most familiar types of tables in print media are stock market results for the day and baseball box scores after a game. Henry Chadwick, a British cricket enthusiast and transplanted American, is called the "Founder of Baseball" because of his promotion and innovations to the game and is credited with the creation of the box score. Writer Stanley Cohen wrote, "The box score is the catechism of baseball, ready to surrender its truth to the knowing eye." Some have suggested that a baseball's box score should be named the "baseball accounting table,"

Figure 9.36

Fact boxes are studies in the visual organization of textual information. As part of a larger story concerned with radiation in space, the fact box uses a reverse, sans serif typeface that makes the title stand out, the leading is tight, but boldface headings instantly identify each section, and careful alignment of the elements gives an organized appearance.
Courtesy of the U.S. Department of Energy's Brookhaven National Laboratory

or BAT. Although they are the least visually appealing of all graphics, tables are useful in presenting data in a logical and ordered way. Headings run horizontally along the top and identify categories of information placed under them in vertical columns, enabling the reader to compare numbers or items easily (Figure 9.37).

Nondata Maps Research supports the widely held belief that Americans generally lack geographic knowledge. One of the reasons that so many maps are published during times of war is that the public needs to be educated about foreign locations. But simple maps also may be used to answer an important journalistic question—they show immediately where a news story has taken place. One of the first maps published in a newspaper was in *The Times* of London

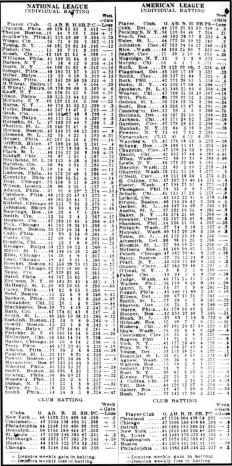

Figure 9.37

An offshoot of a game's box score is the longer table that sums up individual and team standings in both baseball leagues. In this 1919 issue of the New York Tribune, *the neatly aligned columns give the number of games played, at bats, runs, hits, stolen bases, and hitting percentages. "The Georgia Peach," also known as Detroit Tiger Ty Cobb, one of the most celebrated and criticized players in the game, sits atop the American League's list.*
Courtesy of the Library of Congress

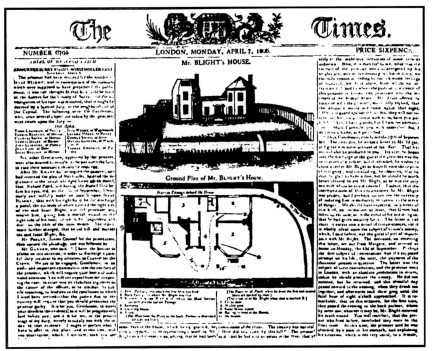

Figure 9.38

One of the first infographics ever printed in a newspaper was the floor plan of a house in which a murder had been committed. The Times *of London in 1806 satisfied curious readers with its illustrations.*
Courtesy of The Times, London

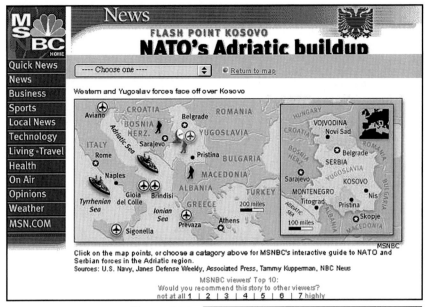

Figure 9.39

In the early years of the web, such a display was impressive. For a news story in 1999 concerned with the conflict between NATO allied forces and Yugoslavia over Kosovo, three locator maps with different scales remind users of msnbc.com where the region is located. In addition, users are encouraged to click on an icon on the map at the left to find more information.
Courtesy of MSNBC and the Microsoft Corporation

Figure 9.40

The British graphic designer Nigel Holmes is one of the most respected informational graphics practitioners in the world. After earning a degree from the Royal College of Art in 1966, he worked for Time magazine for 16 years creating data visualizations. He then resigned to form his own company and work on books concerned with the field. Since 1984 he has written or co-written eight books concerned with news graphics and/or graphic design. His The Enlightened Bracketologist: The Final Four of Everything (2007) shows his skill as a typographical and graphic designer. This diagram explaining the digestion process is a good example of Holmes's bright and easily understandable style.
Courtesy of Nigel Holmes

on April 7, 1806, as part of a story about a murder (Figure 9.38). The simple floor plan of a house printed on the front page revealed, in almost Clue-like fashion, that Richard Patch shot Isaac Blight in the back parlor. It was used for the same reason similar maps are used today—words are too tedious and photographs are impossible to obtain. Maps enable understanding at a glance.

There are two types of nondata maps: locator and explanatory. Locator maps show a geographic location or a road system in a simplified design that lets the reader or viewer know where something of importance has occurred (Figure 9.39). In large cities, television news programs include a traffic report about which highways are heavily congested and identify each one with a circle on a map. If a major news story happens anywhere in the world, a locator map might be the only visual information available until pictures can be taken at the scene. Explanatory maps not only reveal where a news story has occurred but also tell how a series of events has taken place. Usually designated with numbers, events leading to the arrest of a serial murderer, for example, are plotted on a locator map. Readers not only learn where a news story has taken place but also discover the background and time frame of events leading up to it.

Diagrams Some of the most dramatic and artistically rendered informational graphics involve the use of diagrams. Diagrams can reveal the details of how processes and machines work with line drawings and color (Figure 9.40). Because diagrams are complex, designers often prepare them in advance. A team of graphics researchers and artists works with the graphics editor to find verbal and visual resource materials that will ensure accuracy.

Miscellaneous Formats Artists also are asked to produce a variety of designs that don't fit any of the preceding categories. Again, because of the widespread use of desktop computers, print and screen media regularly present these types of graphics to catch the viewer's attention and help explain a story. Miscellaneous formats include sketches, television schedules, calendars, icons and logos, flowcharts, time lines, and illustrations.

Sketches Sensational courtroom trials generate communitywide and sometimes nationwide interest. Most readers and viewers want to know what the participants in a trial look like and how they acted. Many courts, including the Supreme Court and most Federal trials, do not allow still or moving pictures of the proceedings. A sketch artist is a highly specialized individual who is usually hired on a freelance basis by a media organization to produce courtroom drawings during a trial. A good artist reveals not only what the participants look like, but also how they feel about being called to testify. Mona Shafer Edwards is one of the best in the profession. Her book, *Captured! Inside the World of Celebrity Trials* is a collection of her courtroom drawings from the trials of O.J. Simpson to Winona Ryder (Figure 9.41).

To protect the identity of those involved, some judges do not allow sketch artists to reveal identifying facial features. The media must respect the privacy of the people involved when the court orders them to do so or they may be held in contempt of court. In Great Britain, courtroom sketch artists are not allowed to make drawings during a trial; they must make their illustrations later from memory. New York City based illustrator Janet Hamlin was asked by the U. S. Pentagon to make sketches during hearings of Guantanamo Bay detainees. When one of the prisoners, alleged 9/11 mastermind Khalid Sheikh Mohammed, complained that his nose was too large

in her drawing, she made an extra effort to correct the image so he would be happy with his picture. Sketches, however, can be used for more than courtrooms. In an unusual decision, the Trump Administration in 2017 banned cameras in some on-the-record press briefings. During one of former Press Secretary's Sean Spicer's updates, CNN had sketch artist Bill Hennessy cover the event.

Television Schedules A common element is the television schedule. The wide-scale use of cable and satellite broadcasting since the 1980s has made the task of designing the TV program table much more complicated than when there were only three major networks. A large community may have several competing cable companies that offer different services and as many as 50 separate channels. Color coding and alignment aid in the readability of these complex tables.

Calendars Business meetings and other kinds of events often are shown in a calendar format because it is a graphic design that everyone understands. An artist or draftsperson will draw the background template or shell for the calendar and reuse it each month. New information is written in the days of the calendar.

Icons and Logos In the past 30 years, executives have realized the importance of visual symbols that identify their companies and products. Such symbols, or logos, are important visible links to consumers. Graphic designers such as Saul Bass and Paul Rand have created eye-catching icons and logos for some of the most important businesses in the world (Figures 9.42 and 9.43). Print and screen media news graphic artists have extended those ideas to simple line drawings that attract attention to a story, briefly summarize its content, and

W LINK
Figure 9.41
(Weblink: http://goo.gl/R3vJrK) The website of Mona Shafer Edwards not only includes courtroom sketches from such famous cases that involved O.J. Simpson, Mel Gibson, and Michael Jackson, but also includes illustrations related to travel, fashion, and children.

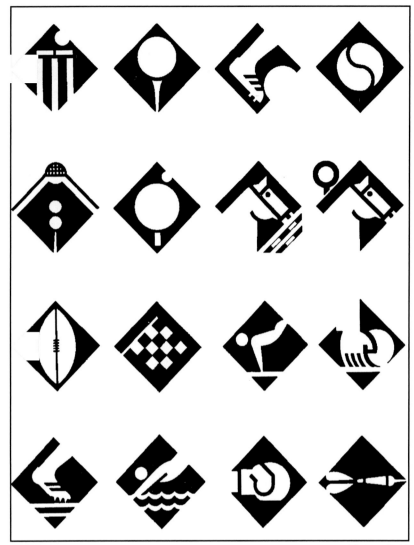

Figure 9.42

Icons and logos communicate vital messages visually, as demonstrated by these examples. A well-designed logo not only presents a clear message but also can provide a memory link to the company, service, or function. While working for Time magazine, Nigel Holmes created pictographs for use with sports stories. The simple, easy-to-understand icons rely on our ability to combine the white background with the black foreground pictures.
Courtesy of Nigel Holmes

Figure 9.43
An icon on a wall in Helsinki, Finland urges pet owners to control the flow from their dogs.
Courtesy of Paul Martin Lester

help anchor a reader or viewer to the page or frame.

Flowcharts Depending on the type of story, an artist may also be called upon to produce a flowchart that shows a corporation's organizational structure, a series of mechanical or chemical processes, or steps in a decision-making process (Figure 9.44). Most flowcharts use a specialized symbol system that must be explained to the novice reader in order for the labels and the connections between them to have meaning. An innovative variation of the classic flowchart is a computer program developed by Jonathan Feinberg, a researcher for IBM and a former drummer with the indie band They Might Be Giants. His program, Wordle (Figure 9.45), creates a word or tag cloud of the most numerous words in a block of text or website (Figure 9.46).

Time Lines Some stories that detail events over a long period of time benefit from a more graphic representation than a chronological fact box. A time line shows significant events along a horizontal or vertical line where important dates are indicated (Figure 9.47). The most effective use of time lines involves a combination of two or more such lines, making relationships between them visually obvious.

Illustrations These are the least factual form of graphic. Good ones instantly attract readers' attention and make them want to read the accompanying story. Illustrations usually exhibit traditional artistic techniques. Illustrators favor pen, ink, brushes, and paints over computers because they more easily can create pieces that have a unique style. However, recent developments in hardware and software make determination of whether an illustration has been created with traditional or innovative tools irrelevant (Figure 9.48).

Data visualizations evolved from simple maps and line charts to complex combinations of visual and textual elements. Many newspapers and magazines seldom use just one type of graphic to tell a story anymore. For a complex story, diagrams and icons might be combined with fact boxes, line and pie charts, and tables. Television producers still hesitate to use many informational graphics because viewers need time to absorb a complex array of information. Web presentations, however, allow viewers the option of repeating pages for better understanding and in an interactive format.

Ethical Perspective

Through accident, ignorance, or intent, visual representations of empirical data can easily mislead unsuspecting and trusting readers and viewers. Critics of the field cite two main reasons why errors and visual distortions occur frequently—few data visualization producers have much experience with statistical information, and many designers believe that if the sole purpose of a piece is to grab the reader's attention, presentation errors and decorative flourishes can be overlooked.

It is the rare staff member in print or screen media who has taken a statistics class. Moreover, infographics production usually isn't offered as a separate university course. Consequently, few individuals are knowledgeable enough about words, numbers, pictures, and computer operations to know when an infographic is inaccurate or misleading.

Edward Tufte advocates more education for producers (Figure 9.49). He has been a consultant for the visual display of empirical data for such corporations as CBS, NBC, *Newsweek*, the *New York Times*, the Census Bureau, and IBM. His self-published books *The Visual Display of Quantitative Information, Envisioning Information, Visual Explanations,* and *Beautiful Evidence* were instant classics

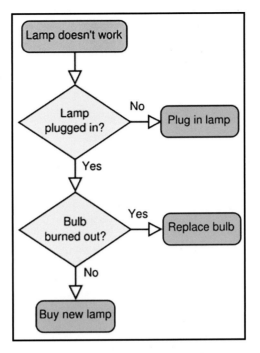

Figure 9.44
Flowcharts can be complex, book-length tools for solving a complicated technical problem, or simple demonstrations to help you figure out what to do if the light in your desk lamp is not working. Meant to be read from the top to the bottom, this flowchart still does not answer the question of how many persons are needed to change a light bulb.
Courtesy of Eric Pierce

Figure 9.45
*(Weblink: http://goo.gl/bDTvR4)
A user can paste from a few words to entire books and get a graphic illustration of the contents in Jonathan Feinberg's Wordle website.*

Figure 9.46
Another type of flowchart is the word or cloud tag. Here, all of the words appearing in this chapter are combined into a word cloud using the Wordle online program. Since the most common words used are presented larger, note the size of the words maps, graphics, information, and data (and yes, figure and courtesy).
Courtesy of Paul Martin Lester

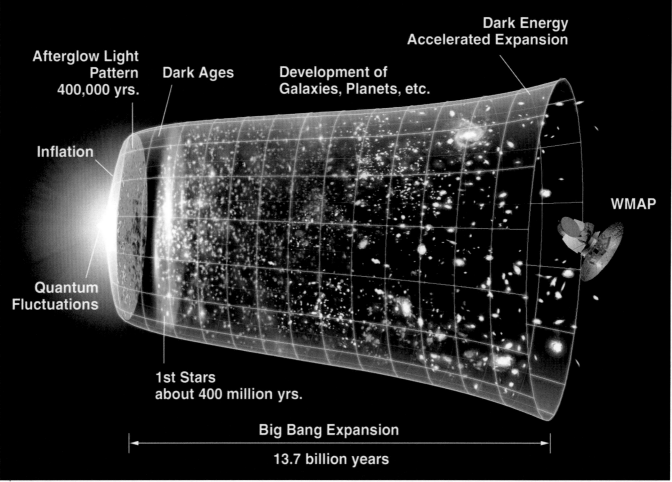

Afterglow Light Pattern 400,000 yrs.

Dark Ages

Development of Galaxies, Planets, etc.

Dark Energy Accelerated Expansion

Inflation

Quantum Fluctuations

WMAP

1st Stars about 400 million yrs.

Big Bang Expansion

13.7 billion years

Figure 9.47

This deceptively simple time line represents 13.7 billion years measured from the "Big Bang" to the present day. Launched in 2001, the Wilkinson Microwave Anisotropy Probe (WMAP) measures and maps the cosmic microwave background radiation, "the oldest light in the universe." The left side of the graphic depicts the earliest time period that can be measured after a time called "inflation" produced a burst of energy and created the universe. The gradually rising vertical height of the time line indicates that the size of the universe is expanding.

Courtesy of NASA / WMAP Science Team

because of the combination of useful information and pleasing graphic design presentations. He travels around the world giving workshops in how best to link graphic design and statistical information.

For Tufte, a high-quality data visualization should have an important message to communicate, convey information in a clear, precise, and efficient manner, never insult the intelligence of readers or viewers, and always tell the truth. Tufte argues for a conservative approach in which the presentation is never more important than the story. "Ideally," he admits, "the design should

disappear in favor of the information."

Tufte calls news graphics loaded with gratuitous decorations or window dressing "chartjunk." Such graphic devices serve merely to entertain rather than to educate readers, he maintains. Tufte is particularly critical of the Microsoft Office popular presentation software PowerPoint. In his second edition of *The Cognitive Style of PowerPoint: Pitching Out Corrupts Within*, he rails against ready-made templates that "usually weaken verbal and spatial reasoning, and almost always corrupt statistical analysis." Anyone who has ever sat through a PowerPoint presentation with a presenter reading every word of multiple bullet points embellished with much too cute clip art graphic images, overly dressed graphic elements, and dizzy transitions knows Tufte is correct.

Charts should accurately reflect the numbers they portray. For example, dollar amounts over many years should be adjusted for inflation and monetary values of different currencies should be translated into one currency value. Because images generally have a greater emotional impact than words, the potential to mislead with visual messages is higher. Inappropriate symbols used to illustrate an infographic can be confusing. A serious subject, for example, demands serious visual representation and not cartoon characters. Such graphic devices may attract attention, but the risk is that the audience will be offended.

Inaccurate charts can be produced inadvertently when the *y*-axis is not based on the number zero. If the numbers of a graph are not based on zero, lines in a chart will be a roller coaster ride of dramatic up and down swings, making the presentation visually misleading. CNN sparked controversy in 2005 when the results of a poll concerned with Terry Schiavo, a Florida woman in a severe degenerative state, were not zero-based. The result was a visual representation that made Democrats appear much more in favor of a court's decision to have her feeding tube removed than Republicans or Independents. After criticism, CNN published a second chart that more accurately reflected the slightly higher results from democrats, but similar responses as the other two groups. The second display was zero-based (Figure 9.50).

Although computers have greatly aided the production of data visualizations, the technology also makes easy the inclusion of decorative devices that distract the reader from the chart's message. Three-dimensional drop shadows, colored backgrounds, icons, and other

illustrations may catch the reader's eye but not engage the brain. Tufte notes the trend in television and computer presentations in which the numbers get lost in animated, colorful effects. Weather maps for television and newspapers sometimes are so crowded with cute illustrations that their informational content is lost. Designers should avoid the temptation to base designs solely on aesthetic or entertainment criteria, a hedonistic approach. They miss an opportunity to educate a reader or viewer whenever they rely on decorative tricks. At best, such gimmicks distract from the message, and at worst

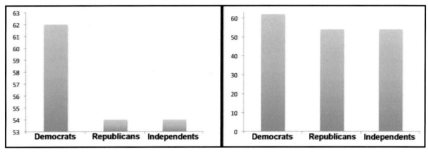

Figure 9.50
CNN was criticized after it presented the results from a telephone survey of adults concerning the Terry Schiavo case, a Florida woman who was in a severe degenerative state for about 15 years. She ultimately died after her feeding tube was removed following a court's order. The question asked of the survey participants was "Based on what you have heard or read about the case, do you agree with the court's decision to have the feeding tube removed?" On the left are the results by political party that was originally presented on the CNN website. However, after users complained about the misleading visual message conveyed by a graph that was not zero-based, CNN corrected the column chart to show a more accurate view.
Courtesy of Paul Martin Lester

they give wrong information. Tufte said it best: "Consumers of graphics are often more intelligent about the information at hand than those who fabricate the data decoration. And, no matter what, the operating moral premise of information design should be that our readers are alert and caring; they may be busy, eager to get on with it, but they are not stupid. Disrespect for the audience will leak through, damaging communication."

Cultural Perspective
The key to understanding data visualizations is to know a visual symbol or sign's context and its possible interpretations.

W
LINK
Figure 9.48
(Weblink: http://goo.gl/XapYgM)
Some of the most aesthetically beautiful images with messages can be found within the pages of printed publications in the form of editorial illustrations.

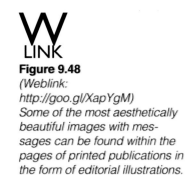

Figure 9.49
Edward Tufte.
Courtesy of Edward Tufte, Graphics Press LLC, Cheshire, CT

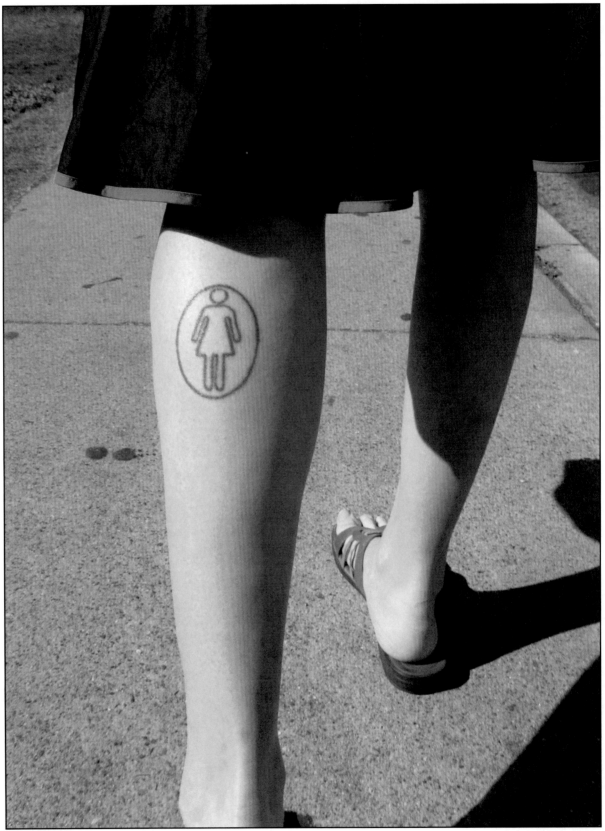

Figure 9.52
Based on the work of Otto Neurath and others in creating Isotype universal images, few of the simple pictures have recognizable women's shapes. One exception is the one used for bathroom doors, tattooed on this woman's leg.
Courtesy of Paul Martin Lester

Austrian statistician Otto Neurath wrote in 1925, "Words divide, pictures unite." In 1936 Neurath introduced a set of pictographic characters he called Isotype (International System of Typographic Picture Education) that he hoped would become a universal visual language and help unify the world. One of the illustrators who worked with Neurath was the German Gerd Arntz who drew more than 4,000 Isotype symbols (Figure 9.51). Traffic and Olympic competition sign designers owe their careers in large part to the efforts of Neurath (Figure 9.52).

The modern version of a universal visual language proposed by Neurath and Arntz has the multiple names of smileys, emoticons, or more widely called, emojis. First seen on Japanese smartphones in the late 1990s, these small pictographs were used in text messages to convey emotions or to communicate more clearly. For example, a "winkie" emoji after a sarcastic text indicates to the receiver that the previous statement should not be taken seriously. The popularity of such social media sites as Facebook, Twitter, and Instagram propelled the pictorial language into the mainstream. In 2015 the public relations department for Chevrolet produced a press release composed entirely of emojis in order to announce its Cruze, targeted for consumers in their twenties who use the language (Figure 9.53). Currently there are almost 3,000 distinct emoji characters with their definitions catalogued by the Emojipedia organization (Figure 9.54). A challenge for communicators is to understand the cultural meanings associated with the tiny, colorful characters. An "OK" hand gesture emoji in one culture means "all is fine," but others may view it as obscene. Nevertheless, people from different cultures may be more united in their common understanding of the information conveyed by the pictures rather than repelled. Data visualization pro-

ducers need to be concerned that mass audiences can understand their work. Carefully choosing the symbolism for communicating a message is vital in data visualization production.

Critical Perspective
Computer technology makes using words and numbers with pictures to produce sophisticated visual messages in the form of informational graphics easier than ever before. Computer hardware and software can make up for a lack of artistic talent. Unfortunately, much of the power of the computer is given to the creation of entertaining, decorative illustrations on subjects of little social importance. The computer can be used to make associations and inferences about seemingly incomprehensible data only if an operator has the skill to work comfortably with numbers.

The best data visualization designs "draw the viewer into the wonder of the data" and represent the true merging of word and image. The convergence of verbal and graphic reasoning should be a prime concern of educators, students, professionals, and consumers. Mark Monmonier in his book *Maps with the News* makes the point that most individuals view news graphics as "a means of analysis, not of communication." A simple locator map, he argues, is equivalent to third grade prose. And yet, a graphic is praised as if it were a thing of wonder simply because it can be produced quickly. If words and pictures are not united in form and function, the typical locator map suddenly becomes ridiculously rudimentary. Locator maps that show meaningful physical relationships, reveal an event's sequences, and explain complicated patterns within a specific area are intriguing and challenging. Data visualizations run the risk of becoming an entertainment medium when only entertainers use computers.

W LINK
Figure 9.51
(Weblink: http://goo.gl/D3I0Y5) Imagine coming up with 100 graphic images related to common objects and/or concepts. Now, expand the collection to produce 4,000 pictures and appreciate the work of Gerd Arntz.

W LINK
Figure 9.54
(Weblink: http://goo.gl/NRmELP) Emojipedia maintains a dictionary for all known characters within several categories, versions, and platforms. Type in a word and get it translated into a emoji symbol.

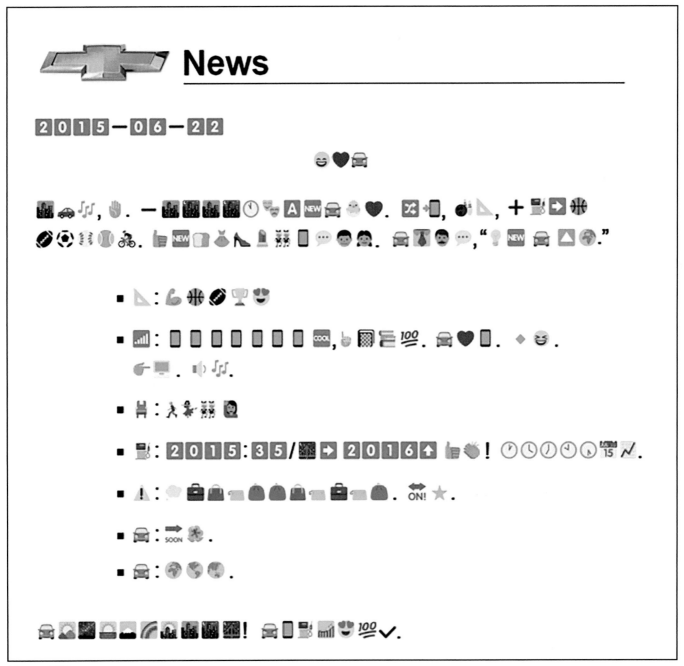

Figure 9.53
Starting with "Words alone can't describe the 2016 Cruze," the press release was the first of its kind. However, as emphasized in Chapter 7, the history of typography is concerned with turning highly symbolic line drawings into characters that can be easily read. Emojis are words.
Courtesy of the Chevrolet Division of the General Motors Company

If there is any hope for newspapers to attract more readers, a news story presented with the traditional treatment of a story and a photograph, whether in print or online, will not suffice. Informational graphics will have to be included to engage viewers and fully explain the cause. An interactive locator map that shows the approximate site of the story, with an interactive time line and a diagram that explains how the story unfolded, are now mandatory parts of a journalism message.

TRENDS TO WATCH FOR DATA VISUALIZATIONS

Showing information in unique, fascinating ways is the work of Seattle-based photographer Chris Jordan (See Chapter Two). Two collections on his website titled "Running the Numbers" present a series of manipulated photographs that when seen from a distance have unique communicative messages, but when viewed close-up become powerful informational graphics that convert raw data into surprising insights. For example, from about 20 feet, you see a pattern of colored dots with two swimming shark silhouettes. Move closer and it is revealed that the image "Shark Teeth, 2009" is composed of 270,000 images of fossilized shark teeth, "equal to the estimated number of sharks of all species killed around the world every day for their fins." Likewise, "Shipping Containers, 2007" becomes "38,000 shipping containers, the number of containers processed through American ports every twelve hours," "Plastic Bags, 2007" becomes "60,000 plastic bags, the number used in the US every five seconds," and "Constitution, 2008" transforms the Preamble to the U.S. Constitution into "83,000 Abu Ghraib prisoner photographs, equal to the number of people who have been arrested and held at the U.S. detention facilities with no trial or other due process of law, during the Bush Administration's war on terror."

An illustration of how informational graphics infiltrates popular culture is a music video from the Norwegian duo known as Röyksopp for their 2002 song "Remind Me" (Figure 9.55). Produced by the French graphics studio H5, the video shows the day in the life of a young professional woman working in London using everyday products with animated diagrams, maps, and charts in a cartoon style known as cel-shading. H5 also produced music videos for such bands as Goldfrapp, Massive Attack, and Super Furry Animals as well as commercials for Audi, Volkswagen, and Cartier. In 2010 H5 won an Academy Award for its 16-minute film, *Logorama* where everything is represented by brand logos (Figure 9.56).

When all media—newspapers, magazines, books, movies, television, and computers—become combined through the web, viewers will not be satisfied with static, traditional displays. Users will want to be engaged, challenged, and awed. It is up to data visualization designers now and in the future to reveal the rich and often hidden mysteries when everyday facts and events are combined in innovative and informative designs.

KEY TERMS FROM THIS CHAPTER

Adjusted for inflation • Analog • Bullet points • Cholera • Digital • Emoji • Engraving • Freelance • Halftone • Isobar • Logos • Noise • Qualitative • Quantitative • Wirephoto

Figure 9.55
(Weblink: http://goo.gl/djuPGm) Set to the tune of the foot-tapping "Remind Me," Röyksopp's music video is an extensive collection of data visualizations that describe a working woman's day produced by the French motion graphics company, H5.

Figure 9.56
(Weblink: http://goo.gl/hcrP22) Winner of an Academy Award, H5's Logorama shows more than 2,500 logos and mascots as a viewer travels around the Los Angeles area. As such, the film is an overt criticism of commercialism. H5 members explain, "Logorama presents us with an over-marketed world built only from logos and real trademarks that are destroyed by a series of natural disasters."

10 Cartoons

Homer, Marge, Bart, Lisa, and Maggie need no introduction. You have known them for more than 20 years (Figure 10.1).

Matt Groening (as he admits, "it rhymes with complaining") created Homer, a beer-and-pork-chop-loving family man and inattentive safety inspector for a nuclear power plant, his stay-at-home wife, Marge, with her blue-colored, beehive hairdo and their three children. Ten-year-old Bart (an anagram for Brat) is easily one of the most popular troublemakers on television, Lisa, the troubled, saxophone-playing, intellectual younger sister, is a favorite of all viewers who are sure that, when born, they were switched with another infant in the hospital, and baby Maggie, the quietly observant and untroubled baby of the family, constantly sucks on a pacifier.

The Simpsons never age, they live by their own set of rules, and are not easily killed—they must be vampires (Figure 10.2).

"The Simpsons" is a result of three powerful television forces—writer-producer James L. Brooks, writer Sam Simon, and Groening. Brooks is a savvy Hollywood veteran. He's the writer and producer of such highly respected motion pictures as *Terms of Endearment* (1983), *Broadcast News* (1987), *Big* (1988), and *As Good as It Gets* (1997). He was also the creator and multi-Emmy winner for such television hits as "The Mary Tyler Moore Show" (1970–1977), "Lou Grant" (1977–1982), and "Taxi" (1978–1979). In 1986 he formed his own production company, Gracie Films. Sam Simon was a writer for such shows as "Taxi," "Cheers," "It's Gary Shandling's Show," and "The George Carlin Show."

In 1987 Brooks and Simon were executive producers for the fledgling Fox television network's comedy series "The Tracey Ullman Show," starring the British comedienne. Groening was asked to produce 20-second cartoons that would air between the live sequences.

Figure 10.2
Bart seems to be the fan favorite as his dolls hang over Marge and Homer Simpson in a toy store at Universal Citywalk in Los Angeles.
**Courtesy of
Paul Martin Lester**

Figure 10.1
(Weblink: http://goo.gl/xTMr7A) The website for "The Simpsons" has everything a fan would love—stills, video clips, and links to merchandise.

Matt Groening was born in 1954 in Portland, Oregon, about a two-hour drive north of Springfield. In 2012 he admitted in an interview that the Oregon Springfield was the cartoon family's hometown. His real-life family resembles his cartoon creation. His father, Homer, was an independent filmmaker best known for his surrealist short, *Basic Brown Basic Blue* (1969) and his documentary, *Linfield Revisited* (1973) (Figure 10.3). His mother is named Margaret and wore her hair in a beehive. His sisters are Lisa and Maggie. "When I was a kid," Groening says, "my friends and I used to put on puppet shows, make comic books, and I decided that's what I wanted to do." Groening did well in school, although he was frequently sent to the principal's office for muttering wisecracks in class. What a shock (Figure 10.4).

A philosophy major at Evergreen State College in Olympia, Washington, he quit school and moved to Los Angeles in 1977 to become a writer. One of his first jobs was a low-paying position for a photocopying shop. His first cartoon series was titled *Work is Hell* sent to his friends about his after school experiences. Groening's clever wit morphed into commercial success with another cartoon, *Life in Hell*. The satirical comic features the characters Akbar and Jeff. When asked if the two characters are lovers or brothers, he answered, "Whatever offends you the most." *Life in Hell* was originally published in the Los Angeles new wave graphics innovator, *WET* magazine. In 1979 he was hired as an assistant editor for the independent newspaper, the *Los Angeles Reader*. The next year his *Life in Hell* cartoon began in the *Reader*. After a collection of individual cartoons was published in a book in 1984, his popularity soared. In 2002, it won the prestigious National Cartoonist Society Reuben Award. Groening still draws one *Life in Hell* cartoon a week—it is syndicated to as many as 250 publica-

Figure 10.4
Matt Groening
Courtesy of Gage Skidmore

tions (Figure 10.5).

James Brooks, a fan of Akbar and Jeff, asked Groening to use those characters for Ullman's show. But because the *Life in Hell* characters are limited in their situations and he didn't want to lose his marketing rights, came up with the Simpson family. Although the Ullman show was a critical success, it was not popular with viewers. Groening's Simpson shorts were a surprise hit. Brooks, Simon, and Groening then decided to produce a separate animated situation comedy. When "The Simpsons" hit the air in 1989 as a separate series, it won an Emmy Award that first year.

To date, "The Simpsons" has won 31 Primetime Emmy Awards, 30 Annie Awards from the International Animated Film Association, and a Peabody Award for television excellence. In 2000 the characters were awarded a star on the Hollywood Walk of Fame next to the musician Kenny G (Figure 10.6). On February 19, 2012 during its 23rd season "The Simpson's" aired its 500th episode with WikiLeaks founder Julian Assange, under house arrest in England, making a guest appearance. Groening's family-ori-

LINK
Figure 10.3
(Weblink: http://goo.gl/BnM6vj) Homer Groening's single-camera documentary is described on YouTube as, "Linfield Revisited is a 16mm color film from Homer Groening. A 1941 graduate of Linfield College in McMinnville, Oregon, Homer Groening 'revisited' the college in 1973 and produced this 28-minute color film, which he narrates. The film was shown by the college's Admissions and Alumni Offices."

LINK
Figure 10.5
(Weblink: http://goo.gl/EAyV5n) The graphic roots for "The Simpsons" are discovered by studying the simple lines and sophisticated humor of the "Life in Hell" cartoons.

Figure 10.6
"The Simpsons" star on Hollywood Boulevard preceded Matt Groening's star placed on the famous sidewalk in 2012.
Courtesy of Paul Martin Lester

ented comedy is the longest running animated program, situation comedy, and scripted prime-time series in television history. In 2016 the show was renewed for a 30th season up to 2019.

As an indication of the scope of the cultural influence of the television show, during its 13th season in the fall of 2001, the *Oxford English Dictionary* added Homer's catchphrase "D'oh." It is defined as "expressing frustration at the realization that things have turned out badly or not as planned, or that one has just said or done something foolish." In 2007 the feature-length motion picture *The Simpsons Movie*, co-written by Groening and Brooks, was released. Its worldwide ticket sales grossed over half a billion dollars. The next year "The Simpsons Ride" opened at Universal Orlando theme park, an IMAX-style motion ride that is (big surprise) a parody of a theme park attraction (Figure 10.7). In 2009 the U.S. Postal Service issued a first class stamp that featured the Simpson family, the first ever given to television characters while the show still aired on prime time. Said James Brooks, "We are emotionally moved by the Post Office Department's selecting us rather than making the lazy choice of someone who has benefited society." Unfortunately, the stamps didn't sell and the Postal Service was left with a $1.2 million bill—one of the only missteps by the producers.

Currently, Groening has backed off from much of the production work for the show and is now an executive producer and creative consultant for the series. Al Jean and Mike Reiss started as writers, and progressed to show runners (making sure each episode with all its component parts—writing, animation, voice-over acting, and so on—get completed). Reiss continues as a consulting producer and Jean is an executive producer for the show. Groening's work load increased after his 1999 futuristic cartoon *Futurama*, which ran on Fox until 2003, was picked up by Comedy Central and began airing new episodes in 2010. The series is in its seventh season. With a $500,000 endowment to the UCLA School of Theater, Film and Television, Groening established a Chair in Animation. In the meantime, he can be seen at comic book conventions signing autographs. He also occasionally plays with a rock band composed of famous authors such as Mitch Albom, Stephen King, and Amy Tan. Groening plays the cowbell.

Reaction to the barely functional cartoon family is as varied as the life experiences and attitudes of the viewers who watch it. If you are a fan of animated films, the cartoon may be appealing because it reminds you of your childhood. If you grew up in a similar home, you may laugh about like situations involving your family. If you enjoy watching the symbols of popular culture being gently nudged off their pedestals,

Figure 10.7
The Simpsons Ride at Universal Studios Hollywood. Bart seems out of character as he holds the rail of the roller coaster car in fright. Did they forget Maggie?
Courtesy of Paul Martin Lester

you will appreciate the humor of the program. But if you think cartoon characters should be reserved for children and their concerns, you probably will be offended at the social satire and adult themes and jokes expressed during the half-hour. Its ultra-violent cartoon-within-the-cartoon, "The Itchy and Scratchy Show" that the Simpson children love, for example, is meant to be a commentary on those that criticize violence in children's animated shows.

"The Simpsons" is drawn in a decidedly elementary graphic style. As Groening says, "I've been drawing this way since fifth grade—people with big eyes and overbites." His *Life in Hell* cartoon also is marked by a minimalist style. "The Simpsons" is composed of such simply rendered images for three important reasons: time, money, and intent. Detailed, realistic drawings require an enormous additional output from animators and cost far more. Spending less time on the visual message allows the producers to concentrate more on the writing and acting with the characters brought to life by Dan Castellaneta (Homer), Julie Kavner (Marge), Nancy Cartwright (Bart), Yeardley Smith (Lisa), and many others by Hank Azaria and Harry Shearer.

Figure 10.8

(Weblink: http://goo.gl/evZxYK) A variation of the "couch gag" seen at the start of every episode of "The Simpsons" created a critical stir when Banksy produced the short video. In an interview, Al Jean, an executive producer, admitted that although the animated cels are finished in South Korea, the working conditions are nothing like Banksy's vision.

Ethicists find fault with an aspect of the program that involves the way the shows are produced. For each episode, an American production company draws storyboards, new characters, and backgrounds. A South Korean animation company completes the frames necessary for each program. From start to finish the process takes about four months. The only reason for this long-distance arrangement is that Asian workers are paid much less than their U.S. counterparts. Even though the South Korean workers acquire specialized skills and money that they might not obtain in any other way, the cost of the exploitation is high. British street artist Banksy created an unforgettable dark opening to the show during the 22nd season in 2010. Although the opening starts as usual, the viewer is soon transformed to an assembly line of similarly dressed Asian children where cels are painted under dire conditions and dirge-like music, live kittens are killed for their fur to stuff toys, a panda bear pulls a cart with Bart dolls, tongue of a dolphin's head is used to seal boxes, and a unicorn's horn punches holes in the middle of CD disks. The Banksy work is an unrelenting satire of all that is exploitive and commercial about the show and animation generally (Figure 10.8).

The show teaches that rich people are greedy, politicians are corrupt, police officials are stupid, teachers and parents are easily manipulated, and children are devious. At the same time, it contains symbols that transcend this one family—Homer's love for bowling, beer, and bacon, Marge's simpleminded support of her sexist husband and ungrateful children, Bart's smart-aleck retorts, Lisa's angst and alienation, and Maggie's . . . no, Maggie is okay. Yet despite their many personality disorders, the Simpson family members manage to support one another and stay together. Although flawed in many ways, the Simpsons all love each other, and given the show's continued popularity, so too do the viewing public.

CARTOONS AND THE SIX PERSPECTIVES

When the manuscript for this textbook was first sent to the publisher, anonymous reviewers approved the work but with one exception—they all had the opinion that a chapter devoted to cartoons was not appropriate for a college-level course. In fact, for most of the history of cartoons, researchers have considered them unworthy of serious attention. It is hoped that by the end of this chapter there is an appreciation of the importance and complexity of the cartoon medium within the field of visual communications.

Personal Perspective

Few academic programs or private art schools offer courses in the production or theory of cartoon art. Editorial cartoonists for financially strapped newspapers are often the first to be let go. Comic strips, comic books, and animated movies are considered by many to be junk for children and unworthy of serious attention. But with the rise in the use of visual messages in all media, the highly respected graphic novel genre, and the rebirth of animated programs sparked by the success of "The Simpsons," this pictorial art form has gained new converts, with serious studies written by social and artistic scholars and private and public educational institutions train students to work in the industry.

Historical Perspective

Since the elaborately animated characters in motion picture, television, and computer programs all started as crudely rendered line drawings, it is important to know how cartoons developed in order to fully analyze present efforts.

Single-Framed Cartoons The historical roots of cartoons can be found in simple, unsigned visual messages that poked fun at others. Scrawled on walls by untrained artists (today we call such examples graffiti), these cartoons reveal an average person's opinion about someone in power that is missing from many mainstream historical documents. There are three types of single-framed cartoons: caricatures, political, and humorous.

Caricatures The first cartoons were caricatures (Figure 10.9). In about 1360BCE, some unknown cartoonist painted an unflattering portrait of Akhenaten, the unpopular father of the Egyptian boy King Tutankhamen. In India, cartoonists made fun of their Hindu god Krishna. Greek terra-cotta vases and wall paintings often were decorated with profane parodies of overweight Olympian gods. Dating from at least 2,500 years ago, ancient Latino cultures used to keep the skulls of their vanquished as trophies. This ritual led to the *Dia de Los Muertos*, or Day of the Dead, a ritual that celebrates those who have passed and the promise of rebirth on All Soul's Day on Halloween (Figure 10.10). Almost every country in the world has a tradition of wearing elaborate, often brightly painted masks during festivals, theater performances, and other rituals (Figure 10.11).

Today, a single-framed caricature is an important illustrative device created by such artists as Sam Viviano, Sebastian Krüger, and Hermann Mejia.

Political Cartoons The founder of the English political cartoon is considered to be William Hogarth. In 1731, he published his most famous collection of drawings, *A Harlot's Progress*. Because he was appalled by the living conditions of the poor of his day, he intended his drawings to be moralistic lessons rather than entertainment (Figure 10.12).

Another British artist, James Gillray was known for his satirical portraits of Napoleon, whom he and other cartoon-

Figure 10.9
At Universal Citywalk in Los Angeles a couple bravely poses for a caricature artist's portrait in front of examples that include the exaggerated features of such celebrities as Richard Pryor, Whoopi Goldberg, former President Barack Obama, and Jay Leno.
Courtesy of Paul Martin Lester

Figure 10.10
One of the most popular El Dia de los Muertos ("Day of the Dead" or "All Souls Day") figures is that of the high society woman, "La Catrina." Popularized by Jose Guadalupe Posada, a Mexican engraver and illustrator, his lithographic calaveras or skulls often satirized the upper class with exaggerated, caricature figures. Here she is used to sell paletas, a fruit-based ice drink.
Courtesy of Paul Martin Lester

Figure 10.11
"Ngil mask from Gabon or Cameroon," Africa, 19th century. Members of the religious and legal secret society known as Ngil wore masks during ceremonies meant to maintain social order and their power. Law-breakers and those accused of sorcery feared for their lives by their rulings. When illuminated by firelight, the mask, with its long shape, double arched eyes, ape-like mouth, and pale color symbolizing the spirit of the dead, were dramatic and fearsome.
Courtesy of Bin im Garten

Figure 10.12

"Plate 1 of Harlot's Progress," 1732, by William Hogarth. This first engraving in the series shows the destitute and tentative Molly arriving in London and being greeted by a syphilitic brothel madam. Leering in the background is the likeness of Colonel Frances Charteris, an actual person nicknamed "The Rape-Master General," as he was convicted of raping a servant girl two years before the cartoon was drawn. He was pardoned, but died soon afterward. Hogarth became one of the most influential editorial cartoonists in history, particularly responsible for sequential narratives that led to comic books and motion picture storyboards. A prolific and popular artist who overcame his humble beginnings, seven years before his death he was named the "Serjeant Painter" to George II, King of England, essentially the monarch's personal artist.

Courtesy of the British Museum

ists called "Little Boney." His strong graphic style combined with a powerful political message influenced many subsequent cartoonists (Figure 10.13).

The most famous American political cartoonist during this period was Thomas Nast. He is responsible for the popular elephant symbol used by the Republican Party, the donkey by the Democratic Party, Uncle Sam and for the popular image of Santa Claus (Figure 10.14).

Nast is also known for his campaign to bring down the corrupt politician William "Boss" Tweed of Tammany Hall during the 1870s. Tweed and his Democratic cronies stole from the New York County treasury. Nast drew more than 50 political cartoons for *Harper's Weekly* criticizing Tweed (Figure 10.15). In 1886 he quit *Harper's* after he clashed with the

Figure 10.13
"The plumb-pudding in danger," February 26, 1805. William Pitt the Younger (left), the youngest Prime Minister of Great Britain wears a regimental uniform and hat and sits at a table with Napoleon Bonaparte carving their piece of the world. With his sharp pen, sharper wit, and fearless opinions, James Gillray is considered to be England's most influential political cartoonist in history. Sadly, after his eyesight began to fail, he started drinking heavily and attempted to kill himself. He died insane in 1815 the year Napoleon was defeated at Waterloo.
Courtesy of the Library of Congress

Figure 10.14
Although Thomas Nast originally penned a portrait of Santa Claus in an 1863 issue of Harper's Weekly, *it proved to be so popular that in 1889 he made the drawing seen here that became the icon for the gift-giving character.*
Courtesy of the Library of Congress

newspaper's new management and eventually ran a magazine he renamed *Nast's Weekly*. After it failed he was rescued financially by Theodore Roosevelt who named him Consul General to Ecuador. But when yellow fever broke out, he caught the disease and died in 1902.

Following in Nast's tradition were newspaper editorial cartoonists Bill Mauldin, Herbert Block, and Paul Conrad.

Mauldin began as a cartoonist for the military's newspaper, *Stars and Stripes* during World War II where his cynical and honest soldier characters Willie and Joe were grudgingly tolerated by the generals and loved by the GIs on the ground. He worked for the *St. Louis Post-Dispatch* and retired from the *Chicago Sun-Times*. His most famous cartoon is a 1963 drawing of the Lincoln Memorial grieving the death of President Kennedy printed in the *Sun-Times*. Seven years after his death in 2003, the U.S. Postal Service issued a stamp

that depicted him with Willie and Joe. During his career, he won the Pulitzer Prize twice for his cartoons (Figure 10.16).

Herbert Block or Herblock was the political cartoonist for the *Washington Post* and invented the word *McCarthyism* to describe the Wisconsin senator's communist witch hunt (Figure 10.17). His drawing of Richard Nixon as a shifty-eyed, unshaven character became an unshakable symbol of that political leader throughout his career. Block won his third Pulitzer Prize for criticizing the Nixon Administration during the Watergate scandal of the 1970s. He died three

Figure 10.15
"A Group of Vultures Waiting for the Storm to Blow Over" – 'Let Us Prey,'" Harper's Weekly, September 23, 1871. The Tammany Ring with William "Boss" Tweed and members of his cabal, Peter B. Sweeny, Richard B. Connolly, and A. Oakey Hall weather a violent storm on a ledge over the remains of New York City.
Courtesy of Harper & Brothers

A GROUP OF VULTURES WAITING FOR THE STORM TO "BLOW OVER."—"LET US *PREY*."

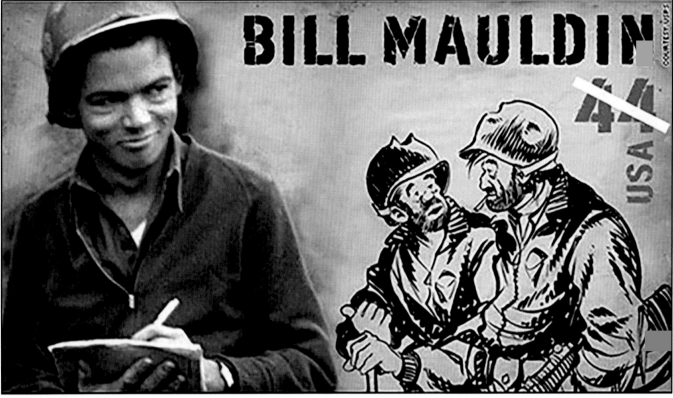

Figure 10.16
Postmaster General John Wanamaker in 1893 thought of the idea for a commemorative stamp. The first honored the World Columbian Exposition. In 2010. Bill Mauldin was so honored.
Courtesy of the U.S. Postal Service

days short of his 92nd birthday about a month after the 9/11 attacks.

Paul Conrad worked for the *Los Angeles Times* for 29 years until his retirement. Winner of three Pulitzer Prize awards, he also took aim at President Nixon during Watergate and was a member, along with Herblock, on Nixon's enemies list. He died in 2010. His stark visual style and direct messages are an outgrowth of his philosophy about cartoons. He once said, "I figure eight seconds is the absolute maximum time anyone should have" to understand a cartoon's meaning (Figure 10.18).

Political cartoons filled with emotionally symbolic visual messages can spark great controversy and violence. In September 2005 after the Danish newspaper *Jyllands-Posten* printed 12 cartoons with most depicting the Islamic prophet Muhammad in satirical or silly ways, many in the Muslim world organized protests, with some that turned

violent. There was also a boycott of all things Danish (Figure 10.19). In open letters to readers, editors for the newspaper defended the publication of the cartoons on free speech grounds, but apologized if anyone were offended by their content. The editorial office of the French satirical weekly magazine *Charlie Hebdo* was attacked in 2011 and 2015 for its depictions of Muhammad on its covers (Figure 10.20). In 2011 the office was firebombed, but no one was injured, but in 2015 armed terrorists entered the Paris office, opened fire, and killed 12 and wounded 11. Free speech advocates and concerned citizens held rallies around the world in support of the magazine around the theme, "Je Suis Charlie" (Figure 10.21).

Humorous Cartoons Harold Ross, a high school dropout who learned journalism while copyediting as an employee of the U.S. government's *Stars and*

"FIRE!"

Figure 10.17
This cartoon from Herbert Block illustrates the hysterical McCarthy era when many patriotic Americans were accused wrongly of being communists. Here, Herblock uses symbolism to make his point: The open-mouthed man with "HYSTERIA" written across his pants and a water bucket spilling its contents suggest a rush to douse the flame of Liberty.
Courtesy of the Library of Congress

Stripes magazine, started *The New Yorker* magazine in 1925. Ross had a gift for hiring excellent personnel. Some of the most famous *New Yorker* cartoonists include Charles Addams, Peter Arno, Roz Chast, Saul Steinberg, Gahan Wilson, and Edward Steed (Figure 10.22). The magazine is credited with having almost single-handedly developed the art of the humorous cartoon to its highest intellectual potential.

Multi-framed Cartoons

The roots of multi-framed cartoons are about as long as caricatures. Egyptian scholars found a burial chamber mural from about 1300BCE that showed two wrestlers fighting one another in several sequential frames (Figure 10.23). More than 1,700 years later in 1067, the Bayeux Tapestry is a huge embroidered cloth wall decoration more than 200 feet long that depicts the Norman conquest of England with figures within sepa-

rate frames or borders (Figure 10.24). Multi-framed cartoons include comic strips, comic books, graphic novels, and animated films.

Comic Strips The first color comic strip was Richard Outcault's *Hogan's Alley*, first published on May 5, 1895, in Joseph Pulitzer's *Sunday World*. The cartoon provided social commentary in the disguise of a collection of orphaned, unkempt children living among the tenement houses in New York City. The central character was a towheaded, unnamed boy in a nightshirt who smoked cigars. A printer in Pulitzer's back shop made the boy yellow to help him stand out in the crowd of children (Figure 10.25).

The dada art movement coincided with the *Krazy Kat* comic strip of George Herriman. Introduced in 1915, the cartoon described a surreal and often violent world of a mean-spirited mouse named Ignatz and an alley cat who loved him (Figure 10.26). Born in New Orleans in 1880 to Creole parents, the family moved to Los Angeles to escape discrimination caused by Jim Crow laws. At the age of 17 he worked as an illustrator for the *Herald-Examiner*. By the 1920s he was famous for his comic strip in publisher's William Randolph Hearst's newspapers, a Broadway play based on his characters, and induction into *Vanity Fair*'s "Hall of Fame." Sadly, at the height of his success, his wife was killed in a car accident and his daughter died a few years later. Nevertheless, the charm of his scratchily-drawn characters endures. In the last scene of Quentin Tarantino's breakthrough motion picture *Pulp Fiction* (1994), the philosophical hit man Jules played by Samuel L. Jackson, wears a blue t-shirt with a graphic of Krazy Kat hitting Ignatz with a brick.

An important innovation in the continuing popularity of comic strips—the serial—first appeared in the 1920s. Adventure stories that continued from

Figure 10.18
(Weblink: http://goo.gl/CzLiiC)
As with the work of Saul Bass (Chapter 8), the genius of Paul Conrad is that he could take a complex topic and distill it down to its most salient graphic properties.

Figure 10.19
(Weblink: http://goo.gl/mysWnd)
For most Muslims, any visual depiction of the prophet Muhammad is forbidden by religious and social conventions. Imagine if your most cherished religious leader was depicted as a bomb carrying terrorist?

Figure 10.20
(Weblink: http://goo.gl/XmRydt)
The French Charlie Hebdo humor magazine is known for its controversial cover cartoons that usually pokes fun at religious leaders regardless of faith—a clash of free speech vs. discretion. Perhaps a golden mean approach could ease tensions between humorists and fundamentalists (See Chapter 6).

Figure 10.22
(Weblink: http://goo.gl/aKBfo2)
Whenever you notice the scratchy drawing style of an Edward Steed cartoon, cover the caption as quick as you can and try to guess what a character says. Once revealed,

Figure 10.21
A man holds a "Je Suis Charlie" sign during a rally of support for the Charlie Hebdo magazine in Strasbourg, France.
Courtesy of Claude Truong-Ngoc

Figure 10.23
Found on a wall of the burial chamber of Baqet III, governor of the Oryx district in central Egypt, is a sequence of about 200 wrestlers in various poses. Estimated to be about 3,500 years old, the images are often cited as one of the earliest examples of multi-framed cartoons.
Courtesy of Olaf Tausch

Figure 10.24
More than 950 years old and measuring about a yard high and more than 75 yards long, the Bayeux Tapestry is one of the finest examples of visual narrative storytelling. Although misnamed a tapestry, it was not fabricated with a loom, this handmade embroidered work tells of the 1066 Norman victory at the Battle of Hastings. After the Norman Conquest, England became ruled by French-speaking royalty, which significantly changed the English language. In this fragment of a panel, English soldiers are killed during the battle.
Courtesy of Dan Koehl

day to day were enormously popular. Many newspapers depended on them for their survival. Richard Calkins and Phil Nowlan produced the 25th century space traveler "Buck Rogers" and Harold Foster brought Edgar Rice Burroughs's "Tarzan" character to visual life. These and other adventure and soap opera serials inspired motion picture and television producers to create storylines that developed through multiple sequels and episodes.

One of the most popular cartoon strips was *Peanuts* by Charles Schulz, originally published on October 2, 1950. His tale of a band of small children and a dog in the minimalist artistic tradition became a symbol for America (Figure 10.27). At its peak the strip reached 300 million readers in 75 countries and

Figure 10.25

As printed in a 1905 edition of the San Francisco Call, *the "Kid from Hogan's Alley" was never as happy as when he was carried on the shoulders of his creator, Richard Felton Outcault and moving to a new paper. An employee of Thomas Edison hired to promote electric lighting in Europe, Outcault's "Yellow Kid" character later was the subject of bidding wars between two powerful publishers of the day—Joseph Pulitzer and William Randolph Hearst—the basis for the term "yellow journalism," or an unethical practice when a subject is paid for an interview. For this illustration, yellow was added to the kid.*

Courtesy of the Library of Congress

Figure 10.27

One of the most beloved cartoon characters in the world is Charles Shultz's Snoopy. In 1969 the beagle, along with Charlie Brown, were the unofficial mascots for the Apollo 10 mission to the moon. Here, Commander Thomas Stafford pats the nose of the dog for good luck on his way to the launch complex.

Courtesy of NASA

Figure 10.26

In this 1918 anniversary issue of The Washington Times, *his Krazy Kat characters surround cartoonist George Herriman, who almost always wore a hat in public to hide his hair and African American heritage. Herriman inspired cartoonists such as Chuck Jones and Tex Avery of Warner Bros.*

Courtesy of the Library of Congress

appeared in 2,600 newspapers in 21 languages. The strip helped make Schultz "the wealthiest contemporary cartoonist in the history of comics."

A current, if at times controversial cartoonist is Garry Trudeau. He began *Doonesbury* in 1968 while a student at Yale. In 1975, Trudeau became the first comic strip artist to win a Pulitzer Prize for his cartoons about the Vietnam War, former president Richard Nixon, and the Watergate scandal. He won an Academy Award in 1977 for his short animated film, *A Doonesbury Special* and another Pulitzer in 1990. Today, the strip appears in nearly 1,400 papers mostly seen on the comics pages.

Comic Books In 1933, Eastern Color published *Funnies on Parade*, an eight-page tabloid-sized collection of cartoons. Maxwell Gaines, a salesperson for Eastern, convinced his bosses to fold the tabloid-sized publication to more resemble a book. The result contained 36 pages and was named *Famous Funnies: A Carnival of Comics*. It is considered the first comic book (Figure 10.28).

Gaines went on to establish Educational Comics (EC) specializing in crime and science fiction stories. After Max Gaines died in a boating accident in 1947, his son, William, took over EC and created in 1952 the irreverent parody of popular culture, *Mad* magazine (Figure 10.29).

Inspired by the success of a separate book of cartoons, action adventure stories soon followed. The first major superhero character, Superman, was the brainchild of two Cleveland, Ohio high school students, Jerry Siegel and Joe Schuster. The two sold all of their rights to the character for $412 (about $6,300 today). In 2012 the check itself sold in auction for $160,000. Originally produced as a comic strip for newspapers, the original Superman was born in Action Comics #1 in 1938. Action Comics eventually became Detective Comics (DC) and introduced such characters as Batman, Wonder Woman, and the Flash. In 2012 issue No. 27 that introduced Batman was sold for $523,000. Another giant in the field, Marvel Entertainment introduced memorable characters from the minds of writer Stan Lee and artist Jack Kirby such as The Fantastic Four and the X-Men. Lee and artist Steve Ditko created The Amazing Spider-Man in 1962, one of the most successful superhero characters that has rivaled Superman's popularity. Stan Lee has worked with comic heroes for more than 70 years. He is unrivaled in terms of his influence over the medium with successes in comics, films, cameo roles, and marketing. Academy Award director Steven Spielberg once told him, "You do pretty much what I do, except my pictures move." Marvel's *The Avengers* opened in 2012 with the characters Black Widow, Captain America, Hawkeye, Hulk, Iron Man, Loki, and Thor.

Comic books (sometimes called "floppies) also can express serious subjects in a nonthreatening way. Author Harvey Pekar's 1976 *American Splendor* (with many issues illustrated by Robert

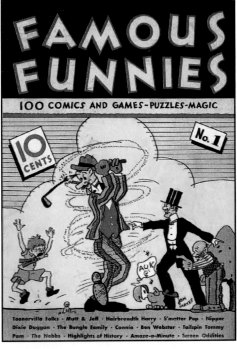

Figure 10.28
Originally, comic books were specially prepared publications produced by newspapers as an advertisement for their comic strips. Max Gaines printed 35,000 copies of Famous Funnies *in 1934 with cover art by John Mayes. The comic book proved to be enormously successful.*
Courtesy of the Grand Comics Database

Figure 10.29
William Gaines began Entertaining Comics as a way to interest adults in reading science fiction and horror comic books. Part of the EC empire were his Crime and Shock SuspenStories issues. Called the "most notorious cover illustration of all time," Johnny Craig's illustration on the 1954 issues #22 Crime Suspen-Stories was part of a Senate committee convened to investigate juvenile delinquency. Chair Sen. Estes Kefauver questioned William Gaines on the cover's appropriateness for children. This cover is a typical example of the genre with its mix of typeface styles, font sizes, and action-oriented illustrations.
Courtesy of CGC Comics

Figure 10.30
One of Robert Crumb's most popular characters is the always frisky Fritz the Cat first published in his publication, R. Crumb's Head Comix in 1968.
Courtesy of Sugar Bear

Figure 10.31
Typical of Japanese manga, this illustration of a schoolgirl shows free-flowing penmanship, large eyes, and youthful innocence.
Courtesy of Kasuga

Crumb) was his effort to tell everyday stories with quirky observations in contrast to the superhero comic books of the day. Crumb's irreverently humorous characters, Fritz the Cat, the Fabulously Furry Freak Brothers, and Mr. Natural poked fun at the hypocrisies he saw in the emerging hippie social movement (Figure 10.30).

In Japan and other Asian countries, comic books are called *manga*. They are so popular with adults that they dominate entire bookstores (Figure 10.31). And yet, in the United States, comic book sales are falling since its high in 2007. Media critics wonder if the reason is the same for other reading materials—younger audiences would rather watch movies, see YouTube videos, and play video games. To buck the trend, in 2011 DC, owned by Warner Bros., brought back all of their superheroes with updated costumes, simplified storylines, and digital downloads. Time will tell if these innovations will save the industry.

Graphic Novels Art Spiegelman showed American readers that a graphic novel could be literature worthy of respect. His retelling of the Holocaust in an animal fable called *Maus* won a National Book Critics Award in 1987, the first time the award had ever gone to a cartoon. Adding additional prestige to the medium, author Alan Moore and illustrator Dave Gibbons teamed to produce *Watchmen*, the only graphic novel honored by *Time* magazine as one of the top 100 English-language books ever written. Brian Selznick's critically acclaimed story, *The Invention of Hugo Cabret* about a lost boy who is found, was magically transformed by director Martin Scorsese into the film, *Hugo* (2011). The fusion of words and pictures were never so obviously transforming. The power of telling stories through visual messages held in the hand in the form of a book is also demonstrated in a three-book series titled, *March*. Written by Congressman John Lewis and Andrew Aydin and illustrated by Nate Powell, the *March* trilogy tells the story of Lewis and the Civil Rights movement. Another powerful work was produced by the Naval Health Research Center. *The Docs* is meant to prepare Navy corpsmen how to deal with the stress of combat (Figure 10.32).

Animated Films The history of animated film is naturally tied to the history of the motion picture. In 1876 Professor Charles-Émile Reynaud of France managed to combine several drawings and a projection system he called a praxinoscope. In 1882 he opened the first public theater for showing animated films, the *Théâtre Optique* (Figure 10.33). Reynaud showed thousands of cartoons, many drawn by his assistant Émile Cohl. Reynaud's setup predated the Lumière brothers' public motion picture showings by 13 years.

In 1879 the photographer and adventurer Eadweard Muybridge introduced his zoopraxiscope that projected sequential stop-motion photographs on rotating discs that provided the illusion of movement (Figure 10.34). Muybridge's invention inspired the American inventor Thomas Edison and his assistant William Kennedy Dickson to develop the Kinetoscope in 1888, marking the start of the motion picture industry.

The founder of the American animated film industry is considered to be the cartoonist Winsor McCay. In 1906, he printed a series of drawings of a trapeze artist inspired from a child's flip book. These sequential pictures inspired him to make animated movies. In 1914, he created *Gertie, the Trained Dinosaur*, a charming, crowd-pleasing animated brontosaurus that happily performed according to McCay's stage instructions (Figure 10.35).

But the master of animation was Walt Disney who grew up on a small farm in Missouri and went on to become

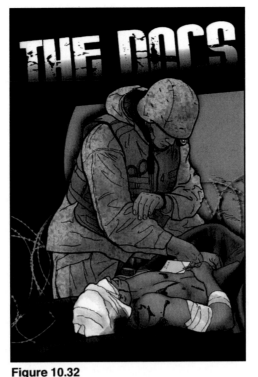

Figure 10.32
Instead of a traditional text-based book that detailed the stresses associated with combat, Naval executives produced a graphic novel, The Docs *to tell the story in pictures. The reason for the cartoon version is simple. As one corpsman wrote, "Comics have always been a hit for the troops while deployed, they would change hands so many times being passed from one to another until a whole unit would have read what was sent to one guy."*
Courtesy of the Naval Health Research Center

Figure 10.33
Charles-Émile Reynaud stood behind a screen and hid from the audience as he would turn wheels that moved his images, creating the animation effect. A lamp illuminated the pictures while a mirror projected them on a screen.
Courtesy of the Library of Congress

W
LINK
Figure 10.35
*(Weblink:
http://goo.gl/8RcGvC)
For some, Winsor McCay's*
Gertie, the Trained Dinosaur *is
the first example in animation
history of live action/cartoon
interaction.*

Figure 10.34

"#29 Mule—Bucking and Kicking," 1896, by Eadweard Muybridge. In 1879 Eadweard Muybridge invented a movie projector he called the zoopraxiscope. The illusion of animation was created by sequential painted pictures and, later, hand-colored photographs that were transferred to glass discs and spun within a cabinet. A lamp illuminated the pictures through a lens with which the images were projected on a screen. Muybridge demonstrated his invention to audiences in America, England, and France. In 1888 he showed it to the American inventor Thomas Edison. And yet, as a still photographer, Muybridge never realized the enormous social and economic implications of what he had invented.

Courtesy of the Library of Congress

the undisputed king of American animation. After graduation from high school and a brief stint as an ambulance driver in France for the Red Cross during World War I, he settled in Kansas City, created advertisements for an art studio, and met fellow artist Ubbe (Ub) Iwerks. After the two were laid off, Iwerks, Walt, and his brother Roy teamed up to create short cartoons based on fairy tales called *Newman Laugh-O-Grams* in 1921 that were shown in local movie theaters (Figure 10.36). The three then moved to

Hollywood in 1923 and made films with the series name *Alice in Cartoonland*, which combined a live-action girl with drawn characters (Figure 10.37). In 1927 the team introduced its first popular animal character, Oswald the Lucky Rabbit for Universal Studios (Figure 10.38). However, when Disney learned that the contract he signed gave the copyright to the studio, he and Ub created a second animal character similar to the rabbit but with smaller ears—a mouse originally named Mortimer. Luckily, the name was changed to Mickey Mouse, the most beloved cartoon character in the world. Mickey debuted in a silent film, *Plane Crazy* in 1928. Later that same year, Disney introduced *Steamboat Willie*, which had a fully synchronized sound track with Disney putting his voice to Mickey (Figure 10.39). The mouse would eventually star in more than 130 cartoons. In 2006 the Walt Disney Co. traded sportscaster Al Michaels to Universal-NBC for Oswald so the rabbit could star in "Disney Epic Mickey 2: The Power of Two," an adventure game for the Wii, PlayStation 3, and Xbox 360.

The first color cartoon, *Flowers and Trees*, won the Disney team its first Academy Award in 1933. *Snow White* (1937), *Pinocchio* (1939), *Fantasia* (1940), *Dumbo* (1941), *Bambi* (1942), *One Hundred and One Dalmatians* (1961), and many others followed. After World War II, Walt Disney concentrated on live-action nature films, the merchandising of his characters, television shows, and theme parks—Disneyland in southern California and, later, Disney World and Epcot Center in central Florida. The crowning achievement for the studio, *Beauty and the Beast* (1991), was the first-ever animated motion picture nominated in the Best Picture category along with the other live-action features by the Academy Awards. It was rereleased as a 3D version in 2012. In 2017 another *Beauty and the Beast* version reached theaters as a live action/animation combination.

Inspired by the absurd violence and cynicism of George Herriman's *Krazy Kat*, Fred "Tex" Avery, Friz Freleng, and Chuck Jones at Warner Bros. studio, created such classic *Looney Tunes* and *Merrie Melodies* characters as Bugs Bunny, Porky Pig, Daffy Duck, Elmer Fudd, Wile E. Coyote, and the Roadrunner (Figure 10.40). The team made more than 800 films.

Other famous cartoon animators provided popular characters. Friz Fre-

leng invented Tweety Pie, Sylvester, and the Pink Panther. Walter Lantz created Woody Woodpecker. Jay Ward produced the popular "Rocky and Bullwinkle" Saturday morning television show with stories that appealed to both children and adults. William Hanna and Joseph Barbera had Mr. Magoo and Huckleberry Hound. In 1960, the team produced the first prime-time television cartoon, "The Flintstones" (Figure 10.41). Paul Reubens aka Peewee Herman was an elementary grade student said, "The whole idea of a cartoon in prime time was exciting." With the success of that Stone Age family, the production company moved the familiar situation comedy genre ahead a few centuries to create "The Jetsons" (Figure 10.42).

Pixar Animated Studios started as a computer division of *Star Wars* (1977) director George Lucas's company, Lucasfilm. After Apple Computer co-founder Steven Jobs bought the division in 1986, it was renamed Pixar. One of the animators that worked for Lucasfilm was the talented John Lasseter. He won an Academy Award for the first all-computer-generated short feature *Tin Toy* (1988) (Figure 10.43). He also directed *Toy Story* (1995), the first feature-length animated cartoon produced solely with computer technology, as well as *A Bug's Life* (1998), *Toy Story 2* (1999), and *Cars* (2006), also all-computer productions. Pixar and Disney collaborated to produce *Monsters, Inc.* in 2001, which featured innovations in computer-generated technology. Another collaboration with Disney was *Finding Nemo* (2003), which won the 2004 Academy Award for best animated motion picture. In 2006 Disney acquired the Pixar Company. John Lasseter became the chief creative officer of Pixar and the Walt Disney Animation Studios. A friend of Lasseter's and an animator for Warner Bros. and Disney, Brad Bird won Academy Awards for Best Animated Feature for *The Incredibles* (2004) and *Ratatouille* (2007). He has also directed

W LINK

Figure 10.36 (Weblink: http://goo.gl/RgqQYx) Walt Disney plays an over-worked animator in this early animated tale. The film is a study of how much work there is involved in creating an animation.

W LINK

Figure 10.37
(Weblink: http://goo.gl/uuRVEN) The live action Alice character trades magical dives with a cartoon character and is involved in various predicaments in this Disney classic.

Figure 10.39

(Weblink: http://goo.gl/p9LXAL) Any visitor to a Disney amusement park who wants to escape the heat of summer finds herself in a movie theater that continually plays the classic film, Steamboat Willie—the first synchronized sound cartoon.

Figure 10.40

(Weblink: http://goo.gl/jqUpna) All of the Looney Tune characters are featured on this Warner Bros. website.

Figure 10.41

(Weblink: http://goo.gl/JcUK1A) Hanna-Barbera studies produced the first prime-time television animated situation comedy, "The Flintstones."

Figure 10.42

(Weblink: http://goo.gl/wQcL9A) "The Jetsons" opening sequence with its catchy song predicted self-driving flying vehicles.

Figure 10.43

(Weblink: http://goo.gl/L4qJRu) Watch for the Pixar logo on the shopping bag and the generic toys hiding under the couch (the author's favorite scene) in Tin Toy. John Lasseter couldn't afford to pay for the use of actual toys, but he could two years later for Toy Story.

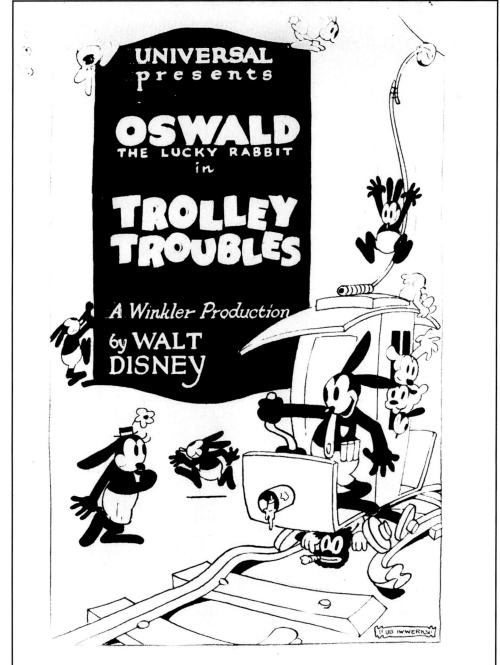

Figure 10.38
Poster for Oswald the Lucky Rabbit in "Trolley Troubles."
Courtesy of Universal Pictures

two episodes of "The Simpsons" and broke into live-action filmmaking when he directed Tom Cruise in *Mission Impossible – Ghost Protocol* (2011). The 12 Pixar feature-length movies have earned more than $6.5 billion worldwide and 10 Academy Awards.

A major producer of both live action and animated films is DreamWorks SKG, which was started by Hollywood heavyweights David Greffen, Jeffrey Katzenberg, and Steven Spielberg in 1994. The company has produced three types of animated movies: hand-drawn cel, seen in *The Prince of Egypt* (1998); stop-motion, through a partnership with Aardman Animations headed by the British animator Nick Park, for *Wallace*

& *Gromit: The Curse of the Were-Rabbit* (2005); and computer-animated, such as *Shrek* (2001), and *Madagascar: Escape 2 Africa* (2008).

Another animation house is the combination of Paramount Pictures and Lucasfilm's Industrial Light and Magic. The collaboration is off to a great start. Their first motion picture, *Rango* (2011), directed by Gore Verbinski, won the 2012 Academy Award for Best Animated Feature Film.

Released in 2017 are such titles as *Captain Underpants: The First Epic Movie (DreamWorks), The LEGO Batman Movie* (DC Entertainment), *Cars 3* (Pixar), *The Boss Baby* (DreamWorks), and *Despicable Me 3* (Universal). There seems to be no end to the production of animated motion pictures as new generations of cartoon fans crave cartoons.

Technical Perspective

Whether cartoons are intended for print or screen media presentations, the cartoonist uses specific devices to convey information to the viewer. The meaning of these graphic conventions often is not obvious because as symbolic codes, they must be learned (Figure 10.44). In order to analyze cartoons, you need to be aware of the various terms used to describe illustrative techniques. Once you know the name of an element, you will notice it more easily. One of the most respected sources to help you understand print cartoon production is Scott McCloud's *Understanding Comics: The Invisible Art* (1994).

There are at least eight separate technical considerations for cartoonists in print and screen media:

Frame Top and bottom boxes or panels often contain narration and story explanations. Different sized frames increase visual interest (Figure 10.45).

Setting The background illustrations might be highly stylized and simple as in

Figure 10.44
Editorial cartoons often are filled with symbols—some understandable, but many dependent for their meaning or a thorough knowledge of the time in which they were produced. Justice gives up her seat for an unknown corrupt politician in this woodcut.
Uncensored Situations, 1966, the Dick Sutphen Studio, Inc.

Figure 10.45
Although Colombian artist and illustrator Patricio Ruales López has been a professional for only a short time, she has developed comic books, book covers for a Spanish publisher, and illustrations for video games for companies based in Canada, Mexico, and the United States. In her "good vs. evil" futuristic action comic Cancro, *the use of differently sized frames—square, horizontal, and small verticals—heighten the dramatic action and compel the viewer to think of the page as a motion picture on paper.*
Courtesy of Patricio Ruales Lopez

Figure 10.46
Little Sammy Sneeze was the print and screen media animation artist Winsor McCay's first regular comic strip. Begun in 1904 in the pages of the New York Herald, *every week his main character, an innocent-looking boy, would be placed in a variety of settings and end with "CHOW," a sneeze that would usually create great havoc. In this series, McCay uses the simplest setting possible, a blank background to emphasize the innocence of the lone child who has no one else but himself to blame for destroying the cartoon's frame with his sneeze.*
Courtesy of Peter Maresca/Sunday Press Books

a *Peanuts* cartoon or realistic and elaborate as in the *Spider-Man* comic strip. The degree to which elements of reality are removed from a cartoon is called *leveling*. Often the artist conveys the seriousness of the cartoon by a high or low degree of leveling (Figure 10.46).

Characters As with the setting, the degree of realism with which the characters are drawn often indicates whether the strip is humorous or serious. *Assimilation* is the term used to describe the technique of exaggerating features, usually for a stereotypical effect. Homer Simpson's large belly and Marge's high beehive are examples. As with any pictorial representation of the human face, expressions connote emotional states that may help explain a character's motives (Figure 10.47).

Motion Lines Mort Walker, creator of the popular strip *Beetle Bailey*, gave names to various movement lines: hites—horizontal movement, vites—vertical motions, dites—diagonal movement, agitrons—wavering or repetitive motions, briffits—little puffs of smoke or dirt, waftaroms—odors that float in the frame, and plewds—sweat beads that pop up on a character's forehead that indicate nervousness (Figure 10.48).

Typography Unlike any other art form, the reader of a comic strip, comic book,

Figure 10.47
The fear of the Frankenstein monster is enhanced with an illustrator's technique that emphasizes his facial and arm gestures in this production of the Mary Shelley horror story. The comic book series based on famous novels debuted in 1941 as Classic Comics, *changed its name in 1947 to* Classics Illustrated, *and ceased publication in 1971.*
Courtesy of Wikimedia Commons

Figure 10.48
Anime demon girls fly through the air with the help of strategically placed motion lines.
Courtesy of Karbo and gamera1985

or graphic novel is asked to supply a dramatic reading of a character's dialogue by means of typographical variations. By recognizing differences in letter size and thickness, the reader becomes an actor, emphasizing important words either in the mind or out loud (Figure 10.49).

Balloons The way dialogue of characters in comic strips is encircled is an example of a complicated semiotic structure. The reader must learn to interpret the symbolism of the various balloon types: unbroken line—normal, unemotional speech, perforated line—a whisper, a spiked outline—loud yelling, little bubbles instead of lines—thoughts by the character, icicles hanging from a balloon—conceited or aloof speech, tiny words within a large balloon—astonished or ashamed emotional speech, a zigzag line—sound from a telephone, TV set, or computer, and the tail of a balloon outside the frame—similar to an

off-camera voice (Figure 10.50).

Action Sequences All the techniques utilized by motion picture directors are also used in cartoons. Close-ups, perspective and framing variations, special lighting effects, montage techniques, and panning and quick-cut editing help move the action from frame to frame. These film techniques once led cartoonist Will Eisner to say, "Comics are movies on paper." Of course, with all the absurd plot lines, killings, explosions, and digital special effects in today's action-adventure movies, we can also say that movies are comic books on film. Not surprisingly, film directors such as George Lucas (*American Graffiti*, 1973, and *Star Wars*, 1977) and Steven Spielberg (*E.T.: The Extra-Terrestrial*, 1982, and *Saving Private Ryan*, 1998) admit that early in their careers they learned about perspective, framing, and plot techniques by being avid adventure comic book readers.

Animation Techniques Almost all the cartoons intended for the print medium are created with either traditional pencil, pen, and ink materials or through computer software. Animated films, however, are made using three major techniques: cel, stop-motion, and computer-generated imagery (CGI).

Cel Animation Also called traditional and hand-drawn animation, this technique is divided into three types: full, limited, and rotoscoping.

Full animation This technique requires 24 frames per second for realistic movement—or for a 10-minute movie, more than 14,000 drawings. The process is enormously expensive and time consuming. Early Disney classics as well as the critically acclaimed *The Princess and the Frog* (2009) used traditional cel animation (Figure 10.51). British animator James Baxter, who was responsible for Belle in the Disney classic *Beauty and*

Figure 10.49
Before the term, "graphic novel" was invented, long-form animated stories were called "picture novels." This 1950 cover for "It Rhymes with Lust" was produced by Matt Baker and Ray Osrin. The dynamic use of typography is a trademark of printed cartoons.
Courtesy of Comicartville.com

Figure 10.50
In this 19th century woodcut, warriors are comically polite, as indicated by the dialogue within the balloons.
**Uncensored Situations, 1966,
The Dick Sutphen Studio, Inc.**

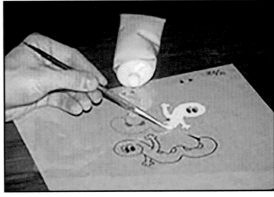

Figure 10.51
An animator applies paint to a traditional acetate cel.
Courtesy of J-E Nyström, Helsinki, Finland

the Beast as well as supervising *The Lion King* (1994), *Shrek 2* (2004), and *Kung Fu Panda* (2008), prefers hand-drawn techniques to the computer for action scenes. Using see-through paper and a pencil, he makes each drawing on a page so he can see how they line up. Baxter explains, "It's basically like making a flip book, page by page."

Another full animation technique, Japanese *anime*, has a distinctive style often noted for its hand-drawn cels with bright colors, supernatural characters,

and out-of-this-planet landscapes. Popular in the United States only in the last ten years, *anime*—like its print counterpart, *manga*—is gaining support. One of the masters of Japanese anime is director Hayao Miyazaki. His critically acclaimed films *Spirited Away* (2001), which won an Academy Award, and *Princess Mononoke* (1997) have reached general audiences around the world (Figure 10.52). In 2009, *Ponyo* Miyazaki's adaptation of Hans Christian Andersen's *The Little Mermaid* received critical success. For

Figure 10.52
(Weblink: http://goo.gl/53SMqy)
Princess Mononoke is a master-ful animated conflict between the forces of urbanization and nature by the Japanese master,

Figure 10.53
(Weblink: http://goo.gl/WzJK3X)
Yellow Submarine achieved critical acclaim for its animated style and ignited a renewed interest in cartoons. Although members of the Beatles offered their support for the project, the group only performed at the end of the movie. Character actors performed the voices for the band members in the film.

Figure 10.55
(Weblink: http://goo.gl/uyaBX2)
Richard Linklater's Waking Life *demonstrates fully the connection viewers can have when actual actors are turned into animated characters through the rotoscoping process.*

Figure 10.54
A wall muralist in downtown Denton, Texas adopts the style as seen in the motion picture, Yellow Submarine.
Courtesy of Paul Martin Lester

40 years Miyazaki thought about adapting Mary Norton's 1952 *The Borrowers* to animation. After he planned and wrote the screenplay, he asked Hiromasa Yonebayashit, an animator for *Spirited* and *Mononoke*, to direct the film named *The Borrower Arrietty*. It was released in Japan in 2010 and was a top-grossing film. The Walt Disney Co. had the script slightly rewritten, hired English-speaking actors to voice the characters, and renamed the movie for a U.S. opening in 2012 as *The Secret World of Arrietty*. The timeless tale of tiny people living under the floor of a house might propel the film into the mainstream.

Limited animation As the name implies, this technique of cel animation uses fewer frames per second for a more stylistic and jerky appearance and can be seen in movies such as *Yellow Submarine* (1968), art directed by the famous poster artist Heinz Edelmann (Figure 10.53). He claimed to never have tried

hallucinogenic drugs (Figure 10.54). The television programs produced by the Hanna-Barbera production company such as "The Flintstones" and "The Jetsons" are other examples.

Rotoscoping This animation technique was invented by Max Fleischer in 1917. Fleisher's animation company produced such classic movie characters as Betty Boop, Popeye, and Superman. With this technique, live action movements were traced by hand frame by frame. The director Richard Linklater used the rotoscoping method with computers to produce the visually arresting films *Waking Life* (2001) (Figure 10.55) and *A Scanner Darkly* (2006). The investment company Charles Schwab also employed rotoscoping for a series of commercials shown in 2009.

Stop-Motion Animation This animation technique describes a wide variety of object manipulations that might

Figure 10.57
Claymation characters from a Russian animated series, "Kuzmich."
Courtesy of Max Sviridov Studios

include models, clay, and puppets.

Model animation Willis O'Brien used the method in his 1925 classic about angry dinosaurs, *The Lost World.* Tooled steel formed the animals' skeletons, which were then covered with foam latex and painted. Animators moved these models slightly and photographed them frame-by-frame to produce the effect of the dinosaurs walking and fighting. The technique also was used in the popular movie *King Kong* in 1933. Ray Harryhausen was 13 years old when his aunt took him to see *King Kong* at Grauman's Theater in Hollywood. The movie so inspired him that he devoted the rest of his life to the animation field. In 1963 Harryhausen's animated work *Jason and the Argonauts* includes a memorable scene in which the intrepid crew of the Argos fights sword-wielding skeletons. The life-like scene inspired future directors George Lucas, Steven Spielberg, and James Cameron (Figure 10.56).

Clay animation Plasticine, the

favorite brand for claymation animators, is commonly used as a character medium because it gives 3D depth (Figure 10.57). In 1953, Art Clockey introduced the popular clay characters Gumby and Pokey in the film *Gumbasia* (Figure 10.58). Clay in the hands of master Nick Park of Aardman Animations (Figure 10.59) becomes a powerful emotional element in which facial gestures reveal the inner feelings of the lifelike characters. Park's *Chicken Run* (2000) earned more than $225 million in global ticket sales while *Wallace & Gromit in The Curse of the Were-Rabbit* (2005) won the Best Animated Feature Academy Award. In 2012 Aardman released *The Pirates! Band of Misfits* in 3-D of course. In 2017 the British actor Peter Sallis who voiced the beloved character of Wallace died.

Puppet animation Similar to clay animations, this technique usually employs wood, rubber, or plastic puppet figures that interact with each other within constructed worlds. One of the

Figure 10.56
(Weblink: http://goo.gl/8aYaCx)
Ranking as one of the best experiences in the cinema, Ray Harryhausen's skeleton scene in Jason and the Argonauts *demonstrates a master craftsperson at the top of his field.*

Figure 10.58
(Weblink: http://goo.gl/kC3y6M)
Clay in the hands of stop-motion animator Art Clokey came to life and inspired generations of other artists including Nick Park. He produced Gumbasia, his first film, as a student at the University of Southern California on a table tennis surface in his father's garage.

Figure 10.59
(Weblink: http://goo.gl/XK9d-QM)
The Aardman studio website contains clips on many of the classic productions and films that describe the stop-motion process. In a word—tedious.

Figure 10. 60
(Weblink: http://goo.gl/TusGmv)
Known for a sinister, Gothic animation style, Tim Burton is a distinctive artist with a confident style.

Figure 10.63

masters is Henry Selick who worked for Disney where he learned stop-motion techniques. After he left to form his own company, his creativity revitalized the Doughboy for Pillsbury commercials. When an innovative film he made for MTV, *Slow Bob in the Lower Dimensions* (1990), got the attention of director Tim Burton, he was asked to direct *The Nightmare Before Christmas* (1993) (Figure 10.60). His latest work is the ambitious *Coraline* (2009) with anima-tor Travis Knight, son of Nike billion-aire Phil Knight. The inherent depth of using puppets is further enhanced by a 3-D version in which moviegoers wear special glasses for an even more realistic view (Figure 10.61). Another stand-out in 2009 was Wes Anderson's *Fantastic Mr. Fox* that puts the viewer into the elaborate and magical world of a fox, his family, and an assortment of wild ani-mals including humans (Figure 10.62).

Computer-Generated Imaging
Computer-generated imaging (CGI) is the most popular choice by many directors and comes in 2-D, 3-D, perfor-mance capture, live action/cartoon, and virtual variations.

Two-dimensional With 2-D effects, animation can be accomplished with traditional animation techniques that are transferred to a comput-er screen, as in the television series "SpongeBob SquarePants" and by vari-ous software applications such as Flash and PowerPoint. Producers of the pop-ular and irreverent "South Park" show on Comedy Central use computers to make it appear to be a child's paper con-struction project. Most animations seen on the web through the Adobe Flash software program employ 2-D methods. A popular web-based animation studio known for its political satires, JibJab, is the work of Evan and Gregg Spiridellis. Their "viral videos" spread around the world via links provided by fans to their

friends (Figure 10.63).

Three-dimensional With 3-D animation, lifelike simulations of body movements are possible. The films *Toy Story*, *Shrek*, and *Monsters, Inc.* have a simulated realism about them that 2-D animation cannot supply. A kind of hybrid between 2-D and 3-D can be seen in the documentary movie *Waltz with Bashir* (2008). Written and directed by Israeli Ari Folman, it tells the story of his experience as a 1982 Lebanon War veteran. To simulate a 3-D look, the animators used Flash, traditional ani-mation, and 3-D computer techniques (Figure 10.64) A related procedure, cel-shading, turns 3-D CGI images into a style that looks like hand-drawn cel animations. The technique is popular for video games, films, television shows, and commercials—examples include "The Simpsons Game," *Hey Arnold!: The Movie* (2002), "Family Guy," and Procter & Gamble's Mr. Clean commercial char-acter (Figure 10.65).

Performance capture Also called motion capture or mocap, this technology creates the most startling example of lifelike human characters and can be found in television commercials, digital computer games, and motion pictures. Sony Pictures Imageworks hired professional baseball players to re-create their body movements for its "MLB 2009: The Show" video game. Using 55 sensors attached to a spandex bodysuit, special cameras captured a player's every move for a realistic effect. *Final Fantasy: The Spirits Within* (2001) from directors Hironobu Sakaguchi and Moto Sakakibara was a quantum leap for technical achievement in mimicking the lifelike qualities of humans (Figure 10.66). Other standouts include *The Polar Express* (2004), *Beowulf* (2007), *Watchmen* (2009), and James Cameron's *Avatar* (2010) (Figure 10.67). The actor Andy Serkis was rendered as Gollum

Figure 10.67
Zoe Saldana performs motion capture for her character, Neytiri in James Cameron's Avatar.
Courtesy of the Fox Movie Channel

and Smeagol in *The Lord of the Rings* trilogy (2001–2003), as the mighty ape in the remake of *King Kong* (2005), Caesar in *The Rise of the Planet of the Apes* (2011), and Captain Haddock in *The Adventures of Tintin* (2011). The latter directed by Steven Spielberg about a reporter looking for a treasure and based on the work of the Belgium artist Hergé is causing worry among members of the Academy Awards. The trouble is how to fit performance capture movies within existing Oscar categories when it is a hybrid between live-action and animation. However, for 2012 the Academy decided to punt—Serkis was not nominated for an acting award. Rest assured, the issue will not go away.

Live Action/Cartoon Combinations
Another common special effect is to combine live action and animated characters in the same scene. This collaboration between humans and cartoons is as old as the stage work of Winsor McCay

and his pet dinosaur Gertie from 1914. Walt Disney tried the technique in an animated series in which a young actress, Virginia Davis, interacted with an animated cat named Julius in the "Alice Comedies" of the 1920s. The 1964 classic *Mary Poppins* featured several scenes in which actors and cartoon characters (Figure 10.68). Walt Disney would often interact with some of his animated characters for his television show that ran under different titles such as "Walt Disney Presents" and "The Wonderful World of Disney" from 1955 to 2008. More recent examples can be seen in *Who Framed Roger Rabbit* (1988), *Space Jam* (1996), *Looney Tunes: Back in Action* (2003), and *The BFG* (2016) (Figure 10.69).

Virtual With sophisticated software and hardware, producers have developed immersive encounters in which users experience being a part of the action as they watch animated versions of people and surroundings by wearing (VR)

W LINK
Figure 10.65
(Weblink: http://goo.gl/hrcKeQ) Created by Seth MacFarlane, a graduate of the Rhode Island School of Design, "Family Guy" exhibits the edgy satire common with such sitcoms as "The Simpsons," "King of the Hill," and "South Park."

W LINK
Figure 10.66
(Weblink: http://goo.gl/MnxkVn) Although many praised the animation details exhibited in Final Fantasy: The Spirits Within, *some critics were put off by a concept known as the "uncanny valley" in which humans are portrayed so realistically that they evoke a creepy emotion. Robert Zemeckis' 2004* The Polar Express *suffered the same criticism.*

Figure 10.68
(Weblink: http://goo.gl/fbsGoY)
Because the author's four-year old twin boys love penguins, they regularly ask to view this scene from Mary Poppins.

Figure 10.69
(Weblink: http:// goo.gl/VFSt5H)
Directed and co-produced by Steven Spielberg, The BFG *(Big Friendly Giant) is a delightful combination of live action and animated characters.*

Figure 10.70
(Weblink: http://goo.gl/8CgxHD)
One of the most exciting and innovative communication technologies for news, education, and entertainment is virtual reality. However, watching the animated production, "Hunger in LA" on a computer screen does not match the experience while wearing a head-mounted display.

Figure 10.71
(Weblink: http://goo.gl/fdhWCx)
The seemingly unlimited creative controls available to an animator is demonstrated by watching The Fantastic Flying Books of Mr. Morris Lessmore.

head-mounted displays. A leader in the field is Nonny de la Peña of Emblematic Group who has created 360 virtual reality programs that engage viewers as no previous medium. One of her first VR animations was "Hunger in LA" that premiered at the Sundance Film Festival in 2012. With a headset such as the Oculus Rift, a user is thrust onto a sidewalk with others waiting in line to receive donations from a food bank. Suddenly, a man in line falls on the ground due to a diabetic episode (Figure 10.70).

Independent animators often employ a combination of many of the techniques described above. For example, Louisiana-based co-directors William Joyce and Brandon Oldenburg in their 2012 Academy Award winner for Best Animated Short Film, *The Fantastic Flying Books of Mr. Morris Lessmore* (2011) (Figure 10.71), used stop-motion miniatures, computer animation, and traditional, hand-drawn 2-D techniques. From Moonbot Studios based in Shreveport, the film is often compared with *The Wizard of Oz* (1939) in its plot and child-like wonderment. The producers also have smartphone apps while in reverse order of what is generally done, a book version of the movie was released in 2012.

Ethical Perspective
Critics most often cite three main ethical issues for cartoons: marketing cartoon characters to children, using too few multicultural characters, and introducing political opinions in comic strips.

Marketing Product tie-ins are as old as comic strips. When the *Yellow Kid* was introduced in 1895, the popularity of the strip sparked one of the first mass-marketing campaigns in the United States. Illustrations reproduced on buttons, metal cracker boxes, and hand fans promoted the cartoon character and the newspaper. But the clear-cut winner of the marketing race and the model for

other cartoonists and studios is Walt Disney. Disney gave up illustrating his motion pictures himself to organize and manage the lucrative product lines inspired by his company's characters. It seemed that every American child had to have a Mickey Mouse doll.

With a popular movie, every animation studio makes an enormous profit on international ticket sales, video rentals, sound track albums, and product licensing agreements (from lunch boxes to dolls). At the same time, Saturday morning television programs and motion picture characters frequently appear in advertisements promoting everything from dolls to bicycles. Animated cartoons are often the most colorful forms of entertainment, with their characters attracting the eyes of young and old. Brightly colored characters sitting on toy store shelves that look exactly like their animated equivalents also attract young eyes and elicit pleading requests to a parent or guardian. Children are particularly vulnerable to such persuasive commercial techniques, but adults also are easily manipulated (Figure 10.72).

Animators should be aware of how their creations are marketed. Four-time Academy Award–winning British animator Nick Park, who produced such cartoon shorts as *Creature Comforts* (1989), discussed in Chapter 1, as well as *The Wrong Trousers* (1993) and *A Close Shave* (1995) with the enduring characters Wallace and Gromit, knows that his Claymation technique provides a lifelike, 3-D depth to his work and also brings out the color of his characters. Park sells cuddly and colorful toys, backpacks, watches, and DVDs on his animation studio's website. An artist with an opposite style, both in its execution and content, is Canadian John Kricfalusi (pronounced "Kris-fa-lose-ee"). His best-known cartoon is the adult-oriented "Ren and Stimpy," drawn in a traditional cel-animation style. It is often criticized for being too violent,

Figure 10.72
The brightly colored Bart and Marge Simpson attract attention to the souvenir shop behind them at the Universal Studios Hollywood theme park.
Courtesy of Paul Martin Lester

W
LINK
Figure 10.73
(Weblink:
http://goo.gl/ozE5DS)
Animator Tex Avery chose not
to be credited for the racist car-
toon, All This and Rabbit Stew. *It*
is unnerving to see the loveable
Bugs Bunny character asking
"What's up doc?" to one of the
most hateful African American
stereotypes one can imagine.

too scatological, and with language too strong for children.

Stereotypes As with other mass media images, Anglo males have almost exclusively dominated comic strip and cartoon visual messages. For example, of the 25 comic strips and five single-framed humorous cartoons that included popular titles such as "Doonesbury," "Garfield," and "Peanuts," on three pages featured in the *Dallas Morning News* for June 15, 2017, there were a total of 57 human characters portrayed: 54 European American (95 percent) and three African American (five percent). There were no other cultural groups shown in any of the strips. Men also beat out women with 36 male characters (63 percent) to 21 characters (37 percent). Such demographics, to do not match the north Texas region. According to the Dallas Chamber of Commerce, the Dallas/Fort Worth area is composed of 49% European American, 28% Latino, 15% African American, and 6% Asian American. No gender figures were shown. Whenever any percentages are much greater or lower than a population's demographics, the reasons for the differences should be considered and if possible, corrected.

In addition, African Americans had to endure extremely offensive racist stereotypes in Bugs Bunny cartoons in the 1940s from *Looney Tunes* and *Merrie Melodies*, distributed by Warner Bros. One particularly disturbing animated short showed a slow-talking, slow-walking, and slow-thinking African American boy resembling Elmer Fudd attempting to shoot Bugs Bunny with a shotgun. The title, *All This and Rabbit Stew*, was originally released in 1941 and directed by Tex Avery, although his name is not in the credits. After media mogul Ted Turner purchased the Warner Bros. collection, he vowed to never show the 11 most racist cartoons on television, although they can be found on DVD collections and other sources, including YouTube (Figure 10.73).

Controversial Themes Many object to serious messages disguised as children-oriented cartoons, often because they do not agree with the political messages. Perhaps the leader in the most offended category is the animated hit "South Park" created by Trey Parker and Matt Stone, now in its 16th season on Comedy Central. Its homemade, paper cut-out look perhaps buffers it against critics whom nevertheless cringe when the actress Sarah Jessica Parker is called a "transvestite donkey witch" or when the word *feces* is used 162 times in a fifth-season episode. Newspapers also have received the wrath from readers. *Little Orphan Annie* frequently criticized President Roosevelt's New Deal politics, and *Pogo* often went after Senator Joseph McCarthy. In the 1960s, underground or alternative comic books were intended to shock traditional audiences and establish a counterculture readership. One cartoonist used to such criticism is Garry Trudeau. "Doonesbury" sometimes offends conservative readers with its liberal perspectives that it is placed on the editorial or opinion page or a website of a newspaper instead of in the comics section. In 2012 many newspaper editors decided not to run his strip that was concerned about a Texas law that requires women who choose to obtain an abortion to undergo a vaginal probe ultrasound. The management for the *Cleveland Plain Dealer* newspaper decided to run the strip, "Garry Trudeau's métier is political satire; if we choose to carry 'Doonesbury,' we can't yank the strip every time it deals with a highly charged issue. His fans are every bit as vocal as his critics. We are alerting readers to the nature of the strips so they can decide whether to read them next week." As cartoons can be enjoyed by persons of all ages, a wide variety of political and thoughtful issues should be a part of the comics pages.

Editorial cartoons filled with emotionally symbolic visual messages can spark great controversy as mentioned earlier with the Danish cartoons. In 2012 Indian political cartoonist Aseem Trivedi was sentenced to a three-year jail term plus fines for criticizing the government in a cartoon published on a website. "India's lost its sense of humor," said Trivedi. "If the government gags its citizens, how are we going to grow? We're going the Taliban and China way."

Cultural Perspective

Many times the Sunday comic pages are a child's first introduction to the magical world of reading. Upon seeing the brightly colored funnies, a child is interested immediately. But cartoon strip characters that are amusing to a child no longer provoke the same response in adults. Part of the reason that comic books are not considered a serious art form is that traditionally they have been intended for younger audiences. One of the most common causes of cultural division between people is differences in age. Consequently, the kinds of comic material you read help identify you as belonging to a particular cultural group. With adult-oriented graphic novels, the gap between young and old is narrowing.

Cartoons are an essential part of any country's culture. The types of cartoon subjects seen in a society reflect the values and beliefs common to the culture at that time. In 2011 China opened its National Animation Industry Park 100 miles from Beijing. The government hopes that Chinese animated movies will compete on an international market. But so far the films made with a Chinese point of view do not perform well in foreign markets. For example, the propagandistic *Xibaipo* (2011), a tale of children caught up in the Chinese civil war, was pulled from American theaters after it only made $100,000 from box of-

fice sales. It may get better. In 2012 it was announced that DreamWorks Animation formed a partnership with Chinese state-owned companies to produce movies under the name of Oriental DreamWorks.

As with many visual messages, cartoons can be studied in terms of society's myths (good vs. evil), their various genres (from westerns to soap operas), and their use of symbolism (both visual and verbal). Large numbers of readers enjoyed the *Yellow Kid* comic strip because the story about a group of lost children, seemingly abandoned by their parents, struck a sympathetic chord with readers, many of whom were immigrants living far away from their families. The threat of world domination by totalitarian regimes beginning in the 1930s inspired comic strips with conservative views or superhuman characters who would fight for the values expressed by the "American way of life," whatever that phrase happened to mean at the moment. Visual symbols expressed in drawings also reflect the culture from which they are produced. Editorial cartoons, much more than any other type of comic, regularly feature symbolic images in the form of religious icons, military designations, and national emblems as a visual shorthand to make the point of the cartoons clear. Consequently, meaning resides in an understanding of these verbal and visual codes.

Critical Perspective

A cartoon, although packaged within a deceptively simple frame, is a complex exercise in semiotic analysis. No other art form, in print or screen media, combines words, pictures, and meaning in such an interwoven way. Like the effects created by motion picture and television images, cartoons form complex intellectual and emotional unions of text and images in a highly personal way. By reading a cartoon out loud, a reader becomes a character in the unfolding frame-by-frame drama. Cartoons have

Figure 10.74
Cartoons can be used to attract a viewer's attention to a social problem. In a program called "Art Attacks AIDS," Mike McNeilly shows his work on the back of a bus stop bench.
Courtesy of Paul Martin Lester

a powerful yet not fully understood effect on those who never outgrow their charm. In corporate advertising, government propaganda, and instructional aids, cartoon art is used because it is a powerful communication medium. To simply label comics as "children's art" and "unworthy of serious attention" is to deny the impact of all words and pictures that communicate a message. Such an attitude also discounts the enormous effect that cartoons have on all generations of readers and viewers.

However, some studies have shown that the effect is not all positive. Watching fast-paced and brightly colored cartoons may be the reason some children have short attention spans. In a study of 4-year-olds, those who watched nine minutes of "SpongeBob SquarePants"

did more poorly on mental functional tests than those who did not.

Nevertheless, cartoons teach us not only how to combine words and pictures in symbolic ways, but also how to confront the significant issues that all societies face (Figure 10.74).

*TRENDS TO WATCH
FOR CARTOONS*
With the global economic downturn combined with a drop in subscriptions, newspaper publishers and their parent corporations have been pressured to reduce their staffs. Two of the first positions to go for many newspapers were the editorial and syndicated comic strip cartoonists. In place of editorial cartoons, newspapers may on occasion print work from artists who reside any-

Figure 10.75
Students in a media culture class came up with 110 of their favorite animated shows rearranged as a Wordle display. Any words remind you of your favorite?
Courtesy of Paul Martin Lester

where in the world on important issues. Nevertheless, this action is a shame as only a local cartoonist can make visual commentaries on local issues. With newspaper page counts being reduced to save money, some publications have made the strips smaller to fit more in the same space, cut long-time comic strips altogether, or run them only on their websites.

Graphic novels on specialized, serious subjects and distributed through major publishing houses, comics stores, and the web will become more common. Sid Jacobson and Ernie Colón produced an achievement in comic book art, *The 9/11 Report: A Graphic Adaptation.* They enhanced the reputation of the medium with their cartoon version of the governmental report requested by the President and Congress. In 2008 the two produced a follow-up, *After 9/11: America's War on Terror.* Personal stories are told as well. Work from cartoon authors such as Lynda Barry, Alison Bechdel, Daniel Clowes, Aline Kominsky-Crumb, the wife of Robert Crumb, Justin Green, and Harvey Pekar help define the genre of

the graphic memoir. In her 2012 publication, *Are You My Mother?* Bechdel, a cartoonist better known for her comic strip, "Dikes to Watch Out For," tells a hauntingly honest story of growing up and surviving a flawed family. Bechdel won a MacArthur "Genius" award in 2014 and is also known for the "Bechdel Test," a tool for evaluating women characters in motion pictures. Another graphic artist to take note of is Emil Ferris after her stunning debut book, *My Favorite Thing is Monsters*, a murder mystery with elaborate drawings in a simulated lined paper notebook.

With courses offered in high schools and colleges, graphic novel production will increase as will interest in cartoons generally. One indication is the popularity of the San Diego-based Comic-Con gathering for creators and their fans. Begun in 1970 with 145 attendees, the annual convention has soared in attendance to more than 125,000. In 2012 the documentary filmmaker Morgan Spurlock released his homage to cartoons and their enthusiasts in *Comic-Con Episode IV: A Fan's Hope.*

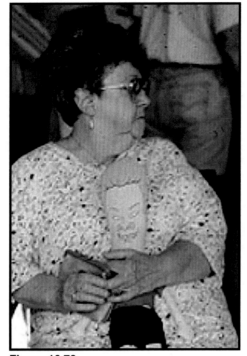

Figure 10.76

An anxious woman at the Indianapolis airport finds a bit of comfort from Mike Judge's Beavis cartoon character.

Courtesy of Paul Martin Lester

The Academy Awards separate category honoring the best achievements in mainstream animation sparks interest among indie producers of short- and long-form animations, and graphic novels produce compelling work. The web is the medium to see animated productions, from established and indie sources (Figure 10.75). For example, the Yahoo web portal in 2012 presented "Electric City" conceived by the actor Tom Hanks. The dramatic series is composed of 20 five-minute episodes with interactive games and additional plot lines available through Facebook and Twitter. However, television is still the medium of choice for most animators. The Cartoon Network, popular among children during the day for its typical selections of classic and current cartoons, changes late at night into a visually stirring collection of animations called "Adult Swim." *Anime* and other styles present mature fare that can be found in such shows as "Agua Unit Patrol Squad 1," "Robot Chicken," and "Squidbillies." The once struggling

network now boasts of 2.2 million viewers a night between 11:30pm and 12:30am. Another popular place for primetime animated sitcoms is Fox television's adult-oriented "Animation Domination" on Sunday evenings with such hits as "The Simpsons," "The Cleveland Show," "Family Guy," "American Dad," and with characters based on the 2004 motion picture, "Napoleon Dynamite." The FX cable channel, named for Fox Extended, airs a critically acclaimed animated series, "Archer." The brainchild of voice actor Adam Reed, the show has been called "James Bond meets 'Arrested Development.'" In 2012 director Kevin Smith produced a reality television show "Comic Book Men" about two store clerks in New Jersey. In addition, MTV brought back its controversial fan favorite "Beavis and Butt-Head" from Mike Judge, also creator of "King of the Hill." This time, the dumb-and-dumber duo will not only make fun of MTV music videos on their ratty couch but also movies and YouTube videos (Figure 10.76).

The web has also increased the number of cartoons being produced, because comic strips, comic books, and animated films have all merged in the new medium. As the status of cartoons improve, they may be used in informational graphics, not for their entertainment value, but to increase the knowledge of viewers about complex subjects.

WORDS IN THE GLOSSARY FROM THIS CHAPTER

Anime • Beehive hairdo • Cel • Cut • Kinetoscope • Live-action • Manga • Montage • Panning • Reuben award • Serial • Short • Sitcom • Viral videos • Virtual reality

11 Photography

Figure 11.1
"Migrant Mother," 1936, by Dorothea Lange. The disturbing and touching storyline of a woman alone with her children during the height of America's Great Depression spurred many to help others. But is she posing or wishing the photographer would leave?
Courtesy of the Library of Congress

Once you see the forlorn face of Florence Thompson, you will never forget her (Figure 11.1). With furrowed forehead, a faraway look, hand cupped to her chin in a gesture of uncertainty, two children shyly hiding their faces in the warmth of her shoulders, and an infant sleeping on her lap, the photograph is more than a simple portrait of a family. Here in black and white is a real-life symbol for all parents struggling to survive and feed their families during the Great Depression and for all uncertain economic times. "Migrant Mother" is probably the world's most reproduced photograph in the history of photography because it makes people care about this mother on a deep, personal level.

But it was a picture that almost was not taken.

Dorothea Nutzhorn was born in Hoboken, New Jersey, in 1895. When she was 12-years-old she took her mother's maiden name of Lange after her father left the family. As a child she suffered from polio that gave her a limp in her right leg for the rest of her life. Although she'd never held a camera, at 14 she wanted to be a photographer, because she said that her disability "gave her an almost telepathic connection with those who suffered." After studying at Columbia University under the photographer Clarence White, she moved in 1918 to San Francisco where she enjoyed the Bay Area's bohemian lifestyle. She married the painter Maynard Dixon and had two sons. She supported her family through her photography studio business. By 1932, she had become an able portrait photographer with a reputation for capturing the personalities of the rich San Francisco matrons of the day.

News reports of the terrible living conditions of rural Americans prompted Lange to want to document their lives. The country was undergoing the worst drought in its history. The stock market crashed in 1929 and farm prices plum-

Figure 11.2
"Family between Dallas and Austin, Texas," 1936, by Dorothea Lange. The Library of Congress' caption for the photograph reads, "The people have left their home and connections in South Texas, and hope to reach the Arkansas Delta for work in the cotton fields. Penniless people. No food and three gallons of gas in the tank. The father is trying to repair a tire. Three children. Father says, "It's tough but life's tough anyway you take it." During the Great Depression, the Farm Security Administration of the U.S. government produced numerous classic documents such as this "Migrant Mother" alternative.
Courtesy of the Library of Congress

meted, throwing millions out of work. In the Midwest, dust storms blew away the once-fertile topsoil. Thousands of farmers from the Great Plains who had lost their land and livelihoods took off in mattress-topped automobiles or hitch-hiked for the promised land—the golden West (Figure 11.2). Lange obtained a job with the State of California to document agricultural labor conditions. She teamed with Dr. Paul Taylor, a professor of economics at the University of California, Berkeley. She would later divorce her husband and marry him (Figure 11.3).

After completion of the project, the head of the Resettlement Administration (RA), Rexford Tugwell reviewed her pictures in Washington and promptly hired her. The RA, later renamed the Farm Security Administration (FSA), was an agency of the U.S. Department of Agriculture. Besides Lange, famous

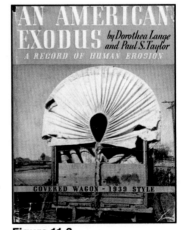

Figure 11.3
The book jacket shows a typical sight along the roads during America's Great Depression—a truck filled with household goods. With Lange's pictures and Taylor's words, the two documented the migration of many from ruined Dust Bowl farms to migrant worker camps out West.
Courtesy of Paul Martin Lester

Figure 11.4

Perched atop her 1933 Ford Model C four-door wagon, Dorothea Lange poses with a Graflex 4 × 5 Series D camera. She was driving this car when she spotted Florence Thompson and her family at the side of the road and used the camera for her famous portrait. A fellow FSA photographer and Lange's assistant at the time, Rondal Partridge took this photograph of Lange in 1935.
Courtesy of the Library of Congress

photographers who worked for the FSA were Walker Evans, Russell Lee, Gordon Parks, Arthur Rothstein, and Marion Post Wolcott.

Tired, hungry, and anxious to get home after a month-long project taking pictures in central California, Lange drove her car north along the cold and wet Camino Real Highway (101) in February 1936 (Figure 11.4). Along the way she noted a migrant workers' camp of about 2,500 people outside the small town of Nipomo. On the side of the road someone had placed a sign that simply proclaimed, "Pea-Pickers Camp." These sights were all too common, with poor people from all over the country forced to stop for lack of money and gasoline for their cars and earn a few dollars pick-

ing local crops.

For 30 minutes, Lange drove toward home and thought about the camp she had passed. Finally, the image of the people she had briefly seen overpowered her desire to get home. She turned her car around and drove back to the camp.

Lange retrieved her press camera, a portable version of the tripod-bound, large-format camera, and immediately found Florence Thompson sitting in the barely adequate shelter of an open tent with her daughters (Figure 11.5). With the crop destroyed by a freeze, there was no work at the camp. An engine chain had broken on their Model T Ford, so they were stuck. Thompson's two sons, along with a man living with Thompson at the time, went to town to get the car fixed, leaving her to care for her daughters.

In notes about the brief encounter, Lange later wrote, "Camped on the edge of a pea field where the crop had failed in a freeze. She said that she had been living on frozen vegetables from the surrounding fields and birds that the children had killed." Lange did not ask her name or anything about her past history. She stayed ten minutes and made six exposures.

When she returned to her home in Berkeley, Lange made several prints and gave them to an editor of the *San Francisco News*, where they were published on March 10 under the headline, "FOOD RUSHED TO STARVING FARM COLONY." Two of Lange's photographs accompanied the story that detailed the situation of the migrants and the efforts of relief workers to bring food and cleanup crews to the camp. The famous close-up was not published. Because of the story and pictures, the camp residents received about 20,000 pounds of food from the government and contributions of cash from the public, but Thompson and her family had left before help arrived.

Back in Washington, Roy Stryker of

Figure 11.5

Photojournalists call the first picture taken at a scene a "cover shot," but not related to a magazine page. If you are asked or are forced to leave, at least you have something. With the older girl avoiding the camera, the younger one smiling for the lens, and Florence Thompson looking back at a daughter hiding behind her, this image is almost a snapshot—not a particularly telling moment.

Courtesy of the Library of Congress

the FSA recognized the historical and social significance of the Thompson portrait immediately. The picture soon became an American classic with a life of its own. Newspapers across the country reproduced it. When John Steinbeck saw the picture, it inspired him to write *The Grapes of Wrath*. In 1941, the Museum of Modern Art in New York City exhibited it. Without question, the photograph made Lange famous. Yet despite her later achievements as a staff photographer for *Life* magazine, her collaboration with Paul Taylor on their book *An American Exodus: A Record of Human Erosion*, and her documentation of Japanese American internees during World War II, she is forever linked to it. Frustrated over that fact, she once complained that she was not a "one-picture photographer." In 1965, Lange died at the age of 70 after a long and event-filled life made possible by her photographic skills and her sensitivity to the important moments in everyday life.

Florence Leona Christie Thompson's life didn't change for the better after the picture was published. Florence Thompson was born to poverty in Native American territory in rural Oklahoma in 1903. Her father, Jackson Christie abandoned the family before she was born. Her mother, Mary Jane Cobb married a Choctaw native and the family lived on a small farm near Tahlequah in eastern Oklahoma. When Thompson was 17 she married Cleo Owens, a logger. The couple had three children, Viola, Violet, and Leroy. Finding little work in their home state, they moved to California in 1922 to work in the sawmills. By 1929 the couple had five children. After Owens lost his job, they moved from field to field to pick peaches until he caught a fever and died at the age of 32. Pregnant with her sixth child, she moved with her children from town to town seeking help from her family. She went back home to Oklahoma for a brief time where she became pregnant again and returned to California with her parents to continue the farm-picking migrant life, traveling from camp to camp. On this trip she met Jim Hill. Although the two never married, they had three children together. In the 1940s she married George Thompson and settled in Modesto with her children.

When she first saw the famous picture in print, she didn't like the image because her family were not looking for work in Nipomo. They had only stopped in the migrant camp because their car broke down. When she couldn't get the picture suppressed, she tried to get Lange and/or the government to pay her for being in the picture. In 1979, 44 years after the picture was taken, Thompson was still bitter about the fact that the photograph made Dorothea Lange famous but didn't improve her life. In a newspaper article, Thompson, living in a trailer complained to a reporter, "That's my picture hanging all over the world, and I can't get a penny out of it." In 1983, Thompson suffered from cancer

and heart disease. She couldn't pay her medical bills. Family members alerted the local newspaper and a national story was published about her situation. Readers who saw the story and remembered the emotional image were moved to send money to her—more than $15,000 ($36,500 today)—before she died. Many of the letters that contained money noted how the writers' lives had been touched by Lange's close-up portrait of "Migrant Mother."

In a 2008 interview with a CNN reporter, Thompson's daughter Katherine (the girl on her mother's right shoulder in the famous photograph) said that the "photograph's fame made the family feel shame at their poverty." And yet, on Florence Thompson's gravestone, next to her husband George at the Lakewood Memorial Park in Hughson, California, about 250 miles north of Nipomo, it reads, "Migrant Mother—A Legend of the Strength of American Motherhood."

In 1998 the US Postal Service issued a 32-cent stamp that featured the famous photograph as a part of its "Celebration of the Century" series. In 2006 the Dorothea Lange Elementary School was dedicated in Nipomo, not far from where the famous "Migrant Mother" photograph was made. In 2017 several residents of Nipomo and other interested persons are helping to erect a historical marker to commemorate the meeting of Dorothea Lange and Florence Thompson who collaborated to produce one of the most enduring photographs in the history of the medium.

Photographic manipulations. A controversial aspect of the photograph was the way it was manipulated in two overt ways. In a later version of the print, part of a hand and a thumb holding a tent flap was painted out of the image (Figure 11.6). But more significantly, the picture was a stage-managed setup by Lange. This fact should not be surprising given Lange's roots as a portrait photographer. Linda Gordon in the *Los Angeles Times* wrote, "Always a portraitist, she never sought to capture her subjects unaware, as a photojournalist might."

When one studies the images of Thompson and her family members in the order they were taken, the collaboration between Lange and the children is especially marked by an obvious degree of stage managing. For example, the initial image shows 14-year-old Viola sitting glumly on a rocking chair inside the tent. Daughter Katherine smiles at the camera while Thompson holds baby Norma and looks behind her for Ruby who hides behind her back. The next picture is a formal and stiff portrait of the family group. Viola is now in front of the lean-to tent sitting awkwardly on the rocker. Inside the tent Ruby, who wears a wool cap, has been coaxed to join the others for a picture (Figure 11.7).

As an experienced image maker, Lange knew that a family portrait with an older girl would not be an emotionally powerful image, so for the next three pictures, Lange moved in close to concentrate on Thompson with her small children. In one, she nurses the baby (Figure 11.8). In another, Ruby rests her chin on her mother's shoulder *without her knit cap* (Figure 11.9). In the third Ruby leans her head more comfortably on the shoulder while grasping the tent pole. With its vertical view that includes the crude camp-life necessities of a kerosene lamp, a tin plate, a suitcase used as a table, a view of the barren ground beyond the tent, and Florence with a wedding ring, this image is a strong document of the Dust Bowl and further demonstrates Lange's photographic artistry (Figure 11.10). Finally, the famous portrait is a close-up of Thompson looking into the distance with the two children told to turn away to avoid the distraction of their faces. Although such overt manipulations of a news photograph would be discouraged today and could get a photojournalist fired, the

Figure 11.6
Compare the lower-right corner of this version of "Migrant Mother" with the untouched photograph that starts this chapter and you will notice the distracting thumb that is probably Thompson's as she holds the tent flap out of the way. The retouched, darkened thumb is a picture manipulation that was common in the day, but would be considered unethical for a news picture today.
Courtesy of the Library of Congress

Figure 11.7
In this formal portrait of the family group, the older Viola strikes a model's pose as she sits awkwardly on the cane rocking chair as (from left) Ruby, coaxed from behind her mother and wearing a wool cap, Katherine, Florence, and baby Norma are inside the lean-to tent. Lange is now obviously stage-managing this situation, an ethical violation for documentary and news photographs by today's standards.
Courtesy of the Library of Congress

Figure 11.8
Wisely, Dorothea Lange quit taking overall scenes and moved in closer to concentrate on Florence Thompson. Although much richer in content than the famous portrait, with the breast-feeding baby, kerosene lamp, and wedding ring, this photograph does not have the same emotional quality as "Migrant Mother." Notice that the edge of the canvas tent flap hangs parallel with the wooden pole.
Courtesy of the Library of Congress

Figure 11.9
Dorothea Lange moves in a little closer. Five-year-old Ruby unnaturally rests her chin on her mother's shoulder, is not wearing her wool cap, and the tent flap has been pulled back, probably by Viola. All of this stage managing was no doubt suggested by Lange.
Courtesy of the Library of Congress

Figure 11.10
If "Migrant Mother" had never been taken, this photograph would have been revered as a powerful portrait of migrant life, with probably as much attention given to it as its famous cousin. Florence looks just as forlorn as in "Migrant Mother" and little Ruby now seems more comfortable with one hand on her mother's shoulder as she grasps the pole with the other, but this image also contains more information with the addition of the simple metal plate and worn trunk used as a table and the outside, forbidding farm field beyond the tent's inadequate shelter.
Courtesy of the Library of Congress

ethics of that time were different.

Lange and Thompson came from different worlds with no common bond except being at the same place at the same time. The camera became the basis for their relationship that lasted a little longer than the shutter was open. For Thompson the person, not Thompson the public icon, the image revealed a bone weary numbness in which she was probably too polite or helpless to refuse being photographed. But she *was* saying "no" in the photograph the only way she could. She looked off as if wishing this "city girl" would move on and leave her alone. The image forever stereotyped Florence Thompson as a homeless matriarch who could survive only with contributions from the public. Never mind that she had worked hard to feed and clothe her family as best she could, given the country's and her family's economic hard times. That is why she was probably upset that the picture was published. As such, "Migrant Mother" is a study not only of Great Depression photography but also a commentary on the ethics of manipulation and the right to privacy of those pictured.

Any great work of art always has many stories to tell. There is the story of the subjects within the frame, why and how it was created, and what happened after it was made public. But one of the most important stories any visual message tells is the one the viewer makes up. The way you interpret an image is the story of your life.

PHOTOGRAPHY AND THE SIX PERSPECTIVES

Photography runs the gamut from simple, amateur snapshots to enormously expensive professional enterprises. Artists use images to express their inner emotions, commercial photographers to sell products and ideas, visual journalists to illustrate the lives of those in the news, and scientists to make an unseen world visible. With equipment that ranges from less than ten dollars to several thousand dollars, photographers take and preserve millions of images every year. A photograph is still considered truthful and believable—so much so that it is used as evidence in courts of law. Time will tell if the notion of "seeing is believing" remains for the medium in the digital era.

Personal Perspective

After learning how to use paint on fingers, a pencil, and a brush, many children are introduced to a simple point-and-shoot camera, often their first contact with the image-making process using a machine. Although their first attempts may be out of focus, blurred, off-center, or incorrectly exposed, they are nevertheless awed by the magic of capturing light and seeing it on a computer screen. Part of the joy of photography is that high-quality pictures can be taken with relative ease—the machine itself is easy to master.

Moments captured by amateur photographers are a combination of space and time that often are prized possessions sometimes preserved in ornate frames and leather-bound albums. Pictures give evidence of a trip once taken, a car long since sold, and a baby who is now a grown woman. We use photographs not simply to show others where we have been, what we possess, or whom we have loved, but to remind ourselves of those important events, things, and people in our lives (Figure 11.11). Not surprisingly, most victims of catastrophic events caused by wind, water, or fire report that after the secured safety of their loved ones, what they most regret and wish could have been preserved from their destroyed houses were their precious photographs.

Historical Perspective

The camera predates the photographic process by more than 2,000 years. The first recorded reference in history of an

Figure 11.11
With the Earth in the background, Edwin "Buzz" Aldrin takes a selfie during a Gemini space walk in 1966. Three years later he was the second person to walk on the Moon after Neil Armstrong. Self portraits or selfies with or without celebrities or landmarks have been a staple for photography since one was taken with the daguerreotype process in 1839. Smartphone cameras have made the genre ubiquitous.
Courtesy of NASA

image effect produced by a darkened chamber, called a *camera obscura*, was by a Chinese writer and philosopher, Mozi who died around 391BCE. Later, Aristotle also wrote briefly about the phenomenon of light that produces an upside-down view of the outside world through a pinhole in one wall. From what is now Iraq, Abu Ali Hasan Ibn al-Hayitham (Figure 11.12), or simply al-Hazen to his Western friends, was the first to use the principle to watch an eclipse of the sun inside a tent in the year 1000 to solidify his ideas about the speed and nature of light for his scientific work *Book of Optics* published in 1021

(Figure 11.13). Artists used the camera obscura as a tool to trace rough sketches of natural scenes on paper or canvas, to be filled in later with paint. In the 2003 motion picture *Girl with a Pearl Earring*, the artist Jan Vermeer shows the maid, Griet, how to see images with the device (Figure 11.14). Art historians have concluded that another 16th Century master, the Italian Michelangelo Merisi da Caravaggio also used a camera obscura as it explains why most of his subjects are left-handed—the image projected would be reversed on a canvas. The camera obscura device led to the idea of using photosensitive materials in place of a

W LINK

Figure 11.14
*(Weblink: http://goo.gl/yJVqHo)
The camera obscura scene in
the* Girl with a Pearl Earring *is
an accurate portrayal of the device and the amazement of seeing an image for the first time.
As a viewer, however, you must
forgive the British accents from
the English Colin Firth and the
American Scarlett Johansson
despite the Dutch setting.*

Figure 11.12
*Abu Ali al-Hasan ibn al-Haytham or al-Ha-
zen. Born in Basra in 965 CE, his scientific
achievements include significant contributions to astronomy, medicine, and visual
perception. He is considered the founder of
modern optics.*
Courtesy of Matt Wronkiewicz

Figure 11.13
*Dr. Charles Savage of the Royal Society, London asserts that this artist's render-
ing is a true representation of al-Hasan's camera obscura set-up and effect.*
Courtesy of The Royal Society, London

canvas (Figure 11.14).

Throughout the history of photography, nine main photographic processes have preserved the views captured
through the camera obscura: heliography, daguerreotype, calotype, wet-collodion, color emulsions, gelatin-bromide
dry plate, holography, instant, and
digital. Before the invention of photography only the wealthy could afford to hire
an artist to paint a picture, which is why
museums are mostly filled with images
of the rich.

Heliography Joseph Nicéphore
Niépce has been called the founder of
photography because he produced the
first permanent photograph, which can
still be viewed. Born to rich and well-ed-
ucated parents in 1765 in the town of
Chalon-Sur-Saône, France, about 350
kilometers southeast of Paris, he became
interested in the many scientific and
technological discoveries of the day. At
the age of 51, Niépce began work that
eventually led to the photographic process (Figure 11.15). Trying to improve
the lithographic process for making
printing plates that had been recently
invented, he discovered that bitumen
of Judea (a type of asphalt) hardened
when exposed to the sun. After the soft,
unexposed parts of the picture were
washed away, the result was a positive
image. Niépce placed his asphalt emulsion on a pewter plate within a crudely
constructed camera obscura and produced the world's first photograph—the
view outside his home—in 1827 (Figure
11.16). It was the first and only photograph that Niépce ever made. The image
now is a part of the Gernsheim photography collection in the main lobby of the
Harry Ransom Center at the University
of Texas at Austin. The faint picture is
encased within a Plexiglas frame where
xenon gas protects it from deterioration.

Niépce named his process heliography (Greek for *sun writing*). The process
never attracted much public attention

Figure 11.15
The Niépce camera, c. 1820-1830.
Courtesy of the Musée Nicéphore Niépce

because the exposure time required was about eight hours, the image was extremely grainy in appearance, it appeared to be out of focus, and the public never learned of the procedure until many years after Niépce's death. Nevertheless, the process did attract the attention of Louis Daguerre, a theatrical artist and amateur inventor who used Niépce's basic work to produce the first practical photographic process.

Daguerreotype Louis Jacques Mandé Daguerre was born in 1789 in Cormeilles, France, just north of Paris. He became famous in that city for his dioramas, illusionary pictorial effects with painted

Figure 11.16
"View from the Window at Le Gras," heliograph, c. 1826, by Joseph Nicéphore Niépce (inverted to match the scene as seen). For photography to become a successful medium for visual communication, inventors needed to use light-recording materials within a camera that (1) could produce a sharp image, (2) stop fast action, (3) could be easily reproduced, and (4) was simple to operate. With this heliograph, considered the first photographic image produced by the French inventor, none of those conditions were met.
Courtesy of the Harry Ransom Humanities Research Center

Figure 11.17

"Boulevard du Temple," Paris, 1838 (inverted to match the scene as seen). A year before the process was announced, Louis Daguerre is credited with this photograph in 1838. A Parisian street scene with horse-drawn carriages and wagons and sidewalk walkers are blurred to invisibility by the 10-minute exposure. It is recognized as the first photograph ever made of a person—a man getting his boots brushed the slightly blurred figure at the bottom-right—and shows the extreme sharpness of the daguerre-otype. Since the process creates a mirror image, the picture has been reversed to recreate the scene from the photographer's point of view. Sadly, the original was destroyed in a fire.

Courtesy of the Phaidon Press

backdrops and lighting changes. An optician who supplied lenses for Niépce's camera obscura told Daguerre about the heliograph experiments. At the age of 64, in ill health and in serious financial difficulties, Niépce reluctantly signed a contract with Daguerre to share information about the heliographic process. In 1833, Joseph Niépce died before seeing the results from Daguerre's experiments, but his son Isidore maintained the partnership. Daguerre switched from pewter to a copper plate and used mercury vapor to speed the exposure time. These technical changes resulted in a

one-of-a-kind, reversed image as if seen in a mirror, of extraordinary sharpness (Figure 11.17). Daguerre *modestly* named the first practical photographic process the daguerreotype (Greek for *picture by Daguerre*).

On January 7, 1839, the French astronomer Arago formally announced Daguerre's invention to the prestigious Academy of Science. Upon seeing the wondrous examples, the American physician and author Oliver Wendell Holmes Sr. dubbed the reversed daguerreotype image a "mirror with a memory. The French government paid Louis Daguerre and Isidore Niépce an annual pension in return for making the process available to the public.

The precious, positive, one-of-a-kind portraits were an instant hit because common people could finally afford to have a picture made of them. Daguerreotypes were often displayed within elegantly crafted miniature boxes made of papier-mâché, leather, or highly finished wood. Samuel F. B. Morse, inventor of the telegraph, opened the first photographic studio in New York City and taught many entrepreneurs the process. With a faster chemical process, a larger lens that let in more light, and a smaller plate size, exposure times were reduced to 30 seconds.

The new process needed a name other than a derivative of Daguerre. England's Sir John Herschel, who earlier had made important discoveries about the electromagnetic spectrum, coined the word *photography* for the new light-sensitive process, from the Greek words that mean *writing with light*. However, the process, as stunning as it was, had two significant drawbacks—it produced a positive image that couldn't be reproduced, and depending on lighting conditions, exposures were too long to stop action.

Calotype Coincidentally, a different photographic process was announced the same month as the daguerreotype. Sometimes referred to as the talbotype, the calotype (Greek for *beautiful picture*) was invented by William Henry Fox Talbot. The process is the foundation for modern photography.

Talbot was born in Dorset, England in 1800. After being educated at Trinity College in Cambridge, he devoted the next 50 years of his life to studying physics, chemistry, mathematics, astronomy, and archaeology. In 1833, while vacationing in Italy, he came to the conclusion that images from a camera obscura could be preserved using light-sensitive paper. After several experiments upon his return home two years later, he produced a one-inch-square paper negative of a window of his house. He then produced a positive picture by placing another sheet of sensitized paper on top of the negative image and exposing it to the sun. The exposure time was about three minutes in bright sunlight. Talbot continued to produce many views of his estate, which were later collected in the first book illustrated with photographs, *The Pencil of Nature*, (Figure 11.18). The work was published without binding to subscribers who were meant to collect all 24 plates and pay to have the pages bound. But due to a lack of interest from the public, only six plates were created (Figure 11.19).

The calotype process never became widespread because of two reasons—its quality when compared with daguerreotypes, and Talbot's insistence on making the process available only to those who paid for the formula. Because a positive image had to print through the paper fibers of the negative view, Talbot's pictures never achieved the sharp focus of daguerreotypes. Furthermore, unlike the daguerreotype process that was released by the French government, Talbot charged interested parties a large sum to learn the secret of the calotype. Consequently, few took him up on his offer. Nevertheless, the process represents the first instance in which the modern terms *negative* and *positive* were used. Once a negative image was created, any number of positive prints could be made. This concept is the basis for modern photography and encouraged economic development of the medium until it was replaced by digital photography.

Wet-Collodion In March 1851, the year Louis Daguerre died, Frederick Scott Archer published his formula for all to read in a popular journal of the day, *The Chemist*. Archer was a British sculptor and part-time calotype photographer.

Figure 11.18

Cover of The Pencil of Nature, *1844, by William Henry Fox Talbot, the first book with photographs included on its pages.*
Courtesy of Paul K.

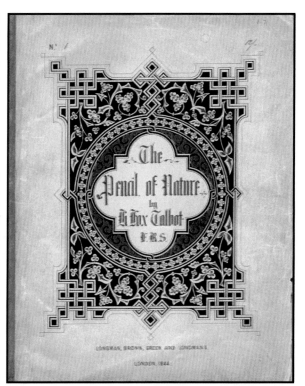

Figure 11.19

"Plate VI—The Open Door," 1844 by William Henry Fox Talbot. What Talbot wrote about the picture is also a call for being more observant generally: "This is one of the trifling efforts of [photography's] infancy, which some partial friends have been kind enough to commend. A painter's eye will often be arrested where ordinary people see nothing remarkable. A casual gleam of sunshine, or a shadow thrown across his path, a time withered oak, or a moss covered stone may awaken a train of thoughts and feelings, and picturesque imaginings." With Talbot's calotype process, photography satisfied one other condition for its popularity—a negative image that could easily reproduce any number of positive prints, but the pictures weren't as sharp as daguerreotypes.
Courtesy of the University of Oxford

He had grown weary of the poor quality of prints obtained from using paper negatives. He suggested glass as a suitable medium for photographic emulsion. The problem with glass, however, was in making the emulsion adhere to its surface. However, the invention of collodion in 1847 solved that problem. A mixture of guncotton or nitrocellulose dissolved in alcohol and ether, collodion was used to protect wounds from infection. When poured on any surface, it forms a tough film. Archer mixed collodion with light-sensitive silver nitrate.

His wet-collodion process produced glass negatives of amazing detail and subtlety of tone that could be used to make hundreds of positive prints. The exposure time was a remarkable ten seconds. Although the process required that the glass plate be exposed while moist and developed immediately, serious portrait and documentary photographers around the world used the wet-collodion process for the next 30 years.

Most of the photographs taken during the American Civil War utilized the wet-collodion process (Figure 11.20). However, with the long exposure times, only before and after battle scenes could be captured (Figure 11.21). This era also saw the introduction of several processes that were popular with the public such as inexpensive wet-collodion tintypes (images on metal plates) and ambrotypes (images on paper), and albumen prints, a process that used egg whites to bind the photographic emulsion to paper, which was usually used to print small calling cards that were handed out between friends and business associates called *carte de visites*.

Color Emulsions Scottish physicist James Clerk Maxwell is credited with producing the first color slide. In a lecture to the Royal Institution in London in 1861, he admitted that his work was influenced by Thomas Young's discoveries about the eye's color perception. Maxwell made three separate pictures of a ribbon through red, green, and blue

Figure 11.20
A stereocard shows a seated Alexander Gardner in front of a horse-drawn darkroom. Gardner, an immigrant from Scotland moved to New York City in 1856. Matthew Brady hired him to cover the Civil War. He later ran Brady's gallery in Washington D.C. and produced a book, Gardner's Photographic Sketch Book *of the Civil War.*
Courtesy of the Library of Congress

Figure 11.21
"Battle-field of Gettysburg— Dead Confederate sharpshooter at foot of Little Round Top,"
1863 by Timothy H. O'Sullivan. Since the famed photographer Mathew Brady was practically
blind by the time of the American Civil War, he hired several photographers to take photo-
graphs for him. One of those was Timothy O'Sullivan, who made this silent study of a young
sniper's body using Frederick Archer's wet-collodion process. Now, the photographic medium
had two conditions met—sharp images that were reproducible. However, the process was still
difficult to use and could not stop movement.
Courtesy of the Library of Congress

colored filters. When he projected the three separate images with the colored light from each filter at the same time and aligned the views, a color slide was the result (Figure 11.22).

Because of the impracticality of Maxwell's discovery, attention soon focused on color print materials (Figure 11.23). In 1903, Auguste and Louis Lumière, important figures in the history of motion pictures, started selling their autochrome photographic plates to the public. The Lumière brothers mixed red, green, and blue colored potato starch grains randomly throughout a photographic emulsion. Although the film was quite expensive for the day, photogrphers immediately favored autochrome because of the quality of the images produced.

Gelatin-Bromide Dry Plate Dr. Richard Maddox of London drastically changed photography and sparked the motion picture medium. A medical doctor and amateur scientist and photographer, he was looking for a substitute for collodion as a photographic emulsion. After experimenting with a number of sticky substances, he tried gelatin, an organic material obtained from the bones, skins, and hooves of animals. The result was a light-sensitive film that could be manufactured, stored, and exposed much later by a photographer.

With his invention, photography was advanced to a point at which it could truly be a successful mass medium. It now had exposure times that could stop fast action, sharply focused images, and a negative that could produce any number of positive prints. All photography

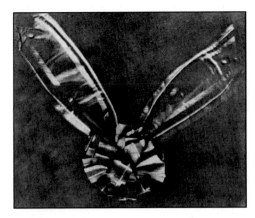

Figure 11.22
"Tartan Ribbon," 1861 by James Clerk Maxwell and Thomas Sutton. The Scottish physicist James Clerk Maxwell had Thomas Sutton photograph a Scottish "tartan" ribbon three times, each with a different color filter (red, green, and blue) over the lens. Ironically for Maxwell, who identified the electromagnetic spectrum, the photographic emulsion used for the picture was not sensitive to the red wavelength. However, the red dye of the day used in the ribbon fluorescently created the "red" color for the film.
Courtesy of the James Clerk Maxwell Foundation

needed was a simple way to use Maddox's dry plate invention.

It was an American who figured out the last step to make photography a popular medium. George Eastman of Rochester, New York invented cameras that used gelatin dry plate films in long rolls. In 1888, he introduced his $25 Kodak camera (in today's dollars, the camera would cost about $650). *Kodak* simply was an easily pronounced and remembered name that he invented (Figure 11.24). With the motto "You push the button—we do the rest," the camera came loaded with 100 exposures. After taking all the pictures, a customer mailed the camera back to Rochester where the round negatives were printed. The camera was reloaded with film and sent back with the prints. Maddox's discovery with Eastman's addition also led to the invention of motion picture film after the American Thomas Edison saw stop-motion images of animals and persons.

Figure 11.23
Russian chemist and photographer Sergey Mikhaylovich Proku-din-Gorsky is shown in a self-portrait next to the Korolistskali River in 1912. Using Maxwell's idea, he produced a method for more easily taking slide photographs that were used to make color motion pictures.
Courtesy of the Library of Congress

Figure 11.24

This Kodak camera advertisement was published in the first issue of Amateur Sportsman, November, 1889. The famous slogan, "You press the button, we do the rest" was George Eastman's message that inspired amateur photography.
Courtesy of Shutterbug

Figure 11.25

A holographic self-portrait of Ventseslav Saynov," 1995. National Polytechnic Museum, Sofia.
Courtesy of Georgy Palpurin

Holography In 1947, Hungarian scientist Dennis Gabor developed holography to improve the sharpness of views obtained with an electron microscope. The unique aspect of holographic images is that they reproduce a three-dimensional view of an object photographed on one sheet of film. Russian researcher Yuri Denisyuk created a slightly different process that is used today to display logos on credit cards, unique jewelry and art presentations, novelty stickers for children, and for publications (Figure 11.25). One of the first mass-produced holographic displays was a picture of an eagle for the March 1984 cover of *National Geographic*, which featured stories on holography, China, Calgary, Canada, and the rhinoceros. During the 2012 Coachella Valley Music and Arts Festival in California, audiences were awed by a dancing holographic image of the rapper Tupac Shakur, shot to death in Las Vegas in 1996. The effect was composed from photographs and video footage projected on a Mylar transparent sheet (Figure 11.26). James Cameron's company Digital Domain (See Chapter 14) and two hologram-imaging companies, AV Concepts and Musion Systems, produced it. With the success of the "performance," look for other uses for holograms.

Instant Edwin Land was a prolific American inventor with more than 500 patents to his name. On a family vacation in New Mexico in 1944, his daughter asked her father "Why couldn't she see the photographs now?" Four years later he introduced his most famous invention—the black-and-white Polaroid 50-second film camera. Instant photography was born. About 15 years later he announced a color version, calling it Polacolor. Once popular with married couples on their honeymoons, and professional photographers to check their compositions before committing to exposures on film, the process has mostly been replaced by digital cameras.

However, artists such as Ellen Carey, Chuck Close, Barbara Crane, David Hockney, Dennis Hopper, Robert Rauschenberg, and Andy Warhol have used Polaroid materials. William Wegman used large-format, 20 × 24-inch cameras to produce fine-quality, one-of-a-kind Polaroid portraits of his Weimaraner dogs (Figure 11.27). Another artist is Stephanie Schneider, who manipulates the colors with heat and pressure to produce striking results (Figure 11.28). The Australian musician Sia Furler used about 2,500 Polaroid images in an animation style for the production of a video for her song, "Breathe Me" in 2004 (Figure 11.29).

Digital Although experiments with devices that could digitize video signals were known since 1968, it wasn't until Willard Boyle and George Smith of Bell Laboratories invented the charge-coupled device (CCD) in 1974 that digital photography took off. The CCD computer chip converted electronic analog signals into digital values. They shared a Nobel Prize in physics in 2009 for their work. In 1975 Eastman Kodak engineer Steven Sasson used a CCD to produce the first digital camera. It took 23 seconds to record a black and white image on a cassette tape for a whopping 10,000 pixels. Today's professional cameras can instantly take and store a single color image of more than 100,000,000 pixels. In 1981 Sony introduced its electronic still video camera, the Mavica (**Mag**netic **Vi**deo **Ca**mera). Its two-inch disc recorded 50 color images that could be viewed on a television screen. However, the camera was not technically a digital camera because it recorded an electronic video signal. Nevertheless, it started the era of digital photography, with all the major camera companies eventually producing true digital models. Except for hardened advocates who love their darkrooms, digital has virtually replaced analog film cameras. And with

smartphones able to take high definition pictures to be saved or sent, photography has never been so popular (Figure 11.30).

Because of the success of digital materials and despite the company's relative success with its DCS and DC line of digital cameras, the venerable company founded by George Eastman has experienced rough economic times. In 2012 filed for Chapter 11 bankruptcy and told the court that it could no longer afford to pay the $3.6 million for its name on the Kodak Theatre in Hollywood, where the Academy Award presentation was held. The motion picture audio pioneer Dolby Laboratories bought the rights and changed the name to Dolby Theatre. The next year the company emerged from bankruptcy and has introduced a deal with Hollywood movie producers to provide motion picture film, introduced a smartphone in 2014, and strangely, in 2017 it reintroduced its popular Ektachrome color film. Eastman Kodak, one of the most significant companies in the history of photography, is stuck in a pre-digital mindset and may cease to exist.

Figure 11.30
A photographer makes a self-portrait with his smartphone's high definition camera with the help of a men's room mirror in Helsinki, Finland. Notice the proper form with the left hand fingers.
Courtesy of Paul Martin Lester

Figure 11.26
(Weblink: http://goo.gl/7mnJL1) For fans of rapper Tupac Shakur who was killed in a drive-by shooting in Las Vegas in 1996, it must have been a surreal experience as a Coachella concertgoer in 2012 to see him perform his song "Hail Mary" with the live singers Snoop Dogg and Dr. Dre.

Figure 11.27
(Weblink: http://goo.gl/UbV2zM) Artist William Wegman began as a painter with works exhibited around the world. While teaching at Cal State University, Long Beach he acquired a Weimaraner dog he named Man Ray and used him in his videos and still photographs.

Figure 11.28
(Weblink: http://goo.gl/79U73H) The German Stephanie Schneider has homes in Berlin and Los Angeles as she creates her own collectable work and album covers for such artists as the Red Hot Chili Peppers and Cyndi Lauper.

Figure 11.29
(Weblink: http://goo.gl/5CnbwE) Music videos are a bit of a lost artform, but Sia's "Breathe Me" motion picture directed by Daniel Askill and shot in a London hotel is evidence of the power of still images.

Figure 11.31

"Firebomb Damaged Sale," 1981. Life and sales go on in Belfast, Northern Ireland despite violent actions from terrorist organizations. A wide-angle lens is used not only to show as much information along the edges of the frame as possible but also to give a viewer the illusion of being in the scene.
Courtesy of Paul Martin Lester

Technical Perspective

You should be aware of five main technical considerations when analyzing your own or someone else's image: lens type, lens opening, shutter speed, lighting, and image quality.

Lens Type Lenses come in three variations—wide-angle, normal, and telephoto—and in two styles—fixed-focal and zoom. A wide-angle lens gives a viewer an expansive, scene-setting view. The visual array photographed also has great depth of field—more is in focus (Figure 11.31). A normal lens mimics the angle of view as seen by the human eyes and is seldom used by professionals. A telephoto lens produces a close-up, narrow perspective of a scene with the foreground and background compressed. It also has a shallow depth of field with little in focus. To save money, many photographers buy a zoom lens that covers all three visual arrays. However, most professional photographers prefer fixed-focal lenses for their improved sharpness and larger apertures.

Lens Opening The opening of a lens is like the pupil in the eye—it regulates the amount of light that enters the camera. If you squint your eyes, your pupils get smaller and more will be in focus. The same is true for a lens. A small opening or aperture will produce an image with much greater depth of field, whereas a large lens opening will have shallow depth of field. Like the choice of the type of lens, a photographer can select elements of a scene she wants a viewer to notice by the choice of lens opening (Figures 11.32 and 11.33).

A new camera technology may make the concept of depth of field obsolete.

Introduced to the public in 2012, the Lytro camera, developed by Stanford PhD graduate Ren Ng, employs digital light field photography that allows a user to focus different parts of a picture *after the shot has been taken*. In 2004 researchers at the Stanford Computer Graphics Laboratory developed a light field camera, but it needed a powerful supercomputer to work. Ng, an alumnus of the Laboratory, simplified the process with a light field sensor built into the Lytro camera. It captures 11 million individual light rays per picture allowing a user to change focus, shift perspective, and switch from 2D to 3D views.

Shutter Speed The amount of time a camera's shutter stays open—its shutter speed—can greatly affect a picture's content. A speed of 1/30th of a second or longer will usually cause blurring of anything that moves. A faster shutter speed will stop motion and is required to overcome shaking of the camera during exposure (referred to as *camera blur*). However, an important feature of many modern cameras is motion stabilizer technology that produces a sharp image during longer shutter speeds and/or jarring conditions such as on a motorboat. An extremely fast shutter speed is necessary to photograph fast-moving subjects without blur. Sports photographers typically use shutter speeds of 1/500th of a second and faster (Figure 11.34). Researchers at the Massachusetts Institute of Technology (MIT) announced in 2011 that they have developed a camera with the fastest shutter speed ever produced. It can record one trillion frames a second and is used in studying the nature of light as it can stop the motion of photons going 670 million miles per hour.

Lighting Photography exists because of light. Knowledge of how lighting is used by photographers is essential in the analysis of an image. There are two kinds of lighting: lighting that comes from

Figures 11.32 and 11.33
"Vinton Cemetery 1, California," (top) and "Vinton Cemetery 2, California," 2002. With a small aperture setting on a camera's lens, objects close in the foreground as well as those in the distance are in focus. However, if a large aperture setting is chosen, a photographer can chose what to emphasize within a picture's frame by controlling focus.
Courtesy of Gerry Davey

available sources and lighting that the photographer brings to a location. Natural lighting, most often called available light, is illumination that already exists within a scene (Figure 11.36). Although its name implies light from the sun, it can also refer to incandescent bulbs, neon light tubes, or fire from a candle. Lighting equipment that a photographer brings to a photography shoot or that is contained within a studio is called artificial lighting. The most commonly used artificial light for location work is the electronic flash.

Figure 11.34
An example of the stopping quality of a camera's shutter is provided by this picture of a young man jumping from a cliff in Mazatlan, Mexico.
Courtesy of Paul Martin Lester

Figure 11.35
The facial features of a woman in an assisted care home in Austin, Texas are softened by muted light from a window in this available light portrait.
Courtesy of Paul Martin Lester

Image Quality Learning how to evaluate the quality of an image in terms of its exposure and contrast is important. A picture that will reproduce well in a publication or for a webpage must have a full range of tones supplied by proper exposure and contrast. As a general rule, a picture is considered properly exposed if it shows detail in the shadow areas and in the light areas. Contrast is defined as the difference between the black and white tones of the image. A low contrast image has little differences in light and dark areas. A high contrast picture has extreme differences.

A recent technological development is high dynamic range imaging (HDR). Through multiple pictures at different exposure settings, the computer technology creates an image with a wider range of tones between the lightest and darkest areas than conventional camera settings (Figure 11.36). The concept of using multiple exposures to create a single photograph can be traced to seascape pictures produced by Gustave Le Gray in the 1850s. Le Gray took a picture of the sky and another of the ocean and combined them into a single print. The process has advanced since then to include software programs and cameras with built-in HDR features. For example, in 2010 the iPhone 4 has HDR included. When the HDR function is selected, the camera automatically takes three pictures at different exposures and combines them for the final image. However, it is this multiple image requirement of the process that makes journalism professionals, including members of the National Press Photographers Association (NPPA) nervous as being a form of picture manipulation.

Ethical Perspective
Visual communicators must be aware of five major ethical concerns whenever images are used. Two of those concerns—visual persuasion and

stereotypes—have been discussed (See Chapters 4 and 5). The three other main ethical issues are showing victims of violence, violating rights to privacy, and picture manipulations.

Victims of Violence After the publication or broadcast of a controversial image that shows, for example, either dead or grieving victims of violence, people often make telephone calls and write letters attacking the photographer as being tasteless and adding to the anguish of those involved. And yet, violence and tragedy are staples of American journalism because readers have always been morbidly attracted to gruesome stories and photographs. It is as if viewers want to know that tragic circumstances exist but don't want to face the uncomfortable details (Figure 11.37).

Gruesome images have a long impact on viewers. Most editors will not publish horrific car wreck pictures, but that doesn't prevent them showing up on

Figure 11.36
"Calton Hill, Edinburgh, 2008." The intense colors and 3-D effect come from using the HDR technique when five different exposures are combined into one photograph. For this image, Davidson set the lens of his Pentax K10D camera to f8 and used different shutter speeds from 1/4000 to 1/15 seconds. Final processing was accomplished with Photomatrix Pro and Adobe Photoshop software.
Courtesy of Paul Davidson

Figure 11.37
The front page of the Bakersfield Californian *is a study in contrasts. Mickey Mouse and Edward Romero's grieving family share the front page. A reader firestorm of 500 letters to the editor, 400 telephone calls, 80 subscription cancellations, and one bomb threat resulted. Many readers probably were sparked to protest publication of the picture because of its insensitive display on the same page as a popular cartoon character.*
Courtesy of John Harte

websites. In 2006 18-year-old Nicole Catsouras of Orange County, California took her father's Porsche out for a joy ride without permission. After speeding more than 100 mph, she lost control of the vehicle, hit another car, and slammed into a toll booth. She died instantly. Her body was so badly disfigured that her parents were told not to take a look. However, anyone with web access could view her nearly decapitated head from pictures taken by a Highway Patrol investigator and put on the web by two dispatchers. In 2012 the family received $2.37 million for the pain and suffering caused by the photographs.

In 2012 the *Los Angeles Times* newspaper published photographs that disturbed many readers. An attack on a Shiite Muslim gathering in Afghanistan in 2011 killed more than 70 people (Figure 11.38). The original caption stated, "Tarana, 12, reacts while surrounded by the bodies of men, women, and children who died after a suicide bomber detonated a bomb during a religious ceremony in Kabul on December 6, 2011. Out of 17 women and children from her family, seven died including her seven-year-old brother Shoaib." Photographer Massoud Hossaini of AFP/Getty Images reported that he was crying when he took the pictures. "I have never experienced that before," he admitted. Many readers were upset by the graphic nature depicted in the image. "I can't believe that you would put a photo like this in your paper," "Put dead children on the front page. You are disgusting," and "Tell me the lifeless image of the toddler in yellow doesn't sicken your stomach" were common complaints. Deputy Managing Editor Colin Crawford of the newspaper responded, "We understand that it is a tough image to look at, but we felt the news value of the photo made it worth publishing. This photo, though gut-wrenching, shows just how many innocents are being killed." With such gruesome content, readers often cite golden rule, veil of ignorance, and hedonism philosophies while journalists justify the picture with categorical imperative and utilitarian arguments (see Chapter 6). It was later announced that the photograph won the Pulitzer Prize—one of the most prestigious awards in journalism.

In 2012 a set of 18 pictures of U.S. soldiers posing with corpses given to the *Los Angles Times* by a soldier caused a public uproar (Figure 11.39). The newspaper published one on the front page in color and another, the more shocking image of a smiling soldier holding the severed leg of an Afghanistan suicide bomber, was printed on an inside page and in black and white—a golden mean approach (see Chapter 6). U.S. military personnel asked the newspaper not to publish the gruesome pictures because they feared retaliation. Readers objected to the publication because they provided "ammunition for the enemy," showed "disrespect [to] our fighting soldiers," and gave "another reason to go after our soldiers." Editor Davan Maharaj explained, "After careful consideration, we decided that publishing a small but representative selection of the photos would fulfill our obligation to readers to report vigorously and impartially on all aspects of the American mission in Afghanistan." Sometimes the public needs to see what their government does in its name.

Print and broadcast journalists have a duty to report the news as objectively, fairly, and accurately as possible. Editors and producers should be mindful that some images, because of their emotional content have the potential to upset many people. However, decisions should be guided, never ruled, by readers and viewers. One solution attempted by some media organizations is to show controversial pictures on a website with a strong disclaimer. That way a user can decide whether or not she wants to click on the link and see the image. This golden mean (See Chapter 6) solution is common with television presentations.

A Right to Privacy Florence Thompson looked away from Dorothea Lange's camera lens in the famous "Migrant Mother" photograph because that was the only way she thought she could protect her privacy. When subjects of news events and their families, through no fault of their own, are suddenly thrust into the harsh light of public scrutiny, they often complain bitterly, as Thompson did the rest of her life.

The judicial system in America has recognized that private and public persons have different legal rights in terms of privacy. Privacy laws are much stricter in protecting private citizens not involved in a news story than they are for public celebrities who often invite media attention. As many as 60 paparazzi if it's Kim Kardashian or Justin Bieber regularly stake out the places where celebrities shop and go clubbing on a 24/7 basis. The general public often justifies such extreme behavior because of the intense interest in the celebrities. Tabloid magazines, television shows, and websites pay as much as $100,000 for an exclusive picture that shows a private moment of a troubled star. Although photographers need to be aware of the laws concerning privacy and trespass, ethical behavior should not be guided by what is strictly legal (Figure 11.40).

Picture Manipulations Since the birth of photography, photographers have manipulated subjects and images to produce the result they desired. Hippolyte Bayard was the French inventor of a unique photographic process who did not receive the attention or pension granted to Louis Daguerre. In protest, Bayard faked his own death in an 1839 photograph. It is the first example of a manipulated image in the history of photography (Figure 11.41).

More recently, digital manipulations are noticed by the public and critics. The police mug shot of O.J. Simpson arrested for the murder of his wife and her friend

W LINK

Figure 11.38
(Weblink: http://goo.gl/x6Yyur)
Massoud Hossaini's Pulitzer Prize winning photograph is difficult to view and study, but it is necessary for these types of images to be published in order to fully understand the tragedies that occur in war zones around the world.

W LINK

Figure 11.39
(Weblink: http://goo.gl/tu3TMR)
The general public should always be willing to see actions that government officials do in their name.

Figure 11.40
Boys play in the grass while women pass near a man with his barrel organ pulled by a donkey in this photograph by Paul Martin taken in 1898. One of the first street photographers, Paul Martin took candid moments of rich and poor people as they played, relaxed, and generally enjoyed the day. Considered to be one of the first photojournalists, Martin's private moments captured on film provided a reord of how British citizens actually lived during the Victoria era.
Courtesy of the Victoria and Albert Museum.

in 1994 was used for the covers of *Time* and *Newsweek* magazines the same week (Figure 11.42). The *Time* cover was criticized for illustrator Matt Mahurin's darkening of O.J.'s facial features, which some said was a slap at all African Americans, and yet *Newsweek* was never criticized for the manipulation of the words on the cover, "A Trail of Blood." Brian Walski of the *Los Angeles Times* was fired for a photo composite he created while a photojournalist covering the war in Iraq (Figure 11.43). No doubt fatigue, tough conditions, and competition were factors responsible for him combining parts of two images into a third. However, there is no good reason for such an ethical

lapse. Credibility is a precious commodity that should be protected with as much fervor as can be mustered (Figure 11.44).

Cultural Perspective
The story of photography, as with any other medium, is never simply about the technical contributions made by scientists and inventors to improve the process. Technological advances allow photographers to communicate the cultural values of the time, but a photographer's style is formed by the culture in which the pictures are made. Studying the images produced within a certain time period is a study of the society from which they come. Throughout the histo-

Figure 11.42
*(Weblink: http://goo.gl/8Cgq6c)
Although most of the criticism
of the O.J* Time *mug shot was
centered on the darkening of
the face by Matt Mahurin, the
typography choices by* Newsweek *editors should be held in
reproach as "Trail of Blood" in
all red is just as sensational.*

Figure 11.43
*(Weblink: http://goo.gl/qSKonx)
Because of the Iraq war picture
combination error, whenever
a photojournalist uses Photoshop to merge elements from
different pictures, it is called a
"Walski." Although fired from
the* Los Angeles Times, *Brian
Walski maintains his own photography business in Denver,
Colorado.*

Figure 11.41
"Self-Portrait as a Drowned Man," 1840 by Hippolyte Bayard. The French inventor Hippolyte Bayard created the first practical photographic process that predated the daguerreotype, had the first public exhibition of photographs, made the first self-portrait, and created the first manipulated picture in the history of medium. Frustrated by not receiving recognition from the French government that Daguerre and Niépce enjoyed, Bayard staged a photograph with a caption that read, "The corpse which you see here is that of M. Bayard. The Government which has been only too generous to Monsieur Daguerre, has said it can do nothing for Monsieur Bayard, and the poor wretch has drowned himself."
Courtesy of the University of Southern California

ry of photography, various photographic styles have reflected the people and their times.

Photographer as Portraitist One of the earliest uses of the photographic medium was to capture the faces of people, both famous and ordinary. Eventually, photography became a great equalizer. Because long exposure times and bright sunlight were required for early photography, Victorian portrait subjects appear to be grim, unsmiling people. In reality, they had to keep still in order to get the best picture possible.

In the 19th century, several photographers created a photographic style that reflected the culture of the times. Scottish calotype photographers David Octavius Hill and Robert Adamson made sensitive studies of ordinary people. Julia Margaret Cameron, one of the few women in visual communication history, made dynamic images of her

Figure 11.44
*A hard-working employee of a California winery is either removed or added to a
scene manipulated by Photoshop software.*
Courtesy of Paul Martin Lester

famous friends: Alfred Tennyson, Sir
John Herschel, Thomas Carlyle, Charles
Darwin, Robert Browning, and Henry
Longfellow (Figure 11.45). Gaspard Felix
Tournachon, or Nadar, as he was known,
matched his bold shooting style with the
strong personalities of the day. Brady is
credited for the daguerreotype image of
President Lincoln that appears on the
redesigned five-dollar bill that was first
issued in 2008 (Figure 11.46). Brady was
one of the most influential photographers in the United States, had portrait
galleries in New York and Washington,
and funded photographers to document
the Civil War (Figure 11.47).

The portrait tradition continues with
August Sander's views of everyday German citizens before World War II, Diane
Arbus's direct and sensitive portraits of
extraordinary subjects, Irving Penn's
series of everyday workers, and Richard
Avedon's large-format images of known
and unknown Americans. Stand-outs
in this genre also include a master of
the celebrity set-up photograph Annie
Leibovitz with such sensitive portraits as
John Lennon and Yoko Ono for *Rolling
Stone* taken on the day of the Beatle's
death, the naked and pregnant Demi
Moore on the cover of *Vanity Fair*, and
Queen Elizabeth II during her state
visit to Virginia (Figure 11.48). Lauren
Greenfield shows revealing portraits of
women in her books *Girl Culture* and
Fast Forward and her documentary films
Thin (2006), *Kids + Money* (2008), and
The Queen of Versailles (2012). Relative
newcomer Suzanne Opton's has made
close-up portraits of American soldiers
who had spent time in Afghanistan and
Iraq. Her "Soldier" series was shown in
print, on websites, and on public billboards (Figure 11.49).

Photographer as Painter Many
painters feared that photography would
soon replace their profession. To hedge
their bets, some artists became photographers who mimicked the style of

Figure 11.45
"Sir John Herschel," 1867, by Julia Margaret Cameron. One of the most respected individuals in the history of photography is the British astronomer and scientist Sir John Herschel. He not only discovered a way to make photographic images so they wouldn't eventually fade if exposed to light, he also invented the cyanotype photographic process later called "blueprints" used by the English botanist Anna Atkins and by architects, created the first picture on glass, and came up with the terms "snapshot," "negative," "positive," and most importantly, the word "photography," Greek for "writing with light." Julia Margaret Cameron, born in India, took up photography when she was 48 years old. She eventually made portraits of many of the most important figures in the worlds of literature and science at that time.
Courtesy of the Metropolitan Museum of Art

allegorical painters to tell a story with photographs in the tradition of paintings of the day. Two photographers who worked in this style during the 19th century were Oscar Rejlander and Henry Peach Robinson. Rejlander's "The Two Ways of Life" used 32 separate pictures spliced together to show the choice two young men must make (Figure 11.50). Robinson's most famous image, "Fading Away," is a combination print using five separate pictures to show a young woman on her deathbed. Contemporary

Figure 11.46
"Abraham Lincoln," daguerreotype (inverted to match the scene as seen), 1864, by Mathew Brady.
Courtesy of the Library of Congress

photographers Vicky Alexander, Richard Prince, and Mike and Doug Starn use "cut-and-paste" techniques to produce elaborate artistic renderings from their own or previously published pictures.

Photographer as Landscape Documentarian Photographers have always enjoyed taking pictures of natural scenes. When the American Civil War ended, Timothy O'Sullivan and William Jackson traveled west to explore and photograph scenic views with their awkward wet-collodion technology. In 1873, O'Sullivan made one of his most famous pictures at the ruins of "White House" at the Cañon de Chelle in Arizona (Figure 11.51).

The power of photography to shape the opinion of others is demonstrated by these views of the land. The images became synonymous with what people thought of as natural and beautiful. Jackson, who lived to be 99 years old, made the first photographs of the Yellowstone area in 1871, which helped convince Congress to set aside the land as the

Figure 11.47
Mathew Brady, 1875. Born in upstate New York, Brady moved to New York City when he was 18 years old and learned the daguerreotype process from the American inventor of the telegraph, Samuel Morse, who had his own studio. Three years later Brady opened his own studio, and by the time of the American Civil War he was the most famous photographer of his day. Despite reservations from friends, Brady hired and outfitted more than 20 photographers, including Alexander Gardner and Timothy O'Sullivan, to document the battles of the Civil War. Controversially, Brady took credit for their photographic work. He spent more than $100,000 of his own money (equivalent to about $2.4 million today) and never recouped his investment. Depressed over his financial situation and the death of his wife, he died penniless in the charity ward of a New York hospital after being struck by a streetcar in 1896. Many of the glass plate negatives of the Civil War were found to be used as windows for the top of his greenhouse.
Courtesy of the Library of Congress

W
LINK
Figure 11.49
*(Weblink:
http://goo.gl/VkJr7b)
The photographic portraits by
Annie Leibovitz always
show a close and honest
connection between the
photographer and the
person pictured.
It is as if there*

Figure 11.49

"Birkholz—353 Days in Iraq, 205 Days in Afghanistan," 2007, by Suzanne Opton. For her *"Soldier"* series, Suzanne Opton photographed nine American soldiers who were between tours in Iraq and Afghanistan stationed at Fort Drum, New York. Of her series, Opton says, *"We all experience strategic moments when we feel most alive. These are the moments we will always remember, be they transcendent or horrific. After all, what are we if not our collection of memories? In making these portraits of soldiers, I simply wanted to look in the face of someone who'd seen something unforgettable."*
Courtesy of Suzanne Opton

country's first national park because the land was viewed, within the photographs, as naturally beautiful. Following in the footsteps of the early landscape photographers, Ansel Adams, Wynn Bullock, and Harry Callahan all have made photographs that record exquisitely nature's beauty and sharpen our sense of wonder of it. Contemporary New York photographer Paul Raphaelson captures hauntingly beautiful post-apocalyptic urban landscapes (Figure 11.52).

Photographer as Artist Many traditional artists have looked down on photography, thinking it a simple craft. Another problem artists had with photography was that any number of images could be made from a single negative.

Therefore, acceptance of photography as a fine art on the same level as painting was slow in coming. One of the most important figures in elevating the medium to a fine art was the American Alfred Stieglitz (Figure 11.53). Not only did he exploit photography's unique technological features, he also opened a gallery that exhibited painting and photography on an equal footing and published a critical journal about photography, *Camera Work*. Married to artist Georgia O'Keeffe, he was a strong proponent of modern art photography and inspired many photographers to build that tradition. Recent photographers who view photography as a way of expressing a deeply personal statement include Lucien Clerque, Yasumasa Morimura, and Sandy Skoglund.

Figure 11.50
Originally a stonemason and painter, Oscar Rejlander, born in Sweden, but lived in England most of his life, took up photography after seeing one of Henry Fox Talbot's photographs. He became one of the most important Victorian photographers in the history of the medium. His most important work, "The Two Ways of Life" was a combination of thirty-two images first exhibited at the Manchester Art Treasures Exhibition of 1857. In the picture, two young men are shown lifestyle extremes—one based on gambling and sexual encounters and the other a combination of piousness, hard work, education, and helping others. Perhaps the choice should be an Aristotelian middle way? **Courtesy of the Metropolitan Museum of Art**

In a reversal of the process, Marc Trujillo makes large paintings that feature a street corner with a gas station, workers in a fast food drive-in restaurant, and passersby in a shopping mall that look like color photographs (Figure 11.54).

Photographer as Social Documentarian Because images have the capacity to spark interest and convey emotional messages, many photographers have used the medium to shed light on social problems in the hope of getting the public to act. In 1877, John Thompson teamed with writer Adolphe Smith for a book about London's poor, *Victorian London Street Life*. Newspaper reporter-turned-photographer Jacob Riis used photography to illustrate his writings and lectures on the slums in New York City (Figure 11.55). In 1890, he published his work in a book, *How the Other Half Lives*. In 1909, Lewis Wickes Hine

managed to help enact child labor laws with his sensitive portraits of children working in dangerous, backbreaking occupations around the country (Figure 11.56).

Following in their tradition, French photographers Eugene Atget in the 1920s, a social documentarian with a view camera, and Henri Cartier-Bresson in the 1930s, with a small, hand-held camera, showed views of ordinary people. Cartier-Bresson captured the "decisive moment"—a term he used to describe the instant when content and composition are at their most revealing.

The FSA photographers documented living conditions of homeless people for the U.S. government during the Great Depression. Photographers for *Life* magazine, most notably W. Eugene Smith, produced photographic stories that illustrated the lives of diverse individuals. James Nachtwey, Eugene Richards, and

Figure 11.52
(Weblink: http://goo.gl/DbrvSG) The stunningly graphic photographs of Paul Raphaelson who specializes in "urban and cultural landscapes" are featured on his website.

Figure 11.51
Stereocard of "Ancient Ruins in the Cañon de Chelle, New Mexico," 1873 by Timothy O'Sullivan. Born in New York City, O'Sullivan was a teenager when he was hired by Mathew Brady to work in his studio. After fighting in the Civil War as a Union Army officer and honorably discharged, he joined Brady's team of photographers to document war participants and the aftermath of battles. One of his most powerful images is the eerily disturbing "The Harvest of Death," taken after the battle at Gettysburg, Pennsylvania, as seen in Figure 8.20. Perhaps disgusted by the death and destruction, after the war O'Sullivan joined several expeditions exploring the western United States and Panama. But after an expedition's boat capsized while exploring the Colorado River, he lost most of his 300 glass negatives. However, the image of the majestic Native American ruins precariously set within a canyon's wall survived. Nine years after he made the photograph, O'Sullivan died of tuberculosis at the age of 42.
Courtesy of the Library of Congress

Figure 11.53

"A Bit of Venice," 1894, by Alfred Stieglitz. One of the most important figures in the history of photography as a practitioner, editor, and advocate, Stieglitz elevated the medium into a respected fine art form. Born in New York to upper-middle-class parents, he studied mechanical engineering in Germany where he happened to enroll in a chemistry class taught by the photographer and inventor Hermann Vogel. Intrigued with the medium, Stieglitz entered and won several competitions. He later promoted photography through two publications, Camera Notes and Camera Work, the Photo-Secession pictorial art movement, and his galleries "291" and "An American Place." Taken while on his honeymoon with his first wife, whom he left in 1923 to marry the American artist Georgia O'Keeffe, who was known for her erotic paintings of flowers, "A Bit of Venice" reveals the ethereal and transformative power of photographs over paintings after you realize that this corner of the canalled city actually existed in the real world.
Courtesy of Allen Memorial Art Museum, Oberlin College

Figure 11.54
"6800 Hayvenhurst Avenue," oil on canvas, 2008 by Marc Trujillo. Although photography is not used in his artistic process, Marc Trujillo's paintings of drive-thru restaurants, big box stores, and shopping malls display a photographic presence combined with a feeling of unease in the style of the American painter Edward Hopper.
Courtesy of Marc Trujillo

Sebastião Salgado are photojournalists who continue in Smith's documentary style tradition. Considered the best of the best, Mary Ellen Mark, who died in 2015, brought the stories of the voiceless from around the world to viewers of her many books and exhibitions. Greg Constantine is an independent photojournalist who travels the world documenting displaced persons with his images used by such groups as Doctors Without Borders and the United Nations Refugee Agency (Figure 11.57). His books, *Kenya's Nubians: Then & Now* (2011), *Exile to Nowhere: Burma's Rohinyga* (2012), and *Nowhere People* (2015) are examples of the best photojournalism can offer (Figure 11.58).

Critical Perspective
Photography was invented at the height of the Industrial Revolution, during which millions of people around the world eventually had more money and

free time to spend taking pictures. Photography, with its emphasis on realistic scenes, freed artists to be more expressive. Impressionism and surrealism, for example, flourished because painters no longer had to render natural scenes exactly on canvas as shown by the artist Édouard Manet (See Chapter 1).

Photography educated people about social problems within their own communities and among native peoples around the world. Visual messages inspired immigrants to learn to read words after pictures hooked them into buying a newspaper. But photography also was used to mislead and misinform. Government agencies in both totalitarian and democratic countries used photography to persuade citizens to adopt a desired point of view.

Photographs entertain and educate. They provide a historical record that relies on the idea that a camera does not lie. Throughout the history of photog-

Figure 11.55
"Bandit's Roost," New York City, 1888 by Richard Hoe Lawrence. Social reformer Jacob Riis was not a trained photographer, so he often hired them to accompany him on his nightly journeys through New York's seedy underworld. He used the pictures in his lectures and for his book, How the Other Half Lives. *This is one of the most famous photographs that he took credit for, "Bandit's Roost," was actually taken by Richard Hoe Lawrence in an alley off Mulberry Street, today located within New York's Chinatown district. About the picture Riis wrote,"The true line to be drawn between pauperism and honest poverty is the clothesline. With it begins the effort to be clean that is the first and best evidence of a desire to be honest."*
Courtesy of the National Endowment for the Humanities

Figure 11.56
"Newsboys Selling on Brooklyn Bridge, 3 a.m.," 1908 by Lewis Wickes Hine. The American sociologist Lewis Hine encouraged his students at New York's Ethical Culture School to use photographs to document the immigrants arriving daily into the city. After he tried it himself, he devoted the rest of his life to documentary photography. Working for the National Child Labor Committee, he made thousands of pictures of children suffering under long hours in dangerous situations throughout the United States so that the images could be used as evidence to persuade members of Congress to enact child labor laws. He also documented the efforts of the Red Cross in America and in Europe, the construction of the Empire State Building, and served as the chief photographer with the government's Works Progress Administration (WPA), which concentrated on how work affects workers.
**Courtesy of the
Library of Congress**

Figure 11.57
"Bihari woman," by Greg Constantine. During Pakistani rule, the Bihari were a prosperous and privileged community, but after a civil war in East Pakistan resulted in the birth of Bangladesh, they were fired from government jobs and lost ownership of their land. Since 1971 more than 300,000 live in 66 refugee camps where they are exploited, harassed, and unwanted.
Courtesy of Greg Constantine

Figure 11.58
(Weblink: http://goo.gl/Gf9LdE) Greg Constantine's website is a clinic in graphic design choices that best feature photographic stories.

raphy, the picture enjoyed far greater credibility than the printed or spoken word. But computer operators who can alter the content of a digitized news picture as easily as an advertising image are undermining the medium's credibility.

TRENDS TO WATCH FOR PHOTOGRAPHY

Photography is undergoing exciting and challenging changes. This era in its history is not unlike the time when the wet-collodion process was replaced by the gelatin bromide dry plate. Of the nine major advances in the technological history of photography, only four have significantly changed the way people think about the medium. The daguerreotype introduced the world to the medium. The wet-collodion process proved

that photography could be a high-quality and reproducible method of communicating visual messages to large numbers of people. The gelatin-bromide dry plate process made photography easy for both amateurs and professionals. Finally, digital photography, which combines the medium with the computer, promises unlimited possibilities for visual communicators. As more of us view photographs on monitors, paper prints are less important. Home computers contain collections of images that can be easily shared through wireless connections. Viewers can share their precious pictures with anyone anywhere in the world. This need to share photographs explains why Yahoo! purchased Flickr in 2005 for $35 million and why Facebook in

2012 bought Instagram, a two-year-old social network sharing application, for about one billion dollars.

Regardless, the stilled moment will always be a vital component of mass communication messages because there is no way to escape its underlying power. As Carina Chocano, a critic for the *Los Angeles Times*, wrote, "Video may dominate the visible world, but still photography trumps it when it comes to administering electric jolts to the imagination."

Examples of the need for still images are easy to find in both the art and documentary worlds. For example, director Steven Soderbergh's trailer for his 2005 motion picture *Bubble* was a tribute to still photography, with spooky images taken within a doll factory (Figure 11.59). David Crawford (Figure 11.60) takes hundreds of still images of persons riding subways throughout the world and then creates stop-motion studies. When seen on a computer, the effect is a moving, still image. A commercial for the Olympus PEN camera used a stop-motion animation technique in which the creators shot more than 60,000 pictures and used about 10,000 photographs that told the story of a man's life in an intriguing and compelling visual array (Figure 11.61). Artists who use the stop-motion technique with still photographs present their work on YouTube. Noah Kalina took one picture of himself every day from 2000 and continues to add to the collection the first day of every month (Figure 11.62). The flash mob fad of a few years ago inspired people to become still photographs. "Frozen Grand Central" has been named one of the top seven flash mobs of all time by AdWeek. In the middle of Grand Central Station in New York City 200 people suddenly freeze amid the startled looks of passersby (Figure 11.63).

For documentary presentations,

Brian Storm maintains one of the premiere websites to see the work of still photographers within multimedia presentations that also include voice-overs, sound, music, and interactive navigation features with MediaStorm.com. With a master's degree in photojournalism from the prestigious University of Missouri and experiences as the former director of multimedia for MSNBC and vice president of News, Multimedia & Assignment Services for the picture agency Corbis, Storm runs a multimedia production studio that presents stories created by journalists throughout the world. He also trains professionals and academics how to make their own multimedia programs. Its "Crisis Guide: Darfur" produced for the Council on Foreign Relations and "Kingsley's Crossing" by Olivier Jobard won Emmy Awards. Other stories tell of the lives of women raped in Rwanda in 1994, drug addicts in a New York City apartment, and the lives of Kurdish people in northern Iraq—stories you rarely can find on paper (Figure 11.64).

With the popularity of social media, photographers find new sources for the stories they want to tell to internet-savvy users. Concerned about the epidemic of opioid addiction and overdose deaths in their town of Martinsburg, West Virginia, wedding photographers Lori and John Swadley used Instagram to publicize their portraits of recovering addicts that go against the usual visual stereotypes in "52 Addicts." Anyone with a camera can make a difference (Figure 11.65). In a well designed, interactive format, MSNBC sponsored photographer Matt Black on his travels around the United States photographing persons who live below the poverty line in "The Journey" (Figure 11.66).

Regardless of how still and moving images are combined and presented, the stilled moment will always be important. A moving image shocks, illuminates, and entertains, but it is fleeting, quickly replaced by another picture. A stilled

Figure 11.59
(Weblink: http://goo.gl/9jU1aE) Director Steven Soderbergh celebrates still photography and the eerie theme of his film, Bubble *in the opening title credits.*

Figure 11.60
(Weblink: http://goo.gl/hZkTHA) David Crawford's "Stop Motion Studies" are not only interesting to view, but reveal cultural differences between subway and train riders from around the world.

Figure 11.61
(Weblink: http://goo.gl/Msu8qs) It is wholly appropriate for a commercial devoted to a camera use the stop-motion animation technique using more than 60,000 photographs.

Figure 11.62
"Everyday," detail, 2009 by Noah Kalina. New York based Noah Kalina is primarily an advertising photographer with clients that include Motorola, Sony, and Neiman Marcus, but he possesses an artist's independent spirit. On January 11, 2000, he started to photograph his face every day, a project that continues. A video of the collection was a YouTube favorite and inspired many imitators.
Courtesy of Noah Kalina

Figure 11.63
*(Weblink:
http://goo.gl/URVeRL)*
The organization Improv Everywhere arranged a practical joke on passersby in Grand Central Station in New York City in which more than 200 individuals turned into still photographs for five minutes.

LINK

Figure 11.65
*(Weblink:
http:// goo.gl/83dw4V)*
Lori Swadley started as a wedding photographer, but after witnessing first-hand the devastation of opioid addiction on the fellow residents of her small town, she decided to devote part of her commercial website for portraits of recovering addicts that defied the common stereotype.

Figure 11.64
The MediaStorm interactive multimedia website is a showcase of the best photojournalism can offer with text, audio, and video presentations. Its homepage contains links to published work, stories produced for clients, and workshops where you can learn visual journalism techniques.
Courtesy of Brian Storm and MediaStorm

Figure 11.66
*(Weblink:
http:// goo.gl/DCuJMu)*
As with other major news entities, investigative reporting with thoughtful words, pictures, and graphic designs can be found on the web.

image, one that freezes time forever in a powerfully arresting moment, will always have the capacity to rivet a viewer's attention so that long-term analysis is possible.

KEY TERMS FROM THIS CHAPTER
Allegorical • Aperture • Bitumen of Judea • Collodion • Contrast • Crop • Darkroom • Depth of field • Dioramas • Doctors Without Borders • Dust Bowl • Electromagnetic spectrum • Emulsion • Flash • Flash Mob • Gelatin • Impressionism • Paparazzi • Plates • Polio • Silver bromide • Visual journalism

12 Motion Pictures

The length of a film should be directly related to the endurance of the human bladder.

Alfred Hitchcock 1899–1980
DIRECTOR, PRODUCER, & AUTHOR

According to the Internet Movie Database (imdb.com), there have been more than 600,000 motion pictures made throughout the world since the first public showing of a motion picture in 1895, or an average of about 5,000 movies a year. Only one of those movies is consistently rated the best film ever.

Citizen Kane (Figure 12.1).

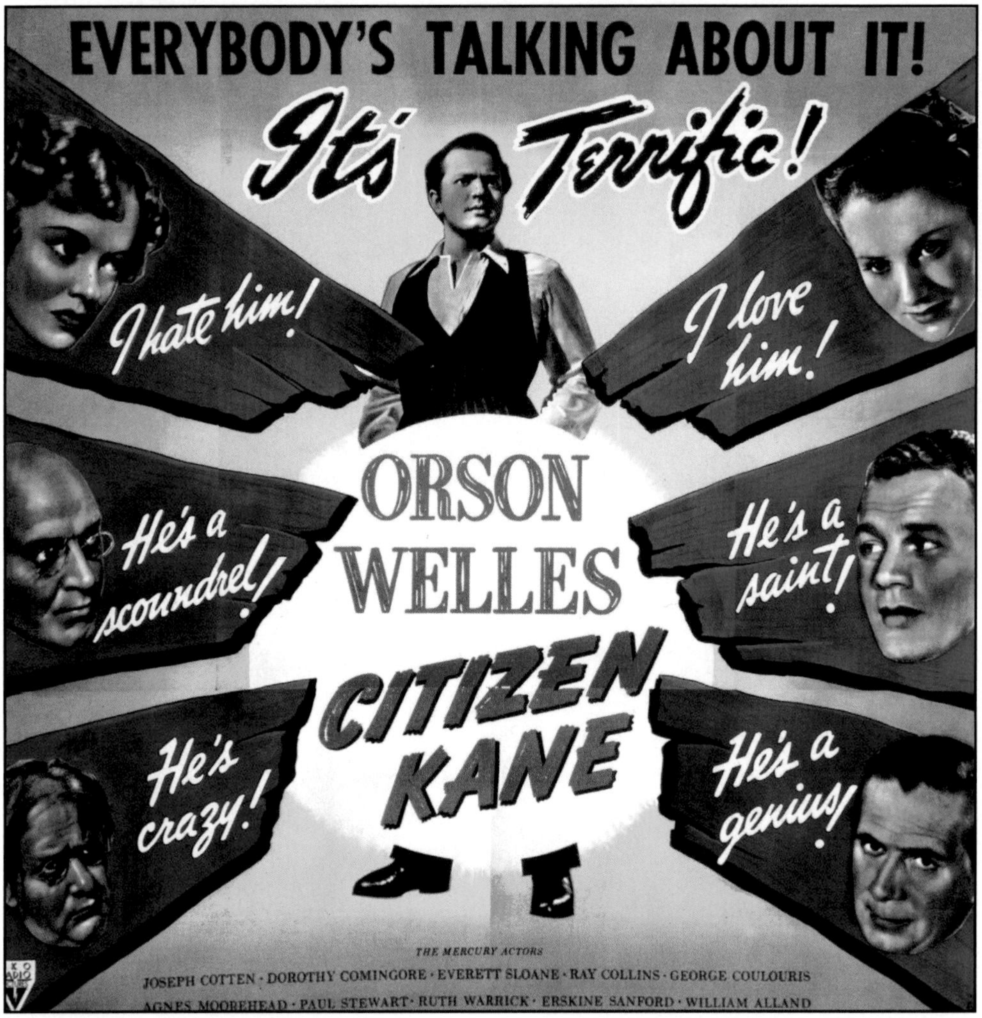

Figure 12.1
A "one sheet" for Citizen Kane *that was obviously not designed by Saul Bass shows the lead characters and their opinions of Kane.*
Courtesy of RKO Radio Pictures

The American Film Institute (AFI), founded in 1967 is a nonprofit organization that helps to preserve the future of filmmaking. In 2007 it polled 1,500 film artists, critics, and historians to determine the greatest movies of all time. The top ten, starting from tenth place, were *The Wizard of Oz* (1939), *Vertigo* (1958), *Schindler's List* (1993), *Lawrence of Arabia* (1962), *Gone with the Wind* (1939), *Singin' in the Rain* (1952), *Raging Bull* (1980), *Casablanca* (1942), *The Godfather* (1972), and *Citizen Kane* (1941).

The AFI website hints at the reason for the movie's exalted position: "[Orson] Welles broke all the rules and invented some new ones with his searing story of a newspaper publisher with an uncanny resemblance to William Randolph Hearst." Orson Welles was fortunate that his first Hollywood movie matched his brash, self-confident personality (Figure 12.2).

But he could not have made such

Figure 12.2
Orson Welles during the filming of Citizen Kane. *Photography by Alexander Kahle.*
Courtesy of RKO Radio Pictures

a respected film alone. He had a lot of help. Herman Mankiewicz, a Hollywood writer for the previous 15 years for more than 50 movies such as *Gentlemen Prefer Blondes* (1928) and uncredited for *The Wizard of Oz* (1939), helped Welles write the screenplay. Joseph Cotten, Agnes Moorehead, and several other radio actors—many making their film debuts—were brought to Hollywood for the picture. Welles also assembled a technical team second to none. Vernon Walker, a photographer for the spectacular movie *King Kong* (1933) coordinated the many special effects in the movie. The film editor, a young RKO staff employee named Robert Wise, would go on to direct *The Day the Earth Stood Still* (1951), *West Side Story* (1961), *The Sound of Music* (1965), and *Star Trek: The Motion Picture* (1979). Mercury Theater colleague Bernard Hermann, who won an Academy Award for his scoring of *All That Money Can Buy* (1941), composed

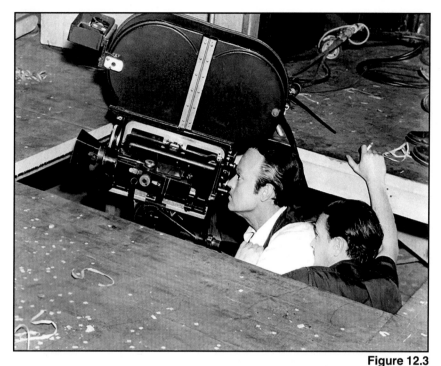

Figure 12.3

Orson Welles and cinematographer Gregg Toland used a hatchet to break through a floor of the studio to bury a camera for an extremely low angle shot.

Courtesy of RKO Radio Pictures

Figure 12.4

Orson Welles in 1937 when he was 22 years old, four years before the release of Citizen Kane.

Courtesy of the Library of Congress

and arranged the music for *Kane* and other productions such as *Psycho* (1960), "The Twilight Zone" (1959–1963), and T*axi Driver* (1976). Famed cinematographer Gregg Toland, who had just won an Academy Award for his work in *Wuthering Heights* (1939), was in charge of photography (Figure 12.3).

Yet despite its best intentions, *Citizen Kane* was a financial disaster. Although praised by critics, mass theater audiences of the day were accustomed to seeing lightweight action and comedic films— not a dark, moody psychological drama with an unhappy ending. Film critic André Bazin wrote that the motion picture was "decidedly above the mental age of the average American spectator." Although nominated for several Oscars, the film won only one award—for best screenplay.

Born on May 6, 1915, George Orson Welles was the second son of a troubled, yet creative, family in Kenosha, Wisconsin. His father, Richard, was a frustrated inventor who died early from alcoholism. His mother, Beatrice, was a strong supporter of women's rights, an excellent rifle shot, and a failed professional pianist.

From an early age Orson attracted media attention. In newspaper articles he was praised as a "boy genius"—at the age of two he could read fluently, at seven he could recite passages from Shakespeare's *King Lear*, and at ten he started producing backyard plays of his own. At 16 years old Welles made a walking tour of Ireland and ended up at the famous Gate Theater in Dublin. He convinced the Irish owners that he was a famous actor from the New York Guild Theater. Consequently, he became the first American actor ever to guest star with the Abbey Players of Dublin. After returning to New York and getting more acting experience, his booming voice landed him radio work (Figure 12.4). For the NBC broadcast "The March of Time," he supplied the voices for the dictators Mussolini and Hitler. He also played the popular mystery character Lamont Cranston on "The Shadow."

In 1938, CBS offered the theater group a contract to produce radio dramas, naming the program "Mercury Theater on the Air." The acting troupe regularly produced classic works such as *Treasure Island* and *Jane Eyre*. But Welles wanted to stage a science fiction piece for Halloween and selected H. G. Wells's *War of the Worlds*. The night before the broadcast, however, he thought the script too dull and rewrote it in a documentary style similar to the "March of Time" news program of the day. The result was one of the most sensational broadcasts ever produced. Despite numerous reminders that the show was a fictionalized account of a novel, millions of radio listeners were convinced that Martians had invaded Earth. People fled in all directions to escape cities, limbs were broken in fights as people tried to get away, and priests were called to hear final confessions (Figure 12.5). One of the readers of the controversy was

Figure 12.5
After the panic caused by Orson Welles' radio broadcast of "War of the Worlds," an unshaven Welles (center) explains to skeptical reporters that he had no idea the fictionalized piece would cause such controversy. Riiiiight.
Courtesy of Acme News Photos

RKO Pictures president George Schaefer. At the time the studio was close to bankruptcy. Schaefer thought Welles could offer a lifeline. With a promise of complete freedom over production and a three-picture deal worth $100,000 ($1.5 million today) each, Schaefer lured Welles to Hollywood to make movies.

After considering and rejecting several ideas, Welles decided to produce a movie that he and screenwriter Herman Mankiewicz had conceived. Originally titled *American*, it was an obviously critical biography of newspaper publisher William Randolph Hearst (Figure 12.6). As a former newspaper reporter, Mankiewicz was familiar with the intricacies of Hearst's financial empire and his personal strengths and failings. As a visitor to Hearst's castle in central California, San Simeon, Mankiewicz had witnessed many of the excesses made possible by the publisher's enormous

wealth (Figure 12.7). Hearst's passion for collecting art objects from around the world, staging elaborate picnics, and supporting his mistress, the actress Marion Davies, all were a part of Mankiewicz's screenplay. Written by Welles and Mankiewicz with editorial supervision by the actor John Houseman during the summer of 1939, the idea for the script might have come from a novel by Aldous Huxley, *After Many A Summer Dies The Swan*. Published that same year, Huxley's book told the story of an egomaniacal newspaper magnate who lived in an even larger castle than San Simeon and who had a mistress. Although Welles always denied the connection between Hearst and Kane, no one was convinced there wasn't one.

Shooting for *Citizen Kane* began on July 30, 1940, and was completed on October 23. Extremely tight security fanned rumors about its connection to Hearst.

Figure 12.6
The American newspaper magnate William Randolph Hearst in 1906 when he was 43.
Courtesy of the Library of Congress

Figure 12.7

The Hearst castle, called San Simeon, now a California historical monument, overlooks the central California coastline and features 30 fireplaces and 38 bedrooms. It is so large there are five separate tours visitors can take. A view of its entrance gives a hint of the castle's excessive opulence. In 2012, for the first time, Citizen Kane *was shown at the castle. The great-grandson of William Randolph Hearst, Stephen T. Hearst, said, "It's a great opportunity to draw a clear distinction between W.R. (Hearst) and Orson Welles, between the medieval, gloomy-looking castle shown in* Citizen Kane *and the light, beautiful, architecturally superior reality."*
Courtesy of the Tony Jin

The film was scheduled to be released on Valentine's Day, 1941, but the opening was delayed after Louella Parsons, Hollywood correspondent for the Hearst newspapers, viewed an early screening. She relayed the message to Schaefer that Hearst would sue the studio if it released the film. Schaefer quickly invited the press for a sneak preview in which the movie received favorable reviews. But because of the threats by Hearst's organization, Schaefer had trouble finding theaters that would show the movie. For the May 1 public openings in New York, Chicago, and Los Angeles, RKO-owned theaters were hastily prepared. When Hearst felt that the published attacks on the film gave it too much publicity, the negative stories ceased, but he allowed no advertising about the movie to appear in any of his newspapers. In a last, desperate attempt to have the film shown, Schaefer sent the picture as a package deal with other RKO movies. Nevertheless, most theater owners did not show the movie.

Despite receiving nine nominations that included Best Picture, Best Director, and Best Actor for Welles, the film was booed at the Academy Awards program. The classic only won one Oscar—for the screenplay he shared with Mankiewicz. In 2011 Welles' statuette was sold in an auction for $861,542. The next year Mankiewicz's Oscar was purchased for $273,087 less.

Welles was labeled a troublemaker, but he continued to direct and act in such highly revered motion pictures as *The Magnificent Ambersons* (1942), *Touch of Evil* (1958), and *Chimes at Midnight* (1965). The prestigious British Film Institute rated him the greatest film director of all time over Alfred Hitchcock, Jean-Luc Godard, and Jean Renoir. The Institute also rated *Citizen Kane* as the greatest movie of all time.

Late in his life, a bit overweight but still in possession of a Shakespearean voice and able to tell insider Hollywood stories, Welles made commercials for Eastern Airlines and Paul Masson wines and appeared regularly on the talk shows hosted by Johnny Carson and Dick Cavett. Two hours after he taped an interview on Merv Griffin's show, Welles died of a heart attack at the age of 70 in his Los Angeles home in 1985. Unlike Kane, no one heard his last word. Welles once said, "Hollywood is a golden suburb for golf addicts, gardeners, men of mediocrity, and satisfied stars. I belong to none of these categories."

The opening of the movie is a metaphor for the entire picture. In a series of tracking shots that begin outside the castle gate of the once stately Xanadu estate showing a NO TRESPASSING sign, the camera moves us closer to a light from Kane's bedroom window, which always maintains the same position in various shots (Figure 12.8).

And just when the window is reached, the light suddenly goes off and Kane speaks his last word, the enigmatic "Rosebud" (Figure 12.9). The scene loudly shifts to a newsreel that serves as an obituary for the publishing tycoon. But toward the end of the footage, the documentary stops and the scene shifts to a smoky room filled with journalists who are given the task to discover, through interviews with his associates, why Kane uttered the word "Rosebud." The rest of the film is divided into four sections in which his banker reveals Kane's early life, his business associate tells about the newspaper empire and details of his first marriage, his former best friend analyzes his personality and the reason for his downfall, and his second wife, in an alcoholic haze, gives details about the frustrated and sad old man Kane had become.

In the end, none of his associates could solve the mystery of "Rosebud." But the audience learns the secret. As workmen burn objects that had accumulated over the years in his castle, the name "Rosebud" on a sled given to Kane

as a boy goes up in flames (Figure 12.10). A symbol of lost youth, missed opportunities, or an acknowledgment of Kane's love of objects over people—viewers are left to make sense of the movie's central riddle on their own.

As with Johannes Gutenberg's invention in which established components were combined into a commercial printing press, Welles didn't invent the film techniques used in the movie. He simply combined many different ideas into one work. Until *Kane*, movies of the day were dominated by snappy dialogue and unusual situations, but the visual messages weren't as important. Orson Welles combined the most recent technical innovations for producing visual messages with choreographed actions by actors to move the plot along on several levels. Gregg Toland took advantage of new lighting and film stock to perfect a technique called "deep focus." With higher-quality lights, faster film, and wide-angle lenses, Toland could have a depth of field that carried from 20 inches to several hundred feet (Figure 12.11). Consequently, Welles was able to exploit this technical advantage in his staging of the actors. Action could take place simultaneously in the foreground and in the background. André Bazin has written that the technique gave viewers much more freedom in deciding which part of the screen they wanted to watch.

Welles also requested that the sets include muslin ceilings so that extreme up-angle perspectives could be used. Few directors ever thought to bother with ceilings for their sets because most shots were at eye level (Figure 12.12). Also, lighting and microphones were hung from the top of sets. Nevertheless, Welles presented a much more realistic visual message with the addition of ceilings. In addition, lighting was high in contrast and usually from behind. The effect dramatically separated the actors from their surroundings (Figure 12.13).

When asked if he knew that he was

Figure 12.8
(Weblink: http://goo.gl/GSkUZv)
From the opening sequence of shots for Citizen Kane, you should be aware that you are watching something special as your eyes become attracted to the light from the castle always positioned in the same location.

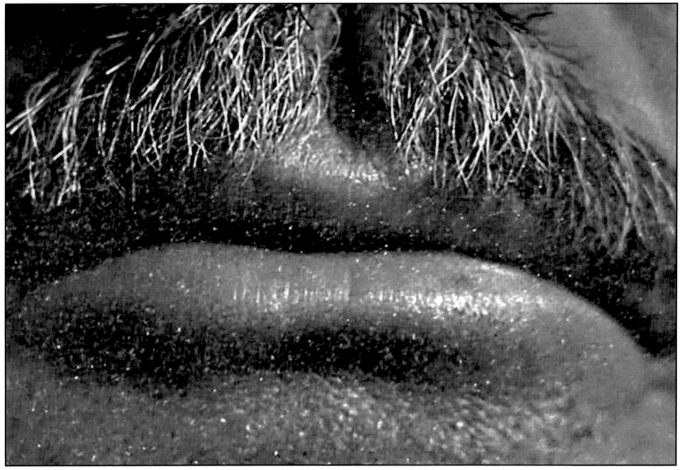

Figure 12.9
One of the most famous dying words ever uttered by a real or fictional person, "Rosebud," is said at the start of the movie by the Orson Welles's character Charles Foster Kane. Close-up photography and enhanced audio effects emphasized this important scene in the movie.
Courtesy of RKO Radio Pictures

Figure 12.10
The mystery of Kane's last word was relatively simple—the name of the sled young Charles possessed as a child.
Courtesy of RKO Radio Pictures

Figure 12.11
The "deep focus" effect created by cinematographer Gregg Toland, as evident in this scene from Citizen Kane, *allowed the viewer more control in selecting which part of a set to watch.*
Courtesy of RKO Radio Pictures

Figure 12.12
Orson Welles and Ruth Warrick on the breakfast montage set in which the ceiling adds realism.
Courtesy of RKO Radio Pictures

making a masterpiece, Welles answered simply, "I never doubted it for a single instant." The trouble with creating a perfect work of art your first time out is: Where do you go from there? Unfortunately, Welles could not improve upon his initial work because such an effort would have been almost impossible for anyone.

David Denby, movie critic for *The New Yorker* magazine, wrote about motion pictures, "Almost every movie, of course, is a fantasy, or a fable, or a fairy tale of one kind or another. In a great movie, though, narrative and technological magic combine to produce heightened intimations of the real, and that

Figure 12.13
Many scenes in Citizen Kane *were shot with high contrast lighting.*
Courtesy of RKO Radio Pictures

ecstatic merging of magic and reality is what imprints the movie on our emotional memory." *Citizen Kane*, as a great movie, will always be remembered.

MOTION PICTURES AND THE SIX PERSPECTIVES

Like any art form, motion pictures reflect the archetypes and myths that are popular within a particular culture at a particular time. All visual messages, movies included, help shape what we think of our society and ourselves. Hollywood stars give us ideals to strive toward as well as behaviors to avoid. Movies tell mythic stories of good versus evil, social order versus anarchy, and group dependence versus independence. These themes strike deep, cultural

chords and will continue because there is almost no other experience that binds humans as social creatures as sitting in the dark watching stories presented through flickering light.

Personal Perspective

Motion pictures began as jerky films of everyday activities, capturing ordinary events to show the capabilities of this new medium. Soon, however, visionaries discovered that motion pictures could be much more than static camera shots. Early in the history of the movies, filmmakers exploited aesthetic, political, and economic advantages. The three primary functions probably explain why so many different terms—cinema, documentary, feature, film, flick, motion picture,

Figure 12.14
"The Horse in Motion," 1878, by Eadweard Muybridge. To publicize the successful technical feat of taking stop-motion images of Leland Stanford's horse "Sallie Gardner," Eadweard Muybridge arranged to have a postcard made for sale by Morse's Gallery of San Francisco. As his unusual name might suggest, Eadweard Muybridge, born Edward Mugger-idge in England, was a unique character in the history of photography. He changed his last name to Muybridge when he started his photographic career in San Francisco and then changed his first name to match that of King Eadweard who was consecrated at Muybridge's hometown in 900 CE. In 1855 he arrived in San Francisco, but had to return to England after he suffered brain damage from a stagecoach accident. Returning in 1866, he became known for his landscapes of Yosemite and was asked to be a photographer for the U.S. Army's expeditions of the Western states. In 1872 Stanford contacted him to take pictures of his running horse. Two years later, he discovered that his wife had a lover, whom he then murdered. During the trial he pleaded insanity because of his earlier head injury. Nevertheless, the jury found the action "justifiable homicide" and acquitted him. Stanford had paid for his defense. The trial is the subject of the 1982 opera "The Photographer" by Philip Glass.
Courtesy of the Library of Congress

movie, picture, show, and so on—have been used to describe the presentation of single-framed, sequential images that move through a machine so rapidly that they create the illusion of movement when projected on a screen.

Historical Perspective
The history of the motion picture can be summed up in one word—adaptation. Innovative inventors, directors, and studio executives worked to make sure that movies would become and remain a popular source of entertainment. When-ever movie sales dipped, the industry

created better stories, turned up the publicity about the stars, and developed innovative technology to attract more viewers.

With the invention of Richard Maddox's gelatin-bromide dry plate process in 1871, fast action could finally be captured on film. One of the first to take advantage of this new medium was the English photographer Eadweard Muybridge. He invented an early movie projector, the zoopraxiscope in 1879. It used rotating glass discs to simulate movement with separate images. Muy-bridge sold collections of images on discs

Figure 12.15
(Weblink:
http://goo.gl/AUbHV5)
*It's only two seconds—about
40 frames—but according to
most experts,* Roundhay Garden Scene *was the first movie
produced in 1888.*

Figure 12.16
(Weblink: http://goo.gl/Zuo631)
*With scratches, lighting, and fo-
cus errors, the moving figure in
white against a black backdrop
in the 1890* Monkeyshines *only
hints and what might be possible with this new medium.*

as well as prints of people and animals in various poses (Figure 12.14).

Just as with Hippolyte Bayard who invented a still photography process but never received the credit he deserved (Chapter 11), another French citizen, Louis Le Prince made a motion picture with a camera of his invention using sequential paper prints to create, according the the *Guinness Book of Records*, the first movie in 1888. Titled *Roundhay Garden Scene*, for about two seconds, it shows relatives and a friend of Le Prince walking playfully in a garden in Leeds, England (Figure 12.15). However, the film never had a public showing because Le Prince mysteriously disappeared from a train and was eventually declared dead. Wait. It gets better.

Meanwhile, in 1888 the American inventor Thomas Alva Edison bought 90 of Muybridge's motion studies. After numerous experiments, he and his assistant William Kennedy Laurie Dickson started to make movies through a Kinetograph device and shown via a Kinetoscope, a peephole viewer. In that same year Edison remarked, "I am experimenting upon an instrument which does for the eye what the phonograph does for the ear, which is the recording and reproduction of things in motion."

But Edison ran into a legal challenge. After Le Prince's disappearance, Edison attempted to take credit for the motion picture camera in order to receive royalties for its use by others. Le Prince's wife, Lizzie and son Adolphe sued Edison in order to prove that Le Prince was the sole inventor. During the subsequent trial, Adolphe, who had helped his father with his films, was never able to show his father's camera equipment and lost the case. Two years later, Adolphe was killed while duck hunting in New York. Thomas Edison was never accused officially of any fowl play.

The first film made by Edison was an 1890 effort titled *Monkeyshines* that could be seen on a revolving cylinder

(Figure 12.16). It was an experimental film not intended for commercial release. The poor quality should remind you of the first photograph made by Joseph Niépce (Chapter 11). Four years later, Edison, Dickson, and director William Heise made the first motion picture to be preserved in the collection of the Library of Congress. The short film was a close-up of a slightly self-conscious Edison mechanic Fred Ott who pretended to sneeze for the camera in *Fred Ott's Sneeze* (Figure 12.17). Within three years, Edison had established Kinetoscope arcades in which phonographs, another Edison invention, could be heard, and 30-second movies could be seen and most of the world forgot about Louis Le Prince.

Dickson made most of the Edison films, which were 50 feet long, with no editing or camera movements. Early Edison movies simply showed dancers, clowns, and other entertainers performing in front of the camera. However, one of the first commercial productions for the public was considered scandalous by social critics of the day. Directed by Heise, *The Kiss* (1896) showed a reenactment of an amorous exchange between two characters in the play *The Widow Jones* (Figure 12.18).

Edison never thought much of the new medium. He was content to offer peephole films in his arcades where he featured what he thought would be more popular phonograph recordings. Consequently, he didn't bother to secure patent rights for his film equipment in Europe. An English scientific instruments maker, Robert Paul, bought a Kinetograph and made an important technical improvement—he replaced Edison's electrified mechanism with a more portable hand crank. In 1894, two French brothers, Auguste and Louis Lumière purchased one of Paul's Kinetographs. The brothers improved the device so that not only could they make films with it but could also use it to process and project the movies.

W
LINK
Figure 12.18
(Weblink: http://goo.gl/XBrzzN)
Six years after the technically
challenging Monkeyshines,
Edison and company produced
The Kiss. *Please be advised*
that its content may not be
suitable for all audiences.

Figure 12.17
Fred Ott's Sneeze of 1894 is the first motion picture in the Library of Congress collection. Ott's
sneeze should be viewed column-by-column starting from the top left. Edison believed if any-
one wanted to watch a motion picture, it would be through a peephole viewer, and the subject
would be fictionalized works.
Courtesy of the Library of Congress

Figure 12.19
Auguste Lumière holds an umbrella so the crochet piece his brother Louis works on doesn't get wet in this photograph dated around 1910. The two invented the concept of an audience watching motion pictures, but gave up making and producing films in 1903 to concentrate on their invention of color film, the autochrome.
Courtesy of Adoc-photos

They named their invention the *Cinéma-tographe*, which soon was shortened to *cinema* (Figure 12.19).

The Lumières' first films were similar to those created by purchasers of video cameras—glorified home movies. Early in 1895, the two previewed their first effort, the 46-second *Les Travailleurs Sortie des Usines Lumière*, with a group of friends and family members (Figure 12.20). On December 28, 1895, the first public audience for motion pictures was treated to ten short films in the basement of the Grand Café in Paris (Figure 12.21). The modern concept of motion pictures—movies seen with an audience—was born (Figure 12.22).

Edison's short films differed from the Lumière works in a fundamental way. Instead of a documentary approach, in which the camera recorded people and situations often without their being aware of its presence, Edison favored heavy-handed staged productions in the fiction genre that could be seen by only one viewer at a time. As it turned out, both the Lumières and Edison had it wrong *and* right. What most of the public did *not* want to see were documentaries through a peephole. But what they clamored for were fictionalized productions shown in a theater.

One of the first to realize the aesthetic potential of movies was George Méliès of France, considered the founder of special effects. The son of wealthy parents, Méliès started his career as a caricaturist, stage designer, magician, and actor. In 1896 he purchased a camera from Robert Paul and made his first movie, *Un Jeu de Cartes* (Figure 12.23). With the public weary of documentaries like those produced by the Lumière brothers, Méliès filled the void when he switched direction and made surreal films inspired by his experiences as a magician and stage performer. His most famous work is the 14-minute classic *Un Voyage à la Lune* (*A Trip to the Moon*) made in 1902. Roughly based on the Jules Verne

Figure 12.20
Unlike Edison, Auguste and Louis Lumière thought motion pictures would be viewed in theaters with large audiences and that the type of films most would want to see would be documentaries. One of the first films by the Lumière brothers is the 1895 film Workers Leaving the Lumière Factory. *Three versions of the scene were made with the latest one the most popular with the public as it showed women in bodices and work-men wearing boater hats. With its objective camera approach, the work has a contemporary documentary style.*
Courtesy of the Lumière Institute

Figure 12.21
On a busy street in Paris, the plaque mount-ed on the wall at the top left commemorates the location of the Lumière brothers' motion picture theater, then called Le Salon Indien du Grand Café.
Courtesy of Paul Martin Lester

stories of *From the Earth to the Moon* and *Around the Moon*, the movie shows a group of professors who take a voyage in a rocket ship that lands in one of the "eyes" of the face on the moon (Figure 12.24) and discovers numerous creatures living below its surface (Figure 12.25). A rare hand-tinted version was restored by Serge Bromberg of France's Lobster Films and shown to rave reviews by an audi-ence at the Cannes film festival in 2011 with a new musical score by the French duo Nicolas Godin and Jean-Benoit Dunckel of Air released the next year (Figure 12.26).

Méliès made more than 500 short films, but when his company went bank-rupt because other producers pirated his movies—Thomas Edison among them—the French Army seized his films, melted them, and turned the celluloid into boot heels. Méliès ended up forgotten and working in a toy store (Figure 12.27).

Figure 12.24
The iconic moon landing in George Méliès' A Trip to the Moon.
Courtesy of Roger-Viollet

LINK
Figure 12.22
(Weblink: http://goo.gl/U5LjFe) Not surprisingly, audiences grew tired of the one-camera, documentary films produced by the Lumière brothers. Con-sequently, the two eventually quit making movies to concen-trate on producing color film in which they were successful.

LINK
Figure 12.23
(Weblink: http://goo.gl/1EXmwg) The 1896 A Card Game *is best seen with the sound muted. Al-though the plot could be more intriguing, in the brief film two men play cards, a friend pours beer into glasses, and a wait-ress watches smiling. The man on the left is George Méliès.*

W
LINK
Figure 12.25
(Weblink: http://goo.gl/t8tPM7)
The 14-minute film from George
Méliès is a delightful fantasy
that foreshadows many of the
special effects seen in motion
pictures today.

W
LINK
Figure 12.26
(Weblink: http://goo.gl/t4eVNQ)
The trailer for Serge Bromberg's
restored color version of the
Méliès classic shows scenes
from the movie and some of the
work involved to produce the
work.

W
LINK
Figure 12.29
(Weblink:
http:// goo.gl/9PYmdb)
Many of the cinematic conventions used in modern motion
pictures were first exhibited in
the film work of Edwin Porter
including his 1903 motion picture, The Life of an American
Fireman.

In Martin Scorsese's *Hugo* (2011), Ben Kingsley plays the special effects master. In a fitting tribute, at the 2012 84th Academy Awards ceremony, the movie won Best Visual Effects, along with four other Oscars in technical categories. Scorsese gave himself a small role as a photographer who takes a photograph of Méliès.

An early innovator in filmmaking who understood the public's desire to see action movies produced outside a studio was the American Edwin Stratton Porter. In 1896, he had left the U.S. Navy and went to work for Edison as a mechanic, electrician, and film operator. He soon left Edison, bought his own camera, made films, rented a theater, and showed his movies under the name of Thomas Edison, Jr. He made his two most famous pictures in 1903—*The Life of an American Fireman* and *The Great Train Robbery*, in which much of the action was shot outside of a studio (Figure 12.28). He also invented the important concept of "cinematic time." Instead of simply leaving the camera on during an entire film, Porter edited scenes to create

Figure 12.27
In addition to the final resting place of The Doors' frontman, Jim Morrison, the Pére Lachaise cemetery in Paris also is the location for the grave of French director George Méliès, adorned with flowers laid by fans of the man who introduced the field of special effects to the motion picture industry.
Courtesy of Paul Martin Lester

Figure 12.28
As a publicity stunt, some theaters showed this hand-painted scene in The Great Train Robbery *in which a cowboy fires directly at the audience. Reportedly, panic ensued.*
Courtesy of the Kobal Collection

interest for the audience (Figure 12.29).

During the silent era, the rise and fall of David Wark Griffith is a metaphor for the entire early time period. Born in Kentucky to a Confederate Civil War hero, Griffith had been a reporter for a Louisville newspaper and had written and acted for the stage when he was signed up as an actor at five dollars a day ($120 today). With his stage experience, Griffith was offered a director's position with Biograph Studios in New York City and then moved to Hollywood. Griffith is best known for the infamous *The Birth of a Nation* (1915). The movie is a demonstration of the maturity of Griffith's film work, but unfortunately tells a mean-spirited and racist story. Originally titled *The Clansman* from Thomas Dixon Jr.'s book *The Clansman An Historical Romance of the Ku Klux Klan*, the movie tells of the history of the United States immediately after the Civil War. When a struggling community is attacked by a ravaging group of African Americans (Anglo actors played with heavy black makeup), the people are saved by white-hooded members of the Ku Klux Klan (KKK) who ride into town on horseback (Figure 12.30).

Compared to the other Biograph movies, *Birth* was an incredible gamble. Most films of the day cost no more than $100 (about $2,300 today) for the total production. *Birth* cost $83,000 (about $1.8 million)—the most ever invested in a motion picture at that time (Figure 12.31). To offset the cost of making the movie, the ticket price was $2—the equivalent of $45 today. Obviously, the movie was intended for wealthy audience members. The three-hour movie premiered at Clune's Auditorium in Los Angeles (the grand movie palace was demolished in 1985) to immediate controversy as Klansmen in full robes helped publicize the movie. The NAACP issued a pamphlet called "Fighting a Vicious Film" and began a boycott of the studio. Many leading politicians and civic lead-

Figure 12.30
In this lobby card for the 1915 movie The Birth of a Nation, *the film's connection with the Ku Klux Klan is unmistakable with the rider and the horse wearing sheets to protect their identities.*
Courtesy of the Epoch Film Co.

W
LINK
Figure 12.31
*(Weblink: http://goo.gl/EzDTzf)
Despite its racist themes, the
three-hour* The Birth of a Nation, *was a technical milestone
and inspired generations of film
directors to go beyond the one-
reel convention.*

ers were unanimous in their condemnation because of the racist message of the
movie. When it was shown in Boston, a
race riot followed, but attendance at road
show engagements was high. Nevertheless, after President Woodrow Wilson
saw it in the White House, he said it was
"like writing history with lightning. And
my only regret is that it is all so terribly
true." Although the KKK had disbanded
in 1869, the film was responsible for the
racist extremist group's revival.

Over the years, *Birth of a Nation*
reportedly made $20 million (almost
$300 million today). In 1919, Griffith,
Charles Chaplin, Douglas Fairbanks, and
Mary Pickford formed their own film
company that they named United Artists
(Figure 12.32). In his later years, Griffith

lost much of the creative energy associated with his early films. In the 1930s,
he tried to make movies with sound, but
his lack of technical experience and his
reputation among studio executives who
viewed him as a quaint, silent movie
dinosaur prevented him from doing so.
For the last 17 years of his life he lived
as a virtual hermit in Los Angeles. He
died in 1948 on his way to a Hollywood
hospital from a hotel where he had been
living alone.

Although making movies has always
been a collaborative effort, the role of the
director is the key to a production. A director turns the words of a screenwriter,
the talent of the actors, and the expertise
of the technical crew into an art form
with a unique visual style. Some of the

Figure 12.32
*Standing behind a seated, camera-aware Charlie Chaplin are D. W. Griffith, Mary Pickford,
and Douglas Fairbanks as they prepare to sign the contract establishing United Artists motion
picture studio in 1919.*
Courtesy of the Library of Congress

most powerful studio executives had humble beginnings. Mack Sennett was an actor under Edison and later worked for Griffith. In 1912, he financed his own production company, the Keystone Film Company of Los Angeles. The studio became famous for its madcap chase scenes involving the Keystone Kops and romantic comedies featuring the sophisticated star Gloria Swanson. Keystone launched the careers of writer-turned-director Frank Capra and comedic actors Harold Lloyd and Charles Chaplin, the most famous silent film star. But when the silent film period ended, Sennett's comedies were no longer popular. Hal Roach was Sennett's biggest competitor. Roach wooed Lloyd away with more money. With his alter ego, whom he called the "Glass Character," Lloyd made more than 100 one-reel comedies that exhibited his acrobatic skills and a sophisticated sense of visual humor (Figure 12.33). Roach went on to direct Stan Laurel and Oliver Hardy in several comedy classics as well as the *Our Gang* children's comedy series, which was popular in theaters and on television.

One of the most famous silent film directors was Cecil B. DeMille, who often clashed with studio executives over his high budgets. His 1923 *The Ten Commandments* cost more than a million dollars ($12.8 million today) to produce. DeMille had been inspired to become a director after watching Porter's *The Great Train Robbery*. He initially worked for Samuel Goldwyn and moved his production facilities to a barn in Hollywood in 1914 to begin making feature films. DeMille was popular with the public because his movies always contained a hint of sensuality as opposed to Griffith's sentimentality.

One of the most influential directors in the history of silent films was the Russian Sergei Eisenstein. Like Orson Welles, Eisenstein was known primarily for his innovative film technique in one motion picture. He studied architecture

Figure 12.33
Suspended above Los Angeles during the filming of Safety Last! in 1923 is Harold Lloyd, one of the most popular physical comedians of the silent era. Lloyd made about 200 pictures, and is best known for his "Glass Character" who thrilled audiences with his elaborate chase scenes and self-performed stunts. Attesting to his popularity, his hand- and footprints, along with the outline of his eyeglass frames (in reality, sunglass frames) are preserved in the cement in front of Grauman's Chinese Theatre on Hollywood Boulevard. In 1994 the U.S. Postal Service issued a stamp that included a caricature of him.
Courtesy of *An American Comedy*

and engineering before being bitten by the theater bug. He gave up his engineering career when he landed a job with an experimental theater where he designed sets and directed plays. He became interested in filmmaking after watching Griffith's use of montage sequences in *Birth of a Nation*. In 1925, he released his classic *The Battleship Potemkin*, which told the story of a 1905 sailors' rebellion in Odessa and the Tsar's brutal reprisal. The movie is probably best known for its famous "steps" scene in which montage and quick-editing techniques created dramatic tension (Figure 12.34). Eisenstein was inspired by the dada art move-

W LINK
Figure 12.35
*(Weblink: http://goo.gl/pkh5zs)
The "Odessa Steps" scene in
Sergei Eisenstein's* The Battle-
ship Potemkin *is one of the most
memorable in film history.*

Figure 12.34
*Adding to the horror of the famous steps scene in the 1925 classic by Russian director Sergei
Eisenstein,* The Battleship Potemkin, *is the abandoned baby carriage that is left on its own
to perilously travel down the steps between dead and dying citizens. In* The Untouchables
*(1987) that starred Kevin Costner, a recreation of the baby carriage scene took place during
a gun battle.*

Courtesy of the Kobal Collection

ment, in which multiple images were shown on the screen at the same time for maximum visual effect. With film pieces as short as 1/16th of a second, the murder of Russian civilians by the Tsar's troops (an incident that probably was not as severe as shown) is one of the best examples of the art of editing in the history of film (Figure 12.35). Eisenstein became a teacher of motion picture art and wrote several books about the power of film as a communication medium before his death in 1948.

Hollywood sensuality on and off the big screen caused many people to become concerned that movies could have a corrupting influence on the morals of the nation. In 1920 Mary Pickford divorced her husband and two weeks later married Douglas Fairbanks. Fans were shocked, thinking Pickford's own personality was the same as her sweet, girl-next-door characters. The actor and director Roscoe "Fatty" Arbuckle was involved in a 1921 scandal. A young

actress died during a party at his rented 12th-floor suite in the St. Francis Hotel in San Francisco and Arbuckle was charged with rape and murder. Even though he was found not guilty, his reputation was ruined because of vicious attacks in the Hearst newspapers.

As a public relations ploy to help dignify the criticized film industry, the Academy of Motion Picture Arts and Sciences (AMPAS) first presented its Academy Awards on May 16, 1929. The treasured eight-pound, gold-plated award originally was called "The Statuette," but when an Academy librarian remarked that the standing man looked like her uncle Oscar, the name stuck. Douglas Fairbanks hosted the event that cost $5 ($63 today) to attend the 15-minute ceremony.

The history of motion pictures is also concerned with producers and directors who learned to exploit the use of sound, color, widescreen views, and 3-D while theater owners tried drive-ins and multi-screen viewing options. As mentioned at the start of the historical perspective, adaptation is the key in understanding movie innovations. From the 1950s adaptation was vital in the attempt to overcome the medium's biggest fear—the growth in popularity of television.

Sound MGM executive Irving Thalberg once said, "Sound is a passing fancy. It won't last." His prediction was made in a wishful attempt to avoid the high costs associated with combining sound with film. Amplified sound that could be heard by large audiences was made possible by Lee De Forest's invention of the audio tube. Based on an earlier idea of Edison's, De Forest created a vacuum tube that eventually led to public address systems, radio, stereo equipment, and television.

The advent of "talking pictures" was delayed because there were two different sound systems that competed for adoption by the studios, theater owners were not convinced of the necessity to fit their movie houses with expensive sound equipment and movie producers were reluctant to replace their silent screen stars, many who were European with accents that were hard to understand.

Sound for movies required that synchronized dialogue, music, and sound effects be recorded during a movie's filming. Two sound systems—the Vitaphone (sound on disc) and the Phonofilm (sound on film)—became available to filmmakers at about the same time. The Vitaphone process was an adaptation of Edison's phonographic cylinder invention in which a recording disc was made when the film was shot. To produce sound during a movie, a theater exhibitor had to run the picture and the disc with two different machines. Occasionally problems arose (considered humorous by early audiences) when the two didn't match or a haphazard projector technician accidentally played the wrong

disc (Figure 12.36).

Phonofilm, the technology that eventually won the competition, was a sound-on-film innovation in which symbols were printed on a side of the film and converted into sound as the movie ran through an equipped projector. Consequently, no separate machine was required because the visual and the audio components of the movie always matched.

Warner Bros. invested heavily in Vitaphone, whereas 20th Century Fox advocated Phonofilm. On October 6, 1927, Warner debuted Al Jolson's *The Jazz Singer* using the Vitaphone process. Although not the first sound picture—there had been earlier experiments with recorded voices and music—*The Jazz Singer* was the first movie in which sound was used in a feature motion picture to tell a story (Figure 12.37). The movie is forgettable except as a footnote in the history of sound presentations, although it included Jolson's famous ad-libbed line, "Wait a minute, wait a minute, you ain't heard nothin' yet." Nevertheless, it made $3.5 million ($42 million today) at the box office and Warner's production head, Darryl F. Zanuck received an Oscar during the first Academy Awards ceremony for the technical achievement.

In a throwback to the silent era of films, the 2011 *The Artist* is a melodrama about a silent film star with a strong French accent who finds it difficult to adjust to "talkies." Played by Jean Dujardine, who won the Best Actor Oscar at the 84th Academy Awards ceremony, he had only two words of dialogue toward the end of the film, "With pleasure." Despite winning the Best Picture award, an honor last given to the silent movie *Wings* (1927) in 1929 during the first ceremony (films from 1927 and 1928 were honored), it is unlikely audiences will demand that actors be silent.

Color Another technical innovation was the use of color. The tedious method of

Figure 12.37
(Weblink: http://goo.gl/SSuZyZ)
Although Euro-Americans during this era regularly performed in blackface, the final scene in the 1927 The Jazz Singer, the first "talkie" and performed by Al Jolson, is jarring for contemporary audiences.

Figure 12.38
(Weblink: http://goo.gl/U8gF9P)
Directed by the troubled Burt Gillett, Flowers and Trees *inspired animators to work exclusively in color—an innovative breakthrough at the time.*

Figure 12.39
(Weblink: http://goo.gl/btUsGg)
The difference between this trailer for Becky Sharp *and any seen today is the emphasis on the technical innovation of using the three-color Technicolor process for the first time in a feature film.*

Figure 12.41
(Weblink: http://goo.gl/cWPu-Vm)
Who knew the innocent Dorothy wore so much makeup?

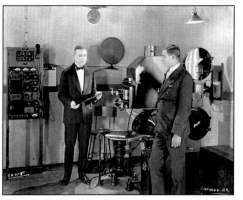

Figure 12.36
Western Electric engineer E.B. Craft holds a Vitaphone recording disc as he poses with an unknown person in this 1926 publicity photograph. It is assumed that Craft did not regularly perform his engineering duties in a tuxedo.
Courtesy of the University of San Diego

hand-tinting individual frames of a motion picture was used commercially as early as Porter's *The Great Train Robbery*. The first full-length movie filmed and projected in color was *The World, the Flesh and the Devil* (1914). The British production used a short-lived, two-projector process called Kinemacolor. A more advanced three-color Technicolor process was introduced in 1932. The next year the Walt Disney Studio won an Academy Award for its all-color animated classic *Flowers and Trees* (Figure 12.38). *Becky Sharp* (1935) was the first live action feature-length film shot with the three-color innovation (Figure 12.39). Public acceptance of color began with the classic fantasy motion picture *The Wizard of Oz* (1939) (Figure 12.40). Audiences reportedly burst into wild applause when Dorothy, played by Judy Garland, opened the door of her drab, sepia-toned Kansas and entered the brightly hued world of Oz after her tornado trip (Figure 12.41). During a "sing-a-long" version at the Castro Theatre in San Francisco in 2012, audience members also "oooed" and "ahhhed" when the screen filled with color.

Widescreen **Another** attempt to lure viewers out of their living rooms or dens

was widescreen movies. AMPAS selected the 4:3 width-to-length aspect ratio as the industry standard for screen presentations in order to avoid costly differences in film stock, cameras, and theaters. The almost square proportions of the film image had to be widened in the 1930s for the Phonofilm process to allow the sound track to run along the side of the film. Eventually, widescreen became the standard presentation format. In 1952, the first commercial widescreen format—Cinerama—was introduced. Although it was a complicated process that required a movie to be shot with three cameras and shown with four projectors (one reserved for the sound track), the widescreen, expansive look was a great success with the public. The next year CinemaScope (later called Panavision) provided directors with a widescreen process that needed only one camera and projector. Some early widescreen hits included *The Robe* (1953) (Figure 12.42), *How the West Was Won* (1962), and *It's a Mad, Mad, Mad, Mad World* (1963) (Figure 12.43). The widescreen trend continues today with the IMAX and OMNIMAX presentation formats that require specially built auditoriums. IMAX theater screens are typically 40 × 28 yards.

3-D Three-dimensional (3-D), drive-in, and multi-screen movies were promoted to compete with television. As early as 1915, Edwin Porter showed 3-D test films to audiences, but nothing became of his early attempt. In Los Angeles, the first 3-D movie shown to a paying audience was called *The Power of Love* in 1922. In the 1950s 3-D took off with *Bwana Devil* (1952) and the first feature-length 3-D motion picture presented in stereo sound, *The House of Wax* (1953). It starred the great horror actor Vincent Price, who went on to make three other 3-D pictures (Figure 12.44). Alfred Hitchcock even filmed a 3-D version of his classic thriller *Dial M for*

Figure 12.40
The theatrical release poster for The Wizard of Oz *emphasizes to audiences that the movie is shot in color.*
Courtesy of MGM

Figure 12.42
The theatrical release poster for The Robe *in 1953.*
Courtesy of 20ᵗʰ Century Fox

Figure 12.43
(Weblink: http://goo.gl/oBs7nK) The trailer for It's a Mad, Mad, Mad, Mad World *(with opening title credits by Saul Bass) emphasizes the madcap energy of this classic comedy directed by Stanley Kramer.*

Figure 12.45
Weblink: http://goo.gl/EdZKFP) Although 3D glasses won't work while watching the trailer for James Cameron's Avatar *(see Chapter 14), in a movie theater the experience of watching the film is enhanced by the immersive effect for some.*

Murder in 1954. Audiences soon grew tired of the passing fad.

The technique is enjoying a comeback with high quality 3-D effects as seen in Henry Selick's animated puppet movie *Coraline*, Disney's first computer-generated 3-D cartoon with Pixar, *Up*, and James Cameron's *Avatar*, all released in 2009 (Figure 12.45). The 3-D technology company RealD 3D supplies comfortable glasses for audience members and installs digital screens for theater operators such as AMC Entertainment, Cinemark USA, and Regal Entertainment Group. In 2017 fan favorites such *The Lego Batman Movie*, *Logan*, *Guardians of the Galaxy Vol. 2*, *Alien: Covenant*, and *Blade Runner 2049* were available in 3-D versions while previously released 2-D hits such as *Star Wars* (1977), *Top Gun* (1986), *Beauty and the Beast* (1991), *Titanic* (1997), and *Monsters, Inc.* (2001) have been converted to 3-D. Perhaps out of reach for theater owners, Peter Jackson's *King Kong 360 3-D*, a ride at Universal Studios Hollywood may be the ultimate 3-D fan experience. With guests wearing 3-D glasses, Kong battles velociraptors and a T. Rex while the tram car shakes violently. Relax. Everyone arrives safely back.

Drive-ins One of the most notable movie directors of this era was Roger Corman, known as the "King of the B Movies." He produced almost 400 motion pictures and gave many in Hollywood their start in the industry, including James Cameron and Ron Howard. Many of his films were only shown in drive-ins. During the 1950s, drive-in movies prospered throughout the country, with more than 4,000 screens across America. Owners of cheap land away from city lights saw drive-ins as a way to put the unproductive real estate to better use. Despite being a haven for lovers and parents with young children, drive-ins, with their colorfully painted front screens,

are hard to find. Today, many are used as convenient open spaces for flea markets (Figure 12.46).

Multi-screens Despite efforts to upgrade movie palaces in downtowns around the world to their opulent grandness, casualties of the war with television are the large, often enchanting movie theaters that could hold up to 3,000 people. With architectural and sculptural curiosities, moody and mysterious lighting effects, and a huge screen behind a heavy maroon or blue curtain, these movie houses were truly magical places that matched the wonder of the motion pictures themselves. Today the trend is against large, single screens because owners can make more money with multi-screen theaters. Some cineplexes have as many as 27 separate theaters under one roof. Managers can receive films via mailed discs, satellite, or internet connections and project them digitally (Figure 12.47).

Multiplexes are here to stay with their stadium seating and convenient showing times. Luxury theaters such as the ArcLight movie complex in Los Angeles and the Mexico City chain Cinepolis Luxury Cinemas. For about $30 a ticket with food and drinks extra, Gold Class Cinemas founded in Australia with theaters in California, Illinois, and Washington state offers "online seating reservations, free valet parking, [and] in-theater food and beverage service with a call button" that makes you feel like William Randolph Hearst watching a movie in his castle. At the LOOK theater in Dallas, promotional content on its website lists several movie watching options, "You can look & dine in our luxury dine-in theatres with service from Ivy Kitchen; savor handcrafted cocktails and take-in fare with your movie in The Lofts; or enjoy our big screen experience in Evolution with power recliners or spend time with the family in the living rooms with power recliners, sofas or armchairs."

Figure 12.44
The typography alone for the one-sheet of House of Wax *is worth the price of admission. Plus, you don't need to wear glasses to enjoy its 3-D effect.*
Courtesy of Warner Bros.

Technical Perspective

As with cartoon and photography media, movies primarily communicate in a visual format. By studying previous works and by being creative, directors have learned to exploit the visual considerations inherent in static or dynamic shots and film choices.

The Shot The basic unit of a movie is the shot, defined as a continuous picture in which the camera doesn't stop. A shot can be as quick as 1/24th of a second—one frame—or can last the entire length of a picture. Graphic designer Saul Bass created the storyboards for one of the most memorable scenes in Hollywood history—the shower murder in *Psycho* (1960). Alfred Hitchcock, using storyboards from Bass, created an impressionistic murder with shocking intensity by using 67 separate editing cuts for

Figure 12.46
Drive-in theaters have been nearly eliminated as places for showing movies, except in a few, mostly rural communities. In 2009 "The Spud" drive-in outside of Victor, Idaho, still serves up first-run movies during the summer season, along with their famous fries.
Courtesy of Paul Martin Lester

Figure 12.47
Typical of most movie centers in large metropolitan areas, the movie complex at Universal Citywalk in Los Angeles includes 19 screens with a giant IMAX theater all with stadium seating.
Courtesy of Paul Martin Lester

the 90-second scene (Figure 12.48). The Swiss American video artist Christian Marclay produced an astounding achievement in editing with *The Clock* (2010). He used thousands of scenes from motion pictures and television shows to produce a 24-hour continuous montage that has been described as mesmerizing. Unfortunately, it seldom is shown (Figure 12.49). On the opposite side of a film with numerous cuts, an incredible technical feat was accomplished in 2002 when the Russian director Alexandr Sokurov used one continuous shot for his motion picture *Russian Ark*. The film traced more than 300 years of Russian history by taking the viewer on a rhythmic, rambling stroll through 33 rooms of the State Hermitage Museum in St. Petersburg (Figure 12.50).

Film Choices Black and white always has been associated with serious, documen-

tary-style subjects, whereas, at first, color was thought to be a distracting attribute better used for fantasies. But black and white can be as colorful and sensational as color. Richard Brooks's haunting retelling of the story of two killers and their capture in the film *In Cold Blood* (1967) and Martin Scorsese's *Raging Bull* (1980), the story of boxer Jake LaMotta, were shot in black and white. The rich tones contribute to a documentary atmosphere in the telling of the brutal stories. Such directors as the indie favorite Jim Jarmusch in his *Stranger than Paradise* (1984), *Coffee and Cigarettes* (2003), and *Broken Flowers* (2005), and the Hollywood iconoclast Francis Ford Coppola in his personal story *Tetro* (2009), known for his colorful classics *The Godfather* (1972) and *Apocalypse Now* (1979), preferred to tell their stories in the less distracting format of black and white. Some directors combine black and white and color for dramatic contrast. Oliver Stone switched quickly back and forth between the two film formats in *Natural Born Killers* (1994). The same technique was employed by Guy Maddin in his wonderfully strange film *The Saddest Music in the World* (2003) (Figure 12.51). To signify the end of the silent era, French cinematographer Guillaume Schiffman shot *The Artist* in color film and then transferred it to black and white for a rich array of gray tones.

Ethical Perspective

Besides the issues associated with the other media discussed, there are three main ethical concerns for the movie industry: stereotypical portrayals, emphasis on violent themes, and the promotion of smoking. However, a fourth concern is taking hold within the industry due to the availability of motion pictures on the internet—copyright infringement.

Stereotypes

In 2001 the Oscars for best male and female actors went to two African Americans—Denzel Washington and Halle Berry for their work in *Training Day* and *Monster's Ball*, a first for the Awards. But since that time such films as *Soul Plane* (2004), *White Chicks* (2004), and *Norbit* (2007) (see Chapter 5) were released. Director Spike Lee said that *Plane* is "coonery and buffoonery," while another critic wrote that the film is "among the most offensive ever in terms of showing African Americans in a negative light." It seems that progress against stereotyping is always tempered by movies that are made to sell tickets and not to advance society (Figure 12.52).

African Americans aren't the only group to feel the sting of stereotyping in motion pictures. Native Americans, although seen in films frequently in the early westerns, almost always were portrayed as murderous savages. Lobbying from Arab groups, upset over the stereotypes in Disney's *Aladdin* (1992) convinced the studio to change offend-

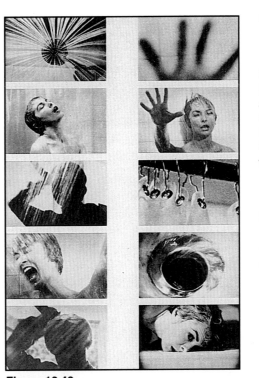

Figure 12.48
One of the most unforgettable moments in motion picture history is the shower murder scene with Janet Leigh and Anthony Perkins in Alfred Hitchcock's 1960 Psycho. *The terror of the scene is enhanced by the quick cuts, but after the Leigh character is killed, a slow transition between the shower drain and her eye is breathtaking. Compare these stills with Saul Bass' storyboards in figure 8.3.*
Courtesy of Saul Bass

ing lyrics in a song, although many other common Arab stereotypes remained. On the other hand, Sacha Baron Cohen's parody *Borat: Cultural Learnings of America for Make benefit Glorious Nation of Kazakhstan* (2006) revealed in a comedic way the stereotypes and prejudices of middle-class Americans. His next film was produced for the same purpose and featured his character Bruno, a gay Austrian fashion writer, in *Bruno: Delicious Journeys Through America for the Purpose of Making Heterosexual Males Visibly Uncomfortable in the Presence of a Gay Foreigner in a Mesh T-Shirt* (2009). The full title didn't fit on theater marquees. Nevertheless, gay activists criticized the film for the character's stereotypical obsession with "anal sex, bondage wear and sex toys."

W LINK

Figure 12.49
(Weblink: http://goo.gl/iTNwFv) Although seen in its entirety, after all it runs for 24 hours, Christian Marclay's The Clock *is a unique visual experience.*

W LINK

Figure 12.50
(Weblink: http://goo.gl/ZJFyRQ) Another one-of-a-kind motion picture treat is Russian Ark *by the director Alexandr Sokurov. Instead of all the quick cuts in television and movie productions, the experience of watching a single, continuous shot in which the camera is choreographed as much as the actors, is mesmerizing.*

W LINK

Figure 12.51
(Weblink: http://goo.gl/dDBxee) Guy Maddin's quirky, David Lynch inspired style in The Saddest Music in the World *is a clinic in the use of color or not.*

W
LINK
Figure 12.52
(Weblink: http://goo.gl/8qtbKs)
Although on a surface level you might be tempted to laugh at the humor shown in Soul Plane, *the stereotypes used to create laughter is reminiscent of* All This and Rabbit Stew *(see Chapter 10).*

Violence Offering the simplistic argument that the violence seen in motion pictures is responsible for all of the social problems in a society is always politically popular. Undeniably, action-adventure movies, always a popular genre, are filled with violent activities. Despite momentary sensitivity among U.S. film producers, violence will continue to be a staple of American films because violent films are enormously popular. One of the main reasons that the number of violent movies has increased is the economic situation of the major studios. Studio executives need big blockbuster hits to maintain the economic health of their enterprises. And since about 80 percent of all movies shown in Europe are from the United States, executives have learned that action-adventure films are popular throughout the world because violence translates across cultures. For example, *Resident Evil: Afterlife* (2010) from Sony and Screen Gems earned $60 million in the U.S. and $236 million in foreign sales.

Criticism of the MPAA's rating system, first established in 1968, became more public after two movies were given different ratings. A ticker buyer must be 17-years-old to see an R-rated movie without an adult while many theaters will not show them. *Bully* (2012), a documentary that follows five bullied children throughout a school year, was given an R rating because of its multiple use of the "f-word" while *The Hunger Games* about teenagers who must kill to stay alive received a PG-13 designation. Obviously, words are viewed as more dangerous than violence by the rating's board. However, after much publicity, Lee Hirsch, the director of *Bully* edited some of the obscenities and the rating was changed to PG-13 to get a wider audience. Hirsch said, "I think this [controversy] has given fuel to a conversation that's long overdue about the double standard when it comes to rating movies."

Smoking in the Movies A five-year content analysis of U.S. motion pictures conducted by academic researchers and reported on the website "Smoke Free Movies" found that 80 percent of the "776 Hollywood and independent movies included tobacco use." About 90 percent of R-rated films, 80 percent of PG-13 movies, and 50 percent of G and PG motion pictures had at least one scene with an actor smoking. Furthermore, the major studios of "TimeWarner, Disney, and Sony accounted for more than half of all movies released with smoking." The number of scenes with characters smoking is higher today than it was during the 1950s, when the health issues related to smoking were not as well known. Because children are highly influenced by seeing stars smoke and the brands they choose, the advocacy group recommended that movies with characters who smoke should have an R rating and that cigarette brands not be visually identified in the films. In 2007 Disney announced it would no longer show characters smoking in its movies and discouraged directors of its Touchstone and Miramax adult labels from showing characters lighting up. In 2008 the six major movie studies announced that they would include anti-smoking public service announcements on DVD versions of any movies that depict smoking. For film companies with an anti-smoking policy, a content analysis revealed that scenes involving tobacco dropped from an average 23 to only one per movie.

Copyright Infringement An open letter presented on the website of the Motion Picture Association of America (MPAA) reads, "As with any business, the people and companies that create music, movies, and other copyrighted material rely on getting a fair reward for their creativity, time and hard work. That happens when people buy these works, but not when they steal them—including by copying or transmitting them without the permission of the copyright owners." Former chairman and CEO Dan Glickman said in 2004 that the organization would combat piracy through three approaches: "improve [piracy deterring] technology, enforce the laws, and educate people." Computer network systems make the downloading of music, movies, and other materials easier than ever before in the history of the medium. Just as movie producers adapted to the competition from television, they will once again need to be creative to overcome the trend toward an all-download future. After the U.S. Congress tabled the Stop Online Privacy Act (SOPA) because of pressure from Google, Wikipedia, and hundreds of other websites (See Chapter 15), the current chairman, Chris Dodd was vehement in his criticism of the legislators and websites.

Cultural Perspective

At least 12 genres, or types of stories created on film, reflect a society's cultural values—comedy, crime, documentary, epic, horror, musical, romance, science fiction, social impact, thriller, war, and western. Here are some standouts in each category:

Comedy: *City Lights* (1931), *Some Like It Hot* (1959), and *Rough Night* (2017)—from sophisticated situations and dialogue to one that shows women can behave as badly as men (Figure 12.53).

Crime: *Scarface* (1932), *Bonnie and Clyde* (1967), and *John Wick Chapter 2* (2017)—from stories with clear good and evil characters to sympathetic psychological profiles of dangerous criminals (Figure 12.54).

Documentary: *Nanook of the North* (1922), *Primary* (1960), and *I Am Not Your Negro* (2017)—balanced reporting is not as valued as advocating a point of view (Figure 12.55).

Horror: *Frankenstein* (1931) (Figure 12.56), *Night of the Living Dead* (1968), and *Get Out* (2017)—from traditional to racist monsters.

Musical: *The Wizard of Oz* (1939), *The Sound of Music* (1965), and *La La Land* (2016)—from unrealistic fantasies to a throwback to an old Hollywood story (Figure 12.57).

Romance: *Gone with the Wind* (1939), *Casablanca* (1943), and *Beauty and the Beast* (2017)—from love in the midst of civil and world wars to another remake of a Disney classic (Figure 12.58).

Science fiction: *Metropolis* (1926), *2001: A Space Odyssey* (1968), and *Woman Woman* (2017)—from thoughtful commentaries about the future to a blockbuster that conveys a feminist narrative (Figure 12.59).

Thriller: *The Maltese Falcon* (1941), *Psycho* (1960), *The Mummy* (2017)—from well-written dramas with fine acting to a movie with fast-paced and intense action scenes that add dramatic effect to an otherwise ordinary story (Figure 12.60).

War: *Apocalypse Now* (1979), *Waltz with Bashir* (2008), and *Hacksaw Ridge* (2016)—the best in this genre are critical examinations of why wars are fought (Figure 12.61).

Western: *Stagecoach* (1939), *The Wild Bunch* (1969), and *The Hateful Eight* (2015)—the best films in this genre question the need for violent actions but understand that it sometimes cannot be avoided (Figure 12.62).

Because motion pictures are primarily visual media, they tell their mythic stories through visual symbolism. Myths are the stories of our culture, whereas symbols are the way those stories are communicated. Motion pictures are cultural

Figure 12.53
Tony Curtis and Marilyn Monroe in a scene for one of the most popular comedy motion pictures, Some Like It Hot *(1959).*
Courtesy of United Artists

Figure 12.54
(Weblink: http://goo.gl/CimsBz) Keanu Reeves reprises his action role in John Wick 2, a tribute to conflict over conciliation.

The truest and most human story of the Great White Snows

A picture with more drama, greater thrill, and stronger action than any picture you ever saw.

REVILLON FRÈRES
PRESENT

NANOOK OF THE NORTH

A STORY OF LIFE AND LOVE IN THE ACTUAL ARCTIC

PRODUCED BY
ROBERT J. FLAHERTY, F.R.G.S.

Pathépicture

Figure 12.55

A good example of a one-sheet promotional poster before the influence of the graphic designer Saul Bass is the one for Nanook of the North *(1922), considered the first true documentary dramatic film. Instead of one central graphic element, three textual descriptions and five illustrations attempt to intrigue a potential moviegoer to watch the black-and-white silent movie.*
Courtesy of PD-US

artifacts. Movies affect us emotionally because the powerful visual messages, on a screen as large as a house and with sound quality that is better than being on a set, tell stories that we understand.

Critical Perspective

Movie attendance has dropped 25 percent since 2002. Many blame the popularity of television and video games, the computer and social networks, poorly maintained theaters, and inferior quality movies. The number of tickets sold annually in the United States immediately after World War II averaged about four billion. In 2011, the number of tickets sold was about 1.28 billion. The movie industry is still profitable because ticket prices have risen, sales of refreshments have increased, and screens have been added to the 5,800 local theaters in the United States. With multiplex suburban theaters, first-run blockbuster movies with huge marketing budgets are sold out the first few weeks of their runs. But after attention wanes, it's hard to find theater seats with someone sitting in front of you.

Today, many forms of entertainment are available to those who can afford them— restaurants, lectures, art museums, music concerts, comedy clubs, shopping malls, traditional theaters, athletic activities, and sporting events. But by far the biggest threat to the existence of motion pictures is in the home, with radio, broadcast television, cable and satellite television, DVRs, board and video games, web presentations, reading, yard work, talking, dinner parties, and sex all keeping people occupied.

Moviemaking is a business. If anticipated blockbusters bomb embarrassingly at the box office, the studio executives responsible sometimes get the axe. This blockbuster mentality, in which most of the profits for a studio are made during the summer months, forces producers to make films that appeal to large audiences. More often than not, proven formulas

Figure 12.56
Theatrical release poster for Frankenstein *(1931). Compare this onesheet with the comic book cover in figure 10.47.*
Courtesy of Universal Pictures

W LINK
Figure 12.57
(Weblink: http://goo.gl/ofAyWf)
Although named Best Picture at the end of the 2017 Academy Awards by actress Faye Dunaway, La La Land *lost to* Moonlight. *Nevertheless, the musical is a heartfelt portrait of the difficulty of being a success*

W LINK
Figure 12.58
(Weblink: http://goo.gl/TF6ZGj)
With its music, lighting, set designs, animation, acting, dancing, and possible gay storylines, with this live action/ animated combination production of Disney's classic Beauty and the Beast, *the franchise is secure.*

W LINK
Figure 12.59
(Weblink: http://goo.gl/VokZZs)
Directed by Patty Jenkins who also led the production of Monster *that won a Best Actress Oscar for Charlize Theron, the superhero* Woman Woman *comes from the folks at DC Comics and Warner Bros. Pictures.*

W LINK
Figure 12.60
(Weblink: http://goo.gl/QfGfpd)
Known for his popular Transformer movie directorial duties, Alex Kurtzman was in charge of the action flick, The Mummy, *first seen in 1932 with Boris Karloff as the Egyptian walking wrap.*

W
LINK
Figure 12.61
(Weblink: http://goo.gl/zjEJvf)
From the moment the opening
notes of The Doors' "The End"
plays until the last frame in which
the title of the movie is finally revealed, Apocalypse Now from
Francis Ford Coppola has little
to do with the Vietnam War, but
is a complex metaphor of power
and loss.

W
LINK
Figure 12.62
(Weblink: http://goo.gl/zCsbLb)
With the ninth motion picture
from director Quentin Tarantino,
his assured visual style in The
Hateful Eight is at its peak in
this period piece filled with sus-
pense, betrayal, and friendship.

from the past—remakes and sequels with sexual and violent themes—do well.

Moviemaking is also, it is necessary to report, an Anglo man's business. The Center for the Study of Women in Television and Film at San Diego State University reported that out of 250 top-grossing movies in 2016, only seven percent had women directors. Also, in 83 years of Oscar awards, less than four percent of the acting awards have gone to African Americans. One reason may be the membership of the Academy. In a 2012 article by the *Los Angeles Times*, a study of 5,112 voting members revealed that 90 percent of those in 14 branches of the Academy are Anglo while 88 percent of actors are Anglo. The executive and writing branches are composed of 98 percent Anglo members. Overall the Academy is 93 percent Anglo and 76 percent male.

Nevertheless, standout women directors include Amma Asante, *Belle* (2013) and *A United Kingdom* (2016), Kathryn Bigelow, *Point Break* (1991), *Strange Days* (1995), and *The Hurt Locker* (2009), that won her Best Director and Best Feature Film Academy Awards (Figure 12.63), Gurinder Chadha, *Bend It Like Beckham* (2002) and *It's a Wonderful Afterlife* (2010), Jane Champion, *The Piano* (1993) and *Bright Star* (2009), Sofia Coppola, *Lost in Translation* (2003) and *Somewhere* (2010). At the Cannes Film Festival, Coppola was only the second woman in the festival's history to win best director for *The Beguiled* (2017) (Figure 12.64), Ava DuVernay, *Middle of Nowhere* (2012), *Selma* (2014), and *A Wrinkle in Time* (2017), Lauren Greenfield, *The Queen of Versailles* (2012), Sanaa Hamri, *Sisterhood of the Traveling Pants 2* (2008) and *Acceptance* (2009), Catherine Hardwicke, *Twilight* (2008) and *Maximum Ride* (2010), Christine Jeffs, *Sunshine Cleaning* (2008), Phyllida Lloyd, *Mamma Mia!* (2008) and *The Iron Lady* (2011), Jennifer Lynch, *Boxing Helena* (1993) and *Surveillance*

(2008), Dee Rees, *Pariah* (2011) and *Mudbound* (2017), Nia Vardalos, *I Hate Valentine's Day* (2009) and *My Big Fat Greek Wedding* (2002), and Lana and Lily Wachowski, *The Matrix* (1999) and *Cloud Atlas* (2012).

TRENDS TO WATCH FOR MOTION PICTURES

The most exciting trend for the motion picture medium involves technology and funding—admittedly not two of the most compelling topics. But high definition (hi-def) camcorders, called "Hollywood's filmless future" offer high resolution, high quality images and audio in a portable format using laptop editing software programs allow independent directors to make high quality movies.

Independent productions ("indies") will continue to be vital to the movie industry. The 2009 Academy Awards Best Picture and winner of seven other Oscars, the much-touted *Slumdog Millionaire*, for example, was a British production, co-financed by a French company, and starred an all-Indian cast. It debuted in only ten theaters, but was marketed wisely by a small studio within media giant News Corp., Fox Searchlight. It also handled such surprise independent hits as *Juno* (2007), *Little Miss Sunshine* (2006), and *Sideways* (2004). Searchlight paid $2.5 million for distribution rights to *Slumdog*. The Paramount Film Group marking its 100th anniversary in 2012 uses its Insurge subsidiary to fund low-budget productions that have turned into big moneymakers such as *Paranormal Activity* series (2007-2015), *The Devil Inside* (2012), and *Dog Tease*, based on Charlie, a talking dog seen by more than 86 million views on YouTube.

Indies are having their way with the help of film festivals such as Sundance in Park City, Utah, and South by Southwest in Austin, Texas, television channels such as the Independent Film Channel, and the Spirit Awards that celebrate "independent, low-budget filmmaking."

The 2017 Sundance Film Festival showed 113 feature films that were selected from more than 13,000 entries from 32 countries. These indie directors seek valuable but hard to get distribution deals with established film studios. Consequently, many indie directors bypass traditional theater distribution and make their films available for internet downloading through video-on-demand (VOD) via cable providers or web services such as Amazon on Demand or YouTube Screening room. Indie standouts for 2017 include *I Am Not Your Negro, A United Kingdom, Lovesong, Raw, Personal Shopper*, and *Wilson* (Figure 12.65).

Renting movies is becoming easier. If willing to pay the price, consumers can download first-run motion pictures through Amazon, Hulu, and Netflix to computers and big screen projectors in a home's media room instantly. Movie producers understand that consumers want more options in watching movies than going to a theater. Although downloads to home televisions, computers, tablets, and smartphones cut into theater sales, Hollywood can still make money from the practice. A savvy move from producers is to change the format of recorded motion pictures so that viewers must buy new systems and their accompanying versions. Similar to sports franchises that alter mascots or logos to sell new sets of fanwear, motion pictures for home and portable viewing have seen transitions from black and white, to color, to videotape, to DVD, to Blu-ray, and to UltraViolet, an online-only format.

Motion picture innovations such as live action players on stage as in *The Rocky Horror Picture Show* (1975) performances, guest lectures from movie producers, critics, and academics, concert performances, live, simulcast operas, and seats installed with computer monitors for value-added information about the film, won't get a mass audience off their couches. The newest experiment, "Aroma-Scope," a scratch-and-sniff experience, is a variation of an idea from decades ago is now called 4D. "Odorama" was a part of John Waters' *Polyester* (1981) with theatergoers able to smell pleasant and rude odors. The latest version was included on cards given to audience members to enhance their experience while watching *Spy Kids: All the Time in the World in 4D* (2011). As with a bad smell that fills a room, this craze will pass.

To remain a viable medium and to get people away from their home entertainment centers, movie producers will need to rely less on blockbuster movies to improve their bottom line and more on smaller, well-made, and compelling stories that are now mostly supplied by independent filmmakers. Theater owners must also think of new ways to enhance the viewing experience, including higher quality and healthier food offerings, Facebook-style friend group special screenings, and better soundproofing so that the explosions from the theater next door are silenced.

Will people continue to go to movie theaters? Of course they will. Humans are social animals and simply enjoy the company of one another too much to stay home for long.

KEY TERMS FROM THIS CHAPTER

Archetypes • Aspect ratio • CinemaScope • Contrast • Indie • Kinemacolor • Kinetograph • Kinetoscope • Ku Klux Klan • Technicolor • Vacuum tube • Zoopraxiscope

Figure 12.63
(Weblink: http://goo.gl/RpPW25) Kathryn Bigelow's thoughtful and suspenseful The Hurt Locker *won six Academy Awards. Bigelow, known for directing* Point Break, Strange Days, The Weight of Water, *and* Zero Dark Thirty, *shows a consistent feminist style in her choices. Her latest,* Detroit *is concerned with the 1967 racially-inspired riot.*

Figure 12.64
(Weblink: http://goo.gl/HtkyWf) Daughter of Francis of The Godfather *films, Sofia Coppola is most known for her work directing Bill Murray and Scarlett Johansson in* Lost in Translation. The Beguiled *is a strange, eerie story about women in charge during the American Civil War.*

Figure 12.65
(Weblink: http://goo.gl/g14PNB) Woody Harrelson has come a long way from his dim-witted yet loveable character in "Cheers" to an impressive filmography that includes Natural Born Killers, The Hunger Games, *and* War for the Planet of the Apes. *In* Wilson, *he plays a character inspired by the*

13 Television

Television is a medium of entertainment which permits millions of people to listen to the same joke at the same time, and yet remain lonesome.

T. S. Eliot
POET, PUBLISHER, &
SOCIAL CRITIC

The tribe has spoken.

If you don't own a TV or don't watch it, you will probably have trouble identifying that catchphrase. In 2017 the show's 34th season featured, as always, Jeff Probst speaking the words toward the end of each episode of the CBS consistent hit, "Survivor" (Figure 13.1). The implicit meanness of the phrase, which no contestant wants to hear because it means you are voted off the game, says a lot about the state of television programming and modern society as well. The phrase also signifies that reality or unscripted television has come a long way from "Smile. You're on Candid Camera," the innocent ending to a mild practical joke in the 1950s classic.

Reality television includes an astonishing number of unscripted programs. Besides the traditional offerings such as news, sports, and talk shows, included in the reality mix are programs based on documentaries, historical re-creations, dating, law enforcement and military subjects, makeovers, life changes, docusoaps, hidden cameras, games, spoofs, talent searches, fantasies fulfilled, cooking, commercial sales, and situation comedies where actors ad-lib dialogue without a script.

Since 2000, the television genre has been a ratings powerhouse with reality shows such as "Who Wants to be a Millionaire?" in 2000, "Survivor: The Australian Outback" in 2001, and "American Idol" from 2005 to the present attracting more viewers than most other shows. There is even a reality show channel. In 2008 the media giant Time Warner converted its Court TV channel to TruTV that features sports, trial coverage and commentary, "caught on video" programs, and other reality shows such as "Lizard Lick Towing," "World's Wildest Police Videos," and "Cops."

Realitytvworld's website has a list of about 1,000 programs. There are

Figure 13.1
"Survivor" host Jeff Probst interviewed at the ET Post-Emmys Party, Walt Disney Concert Hall, 2008.
Courtesy of Kristin Dos Santos

so many shows that there are subgenres within groups. The documentary category, for example, contains rural or blue-collar reality TV shows such as "Bayou Billionaires," "Deadliest Catch," "Hillbilly Handfishin'," "Ice Road Truckers," "Lady Loggers," "My Big Redneck Vacation," "Swamp Wars," and "Rocket City Rednecks" while the singing contestants genre is replete with "American Idol," "The X Factor," and "The Voice." Some critics write that too many shows within a single category will cause viewers to lose interest. For example, in 2012 for the first time, "Idol," which has been called the "Death Star" for eliminating any competition lost for the first time in its time slot to the CBS hit "The Big Bang Theory." Fox officials blamed the reversal of fortune to another reality category—NBA basketball on cable.

To prove the point, according to Nielsen Media Research for the 2016 season, the top ten primetime regularly scheduled programs were "The Big Bang Theory," "NCIS," "NBC Sunday Night Football," "Walking Dead," "Bull," "NCIS:

New Orleans," "Sunday Night Pre-Kick," "Designated Survivor," "Thursday Night Football," and "Blue Bloods." Only the three sports programs could be loosely called reality shows.

The founder of reality programming is Allen Funt. During World War II while serving in the Army Signal Corps, he experimented with portable radio equipment and put his skills to work after the war. He was a writer for "Sweetheart Soap," which was First Lady Eleanor Roosevelt's radio program, came up with funny skits for the popular "Truth or Consequences" show and headed what he called "the stupidest show in radio," a program called "Funny Money Man," which was turned into a syndicated comic strip. His interest in gags that made fun of ordinary persons led to "Candid Microphone," which aired on the ABC Radio Network in 1946. The next year he took his show to television where it eventually became the smash hit "Candid Camera" in 1953. At one time or another it aired on all three major networks. The show originally consisted of good-humored practical jokes pulled on unsuspecting individuals. When the joke had run its course, the catchphrase, "Smile, you're on Candid Camera" would be spoken amid laughter (Figure 13.2). But not everyone laughed. In an era in which security cameras were not common, few appreciated the joke played on them. For every scenario that aired, about 20 were rejected because the person did not smile or sign a necessary release form.

The first documentary-style reality show seen in America, "An American Family," was broadcast on the Public Broadcasting Service (PBS) network in 1973. Directed by Alan and Susan Raymond, the 12-part series followed the highs and lows of an actual family—Bill and Patricia Loud of Santa Barbara, California and their five children (Figure 13.3). The series became controversial as the family dealt with highly personal

Figure 13.2
Allen Funt on the Dick Cavett interview show in 1972.
Courtesy of ABC Television

Figure 13.3
A family portrait of the Louds of Santa Barbara, California, doesn't reveal the hidden tensions that "An American Family" on the PBS network showed. The series was the first documentary-style reality program on television.
Courtesy of the Public Broadcasting Service

issues including an impending divorce and their son Lance's homosexuality. It used nonintrusive camera techniques similar to today's "Survivor." In 2002 *TV Guide* magazine listed the program as number 32 of the "50 Greatest TV Shows of All Time." The family reunited 30 years later for "A Death in An American Family" which documented Lance's addiction to crystal meth and his struggle with HIV/AIDS.

In March 1988, the Screen Actors Guild (SAG) and the Writers Guild of America (WGA), two important Hollywood unions that represented thousands of actors and writers, went on strike. The SAG strike lasted less than a month, but the WGA strike lasted five months and devastated the fall lineup of scripted shows. Since television producers did not have shows to air, many popular programs delayed their start until December. However, innovative executives realized, as some already knew, that there could be programs without the need for actors or writers.

Two hits begun in 1989 required little writing and acting, "Cops" and "America's Funniest Home Videos." "Cops" used actual footage from videographers riding along with police units. It was the brainchild of John Langley and Malcolm Barbour who pitched the concept to Stephen Chao, a Fox television programming executive who liked the raw edge of the show, its inexpensive production costs, and its appeal to a young, male demographic valuable to advertisers. Fox, the network that gave "The Simpsons" the green light, is known for being innovative when it comes to programming. "Cops" garnered four Emmy nominations and concerns from social critics about stereotyping African Americans and southern Anglos. "Funniest Home Videos" was produced by Vin Di Bona for the ABC network and was based on a popular Japanese show, "Fun TV." Each week the studio audience votes

for a top video, with an end-of-the-season winner receiving a $100,000 prize.

"Home Videos" put entertainment producers on notice that everyday persons with their video camcorders were potential contributors to their shows. In 1991 this trend led directly to what is considered to be "the most famous home video of all time," the beating of Rodney King by members of the police force, taken by amateur George Holliday. King was a recently released convict whose alcoholic father died at age 42. Holliday was an upper-middle-class son of an oil executive, who had been born in Canada but lived most of his life in Argentina. King was out of work and angry. Holliday was a manager of a plumbing company and contented. King was beaten severely by members of the Los Angeles Police Department (LAPD). Holliday was watching the beating through the viewfinder of his new $1,200 (about $2,000 today) Sony Handycam (Figure 13.4). King was African American. Holliday was Anglo. Excerpts were shown throughout the world, and when the police officers were initially found not guilty in April 1992, many blamed the video for causing unrest that led to the worst civil disturbance in the history of the United States (Figure 13.5).

The violence claimed 54 lives, caused 2,300 injuries, resulted in hundreds of arrests, and cost more than $1 billion ($1.6 billion today) in property damage. Since the 1992 riots, King has had various run-ins with law enforcement due to drinking and accusations of domestic violence. He became an alumnus of the reality TV genre in 2008 when he appeared on VH1's "Celebrity Rehab with Dr. Drew" and in 2009 on "Sober House." In 2011 King was arrested in California on suspicion of driving under the influence. Coinciding with the 20th anniversary of the Los Angeles riots, with co-author Lawrence J. Spagnola, King published a memoir, *The Riot Within: My Journey from Rebellion to Redemption*. When

Figure 13.4
Shown on KTLA television station, this high-contrast and blurry still image taken from George Holliday's videotape shows a Los Angeles police officer about to hit the crouched form of Rodney King in front of his automobile.
Courtesy of the Public Broadcasting Service

W LINK
Figure 13.5
*(Weblink: http://goo.gl/FMF8Sy)
The eight-minute video shot by George Holliday of Rodney King's beating and arrest is an early example of the recent citizen journalist trend in which amateur videographers capture news events. The difference is that instead of a camcorder, a smartphone is used.*

W LINK
Figure 13.6
(Weblink: http://goo.gl/urTwwh)
The first season of MTV's "The Real World" is a product of its early 1990s era—a time capsule of fashion, interests, and controversies.

asked what he thought when he saw the videotape of the beating he replied, "I'm so glad I made it through. Now I laugh, I smile, when I see it." The laughter didn't last long. In 2012 his fiancée found him at the bottom of his swimming pool. An autopsy discovered alcohol, cocaine, marijuana, and PCP in his body. After his death his daughter, Lori tried to bring peace between the LAPD and the African American community.

In 1992 television producers and audience members were introduced to the strange world of voyeurism. "Real World: New York," the first reality-based series to appeal to an enormous television audience, was premiered on MTV (Figure 13.6). Co-created by soap opera producer ("As the World Turns" and "Search for Tomorrow") Mary-Ellis Bunim and documentary filmmaker Jon Murray, "The Real World" featured a familiar scenario of several strangers living together in a beautifully furnished house in a major city while viewers watched how their relationships disintegrated or

prospered. After a long battle with breast cancer, Bunim, 57, died in Burbank, California, in 2004. Nevertheless, Murray continues to produce reality-based programs. In 2009 MTV aired *Pedro*, a movie based on the "Real World: San Francisco" cast of 1994, which featured the sad but inspirational story of Cuban American HIV/AIDS victim Pedro Zamora.

In 2009 the genre was criticized for seemingly exploiting willing, yet naïve participants by airing their public confessions and unusual behavior. Shows such as "The Bachelor" and "The Bachelorette," "The Real Housewives of New Jersey," "Jon & Kate Plus 8," and "Octomom: The Incredible Unseen Footage" invite ethical concerns. In 2017, ABC's spinoff, "Bachelor in Paradise" quit production after allegations of sexual assault were made public.

Despite the criticisms of American reality television, the title of "king of reality TV" has to go to a British citizen, Mark Burnett, 49, who almost

Figure 13.7
King of reality television, Mark Burnett at his Hollywood Walk of Fame ceremony, 2009.
Courtesy of Angela George

single-handedly defined the reality genre. His list of hits is impressive: "The Celebrity Apprentice," "Shark Tank," "The Voice," and of course, the winner of them all, "Survivor."

Mark Burnett was born in England in 1960 (Figure 13.7). At 18 years old he joined the British Army Parachute Regiment. He fought in Northern Ireland and in the Falkland Islands. After his discharge in 1982, he left for America. Since he had only $600 (about $1,500 today) in his pocket, he stayed with friends in southern California. He hoped he might become a mercenary who helped train Central American military forces in the ways of weapons, explosives, and tactics. But a talk with his mother convinced him to pursue a less romantic lifestyle—at least for the time being. Instead, he was hired as a babysitter for a Beverly Hills couple with a young son and then as a nanny for two boys in Malibu. His selling point to the parents was that he could do the dishes and be a bodyguard to his young charges. Not surprisingly, "Commando Nanny" was the name of a scripted pilot he sold to the WB network based on his early experiences living in Los Angeles.

His love for physical challenges and salesmanship came in handy when in 1992 he joined a team of fellow adventurers for the grueling "Raid Gauloises," in which four-person teams from around the world competed in a variety of athletic tests for five to seven days over four continents. Seeing the potential of "Raid" as a television program, Burnett sold the idea of his renamed "Eco-Challenge" to MTV executives with teams who biked, rafted, and climbed their way around Moab, Utah, in 1995. With the success of the show, Burnett was on his way to becoming a full-time television executive.

"Survivor" has its roots in Burnett's home country. In 1988 British television producer Charlie Parsons conceived of a show he called "Survive!" in which

four contestants were shipwrecked on a desert island. The concept was inspired by William Golding's 1954 novel *Lord of the Flies*. In 1996, Burnett talked with Parsons at a party and discussed buying the U.S. rights to the program. Burnett pitched the show to all the major networks without success. Finally, CBS reconsidered and gave it a try.

The first U.S. "Survivor" aired during the summer of 2000. It became more than a hit—it was a cultural phenomenon as it was watched by about 70 million viewers and earned more than $50 million for Viacom, the parent company of CBS. It gave its 16 contestants their 15 minutes of fame and then some. It also made a star of host and tribal master Jeff Probst who won Primetime Emmy Awards four years in a row from 2008 for "Outstanding Host for a Reality Program." Since 2010 he has been an executive producer for "Survivor." In 2012 he hosted a one-hour daytime talk show for CBS. The next year it was canceled.

The star of the first "Survivor" and winner of the $1 million prize was a "gay, overweight corporate trainer from Newport, Rhode Island," Richard Hatch. Later, he was sentenced to a 51-month sentence after he was convicted for not paying taxes on his winnings. After spending three years in prison, his comeback on Donald Trump's "Celebrity Apprentice 4" in 2011 was cut short when he was arrested again for violating the terms of his release. He asked for a court-appointed lawyer since he claimed he was "destitute." Always a survivor, in 2016 Hatch was on "The Biggest Loser: Temptation Nation."

In many ways, "Survivor" and other game-oriented reality programs feature the best and worst elements about television and American society. The people chosen for the unscripted program, the situations and challenges they must overcome, and the dramatic camerawork and careful editing help sustain interest for 13 one-hour episodes. Each season epitomizes all the elements needed for a top television program when characters, situations, words, pictures, and audio come together within the confines of the screened medium and are combined with the comfort of watching the show at home.

Despite the high ratings, there are critical views of the television genre. "You're watching people caught in the act of being on a reality show," writes critic John Jeremiah Sullivan. "This is now the plot of all reality shows, no matter their cooked-up themes." He goes on to make a point that reality TV is nothing more than a mirror of American culture, "There have been more tears shed on reality TV than by all the war-widows of the world. There are simply too many of them—too many shows and too many people on the shows—for them not to be revealing something endemic. This is us, a people of savage sentimentality, weeping and lifting weights."

TELEVISION AND THE SIX PERSPECTIVES

Television is easy to criticize. Former Federal Communications Commission (FCC) chair Newton Minow in a 1961 speech called the medium "a vast wasteland." In some cultures, it is hip to criticize "the boob tube." Mark Miller, in his book *Boxed In*, writes that "a great deal of the time when we are watching TV we know that it is stupid and enjoy the feeling of superiority." Nevertheless, despite the popularity of watching programs on the web, television is still considered the most influential and prevalent medium of visual communication in the world. All that producers of shows and their advertisers ask is that you "Stay Tuned."

Personal Perspective

Mark Frost, co-creator with David Lynch of the "Twin Peaks" television series, admits, "In this country, television is used primarily as a narcotic to prepare people for the commercial." David Chase, the

creative force behind HBO's successful series "The Sopranos," also has a dim view of television. In a 2004 interview Chase said, "Television is at the base of a lot of our problems. It trivializes everything. So there's no more mystery, we've seen it all 50,000 times. And in order to make the boring interesting, everything is hyped." Tough words from someone who has been so successful with the medium.

Viewers use a remote control device to flip from one program to another in the sometimes frustrating effort to find something interesting to watch. Called *channel grazing*, the curious habit of discovering a good program without the aid of a television guide evokes the wide-open plains of the Old West—the metaphor of a better life over the next hill or around the bend. That promise of a better program through the next push of a button is where television gets its power.

In the early history of the medium, viewers were content to be intrigued by the low-quality flickering pictures. With few stations and programs, people watched whatever was broadcast because they were easily fascinated. Today, viewers are more choosy, demanding constant entertainment. The reason is simple—television actually is radio with pictures, and radio has roots deep in vaudeville theater. Consequently, television always was meant to be more of an entertainment than an educational medium. The high ideals and educational hopes came later. If you learn something from "The Big Bang Theory" or "Masterpiece Classic" it is only because entertainment has been made educational. Conversely, producers of more serious television fare hope that they make education entertaining (Figure 13.8).

Whether you don't watch television at all or watch it for several hours each day, one conclusion is clear: TV is a medium in which the viewer is charged with the task of making sense of it all. Jack

Figure 13.8
An ever-present television set is left running in a motel room.
Courtesy of Paul Martin Lester

Perkins said of the Arts & Entertainment cable network that it "shows the entire scope of television, which is, of course, the entire scope of life." Television *is* life because it reveals much about the lives of those inside and outside the screen. Whether conscious of television's effect or blissfully unaware, people eventually succumb to the enticing images that flicker across the glowing glass or plasma frame.

Probably the chief reason why television is so routinely criticized is the queasy feeling that comes from the thought that despite all the great moments presented—all the news, drama, comedy, and sports—television never has lived up to its potential. One source that helps to improve the medium's credibility is the Archive of American Television. It provides one of the best resources for the appreciation of television in a collection that contains more than 1,000 hours of interviews with producers, performers, and production personnel (Figure 13.9). Regardless, there is always a feeling that television should be something more—something better.

Historical Perspective

In the 1930s when Hollywood executives first learned about the new medium of television, they laughed at the idea of a radio with pictures. In the 1940s they were concerned enough to reduce ticket prices and offer double features. In the 1950s the war was over—television had become the single most popular form of entertainment for Americans. The laughing stopped.

1920s The birth of modern television began in 1922 after two scientists with Western Electric, the research arm of AT&T, improved upon the cathode-ray tube (CRT), a vacuum tube that fires a beam of electrons onto a florescent screen. By 2010, CRTs have been replaced by LCD (Liquid Crystal Displays) flat panels. That same year, an Idaho high school student, Philo (or Phil, as he preferred) Farnsworth, 14, inspired by the rows of upturned soil after plowing his family's field, invented a model for television (Figure 13.10). Five years later, he transmitted a vertical black line on a CRT that moved back and forth like his plow against a lit background. He called his device an "image dissector." In 1928, he demonstrated his invention to investors at his San Francisco laboratory by showing them a transmission of, perhaps fittingly, a dollar sign. The next year his wife Elma, known as "Pem," posed for a live image with her eyes closed because of the bright light needed for the picture. Farnsworth later established research centers in Indiana and his birth state of Utah. He is credited with 300 U.S. and international patents contributing to advances in radar, the electron microscope, and the astronomical telescope (Figure 13.11).

1930s Because of the interest in television, GE, RCA, and Westinghouse scientists merged their research operations in 1930. Russian immigrant Vladimir Zworykin headed the television team. He visited Farnsworth and was impressed enough to have his engineers produce a copy. In their laboratory in New Jersey,

Figure 13.11
Philo Farnsworth in 1929.
Courtesy of the Library of Congress

the scientists improved on Farnsworth's invention with what they called the iconoscope electronic scanning tube for television. RCA's variation of television was more practical than Farnsworth's process because it required less light. Nevertheless, the first transmission was a crude, 60-line reproduction of a small cartoon drawing of the popular character Felix the Cat, the work of Australian cartoonist Pat Sullivan and American animator Otto Messmer (Figure 13.12).

The iconoscope was soon improved with a 441-line picture scanner. The success of these experiments led David Sarnoff, president of RCA, to decide in 1932 to invest heavily in this new technology. It was Sarnoff who came up with the word *television*. During the 1936 Summer Olympics in Berlin, Germany, two companies used the RCA and Farnsworth systems to televise a total of 72 hours of sporting events. The New York World's Fair in 1939 first introduced the American public to the new medium (Figure 13.13).

W LINK
Figure 13.9
(Weblink: http://goo.gl/a4JS6v) The Archive of American Television is a treasure chest filled with information, history, and interviews.

W LINK
Figure 13.10
(Weblink: http://goo.gl/GRzJk9) A short, grammatically-challenged documentary of Philo Farnsworth, The Most Famous Man You Never Heard Of, *produced by his great granddaughter Jessica, starts with his appearance in the televised guessing game "I've Got a Secret," in which none of the panelists guessed his name.*

Figure 13.12
As with the first photograph and motion picture, one of the first television transmissions is a crude prelude for what was to come. One of the first experiments with television technology was the transmission of the popular cartoon character of the day, Felix the Cat. Creator Otto Messmer got his start producing fashion illustrations when animated films fascinated him. He worked for an advertising agency making animations and was noticed by Pat Sullivan who hired him for his studio, where Felix was born. The high contrast character was perfect as a test of the new television system from RCA.
Courtesy of the David Sarnoff Library

1940s Concerned about competing technologies that would delay the spread of television, the Federal Communications Commission (FCC), a U.S. regulatory body overseeing radio and television, authorized sets to contain a 525-line electron scanner for black-and-white transmission in 1941. World War II temporarily halted advances in television because of the need for the country to concentrate on the war effort. During the war years, only six stations were broadcasting to about 10,000 sets in the United States. Most of them were in bars, bowling alleys, appliance store windows, and the homes of wealthier families. Broadcasting was limited to a short time in the evening. Radio employees re-created their popular programs, announced some news, and narrated sporting events.

After the war, attention once again turned to television, and commercial broadcasting began in earnest. NBC, CBS, and ABC dominated the market because of the expense of establishing a network and the limited number of stations operating in any one area. The popular vaudeville-style variety shows of Milton Berle and Ed Sullivan were typical broadcasts (Figure 13.14).

1950s Many writers have dubbed the 1950s the "golden age" of television because of technological and programming innovations. One fact is clear: During the decade, television gained a tremendous number of viewers and became a true mass medium.
Fifteen million homes in the United States had television sets by 1956 while 500 broadcast stations in the United States were generating more than $1 billion ($8 billion today) in advertising sales. In addition to movie stars, theater actors were persuaded to perform on television in the mid-1950s. For example, the "I Love Lucy" show was a landmark production in 1951 for many reasons. Produced by Lucille Ball and

Figure 13.13
More than 44 million people attended the 1939 New York World's Fair held in Flushing Meadows, the author's birthplace. Part of the attraction was the NBC exhibition that featured television. President Franklin Roosevelt delivered an opening day speech that was televised by NBC for about 1,000 viewers watching on 200 sets in the New York area.
Courtesy of the David Sarnoff Library

Desi Arnaz through their Desilu production company in studios purchased from the failed movie studio RKO, the situation comedy was filmed with three cameras in front of a live audience and was enormously successful. Filmed productions meant that the shows could be shown again and again as reruns for additional profits (Figure 13.15).

In 1958 a quiz show scandal rocked the television industry. A congressional investigation discovered that contestants had been coached with the correct answers in order to make the programs more dramatic. The networks canceled many quiz shows after Charles Van Doren testified that he had been given the answers for the show "Twenty-One" (Figure 13.16). Quiz shows soon returned to daytime television, but under much stiffer regulations. The controversy was examined in the 1994 movie *Quiz Show*, directed by Robert Redford (Figure 13.17).

Color, videotape, and cable were introduced in the 1950s. CBS and RCA proposed two different systems for camera and receiver color. The FCC tried to delay the switch to color, fearing that the transition would be too expensive. Nevertheless, the FCC approved RCA's color

Figure 13.14
"The Ed Sullivan Show" was one of the most popular variety shows on television. Broadcast from 1948 to 1971, it was hosted by the genial yet awkward host Ed Sullivan. Elvis Presley and The Beatles are among the countless acts that were introduced to the American public on the show. Today the theater where the show originated is named after Sullivan and is where "The Late Show with Stephen Colbert" is produced.
Courtesy of Alex Lozupone

technology as the industry standard. The first color television set was introduced in 1954 at a cost of $1,000 (about $8,000 today). Because of the high cost of the sets and the time required for stations to convert to color, they were not immediately popular.

A southern California company, Ampex, that was more known for its sound equipment, began working on a videotape system. At the National Association of Broadcasters (NAB) annual convention in Chicago in 1956, Charles Ginsburg demonstrated the new method for recording programs. The convention

Figure 13.15
Publicity photo of the "I Love Lucy" cast: William Frawley (Fred Mertz), Desi Arnaz (Ricky Ricardo), Vivian Vance (Ethel Mertz), and Lucille Ball (Lucy Ricardo).
Courtesy of CBS Television

was set up with closed-circuit television for those not able to get into the auditorium. Ginsburg tapped into the system, recorded a few minutes of the proceedings, and played the tape back for astonished attendees. Within days of the NAB convention, Ampex received about 50 orders for its $74,000 videotape system (about $600,000 today). CBS was one of the first customers and began rebroadcasting its nightly news program called "Douglas Edwards and the News" to its West Coast affiliates at a normal viewing time (Figure 13.18). Another innovation of using videotape was that it allowed high-quality reproductions of programs,

so that huge amounts of money could be made from showing reruns of previously aired shows. Desi Arnaz no longer had a monopoly with his filmed reruns.

1960s During this decade, more than 90 percent of the homes in the United States had at least one television set. In 1967 the public became aware of the potential for videotape technology to add to their viewing pleasure when instant replay was introduced during a Super Bowl football game. With the advent of instant replay technology for sports programs, ABC became a leading network. In addition, new sports leagues were formed to take advantage of the tremendous profits by selling commercials during televised sporting events. Cable companies flourished, with more than 650,000 subscribers and 640 different cable firms. Cable or pay television began as a way to bring television to communities in Pennsylvania that were nestled among mountains that prevented over-the-air reception. The cable company received television signals and then piped them into individual homes through coaxial cable links. Customers paid about $10 a month for the service (or about the price of cable today, $80). Besides better reception, viewers with cable could get many more channels and commercial-free sporting events and movies. In 1962, AT&T and NASA collaborated to develop and launch the first communications satellite, Telstar I. With other launches, live same-time programming across the United States became popular.

Action-adventure dramas produced outside of theater studios were the most popular shows. One of the most controversial was the Desilu production of "The Untouchables." With its Elliot Ness–inspired stories, car crashes, and flying bullets, the show, according to a Senate subcommittee, was "the most violent program on television" (Figure 13.19). Concerned that Congress might

W LINK

Figure 13.17
(Weblink: http://goo.gl/pzzUYq)
The mature directorial style of
Robert Redford, known for his
movie acting and starting the
Sundance Film Festival, is clear
in this trailer for Quiz Show.

Figure 13.16
Host Jack Barry of the tainted television quiz show "Twenty-One" turns toward contestant
Charles Van Doren as fellow contestant Vivienne Nearing looks on. Canceled in 1958 after a
congressional investigation discovered that the show was rigged, the "Twenty-One" scandal
had a lasting effect on all television game shows and their participants. Jack Barry was forced
into exile and didn't work again on television until a decade later. Nearing, who at the time
was a lawyer for Warner Bros. and beat champion Van Doren, was disbarred for six months
after being convicted of lying to a grand jury about the show. Charles Van Doren resigned
his position as an assistant professor at Columbia University, but he became an editor for the
Encyclopedia Britannica, author of several books, and is now an adjunct professor at the University of Connecticut, Torrington, for the English department. Sponsor-controlled involvement
in the playing of game shows was eliminated, and contestants were forbidden to have any
off-camera personal conversations with a host.
Courtesy of the Library of Congress

Figure 13.18
Begun in 1944 by the Russian-born engineer Alexander
M. Poniatoff, Ampex (his initials combined with "EX" for
excellence) is an electronics company more known for
its audio equipment. However, the VR-1000A shown
here was the first videotape recorder introduced by the
company in April 1956 and was developed by Charles
Ginsberg and Ray Dolby. One reel of tape cost $300
($2,400 today), and the entire machine was priced at
about $100,000 ($803,000 today). The first broadcast
using the new machine was from the CBS network.
Courtesy of Karl Baron

Figure 13.19

The cast for the first showing of "The Untouchables" on Desilu Playhouse, a production company created by Desi Arnaz. From left: Bob Osterloh, Eddie Firestone, Robert Stack, Keenan Wynn, Peter Leeds, Abel Fernandez and Bill Williams. Keenan Wynn is the son of Ed Wynn; only Robert Stack and Abel Fernandez went on to the television series which aired on ABC.
Courtesy of CBS Television

seek censorship through legislation, network executives moved most of their production facilities to California, where Hollywood was responsible for mass appeal, inoffensive sitcoms such as "Mr. Ed," "Gilligan's Island," and "The Beverly Hillbillies."

Although most of these entertainment programs were criticized, news and sports during the politically troubled 1960s were experiencing their own golden age. With satellite and videotape technology, news programs could cover many social and political events. The 1960 televised presidential debate between John Kennedy and Richard Nixon demonstrated to political managers the importance of a candidate's image on television for the first time (Figure 13.20). Vivid images of assassinations, civil rights marches, political speeches, and the Vietnam War had a tremendous impact on viewers who watched them on their home screens. The effect of bringing the outside world's problems into the

home was that the social problems protested in the 1960s could not be ignored.

1970s In this decade, the federal government became much more proactive in regulating television content. Congressional action banned cigarette commercials from television in 1972. (To avoid a similar fate, beer company advertisements never show a person actually drinking.) In that same year, cable became competitive with the broadcast networks when Home Box Office (HBO) started to air second-run movies. On regular television, spin-offs, or shows based on characters from previously broadcast programs, proliferated. For example, the popular sitcoms "All in the Family" and "The Mary Tyler Moore Show" resulted in 15 separate spin-offs and gave independent television production companies, Tandem for "Family" and MTM Productions for "Moore," as much financial clout as the movie studios.

During this era, professional electronic news gathering (ENG) videotape trucks were equipped with all the switching and editing equipment found in a station's control room. Large ENG trucks became common sights outside sports stadiums when games were televised. When the technology became linked with satellites and the equipment grew smaller, local news stations could send news teams to cover events anywhere in a city or the world. To further increase the popularity of home video recording equipment, in the 1980s Sony introduced its Video 8 camera (the palmcorder). It was a small, lightweight camera that used high-quality 8-mm tape.

1980s An economic downturn during this decade caused companies to merge to save money. Capital Cities Communication bought ABC, General Electric purchased NBC's parent company RCA, and Westinghouse purchased CBS. Cost-cutting measures at all three net-

Figure 13.20
During the 1960 presidential campaign, Senator John F. Kennedy and Vice President Richard M. Nixon agreed to have one of their debates televised for the first time. Broadcast from NBC studios in Washington on October 7, 1960, surveys conducted afterward indicated that those who heard the debate on the radio thought Nixon had won, whereas those who watched it on television thought Kennedy came out ahead. Consequently, the visual image of candidates became a serious consideration for politicians and their handlers even though the next televised presidential debate didn't occur until 1976, between Governor Jimmy Carter and President Gerald Ford.
Courtesy of United Press International

works resulted in fewer highly trained journalists in their news divisions. This move allowed Ted Turner's 24-hour news channel, the Cable News Network (CNN), to become the preeminent source for worldwide news. To further protect their investments, television networks, cable companies, and movie studios formed partnerships. In 1985, Australian tabloid mogul Rupert Murdoch bought half control of the movie studio 20th Century Fox. Two years later the Fox Broadcasting Company, a fourth broadcasting network, introduced one night a week of Fox-produced shows to its 105 independent stations. With the success of "The Simpsons" and "Cops," its programming, once dominated by reruns, expanded to include several original productions.

1990s This decade saw the introduction of new cable networks, direct-broadcast satellite channels, and more importantly, the web with information about various programs available from a user's computer. With this competition, viewership of the traditional broadcast networks decreased to 50 percent. Pressure from television critics forced the industry to rate their programs from TV-G for all to TV-MA for mature audiences. V-chips installed in sets allowed adults to electronically supervise shows watched by children. By the end of this era, many watched videos on the web instead of through their television sets.

2000s and Beyond A technological shift as fundamental as the move from black-and-white to color television sets was the transition from analog to digital broadcasting and receiving. Implementation of the switch to high definition, digital television (called HDTV or simply DTV) was delayed several times while regulators worked with manufacturers to make sure the technology was the best possible and the government worked with various agencies and public groups to make sure citizens were informed fully of what would be needed for the transition to digital. Despite all the publicity about the switch, anywhere from one to three million lower-income, elderly, disabled, young, and non-English speaking U.S. households lost their television signal because they watched television via an antenna and failed to get a converter box for the DTV digital signal.

Equally transforming to the history of television is the way viewers can now watch their favorite programs. Seth MacFarlane, the creator of the animated situation comedy "Family Guy" on the Fox network, said, "I think what we're seeing right now is a great cultural shift of how this country watches television." He was referring to the trend toward seeing shows on a computer. More viewers will forego watching programs on their actual television sets and use their computers and smartphones as higher quality wireless internet connections become the norm. The trend is happening now with younger viewers who overwhelmingly watch television shows through internet sources. Can we still call the medium television?

Technical Perspective

Movie studio executives laughed when they first saw television because they never believed that the small, fuzzy black-and-white picture, with its poor audio component, would ever be a serious threat to their industry. What they did not imagine was how resourceful technicians would be in improving the medium. Over the years, cameras, transmission modes, and receivers have been continuously refined.

Cameras

A video camera's controls are similar to those of a still camera, and shot considerations are determined in the same way as those in motion pictures. A camera has a tube or microchip, called a *charge-coupled device* (CCD). It converts the image into an electrical equivalent. When a television operator focuses on a subject with the camera's lens, the picture strikes a layer of photosensitive material consisting of dots, which emit an electrical charge. A dot in a light part of a picture sends a higher charge than one in a darker part of the image. All the electrical charges from the dots strike a target and compose an electrical version of the image in the form of 525 lines (or 636 or 840 lines for non-U.S. systems). An electron gun in the back of the camera generates a steady stream of electrons that scan the target. In the U.S. system, the electron scanning starts with the odd-numbered lines and repeats the process with the even-numbered lines. The two scans take 1/30th of a second, or accomplishes the scanning at a rate of 30 frames a second (Figure 13.21).

Transmission Modes

Television signals can be sent to a home through the air and picked up from rooftop antennae and satellite dishes or by telephone lines and coaxial or fiber optic cable. Originally a home required a large roof-mounted antenna to pick up the audio and video signals sent by a broadcast television station. The sound signal was sent via an FM radio frequency. The pictures came from either VHF or UHF channels on the electromagnetic spectrum. Both VHF and UHF are known as line-of-sight carrier waves. The more powerful VHF stations can usually go around barriers such as buildings, mountains, or large weather systems, but UHF channels are susceptible to interference. The broadcasting of television programs by

VHF and UHF stations first introduced television into people's homes. However, such methods are obsolete since the switch to DTV.

Since the 1970s, consumers have been able to buy large and expensive receiving dishes and point them in a southern direction to capture television images from a satellite in a geosynchronous orbit around the earth. People living in rural communities, where broadcast stations didn't reach and the distance was too far for the local cable company to string wire to their houses, first used these dishes (Figure 13.22). But viewers in cities learned that they could receive hundreds of channels from all over the world and many premium cable networks (e.g. HBO, Showtime, the Playboy Channel, and others) without having to pay a monthly charge. Direct broadcast satellites (DBSs) are the new generation of reception technology that use digital transmission to send hundreds of channels to 18-inch-diameter, window-mounted dishes with high-quality images and sound. For example, DirecTV and the Dish Network have high-powered satellites in space that enable home users to receive hundreds of television channels.

However, most viewers of television don't use an antenna. The most common home connections for television are through cable. Coaxial cable comprises two wires that are separated by insulation. One cable transmits the sound while the other transmits the picture. A cable company pays a fee to receive signals from program producers via a large satellite dish. The coaxial cable connects the operator's facility to a person's home. Depending on the services desired, a home can receive anywhere from 50 to 500 channels. If needed, the cable company supplies a converter box that connects to the television set and changes the cable signal so that the receiver can show the images. However, most new TV sets are "cable-ready," having a

Figure 13.21
Football television coverage greatly improved with the advent of the hanging camera overlooking the action on the field by Skycam. Photograph taken at a football game of University of California, Berkeley vs University of Tennessee in 2007.
Courtesy of Leonard G.

Figure 13.22
Many people living in rural communities are too far away to receive television broadcast signals and find that getting a cable connection is too expensive. Consequently, they are forced to buy satellite dishes. This photograph is a study in contrast. A woman outside Bloomington, Indiana, burns her own trash—an ancient chore—amid two satellite dishes. She explains, "I have two TVs."
Courtesy of Paul Martin Lester

built-in signal converter.

Receivers High-definition digital television (HDTV or DTV) presents pictures as sharp as high-quality photographs—ten times the picture resolution obtained by traditional analog television broadcasts. In addition, the sound is of DVD quality. In order to receive the digital signal, home users either are connected through their cable company or have a set-top box that converts the digital signal from an antenna to an analog version for a TV set.

With digital transmissions, television sets are interactive computers in which users can order shows when they want to view them, watch sporting events from specific cameras on the field, learn more information about a program's topic through the web, order products seen in shows, and so on. In 2009, plasma slim-screen DTV manufacturer Fujitsu offered a 50-inch monitor for $4,499. Today you can buy a television for the same size for less that $700. The ultimate big screens are HD monitors that hang over the playing field of the Dallas Cowboys football stadium (Figure 13.23). The largest in the world—60 yards wide and 20 yards tall—they use 36 million LEDs (Light Emitting Diodes) that show 25,000 square feet of football action. This Mitsubishi Electric Diamond Vision System cost $40 million.

Ethical Perspective

If you let water gush into a kitchen sink for hours, keep all the lights on during the day, or leave the doors and windows wide open at your home, chances are that eventually you will be criticized for such careless behavior. But a television set left on, even when no one is watching, is a cultural standard. Over a 20-year period, the average household will have a television set operating for almost six years.

A 2004 study of 2,600 kids from birth to age seven found that for every hour preschool children watch television, their chances of acquiring a form of attention deficit disorder (ADD) go up to about 10 percent. Another study conducted by the Kaiser Family Foundation found that 36 percent of the 1,000 families surveyed had the TV on all day, and 43 percent of children between four and six years old had a TV in their bedrooms where they could watch programs unsupervised. Not surprisingly, it has been found that children who watch 10 or more hours of television a day have lower reading scores than those who watch less TV. The American Academy of Pediatrics recommends that children under the age of two not watch any television.

It is no coincidence that a television set usually sits in the most comfortable room in a home. Although an impersonal appliance, it evokes the same emotional response as a favorite chair, a soft pillow, or an interesting friend. Television characters become comfortable personalities whom we invite into our lives. Talk-show hosts and nightly newscast announcers look right into the camera and talk directly to us. The television set must remain on—no one wants to offend a friend (Figure 13.24).

Television demands a price for its friendship. The cost is acceptance of the image of the moment as real and representative of society as a whole. Such a belief comes from the cultural notion

Figure 13.23
Dallas Cowboy player Jason Witten towers over the field before a game with the Baltimore Ravens in 2016. With television monitors this large, fans at a game must decide whether to watch the screen or the players on the field. The Cowboys won, 27-17.
Courtesy of Paul Martin Lester

Figure 13.24
In a corner of an apartment that is friendly to cats and flying horses, a news report on a cathode-ray style television set concerned with violence in the Mideast goes largely ignored.
Courtesy of Paul Martin Lester

Ratings Lynn Gross, in her textbook *See/Hear: An Introduction to Broadcasting*, writes that an unnamed television executive once said, "There are only two rules in broadcasting: Keep the ratings as high as possible and don't get in any trouble." The only networks that sell entertainment in the tradition of Hollywood are the premium cable channels. All other networks, especially the "big four," rely on ratings. Shows need not only large audiences but also viewers who are younger, upscale, and likely to buy the advertised products. An emphasis on ratings relegates high-quality broadcasting to the low-rated Public Broadcasting Service (PBS), which depends on government support and viewer and corporate donations.

Stereotypes Expecting television programs to be completely free from some kind of stereotyping of individuals is unreasonable. Someone, somewhere, is bound to object to a media characterization. But because of the enormous scope and influence of television, producers need to be especially sensitive to characterizations that have the potential to cause harm. The problem is that Anglo producers often are unaware of the concerns of those from other cultures. One way of ensuring sensitivity to cultural awareness is by hiring people from diverse cultures. The National Association for the Advancement of Colored People (NAACP) released a report in 2008 that chastised the industry for its Anglo-centric programs. But a surprising development of all the reality television shows is the diversity that can be seen on the programs. Asians, African Americans, and Latinos are often featured contestants in such shows as CBS's "The Amazing Race" and "Survivor," ABC's "Dancing with the Stars," and Fox's "Hell's Kitchen" and "American Idol." However, two exceptions are ABC's "The Bachelor" and "The Bachelorette." According to the *Los Angeles Times* "neither show's main

that education and learning are bitter-tasting medicines that end once you are out of school. Acceptance of this idea comes from laziness and peer acceptance. Television is seen only as a form of entertainment, meant to give a laugh or a thrill. For many, serious, sensitive social issues do not belong on television. Such programming is considered boring, high-minded, and elitist.

Entertainment and education have been merged into something called "edutainment." Programs and commercials all have the same interest level and visual style. Fiction and nonfiction in drama and news shows are jumbled together. Small, insignificant issues become important trends because the medium blows them out of proportion. Vital, important concerns get reduced to a small screen. Simpleminded stereotypes about people and generalizations about communities are reinforced. As much as we love television, it is a medium that we love to hate—especially for its reliance on ratings, stereotyping, and sexual and violent themes.

role has ever been filled with a person of color." However, that color barrier was corrected in 2017 of season 13 when an African American Dallas lawyer Rachel Lindsay offered the red roses.

Sexual and Violent Themes A recent study of viewer behavior estimated that an American child who watches three hours of television a day will see 8,000 murders and some 100,000 other acts of violence by the time she is 12 years old (Figure 13.25). However, television critic Howard Rosenberg makes the point that, although the medium shows thousands of acts of violence, television also displays just as many acts of kindness. "Television violence," Rosenberg writes, "is too simple a solution for violence in the country. It's human nature to seek easy answers to complex questions. Rather than acknowledge the root causes of violence as being deep and complicated, there's a tendency on the part of many to automatically blame television." Sexual aggression and other violent acts committed by members of a culture are partly a result of societal factors—the easy availability of guns, few employment and educational opportunities, and family hardships—and not simply violent portrayals on the screen.

The best defense against gratuitous sex and violence, as well as stereotyping and an emphasis on ratings, is to make intelligent viewing choices. Parents should monitor the viewing habits of their children and explain scenes that disturb them. Offensive shows should not be watched, and uplifting shows should be supported. Because the content of television programs is a result of the collective will of at least part of the culture, each viewer has an ethical and moral responsibility to ensure that positive values are communicated through the media.

Cultural Perspective
Television is a mix of four preceding media: theater, radio, motion pictures, and,

perhaps more importantly, the comic book. From the theater came the familiar stage sets so common in sitcoms. The vaudeville theater also contributed the idea of variety acts. Radio brought its characters, personalities, and story-telling ideas—and the technology to broadcast programs to homes. From motion pictures, television producers learned how to tell their stories in a visual format with the use of multiple cameras and editing techniques. Finally, the comic book gave television its most important concept. Except for made-for-television movies, the basic unit of television isn't an individual program but a continuing series of episodes with the same characters in comfortable surroundings. From week to week and from episode to episode, viewers live with television actors and their problems over a period of several years. Consequently, television is more a medium of personalities than stories. The screen is a poor place for dramatic action and spectacles. But subtle character development reinforced by close-up shots that fill the frame with the face of a friendly actor works well for television.

In his book *TV Genres*, Brian Rose lists 18 different types of programs that have been shown on television since its inauguration: police, detective, western, medical melodramas, science fiction and fantasy, soap opera, made-for-television movies, docudramas, news, documentary reports, sports, game shows, variety shows, talk shows, children's programming, educational and cultural shows, religious programming, and commercials. Any classification scheme is bound to omit some types. For example, legal melodramas, adult programming, reality-based shows, instructional courses sponsored by local colleges, infomercials, home shopping programming, music videos, and web access and services also are important categories.

The reason for the large number of categories for television, as compared

W LINK

Figure 13.25
*(Weblink: http://goo.gl/NvD789)
A violent scene on HBO's "The Sopranos" was one of many plot lines on the critically acclaimed television show.*

with the number of categories for motion pictures, is that television is an intimate medium. Television images come right into the homes of viewers, whereas movies when watched in a theater are generally a one-time experience separate from everyday home life. Consequently, television is able to explore many more commonly held cultural beliefs and values within a much more varied array of formats than motion pictures.

Critical Perspective

Television caused serious declines in all other mass communications media. But the media that survive are those that can adapt to the challenge offered by television. Many magazines in the 1960s and 1970s, such as *Colliers, Saturday Evening Post, Life,* and *Look,* ended publication because national advertisers preferred television. With advertisers tightening their belts since the 2008 economic downturn, present conditions are not much better. The Magazine Publishers of America reported that the industry suffered a 20 percent loss of revenue for the first three months of 2009 compared to the previous year. In response, newsmagazines such as *Time, Newsweek,* and others produce thoughtful, in-depth stories that try to take readers "beyond the headlines" of the 24/7 internet and cable television news channels. Newspapers also suffered severe declines because of television, with some offering web-only presentations and others quitting publication all together.

Polls show that 50 percent of those less than 35 years of age prefer to learn about news events from television. But the news shows they are watching are more likely to be produced by MTV or Comedy Central. Many newspapers have folded, but others have hung on because of chain ownership, a more feature-oriented approach, zoned editions, colorful graphics, and engaging interactive web presentations. Radio quit airing dramatic serials and concentrated on obtaining specialized audiences for specific kinds of music and programs. Motion pictures made their screens larger, their pictures more vivid, the sound clearer, and the seats more comfortable. But more important, Hollywood swallowed its pride and accepted the power of television. It now works with TV producers instead of against them. Most sound stages on movie backlots are devoted to television production.

Commercial television emphasizes mainstream political, economic, and cultural values—and champions consumerism. It is no wonder that television can be both addicting and alienating. A research study released in 2009 found that the more time teenagers watch television, the more depressed they are as older adults. Wars and other personal tragedies reduced to a small screen suddenly segue into a commercial. These curious transitions occur because the bottom line for television executives isn't to sell programs to audiences but to sell audiences to advertisers.

Until that system of funding changes, few innovations will occur in the types of shows the medium offers. But for the first time in its short history, television is getting serious competition from other media, which may fundamentally alter the way television is presented. More people than ever are spending less time watching network offerings, preferring cable programs, DVD and DVR movies, video games, and the web. The reason cable and alternative video sources are successful is that they rely on the diversity of audience interests—not advertisers' preferences.

As we gradually become a society that doesn't write letters and is dependent on visual signs and language, television can remind us, if we let it, that it is an important part of the making of history. More and more, we will be connected to the past by the images we have made. They become what we call our collective memory that will be passed to future generations. Television may be "a vast wasteland," but it allows a lot of space for the creation of memorable visual messages if a culture demands value from it. Viewers need to graze less and learn to settle for more.

TRENDS TO WATCH FOR TELEVISION

The old-fashioned idea of television as a one-way, anesthetizing viewing experience soon will be an anachronism. The days of videotape and DVD presentations may be numbered, as viewers become users able to download any program from web-based menu choices. Videotapes and the rental companies that stocked them are a medium of the past (Figure 13.26).

Television is being replaced by large, flat-screen, high-resolution digital computer monitors in which viewers can watch almost any program or movie made at any time, connect to the web to watch or learn more about a presentation, and talk to a friend over the telephone, all with the same device. LG's 55-inch organic light-emitting diode (OLED) television set weighs less than 17 pounds and provides "the ultimate in vividness, speed and thinness, with true-to-life picture quality, enhanced color accuracy and motion picture quality." Apple TV and Google TV connect a computer to a television monitor for easy viewing of movies and television programs. Sony's EX line has built-in Wi-Fi. Samsung's Smart TVs have a voice-activated command feature. Content providers such as CBS Interactive, Crackle, HBO Go, Hulu, YouTube, Xbox, Zvue, and many others allow users to access current, canceled, and original television shows and movies through computers, smartphones, tablets, and television sets, (Figure 13.27). Since 2012 Netflix and Amazon have produced several original popular and critically acclaimed series providing competition to HBM and Showtime. For Netflix, hits

Figure 13.26
An array of obsolete DVDs become artwork when attached to a chain link fence next to Fingerprints, a music store in Long Beach, California that still sells vinyl records.
Courtesy of Paul Martin Lester

include "House of Cards," "Love," and "Stranger Things," while Amazon has produced "Transparent," Sneaky Pete," and "Catastrophe."

In addition, 3-D televisions has gained in popularity because more 3-D programming is offered. For some systems, users do not have to wear glasses. ESPN telecasts more than 200 sporting events in 3-D. A Nintendo video game console, smartphones from LG and HTC, and television sets from Toshiba, Panasonic, and Sony are glasses-free. The average price for TV sets is about $1,000 with seven million purchased in 2012. In addition, the availability of 3-D digital cameras for consumers should increase sales of 3-D television sets.

As videotaped movies and programs for rent or sale are a quaint anachronism, so too will be DVD rentals. Blockbuster teamed with TiVo and the Dish Network to deliver movies on demand—users could collect and watch their favorite shows from the comfort of their homes on television, computers, game players

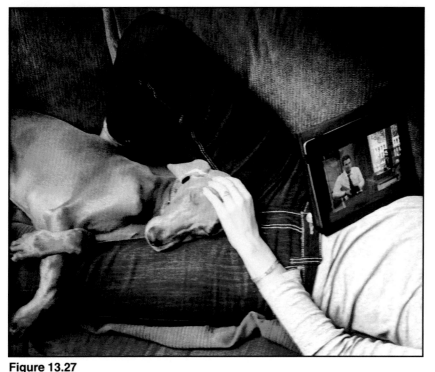

Figure 13.27
Nothing could be finer than watching TV with your Weimaraner on an Apple iPad 2 whenever you decide is the right time.
Courtesy of Paul Martin Lester

such as Xbox, or on a smartphone.

Since many people carry and use video and digital cameras as part of their smartphones, news organizations can now show dramatic video of tragic events shot by amateurs. Reality-based television programs and electronic video monitoring systems are common uses for the equipment. Security systems at homes and businesses record the actions of every passerby. Police officers have digital cameras in their patrol cars to monitor the actions of those detained or arrested. News teams hide cameras in their clothing to record illegal practices for the visually oriented nightly newscasts.

Sometimes gruesome shootings during convenience store robberies captured by digital monitoring equipment are aired on newscasts. Made possible by the digital revolution, the spread of sensational news is a chief concern of many of television's social critics. An upside is the monitoring of the bad behavior of military personnel, police officials, and celebrities by so-called citizen journal-

ists. For example, military excesses in Syria, American troops urinating on dead insurgents in Afghanistan, police officers opening fire on suspects, and a racist rant from a comedian have been captured by individuals with smartphones and uploaded to YouTube for the world to watch.

The 68th Primetime Emmy Awards in 2016, one of the most prestigious given to television programs, is another indication of traditional television's downfall. Out of 156 nominations, programs shown on traditional broadcast networks (ABC, CBS, NBC, Fox, and PBS) were nominated 34 times, basic cable channel shows (FX, AMC, Comedy Central, BBC America, Lifetime, and USA) were nominated 51 times, pay cable channel shows (HBO and Showtime) were nominated 48 times, and web-based providers (Netflix and Amazon) were nominated 23 times. HBO led the entire field with 40 which is significant, but the headline should be the gains in web programming.

With cable as a model for future programming, television channels will necessarily become as content-specific as specialized magazines. NBC, CBS, ABC, and Fox can survive the competition from cable networks by sticking with a concept originated by the early motion picture studios—the star system. The big four can differentiate from all the other channels (as many as 1,500) by establishing a stable of well-known performers who are cast in familiar situations and dramas, always the most successful television strategy.

KEY TERMS FROM THIS CHAPTER
15 minutes of fame • Ad-lib • Analog • Big Four • Coaxial cable • Digital • Electron scanner • Federal Communications Commission (FCC) • HIV/AIDS • Iconoscope • On-demand • Pilot • Screen Actors Guild (SAG) • Situation comedy • Soap operas • Tabloid • Vaudeville theater • Writers Guide of America (WGA)

14 Computers

Computers are useless.
They can only give you answers.

Pablo Picasso, 1881–1973
PAINTER, SCULPTOR,
& POET

Two memorable characters in motion picture history never complained about long working hours, makeup sessions, or the quality of the catered lunches. That's because they never spoke for themselves, were never paid, and never ate anything. The other actors never even saw them during filming—not until the movie was finished.

One was a gentle, compassionate, and positive living force. The other was a violent, insensitive, and cold-blooded killer. The smiling, rippling water snake, termed "water weenie" by the crew, that was featured in the motion picture *The Abyss* (1989) and the murderous T-1000 liquid-alloy robot in *Terminator 2: Judgment Day* (1991) introduced theater audiences not only to memorable visual messages but also to computer images.

The success of those computer creatures, one critically and the other economically, was attributed to director James Cameron, an innovator in the use of CGI (omputer-generated images). When he needed to show the last moments of those who lost their lives on an ocean liner, he didn't use only live actors. Cameron employed the knowledge he had learned from his previous motion pictures by creating computer imagery for his movie *Titanic*, which earned 11 Academy Awards including Best Director and Best Picture in 1998. In 2012 a 3-D version was released. Criticized for his effort, he responds, "When we converted *Titanic* to 3-D, it took us 60 weeks, $18 million, and 300 artists to do it right" (Figure 14.1). No matter. Cameron will be more admired for breaking new ground in merging the analog and digital worlds with his performance capture, 3-D, out-of-this-world experience, *Avatar* (2009) (Figure 14.2).

Figure 14.1
The one-sheet poster for the 2012 re-release of Titanic, *the 3-D version highlights the ill-fated lovers. James Cameron said, "Doing it in 3-D makes it seem more real, more visceral, more immediate. The drama, the romance, the jeopardy—all of those things will be increased by the 3-D." Cameron was wise not to work on a sequel.*
© 20th Century Fox/Courtesy of the Everett Collection

Figure 14.2
From left, Sigourney Weaver, Joel Moore, director James Cameron, and Sam Worthington watch a scene on a computer monitor on the set of Avatar.
Mark Fellman/TM & © 20th Century Fox. All rights reserved.
Courtesy of the Everett Collection

Born in 1954 in Kapuskasing, Ontario, Canada, about 700 miles north of Detroit, Cameron had an early fascination with science and movies. When his family moved to Fullerton, California, in 1971, he started making short films while attending school. After he saw *Star Wars* in 1977, Cameron was inspired to write a science fiction script. He raised the funds needed with two friends to make the little-seen, 12-minute science fiction thriller *Xenogenesis* (1978) (Figure 14.3).

The care taken with the special effects piqued the curiosity of director and producer Roger Corman, who hired Cameron as a model maker. Two years later he was promoted to art director for Corman's big budget movie, *Battle Beyond the Stars*, which starred Richard Thomas, George Peppard, and Robert Vaughn (Figure 14.4). After the director hired for the horror film *Piranha II: The Spawning* (1981) quit unexpectedly, Cameron was asked to take over in his directorial, but forgettable, debut.

Although certainly not an auspicious beginning, Cameron's career moves following this start were the envy of Hollywood. In quick succession he was responsible for the low-budget *The Terminator* (1984) that earned more than $78 million. The sequel to Ridley Scott's *Alien* (1979), *Aliens* (1986), that was a critical and box office success, *The Abyss* (1989) that won an Academy Award for Best Visual Effects, *Terminator 2: Judgment Day* (1991) that smashed box office records around the world and won four Oscars, and then the motion picture that inspired his "King of the World" moment at the ceremony, *Titanic* (1997), that is estimated to have made more than $1.8 billion in global box office receipts and won a record-tying 14 Oscar nominations (Figure 14.5).

The lessons learned in the making of *The Abyss* and *Terminator 2* taught Cameron that any situation with any type of character that could be imagined could be realized on the big screen. Furthermore, the success he experienced with his CGI-enhanced motion pictures taught others—writers, directors, and producers—that with good stories and experienced actors, movies with special effects could be great successes.

The 140-minute *Abyss* was a moderate box office success about an underwater oil rig crew led by actors Mary Elizabeth Mastrantonio and Ed Harris. After the military recruits the aquanauts to retrieve a nuclear weapon from a damaged submarine, the plot twists when they discover an underwater civilization at the bottom of the ocean.

Computer-generated imaging technology took a breathtaking leap forward in the form of a creature that investigates the crew's vessel. Computer innovator Mark Dippé called the shimmering, water-filled pseudopod "one of the most significant pieces of computer animation done up until that time." The water entity is an astonishingly realistic water snake that playfully mimics the startled faces of Mastrantonio and Harris. When Mastrantonio pokes a finger into the being's "face," the computer-generated rippling effect adds to the realism of the moment (Figure 14.6). Dennis Muren of George Lucas's special effects company, Industrial Light and Magic (ILM), who worked on the effects for his *Star Wars* movie, created the "water weenie," which helped win him an Academy Award.

In the first *Terminator* a murderous cyborg played by the former California Governor Arnold ("I'll be back") Schwarzenegger is transported to the past from the future by advanced computers that have taken control of the world from their human programmers. The robot's mission is to kill a woman who is to give birth to a son who will eventually lead a revolution against the machines. He's unsuccessful. In *Terminator 2: Judgment Day*, Linda Hamilton trains her son, portrayed by Edward Furlong, to take a leadership role in the

Figure 14.3
(Weblink: http://goo.gl/osPNqX) Xenogenesis is a peculiar condition in which descendants are nothing like their parents just as James Cameron's first film, Xenogenesis is nothing like Star Wars.

W LINK

Figure 14.4
(Weblink: http://goo.gl/Gh2wsF) Roger Corman is one of the most prolific and respected independent filmmakers in Hollywood. Along with James Cameron, he started the movie careers of Francis Ford Coppola, Ron Howard, Martin Scorsese, and Jonathan Demme. In 2009 he received an honorary Academy Award.

W LINK

Figure 14.5
(Weblink: http://goo.gl/A6EoqC) During the 1998 Oscar ceremony actor and presenter Warren Beatty got it right and correctly announced James Cameron's win as Best Director for Titanic.

Figure 14.6
In the movie The Abyss, *computer-generated image technology comes of age in the form of a lifelike pseudopod sent from a race of underwater creatures to investigate the crew of an underwater oilrig and to mimic the face of actress Mary Elizabeth Mastrantonio. Created by the artists at George Lucas's Industrial Light and Magic facility, it is considered the first computer-generated character in motion picture history.*
© 20th Century Fox/Courtesy of the Everett Collection

**W
LINK
Figure 14.7**
*(Weblink:
http://goo.gl/vHQxWB)
Actor Robert Patrick had trouble finding roles after playing the T-1000 robot in Terminator 2: Judgment Day because he was typecast as a villain.*

upcoming rebellion. But images of a nuclear war eventually drive her insane, and she is committed to a mental hospital. Meanwhile, in the post-nuclear-war future, her now-grown son sends a reformatted Schwarzenegger robot back to the past. But this time it is programmed to protect the boy (himself) and his mother because the evil computers (are you following this?) have sent a new and improved model—the liquid metal, metamorphic cyborg, played in human form by Robert Patrick—to kill the family and anyone else who gets in its way (Figure 14.7). The T-1000 chrome robot in *Terminator 2* was one of 45 special CGI effects used in the blockbuster movie (Figure 14.8). Some of the most riveting scenes occur in the insane asylum

in which the T-1000 character assumes the shape of a section of linoleum floor, makes his hands turn into deadly swords, has his "face" sliced in two by the force of Schwarzenegger's weapon (but it quickly reconstitutes itself), and changes back and forth between a uniformed police officer, a hospital security guard, and the chrome-colored, metal monster.

The over-the-top visual effect, however, is when the cyborg oozes through the bars of a security gate to attack Hamilton, Furlong, and Schwarzenegger. Filming Patrick and the bars separately, a computer model of the actor's face was matched with the live action film to create the through-the-bars scene. The movie, unlike any other that used CGI

Figure 14.8
Fire can't stop him. A view of the T-1000 cyborg character in the movie Terminator 2: Judgment Day. *Note how the use of light and shadow aids in creating the illusion of depth for the computer-generated images.*
Mary Evans/Ronald Grant/The Everett Collection

woke up Hollywood executives to the potential of computer graphics.

After *Titanic* he created and wrote the television series "Dark Angel" for the Fox network, about a genetically enhanced young woman who works for a messenger service in Seattle after a magnetic bomb destroys every computer in the world. It was canceled after two seasons. In 2002 Cameron helped create a television documentary, "Expedition: Bismarck," that told of the demise of the famous battleship. The next year he produced an IMAX documentary titled *Volcanoes of the Deep Sea* and directed *Ghosts of the Abyss*, a 3-D IMAX semi-documentary that takes a cam-

era around and into the actual *Titanic* where they find, well, ghosts. Although he has personally terminated his fascination with the Terminator character, the franchise lives on with *Terminator 3: Rise of the Machines* (2003), *Terminator Salvation* (2009), and the Fox television series "Terminator: The Sarah Connor Chronicles." Continuing his fascination with the visual cue of depth (See Chapter 2), Cameron's 2009 futuristic film *Avatar*, shown with a 3-D system he helped develop, was one of the most ambitious and expensive performance capture animated films ever produced. The movie cost more than $500 million to make, but earned box office receipts of more than

Figure 14.9
(Weblink http://goo.gl/aWchex) Simulation of a Two-Gyro gravity-gradient Attitude Control System is a title and with content only an engineer would love.

Figure 14.10
(Weblink: http://goo.gl/6MvYrb) Although the degree of artificial intelligence the HAL computer exhibits is futuristic, look at the computer monitors in this clip to see the unsophisticated 1960s style of graphics.

Figure 14.11
(Weblink: http://goo.gl/AL4yjd) Six years after 2001: A Space Odyssey, *computer graphics as seen on monitors had not advanced that much as noted in this scene from* Star Wars.

Figure 14.13
(Weblink: http://goo.gl/B2zVp6) In this clip from The Last Starfighter, *the commander voices a memorable phrase that ranks with "Rosebud" in* Citizen Kane.

$1.3 *billion* worldwide. There are plans for four *Avatar* sequels, tentatively titled *Avatar 2, Avatar 3, Avatar 4*, and *Avatar 5* until 2025. Guess he really likes that Avatar name. For a National Geographic special he piloted a submersible submarine seven miles below the surface of the Pacific Ocean to the Mariana Trench, the lowest point on Earth. In his mind, Cameron links his quest to discover new worlds and moviemaking. "I think it's the explorer's job to go and be at the remote edge of human experience and then come back and tell that story. So I don't see them as that separately." Sounds like a real-life *Abyss*.

Although many directors have produced motion pictures with astounding special effects since James Cameron's *The Abyss*, the field of CGI would not be where it is today without his groundbreaking work.

CGI: A Brief History

The history of computer-generated images for film goes back to 1961 when a student at the Massachusetts Institute of Technology (MIT), Ivan Sutherland, created a computer-drawing program called Sketchpad that allowed a user with a light pen to draw simple shapes on a computer screen. Two years later Ed Zajac, a researcher for Bell Laboratories (now Lucent Technologies), produced one of the first computer-generated motion pictures—a simulation of a trip around the Earth that a satellite might take (Figure 14.9).

The first major motion picture that included any computer graphic effects was the 1968 Stanley Kubrick classic, *2001: A Space Odyssey.* Simple lines and letters on monitors controlled by the HAL computer were the best computer graphics could achieve at that time (Figure 14.10). Eight years later the robotic fantasy thriller *Futureworld* presented a brief line drawing of a human head on a computer terminal and in 1977 technology hadn't advanced much further

when George Lucas directed *Star Wars*, summarized in the original trailer as "A story of a boy, a girl, and a universe." The movie presented simple computerized plans for the Death Star displayed on a large screen during a briefing about battle strategies to star fighters. All of the fight scenes seen in outer space in the original release were made with models (Figure 14.11).

The first movie to feature the extensive use of computer graphics was the Disney box office disappointment *Tron* (1982). About 20 minutes of the film, much of it during the Light Cycle race, was produced with computers (Figure 14.12). *Newsweek, Time,* and *Rolling Stone* hailed computer graphics as an important advance in motion picture production. However, the technological benefits were delayed because the public wasn't interested in a story about a computer programmer who was trapped inside a computer. Nevertheless, John Lasseter, who later went on to become CEO of Pixar Animation Studios, said, "Without *Tron*, there would be no *Toy Story*."

In 1984, *The Last Starfighter* was praised for its digital spacecraft dogfights (Figure 14.13). But again, as in *Tron*, the public wasn't interested in a teenage video game player who saves the universe. Two years later the creative genius Jim Henson, best known for his Muppets and George Lucas created the visually stunning fantasy *Labyrinth* that featured computer-generated effects that helped propel the story line.

If the plots sometimes suffered, at least the technology improved. In 1990 Arnold Schwarzenegger starred in the science fiction action thriller *Total Recall*. It has the distinction of being the last major Hollywood movie in which most of the special effects were achieved through miniature models. An exception was an X-ray security view of Schwarzenegger's skeleton. The 42-second effect created by MetroLight Studios

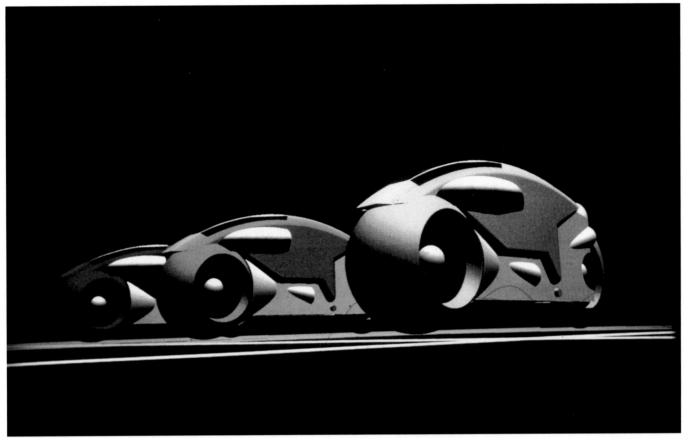

Figure 14.12
With industrial designer Syd Mead as visual consultant for the motion picture Tron *(1982), the Light Cycle racers had a futuristic look. Mead also worked on another science fiction classic,* Blade Runner *(1982) for which he won an Academy Award.*
Courtesy of Walt Disney Pictures/Mary Evans/Ronald Grant/Everett Collection

helped win a Special Achievement Academy Award for the film (Figure 14.14). A year later in a Michael Jackson music video for his song "Black or White," the seamless and breathless transition from one diverse face to another using morphing software at the end of the six-minute-plus film was expertly maneuvered by director John Landis (Figure 14.15). The effect was repeated in a 2012 episode of "Glee."

Two years after the release of *Terminator 2*, a motion picture based on a novel by Michael Crichton and directed by Steven Spielberg astounded moviegoers with CGI dinosaurs on the screen so believable that many thought they had to live somewhere in this world. Stan Winston, the late great makeup and effects artist won an Academy Award for Best Visual Effects for *Jurassic Park* (1993) (Figure 14.16).

Following Cameron's sinking of the *Titanic*, Pixar filmmaker John Lasseter was executive producer for the 2001 hit *Monsters, Inc.* The movie featured several innovations in computer animation technology, mostly related to how hair and clothing were rendered. The action sequence within the Harryhausen restaurant, named in tribute to Ray Harryhausen, a pioneer in movie animated effects, is a stand-out. The fur of Sulley, an 800-pound monster and the clothing of the human girl Boo were simulated to a level not previously achieved in cartoon animation. One of the reasons computer cartoons of the past had a plastic, unrealistic look, Lasseter explained, was because "the more organic something is, the harder it is to do." Despite advances in computer power, animators re-created each strand of Sulley's fur coat—about -three million of them (Figure 14.17).

Figure 14.14
(Weblink: http://goo.gl/sxdnjy) Who knew Arnold Schwarzenegger's bones were the same size as anyone else?

Figure 14.15
(Weblink: http://goo.gl/rqxoka) The 11-minute music video of Michael Jackson's "Black or White" turns memorable at about the five-minute, 30-second mark when morphing technology is used in an aesthetically pleasing and seamless way.

Figure 14.16
*(Weblink:
http://goo.gl/UDYavP)*
Unlike the promise that CGI could do no wrong as touted by the producers and fans of Disney's Tron, the dinosaurs in Jurassic Park wowed audiences and helped make the movie a blockbuster which furthered the progress of CGI.

Figure 14.17
The work required to render Sully's fur through computer software was well worth the time and expense to maintain the illusion of reality within an unreal animated world.
Monster's Inc., James P. Sullivan (aka 'Sulley'), 2001/Courtesy of the Everett Collection

It took two years to write the software required for the clothing used in the film in order to achieve a natural and lifelike appearance. Lasseter wanted theatergoers to say, "Oh, we know it's not real, but it sure does look real."

Such realism comes at a high cost. The skills necessary to render believable CGI effects to an ever-increasingly sophisticated audience are enormously expensive to produce. Before *Avatar*, director Sam Rami had the distinction of making one of the most expensive motion picture in the history of Hollywood, *Spider-Man 3* (2007) (Figure 14.18). Largely because of the extensive use of CGI effects, the film cost more than $350 million. The time needed to render complex digital effects adds to the cost. In 2017 the usual price to make a CGI-heavy movie is about $200 million as with such films as *The Fate of the Furious*, Pir*ates of the Caribbean: Dead Men Tell No Tales*, and *Transformers: The Last Knight*. The opening CGI tracking shot in *Hugo* (2011), Martin Scorsese's 3-D adaptation of Brian Selznick's graphic novel shows a sweeping view of Paris and ends at the Gare Montparnasse train station where most of the action of the movie takes place. The short scene took about a year to complete with more than 1,000 computers needed to process *each frame* (Figure 14.19).

Animated characters such as Dobby, the house elf in *Harry Potter and the Chamber of Secrets* (2002) and Gollum/Smeagol in Peter Jackson's *The Lord of the Rings* trilogy were created by vastly different methods. Dobby was manufactured through traditional object animation techniques by George Lucas's Industrial Light and Magic using a rubber model and the stop-motion technique (See Chapter 10). Director Chris Columbus "wanted Dobby to be a character that felt very real and one that the audience would fall in love with." For the *Rings* characters, Andy Serkis interacted with his fellow cast members wearing a suit covered with tiny dots that were picked up with a digital camera, creating a more lifelike effect with the performance capture process. Serkis' performance as Caesar the head ape in *Rise of the Planet of the Apes* (2011) led many to conclude that it is inevitable that an actor will receive an Academy Award without his likeness ever being seen in a motion picture (Figure 14.20). Andy Serkis shows the same acting chops in the 2017 sequel, *War for the Planet of the Apes*. To date, he has not been nominated for an Oscar.

Determining whether any image—for print or screen media—is a picture of a live action actor or whether it is a completely computer-generated fabrication is almost at the point in which the difference is impossible to detect. Within the context of entertainment, viewers who want to be thrilled, writers and directors who want to turn their imaginations into screen reality, and producers who don't want to hire so many actors wait for the next generation of CGI with great anticipation. Agents, actors, stunt personnel, prop people, makeup artists, and even caterers are among those who will not be thrilled by such advances.

COMPUTERS AND THE SIX PERSPECTIVES

The renowned artist Pablo Picasso growled his contempt of computers in the quotation that starts this chapter in 1968, the year the semiconductor chip company Intel was founded. Picasso, consequently, only knew of computers as large, vacuum-tube-filled mainframes that used paper punch cards to input data. They were not tools for artists. Intel would later create chips that revolutionized the personal computer and used within Apple, Dell, HP, Lenovo (formally IBM), and other machines. Today, Picasso would no doubt explore and embrace the freedom and innovation made possible by digital technology.

Figure 14.18
(Weblink: http://goo.gl/euBSYA) Although most critics panned the film, when all the box office sales were added from showings around the world, Spider-Man 3 *earned almost $1 billion largely because of heavy CGI scenes as shown in this clip.*

Figure 14.19
Weblink: goo.gl/FQ7QpK) The train station tracking shots shown in this Hugo *clip get their charm from the smooth moves of the camera, rich lighting, filled compositions, and CGI mastery.*

Figure 14.20
The life-like, human expression on the face of the cartoon animated character Caesar in Rise of the Planet of the Apes *is a result of the high quality acting of Andy Serkis and performance capture technology.*

Personal Perspective

Science fiction author and scientist Arthur C. Clarke once said, "Any significantly advanced technology is indistinguishable from magic." Computers, with the ability to create, access, and manipulate words, numbers, and images, certainly qualify as magical machines. The near future will be known for the way in which words and pictures are used together as equal partners in the communication process—a Convergent Era, in which all forms of communication are included through web access. Whatever the new era is called, computer technology clearly has grown to such an extent that imagining a world without them is difficult. From buying groceries to watching a movie, innovations brought about by the computer affect our lives for better or worse.

Historical Perspective

The history of computers has its roots with complex calculators. In 1901 under the waters off the Greek island of Antikythera, a mysterious object was found. It took almost 100 years for researchers to discover the secret of this barnacle-encrusted metal tool—it is the first mechanical calculator able to accurately predict various astronomical positions (Figure 14.21). Members of an ancient civilization created it more than 2,100 years ago. One scientist said that the device was "more valuable than the Mona Lisa."

Charles Babbage of London is known as "the founder of computing." In 1822 he designed a steam-powered, program-controlled calculator he called a "difference engine." He claimed that his machine would mechanize the thought process itself. The huge, noisy contraption had pulleys and wheels that were used to make calculations that weighed about 15 tons. Trouble is, he never completed it. That's because he switched

Figure 14.21
A fragment of the 2,100-year-old Antikythera Mechanism is an astonishingly advanced device fabricated to calculate the position and movements of the sun, moon, and planets. With as many as 72 gears, the calculator was more complex than most intricate clocks.
Courtesy of Marsyas

gears and started working on an improved design he named the "analytical engine." His new plan was theoretically capable of storing 1,000 numbers of 50 decimal places each on punched cards, but once again it never got much beyond the lab bench stage. Nevertheless, his assistant, Augusta Ada King, Countess of Lovelace, daughter of the poet Lord Byron, is considered the first computer programmer because she wrote instructions for Babbage's engine and foresaw that the machine had capabilities beyond calculations. She also invented the term "artificial intelligence." In 1991 a difference engine was constructed based

on Babbage's design and successfully completed complex calculations beyond the capabilities of most pocket calculators. Babbage's machine and his brain are preserved at the Science Museum in London (Figure 14.22). In 2011 Science Museum officials announced a 10-year, multimillion-dollar project to recreate Babbage's analytical engine.

Herman Hollerith, an American, had more success with his device. He invented the first electric calculator, which was used for the enormous task of compiling the decennial U.S. Census. Hollerith invented an electromechanical system that could count and sort data from punched

Figure 14.22
Charles Babbage was never able to secure the funding to build his calculating machine during his lifetime. However, the Science Museum of London built a mechanism in 1991 based on the plans of his "Difference Engine No. 2" that could perform calculations with numbers up to 31 digits—more advanced than the average pocket calculator.
Courtesy of Geni

cards. Hollerith's device was first used for the 1890 Census (Figure 14.23). After favorable reviews, orders came from all over the world from governments, banks, insurance companies, and other institutions that required quick tabulations. In 1911, Hollerith had too much business to handle alone so he merged his company with three others to form the Computing-Tabulating-Recording Company (CTR).

A salesperson for the National Cash Register Company, Thomas J. Watson needed a job and a good lawyer—he was found guilty as part of a conspiracy to run other cash register companies out of business. Luckily, an Appeals Court

ordered a new trial, but it never took place. Despite his conviction, a friend of Watson's gave him a job as general manager of CRT and when the president of CTR died, Watson was named to replace him (Figure 14.24).

In an effort to expand its business, in 1924 CTR changed its name to International Business Machines (IBM). The company grew tremendously during World War II and became the world's top producer of office equipment and data-processing machines for government and business applications (Figure 14.25). After Watson retired, his son, Thomas Watson, Jr., succeeded him.

IBM introduced its personal com-

Figure 14.23
Herman Hollerith's tabulating machine with a sorting box added later as seen in the Computer History Museum, Mountain View, California. Information collected through interviews and other means was transferred to punch cards that were then input into Hollerith's device.
Courtesy of Adam Schuster

puter in 1975. Called the 5100 Portable Computer, it weighed about 50 pounds, came in 12 models, and cost as much as $19,975 (more than $85,000 today). Not surprisingly, only about 15,000 were sold. Consequently, Watson never thought computers for home users would be profitable. However, after Apple's success with its Apple II personal computer released in 1977, IBM officials decided to try the personal computer market again. In 1981, it introduced the IBM PC, which was an instant hit. Through the company's worldwide distribution system, it sold more than

800,000 computers the first year. In 1984 the PCjr nicknamed "Peanut" was IBM's first attempt to sell to the home computer market. It was named "One of the biggest flops in the history of computing." It was discontinued the next year.

Nevertheless, the letters "PC," standing for "personal computer," became synonymous with IBM desktop computing. IBM also allowed other companies to use its computer technological specifications to make their own products. The "clones" spread further the concept of the PC for home and office users. In 2004 IBM sold its personal computer business to

Figure 14.24
Thomas Watson, Sr.
Courtesy of Paul C. Lasewicz

Figure 14.25

Thomas Watson, Jr. (left) poses with President Jimmy Carter, January 20, 1978.
Courtesy of the White House

a Chinese company, the Lenovo Group, essentially ending their interest in the consumer computer market.

In a throwback to the early years of IBM computing, in 2011 the company introduced an artificial-intelligence computer system named Watson in dramatic fashion by challenging two of the most successful winners of the game show "Jeopardy!" Ken Jennings and Brad Rutter played a two-game match against Watson—it won by more than $50,000. The trouncing made Jennings remark, "I for one welcome our new computer overlords."

Before computers could be popular with the public, they had to have their own high-quality monitors, be small enough to conveniently fit on a desk, be relatively low in cost, and contain software programs that were useful and fun. An important innovation for computers, which eventually led to visual displays, was the combination of computer and the cathode-ray tube (CRT). At Manchester University in England, F. C. Williams and colleagues in 1948 used CRTs similar to those in television sets for their Manchester Mark I computer. The last room-sized computer of note that used vacuum tubes was the UNIVAC (for UNIVersal Automatic Computer). The SAGE (for Semi-Automatic Ground Environment) military project in 1955 expanded the computer monitor concept to include a handheld controller that later became known as a mouse. An operator seated in front of a large CRT monitor could aim a light pen at a specific point on the screen. The computer would then supply information about that plane and its location (Figure 14.26).

Early room-sized computers were hot and heavy because they operated through hundreds of integrated glass vacuum tubes that often burned out and had to be regularly replaced. One of the most important discoveries in the 20th century was announced to the public

Figure 14.26
The SAGE computer system was designed as an early warning defense system in the event of enemy attack. It was one of the first to use a monitor. Science fiction author Larry Niven (The Mote in God's Eye with Jerry Pournelle) admires a SAGE operator's console, at the Computer History Museum in Mountain View, California. Note the pistol-like device attached to a heavy cord under plexiglass below the monitor. That item was a precursor to a computer mouse.
Courtesy of Roland Dobbins

in 1948 with almost no coverage by the media. A team of scientists working for Bell Telephone Laboratories invented the transistor—a semiconductor with the same function as a vacuum tube but made of silicon, the chief component of sand. As opposed to tubes, silicon transistors didn't get hot, cost pennies to make, and could be as small as a pencil's eraser (Figure 14.27). In 1956 the Nobel Prize in physics was awarded to the three-person Bell inventor team of William Shockley, Walter Braittain, and John Bardeen. One of its first applications was for hearing aid amplifiers in 1953. The next year transistor radios were introduced.

In 1958, Jack Kilby with Robert

Noyce came up with the idea of linking several transistors together on an integrated circuit board. This innovation allowed complex computer operations to occur in a vastly reduced space and at much faster speeds (Figure 14.28). In 1970 Kilby received the National Medal of Science in a ceremony at the White House for his important invention. Because of transistors linked on circuit boards, room-sized computers, commonly referred to as mainframes, were soon replaced with much smaller, faster, and cheaper machines (Figure 14.29).

At the time when computer companies such as IBM were concentrating on business computers, an underground amateur computer movement of in-

Figure 14.28
In 1958 while working for Texas Instruments, Jack Kilby along with Robert Noyce linked numerous transistors on a circuit board to give computers added speed and reliability.
Courtesy of International Business Machines, Inc.

Figure 14.27
Advances in computer technology reduced machine cost and size and increased machine power and speed. The most important advances were from the vacuum tube (left) to the transistor (center) to the tiny silicon chip (the small square speck).
Courtesy of International Business Machines, Inc.

terested hobbyists and entrepreneurs gathered to promote the technology. Many members of computer clubs wanted to build their own machines. To fill that need, a Floridian dentist, Edward Roberts, sold computer kits to amateurs. A *Popular Electronics* cover story in 1971 about his Altair 8800 computer helped launch the personal computer industry (Figure 14.30). After the article was published, Roberts immediately received thousands of orders. However, the computer was a simple design that could be used only to play uncomplicated games. To become a more fully functional machine, it needed a built-in program that would allow the computer to understand commands from a user. When Harvard student Paul Allen saw the article about the computer at a newsstand, he was intrigued and showed it to his friend, freshman William Henry "Bill" Gates. They called Roberts to offer their ser-

Figure 14.29
Look closely around the 5-minute mark on the pocket watch and notice the small silicon chip circuit boards. They greatly reduced the size and cost of computers without sacrificing speed or accuracy.
Courtesy of International Business Machines, Inc.

vices in writing a basic program. Roberts hired Allen, and Gates dropped out of college to become a freelance computer software writer.

Allen and Gates eventually teamed up and formed the Microsoft Corporation, which became America's largest and most successful software company. Their first major client was IBM, who made one of the poorest business decisions in history when it gave the contract for writing its operating system to Microsoft instead of creating its own. Microsoft's Windows operating software and graphical interface, which many thought resembled Apple's user-friendly appearance, was popular mainly because at that time about 97 percent of all the desktop computers in the world were IBM or their clones. The two were paid a royalty for every PC that used the software, making them rich beyond their dreams.

Allen left Microsoft in 1983 to pursue other business interests. With his stock in Microsoft, Allen started Charter Communications Corp., the nation's third-largest cable operator, and bought the NBA's Portland Trailblazers and the NFL's Seattle Seahawks. *The Chronicle of Philanthropy* in its 2011 list of the "50 Most Generous Donors" put Allen in third place with $335 million given to arts and cultural organizations. He has been named on the list for the past 10 years (Figure 14.31).

Gates stayed with Microsoft to become at one point the richest person in the world, personally worth an estimated $60 billion. According to *Forbes* magazine he is currently the second richest in the world (Figure 14.32). In 2000 he started working part-time for Microsoft and devoted more of his efforts to the Bill & Melinda Gates Foundation, a charity organization founded with his wife. It is the fourth largest private foundation in the world. In 2008 at the age of 52, Gates retired from Microsoft to concentrate more on his charity work. It

Figure 14.30
The Altair 8800 computer with an 8-inch floppy disk. The device led Bill Gates and Paul Allen to eventually found the Microsoft Corporation.
Courtesy of Michael Holley

is estimated that the Foundation donates $1.5 billion annually for such causes as HIV/AIDS research, vaccines and immunizations, assistance to the poor, agricultural development, and educational programs worldwide.

Inspired by Roberts's Altair homemade computer, the Homebrew Computer Club was formed and located in Silicon Valley (named for the many computer companies established south of San Francisco). Homebrew started with about 30 members who met for the first time in 1975 near Stanford University. Soon its membership was more than 500. Present at the first meeting was a young computer genius named Stephen Wozniak.

"Woz," as his friends know him, built a transistorized calculator when he was 13 years old. Although he attended colleges in Colorado and California, he dropped out. No worries. He obtained a job with the Hewlett-Packard (HP)

Figure 14.31
Paul Allen and the Underthinkers perform at the Allen Institute for Brain Science's 10th Anniversary Gala, 2013.
Courtesy of James W. Larsen, Jr.

Figure 14.32
Wearing matching outfits, Bill and Melinda Gates are spotted during their visit to the Oslo Opera House in June, 2009.

Company, recognized as the first Silicon Valley computer company. Woz helped design mainframe computers for HP. In 1971, he met Steven Jobs, a 16-year-old, long-haired, and somewhat shy HP summer employee. Jobs left HP to attend Reed College in Portland, Oregon. Later, Jobs got a job as a technician for the video games company Atari. After a life-changing trip to India, Jobs met up again with Woz at a Homebrew meeting. In the meantime, Wozniak had made a simple computer that could be plugged into a television set to play video games. Jobs immediately searched for funding so the computer could be marketed to the public. He sold his Volkswagen bus, borrowed $5,000 from a friend and additional funds from multimillionaire A.C. "Mike" Markkula, and on that basis the two Steves formed the Apple Computer Company (Figure 14.33).

In 1975, the two introduced their Apple I computer, but only sold 175 machines at $500 each (about $2,000 today) (Figure 14.34). While Wozniak worked on a more sophisticated model, Jobs cured his shyness and found additional financial backers. In 1977, the Apple II computer was introduced and became an enormous success. In the first year, sales of the $2,000 computer ($7,500 today) totaled $775,000. When Apple's stock went public in 1980, Wozniak was personally worth $88 million ($333 million today) and Jobs was $165 million ($625 million) richer by the end of the first day of over-the-counter trading. The next year annual sales had reached $335 million ($793 million today) making Apple Computer one of the fastest-growing firms in American history.

After almost losing his life in an airplane crash, Steve Wozniak stopped working at Apple in 1981. He enrolled at UC Berkeley and earned an undergraduate degree. He sponsored music festivals, developed the first universal remote control device for television sets, taught fifth grade students at a school near where

Figure 14.33
Holding the first Apple I circuit board are the two Steves—Stephen Wozniak (left), the technical genius, and Steven Jobs, the innovative thinker and marketing wizard.
Courtesy of Apple Computer, Inc.

Figure 14.34
The original 1976 Apple 1 Computer in a briefcase. Notice the cassette tape recorder that was used to run the computer's software. A television set was used as a monitor.
Courtesy of the Sydney Powerhouse Museum

Figure 14.35
Steve Wozniak in 2005.
Courtesy of Al Luckow

he lived, and funded various charitable organizations. In 2009 Wozniak competed on the eighth season of the reality television show "Dancing with the Stars" with teammate Karina Smirnoff, a world champion professional dancer. However, he was hampered in his effort after he injured his foot and had to wear a removable cast (Figure 14.35).

In 1983, Jobs brought in former Pepsi-Cola executive John Sculley to be Apple's CEO. During the Super Bowl telecast the next year, viewers watched what was called the greatest commercial of all time, produced by motion picture director Ridley Scott (*Alien*, 1979 and *Blade Runner*, 1982). With an obvious link to George Orwell's novel *1984*, the advertisement presented a "Big Brother" (i.e., IBM) theme in which computer operators all looked alike and worked in drab surroundings. Suddenly a young, athletic woman wearing running clothes and carrying a sledgehammer runs toward the giant screen. When she throws the hammer at the picture of the leader, the screen crashes to reveal behind it the latest revolution in computing—the Macintosh.

Produced by the advertising firm of Chiat/Day and featured in the documentary *Art & Copy* (2009), the commercial was critically acclaimed because it had such a different visual look than most advertising of the day. It only ran once at the end of the third quarter during the Super Bowl game between Washington and the LA Raiders, but lives on through the web. The Macintosh sold for less than $2,000 (about $4,000 today) and contained a graphic interface that made many of the functions of the computer intuitively simple for the average person. In the first 100 days of its release, 70,000 were sold. It was an immediate hit with visual communicators (Figure 14.36).

Desktop publishing was born with the Macintosh computer and the LaserWriter printer introduced in 1985. However, Jobs left Apple in 1985 to start another computer company, NeXT, after a power struggle between Sculley and himself. The next year he purchased the computer graphics division of George Lucas's Lucasfilm, which became the Pixar Animation Studios. Pixar was later acquired by the Walt Disney Company in 2006 and is considered one of the most successful animation studios in Hollywood.

By 1996 Apple was struggling financially. After Sculley left the company, Jobs returned the next year and guided Apple to several computer and portable gadget triumphs. In 2001 a slick, modern, and easy-to-use portable music player, the iPod, was introduced. Coupled with Apple's iTunes software for transferring music and videos, the device was an enormous success. The next year saw Apple's launch of the iPhone. The portable touch screen device plays music and videos like an iPod, links to the web, takes photographs, is able to play thousands of applications for educational and entertainment purposes, and, oh yes, acts like a telephone on occasion. Then, in 2010 another launch success— the iPad was able to view apps, books, and web content. The first day they were offered, more than 300,000 were sold. In 2011 the iPad 2 was a thinner, lighter, and faster version with a longer-lasting battery. Also that year, the iPhone 4s was released with Siri, a voice-activated command and response system. Since 2011 when Tim Cook took over the reigns at Apple, the company has introduced the Apple TV, the iCloud, the MacBook Air, the Apple watch, the seventh generation of the iPad, and the iPhone 8.

In 2017 Apple opened its new home office in Cupertino, California, Apple Park. At a reported cost of about $5 billion that took eight years to complete, the 2.8-million-square-foot circular, spaceship-like structure will house about 12,000 employees (Figure 14.37). The design of the headquarters was accomplished by Jonathan Ive who has over-

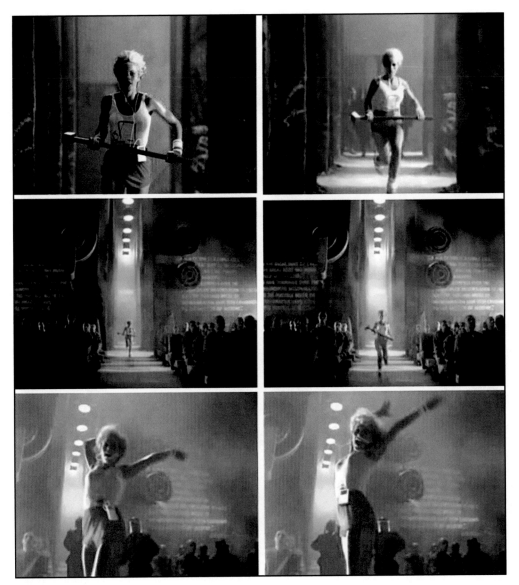

Figure 14.36
It has been called the greatest commercial ever shown. Still frames from the Ridley Scott directed ad for Apple's Macintosh computer shows the stark contrast between the status quo (IBM signified as drag, similar, sitting toilers) and the future of personal computing (Apple as a bright, energetic, athletic trouble-maker).
Courtesy of Apple Computer, Inc.

seen the look of every Apple product since 1997. The building features sliding glass doors at the entrance each weighing 440,000 pounds, shock absorbers in case of earthquakes, 805,000 square feet of solar panels so the entire structure runs on sustainable energy, and 9,000 planted trees in the center, many of them fruit including, of course, apple trees.

In 2003 Jobs was diagnosed with a rare, cancerous, neuroendocrine tumor on his pancreas. Although the type of

cancer is usually treatable because of its slow growth rate, according to Walter Isaacson's biography *Steve Jobs*, the Apple head delayed surgery for nine months while he tried alternative treatments—a vegan diet, acupuncture, herbal remedies, and advice from a psychic. Appearing thin and weak at a conference two years later, speculation about his poor health flooded the media. In 2009 it was revealed that he received a liver transplant from the Memphis, Tennessee

Figure 14.37
An aerial view of Apple Park nicknamed "The Spaceship" while under construction.
Courtesy of Apple Computer, Inc.

Methodist University Hospital Transplant Institute with an "excellent prognosis." But by August 2011 during his third medical leave, he resigned as CEO of the company. Tim Cook, with Apple since 1998, was named CEO. Although weak, Jobs managed to work a few days at the company's headquarters and the rest of the week from home.

On October 5, 2011, Steve Jobs died. He was 56-years-old. His last words spoken to his family at home were reportedly, "Oh wow. Oh wow. Oh wow."

In the days following his death there was an outpouring of sympathy, memories, and sadness expressed through print, television, and websites.

Part of Apple's statement read, "Steve's brilliance, passion and energy were the source of countless innovations that enrich and improve all of our lives. The world is immeasurably better because of Steve" (Figure 14.38).

Technical Perspective
A computer has five basic components: memory, the central processing unit (CPU), switching devices, peripherals, and software (Figure 14.39).

Memory This necessary part of a computer, also called storage, comes in two types: short-term memory that aids computer operations while you are using

Figure 14.38
Weeks after Steve Jobs' death, the Apple Computer website showed this simple visual message.
Courtesy of Apple Computer, Inc.

the machine and permanent memory that resides within the computer and on separate recording devices. As a general rule for visual communicators, computers should have as much short-term and permanent memory as possible. You want to run more than one program at a time quickly and save all of your images, movies, and music. For processing high-resolution still and motion picture images, you need at least four to eight gigabytes (GB) of short-term memory (also called RAM, DRAM, and SDRAM), 320GB within a computer, a 500GB external hard drive, and at least a 1GB portable jump or flash drive. The large external hard drive is necessary in order to make regular backups of your work in case of a computer crash. Another alternative for data is to sign up for storage on a cloud system in which almost unlimited space is reserved for your work.

CPU The faster its chip or clock speed, the faster a computer can process information, and the more you will be able to accomplish. Fast, efficient chips also allow you to easily run more than one program at the same time. This capability is useful when editing digital images for still or moving presentations and playing graphic-intense video games and virtual reality presentations. Currently, the Intel Core i7-7700K processor has a chip speed of 4.2 gigahertz, or 4.2 billion operations a second.

Switching Devices These are simply cords that connect the CPU with all other functions of a computer. They can be telephone-type links or complex 64-pin devices called *small computer systems interface* (SCSI, pronounced "scuzzy")

Figure 14.39
An educator for an arts, technology, and emerging communication school uses a CyberPower PC with an Asus HDMI monitor, a Vuze camera (on the small tripod, and an Oculus Rift head-mounted display for VR 360 capturing, rendering, and presenting along with a MacBook Pro with an Apple Cinema HD display for all other purposes.
Courtesy of Paul Martin Lester

connectors. Program instructions and other information are sent through a switching device to the CPU and out to a monitor or printer depending on the need of the user. The Universal Serial Bus (USB), manufactured by Intel, and Firewire, an Apple product, are devices that have revolutionized peripheral connections by making them faster, more versatile, and easier to obtain. But computers without wire connections are the wave of the future. Apple's thin notebook computer, Air, for example, does not contain a Firewire port but relies on a wireless connection.

Peripherals The three types of peripherals are those that send data to the CPU (e.g., keyboard, mouse, tablet, voice, and scanner devices), those that deliver data from the CPU to a monitor and printer, and those that offer two-way communication between one computer user and another, such as through direct line, e-mail, and web applications.

Software Without software, a computer, with all its storage, CPU, switching devices, and peripherals, is only good as a place to stick yellow Post-it Notes. A visual communicator must be comfortable writing and editing words, creating and manipulating still and moving images, working with numerical output, and sorting and finding information on the web. You must also have a working knowledge of audio production and be able to put all the elements together in graphic designs for both print and screen presentations. Therefore, you should be familiar with at least eight programs: a word processing program such as Word, an illustrator program such as Illustrator, picture manipulation software such as Photoshop, spreadsheet software such as Excel, a page layout program such as InDesign, a presentation program such as PowerPoint, motion picture editing software such as Final Cut Pro, and a web editor such as Dreamweaver. In addition, you should be familiar with CSS for proper web page construction and a bit of software coding such as found on the website Processing.org to create interesting still and motion graphics.

Ethical Perspective
As with photography, motion pictures, and television, computer games have been accused of displaying scenarios that feature gratuitous sex, violence, and stereotypes. Many critics are concerned that children become obsessed with playing video games at home and thus are slow to learn how to interact socially with other people. As pressing as those issues are, there are also concerns about image manipulation.

Violent Themes Computer games began innocently with simple graphics. The first interactive computer game is considered to be "Spacewar!" by MIT student Steve Russel in 1962 that predated Ed Zajac's satellite simulation by two years (Figure 14.40). In 1971, the first arcade game, "Computer Space," helped launch Atari (Figure 14.41). The next year a home system named Magnavox Odyssey was introduced which plugged into your TV set so you could play a type of table tennis game with a ball of

light and two simulated paddles, along with 11 other so-called educational and entertainment games (Figure 14.42). The arcade version from Atari followed, and "Pong" could be found in many bars across the United States (Figure 14.43).

Gradually, games became more sophisticated in their story lines and their technology. As a result, realistic and often violent games were produced in 1993, such as "Super Street Fighter II" (Figure 14.44). With "Grand Theft Auto" in 1997, violent games were established as a popular and lucrative staple of the industry (Figure 14.45).

Using the fastest processing chips available, the newest game systems are much more lifelike than anything seen previously, but they don't mean much without the software. Increasingly, software involves interactive "shooter" games. Social critics raise important concerns about children who become obsessed with video game playing. Users often forsake homework, friends, family, and even meals as they move through the fantasy scenes alone or with others connected through online play.

Most games are criticized because they reward a player for committing some kind of violent act. The object of most video games is to "kill" as many other characters as possible with an often creative assortment of weapons and tactics. Critics point out that the games teach a child, as do violent examples in other media, that conflicts are easily resolved, not through compromise, but through direct, violent action. They believe that game violence has a higher potential for contributing to adverse personality disorders among children than do motion pictures or television because a child is actually responsible for the actions in the game, rather than being a passive viewer.

After two young men killed 13 people and themselves at a Littleton, Colorado, high school in 1999, it was discovered they obsessively played two "first-person

Figure 14.40
(Weblink: http://goo.gl/41fL7B). Although laughably primitive by today's standards (as all first instances of visual communication innovations are), at least no one was injured in the playing of the game.

Figure 14.41
(Weblink: http://goo.gl/QRbSAu). Nine years after "Spacewar!," "Computer Space" was the first coin-operated arcade game. It was developed by the founder of both Atari, Inc. and the Chuck E. Cheese restaurant chain, Nolan Bushnell.

Figure 14.42
(Weblink: http://goo.gl/zqZ1Qo). Meant to be played on Magnavox televisions, Odyssey was the first game console for home use introduced by Ralph H. Baer in 1972. At a cost of $99 or about $300 today, the unit was not a commercial success.

Figure 14.43
(Weblink: http://goo.gl/bS42EX) The table tennis simulated arcade game, "Pong," was developed by Atari employee Allan Alcorn after a suggestion from Nolen Bushnell who saw a similar game played on a Magnavox Odyssey. The game became a huge commercial success with versions for arcades, bars, and the home.

W
LINK
Figure 14.44
(Weblink: http://goo.gl/WSQmzU)
"Super Street Fighter II" was a head-to-head combat-style video game from the Japanese company, Capcom.

W
LINK
Figure 14.45
(Weblink: http://goo.gl/VR79CV)
Published by Rockstar Games, the "Grand Theft Auto" franchise has been named by The Guinness World Records as the most controversial series in gaming history with more than "4,000 articles published about it, which include accusations of glamourizing violence, corrupting gamers, and connections to real life crimes." However, in this first, graphically unsophisticated version, no content alarm bells were set off.

W
LINK
Figure 14.46
(Weblink: http://goo.gl/92xrhf).
As a user runs through a maze with pulse-pounding music in the first person shooter game "Quake II," each adversary killed is accompanied with moans and blood.

W
LINK
Figure 14.47
(Weblink: http://goo.gl/TJ6NZ3)
In "Mortal Kombat Gold" a user is encouraged to complete a kill with the narrator urging, "Finish her."

shooter" video games, "Doom" and "Quake" (Figure 14.46). Consequently, Disney banished all violent video games from its theme parks and hotels. Another game that raised alarms of concern was "Mortal Kombat," which featured decapitations and spinal cord and heart removals (Figure 14.47).

In 2009 Common Sense Media, a computer game watchdog group, warned the public of "Grand Theft Auto IV," developed by Rockstar Games and published by Take-Two Interactive Software (Figure 14.48). Common Sense spokesperson Marc Saltzman said that because of the game's heavy violence, it "should be kept away—far away from children." And yet, "Grand Theft Auto: Chinatown Wars" from Rockstar, filled with violence, mobsters, foul language, and drug references, was released for Nintendo's handheld model, the DS, a popular platform for children. After the game company was sued, the U.S. 9th Circuit Court of Appeals upheld a lower court's ruling that such games cannot be banned from those younger than 18 because of First Amendment free speech protection. Nevertheless, in 2009 Midway Games, the maker of "Mortal Kombat," filed for bankruptcy.

In the controversial related to inappropriately excessive sex and violence for younger audiences, it sometimes gets lost the talent and exceptional artistry demonstrated by game producers. The trailer for "Dead Island," a first-person zombie horror game released in 2011 produced by Techland for Windows, PlayStation 3 and Xbox 360 play systems, received attention for its emotional content and aesthetic beauty. A critic for *Wired* magazine wrote, "It may be the best video game trailer I've ever seen; gorgeous, well-edited and emotionally engaging." In a reverse time sequence (there are versions available in which users can watch the film in normal time), the trailer tells the story of a vacationing family who must battle zombies

and a young girl who becomes infected. Produced by the British animation studio Axis, the trailer is a separate teaser unrelated to the game itself. However, the independent movie studio Lionsgate bought the rights to make a movie from the trailer (Figure 14.49). In 2016 Techland introduced a sequel named "Dead Island Riptide" with an equally aesthetically beautiful trailer (Figure 14.50).

Nolan Bushnell noted honestly that the success of violent games "is all about matching risk and reward. To shoot someone, you have to expose yourself—that's a risk—and the reward is a kill." He also predicted that the future of gaming will be augmented reality. "You'll design a game where there are eight evil monkeys over in the Bank of America building, but you can see them only through your iPhone."

Sexual Themes Many interactive games feature soft pornography, as opposed to hard-core pornographic adult themes. Still, the games are hopeless stereotypical and misogynistic. Women characters take their clothes off and perform sexual services in response to a mouse-generated command. Digitized images and audio effects give the illusion of a one-on-one encounter. One of the first sex-oriented "games" was "MacPlaymate," created by Mike Saenz. As the user clicked a mouse on various parts of the main character's cartoon clothing, Maxie would oblige by undressing. The program also contained a "panic button." If someone came into the room unexpectedly, the user could quickly switch the screen to a simulated spreadsheet program. Saenz also produced one of the most popular adult games, "Virtual Valerie 2." An enhanced animated version of the Maxie line drawing was described in promotional material as "the ultimate in cyberotica and the embodiment of every red-blooded technophile's deepest desires."

In the movie *The Lawnmower Man,*

Figure 14.51
As part of the plot of The Lawnmower Man, *two characters have sex within a virtual reality computerized environment.*
Courtesy of the Everett Collection

W LINK

Figure 14.48
*(Weblink: http://goo.gl/8GcDyh)
Compared with the benign version from Figure 14.45, the advanced computer graphics of "Grand Theft Auto 4" boosts the realism and the social concern as a user shoots police officers during a street fight.*

W LINK

Figure 14.49
*(Weblink: http://goo.gl/ay44Gn).
The aesthetically beautiful images, the sorrowful sound track, and the off-putting reverse chronology .*

W LINK

Figure 14.50
*(Weblink: http://goo.gl/RNoL6Q)
You can almost forgive the ultra violent theme when the images are so pleasant to watch.*

W LINK

Figure 14.52
*(Weblink: http://goo.gl/Bj5VdM)
The Feminist Frequency blog started by media critic and activist Anita Sarkeesian in 2009 "analyzes modern media's relationship to societal issues such as gender, race, and sexuality" with thoughtful stories and insightful images.*

from a short story by Stephen King, the lead character has virtual reality sex with his girlfriend (Figure 14.51). The movie was forgettable, but the scene inspired many stories in the media. Some writers have predicted that VR sex between partners thousands of miles from each other but linked through an online network may be the "killer app"—jargon among program developers for an application that everyone will want to have.

Not surprisingly, the porn industry has developed several VR titles. Google "VR porn" and then explain to your partner that you accessed the websites purely for research purposes. If you have the inclination, time, and funds, you can purchase a full-body "sex suit" as seen in *The Lawnmower Man* and experience VR intercourse from a device developed by the Japanese company Tenga. More insidious are titles that promote stereotypes, sexism, and misogyny. For example, Sean Buckley of engadget.com writes that "Dead or Alive Xtreme 3"

rewards users for committing sexual assaults. As reported by media critic Anita Sarkeesian, there are many other games that promote harmful female stereotypes and violence toward women. She became known after she criticized the gaming industry for its male-dominated storylines under the banner heading, "Gamergate." Her feminist perspective on misogynistic games as expressed through her video blog and speeches, is an important voice that provides an ethical foundation for digital productions (Figure 14.52).

A serious consequence of the increased realism of humans in computer games and presentations is the issue of where you draw the line between innovative presentations and child pornography. Responsible industry executives have established guidelines for adult themes. They state that no underage models, animals, sadistic and masochistic (S&M) practices, or violence toward women are to be featured in these programs. But they are only guidelines with which compliance is voluntary.

Image Manipulations The manipulation of still digital photographs is a valuable tool for photographers who can easily and without chemicals perform all the functions that traditionally were reserved for darkrooms (See Chapter 11). However, critics are concerned that manipulations are going beyond simple cropping or color balance adjustments and altering the content of news editorial pictures. Computer technology allows taking parts from one film and combining them with another. For example, a Coca-Cola commercial featured living musician Elton John singing with several dead entertainers including Louis Armstrong, Humphrey Bogart, and James Cagney. Fred Astaire appeared to dance with a vacuum cleaner in a Dirt Devil commercial and John Wayne asks for pretzels in a Coors Light ad.

Advertising manipulations are less of a concern than those for journalism presentations. Much of the apprehension over digital still and moving image manipulations is because the *original* often is altered. Once a picture is changed, it is changed forever. Photographic credibility—the idea that seeing is believing—may be a naive, old-fashioned concept. But *every* image in the mind's eye, every subject before a camera's lens, and every still and moving picture produced in the dark or light is manipulated. Because more people are learning how images are produced, fewer and fewer believe in the inherent truthfulness of a picture anymore.

When a picture's content no longer is credible, context and the words that accompany a photograph will become more crucial to deciding what should be believed. The credibility of a picture may rest more on a media outlet's reputation and the text used to explain an image than the picture itself in this computer manipulation age. Computer technology didn't start the decline in the credibility of pictures, but it has hastened it.

Cultural Perspective
Although many companies make desktop computers, Apple and IBM used to dominate the industry. Various publications carried stories that pitted the counterculture gurus with their long hair, beards, and sandals against the establishment executives with their white shirts, conservative ties, and blue suits. Steve Jobs would park his motorcycle next to several arcade games and a grand piano in the lobby of Apple Computer. Uniformed security guards greet visitors to IBM sites. But never is the contrast between the two companies as clear as in their two logos.

The first Apple logo, probably one of the worst in logo history, was a black-and-white line drawing of Sir Isaac Newton sitting under a tree reading a book. Jobs and the third founding member of Apple, Ronald Wayne, drew the original logo (Figure 14.53). Above Newton's head is an apple that has just become detached from the branch and is on its way to inspire Newton to theorize about the law of gravity. Around the picture is the strangely cryptic quotation, "A mind forever voyaging through strange seas of thought—alone." The quote is from Book Three of William Wordsworth's *The Prelude* where he described the look of Newton's marble statue while a student at St. John's College, Cambridge. Incidentally, Wayne couldn't risk losing his personal assets if Apple wasn't a success so he sold his share of the company for $800 (about $3000 today). Oops.

Soon, however, the company changed the logo, in the tradition of Saul Bass (See Chapter 8) to a symbol that could be easily condensed into one, simple visual message. Rob Janoff, an experienced graphic artist designed the rainbow colored Apple with a bite taken out in 1976 (Figure 14.54). The logo had several possible interpretations that included a nod to Newton and the apple's

Figure 14.53
The original Apple Computer logo was a confusing array of text and graphics—not the kind of symbol that can be easily reduced and remembered by consumers. Nevertheless, the design introduced the world to the connection of the computer firm to apples.
Courtesy of Apple Computer, Inc.

Figure 14.54
One of Apple Computer's most enduring trademarks was a round, organic, colorful logo that emphasized the computer's ease of use, enjoyment, and slightly irreverent company philosophy.
Courtesy of Apple Computer, Inc.

role in his inspiration, that knowledge was the pot of gold awaiting a user at the end of the Apple rainbow, or that the computer was the "forbidden fruit" and more fun than an IBM PC. It has also been speculated that the rainbow logo was a tribute to one of the founders of modern computing, the gay mathematician Alan Turing who died after eating an apple that contained cyanide.

In 1998 the logo was changed to a solid color apple shape, perhaps reflecting the company's maturity in the business world. Regardless of its many interpretations, the logo perfectly summarized Apple Computer—bright, innovative, visual, and a bit anti-establishment. However, it has not been without controversy. In 1978, Apple Corps, a company begun by the Beatles, sued Apple for trademark infringement. The computer company paid $80,000 and agreed to never get into the music business. But after iTunes was launched, Apple Corps took the company back to court. This time the settlement was pricier as Apple Computers paid $26.5 million in 1991 to settle the suit. After complaints that you can't do that and you never give me your money, in 2008 after working what seemed like eight days a week, the two parties decided to not go down a long and winding road and let it be. The Beatles song catalog became available on iTunes two years later.

The IBM logo is a contrast in style (Figure 14.55). Designed by Paul Rand and architect Eliot Noyes in 1956, it originally comprised three black capital letters in a serious square serif typeface. Rand added the blue color and the distinctive horizontal stripes later because, as he wrote, "since each letter is different, the parallel lines, which are the same, are the harmonious elements that link the letters together." But for others, the stripes reminded them of a prison uniform. The logo is a no-nonsense, conservative design and, like the Apple logo, visually complements the underly-

ing philosophy of the company. Interestingly, Rand, who was also responsible for the logos of such companies as ABC, Westinghouse, and UPS, posed for the grammatically challenged "Think Different" campaign from Apple Computers in 1998.

Despite the strict lines of the IBM logo, the stereotypical image of an individual (usually a male) with mussed hair, glasses held together at the bridge of the nose with tape, about ten pens and pencils carried in a shirt pocket protector, wrinkled clothing, and a laugh similar to a donkey's bray is identified in this culture as that of the "computer nerd." This stereotype emerged during the time when research scientists and technicians dominated the computer industry. Fortunately, the geek look has been upgraded a bit. Think of Jim Parsons' character Sheldon Cooper and his fellow Caltech theoretical physicists in "The Big Bang Theory."

The general public was all too eager to make fun of these intelligent yet socially awkward individuals because the technology scared or intimidated most people. No culture ever generated a "printing press nerd" or a "typewriter nerd" because those machines never evoked the fears equal to that of computers.

During the 1950s, audiences were frightened by a computerized robot featured in *The Day the Earth Stood Still* (1951) that was so powerful it could halt the flow of electricity to every machine on the planet. Fear computers, in which people would have no control over the powerful machines they had created to protect them, fueled such movies as *Failsafe* (1964), *Dr. Strangelove or: How I Learned to Stop Worrying and Love the Bomb* (1964), the *Terminator* movies, *Ex Machina* (2015), and *Ghost in the Shell* (2017). In Arthur C. Clarke's *2001: A Space Odyssey* (1968), the benign, protective, and slightly condescending computer HAL (each letter in the name

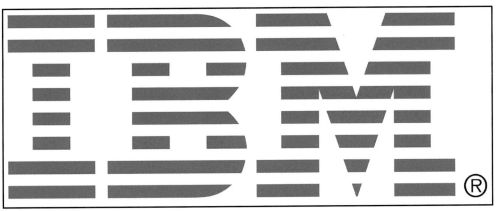

Figure 14.55
Paul Rand's IBM trademark presents bold, uppercase, square serif letters linked by horizontal blue lines. The logo symbolizes the company's powerful position in the industry and its world-wide networking capabilities.
Courtesy of International Business Machines, Inc.

Figure 14.56
The popularity of The Matrix *movies is based on viewer fears of computers. In this publicity photograph from the movie, the character Neo, played by Keanu Reeves, sees three human shapes within the computer environment known as the matrix.*
***The Matrix,** 1999. ©Warner Bros./Courtesy of the Everett Collection*

W
LINK
Figure 14.57
*(Weblink: http://goo.gl/tjQitD)
The E-Sports Earnings
website "is a community-
driven competitive
gaming resource
based on freely a
vailable public
information."*

is one up from the letters IBM) suddenly turned into a psychopathic killer. *The Matrix* trilogy (1999–2003) featured a world in which computers use human bodies as batteries. To occupy their minds, the machines created an elaborate virtual world (Figure 14.56).

Real-life serial killers are often described in media reports as having the "calculating mind of a computer." With the idea of computers as so forceful that they control every aspect of a person's life, stereotyping the creators and operators of these mighty machines as impotent and unattractive isn't surprising.

The desktop publishing revolution helped end the nerd stereotype and the negative view of computers. The image of a sterile, serious, and a bit obsessed IBM executive has been replaced by the image of a passionate, relaxed, and a bit obsessed Apple user.

With easy-to-operate computers and software programs, anyone can learn how to operate the machine. Desktop publishing educated the average user about the difference between a software program and the task of computing. No longer does a computer user need to know how to write a program that makes a computer operate. Similar to the time when George Eastman invented roll film cameras so that anyone could enjoy photography, the diversity of tasks that can be performed relatively easily on a computer makes it a tremendously popular machine. The mystique of the computer is lessened further when elementary school children can write papers, process still and moving images, and make presentations for assignments. With computer chips now essential for the operation of such diverse machines as wristwatches, microwave ovens, and automobiles, computers and their users are admired by the culture that embraces such technology. A computer, especially in the home, is a status symbol—not nerdism. Its owners are considered to be forward thinking, progressive, and men-

tally sharp. The same terms were spoken about those in the 1950s who had a television set at home. Because almost everyone has a TV, the symbol today of an upwardly mobile family is the computer in the extra bedroom.

One way computer technology gains respect from the general public and especially parents who see their children absorbed by computer games is the growing trend of professional game players who compete solo or in teams for millions of dollars in prize money. E-Sports are gaining in popularity on a daily basis. For example, "Dota 2," a multiplayer online battle arena game developed by the Valve Corporation, awards the most prize money, more than $100 million for its 1,972 players in 754 tournaments. The Overwatch Pacific Championship held in Taipei, Taiwan in 2017 awarded $272,240 in prize money. The six players known as "Flash Wolves" netted $98,400 for their first place win. Top players can easily earn six-figure salaries (Figure 14.57).

Critical Perspective
Without question, computers represent a major technological breakthrough on a par with Gutenberg's printing press. All the media are becoming dependent on computers, and this convergence ensures that the world will never return to a pre-computer time. But computers simply are machines that reflect the culture that makes them. As with other means of expression, if a society accepts violence, sexism, and the perpetuation of cultural stereotypes, that type of content will pervade the digital medium. A society always gets the media images it deserves.

Computerphiles advance the simplistic notion that more computer technology can solve all the evils of the world. But capitalistic, free-market democracies have consistently demonstrated that almost any innovation divides people into those who can afford to use it and those who cannot. For example, some schools are better equipped to teach and some restaurants have higher-quality entrées because of the economic status of those who live nearby. Many experts look to the web to help solve many of society's problems. As more people are educated through technology, so the argument goes, the world will become a better and more tolerant place. At present, half of all the messages on worldwide electronic information networks are simple notes that could just as easily be sent by telephone or postcard. No wonder the U.S. Postal Service reported in 2012 a loss of $3.3 billion. If computers turn out to be simply low-cost text alternatives with unfair access, a potentially great societal benefit will be lost.

Computers as they are presently known eventually will become as quaint and old-fashioned as manual typewriters and as ubiquitous as smartphones. American Alexander Bell or most anyone else could ever imagine that the telephone would eventually be the most advanced achievement in communications technology. Handheld computers that provide voice, text, and imagery that link to powerful worldwide networks are instigating a new revolution in communications technology and are also helping to eliminate an ancient human skill—writing by hand (Figure 14.58).

In 1982 the video game company Electronic Arts (EA) started a revolution in game culture with its debut magazine advertisement that asked the intriguing question, "Can a computer make you cry?" The ad included a promise for the production of "Software worthy of the minds that use it" (Figure 14.59). Thus began a quest to inculcate John Rawls' concept of empathy (See Chapter 6) into the world of gaming. EA Founder Trip Hawkins subsequently raised about 10 million dollars for the organization, "Teach Empathy Through Games" for 10-year-olds. In the game, "IF... The Emotional IQ Game," Hawkins explains,

Figure 14.58
Two women are seen text message on their handheld devices while sitting in a coffee shop. Let's hope they're not texting to each other.
Courtesy of Paul Martin Lester

"'IF' was inspired by the Kipling poem of the same name and takes place in a game universe where everything is connected through The Energy Field (so you really need empathy) and where rival dogs and cats are fighting over control but really need to understand and accept each other."

Can media productions, whether through traditional or emerging media, make a user more empathetic? When visual productions are most immersive as with AR and VR technologies, many think so. For example, as a tool in public relations, Cathe Neukum of the charity organization, International Rescue Committee believes virtual reality technology aids in education and leads to donations. "Four Walls: A Virtual Reality Experience" with the actress Rashida Jones allows a user to be with a Syrian woman and her child in their refugee camp in Lebanon. Neukum says, "We can't bring donors or people to the field, but we bring the field to donors and our constituents and our supporters. That's what's so great about VR, that's what makes it, I think, such an important tool for charities. The VR experience *puts you in the shoes of someone* who goes through a journey that ends in homelessness." The

CAN A COMPUTER MAKE YOU CRY?

■ Right now, no one knows. This is partly because many would consider the very idea frivolous. But it's also because whoever successfully answers this question must first have answered several others.

● Why do we cry? Why do we laugh, or love, or smile? What are the touchstones of our emotions?

▲ Until now, the people who asked such questions tended not to be the same people who ran software companies. Instead, they were writers, filmmakers, painters, musicians. They were, in the traditional sense, artists.

■ We're about to change that tradition. The name of our company is Electronic Arts.

SOFTWARE WORTHY OF THE MINDS THAT USE IT.

We are a new association of electronic artists united by a common goal – to fulfill the enormous potential of the personal computer.

● In the short term, this means transcending its present use as a facilitator of unimaginative tasks and a medium for blasting aliens. In the long term, however, we can expect a great deal more.

▲ These are wondrous machines we have created, and in them can be seen a bit of their makers. It is as if we had invested them with the image of our minds. And through them, we are learning more and more about ourselves.

■ We learn, for instance, that we are more entertained by the involvement of our imaginations than by passive viewing and listening. We learn that we are better taught by experience than by memorization. And we learn that the traditional distinctions – the ones that are made between art and entertainment and education – don't always apply.

TOWARD A LANGUAGE OF DREAMS.

In short, we are finding that the computer can be more than just a processor of data.

● It is a communications medium: an interactive tool that can bring people's thoughts and feelings closer together, perhaps closer than ever before. And while fifty years from now, its creation may seem no more important than the advent of motion pictures or television, there is a chance it will mean something more.

▲ Something along the lines of a universal language of ideas and emotions. Something like a smile.

■ The first publications of Electronic Arts are now available. We suspect you'll be hearing a lot about them. Some of them are games like you've never seen before, that get more out of your computer than other games ever have. Others are harder to categorize – and we like that.

WATCH US.

We're providing a special environment for talented, independent software artists. It's a supportive environment, in which big ideas are given room to grow. And some of America's most respected software artists are beginning to take notice.

● We think our current work reflects this very special commitment. And though we are few in number today and apart from the mainstream of the mass software marketplace, we are confident that both time and vision are on our side.

▲ Join us. We see farther.

EA
ELECTRONIC ARTS

Figure 14.59

The ground-breaking 1982 print advertisement from Electronic Arts attempted to inspire computer gamers to create work that promoted empathy rather than conflict. Nevertheless, the games that sell the most for the company in 2017 are not the most highly evolved philosophically: "Madden NFL 17," "EA Sports FIFA," "Ultimate Fighting Challenge," "Battlefield," and "Titan Fall." Empathetic attitudes are fine, but the public generally desires clashes.

Courtesy of Jordan Maynard

description is the personification of the veil of ignorance philosophy.

TRENDS TO WATCH FOR COMPUTERS

Two months before his resignation from Apple, Steve Jobs announced his last Apple venture, the iCloud. Although Amazon and Google have their own versions, the popularity of the Apple brand could make the concept viable. The idea is that a computer should be a simple device (like tablets from Amazon, Apple, or Google) with emails, photographs, videos, music, and documents stored on a virtual hard drive and assessable through a wireless connection. Safety from hackers and privacy considerations are stumbling blocks to be overcome. However, the name brand efforts are eclipsed by an idea from Drew Houston, a 29-year-old computer programmer and entrepreneur and Arash Ferdowsi who invented Dropbox. Every day, an incredible 325 million files are uploaded to the Dropbox server making Houston's personal net worth an estimated $600 million.

U.S. video game sales reached $8.8 billion in 2011. In five years the total came to $30.4 billion with the global figure at $91 billion. Motion picture sales in 2016 lagged far behind with $11.3 billion. Social, online, and mobile games such as "FarmVille" on Facebook, "World of Warcraft," and Android and iPhone smartphone games are expected to grow. The multiplayer online game of "Warcraft" has made more than $3 billion for Blizzard Entertainment.

A relatively new player of video games is from Apple. Although its iPhone and iPod Touch devices play more than half a million apps that include educational, social networking, and travel uses, 75 percent of the apps that are sold are games. Their popularity is causing game producers to develop cheap, faster programs for the small screens. The multibillion-dollar video game industry will prosper even more from independent producers. Major companies such as Microsoft and Sony Corp. are signing up amateur creators to produce games for their Xbox 360 and PlayStation 3. Nevertheless, the top ten games sold in 2016 are from the companies Activision Blizzard, Ubisoft Entertainment, Bethesda Softworks, and Electronic Arts. Of the top ten, most have violent combat themes: "Call of Duty: Infinite Warfare," "Battlefield 1," "The Division," "NBA 2K17," Madden NFL 17," "Grand Theft Auto V," "Overwatch," "Call of Duty: Black Ops III," FIFA 17," and "Final Fantasy XV." However, the rush is on for all producers to create games for virtual reality systems.

Educators are experimenting with computer-human interfaces in the form of online classes. Students, their professors, and guest speakers can be located anywhere in the world and connect through online virtual classrooms. Classes with more than 100,000 students are not uncommon through such online course organizations as Udacity, begun by former Stanford professor Sebastian

Thrun, edX founded by educators from Harvard and MIT in 2012, and Khan Academy, created in 2006 by MIT and Harvard Business School graduate Salman Khan (Figure 14.60).

Another program that has been used by educators is Second Life (SL), an avatar-based virtual social community launched in 2003 by Philip Rosedale of San Francisco's Linden Lab. Residents can walk, fly, drive a vehicle, and teleport to rural and urban simulated environments to engage in all kinds of activities. With a credit card, residents can accessorize their avatars with hair, skin, clothing, and a sexy walk. With a premiere account (SL is otherwise free to join), residents can buy land, build stores and homes, and sell their creations to other users of the program. Roughly inspired by Neal Stephenson's 1992 science fiction classic *Snow Crash* about a user-dominated virtual reality, Second Life currently has more than 15 million registered users.

Although essentially an elaborate chatroom, SL combines the visual cues found in the real, analog world (color, form, depth, and movement) with an interactive communicative experience. In that sense it is possible to make the learning and teaching experience more real for online students than with the virtual classroom chat-based discussions. Presently there are over 150 educational institutions that have a presence on SL with many offering live, synchronous classroom instruction (Figure 14.61).

The colossal elephant in any room— whether real, virtual, or imagined—is the technology and the uses put to augmented and virtual realities. Augmented or mixed reality (AR) involves a user to wear a device that superimposes images on her actual world—information is projected on a scene and augments the experience. One of the first examples of AR was introduced at a 2009 Technology, Entertainment, and Design (TED) conference when Pranav Mistry of MIT's

Figure 14.60
(Weblink: http://goo.gl/BnLrc7) The Khan Academy online course website has access to classes for almost every interest and need.

Figure 14.61

*Moments before a visual communication lecture class offered on Second Life,
the students' avatars sit on rugs, comfortable couches, and "air chairs" while the
professor in the foreground waits for the rest of the class to arrive.*
Courtesy of Paul Martin Lester

Fluid Interfaces Group demonstrated a $350 wearable computer that includes a webcam attached to a small portable projector with a wireless connection to a smartphone and web access that can project images and other types of information on any surface (Figure 14.62). Called "Sixth Sense," a user could form her hands into a framing gesture to take a picture, use a finger to make a circle on a wrist that turns into a watch, project numbers on fingers to make a phone call, and get product information by simply looking at an item on a store's shelf (Figure 14.63). In 2012 Google released its version in a YouTube video, "Project Glass: One day…." However, consumers were not enthusiastic. However, in 2016 Microsoft announced its version of a wearable computer called HoloLens. Reviewers who have used the device call it a "game changer." In the not too distant future these wearable computers may become what we call smartphones (Figure 14.64).

As opposed to mixed reality, virtual reality uses a head-mounted display that has the effect of immersing a user into another world (Figure 14.65). The virtual reality storyteller and leader in the field,

Nonny de la Peña, created one of the first news experiments that attracted attention in the industry. Funded by USC's Annenberg School for Communication and Journalism and its MxR interaction lab, it was based on actual video footage, but with animated, cartoon avatars. "Hunger in Los Angeles" gave users with a virtual reality headset the opportunity to experience waiting in a church-sponsored food line and reacting to a man going into a diabetic seizure. Author Bryan Bishop described the experience (Figure 14.66). "As I took the headset off I was quiet; shaken," Bishop wrote. "I asked de la Peña about the diabetic man's fate, and she assured me that he had survived the attack. I was frankly surprised at how much I actually *cared*."

Currently, virtual reality dominates news stories and the public's imagination. Media entities such as "Frontline," ABC, *The Los Angeles Times*, *USA Today*, *The New York Times*, *The Washington Post*, *The Des Moines Register*, *Time* magazine, VICE, the Verge, and Ryot, games from HTC Vive, Oculus Rift, and PlayStation VR, as well as educational institutions such as the Newhouse School at Syracuse University, Columbia University's Graduate School of Journalism, Stanford University's Virtual Human Interaction Lab, the Reynolds Journalism Institute at the University of Missouri School of Journalism, and the School of Cinematic Arts at the University of Southern California (USC) have created critically acclaimed VR motion pictures.

Most notably, "Harvest of Change" detailed life on a family farm in Iowa produced by staff members of *The Des Moines Register* (Figure 14.67). *The New York Times* distributed more than one million Google cardboard virtual reality viewers to subscribers and smartphone users to watch documentaries such as "Walking New York," a tour of the wonderfully crowded streets of my home town and "Seeking Pluto's Frigid Heart,"

Figure 14.62
With a relatively inexpensive investment in equipment, software, and instructions generously provided by the Sixth Sense team at MIT, a DIY user can build the interactive computer system.
Courtesy of Pranav Mistry, MIT Media Lab

LINK

Figure 14.63
(Weblink: http://goo.gl/hs9c8f)
The Sixth Sense application from researchers at MIT is explained through this informative TED talk.

LINK

Figure 14.64
(Weblink: http://goo.gl/B1tCby)
Tech reviewer James Mackie is an enthusiastic advocate of the Microsoft HoloLens and AR.

Figure 14.65
"Hospital Corpsman 2nd Class Tim Sudduth, from Vashowish, Wash., demonstrates the Virtual Reality (VR) parachute trainer, while Aviation Survival Equipmentman 1st Class, Jackie Hilles, from Ekland, Penn., controls the program from a computer console. Students wear the VR glasses while suspended in a parachute harness, and then learn to control their movements through a series of computer-simulated scenarios. The computer receives signals from the student as they pull on the risers that control the parachute. Navy and Marine Corps aviators receive state of the art training at the Naval Survival Training Institute."
Courtesy of the US Navy and Chief Photographer's Mate Chris Desmond

Figure 14.66

(Weblink: http://goo.gl/RHVeSz) Immersive journalism is the phrase now being used for a new form of storytelling using virtual reality head-mounted displays.

Figure 14.67

(Weblink: http://goo.gl/pdD7sQ) "Harvest of Change" from The Des Moines Register immerses you on a family's farm in Iowa.

a view of the dwarf planet from the New Horizons spacecraft. Film director Spike Jonze worked with the United Nations for a documentary titled "Clouds Over Sidra," that featured a 12-year-old Syrian girl's experience at a refugee camp in Jordan. Jonze, a creative director for VICE and Chris Milk, a digital artist teamed to produce "the first-ever virtual reality news broadcast" titled, "VICE News VR: Millions March," an eight-minute film that featured New York City protesters concerned with police violence. Ryot in conjunction with the news website *The Huffington Post* produced "Protect the Sacred" about the Standing Rock, North Dakota pipeline protest in 2D, 3D, and anaglyph (blue and red filtered sunglasses) 720 degree versions. *The New York Times* was one of the first media entities to use virtual reality technology with a smartphone app to immerse viewers into news stories. In *The New York Times'* 11-minute film, "The Displaced," three children from South Sudan, the Ukraine, and Lebanon are "driven from their homes by war." The experience of riding a bicycle from the perspective of a child is exhilarating and emotionally connecting. Rawls' empathic philosophy, the veil of ignorance, is again evoked (See Chapter 6).

On the academic side, university programs have collaborated with VR startups and news organizations to train a new generation of immersive storytellers. From assignments offered within traditional photojournalism classes such as at the University of Texas at Dallas to entire courses concentrated on AR and VR production as those offered at Syracuse University, students learn to use the technology to engage viewers as never before. As universities offer more immersive storytelling courses and deliver their graduates to industry innovators, additional uses for MR and VR will be discovered with users demanding more. In the end, it will be up to consumers to decide whether MR, VR, or a hybrid will ultimately be the favored platform for immersive storytelling.

KEY TERMS FROM THIS CHAPTER
Atari • Augmented reality • Chief executive officer • Chip speed • Convergent Era • Crash • DRAM • Killer app • Mainframe computer • MIT Media Lab • Mouse • Operating system • Over-the-counter stock • Punch cards • RAM • SDRAM • Silicon Valley • Synchronous classroom • Tablet • Transistor • Vacuum tube • Virtual reality

15 The Web

Have you ever heard a friend ask for a "Coke" to mean any flavor of carbonated sugar water, a "Kleenex" referring to any thin paper handkerchief substitute, or a "Band-Aid" for any sterile adhesive? A product is a huge success when its trademark name becomes the generic term for all products of its type. (Other famous brands include Frisbee, Q-Tip, RollerBlade, and Taser.) Whenever the brand name also becomes a verb, there's a cultural phenomenon going on (Figure 15.1).

All these products pale in comparison to another—one you can't even hold in your hand. It's a noun, it's a verb, and it's the search engine, Google (Figure 15.2).

Google is the name of one of the easiest, fastest, and most popular search engines available on the web. In 2011 there are more than 90 billion searches made with it a month. A simple, uncluttered opening page with a cheery logo, an empty box to type in your keywords, a minimum number of buttons, and plenty of eye-pleasing white space, Google is a welcome change from most other overly busy and too-eager-to-please search portals. Despite its humble appearance, it operates at a blinding speed. Most searches on Google, no matter how complex, take less than a second to complete as it looks through its database collection of more than six billion web pages.

Admittedly, Google owes much of its success to its catchy name. Some say it comes from "Googleplex Star Thinker," a computer character in *The Hitchhiker's*

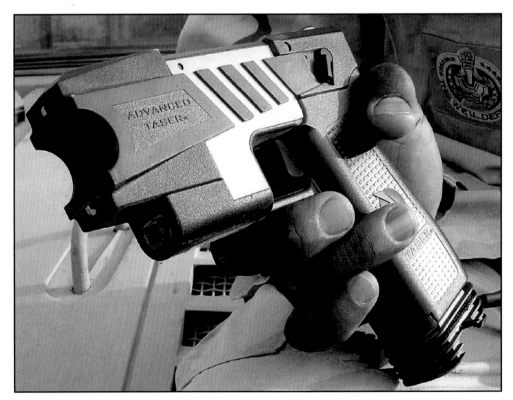

Figure 15.1
Noun and verb. The M26 Taser stun gun is the military and police version of the commercial weapon. Invented in 1974 by NASA scientist Jack Cover, the name is an acronym for Tom A. Swift's Electric Rifle—a weapon that appeared in a young adult adventure novel that featured Tom Swift. The gun fired bolts of electricity described by author Victor Appleton in 1911. As a less-than-lethal weapon, the Taser is a noun, but if you are ever unfortunate enough to have it used on you as a verb, it is hoped you have a good lawyer.
Courtesy of the U.S. Army

Figure 15.2
While still in its testing (beta) phase in 1998, Sergey Brin created the Google logo on a computer. He added the exclamation mark to mimic and perhaps challenge Yahoo! The no-nonsense, yet playful appearance of the home page immediately appealed to search engine users because of its uncluttered appearance and its speed at finding information.
Courtesy of Google

Guide to the Galaxy by Douglas Adams who could "calculate the trajectory of every single dust particle throughout a five-week Dangrabad Beta sand blizzard." Perhaps as a tribute to Adams, the home office for Google is called the Googleplex. However, Sergey Brin and Larry Page, the two visionary Stanford University students who created the search engine, say it comes from a mathematical term that refers to a number that is a 1 followed by 100 zeros, a "googol." That number is larger than all the atoms that make up the universe. So, googol became Google, a worthy name for a large-scale, worldwide search engine.

There have been many two-person teams in the history of computer innovations: Bill Hewlett and Dave Packard (HP), Paul Allen and Bill Gates (Microsoft), Stephen Wozniak and Steven Jobs (Apple), and David Filo and Jerry Yang (Yahoo!), to name a few. Perhaps that fact is an indication of the complicated nature of computer technology. Each one alone probably could never have achieved what the two accomplished together. And so it is with Sergey Brin and Larry Page. Both come from highly intelligent and motivated parents, showed early interest in computers, are under 45 years old, and are Stanford University

dropouts (Figure 15.3).

Sergey Mikhaylovich Brin, a native of Moscow in the Soviet Union, moved when he was six-years old with his family to College Park, Maryland, the home of the University of Maryland, where his father was a math professor and his mother was a scientist for NASA. Later, he received an undergraduate degree from the same university. In 2007 he married Anne Wojcicki, a biotech analyst. The two have a son and a daughter, but were divorced in 2015. Wojcicki co-founded the personal genome service, 23andMe where you can send in a sample of your DNA and get an analysis for $399. In 2008 *Time* magazine named it the "invention of the year." Through this process, Brin, whose mother has Parkinson's disease, discovered that he has a 20 to 80 percent chance of also developing Parkinson's the condition later in his life. However, he sees the genetic defect as a bug in his personal code that can be corrected. In 2017 he was considered the 13th richest person in the world with an estimated worth of about $40 billion.

Lawrence Edward Page is the son of Michigan State University computer science professor, Dr. Carl Page. When he was six years old he received his first computer. He earned a bachelor's of science degree in engineering at the University of Michigan and distinguished himself by building a programmable printer out of Lego toy blocks. In 2007 he married Lucinda Southworth who has a master's of science degree from Oxford University. In 2013 Page announced that his vocal chords are paralyzed probably because of a rare autoimmune disease called Hashimoto's thyroiditis. The condition prevents him from participating in conference phone calls. In 2017 he was considered the 12th richest person in the world with an estimated worth of about $41 billion.

Brin and Page met in 1995 when Page was visiting the campus of Stanford University. Brin was one of a group of

Figure 15.3
Larry Page (left) and Sergey Brin, 2008.

students assigned to show him around. They hit it off and started sharing ideas. The first Google database resided in Page's dorm room. The hard drive contained about 30 million web pages. When they moved their operation to a friend's garage in 1998, they dropped out of school and started to work for the company full-time. One of the persons who encouraged them was David Filo, co-founder of Yahoo!

By 2001 Brin and Page thought it was time to impose a grown-up structure to their company. They became co-presidents, with Brin concentrating on Google's worldwide growth and Page in charge of new product development. To run the day-to-day operations, Eric Schmidt was named chair of the board and CEO. Schmidt had both master's and PhD degrees from the University of California, Berkeley, was on the research staff at the famous Xerox Palo Alto Research Center, and was an executive with Sun Microsystems and Novell. Schmidt guided the young company through enormous growth. But in 2011 he stepped down as CEO. Page took his place. Don't feel bad for Schmidt. Google gave him a parting gift of $100 million. In 2017 he was named the 119th richest person in the world with an estimated wealth of $11 billion. Page, considered the Edison of Google, more comfortable inventing applications and supervising engineers, is nevertheless expected to help the company compete against its formidable rival, Facebook.

Today, Google's offices, reminiscent of the early years at Apple Computers, are located in Mountain View, California, in Silicon Valley, and are filled with perks to keep their employees happy and on the site working (Figure 15.4). They can eat in one of 11 cafeterias, enjoy one of two swimming pools, get a massage from a therapist, have their laundry cleaned for free, and can play pool, a baby grand piano, volleyball, or roller hockey.

Google makes money two ways: from advertisements that are above or to the side of the main result listings, and from selling search services to other companies. Similar to Microsoft, with all its profits, Google can afford to develop all kinds of applications or buy companies it likes. Its new browser, Google Chrome searches the web can be searched even faster and easier while its Chrome OS (Operating System) is a direct competitor to Microsoft's OS, Azure. In 2009 the company announced that its popular video sharing website, YouTube, made deals with a number of companies including CBS, the BBC, Sony, MGM, and Lionsgate to provide programs on its "YouTube Shows" section for the price of watching a brief opening commercial. Potentially, the search engine company may change the way we watch television and movies. More pointedly, consumers living in Kansas City, Missouri were the first to have access to Google's video, a pay-television service with similar content as cable television but with the added benefit of fiber-optic internet access 100 times faster than current systems.

In 2011 Google bought the Zagat restaurant review guide so it can tap into local advertising. The same year Google Wallet was introduced that lets a smartphone thought an app act as a credit card. Could this be the end of paper money?

What do you think about an end to driving as we know it? After more than 140,000 miles driven in California with Google's robot cars on actual roadways, in 2012 Nevada's state legislature gave the okay for driverless Google cars. With an $80,00 laser scanner on the roof and a wrap-around radar and camera system, the autos literally drive themselves. The state's Department of Transportation is working on the legal issues and specialized license plates necessary for consumers. Self-driving or autonomous cars are a reality with Tesla Motors and Uber, the car transportation company, experi-

Figure 15.4
A view of the Googleplex, the Google headquarters in Mountain View, California.
Courtesy of Pancakes from Heaven!

menting with their versions.

Google searches by users make up about 65 percent of all the daily hunts for information that happen on the web. With income from advertising and search services, the company earns $80.5 billion a year and is worth about $101.8 billion. According to *Forbes* magazine, that figure makes Google the second most valuable brand in the world, with Apple first and Microsoft and Facebook, in third and fourth places.

Some of the fun of using Google is to notice the changing logo at the top of the page. Based on an original idea from Sergey Brin, Ruth Kedar, an artist and designer, used the roman typeface Catull to design the original Google logo. Sim-

ilar to the first colored Apple logo (See Chapter 14), the letters use the primary colors of red, green, and blue, with a yellow "o" to signify that the company doesn't follow the rules. A delightful aspect of the simple, uncluttered Google home page is the variations of its logo for special anniversaries or occasions. Dennis Hwang, a graphic artist born in Tennessee but raised in South Korea, started creating his own logos for the page in 2000 when Brin and Page wanted something a bit "more fun." Nicknamed "Google Doodles," Hwang definitely enjoys his work. He claims to love each letter in "G-o-o-g-l-e" equally, but he does favor the "O" (which has become a "Halloween pumpkin, a Nobel Prize

Figure 15.5

The graphic designer for Google, Dennis Hwang, obviously enjoys playing with the logo to make "Google Doodles." From previous chapters of this textbook, it should be obvious that the grid-like Google at the top is a tribute to Piet Mondrian, while the multiview design is a nod to the painter Pablo Picasso. Other famous persons from Albert Einstein to Andy Warhol, as well as important dates such as Bastille, Veteran's, and Valentine's days have been Doodled.
Courtesy of Google

medal, the South Korean flag symbol and the planet Earth") and "L" (which has been used as a "flagpole, the Olympic flame cauldron or a snow ski"). For Piet Mondrian's birthday the logo mimicked one of his paintings using simple colored grids, whereas a tribute to Pablo Picasso used multiple faces in the "OOs" (Figure 15.5). Today, Ryan Germick is head of the Google doodle team and works with six illustrators and engineers to produce the illustrations that sometimes take several months to finish. In 2012 *Time* magazine called doodles Google's "most engaging innovation and its most effective advertising tool."

Critics have challenged the highly publicized corporate ethos of Google, "Don't be evil." Privacy, monopolistic tendencies, and other issues have been concerns. Google has also been controversial at various times for mixing editorial and advertising content. Links that appear as a result of a user's search can be considered Google's editorial content, and commercial sites that pay Google to have their related links presented above and to the right are advertising. Sometimes the two get confused.

For example, when the first links presented after a search for the word "Jew" were to anti-Jewish websites, Google quickly added a disclaimer to explain why such results occur and pointed users to "informative and relevant" sites. But when lawyers representing the Church of Scientology asked Google to stop linking to what they considered to be an anti-Scientology site, the offending links were removed. The strict policy of not allowing "the advertisement of sites that promote hate, violence, racial intolerance, or *advocate against any individual, group, or organization* [emphasis added]" also disallows individuals and groups with political messages. In addition, after a request from the People's Republic of China, Google instituted keyword filters for its Chinese version to prevent users from obtaining information the government didn't want known.

Privacy issues have dogged Google, especially after the introduction of their e-mail service, Gmail that was launched as a beta release in 2004 and made available to the public three years later with 1GB of free space. By 2017 a user receives 15GB of free space and can pay up to $300 a month for 30TB of space, or approximately the equivalent of 13 trillion single-spaced typewritten pages, 6,500 DVDs, or the capacity of 24 human brains.

It should be remembered that Google is not simply offering this service out of the goodness of their hearts. Your e-mail messages are analyzed and advertising links are added pertaining to the content in your texts. For example, if you mention a motorcycle in a text message to a friend, a link to Harley-Davidson might appear to the side. If you were writing about a friend who was involved in a motorcycle accident, you might not be in the mood to buy one. Google explained that it tries to refrain from placing ads next to sensitive e-mail topics. However, that response seems to imply an actual person is reading and evaluating your e-mail messages. In 2011 Google agreed to an independent audit of its privacy practices for the next 20 years demanded by the FTC for Google's privacy violations with its web-based e-mail system, Buzz. Now discontinued, Buzz was an attempt to compete with Facebook but it turned into a rare misstep from the web giant.

After complaints from competitors, regulators, state attorneys general, and foreign governments, in 2011 the Federal Trade Commission (FTC) started an investigation of whether Google's profound monetary superiority has been an unfair advantage. The next year the company settled with the US regulatory commission and promised to change its business practices to be more fair toward competitors. However, in 2017 Google was levied a record fine of $2.7 billion

because of a European Union antitrust ruling for "unfairly favoring some of its own services over rivals" in web searches. Perhaps Google learned its lesson and will do no evil. Nevertheless, the ruling is being appealed by the company.

Is Google and web searching too popular? In a recent poll, 71 percent of middle and high school students reported that they used the internet as their main source for research. Google leads all other search engines with products such as Google Earth with its Mars, Moon, Ocean, and Sky programs, Gmail, News, the digitization of health records and books, and many other applications. Either because of convenience or laziness, many no longer visit libraries to check out books on a particular topic. Reliance on digital rather than analog materials for everything from school papers to textbooks showcases how important the web has become for everyone with a computer or access to one. With such popularity comes enormous influence. On January 18, 2012 an extraordinary act of protest occurred on the web that was led by sites such as Google, Wikipedia, Boing Boing, Reddit, Craigslist, and about 10,000 others. Sparked by a legislative bill known as the "Stop Online Privacy Act" or SOPA, at first glance the proposed legislation seems reasonable. The proposed law is meant to stop the trafficking of intellectual property and counterfeit goods—such as motion pictures and music which is why Hollywood and the Motion Picture Association of America is for it. The problem for critics is that the way the bill was written, it could also potentially shut down informational websites such as search engines, video repositories such as YouTube, and picture collections such as Flickr. Several websites blacked out their logos, directed users to additional information, and asked for signatures for an online petition. Google collected more than seven million signatures while Wikipedia reported that eight million users looked

Figure 15.6
On January 18, 2012 the logo on the Google website was blacked out to show the company's contempt for the "Stop Online Privacy Act" proposed by the U.S. Congress.
Courtesy of Google

up their governmental representatives. As a result of the support from the web community, it is doubtful the law will be passed (Figure 15.6).

Another concern for internet users is a concept called "net neutrality." Should web use be an open, neutral system as it is now in which all users have equal access to the information provided or should they be billed for specific services and faster access speeds as with cable television? In 2015 the Obama Administration enacted legislation to protect net neutrality. However, the current Trump Administration wants to repeal those regulations. July 12, 2017 was named Net Neutrality Day by Google, Netflix, Facebook, Twitter, and about 80,000 other websites. Their sites included a plea for all users to contact members of the Federal Communications Commission to voice opinions about the Trump plan.

THE WEB
AND THE SIX PERSPECTIVES

The first edition of this textbook published in 1995 had a chapter titled "Networked Interactive Communication." About two weeks before the manuscript was sent to the publisher, it was decided to add a paragraph about a computer-based technology that was starting to get media attention, "The World Wide Web."

Personal Perspective

The web is an important medium of communication because it is a convergence of all that has come before it. It gets its immediacy from radio and television, its totality of information from print, and its visual and audio qualities from motion pictures—and yet it is more than all those media. When the first automobile was introduced, no one predicted fast cars, the interstate road systems, highway deaths, mechanic garages, parts stores, the suburbs, pollution, reliance on foreign oil, global warming, and drive-through fast-food restaurants

and liquor stores. One hundred years from now people will no doubt chuckle about how the web was used today.

Whether it is considered the future of mass media or a colossal waste of time and resources, the web has earned its place as a valuable resource for information, entertainment, and blatant commercialism—just as with all media.

Historical Perspective

After World War II, the Cold War set in, a political "war" mainly between the United States and the Union of Soviet Socialist Republics. Its most terrifying moment was the Cuban missile crisis of 1962 when it was discovered that the Soviet Union was storing nuclear weapons on the island nation 90 miles from Key West, Florida (Figure 15.7). Concerned that there well might be a nuclear war in which major cities were destroyed, the U.S. military started to consider alternative communication methods. With the help of the RAND Corporation, a governmental think tank, the Defense Department's Advanced Research Projects Agency (ARPA) started to discuss a communications network via computers. The concept was that if communication was wiped out in some areas, the network could re-route messages around the blank spots. In 1969 the first e-mail message was sent between researchers at UCLA and the Stanford Research Institute using a computer network called the ARPANET.

Coincidentally, others realized the need for networked communications. During the 1970s, powerful IBM and other mainframe computers were popular at government, business, and university research sites around the world. With all the activity generated by these machines, scientists soon realized that they needed communications links among these centers so that computer operators could transfer data and talk with each other electronically. Consequently, more and more computer users

Figure 15.7
An icon of the Cold War era is this aerial photograph taken by Major Richard Stephen Heyser during one of his five flights over Cuba in his U-2 spy photographic plane. It shows a Soviet truck convoy transporting nuclear missiles near San Cristobal, Cuba, on October 14, 1962. After a U.S. naval blockade of the island country and America's agreement to remove its missiles from Turkey along the Soviet border, the Soviet government removed the weapons. Called the "Cuban Missile Crisis," it was the closest the two superpowers have come to a nuclear war and inspired the U.S. military to create an alternative communications network that eventually became the internet. Heyser died at the age of 81 in 2008. It's not known whether he had an e-mail address.
Courtesy of the U.S. Air Force

started using the ARPANET for work-related and personal messages (Figure 15.8). By 1983, the system had become so popular that it was divided into two—the original ARPANET for university use and MILNET for the military. When satellite links were added to the system, international communication became possible. ARPANET's name was changed to the International Network, or internet. Based on the *CIA World Factbook*, in 2011 the United States topped the list of worldwide internet hosts with 439 million, while the rest of the world has an estimated 355 million providers. Second place is Japan with about 55 million hosts. North Korea has three service providers.

Gradually, users of the internet started to see commercial applications for this new communications technology. The first commercial use of networked computers was named *videotex* (called teletext or viewdata in Europe). Videotex was the name for communications systems that delivered information over a broadcast television signal to a person's home. With a small keypad and a television set-top box, a home user could control which frames were viewed. Hundreds of televised "pages" that contained screens for news, shopping, and other kinds of information could be accessed. In 1974, the British Broadcasting Corporation (BBC) began Ceefax, a one-way,

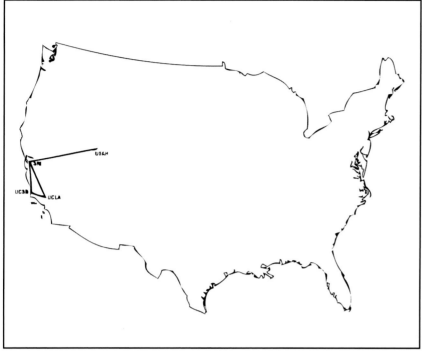

Figure 15.8
Unlike telephone conversations that relied on a party-to-party single connection, the ARPANET (Advanced Research Projects Agency Network) divided communications into discrete packets that could be sent independent of each other through a variety of routes and reassembled so that routing of the message could still take place in case of a major catastrophe. This map shows the extent of the network in 1969, with the four original nodes (also called hosts or service providers) and their connections based at university institutions: UTAH (University of Utah), SRI (Stanford Research Institute), UCSB (UC Santa Barbara), and UCLA (UC Los Angeles).
Courtesy of Paul Martin Lester

text-only teletext system. British users received news and information scrolled along the bottom of their television screens (Figure 15.9). In 2012 the service ceased operation.

In 1979, the British Post Office (known as British Telecom) began the first truly interactive system, Prestel (from Press Telephone). The Prestel system connected computer databases to the home through telephone lines. Users received about the same type of information as with Ceefax, but they could control what they wanted to read. Michael Aldrich invented and sold a computer he called a "teleputer" that could receive television programs using the Prestel system. However, Prestel proved unpopular as consumers had to buy a separate set-top box and pay extra telephone charges for the service (Figure 15.10).

One of the most successful communications systems in the world was Minitel from the French government. Begun in 1981 by the French Telecom telephone company, it provided low-cost computers to every telephone subscriber in France. The government saved millions of dollars by not having to print telephone directories because users obtained phone numbers through their home computers. Canada, Ireland, South Africa, and other countries experimented with versions of the Minitel system. However, the web made the system archaic. In 2009 the French Minitel service was discontinued.

In the United States, pay-for-use videotex services were never popular. A videotex system was tried in 1979 using terminals sold at Radio Shack stores and content provided by CompuServe, the first major online system in the United States. Two years later, the Knight-Ridder newspaper chain with content from the *Miami Herald* and technology from AT&T provided a videotex service called Viewtron to users in Coral Gables, Florida, an affluent suburb of Miami. In the initial experiment, users weren't asked to pay for the videotex terminals or the service. But beginning in 1983, home viewers had to pay $300 (almost $700 today) for a computer terminal and a monthly service charge of about $30 (about $70). After investing more than $50 million (more than $110 million today) in the electronic information experiment, Knight-Ridder abandoned the project (Figure 15.11).

Bulletin board systems (BBS) were initiated in 1978 by Chicago computer programmers Ward Christensen and Randy Suess with information that could be accessed through telephone lines. At first, BBS were an added feature to users of homemade computers such as the Altair 8800 (See Chapter 14). After IBM and Apple desktop computers became popular in the early 1980s, the use of these communication systems took off.

Figure 15.9
Users of the BBC's Ceefax teletext system were able to access news, games, entertainment, and other information from their television sets.
Courtesy of Ceefax

Figure 15.10
Prestel users were able to interact with the information available on their television sets through a keyboard and docking station connected to a phone line.
Courtesy of Dr. R. Becker

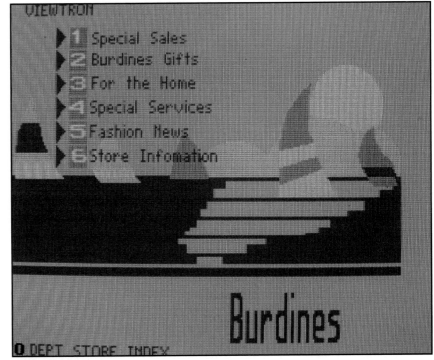

Figure 15.11
More visually interesting than the Antiope system, the graphic look of the Viewtron Videotex Service was still simple by today's web standards. Nevertheless, the service made it easy for Miami-area users to shop online at a Burdines department store.
Courtesy of Paul Martin Lester

Figure 15.12
*(Weblink: http://goo.gl/Y6TT8P)
As described by its creators,
"Monochrome is a long-established BBS with unique discussion, chat and messaging
features. Mono (to its friends)
is the traditional country pub of
the Internet. There's a friendly
bunch of regulars, and the conversations cover pretty much
everything."*

Figure 15.13
*(Weblink: http://goo.gl/Hc4hjv)
Perhaps more equivalent to a
fantasy board game, "Lands of
Stone" is nevertheless an engaging online experience described by its administrators as
"a real time game in which you
can interact with other users."*

At their height there were more than 100,000 boards worldwide. These BBS ranged from local text-only systems with a handful of users to worldwide networks that had millions of subscribers. They offered a wide range of services that included news, information, shopping, banking, software downloads, chatting, and making airline reservations. Before the web, some of the most popular BBS were America Online, CompuServe, Delphi, Genie, Prodigy, the Source, the WELL, and ZiffNet.

In the United Kingdom, the Monochrome BBS is still popular for "interactive chat, offline messaging and discussion files" (Figure 15.12). Users also enjoy playing text-based role-playing multi-user dungeon (MUD) games such as "Banished Lands," "Discworld," and "Lands of Stone" (Figure 15.13). Because a videotex system or a bulletin board stored its data at a central location, users could only access what was made available to them. These systems, in other words, were similar to DVD interactive programs—what was on a disc was all you could get.

Soon, however, a unique communications technology would change that limiting concept—the web.

In 1989, British computer scientist Timothy John Berners-Lee with Tim Cailliau, a Belgium computer scientist, used a NeXT computer while working for the European Laboratory for Particle Physics (CERN) in Geneva, Switzerland. They developed a computer language called Hypertext Transfer Protocol (HTTP) which created files that could be accessed from the internet. In 1991 HTTP was used for the first web browser that Berners-Lee called the WorldWideWeb (Figure 15.14). For his innovations in mass communications, *Time* magazine in 1999 listed him as one of the most influential persons of the 20th century and in 2004 the Queen of England knighted him. In 2017 the Association for Computing Machinery named him the recipient of the prestigious Turing Award "for inventing the World Wide Web, the first web browser."

In 1993, interest in the internet expanded tremendously because of what was called its killer app—the Mosaic software program. Marc Andreesson and Eric Bina developed it while students at the University of Illinois (Figure 15.15). The web browser made accessing and downloading internet files that contained still and moving pictures with audio as simple as clicking a computer's mouse. Web browsers turned the text-dominated internet into the colorful, content-filled surfing explosion that it is today. Apart from the program's graphic capabilities, much of the appeal of browsers comes from the fact that they allow a person to create and use a hypertext link to discover a seemingly inexhaustible amount of interrelated information and services.

After administrators at the University of Illinois demanded that Andreesson give the browser to the school, he quit to form his own company he called Netscape. In 1995 he sold it to AOL, now owned by the media giant Time Warner. Now a Silicon Valley venture capitalist, one of his investments announced in 2010 is a web browser called RockMelt. It is hoped that its ease in incorporating the social media of Facebook and Twitter into web searching will make it a success.

In 1995 Microsoft introduced its Internet Explorer (IE) web browser. By 2003 IE was the clear winner of the browser war because of its advantage in having its software residing on 95 percent of the computers worldwide.

However, other web browsers have overcome IE's dominance. Apple's Safari released in 2003, the Mozilla Corporation's Firefox launched in 2004, and Google's Chrome introduced in 2008 were strong competitors of Internet Explorer. As of 2017, StatCounter reports that IE lost the race. Chrome is used by

Figure 15.14
Sir Tim Berners-Lee in 2008.
Courtesy of the John S. and James L. Knight Foundation

54 percent of web users, Safari by 15 percent, UC Browser (a Chinese company) by eight percent, Firefox by six percent, and all others (Opera, Android, Edge) by 17 percent (Figure 15.16).

Although today it is common to use the web to find almost anything imaginable, the practice of searching online is relatively new. "Archie" was the name for the first computer-based networked data organizer. Alan Emtage and Bill Heelan, students at McGill University in Montreal created it in 1990. It was named either for its closeness to the word "archive" or after the teenager-inspired comic book *Archie*. In 1991 a team of University of Minnesota students introduced "Gopher," named after the school's mascot. It was a menu-driven document retrieval program for the internet. Its search engine was called "Veronica," another character from the *Archie* comic book—thereby solidifying the link between computer users and cartoons.

Developers—from amateurs with their poorly designed home pages to professionals with their poorly designed online brochures—created millions of web pages. However, without knowing

Figure 15.15
On the campus of the University of Illinois is this historical marker indicating where the first web browser was created.
Courtesy of Ragib Hasan

Figure 15.16

Not surprisingly, the Chrome web browser is an exact graphic twin of its cousin, the Google search engine.
Courtesy of Google

what specifically to look for, finding useful content was often a frustrating experience until the first successful organizer for much of the web was invented—Yahoo! The exclamation mark was added because several other companies had already trademarked the word Yahoo (for the rest of this chapter the exclamation mark will not be included). In 1994 two Stanford University students, David Filo and Jerry Yang, created the popular data retrieval program (Figure 15.17). Initially a class project named "Jerry's Guide to the World Wide Web," Yahoo (aka "Yet Another Hierarchical Officious Oracle") was a collection of web pages that were divided into logical categories, as with the Library of Congress and Dewey book catalog systems. Initially, anyone with a website had to request that it be included into the Yahoo database. Once it was accepted, the web pages were entered manually. Yahoo was enormously popular and respected as a great idea. With its success, data organizer programs such as Archie and Gopher became obsolete.

When Filo and Yang announced their public stock offering in 1996, they raised more than $30 million ($42 million today). With the money, Yahoo was turned into a more commercial

web portal, a type of webpage that offers news, entertainment, and e-mail, as well as search services. The company also was able to purchase other web entities such as GeoCites, other search engines Inktomi and AltaVista, and the picture-sharing site Flickr.

Despite its aggressive marketing plan, Yahoo made some missteps. In 2007, executives allegedly gave private e-mail registration information to the Chinese government about a dissident. He was later caught and sentenced to ten years in prison. Boycotts of all Yahoo products and services were formed by a number of worldwide organizations. Sensing vulnerability and wanting to get more into the search engine market, the next year the giant Microsoft Corporation made a bid to buy Yahoo for $44.6 billion, but the offer was turned down. Many in the industry thought that decision was a mistake. The company subsequently had to lay off employees due to the economic downturn of 2008. Co-founder Jerry Yang resigned as CEO in 2009 and agreed to serve on the board of directors for the company. Yahoo's slide continued. In 2012 Scott Thompson, the former head of PayPal agreed to be Yahoo's fourth chief executive in five years. One of the first moves made by Thompson was to accept Jerry Yang's resignation from the board of directors. He then announced the layoff of 2,000 employees, or 14 percent of the entire Yahoo workforce. Four months later, Thompson was out. In another public relations fiasco, he resigned after it was learned he lied on his resume that he had a computer science degree. With its stock price stagnant, in 2016 CEO Marissa Mayer shed 15 percent of the company's workforce. That same year it was announced that Yahoo suffered a massive hack that compromised the security of about one billion users. In 2017 the telecom company Verizon bought Yahoo for $4.48 billion.

Since Yahoo, search engines for

Figure 15.17
Yahoo co-founders Jerry Yang (left) and David Filo in 2007 (Combination image).
Courtesy of Mitchell Aidelbaum

the web have evolved from simple file finders created by innovative graduate students to sophisticated full-service portals maintained by major corporations such as Microsoft. Ask.com was started up in 1996 by two California entrepreneurs, Garrett Gruener and David Warthen, with a programmer, Gary Chevsky, and a logo designed by Marcos Sorensen. It was originally named "Ask Jeeves," after the butler from stories by P.G. Wodehouse. In 2006 the butler was fired and replaced by a more modern logo after the media conglomerate InterActive Corp. (IAC), run by Barry Diller, purchased it. When he headed the Fox Broadcasting Company, Diller gave a green light to Matt Groening's series, "The Simpsons." "Jeeves" was unique in that you could simply type a question rather than worry about using an exact keyword. Microsoft introduced Live Search in 2007. Two years later it was replaced by Bing to further compete with Google. Bing is marketed not as a search engine necessarily, but a "decision engine."

Hunting and gathering is as old as history, but other more creative design-

ers of search engines have expanded the definition of the web genre. While visiting Hawaii in 1994, American computer programmer Ward Cunningham was told to take a "wiki wiki," the name for the shuttle bus that travelled between terminals at the airport. *Wiki* is Hawaiian for fast. After he returned home, Cunningham named his online database the WikiWikiWeb, the first that allowed others to contribute information. Since then, user-supplemented databases or wikis are common. The most successful wiki by far is Wikipedia, an online encyclopedia with more than 10 million topics that are constantly updated by about 75,000 contributors. Begun in 2000 by Jimmy Wales and Larry Sanger of the online encyclopedia company Nupedia, Wikipedia is now an entity of the not-for-profit Wikipedia Foundation and used as a resource in learning about a vast array of subjects by college students and others worldwide.

Delocator began in 2005 after its creator, xtine burrough (she prefers her name lowercase), was frustrated that she couldn't find an independent coffee shop in Soho, New York City amid all the Starbucks stores on seemingly every corner. With programmer Jim Bursch, the result of their efforts is a search engine in which you can type in a zip code and a distance radius and receive a list of Starbucks and non-Starbucks coffee shops (Figure 15.18). Since the initial launch, a user can also find independent bookstores and movie theaters. A unique feature of the site is that users can add reviews, comments, and photographs for each entry. This concept of adding user-generated content to build a sense of community is a key element in the so-called Web 2.0.

When this book's first edition was written in 1993, the internet had about 15 million users worldwide. Thirty years later there are an estimated 1.5 *billion* users, or about 24 percent of the Earth's population. In the past ten years, those living in Africa and the Middle East have had the highest percentage of web use growth. Also, in 1993 the communications tool was called the all-capitalized "World Wide Web." Today, the web, as with the internet, are commonly spelled with lowercase initial letters like photography, movies, and television, and the "www" prefix for web addresses, called the Uniform Resource Locator (URL), is no longer necessary with most browsers. Rather than a demotion in status, the change indicates that the web is a democratizing, universal communications tool that has profoundly changed mass communications.

Technical Perspective
Early in its history, those who envisioned the communication system known as the web realized that there needed to be a set of rules for those who create websites so that files could be viewed on any type of web browser and on any kind of computer. Tim Berners-Lee's simple software language HTML ensured that a web browser can request information from a web server so that you can see all the words and images on your own comput-

er screen. For any website that has been downloaded to your computer, you can view the HTML source code and study how the site was created. A popular HTML editor from Adobe—*Dreamweaver*—makes the task of website creation much easier than writing software code from scratch.

Since the development of HTML, other valuable software tools have been created that enhance the efficiency and functionality of websites. These include Application Programming Interface (API), which helps in the creation of web-based software applications, and Cascading Style Sheets (CSS), in which specifications regarding colors, typefaces, fonts, and layout for a set of web pages can be housed within a separate file. In addition, the Extensible Markup Language (XML) Java, developed by James Gosling of Sun Microsystems in 1995, JavaScript, created by Brendan Eich of Netscape the same year, and its professional programming big brother, AJAX, allow developers to create applications that can more easily be shared between different computers and operating systems.

The technical information to create a website is beyond the scope of this book, but lessons can easily be found on the web and on bookstore shelves. However, you should be aware of how to analyze a website to make sure the information contained within it is credible. Researchers at the Stanford Web Credibility Project conducted a three-year project surveying more than 4,500 persons and came up with ten guidelines that improve a website's credibility. The ten items are as follows:

1. Make it easy for the user to verify the accuracy of the information,
2. Identify the organization that sponsors the site,
3. Note any experts who provide information,
4. Detail the backgrounds of those

Figure 15.18
An alternative way of thinking about web search engines can be found with a website known as Delocator.net created by web artist and educator xtine burrough. Alternative coffee houses, with users adding pictures and brief descriptions, can be found by typing in your zip code. The coffee shop background image and dark green logo are perhaps meant to evoke a Starbucks alternative.
Courtesy of xtine burrough

involved with the site,

5. Make contact information readily available,
6. Make sure the use of typography, images, and graphic design elements looks professional,
7. Include navigational elements so that the site is easy to use,
8. Update the site often and report the last update,
9. Avoid advertisements, and
10. Remove spelling, typographical, and linking errors.

One of the best examples of web design, technology, and credibility is the "Frontline" website, produced by PBS's affiliate WGBH in Boston. Since 1983, "Frontline" has been one of the best programs on television to view investigative documentaries. *Newsday* calls the program

"television's last fully serious bastion of journalism." The website is also an excellent example of the synergy among all of the media elements discussed in previous chapters (Figure 15.19).

Typography The typographical presentations include headlines, text blocks, and captions printed in an easy-to-read sans serif typeface. Colored text, boldface, and backgrounds signal special areas and features so that a user can easily find them.

Graphic Design The home page for the site is divided into discrete sections with each one clearly separated from another by colored backgrounds. Words and images are neatly displayed in a gridlike approach that denotes a serious attitude among the producers to the content of the site.

W
LINK
Figure 15.19
(Weblink: http://goo.gl/B2VckN) As with its website, the PBS-affiliated "Frontline" television show is a leader in the field of investigative reporting.

Photography The mostly color still images, tightly cropped for added impact, and the images from main story sliding automatically across the top of the page give a user a clear idea of what to expect after a mouse click.

Motion Pictures Users have the option to run the digital video in a small screen off to the side of a desktop or fill the monitor with the picture.

Television Using Adobe's Flash software player, investigative reports as seen on television can be watched on a user's computer screen at any time.

Computers Unlike a motion picture or a television program, users can choose their own path through the website. Built-in interactive features allow users to search for specific information and programs and link to other websites and databases.

Ethical Perspective
As can be imagined with a medium barely two decades old, there are many ethical and legal issues that are worthy of serious discussion that have not yet been resolved. Every concern pointed out in the previous chapters' ethical perspective sections can certainly be applied to the web. For visual communicators, one of the most important issues is that of free speech versus governmental censorship. Social critics have sometimes described the web as a huge, unregulated book or DVD store in which a child can suddenly wander into a back room where all the pornographic magazines and lewd materials are shelved. But besides access to sexually explicit sites, there is also easy access to hate speech.

With Google's SafeSearch Filtering feature set to the most adult setting of "Do not filter my search results," the word "sex" resulted, as can be imagined, in more than 62 million hits, with every-

thing from links to free pornographic videos to a sex education website for teens sponsored by Rutgers University. The phrase "white power" produced more than a million websites that included pictures of swastikas and young men giving Nazi salutes. With Google's SafeSearch set to "strict filtering," a search for "sex" resulted in the Rutgers website, numerous links concerned with the television show "Sex in the City," and sexual predator criminal cases. Interestingly, switching to strict filtering didn't make much difference when "white power" was searched. The results were a similar array of Aryan supremacy websites and images, as if no filtering had been applied. The lesson might be that web culture is more concerned with sex than hate. Regardless, as with all media, parents need to be responsible for the materials their children watch. But in a public setting—as in a university or library—adults should be given the opportunity to view a wide variety of materials available on the web.

Social media staples such as texting to friends, sharing pithy observations, updating a status, uploading a picture, and so on is almost always noncontroversial and ethical. Unfortunately, the 2016 presidential campaign demonstrated how fabricated posts easily manipulate the media and the public with President Trump repeatedly labeling traditional news sources, without evidence, as phony. However, many news reports *were* fabricated. Fake news accounts from some social media websites were comprised of fictionalized accounts and contained invented quotations, digitally altered photographs and video, and presented within a graphics layout made to appear credible. For hedonistic, attention-getting, and non-satiric purposes, these politically motivated producers created "news" in order to sway public opinion.

les in 1953, 1978, and 1998

Paul Martin Lester

Professor
Department of Communications
H-324F
Cal State Univ, Fullerton
Fullerton, California
92834
Office Phone: 714 278-5302
Main Office: 714 278-3517
FAX: 714 278-2209
E-mail: lester@fullerton.edu

Courses
Pictures
Writings
Biography

My Bookmarks
Photojournalism Resources

Ethics Home
New Media
Viscom Home

Search this Site

Figure 15.21
Thanks to the Internet Archive, AKA the "Wayback Machine," the author was able to retrieve one of his first websites, mostly a collection of bookmarks, dated December 3, 1998.
Courtesy of Paul Martin Lester

Figure 15.20
(Weblink: http://goo.gl/NzJHGR) The Webby website reports that the number of internet users is about 3.6 billion, or roughly half the world's population and that they use more than one billion websites. In 2017 the organization honored 407 winners.

Cultural Perspective

Alexa Internet ranks the most popular websites among actual users by country worldwide. Currently the top ten worldwide sites in order from the top are Google.com, Facebook.com, YouTube.com, Yahoo.com, Baidu.com, Wikipedia.org, Blogspot.com, Live.com, Twitter.com, and Amazon.com. Only Wikipedia is a non-commercial site. Consistently, the web has moved far away from its research institution roots, but there are indications that the focus is changing back to education. One of the places to find many non-commercial and alternative sites on the web is the annual Webby Awards. Established in 1996 and presented by The International Academy of Digital Arts and Sciences, with judges such as internet inventor Vint Cerf, musicians Beck and David Bowie, and Matt Groening of "The Simpsons," the Webby awards honor those who create websites in almost 70 categories, from Activism to Weird (Figure 15.20).

There has been a dramatic shift in the way the web works and is thought of by users and programs since its introduction in 1993. Mimicking release iterations of software products, the initial version of the medium is sometimes called Web 1.0. Non-users often criticized this form of the web because, for the most part, individuals and corporations simply displayed the equivalent of a flyer, brochure, and/or business card in simply designed home pages with bad typography and spinning animations. The most sophisticated element on a page might have been a visitor sign-in logbook. Irish blogger Joe Drumgoole, CEO and founder of Putplace, a website in which users can store their digital belongings, writes that The Web 1.0 was about reading. It was often said that persons and companies created websites regardless of whether they were functional or viewed by anyone, so that they could *say* they had a website. The web, then, started as a static, page-driven family or corporate tool with little user input or influence on the information (Figure 15.21).

A move in changing the way the web was regarded happened in 2004 when Tim O'Reilly of O'Reilly Media sponsored a Web 2.0 conference in San Francisco to spark development of what he thought should be the next generation. For Drumgoole of Putplace, Web 2.0 is about writing and sharing. For many, user-generated content sites such as Blogspot, Delocator.net, Facebook, Flickr, YouTube, Wikipedia, and Wordpress epitomize this next generation of websites. With these websites you can easily share your ideas, bookmarks, personal stories, pictures, videos, and knowledge with others. With web feed formats, or Really Simple Syndication (RSS) utilities such as podcasts for audio or digital video file sharing and blog sites on any subject imaginable, good ideas get distributed at the speed of light.

Of the ten most used global websites mentioned previously, Baidu, Blogger, Facebook, Twitter, Wikipedia, and You-Tube are Web 2.0 applications. Another popular example of this interactive web is the auction site eBay. Begun in 1995 by French-born Iranian computer programmer Pierre Omidyar to sell used items online, eBay is one of the most successful auction sites with versions throughout the world. The company also owns PayPal for transactions, Skype for telephone calls, StubHub for tickets, and Kijiji for classified advertising, all with the .com suffix.

For many, Web 2.0 is also about creating social communities based on common interests. For others it is a way to take back the web from the large corporations. For visual communicators, the web is wide open. Just about any-thing conceptualized can be visualized. The one-way, force-feeding of tightly controlled words and images for mostly commercial purposes is being replaced by a two-way, more open user culture. Consequently, graphic designers and visual artists team up with computer programmers to create platforms for the web. Yelp is an application that aids users in their search for reviews. Many of these collaborations are commonly called "mashups," so named because they combine two or more existing applica-tions to create a distinct service. One of the first mashups was a combination of the popular craigslist.com classified advertising website and Google Maps called HousingMaps.com, in which users could find out about places to live pin-pointed on a map of the area desired.

Michael Mandiberg, with assistance from New York City's Eyebeam, a center for the creation of experimental digi-

tal tools that "challenges convention, celebrates the hack, educates the next generation, encourages collaboration, freely offers its contributions to the com-munity, and invites the public to share in a spirit of openness," is a strong advocate of mashups. He is the creator of such websites as TheRealCosts, a Firefox plug-in that "adds CO_2 emissions information to airfare websites" and HowMuchIt-Costs.us that uses data from Google Maps and gasoline efficiency data from automobile manufacturers to calculate CO_2 coats for air or car travel. His as-sertion that "Platforms *are* the internet" has become a "meme," a cultural concept that has spread quickly throughout the internet because of user conversations through such social networking sites as Reddit, Facebook, Twitter, and YouTube.

Steve Lambert, CEO of AntiAdverts-ingAgency, elicited programmer friends to create a mashup of AdblockPlus. org and the Firefox web browser. His program replaces sometimes annoying website advertisements found on brows-ers with artwork from his site Add-Art. org. About his mashup, Lambert said, "It is very much a hack. It makes Firefox do what it wasn't designed to do." These innovative mashers combine an artist's eye with an anti-establishment, activist urgency.

Another use of the technology was in 2009 when President Obama gave the first online town hall meeting from the White House through streaming media. Prior to the webcast, more than 100,000 e-mail and video questions were sent to the president's website at whitehouse. gov. From this input, 3.6 million votes from users determined which ques-tions the President would answer. You could watch the live broadcast on your computer. Although Obama's answers didn't make much news, the fact that the technology was used for the first time to connect persons with the government was featured on newspaper front pages and led many television news programs

(Figure 15.22). As of this writing, President Trump has not offered such an online opportunity except to respond to his Twitter tweets that usually criticize the news media or an individual who he thinks as slighted him. Sad.

Critical Perspective

Science fiction writer William Gibson first used the word *cyberspace* to describe the ethereal world of the electronic highway where unusual and unlimited communication links are available. He used the word in a short story called "Burning Chrome" published in *Omni* magazine in 1982. Two years later his classic *Neuromancer* introduced the word to popular culture. Space on the electronic highway comprises not asphalt or concrete, but electricity and light. Writer John Perry Barlow described cyberspace as having a lot in common with the 19th century West. "It is . . . vast, unmapped, culturally and legally ambiguous, verbally terse, hard to get around in, and up for grabs. . . . To enter it, one forsakes both body and place and becomes a thing of words alone. . . . It is, of course, a perfect breeding ground for outlaws and new ideas. . . ." Perhaps that critique was true at the beginning, but new media web designers are changing the face of the medium.

Nevertheless, the sheer popularity of the web causes concerns. As more users download and upload movie clips, use social networking sites, and play online multiplayer games such as "World of Warcraft," internet traffic delays are clogging up the system for all. For example, the Irvine, California-based Blizzard Entertainment that produces "Warcraft" enjoys a fan-base of 11.5 million users with each playing the game about 20 to 30 hours a week. Three popular programs—Facebook, Skype, and YouTube—make the point.

The networking social website Facebook started as a program called Facemash by Harvard computer science

Figure 15.22
President Obama's Online Town Hall meeting was the first of its kind in the history of White House press conferences. Using Web 2.0 technology, anyone could ask questions in text or video formats, vote on their favorite questions, and then watch the President give responses live on the internet from a computer.
Courtesy of the White House

major Mark Zuckerberg in 2003 when he was 19. It soon became popular with other Ivy League students at Columbia, Stanford, and Yale. In 2012 its 800 millionth user was registered, with more than 75 percent of its members living outside the United States. The success of the social network, the same name as the movie in 2010 about Facebook that won three Academy Awards, helped make Zuckerberg richer than the Google guys. In 2012 Facebook expanded its internet presence and member options by teaming with the music-sharing service Spotify, the video services Hulu and Netflix, and Skype, to provide video chat with members. The same year, the company made headlines around the world when it offered its stock for public purchase. Facebook raised about $20 billion with the IPO (Initial Public Offering) with a market capitalization of $100 billion, made 1,000 of its employees instant millionaires, and raised the 28-year-old Zuckerberg's personal wealth to more than $20 billion. In 2017 the 33-year-old's net worth is $64.1 billion.

Skype, a software program that allows users to make free telephone calls to each other using the internet, was begun in 2005 by entrepreneurs mostly based in Tallinn, Estonia. In 2009 on average more than 17 million users were online with Skype at the same time.

YouTube was founded by three friends who worked for the online payment company PayPal in 2005. Now owned by Google, it currently uses more bandwidth space than the entire internet in the year 2000. YouTube's use will increase as the quality of the interface and videos improves and as the website competes with television.

The web has brought human civilization to a great crossroads. Do we use the new tools of communication to perpetuate the same old themes of commercialism that make us feel better about ourselves, better than someone else, to use violence to resolve conflicts, to engage in sexual objectification to devalue relationships, and to display stereotypes to promote the dominant culture's way of life? Or do we use the technology to learn from one another in the hope of creating a world in which ideas are valued more than physical attributes?

Will you use the web to find the most titillating stories, pictures, and digital video found on websites such as Rotten.com, which displays autopsy photographs, or will you use it to take one of hundreds of college courses offered online? In either event, we live in an extremely exciting and challenging time in the history of communication—both in interpersonal relationships and the mass media.

*TRENDS TO WATCH
FOR THE WEB*

Back in 1968, the future-thinking South Korean video artist Nam June Paik declared, "Paper is dead . . . except for toilet paper."

In 2008 the global economy was rocked by one of the worst economic downturns in recent history. In the United States, bank failures, housing foreclosures, and unemployment numbers made many compare the situation with the Great Depression of the 1930s.

Newspaper companies, already suffering from a steady decline in subscribers and advertising revenue and a steady rise in newsprint costs, are in crisis. Major chains and daily newspapers including the Tribune Co., publisher of the *Chicago Tribune*, the *Los Angeles Times*, and the *Baltimore Sun*, the Journal Register Co. that owns 20 daily newspapers across the country, as well as newspapers such as the *Philadelphia Inquirer*, the Minneapolis *Star Tribune*, and the Sun-Times Media Group that publishes the *Chicago Sun-Times* and several suburban newspapers have filed for bankruptcy. The *Rocky Mountain News*, first published in 1859, quit publishing. In 2009 the *Seattle Post-Intelligencer* was converted to an online version. For years, many advocates and critics of the newspaper industry have been saying that the web is the best hope for the newspaper industry.

The Knight-Ridder newspaper chain, the same company that was part of the videotex experiment in Florida in the 1980s, introduced one of the first online newspapers in the world, the *San Jose Mercury News'* Mercury Center. The newspaper was first introduced on the AOL bulletin board in 1993. In 1997, the newspaper chain introduced Real Cities network with 40 newspaper sites that contained news, information, and entertainment options from selected communities on the web. At the present time almost all of the 1,400 daily newspapers in the United States and most around the world have a version of their paper on the web. Given the trend toward a younger demographic of television and online news users, newspapers on paper, a technology dating from the 16th century, may be on its way out. What we think of as "news," however, will survive as content from news-providing entities, whether major corporations or enterprising individuals, will still be produced.

Perhaps traditional publishing entities would be wise to learn from popular online tabloid entertainment gossip sites such as TMZ, owned by the media giant Time Warner. Short for "Thirty Mile Zone," a term used to describe a thirty-mile radius that includes where many Hollywood stars live and the motion picture and television production facilities where they work, TMZ is criticized for paying for tips from the general public, many received via Twitter, and financing still and video paparazzi. Nevertheless, the website scooped all other media in the world to be the first to announce the death of singer Michael Jackson in 2009.

It seems absurd during this present era of mass communications to think of television and newspapers as anything but separate. Television requires a complex machine that usually is the focus of the furniture within a room to comfortably watch the programs provided by a content provider. A newspaper, on the other hand, is a portable collection of paper sheets printed by inked presses, folded together, and physically delivered to homes, businesses, and pay-per-copy sidewalk boxes. When you are finished watching a television show you turn off the set. When you are done with a newspaper, you should throw it in a recycle bin, leave it for someone else, or place the sheets on the floor for your new puppy—an action you cannot take with a television set.

Web innovations have changed forever the perception of television and newspapers as being separate. In fact, on the web there is little difference between a newspaper, radio, television, and the web as evidenced by the *Los Angeles Times* (Figure 15.23), NPR (Figure 15.24), CNN (Figure 15.25), and Yahoo (Figure 15.26). All provide news, information, entertainment, and advertisements using still and moving images and audio with links to more. For the first time in mass communications history, the plural "media" have been transformed into the singular "medium" called the web. Those in the newspaper

industry simply need to think of how to attract viewers and advertisers who will be willing to pay for their product.

A "value-added" concept, similar to Apple's iTunes model in which users pay a few extra cents for engaging, interactive, and user-contributed presentations they choose to view about their neighbors and the world, is a model that will save the news and the journalism profession. News Corporation founder and media mogul Australian Rupert Murdoch exclaimed, "People reading news for free on the web, that's got to change." Publishers such as the Hearst Newspapers, The New York Times, Time Inc., and others have plans to charge users slight fees for stories. The Associated Press plans to charge websites, not readers, for the use of their stories. At Global Post, a news site with 65 reporters around the world, free major news items are supported by advertisements, but "passport" subscribers who pay $199 a year could get access to "correspondents, conference calls and meetings with reporters, and breaking news e-mail messages from those journalists." Passport subscribers could also suggest story ideas. However, few took the Post up on its access deal even after the cost was reduced to $99 and then less than $30 a year. In 2015 the news organization was acquired by the PBS Boston station, WGBH and produces video segments for "The PBS NewsHour."

Some web advocates and futurists are already planning for the next web generation. Web 3.0, sometimes referred to as the "semantic web," will be an example of human-computer interaction in which a user's specific needs are coupled with an advanced artificially intelligent computer agent that will not only deliver information that is salient for a specific user, but will anticipate that person's requirements and desires. Apple's iPhone 4s was the first with a personal assistant called Siri is a first indication of the promise of Web 3.0.

Figure 15.23
*(Weblink: http://goo.gl/5LSXHC)
A newspaper shows little difference between a radio, a television, or a portal.*

Figure 15.24
*(Weblink: http://goo.gl/Nh3wcj)
A radio shows little difference between a newspaper, a television, or a portal.*

Figure 15.25
*(Weblink: http://goo.gl/YBpwpT)
A television shows little difference between a newspaper, a radio, or a portal.*

Figure 15.26
*(Weblink: http://goo.gl/j3MiMc)
A portal shows little difference between a newspaper, a radio, or a television.*

The future of the web may be shown by a bit of science fiction. Imagine receiving an unexpected e-mail from an old friend inviting you to attend your high school reunion in your hometown 1,000 miles from where you presently live. Before you can reply to your friend, a pop-up screen appears on your desktop with information based on your schedule and bank account balance for flight, hotel, rental car, and dinner reservations that can be booked if you select the "OK" box.

Or imagine that you're sitting in your political science class and your professor explains the five-page paper you have to write that is due in two weeks. The next time you open your computer, a list of topics and suggested sources are waiting for you. Sorry, you still have to write the paper yourself.

Or imagine waking up each morning and your computer has an array of stories and/or images queued for you on the platform of your choice—portable player, radio, television, or computer—at home, in your car, or at the office. That is the promise of the Web 3.0. Your computer will have total access to your calendar, files, e-mails, web searches, bank accounts, medical records, shopping history, current circumstances including what you own or lease, personal habits and preferences, and on and on. With that information, your computer will be able to make a thousand choices for you. Privacy issues are not a concern because with Web 3.0, the computer *is* you.

Information highways, with or without wires, are as valuable and necessary for communications as backwoods trails, shipping lanes, telegraph wires, railroad lines, roadways, and airline flight paths. The challenge for government agencies, corporate executives, creative producers, artists, educators, and concerned citizens is to ensure that everyone can ride the information highways as easily as those made of asphalt.

The author's great-grandmother lived to be 100 years old. She once admitted that she laughed when she first heard about automobiles. When asked why she found cars so funny, she replied simply, "How could everyone have their own train?"

It's human nature to evaluate and anticipate technology based on previous experiences, but we should also pay attention to individuals who help us see the future. The French artist and novelist Albert Robida and the British cartoonist George du Maurier envisioned a device that combined the telephone, television, and the web in which users watched 24-hour news and plays, had interactive communications, and took university courses all on a big screen in what was called the téléphonoscope. This innovation was proposed 140 years ago (Figure 15.27).

The future of mass communication may have little to do with our understanding of the past or present. The best plan for anticipating the future is to keep learning with an open mind so that you will be prepared, to paraphrase Aldous Huxley, for the brave new (visual) world.

We can only hope that it is a world in which everyone is, can be, and wants to participate.

KEY TERMS FROM THIS CHAPTER
Beta • Blog • Browser • Chief executive officer (CEO) • Cloud computing • Cold War • Computer agent • Cyberspace • Download • Electronic highway • Hack • Hit • Homepage • Hypertext • Killer app • Meme • Multi-User Dungeon (MUD) • Podcast • Portal • Search engine • Server • Silicon Valley • Streaming media • Uniform Resource Locator (URL) • Xerox Palo Alto Research Center (PARC)

Figure 15.27
Described as an "electric camera obscura," the telephonoscope is illustrated in a parody of Thomas Edison and his inventions created by the cartoonist George du Maurier in an 1878 issue of Punch magazine.
Reproduced with permission of Punch Ltd.

16 The More You Know, The More You See

Google the title of Aldous Huxley's *The Art of Seeing* (yes, use the search engine as a verb) and in about half a second you will be able to link to more than 400,000 results. It will take you considerably more time to visit the websites offered, but such a task would be a worthy assignment. That's because the phrase is associated with philosophical to practical uses that cover the three types of visual messages—mental, direct, and mediated. In short, "the art of seeing" is one of the most important endeavors we should learn as humans, and it should not be surprising that its use is reported so often in a web search. No wonder Huxley's book helped inspire this one (Figure 16.1). He, like many other educators, philosophers, and scientists realized that true seeing is not exclusively a product of light, the eyes, and the brain. To turn sight into insight you need an active, aware mind.

California photographer Pete Eckert understands more than most the art of seeing (Figure 16.2). In a career that has spanned more than 20 years, Eckert has created a body of work that includes sensual portraits of friends and frenetic tributes to light that has been praised by museum curators, awards judges, magazine editors, and collectors. In 2011 he photographed Miss June 2004, Hiromi Oshima for *Playboy* magazine. To other photographers who sometimes have difficulty finding images to focus upon he advises, "If you can't see, it's because your vision is getting in the way."

Eckert should know. His vision never gets in the way of his work. He's blind.

Before he realized he had trouble with his eyes, he graduated from the Art Institute of Boston in 1979 majoring in sculpture and ceramics and worked as a carpenter's apprentice. Four years later he was diagnosed with retinitis pigmentosa, or "tunnel vision," a condition that gradually narrows your field of view until you become blind. Nevertheless, he graduated from San Francisco State University in 1984 with two degrees—one in sculpture and the second in design and industry. As his eyesight continued to dim, he thought it best to get a business degree. He received an MBA from the University of Hartford in 1989. Wanting to challenge himself even more, he studied taekwondo, received his first degree in that martial art in 1993, and developed techniques appropriate for blind persons.

After he became totally blind in 2000, he took up photography full-time. His main method is to keep the shutter open for several seconds in a darkened room or outside at night and with a variety of light sources—flashlights, lasers, lighters, and candles—he creates his photographs (Figure 16.3). As can be imagined, Eckert has much to teach the sighted about seeing. He explains, "The human brain is wired for optical input, for visualization. The optic nerve bundle is huge. Even with no input, or maybe especially with no input, the brain keeps creating images. I'm a very visual person, I just can't see."

Pete Eckert personifies Huxley's mantra, "The more you know, the more you see." The phrase is not simply a good idea—it is a simple fact of human nature. The eyes of a police officer on the lookout for criminal activity and the eyes of a youngster playing a console game are basically the same. Although there is no such thing as superhuman eyesight, a police officer knows how to find and catch a felon in the real world. A teenager, on the other hand, is better able to hunt down bad guys in a computer game. If the situations were reversed, the officer and the youth would be lost in each other's unfamiliar environments.

Huxley understood that clear seeing is a combination of how much you know and how you feel at any particular moment. Your cognitive state is a vital link in the visual communication process

Figure 16.1
The Art of Seeing *by Aldous Huxley inspired the theme used in this textbook.*
Courtesy of Northwest Press Books

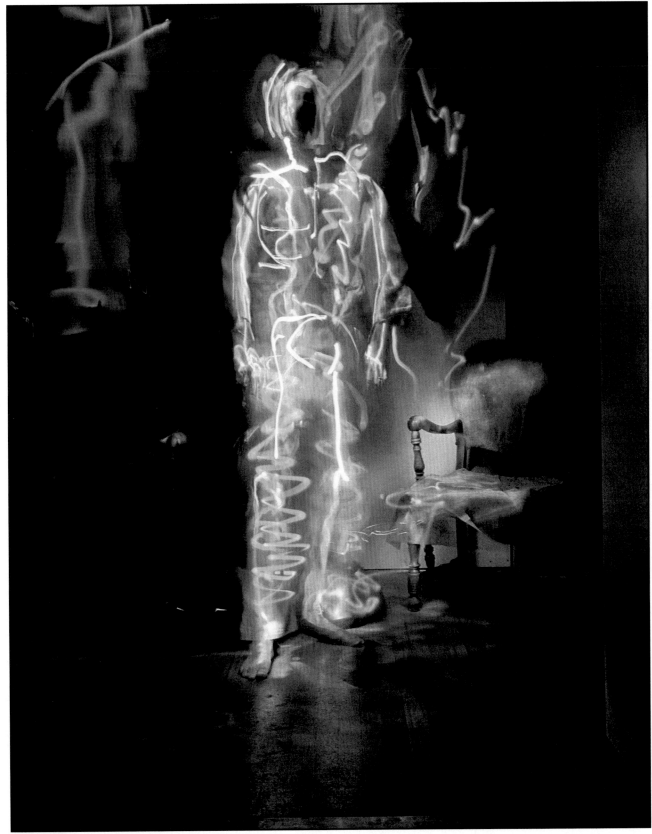

Figure 16.2
"Electro Man." With various non-traditional lighting techniques that include candles, flashlights, and lasers, San Francisco–based photographer Peter Eckert paints with light to create eerily ethereal human forms set within complex, urban scenes.
Courtesy of Pete Eckert

Figure 16.3
(Weblink: http://goo.gl/Aq3Jys)
Read the fascinating story of
Pete Eckert's life and then view
is wondrous photographs on
his website.

(See Chapter 3). As he noted:

> The most characteristic fact about the functioning of the total organism, or of any part of the organism, is that it is not constant, but highly variable. Sometimes we feel well, sometimes we feel poorly; sometimes our digestion is good, sometimes it is bad; sometimes we can face the most trying situations with calm and poise, sometimes the most trifling mishap will leave us irritable and nervous.

This non-uniformity of functionality is the price we pay for being living, self-conscious organisms, unremittingly involved in the process of adapting ourselves to changing conditions. Our organs of vision—the sensing eyes, the transmitting nervous system, and the mind that selects and perceives—is no less variable than the functioning of the organism as a whole.

This book, as strange as it may seem, isn't only concerned with seeing. Visual communication requires a two-way path between producer and receiver. Consequently, the focus of this work has more to do with *remembering* than seeing. If you learn to analyze a visual message in terms of its inventory, composition, visual cues, gestalt laws, semiotic signs and codes, cognitive elements, purpose, and aesthetics, and consider your personal reaction, its historical context, how it was made, any ethical responsibilities of the producer and presenter, and its impact on society, you should be able to create and use memorable pictures. Through the analytical process, you learn what it takes to remember an image.

More often than not, images that are remembered are the ones that combine aesthetically pleasing design elements with content that matters. Many of the pictures reproduced in this book satis-fy both criteria. The trouble is, works that combine both aesthetic beauty and meaning are either enormously difficult to produce or a result of great luck. In addition, because emotional and intellectual attributes are culturally bound, the two seldom agree. Appreciating cultural similarities and differences are keys in effective mass communication through words and pictures.

Learning Words

Most persons are taught to read by converting pictures into words. In reality, the two are the same. As we learned in Chapter 7, words are composed of highly symbolic line drawings. To teach how to interpret the symbolic markings of a letter, most children's books start with the alphabet. In English, the first page shows a picture of an apple and the sentence, "A is for Apple." As a page is turned, each letter of the alphabet is supported by a picture. After much practice, we no longer have to think of an actual red, juicy apple when we see the letter "A." Before anyone learns to read and write, the image and the letter must fuse in our mind. Some, however, never learn that mental trick.

Once called "hobos," homeless travelers who cannot read or write English and want to communicate with others in a written form, have created a unique symbol set that appears to be, by those who don't understand, strange markings without meaning. In reality, as with graffiti on walls, these lines are a complicated language (Figure 16.4).

There are also individuals who have minds that don't need the words that most of us take for granted. Early in her life, Dr. Temple Grandin was labeled as having a primitive mind. It wasn't until she was an adult that she was accurately diagnosed with Asperger's syndrome (AS), a form of autism in which individuals are nevertheless highly functional. Today she is a professor of animal science at Colorado State University

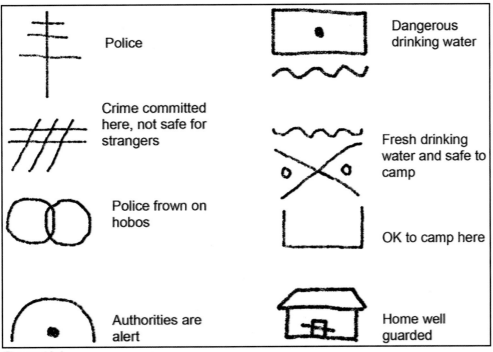

Figure 16.4
Called "hobo signs," these pictographs communicate messages for illiterate individuals.
Courtesy of the National Cryptologic Museum

and a leading advocate for the ethical treatment of animals and the author of several books. Grandin advised Dustin Hoffman for his role in the 1988 movie *Rain Man* while Claire Danes played her in the 2009 biopic *Temple Grandin* for HBO (Figure 16.5). Yet despite her extraordinary communicative skills, she does not think like most of us.

Grandin's mind is predominantly visual and pre-verbal, not dominated by thoughts that most of us consider "thinking." Her visual mind gives her an ability to empathize with animals that resulted in her revolutionary redesign of slaughterhouses to make them more humane. It also led to her writings that have helped autistic individuals and their caregivers.

Although Grandin is primarily a visual thinker, she is obviously a highly literate and verbal individual who would admit that although words are a second language, she would not be able to fully function in their absence. A world totally without language is one in which colors, forms, depth perspectives, and movements can be recognized and com-

Figure 16.5
Actress Claire Danes and Dr. Temple Grandin pose at the premiere of HBO's biopic, Temple Grandin *in New York City in 2010. Danes won an Emmy for Outstanding Lead Actress in a Movie for her moving portrayal of Grandin.*
Courtesy of Gregorio T. Binuya/Everett

pared, but meaning is largely lost. An image without a verbal accompaniment is similar to an amorphous, meaningless shape. Language gives meaning and substance to pictures.

When someone writes an "A" to someone who cannot read the language, it is simply a picture, different than a face or a house, but still just another image drawn with a pen on paper. Soon we learn that combinations of these letter-pictures mean more complicated things. When the drawings

APPLE

are combined, they form another picture, which we learn stands for the name of the fruit. Of course, other languages use different letter pictures for the same word that don't look anything like APPLE (Figure 16.6).

MOLLA	Albanian
ةحافت	Arabic
蘋果	Chinese (Traditional)
苹果	Chinese (Simplified)
JABUKA	Croatian
MANSANAS	Filipino
OMENA	Finnish
POMME	French
ΜΉΛΟ	Greek
תפוח	Hebrew
MELA	Italian
リンゴ	Japanese
'EPIL NAHMEY	Klingon
사과	Korean
JABŁKO	Polish
ЯБЛОКО	Russian
MANZANA	Spanish
ELMA	Turkish
QUẢTÁO	Vietnamese
I-APULA	Zulu

Figure 16.6
One of the most common fruits in the world has a rich variety of pictorial variations.
Courtesy of Paul Martin Lester

When combined with other letter pictures they become word pictures that can spark images in our minds. We further learn that these word pictures, when combined with other word pictures, form sentence pictures, and so on. To a pre-literate child, as with cave and graffiti artists, there is no difference between words and pictures.

As we age and become culturally indoctrinated, the mystery and magic of seeing the world visually is diminished. We are taught to make distinctions between words and pictures and to not think of them in the same way. We are taught that although we can gain meaning from each, reading words is valued more than reading pictures. We are taught that pictures play a separate and subservient role to the words. And although we are taught how to *make* pictures with our colored pencils, watercolor paints, and cameras, we get much more instruction on how to form, with our large lead pencils, the lines and curves that make letters, words, sentences, paragraphs, and textbooks.

We are taught to read stories, but we are never taught how to read images.

A Mental Exercise

Let's use our imaginations and think of archeologists about 1,500 years from now uncovering the buried ruins of one of today's cities (Figure 16.7). In the year 3518 scientists will no doubt find text on walls, storefronts, traffic signs, and so on in the languages we know and use today throughout the world. But just as much of the thoughts expressed in ancient cuneiform texts are lost today, words of the distant future may not be understood by 36th century scientists because the languages of today and the technologies that saved them will eventually become obsolete and forgotten.

As Jean-François Champollion and Thomas Young helped decipher the Rosetta Stone (See Chapter 7), there may be energetic and tenacious researchers with

Figure 16.7
One of the worst environmental disasters in the US, the Berkeley Pit in Butte, Montana.
Courtesy of NASA

laser-enhanced robotic hand spades. But with each area of the ruins uncovered, their frustration mounts. That's because after several months of digging in the dirt, all they find along the viaducts and abandoned highways in the old city are alien and simple line drawings that they assume relate to some form of written communication. They cannot read these strangely shaped pictures. Just before all hope is lost, one of the archeologists yells. Their disappointed suddenly turns to joy as they uncover messages they instantly recognize and can easily read. For amid the buried rubble of a civilization long past are elaborate and brightly colored symbols that have lasted through the centuries.

Street art, the often despised and criminalized form of visual communication, will in the future become the one, universally accepted language. In today's world, multi-colored spray-painted messages are labeled vandalism, graffiti, or tagging, depending on the speaker. These visual messages are actually a complex written form of communication that may mean the mark of a territorial border, a plea for understanding and hope for the future, grief for a killed loved one, anger toward an enemy, a show of playfulness and humor, an act of criminal vandalism, or simply an individual expression that signals the writer's existence. As with any communicative system, if you do not know the language, you will have trouble deciphering the message (Figure 16.8).

In this fictitious scenario, the future of mass communications will not rely on the preservation of pencils, pens, paper, computers, hard drives, wireless clouds, or satellites. In the vast, inconceivable future our so-called advanced human representatives will understand ancient civilizations only because of paint applied to walls. In the end, taggers with spray cans and multi-colored index fingers may be the only ones who will spread the message of our lost civilization.

Is it any wonder why humans created pictures on cave walls thousands of years before images were formed into words?

Reading Images Becomes the Norm

The transition from a verbal to a visual way of thinking is not without warnings from traditionalists. Social critics blame everything from the rise in the crime rate to the deterioration of educational institutions on the concurrent rise in the number of mediated images that can be seen daily. Young persons cling to visual symbols on walls, clothing, stickers on laptops, and in videos on tablets because words are associated with old ways of communicating. Words for many are repressive and only good for short bursts of text on smartphones. Pictures are fresh, fascinating, easily understood within a particular culture, and can be made into personal forms of expression.

Educators and newspaper publishers

Figure 16.8
Graffiti on a London wall shows a combination of several different tags, the personal logos or signatures from writers, and a "throw-up," a quickly spray-painted two-color drawing. At least seven writers have tagged this small space, and yet they didn't draw over the graphic eye in the center.
Courtesy of Paul Martin Lester

Figure 16.9
The last Saturday night of every month in Edinburgh, Scotland is known as Madchester, a club night when bars offer discount drinks, guest DJs, and other entertainments. These two posters no longer communicate literal information about the bar scene but are examples of artwork that fill our world with visual messages.
Courtesy of Paul Martin Lester

both express the same complaint—the younger generation is not a reading generation. But maybe there is little written that they want to read. Maybe they feel there was no point in reading when there are no jobs that require reading. Maybe their parents don't read and don't support the habit in them. Or maybe they *are* reading, but adults don't understand what they like to read. Messages *are* being read, but visual language means nothing to those who can only read words.

Let's face it. We live in a mediated blitz of images. They fill our newspapers, magazines, books, clothing, skin, billboards, theaters, television screens, and monitors as never before in the history of mass communications (Figure 16.9). We are becoming a visually mediated society. And that fact is changing us. For many, understanding of the world is accomplished not by reading words, but by reading images.

Although it is still unclear what the economic, social, and educational effects this visual culture will have upon the world, ironically, the use of images may foster a return of the word's importance. Or rather, a communication medium in which words and pictures have equal status may be a result of the recent explosion in pictures.

Words and Pictures as One

One of the most tired and ill-conceived clichés in photography is "a picture is worth a thousand words." Type the phrase in Google and you will get almost 600,000 results. Go ahead. I'll wait. Back? Good. But the often-quoted phrase seen in many student essays is actually phony and not even comprised of the original words. Fred Barnard, an advertising executive in the 1920s for the Street Railways Advertising Company, was trying to convince advertisers in a *Printer's Ink* trade magazine ad that pictures get a busy streetcar rider's attention and should be included with text messages. To add some of Aristotle's pathos, Barnard added a picture of a boy with a big smile (Figure 16.10). For credibility, or ethos to his argument, a bit of phony ancient philosophy was added: "CHINESE PROVERB One picture is worth ten thousand words." Meaning that a picture of a boy's smile enjoying his mother's treat is equal to 10,000 words explaining the benefits of baking powder. Over time, of course, it took 9,000 fewer words to describe a photograph. But whomever Barnard hired to create the Chinese translation got the proverb a bit wrong. Instead of stating that a picture is *worth* ten thousand words, the literal translation is, "A picture's meaning *can express* ten thousand words." Worth implies a crass, commercial connection, while the meaning of something is subjective and often personal. To say that an image is worth any number of words is a false equivalence. But meaning puts words and pictures on a respectful, equal footing. When all members of society, whether at home, in school, or on the job, use computers for word *and* picture processing, the switch is made from passive watching to active using. There will no longer be the barrier between the two symbolic structures. Words and pictures will become one powerful and memorable mode of communication just as in their beginning on cave walls.

Through the years, many have expressed opinions on the nature of words and pictures. Documentary photographer Lewis Hine (See Chapter 11), who often used words to accompany his photographs, once said, "If I could tell the story in words, I wouldn't need to lug a camera." It is beyond question that words and pictures are different symbolic structures. But each possess a language that some can interpret better than others. Photography philosopher John Berger admits "photographs supply information without having a language of their own. Photographs quote rather than translate from reality." Sol Worth, author of *Studying Visual Communication*, wrote of a compromise between the two points. "Pictures are not a language in the verbal sense. Pictures have no lexicon or syntax in a formal grammarian's sense. But they do have form, structure, convention and rules."

The writer William Saroyan, who won a Pulitzer Prize for his play *The Time of Your Life* (1939) noted how the meaning of images comes from the mind when he remarked, "One picture is worth a thousand words. Yes, but only if you look at the picture and say or think the thousand words." Suzanne Langer, known for her book *Philosophy in a New Key: A Study in the Symbolism of Reason, Rite, and Art* (1942) wrote that because language names relationships rather than illustrating them, "one word can take care of a situation that would require a whole sheet of drawings to depict it." For her, one word can mean a thousand pictures.

Words and pictures are intricately linked for educational and persuasive contexts. Words printed with a photograph signal the importance of the subjects within the image. Words beside a picture in an advertisement explain a product and its attributes clearly to a potential customer. Wilson Hicks, an influential picture editor for *Life* magazine, wrote in his book *Words and Pictures*

Figure 16.10
The origination of the photography cliché "a picture is worth a thousand words" comes from this advertisement created by Fred Barnard, the National Advertising Manager for the Street Railways Advertising Company. Barnard's argument for using illustrations in ads is that words fade from memory, but the picture of the boy's smiling face will make a lasting impression on busy streetcar riders.
Courtesy of Paul Martin Lester

(1952) "It is not correct to say that either medium supplements the other. The right verb is 'complements.'"

Despite occasional problems in discerning the meaning of pictures and words in publications, the combination of the two symbolic systems is one of the most powerful communicative strategies known. Hicks wrote that when words and pictures are equally expressive, the two become one medium where "the meaning of the work can be achieved in one perceptual act." Philosopher and author John Berger also celebrated the word and picture collaboration:

> In the relation between a photograph and words, the photograph begs for an interpretation, and the words usually supply it. The photograph, irrefutable as evidence but weak in meaning, is given meaning by the words. And the words, which by themselves remain at the level of generalization, are given specific authenticity by the irrefutability of the photograph. Together the

two then become very powerful; an open question appears to have been fully answered.

Psychologists have found that concrete nouns are much more effectively remembered as an aid to recall than abstract ones. The concrete nouns of ball, book, bottle, baby, and so on are easier to visualize in the mind because of their link to real objects. This fact explains why early writing was iconic—animals on walls and objects pressed in clay. Abstract concepts of freedom, peace, ethics, love, and so on are harder to link to a single image. As the Greek poet Simonides wrote, "Words are the images of things." Aristotle wrote even more succinctly, "There can be no words without images."

Words and Pictures Combined in the Mind

When you carefully analyze a visual message, you consciously study each visual symbol within that picture's frame. The act of concentration is an important verbal exercise. Without thinking of the signs within an image, there is little chance of it being recalled in the future. The picture is lost from your memory because you have learned nothing from it. Images become real property of the mind and remembered only when language expresses them. Linguistic experts do not need to argue that images have no alphabet or syntax because such assertions are true. The alphabet and the syntax of images reside in the mind, not in the picture itself.

Ironically, ancient societies without a written language had better recall of objects and events because their mental symbol systems had to be highly developed. They passed on their knowledge to future generations in the form of songs and dances. Writing and the literacy that spread throughout the world decreased the need for memory. Once an event is recorded on paper, it does not have to

W
LINK

Figure 16.11
*(Weblink:
http://goo.gl/1NFQL9)
One of the most enduring
photographs of the 1980s
was taken by Associated
Press photographer Jeff
Widener. The contrast
between the average-
sized man and the
mechanical menace of a
Chinese tank emphasizes
the tension in this
composition.*

be remembered exactly as it originally happened. Consequently, the need for a complex system of visual signs within the mind decreased over time as words dominated communication. Memorable images, whether imagined, directly experienced, or seen through a mediated format, are those that you think about often. They are usually simple compositions with immediate impact. They are images that trigger the emotional and rational aspects of your mind. They are pictures you recall again and again long after the original object of perception has faded from your retinas.

Because images cross all international borders, they become more easily understood by almost everyone. Words are easily forgotten, but pictures stay in our minds. We may not remember many of the facts that led to the brief student uprising in China's Tiananmen Square in 1989, but you can never forget the image of the lone protester standing defiantly in front of a line of menacing, green Chinese tanks (Figure 16.11). If you have seen the still picture or video, you remember it not only because it is a highly emotional image, but also because you have thought about the image in your mind with words. Words and pictures become one powerfully effective communicative medium inside your head. It shouldn't be a surprise that our minds are used as a model and metaphor for our communications technology. Computers and the web, more than any other innovations, are responsible for the sudden increase in images.

Toward a Universal Language
In his classic works *The Gutenberg Galaxy: The Making of Typographic Man* (1962) and *Understanding Media* (1964), Canadian media critic and philosopher Marshall McLuhan wrote of the power of electronic communication to unite the world (Figure 16.12). Because this contact is practically instantaneous, it's as if we are all living in one, singular town-

ship—a global village (Figure 16.13). McLuhan's metaphor is often employed to describe the power and the promise of the web to contradict the presumed economic imperialism of globalization.

Globalization fails if it turns into cultural imperialism that is concerned only with spreading one country's cultural values—for better or worse—throughout the vast regions of the planet. Turkey probably doesn't need more McDonald's cheeseburgers and Tokyo has plenty of Starbucks coffee shops (Figure 16.14). Likewise, those living in poverty don't need to be further exploited and stigmatized through sweatshops that churn out clothing, shoes, electronic equipment, and cartoon animations. McLuhan's form of globalization, his global village, was not seen as a way to bring harmony to the world, but, as he said, to have "extreme concern with everybody else's business."

When words and images have equal status within educational institutions and all media of communication, the cultural cues that define a society will not only be more efficiently passed from one generation to the next, but within *this* generation, here and now, diverse cultures will more clearly be able to understand each other. As with the de stijl artists with their peaceful, grid-like designs and Otto Neurath's Isotype language, many throughout history have hoped to unite the planet through verbal and visual messages. The Austrian semiotician Karl Blitz, who later changed his name to Charles Bliss, developed a visual language similar to Neurath's concept. After surviving the Dachau concentration camp during World War II, he invented his Blissymbolics pictograph system inspired from Chinese ideograms. In 1949 Bliss published the three-volume work *International Semantography: A Non-alphabetical Symbol Writing Readable in all Languages.* Although his 900-symbol visual language failed to bring about increased world understanding as he had hoped, in the 1960s it was found that children with severe cerebral palsy could be taught to communicate using Bliss's symbols.

Understanding and respecting each other's ways of communicating through words *and* pictures is a way for a positive form of globalization to occur. We *will* be concerned and care about everybody else's business because we will know each other a little better by the images we are able to view. As the noted photographic historian and collector Helmut Gernsheim wrote, "Photography is the only 'language' understood in all parts of the world, and bridging all nations and cultures."

Light in All its Meanings is the Key
Regardless of whether a presentation is meant for print or screen media, words and pictures have a better chance of being remembered if they are used together. That union is possible because of light. In fact, light links all the information presented in this book. The visual cues of color, form, depth, and movement quickly sort light into helpful or harmful classifications. Gestalt, constructivism, semiotics, and cognitive theories help explain why some light messages are remembered longer than others. Techniques used in advertising, public relations, and journalism help explain how light can so effectively attract, repel, and persuade. Light without reason or compassion produces pictorial stereotypes that mislead and harm.

Light forms the visual messages seen or discussed in all the chapters of this book.

From colorful iconic drawings of animals on cave walls came the symbolic marks of letterforms that Johannes Gutenberg used with his commercial printing press, and typographical designers of today employ to turn words into artistic expressions.

Saul Bass taught us that an entire

Figure 16.12
Canadian author and educator Marshall McLuhan in 1945.
Courtesy of Josephine Smith and the Library Archives Canada

W LINK
Figure 16.13
(Weblink: http://goo.gl/MJRCDp)
As with most interviews with Marshall McLuhan, his vision of the future for the combination of culture and technology was ahead of his time.

Figure 16.14
A McDonald's poster in Istanbul, Turkey proves that although the words are slightly different, the pictures remain the same.
Courtesy of Paul Martin Lester

motion picture's marketing image in print and its opening title sequence should be linked. Graphic designers use the art movements of art nouveau, dada, art deco, punk, new wave, pop art, hip-hop, de stijl, bauhaus, and many others to make designs, regardless of the media, that respect word and picture combinations.

USA Today's weather map not only inspired renewed interest in weather and its reporting, it also helped spur the entire data visualization profession. Innovative and technically savvy designers turn dull listings of numbers into displays that reveal significant details about the way the world works.

Evolving from short animated cartoons in a live action comedy program, Matt Groening's enduring Simpson family is the longest running prime-time show in television history. It inspired the present day renaissance of animation we see today in print and on screens.

From the first photograph, a fuzzy view of buildings in France, to Dorothea Lange's timeless portrait of a mother's concern for her future during the Great Depression. Photographers now can try to duplicate her achievement with their smartphone cameras.

The motion picture medium started with a short film of a fake sneeze by an assistant to Thomas Edison and was transformed by Orson Welles's classic *Citizen Kane*. Movies can now be shown in 3-D onto multi-story screens, but the story still matters for the success of the show.

A vaudeville act converted to radio and transformed into an audio and visual experience became television. It started as a crude, hard-to-see means of entertainment for the wealthy to become the most pervasive and powerful medium in the world.

Computers began as complex room-sized calculators and are now indispensable pocket-sized tools for everyday and magical uses.

Finally, the web was invented as a communication method in case of a nuclear holocaust and has become the one invention that has significantly altered and may replace most all the other media.

Light in the form of typography, graphic design, informational graphics, cartoons, photography, motion pictures, television, computers, and the web makes us sad, angry, happy, tense, calm, smart, dumb, loving, cynical, or bored—but by all means, it always makes us something.

Light.

The light of day, the light of reason, and the light of compassion made us who we were, makes us who we are, will make us who we will become, and will determine how we will be remembered. Louisiana photographer Clarence John Laughlin was an artist with words and pictures who observed and captured light as if he could create it (Figure 16.15). He summed up the reverence visual communicators have for what illuminates them when he wrote, "One of my basic feelings is that the mind, and the heart alike . . . must be dedicated to the glory, the magic, and the mystery of light."

Seeing because of the electromagnetic energy we call light is certainly a major component in visual communication, but there are other ways to understand ourselves and the world. Aldous Huxley might agree that his "the more you know, the more you see" phrase should be expanded:

> The more you know,
> the more you hear.
> The more you know,
> the more you smell.
> The more you know,
> the more you taste.
> The more you know,
> the more you feel.
> The more you know,
> the more you are you.

Today's communicators have the tools necessary to activate all the senses with words, pictures, and sounds. When you do, memorable messages—the only ones that challenge and enrich a person's life—should be the result (Figure 16.16).

KEY TERMS FROM THIS CHAPTER
Globalization • Lexicon • Syntax

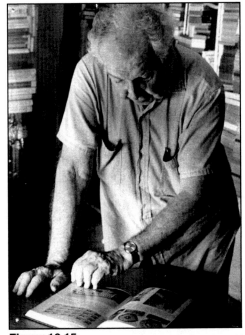

Figure 16.15
Clarence John Laughlin studies the pages of one of about 30,000 books he had within his crowded Pontalba apartment in Jackson Square, New Orleans in 1978. After his death in 1985, Louisiana State University purchased his library.
Courtesy of Paul Martin Lester

Figure 16.16
In this photograph taken by Jack Delano of the Farm Security Administration (FSA), light is a physical substance that has texture, weight, and can almost be touched (try it) as it streaks from windows of the waiting room of Union Station, Chicago in 1943.
Courtesy of the Library of Congress

Glossary

15 minutes of fame: The phrase coined by pop artist Andy Warhol in 1968, "In the future everyone will be world-famous for 15 minutes," as a commentary is concerned with the rise of the entertainment industry and the discounting of celebrity status (13).

9/11: On the morning of Tuesday, September 11, 2001, 19 members of the terrorist group al Qaeda hijacked four airplanes that were used in attacks on American property and civilians. The twin towers of the World Trade Center in New York City were hit and destroyed as well as a significant portion of the Pentagon in Arlington, Virginia. A fourth airliner, bound for the Capitol or the White House, was overtaken by passengers and crashed in a field outside Shanksville, Pennsylvania. Nearly 3,000 victims were killed, and billions of dollars in damages resulted (1).

Abstract: A form of expression that may use the standard tools employed by artists of other forms of art but does not employ elements that are easily identified as being from the real world. The most obvious examples are paintings whose main subject matter are geometric forms (1).

Ad-lib: An abbreviation of the Latin *ad libitum* meaning "at one's pleasure," it refers to the dramatic technique in which actors are asked to improvise dialogue with their own, unscripted words and actions based on what they think their characters would say and do (13).

Adjusted for inflation: A comparison of the rise or fall of the price of goods and services for a time period based on the Consumer Price Index. The greater the difference in two dates, the more the comparison reflects the actual costs to citizens at the time (9).

Advertising campaign: A term used whenever an advertising agency develops a series of messages for a particular product or service within a set time frame (2).

Allegorical: Developed first by the Greeks with their mythic stories and later employed by interpreters of the New Testament, this analytical technique gives literal, sometimes ordinary events significant symbolic meaning (6).

Alloy: A solid solution of one or more elements combined to enhance the properties of both for a specific purpose. For example, steel is made stronger by an alloy of iron and carbon (7).

American Institute of Graphic Arts (AIGA): First organized in 1914, it is a professional and student organization composed of typographers, graphic designers, photographers, and other media artists. AIGA currently has more than 20,000 members in 65 worldwide chapters (7).

Analog: The term can apply to numerical information that is represented by measureable quantities, such as lengths or electrical signals, as well as real-world activities without the aid of a computer (7).

Anime: A term for Japanese-inspired animated cartoons (10).

Anorexia nervosa: A serious psychiatric eating disorder marked by extremely low body weight. About 90 percent of those affected are women (4).

Aperture: The opening or hole of a lens that allows light to travel through it. As the opening gets smaller, the image is more sharply focused (11).

Archetypal or archetypes: The Swiss psychologist Carl Jung and the American mythologist Joseph Campbell theorized the existence of universal stories through a "collective unconscious" that contain original models that inspire other things or ideas and teach about the commonalities of human nature (6).

Aspect ratio: The look or appearance of a screen or frame. Film and television screens originally used an aspect ratio of 4:3 in which the screen is four units across by three down. Movie theaters and digital television sets now use a ratio of 16:9 for a widescreen or letterbox view (12).

Assimilation: Sometimes termed "The Melting Pot," the blending of diverse cultural groups into the dominant society (5).

Atari: An arcade game company founded in 1972 that created the popular tennis-like game "Pong." Atari is a Japanese word meaning *to hit the target* (14).

Augmented or mixed reality: Technology that superimposes computer functions and/or information upon a user's actual world (4).

Aztec culture: Refers to a group of ethnic peoples of central Mexico that dominated the region for about 300 years from the 14th century (5).

Banner: A form of advertisement or a title for a newspaper story that displays a message across an entire printed or web page (2).

Beehive hairdo: An elaborately high and teased head of hair invented in 1958. It was originally called a "B-52" after the shape of the front of an Air Force bomber of the same name (10).

Beta: A prototype version of a software product usually released to a select few for testing and comments before a general release to the public (15).

Big Four: Originally the "Big Three," referred to the American broadcast companies of ABC (American), CBS (Columbia), and NBC (National). The Fox Broadcasting Company was added to the list in 1986 (13).

Binocular vision: The act of using both eyes or two lenses at the same time (2).

Bitumen of Judea: Also known as asphalt, it is a sticky, molasses-like form of petroleum mainly used for paving roads. It was used in early photographic processes, most notably for heliography because it hardens from 10 minutes to several hours, depending on the amount of light it receives (11).

Blog: A contraction of the word weblog (web log), it was invented by the American computer programmer Jorn Barger to describe his activity of listing what he had read each day as "logging the web." Later, weblog was shortened to blog and now refers to any website that provides commentary in any form (text, audio, and/or video) with feedback possible from readers (3).

Bolshevik: A faction of the Marxist political party founded and led by Vladimir Lenin that took control of the Soviet Union during the 1917 Russian Revolution (6).

Broadsheet: Originally referring to one, large sheet of paper for the printing of news first used by a Dutch paper in 1618, it is the largest of the newspaper page formats that can be 22 inches or longer (3).

Bronze Age: An era of prehistoric times, estimated to be about a 2,000-year period from 3300 to 1200BCE in which alloys, particularly the melting of copper and tin to create bronze, were used for art objects, weapons, and other items (7).

Browser: A software application intended for the purpose of retrieving information available from the web (15).

Bullet points: Named for the tip of a rifle's projectile, it is a graphic mark used to stress an item in a list (9).

Calligraphy: Greek for "beautiful writing," it is a style of handwritten letters originally used by Chinese scribes and can be found on the bones of animals and shells of tortoises dating from the 14th century BCE (7).

Caption: Informational text accompanying a picture (4).

Carrier wave: An electromagnetic frequency that can be used to transmit text, sounds, and images over long distances (13).

Cel: Short for celluloid, it is a clear sheet on which hand-drawn animated cartoons are created. Disney's *The Little Mermaid* (1989) was one of the studio's last films to use cels in its production (10).

Chief executive officer (CEO): A high-ranking corporate employee who is responsible for the overall management of a company (14).

Chip speed: Sometimes called clock speed, it is a measurement of a computer processor's efficiency in calculating math, logic, and data functions (14).

Cholera: A highly infectious bacteria transmitted to humans through contaminated food and water. At the first sign of symptoms, a patient experiences a drop in blood pressure and can die within three hours without treatment (9).

CinemaScope: A widescreen motion picture format that used special lenses to project the picture onto the screen. It was popular for 14 years from the release of *The Robe* (1953) (12).

Closure: In graphics, it is the perception of elements within a layout when they are not a part of the design. For example, a circle or line with gaps can be perceived as being whole. It is related to the gestalt law of continuation (3).

Cloud computing: A concept that can mean using an inexpensive computer and accessing software programs from an internet source whenever they are needed, or it can also mean the extent of a wireless reception area (15).

Coaxial cable: A transmission line comprising a wire (usually) surrounded by another wire that is insulated (13).

Cold War: The name of an era in which there was serious political tension between the United States and the Soviet Union from the end of World War II until the fall of the Soviet Union in 1991 (15).

Collodion: A substance produced when highly flammable nitrocellulose is dissolved in ether. It was used as a temporary dressing for wounded American Civil War soldiers and as a photographic emulsion to coat glass plates by photographers who might have taken pictures of those injured soldiers (11).

Composition: The arrangements of visual elements within a frame. In a 1957 interview, the photojournalist Henri Cartier-Bresson defined his concept of the "decisive moment" as the instant when "Your eye must see a composition or an expression that life itself offers you, and you must know with intuition when to click the camera" (2).

Computer agent: A software program that performs its tasks in the background, often with the user unaware of its operation (15).

Consumerism: Any economic policy or habit that emphasizes consumption, usually with the assumption that such activity produces happiness (8).

Contrast: The relative extent of the difference between light and dark areas in a picture (11).

Convergent Era: A concept proposed by MIT professor Henry Jenkins in which the mass media are combining both technically and socially. As he puts it, "We are living in an age when changes in communications, storytelling, and information technologies are reshaping almost every aspect of contemporary life—including how we create, consume, learn, and interact with each other. A whole range of new technologies enable consumers to archive, annotate, appropriate, and re-circulate media content and in the process, these technologies have altered the ways that consumers interact with core institutions of government, education, and commerce" (14).

Copy: The words or text supplied by a writer for a print or screen media graphic design (4).

Cortex: See Visual cortex (2).

Crash: Whenever a software application or operating system stops working and freezes a computer. Oftentimes the only remedy is to restart the machine. However, if the hard drive has failed, data may be lost. It is always a good idea to regularly back up data onto an external hard drive (14).

Crop: To remove the edges of a picture (6).

Cultural relativism: The philosophy that states that a person's attitudes, beliefs, and activities should be understood within that person's own cultural understanding and values without input from ideas from other cultures (3).

Cut: The smallest portion of a film, the name is a holdover from when film was a physical object requiring the slicing of it for editing purposes. Several short cuts in a motion picture scene can add dramatic tension, whereas a long stretch of film without cuts can convey a calm, hypnotic rhythm (8).

Cyberspace: From the Greek word for "rudder," it refers to the various global communications technologies that make such tools as the internet and the web possible (8).

Dark Ages: A period of time in Western European history from the fall of the Roman Empire until the invention and widespread use of the commercial printing press, from about 476 to 1500 CE (7).

Darkroom: A specialized space with plumbing and controlled lighting to allow the processing of negatives and printing of photographs in the dark, or with non-photosensitive safelights (11).

Death penalty: A government's sanctioned murder of another person because of a major offense or capital crime (4).

Depth of field: A term used in image making that describes the relative extent to which a scene is in focus. With a small aperture and longer shutter speed, the elements in the foreground to the background are more in focus than if a large aperture and a quick shutter speed were employed (6).

Digital: Within this book's context, it is any information or practice that must use a computer for its inception and presentation. Editing a document or a photograph is digital; holding a printout is analog (9).

Dioramas: Full- or small-scale models of usually a historically or environmentally significant event often seen in museum displays. They originated in France in 1822 by the co-inventor of the daguerreotype photographic process, Louis Jacques Mandé Daguerre. He created elaborate staged illusions in which audience members thought they were viewing reality. Modern examples can be found in the "Universe of Energy" pavilion at Epcot outside Orlando, Florida, "Pirates of the Caribbean" ride at Disney World and Disneyland, and in the movie *Night at the Museum: Battle of the Smithsonian* (2009) (11).

Discrimination: To act in a prejudiced or biased way toward people (usually) who have apparent, but not essential, differences (5).

DIY (do-it-yourself): A self, home, and world improvement philosophy that advocates creating and repairing things without resorting to paid experts. Activities that fall under the DIY umbrella can also include music recordings, website creation, and zine production (7).

Doctors Without Borders: A worldwide volunteer organization founded in France in 1971 composed of physicians, nurses, and journalists that provides aid to persons in need and publicizes their plight and recovery. As stated in the relief organization's website, it is "committed to bringing quality medical care to people caught in crisis regardless of race, religion, or political affiliation [and acts] independently of any political, military, or religious agendas" (10).

Download: Refers to the act of transferring information— whether textual, audio, and/or visual—from one computer to another. To download means to receive, to upload means to send (15).

DRAM (dynamic random access memory): A form of computer memory that can contain a lot of information but is lost once the power supply is turned off (14).

Dust Bowl: An environmental catastrophe occurring in the United States for a decade starting in about 1930. Severe and continual drought conditions coupled with inefficient and ill-conceived farming methods (e.g., deep plowing, lack of crop rotation) affected more than 156,000 square miles of land, larger than the state of Montana, and was centered in the Oklahoma and Texas panhandle regions. Much of the topsoil of the region was blown away in powerful windstorms that blackened East Coast cities. The soil eventually was deposited into the Atlantic Ocean. More than half a million persons were left homeless, with more than 100,000 families arriving in California to find work (11).

Editorial picture: A photograph usually taken by a photojournalist for use within a news context (1).

Electromagnetic spectrum: Named by the Scottish physicist James Clerk Maxwell, who also invented the first color photography process, it is a range of wavelengths, some as long as the height of the tallest buildings in the world that support radio broadcasts and others as small as atomic nuclei known as gamma rays (2).

Electron scanner: A process in microphotography that uses beams of electrons instead of visible light, as with most microscopes, to provide extremely close-up pictures (13).

Electronic highway: An early metaphor to describe the internet. See cyberspace (15).

Emoji: Also known as a smiley and an emoticon, it is a small pictograph used in text messaging to convey addition meaning and/or context (9).

Emulsion: For analog photographic films, it is a layer that contains light-sensitive material within a medium of collodion, starch, or gelatin on a sheet of metal, glass, paper, or plastic (11).

Engraving: A technique used for printing illustrations that employs a steel tool called a burin to carve an image onto a metal plate. The plate is then used in the printing process (7).

Existentialist: A type of analysis that tries to find meaning by concentrating on actual human existence as an observer and participant of the world and espoused by such philosophers as Søren Kierkegaard, Friedrich Nietzsche, Jean-Paul Sartre, Simone de Beauvoir, and Albert Camus (6).

Fascism: Perhaps best exemplified by Mussolini's pre– World War II Italian government, it is an authoritative ideology that is in constant conflict with its own citizens and other countries (3).

Federal Communications Commission (FCC): Established by the Communications Act of 1934 to regulate radio and television broadcasts and interstate wire, satellite, and cable, its five commissioners are selected by the president and confirmed by the U.S. Congress (13).

Feminist movement: Begun in the 19th

century by women advocating the right to vote (that privilege was granted in 1920), it progressed in the 1960s to include protest against cultural restrictions placed on women including unfair pay structures compared with men; currently the movement attempts to celebrate the achievements of women in order to expand its political membership (2).

Flash: A technique used in photography in which artificial light is supplied by flash powder, bulbs, cubes, and/or electronic units (1).

Flash Mob: A public gathering of seemingly unrelated persons who nevertheless perform a coordinated performance (11).

Freelance: To sell work or services to clients without permanent employment status (9).

Freudian: Relating to an analytical technique inspired from the writings of the Austrian psychiatrist Sigmund Freud in which a person's subconscious mind is evoked in order to discover personal meaning for symbolic signs (6).

Functionalism: An analytical philosophy in which an object's role in society is valued more than its composition (8).

Gallup poll: Developed by the American educator and statistician George Gallup in 1935, it charts the public's opinion on a variety of political, social, and economic issues (5).

Gelatin: A by-product of the meat and leather industries, it is a clear protein substance derived from the bones and internal organs of cattle, pigs, and horses that is used for a variety of purposes including photographic film (11).

Genre: A particular type of written or visual work (2).

Gesture: A form of nonverbal language that is used for communicative purposes, such as a finger to the mouth to indicate quiet or a wink when flirting (2).

Globalization: A condition of cultural and/or economic development in which a local trend becomes accepted on a worldwide scale (16).

Hack: An activity by a hacker in which a computer program is changed from its original purpose either for a positive or a malicious reason (15).

Halftone: A printing technique for photographs in which the image is converted to tiny, differently sized dots through a screen, reproducing the tones on a printing press. First conceived by photographic inventor William Fox Talbot in the 1850s, the process was practically introduced by Stephen Horgan and later perfected by Frederic Ives, George Meisenbach, and Louis and Max Levy (2).

Hijab: Unlike a chadri or burqa in which a woman's entire body is covered, from the Arabic word meaning "to cover," a hijab is a head covering or scarf worn by Muslim women as a symbol of their religious and cultural heritage (5).

Hit: Usually refers to a successful web destination from using a search engine, but can also mean a request from a user to download a file (7).

HIV (Human Immunodeficiency Virus)/AIDS (Acquired Immunodeficiency Syndrome): AIDS is a chronic, life-threatening pandemic disease caused by HIV. First recognized in 1981, it is estimated that more than 2.1 million persons have died from the virus, about 300,000 of them children. Currently about 40 million persons worldwide have HIV/AIDS supported by expensive medications that slow its growth. There is no known cure (4).

Homepage: Usually the first page that is presented on a website (15).

Hospice: A form of medical care available usually within special wings of hospitals reserved for terminally ill patients with a diagnosis of less than six months to live in which the physical needs, including pain management and emotional wants of the patient and friends and family, are supplied (4).

Hypertext: One of the chief differences between print media and the web, it is text that is usually underlined to indicate a hyperlink where additional information is available from some other webpage or website (15).

Iconoscope: An early television camera tube developed by the Russian-born scientist Vladimir Zworykin for RCA that was used by German technicians to televise the 1936 Olympic Games and employed in American sets until it was replaced in 1946 by the highly light-sensitive image orthicon tube (13).

Impressionism: Inspired and influenced by the new invention of photography, Impressionist artists such as Claude Monet, Pierre-Auguste Renoir, and Edgar Degas broke many established "rules" of fine art with their choice of colors, brush strokes, and outdoor, natural settings (1).

Indie: An abbreviation of "independent," it is a term used mostly for music and filmmaking producers who sidestep major companies to create and distribute their art on their own. Indie also refers to a free, break-the-rules kind of attitude (12).

Islam: Based on the teachings of the Islamic prophet Muhammad who died in 632 CE, it is the second most prevalent religion in the world after Christianity. It is a monotheist religion with its religious history, principles, and social rules outlined in its holy book, the Qur'an. A person who practices Islam is called a Muslim (5).

Isobar: In meteorology, it is a line that indicates equal barometric pressure on a map (9).

Jungian: Inspired by the Swiss psychiatrist Carl Jung, it is an analytical method that attempts to understand symbolic images and concepts through the analysis of human archetypes and myths (6).

Killer app: A computer application that is such an innovative and desired program that it is an instant public success. Spreadsheet, banking, and communications software are popular examples (14).

Kinemacolor: A two-color (usually red and green) filter system for the taking and projecting of color motion pictures. It was the first color movie technology and was invented by British George Smith in 1906 (12).

Kinetograph and Kinetoscope: Although the American inventor Thomas Edison first thought of the technology, two of his employees, William Kennedy Laurie Dickson and William Heise, invented the movie camera and viewer. As a camera, the Kinetograph recorded images on long rolls of 35-mm-wide photographic film supplied by George Eastman's Kodak company, and mounted on perforated cylinders. Viewers watched the films through a peephole of a Kinetoscope (10).

Ku Klux Klan: A United States domestic terrorist organization founded in 1865 with veterans from the Confederate Army that was anti-Catholic, anti-Semitic, anti-Communism, and racist. By the 1870s the Klan was mostly suppressed due to the federal government's prosecution of members' crimes. However, with the popularity of and controversy surrounding D. W. Griffith's film *Birth of a Nation* that celebrated the Klan, membership increased so that by the 1920s it claimed more than six million members. Today the estimated membership is about 6,000 (3).

Layout: The arrangement of all graphic elements for print or screen media (2).

Lexicon: Compared with the word "font"

that refers to all the graphic variations of a typeface, it is all the words and expressions that make up a vocabulary (16).

Life **magazine**: A name for a publication with three major iterations—as a humor magazine from 1883 to 1936, a weekly news magazine from 1936 to 1972, a monthly from 1978 to 2000, and finally a weekly newspaper supplement from 2004 to 2007 when it quit publishing. During its second heyday, publisher Henry Luce helped make it one of the premiere places to see the best of photojournalism (4).

Literal: A term that refers to concepts and objects that are easily understood (1).

Lithography: A printing method that allows artwork and type to be printed at the same time (7).

Live-action: Works that are performed during the taping of television shows and the filming of motion pictures by human actors (10).

Locative: A type of augmented reality in which a user of a smartphone or tablet can find information, store locations, and people based on location (4).

Logo: A distinctively identifying symbol for a company, publication, or screen presentation (2).

Long-term memory: In physiological terms, thoughts that stay in a person's mind from a few days to as long as a lifetime (1).

LP (long playing) record: A round vinyl phonograph album about 12 inches in diameter that played music stored in an analog format when amplified through a needle and spun on a turntable (4).

Mainframe computer: Originally large, room-sized computers capable of complex and fast calculations for government and corporate purposes. Personal computer networks are gradually replacing them (14).

Manga: Graphic novels, often containing violent and sexual content, that are popular in Japan and other Asian countries (10).

Marxism: A political philosophy originating from the German economist Karl Marx and the German social scientist Friedrich Engels that presents a non-capitalist and non-religious view of how the world should work (6).

Maya: With its capital in the Yucatán Peninsula, the Maya civilization spanned from southern Mexico to western Honduras from about 2000BCE until the arrival of the Spanish Conquistadores about 900CE. At its height the society was one of the most complex cultures in the world with advances in art, architecture, writings, and political systems (7).

Meme: Invented by the British evolutionary biologist Richard Dawkins in his book *The Selfish Gene* (1976), used to describe the spread of musical, fashion, and religious ideas. It can be a familiar phrase or popular cultural concept such as the YouTube video of a piano-playing cat featured on the 2009 "MTV Movie Awards" show or "All your base are belong to us" from a poorly translated bit of dialogue from the Japanese Sega video game "Zero Wing." (8).

Microelectrode: An electrode with an end so small it doesn't damage a cell's outer membrane that is used for monitoring electrical impulses (2).

MIT (Massachusetts Institute of Technology) Media Lab: A department of the School of Architecture and Planning, its personnel have a reputation for innovations in communications including an initiative to develop a $100 laptop computer to improve educational opportunities for children around the world (14).

Moiré pattern: From a French word for a type of textile, it refers to visual interference that creates the illusion of internal vibration when an illustration with a set of parallel lines overlays another at a slight angle (2).

Montage: An artistic composition of several different parts (8).

Mouse: Named by researchers at the Stanford Research Institute because of its small size and cord that looked like a tail, it is a sophisticated pointing device that allows a user to interact with software programs on a computer (8).

Mug shot: A head-and-shoulders portrait of a person usually looking into a camera's lens and displayed at a small size on a page whether for print or screen media (2).

Multi-User Dungeon (MUD): Online game playing with often-unknown partners on their computers anywhere in the world. An outgrowth of the board game "Dungeons and Dragons," the first MUD was named "Colossal Cave Adventure." Created by computer programmer and spelunker Will Crowther in 1975, the game's pathways are based on the Mammoth Cave system in Kentucky that he used to explore (15).

Multiple exposure: Usually with a camera, taking more than one picture within the same frame (2).

Muslims: See Islam (5).

Mythical: A form of analysis that evokes stories in words or pictures that persons in a culture understand because of their deeply held and common emotions (6).

News photograph: See editorial picture (1).

Noise: In visual communication, it can refer to the amount of grain that is noticed in a film or photograph as well as the number of elements within a frame or as part of a layout that distract from what should be the primary subject matter (9).

Olmec: A Mexican civilization occupying the south central part of the country for about 1500 years from 1200BCE. Best known for their huge stone head artworks, they also performed ritualized body piercing and played ballgames in which the losing team was sometimes executed (7).

On-demand: Any number of user-controlled features that include watching video, working on a computer, using software, or printing whenever it is convenient (13).

Operating system (OS): A software program that manages a computer's communication between an application and its hardware. Popular systems include Mac OS X, Windows Vista, Linux, and GNU, a free program created by the American developer and hacker Richard Stallman (14).

Over-the-counter (OTC) stock: As opposed to exchange trading by large organizations such as the NASDAQ, New York, or London exchanges, it is the buying and selling of stocks directly from one party to another (14).

Pan or panning: A film technique in which the camera is moved horizontally (2).

Paparazzi: Usually freelance still photographers and/or videographers that take photographs and video of celebrities during public and sometimes private events (11).

Pater Noster House: With its slogan "Where Hope Comes Home," it is a 28-year-old licensed home located in Columbus, Ohio, that offers transitional housing for those with HIV/AIDS (4).

Petroglyphs: Images made by scratching or carving into rock surfaces (7).

Phenomenological: Espoused by the philosopher Edmund Husserl and his student Martin Heidegger, it is an analytical method similar to existentialism in which the phenomenon is used as a way of understanding all human knowledge (6).

Photoshop: A software program usually reserved for editing still photographs created by the American software developer Thomas Knoll and introduced by Adobe in 1990 for Macintosh computers only. It has since been developed for almost all platforms and is the most popular program for photographic manipulation in the world (2).

Pictographs: Also called pictograms, they are pictures that closely resemble a physical object they are meant to represent. In that way, they are similar to the semiotic iconic sign (7).

Pilot: A provisionary episode produced in the hope that a television series will be approved and financed (13).

Platen: Originally a wooden and later a metal weight pressed over a sheet of paper above an inked typeface surface during the printing process (7).

Plate: Made of paper, plastic, metal, stone, or other materials, an image on its surface is inked and transferred to paper directly, or in offset printing, transferred to a rubber surface that is then used to print the picture on paper (11).

Podcast: A digital media file that can contain still images, audio, and video that can be downloaded to a computer or portable player. A user can select a single program or subscribe to a producer's work so that presentations are automatically downloaded on a regular basis (3).

Polio: Short for poliomyelitis, it is a highly contagious viral disease that can cause severe symptoms, from stiffness of the neck to paralysis, but only in about 5 percent of those affected. Since the medical researcher Jonas Salk introduced a polio vaccine in 1955, the disease has been essentially eliminated. However, in countries such as India, Nigeria, and Pakistan, the incidence of infection is still about 1,500 a year (11).

Portal: Sometimes called a gateway, it is a major starting site for mainly commercial website users (15).

Poster child: A young person with a debilitating disease selected to have her picture included on posters in addition to making public appearances in order to generate sympathy and publicity to raise funds from the general public in order to provide for the treatment and research for the condition (5).

Prejudice: Bias for or against a person or idea without knowing all the facts (5).

Public service announcement (PSA): Usually a radio, television, or web non-commercial message that raises awareness about a specific topic (2).

Ptolemy V: After his father died, he became Emperor of Egypt at the age of five in the year 204BCE. Known for his cruelty in suppressing a rebellion and his skill at hunting, his main claim to fame comes from a scribe who wrote on the Rosetta Stone of a tax break he gave to a religious group (7).

Punch cards: Perforated stiff paper sheets with holes that defined quantitative data that could be input into early calculating machines and then computers. First used in 1725 in France for controlling the complex patterns of textile looms, their use could still be found by graduate students using university mainframe computers as late as 1985 (14).

Qualitative: Evaluations of information such as from interviews, original written sources, and transcripts (9).

Quantitative: Measurements such as time, distance, weight, public opinions, and demographics that can be defined by a specific unit and thus calculated, and conclusions made about any relationships between the measured elements (9).

Racial profiling: Discrimination usually conducted by law enforcement officials that is based on the assumption that some races are more suspicious or dangerous than others (5).

RAM (random access memory): A type of storage that is accessed quickly and is used to run software programs during a computer's operation; once the computer is turned off, the memory is erased (14).

Random dot stereogram: Two images composed of dots that when viewed by focusing behind them generate a 3-D image in the mind. First created by the Hungarian scientist Béla Julesz in 1959, his student Chris Tyler in 1979 used the principle to make the effect with a single image, called an autostereogram (2).

Realism: An artistic style in which actual scenes found in life were preferred over mythical or fantastical constructs. The Italian Michelangelo Merisi da Caravaggio in the 16th century as well as trompe l'oeil artists were advocates of the art genre (1).

Renaissance: An era of intense cultural growth for about 300 years dating from the 14th century that began in Italy and then spread to the rest of the Western world largely because of the advent of Johannes Gutenberg's commercial printing press (2).

Retinas: A lining of tissue within the back of each eye that contains the photosensitive cells known as rods, sensitive to low-light situations and movement, and cones, used for sharp focus and color perception (2).

Reuben award: An honor given to the "Cartoonist of the Year" by the National Cartoonist Society. Named after Rube Goldberg, a Pulitzer Prize–winning political cartoonist, best known for his humorous comic strip in which he devised overly intricate and complex devices in order to complete an ordinarily simple task. The first recipient was given in 1946 to Milton Caniff for his strip "Terry and the Pirates" (10).

Rhetorical: An analytical methodology often used in persuasion scenarios in which often intriguing questions are asked and concepts pondered without the expectation of receiving an answer (6).

Rituals: A wide variety of acts made by a single individual or a group usually performed on certain dates or for some known cultural reason such as birthday parties, weddings, and funerals (3).

Roman Empire: During its heyday in 117 CE, the Italian-based realm ruled north to England, south to Egypt, east to Mesopotamia, and west to northern Africa. Starting with ancient Rome in the 10th centuryBCE and continuing through the Roman Republic that dated from about 510BCE and had a monarchy that could be influenced by its citizens until it was overthrown through civil wars, the Roman Empire had a single emperor that ruled dictatorially. The Empire had enormous influence over architecture, language, and political thought until its demise in 1453 when the Ottoman Turks captured Constantinople (7).

Rule: A thin, usually horizontal line used in layouts to graphically separate different sections (8).

Sarcophagus: Any stone coffin, but usually Egyptian (7).

Screen Actors Guild (SAG): A union affiliated with the AFL-CIO begun in 1933 that represents about 120,000 actors in "motion pictures, television, commercials, industrials, video games, Internet and all new media formats" (13).

Scribe: A person employed as a copyist of manuscripts (7).

SDRAM (synchronous dynamic random access memory): A quick, powerful, and stable technology for delivering data for computer operations (14).

Search engine: A software application

that allows a user to find information on the web through keyword input (15).

Secularism: A manifestation of the concept of the separation between church and state, it is the idea that government agencies and their decisions should not be guided by religious beliefs (7).

Serial: A continuing plot for radio, television, and web stories that reveal more plot twists as a season unfolds (10).

Serif: Seen in all the typeface families except sans serif, a continuation of a letter's stroke that comes from the cursive writing style in which handwritten letters were joined (7).

Server: A broad term that can mean a software program that is a part of a dedicated computer that accepts data requests from users' web browsers (15).

Sharia law: The moral and religious code of Islam as interpreted in the *Quran*. However, as with most religious texts, the interpretation depends on whether you are modern, traditional, or fundamental in your orientation (5).

Short: In the early history of Hollywood, it was typically a two-reel film less than 25 minutes long. Today these "short subjects" are less than 45 minutes. The "Festival des Très Court" is an annual film festival founded in Paris highlighting films of three minutes or less (10).

Short-term memory: Lasting only a few seconds, it is the ability of humans to store brief bits of verbal and visual data such as phone numbers and visual arrays that sometimes are used in the making of long-term memories (3).

Shot: A single photographic image or continuous take in motion pictures (2).

Shrine: Usually a religiously sacred place worshipped by those who believe in its historical significance, although it can refer to any setting where heroes and idols are remembered with wonder and admiration (3).

Sidebar: Similar to a fact box infographic, it can be a text-related story, pictures, or a collection of hyperlinks, usually graphically separated from the main article for print and online publications (3).

Silicon Valley: Originally used in a trade magazine in 1971 to describe the burgeoning semiconductor industry centered south of San Francisco near San Jose, California, the Silicon Valley is home of some of the world's leading high technology companies including Adobe Systems, Apple, Inc., eBay, Google, Hewlett-Packard, Intel, and Yahoo! (14).

Silver bromide and nitrate: Crystalline halides (others are silver with chloride, iodide, and fluoride) used in black and white photographic film and paper because they turn dark when exposed to light (11).

Situation comedy (sitcom): A television episodic genre for animated or live-action actors in which continuing characters are presented with different and hopefully humorous conditions from week to week (8).

Slander: Unlike its print and broadcast counterpart libel, it is defamation of a person's character that is made orally and in public (7).

Soap operas: A television genre that features long-running, continual story lines, usually shown during the daytime hours (13).

Social symbols: Verbal and nonverbal signs that have meaning to individuals in public settings that aid in human communication. Examples might be a greeting, handshake, kiss, or a brand name on a T-shirt (3).

Stereotype plate: A technology of early hot press printing that is a cost-saving procedure in which a mold of papier mâché or plastic is cast for an entire block of type that can be reused without setting individual letters by hand (7).

Storyboard: A cartoon version of a film used as a way to organize individual frames of a motion picture originally developed by the Walt Disney Studio in the 1930s. Directors such as James Cameron and Joel and Ethan Coen use storyboards almost exclusively in the preparation for shooting (8).

Streaming media: In order to speed the delivery of multimedia programming through an internet network, an end-user can enjoy the material from the beginning instead of waiting until the entire piece is downloaded (15).

Structural: A form of analysis in which elements are studied based on their relationships with each other rather than their history (6).

Stylus: A device for writing first used by cuneiform scribes with the tips of reeds and bones pressed into soft clay. Later, inked quills from the wings of birds and pencils, crayons, fountain and roller ball pens, and computer touch screen markers were employed (7).

Substrate: The first layer in which all others are included (7).

Symbolic: A form of analysis that stresses any aural, verbal, or visual element that represents some other, non-literal meaning for the viewer (1).

Synchronous classroom: A type of online instruction in which the instructor and students use a "virtual classroom" chat room to have same-time discussions and meetings just as with a face-to-face class (14).

Syntax: All of the rules and conditions that describe how sentences should be constructed (3).

Tablet: Any flat pad or panel used for the production of a presentation (14).

Tabloid: Originally a pharmaceutical term to describe a pill that contains compressed medicine, it is a newspaper and television format usually known for its exploitation of sensational news and entertainment stories. However, it can also refer to smaller sized newspapers that are traditional in content (3).

Teasers: These are eye-catching photographs and/or text blocks that hint at a story on an inside page that might be of interest to a reader (3).

Technicolor: A proprietary color process named for MIT, where one of the inventors, Herbert Kalmus, received his undergraduate degree. It was widely used for motion pictures from 1922 until 1952, first as a two-color system and then as a full-color process by Walt Disney Studios for its animated cartoons and for *The Wizard of Oz* (1939) (12).

Terrorists: Those who espouse a philosophy of terrorism that usually involves committing violent acts against innocent citizens for the purpose of disrupting social and economic activities (5).

Transistor: A semiconductor device used for the sending and amplification of an electrical signal (14).

Type mold: Similar to casting, it is a hollow block of metal for making typefaces that contains the shape of a letter that is created after a liquid alloy is poured into it and cooled (7).

Uniform resource locator (URL): The address for a website (15).

Uruk, Iraq: An ancient city of Mesopotamia in which about 80,000 residents lived around the year 2900BCE and located about 150 miles southeast of Baghdad. Home of King Gilgamesh and thought to be the inspiration of the Garden of Eden as told in the Bible, the city was abandoned around 100 CE. Baghdad's National Museum of Iraq was looted of priceless artifacts from the region during the beginning of the Iraq War in 2003 (7).

Vacuum tube: A sealed glass or metal tube once commonly used in electronic devices (12).

Vaudeville: Any stage show that consists of a variety of entertainment genres—songs, animal acts, and comedy sketches (5).

Vellum: French for *calfskin*, a tough and lasting substrate mainly reserved for printed materials made from the flesh of mammals, particularly cattle. Copies of Johannes Guttenberg's Bible printed on vellum have outlasted those he made with paper (7).

Viral videos: Similar to a meme, a video clip that becomes wildly popular through e-mail and instant message sharing. Examples include a digital short titled "Dick in a Box" first shown on "Saturday Night Live;" the Scottish church singer Susan Boyle's surprising debut on "Britain's Got Talent;" and the "Star Wars Kid," 14-year-old French Canadian Ghyslain Raza's personal video that he made while pretending to fight with a light saber (10).

Virtual reality: A term used to describe a technology that simulates an actual, living experience for the user (8).

Visual array: The elements you can see with both eyes open under normal lighting conditions. For an adult, the angle of view is approximately equivalent to a 24-mm wide-angle lens (2).

Visual journalism: A profession in the mass communication field with journalists who work with words, images, and graphic designs for print and/or screen media (9).

Visual perception: Understanding in a literal and symbolic sense what it is your mind is focused upon within a visual array (3).

Wavelength: The distance between two crests of a waveform with a trough between them. A wave that is more energetic or has a higher frequency has a shorter wavelength than one with a lower frequency and longer wavelength. The distance for a wavelength of the color violet is about 400 nanometers (or 0.000016 of an inch), whereas red is longer at about 700 nm (0.000028 of an inch) (2).

Web perfecting press: The name for the extremely fast and efficient rotary printing press invented by the American Richard Hoe in 1843 in which words and images are placed on a curved cylinder (7).

Western culture: Sometimes known as Western civilization, it is a culmination of art, custom, religion, and technology commencing from Western Europe and including immigrants to other parts of the globe, most specifically in the Americas and Australia (1).

Wirephoto: A method for sending photographs via telegraph or telephone lines introduced by Western Union in 1921 and used by the Associated Press (AP) news agency to quickly send images to member newspapers until 2004 when the web made the technology obsolete (9).

World Press Photo: A non-profit organization founded in 1955 and based in Amsterdam that promotes the best of photojournalism through its annual contest (4).

Writers Guild of America (WGA): A United States– based labor organization with its eastern branch representing television and motion picture writers who live in the New York City area and the western branch for the same in southern California. Begun in 1921, it has about 8,000 members (13).

Xerox Palo Alto Research Center (PARC): Founded in 1970 in California's Silicon Valley as an experimental lab supporting innovations in computing, scientists at the Center developed the laser printer, the local area network known as the Ethernet, and the graphical user interface (GUI) that inspired Apple Computer engineers to include it in their Macintosh—one of the most important features in its computers. Much later, Xerox sued Apple for copyright violation, but the suit was dismissed due to the expiration of the statute of limitations (15).

Y-Not: To complete the English alphabet I added this entry to the glossary. Email me your "y" entries with their definitions for extra credit.

Zapf Dingbats: Created by the German typeface designer Hermann Zapf, who also invented the popular roman family typeface of Palatino and the sans serif Optima, it is a miscellaneous set of graphic symbols seldom used by graphic designers. (7).

Zapotec: A pre-Columbian (before the arrival of Christopher Columbus) civilization centered in south central Mexico dating from about 500BCE. Known for their elaborate tombs and jewelry, they also developed a written form of communication with symbols representing the syllables of their language that influenced the later cultures of the Maya and Aztec (7).

Zoom: A film technique in which a camera is connected to a special lens so that its focal length can change from a wide to a close-up view (2).

Zoopraxiscope: One of the first devices for showing animated images invented by Eadweard Muybridge in 1879 (12).

Bibliography

*I'm not a creature of habit. I like
to find things from unexpected
sources.*

*Norman Foster, 1935 -
ARCHITECT
& PHILANTHROPIST*

Weblink: http://goo.gl/RA1Csp

Biography

Dr. Paul Martin Lester is a Clinical Professor with the School of the Arts, Technology, and Emerging Communication at the University of Texas at Dallas.

After an undergraduate degree in journalism from the University of Texas at Austin and employment as a photojournalist for the *Times-Picayune* newspaper in New Orleans, Lester received a Master's from the University of Minnesota and a Ph.D. from Indiana University.

He is the author or editor of several books including: *Visual Ethics: A Guide for Photographers, Journalists and Filmmakers, Digital Innovations for Mass Communications: Engaging the User, Visual Communication on the Web* with xtine burrough, *Images that Injure Pictorial Stereotypes in the Media Third Edition* with Susan Ross, *On Floods and Photo Ops: How Herbert Hoover and George W. Bush Exploited Catastrophes, Visual Journalism: A Guide for New Media Professionals* with Chris Harris, *Desktop Computing Workbook A Guide for Using 15 Programs in Macintosh and Windows Formats,* and *Photojournalism An Ethical Approach.*

For four years Lester was the editor of *Journalism & Communication Monographs* published by Sage and for five years the editor of the *Visual Communication Quarterly* published by Taylor & Francis. For several years, he co-wrote a monthly column, "Ethics Matters" for *News Photographer* magazine for the National Press Photographers Association (NPPA). In 2015 he was honored by the NPPA with the Kenneth P. McLaughlin Award of Merit for "rendering continuing outstanding service in the interests of news photography."

Lester has given speeches, presentations, and workshops throughout the United States and in several countries.

Weblink: http://goo.gl/4Pr1q9

Made in the USA
San Bernardino, CA
17 July 2019